# SWIFT

## POETICAL WORKS

*Oxford University Press, Ely House, London W.1*

GLASGOW NEW YORK TORONTO MELBOURNE WELLINGTON
CAPE TOWN SALISBURY IBADAN NAIROBI LUSAKA ADDIS ABABA
BOMBAY CALCUTTA MADRAS KARACHI LAHORE DACCA
KUALA LUMPUR HONG KONG TOKYO

*Quivis speret idem.* Hor.

Frontispiece from *Works*, Vol. II, Dublin 1735

# SWIFT

## POETICAL WORKS

*Edited by*

HERBERT DAVIS

*London*
OXFORD UNIVERSITY PRESS
NEW YORK TORONTO
1967

## JONATHAN SWIFT

Born Dublin, 30 November 1667
Died Dublin, 19 October 1745

© Oxford University Press, 1967

*Printed in Great Britain
by The Camelot Press Limited,
London and Southampton*

# CONTENTS

# Preface

IT IS thirty years since the imposing edition of Swift's *Poems* by Harold Williams was published, in three volumes, by the Clarendon Press. Twenty-one years later a second revised edition added some new material provided by the discovery of two important autograph manuscripts, some contemporary transcripts, and further information biographical and bibliographical. The text of the poems was printed from a variety of sources—autograph manuscripts, contemporary transcripts (some in the hand of Stella), and the earliest authoritative printed editions. This has meant great variety of usage in spelling, punctuation, and capitalization. But this method has certain obvious advantages, as it provides us with plenty of examples of all the different forms in which Swift's verses have survived—early drafts in his own hand, copies by his friends, printed half-sheets or small pamphlets as they first appeared in Dublin or London, more formal versions, sometimes corrected and revised to be included in his *Miscellanies*, or in that collected volume of Poems, printed as the Second Volume of his *Works*, by George Faulkner in Dublin, in 1735. In the introductory notes to each poem in Williams's edition all the available information is brought together concerning its composition and subsequent publication: we are always informed which copy-text has been chosen; and, with one or two particular and necessary exceptions, the practice is adopted throughout of reproducing that text exactly, and recording all variants in the textual apparatus. Some would not always agree with the editor's choice of copy-text; some would now, I think, in the light of recent new indications of the part Swift himself played in changing the contents and in supervising the *Poems* of 1735, be inclined to give greater weight to the authority of that text.

The present edition in one volume is, however, not intended to provide a new text of the poems; it rests firmly on the authority of this great achievement which grew out of the exhaustive and tireless researches in which Harold Williams had occupied himself for many years. But as there is not room to include his textual apparatus, it has been necessary to incorporate into his text from the variants he records the later corrections of the author, which sometimes involve additions or deletions of whole stanzas. Wherever Williams had provided two versions of the text, e.g. *The History of Vanbrug's House* and *Baucis and Philemon*, taken from the original drafts in Swift's autograph and from the later publication in the *Miscellanies* of 1711, those two versions have been printed separately here, with the later corrections of 1735 incorporated into the text of 1711. Again, Swift's *Answer to a Scandalous Poem* (i.e. Sheridan's *New Simile for the Ladies*) is also printed both from the autograph manuscript and from the much revised and shorter version printed in Dublin in 1733. The source of the text of each poem is given in a footnote. Explanatory notes from the early printed editions, which were either provided by Swift or at least printed with his approval, are included here as footnotes.

The order of the poems has been altered. Since so much of Swift's verse is occasional, and since the editor had succeeded in establishing the date of composition for nearly all of the poems, there seemed to be some advantage in a chronological arrangement throughout according to the date of composition. There are three separate sections at the end for Riddles, Poems of Doubtful Date, and a few of the more likely Attributions.

There have been some omissions of poems which cannot now be regarded as Swift's work—the *Ode to King William* in four-line stanzas and the *Epigrams against Carthy*; a few have been moved to the section of doubtful Attributions; *Apollo's Edict* has been given back to Mrs. Barber, since it certainly appeared with Swift's approval in her *Poems on Several Occasions*, 1734. The very large section which Williams included in his Third Volume under the title *Trifles*, mainly consisting of verses by Swift's friends, Sheridan, Delany, and the Jacksons, and often no better than rhymes strung together as fast as possible in a sort of competitive game, is represented here only by a few of the better pieces, inserted in their place chronologically, such as *Mary the Cook-Maid's Letter* and *To Quilca*, both of which Swift had thought good enough to be included in *Poems*, 1735.

From the Clarendon Press edition, part of two sections of

the Bibliographical Summary, containing manuscript and printed sources for the poems, have been included and brought up to date.

The curious frontispiece and the Advertisement have been reproduced from the Dublin edition of the *Poems*, 1735. There can be no doubt, I believe, that this Advertisement was written by Swift himself; it may well serve therefore as a Preface to this volume of his complete poetical works.

I am greatly obliged to Mr. David Woolley, a friend of Sir Harold Williams and for many years much concerned himself with Swift studies; I have had the benefit of his suggestions in planning the volume, and his generous help in checking the proofs.

*January 1967*                                 HERBERT DAVIS

In view of the late Professor Davis's championship of the authority of Faulkner's edition of Swift's *Works*, Dublin, 1735,[1] very particular interest attaches to the recent discovery of a copy of Volume II in its uncancelled state. This has been admirably described and analysed by Miss Margaret Weedon in 'An Uncancelled Copy of the First Collected Edition of Swift's Poems', *The Library*, Fifth Series, Vol. XXII, No. 1 (March 1967), pp. 44–56. The cancellanda reveal that no less than five poems[2] were dropped from the published volume, three[3] were partially cancelled to permit discreet alteration of the text, and six[4] underwent minor revision in the course of re-setting; and nine poems, only one of which appears previously to have been printed, were provided for the cancel leaves. The substantive variants now supplied by the leaves in their original state have been incorporated in the text of this edition, in the belief that they provide, quite strikingly, evidence of Swift's primary intentions in 1734.

*June 1967*                                     DAVID WOOLLEY

[1] See the 'new' anecdote, no. *132*, in Spence's *Anecdotes*, ed. J. M. Osborn, Oxford, 1966, i. 55: 'Swift's edition [was] under his own eye', Pope *August* 1735.

[2] A Dialogue between Mad Mullinix and Timothy; [An Epistle] To a Lady; Epigram on Fasting; Traulus the First Part; Traulus the Second Part.

[3] The Author upon Himself; An Excellent New Song on a Seditious Pamphlet; To Mr. Gay.

[4] On Cutting Down the Old Thorn at Market-Hill; The Description of an Irish-Feast; On Reading Dr. Young's Satyrs; Cassinus and Peter; In Sickness; Desire and Possession.

# A Bibliographical Summary[1]

## *A*

## MANUSCRIPT SOURCES

### INCLUDING PRINTED VOLUMES WITH ANNOTATIONS

### I. *LIBRARIES*

TRINITY COLLEGE, DUBLIN. MS. 879 [I. 5. 1–3]: *The Whimsical Medley*: Three quarto volumes, containing transcripts of contemporary verse, latter part of the seventeenth and early part of the eighteenth century, made for Theophilus, first Lord Newtown-Butler. MS. 1050 [I. 4. 7]: Contemporary transcript of 'The Legion Club' on seven octavo leaves. Two volumes (Press 3, and Press A. 7. 6³⁸) containing manuscript miscellanies.

ROYAL IRISH ACADEMY, DUBLIN. MS. 24. C. 31: A small quarto volume, bound in vellum, containing transcripts of verses in an unidentified hand. In the same volume are a letter (7 Oct. 1737, to Lord Mayor Walker), and accounts relating to 1734–5, both in Swift's hand.

FORSTER COLLECTION, VICTORIA AND ALBERT MUSEUM, SOUTH KENSINGTON. The valuable collection made by John Forster in preparation for his *Life of Swift*. Contains many MSS. in Swift's hand; papers by Percy, Malone, and others; transcripts, collations, and notes by Forster. Also a copy of Hawkesworth's *Life of Swift*, 1755, with marginal annotations by Dr. Lyon.

BRITISH MUSEUM, LONDON. Add. MSS. 4804–6: *Journal to Stella* and correspondence. Add. MS. 39839: Swift and Vanessa correspondence. Also a few further MSS., Add., Lansdowne, Harley, and Stowe; including the Marmaduke Coghill and Edward Southwell correspondence, which throws some light on the history of verse pieces.

GOLDSMITHS' LIBRARY, SENATE HOUSE, UNIVERSITY OF LONDON. A copy of the *Hibernian Patriot*, 1730, with a couplet added in the hand of Lady Acheson (?).

BODLEIAN LIBRARY, OXFORD. MS. Malone 37. On ff. 68–98 contains matter which appeared in Barrett's *Essay on the earlier Part of the Life of Swift*, 1808.

UNIVERSITY LIBRARY, CAMBRIDGE. Contemporary transcripts in the Bradshaw Collection. See pp. 769, 801.

[1] Page references throughout this Summary are to *The Poems of Jonathan Swift*, ed. Harold Williams, 1958 (see p. xxvii).

JOHN RYLANDS LIBRARY, MANCHESTER. English MS. 659. See pp. 662–4, 680.

SIR WALTER SCOTT'S LIBRARY, ABBOTSFORD. Principal Library, Press N. Shelf 7: A 12mo volume containing transcripts of poems by Swift in an unidentified hand. The volume was presented to Scott by a Mr. Bembridge, as being in Swift's hand. The copies are certainly neither by Swift, nor by Stella, as Scott conjectures. A collection made about the middle of the eighteenth century. The volume has no textual value.

PIERPONT MORGAN LIBRARY, NEW YORK. Contains the valuable Fountaine MSS., for nearly two hundred years preserved at Narford, in Norfolk. Five poems in this collection are in Swift's hand. See further pp. 61, 78, 85, 88, 122. Manuscripts from the Ford papers are also in the library. See p. 744.

HARVARD COLLEGE LIBRARY, CAMBRIDGE, MASSACHUSETTS. MS. Eng. 218. 2: Orrery Papers. MS. Eng. 218. 14: A copy of Orrery's *Remarks*, 1752, annotated by the author. Also MS. Eng. 629 F: A verse miscellany.

HENRY E. HUNTINGTON LIBRARY, SAN MARINO, CALIFORNIA. Two miscellaneous volumes of Swiftiana salvaged by James Smith, after the death of Theophilus Swift. See the 'Advertisement', p. ix, to Scott's second edition of Swift's *Works*, 1824. Also a volume of annotated broadsheets and manuscripts (113198–259) first used by W. R. Wilde in his *Closing Years of Dean Swift's Life*, and mistakenly supposed by him to be in Swift's hand. See George P. Mayhew, *Rage or Raillery, The Swift MSS. at the Huntington Library*, with a Foreword by Herbert Davis. San Marino, 1967.

## II.  *PRIVATE COLLECTIONS*

MRS. BAKER, MALAHOW, NAUL, CO. DUBLIN. A copy of Harward's *Almanack*, 1666, with transcripts of poems erroneously supposed to be in Swift's hand. For a description of this volume and its contents see pp. 1058–63. This book was formerly in the possession of the Christie family, at Newtown House, Swords, Co. Dublin.

SHIRLEY LIBRARY, LOUGH FEA, CO. MONAGHAN, IRELAND. A set of Faulkner's edition of Swift's *Works*, six volumes, 1737–8, with textual annotations in Swift's hand. It is doubtful whether any of the notes or markings are by Swift, save those in vol. ii, which contains the verses, and even these are of little textual importance. The set is of value, however, in showing that Swift substantially approved of Faulkner's edition.

SIR SHANE LESLIE, BT., GLASLOUGH, CO. MONAGHAN, IRELAND. A

commonplace book belonging to Florence O'Crowley, an Irish priest, and evidently in use by him from about 1736 onward. See further *The Irish Book Lover*, vol. xxi, no. 3, July–August, 1933. Contains transcripts of Swift's 'Advice to a Parson' and epigram on Hort (pp. 807–9). Also ascribes to him three doubtful pieces. See pp. 1115, 1137, 1138.

DUKE OF BEDFORD, WOBURN ABBEY, BEDFORDSHIRE. A volume containing transcripts of Swift's poems carefully written by Stella. This book has eighty-five leaves, not counting binder's fly leaves, two in number. The format is small quarto, the leaves measuring 19·8 × 15·5 cm.; and the binding is eighteenth-century calf with gilt back.

The volume contains a note by the fourth Duke of Bedford: 'This Manuscript was given me, by Sʳ Archibald Acheson at Bath 9ᵇᵉʳ 2ᵈ 1768. It was given to his Father, by the Dean of Sᵗ Patrick, and is of the hand writing of Stella, Mʳˢ Johnson.
B.'
Only forty leaves have been used for the transcripts. The book contains nineteen pieces, of which eighteen are copies by Stella. The last piece, 'On the five Lady's at Sots-hole and the Doctor at their head', is in a different and unidentified handwriting.

DUKE OF PORTLAND, WELBECK ABBEY, NOTTINGHAMSHIRE. Several contemporary transcripts of poems by Swift among the Harley Papers. Now deposited in the British Museum and Nottingham University Library.

MARQUIS OF BATH, LONGLEAT, WILTSHIRE. Portland Papers, vols. xi, xiii, xvii, xviii, xix, xx. Verses in Swift's autograph, and contemporary transcripts.

ROTHSCHILD LIBRARY, TRINITY COLLEGE, CAMBRIDGE. Letters and papers belonging to Charles Ford, Swift's friend, passed, on Ford's death, into the possession of Sir John Hynde Cotton, his executor, and were long preserved at Madingley Hall, Cambridge. They came, through the Cotton family, to Mrs. Rowley Smith of Shortgrove. See *Letters of Jonathan Swift to Charles Ford, ed.* D. Nichol Smith, 1935, p. vii. Among these papers are six of Swift's poems, two, 'The Bubble' and 'To Charles Ford Esqʳ. on his Birth-day', in Swift's hand, and four in the handwriting of Charles Ford. See pp. 78, 248, 309, 459, 744. Swift autographs of 'Atlas', p. 159; and 'The Grand Question Debated', p. 863.

A copy of the Pope and Swift *Miscellanies*, 4 vols. 1727–32, with many corrections in Swift's hand. Previously in the libraries of Viscount Powerscourt, and of Mr. W. G. Panter, The Bawn, Foxrock, Co. Dublin.

YELVERTON RECTORY, NORFOLK. Among papers formerly at Yelverton, which had come down from the family of Sir William Temple, were 'A description of Mother Ludwell's cave' (see p. 1068), and a contemporary copy of 'The Journal'. See p. 276.

BROADLANDS, ROMSEY, HANTS. Among Lord Mount Temple's MSS. were copies of 'Apollo to the Dean', and two sets of verses written on the windows of St. Patrick's Deanery. See pp. 259, 262.

The late SIR HAROLD WILLIAMS. Collection now in CAMBRIDGE UNIVERSITY LIBRARY. Two contemporary manuscripts of 'The Legion Club'; and two copies of Faulkner's editions of 'Verses on the Death of Dr. Swift' with the blanks, in text and notes, completed in contemporary hands. Also a copy of the first edition of 'On Poetry: A Rapsody' with the rejected lines added in the hand of Lord Orrery. See pp. 551, 827.

MRS. CARTWRIGHT, AYNHO. Contemporary transcripts of several poems. See pp. 63, 161, 343, 374, 683.

MISCELLANEOUS. A few other manuscripts have been used—the holograph of Swift's lines 'From Catullus' (see p. 679); lines written in a copy of Le Sage's *Devil upon Two Sticks* (see p. 1139); and lines in a copy of Pope's *Iliad* (see p. 1136).

## B
## MISCELLANIES, COLLECTED WORKS, &c.

1692 The Supplement to the Fifth Volume of the Athenian Gazette; . . . *London, Printed for John Dunton* . . . [1692].

The Gentleman's Journal: Or the Monthly Miscellany [Feby., June, and July, 1692]. Ed. P. A. Motteux.

1707 The Muses Mercury: Or The Monthly Miscellany. . . . *London, Printed by J. H. for Andrew Bell,* . . . *1707.* [April–June, 1707.]

1709 Baucis and Philemon; A Poem On the ever lamented Loss Of the two Yew-Trees, In the Parish of Chilthorne, . . . Together with Mrs. Harris's Earnest Petition. . . . *London: Printed and Sold by H. Hills* . . . *1709.* [Another edn. 1710.]

The Works of the Right Honourable The Earls of Rochester, And Roscommon. . . . The Third Edition. To which is added, A Collection of Miscellany Poems. . . . *London:* . . . *E. Curll,* . . . *1709.*

Poetical Miscellanies: The Sixth Part. . . . *London, Printed for Jacob Tonson,* . . . *1709.*

The Tatler. . . . *Sold by John Morphew* . . . [No. 9, 30 April,

1709; No. 238, 17 October, 1710; and No. 301, 13 March, 1710–11].

1710 A Meditation upon a Broom-Stick, And Somewhat Beside; Of the Same Author's. . . . *London: Printed for E. Curll, . . . 1710.* [The B.M. Copy of this pamphlet (C. 28. b. 11⁵) has on the title a note in Curll's handwriting: 'Given me by John Cliffe Esq.; who had them of the Bp. of Killala, in Ireland, whose Daughter he married & was my Lodger.—E Curll'.]

1711 Miscellanies in Prose and Verse. *London: Printed for John Morphew, . . . MDCCXI.* [The first authorized collection of Swift's prose and verse. 2nd ed. 1713.]

Miscellanies by Dr. Jonathan Swift . . . *London, Printed for E. Curll, . . . 1711.*

1714 A Collection of Original Poems, Translations, and Imitations, by Mr. Prior, Mr. Rowe, Dr. Swift, And other Eminent Hands. . . . *London: Printed for E. Curll, . . . 1714.*

1718 Letters, Poems, and Tales, Amorous, Satirical; and Gallant. . . . *London: Printed for E. Curll . . . 1718.*

1719 Ars Punica, sive Flos Linguarum: The Art of Punning; Or the Flower of Languages; . . . *Dublin: Printed by and for James Carson, . . . 1719.* [Also London edns., *Roberts,* in the same year.]

1720 A Defence of English Commodities. . . . To which is Annexed, An Elegy upon the much lamented Death of Mr. Demar, . . . *Printed at Dublin: And Reprinted at London, by J. Roberts . . . MDCCXX.*

The Swearer's-Bank: . . . (With The Best in Christendom. A Tale.) Written by Dean Swift. . . . *Reprinted at London by J. Roberts. . . .*

Miscellaneous Works, Comical & Diverting: By T. R. D. J. S. D. O. P. I. I. In Two Parts. I. The Tale of a Tub; . . . II. Miscellanies in Prose & Verse, . . . *London, Printed by Order of the Society de propagando, &c. M.DCC.XX.*

1721 Miscellanies in Prose and Verse. The Fourth Edition, . . . *Dublin: Printed by S. Fairbrother, . . . 2721 [sic].*

A Miscellaneous Collection of Poems, Songs and Epigrams. By several Hands. Publish'd by T. M. Gent . . . *Dublin: Printed by A. Rhames, 1721.* 2 vols.

1722 Miscellanies, Written By Jonathan Swift, D.D. . . . The Fourth Edition. *London: Printed in the Year M.DCC.XXII.*

1724 Miscellaneous Poems, Original and Translated, By Several Hands. . . . Published by Mr. Concanen. . . . *London: Printed for J. Peele, . . . MDCCXXIV.*

1725 Fraud Detected. Or, The Hibernian Patriot. . . . *Dublin: Re-printed and Sold by George Faulkner . . . 1725.*

A New Collection Of Poems On Several Occasions, By Mr. Prior, and Others. . . *London: Printed for Tho. Osborne, . . . MDCCXXV.*

1726 Miscellanea. In Two Volumes. Never before Published. . . . *London: Printed in the Year, 1727.* [Published July, 1726.]

Whartoniana: Or Miscellanies, In Verse and Prose. By the Wharton Family, . . . *Printed in the Year, 1727.* 2 vols. [Published September, 1726. Re-issued as The Poetical Works of Philip Late Duke of Wharton.]

1727–8. Miscellanies In Prose and Verse. The First Volume. *London: Printed for Benjamin Motte, . . . M.DCC.XXVII.*

Miscellanies. The Second Volume. *London: Printed for Benjamin Motte . . . M DCC XXVII.*

Miscellanies. The Last Volume. . . . *London: Printed for B. Motte, . . . 1727.* [The 'First' and 'Second' volumes were published in June, 1727; the 'Last' volume in March, 1728. The first three volumes of the famous Pope and Swift *Miscellanies*, and edited by the former. They were variously reprinted; and continued with 'The Third Volume', 1732, and 'Volume the Fifth', 1735.]

1728 Miscellanies In Prose and Verse. In Two Volumes. . . . *London Printed, and Re-printed in Dublin, By and for Sam. Fairbrother, . . . 1728.* [Reprinted 1732; a third volume added in 1733, and a fourth in 1735.]

Gulliveriana: Or, A Fourth Volume of Miscellanies. . . . *London: Printed for J. Roberts, . . . M.DCC.XXVIII.*

The Intelligencer. Numb. I Saturday. May, 11, To be Continued Weekly, *Dublin: Printed by S. Harding, . . . 172[8].* [Continued for twenty numbers inclusive. London collected editions, *A. Moor, 1729, Francis Cogan, 1730.*]

1729 Miscellaneous Poems, By Several Hands: . . . Publish'd by Mr. Ralph. *London: Printed by C. Ackers, . . . MDCCXXIX.*

1730 The Metamorphosis Of The Town: . . . To which is added, The Journal of a Modern Lady. . . . By Dr. Swift. . . . *London: Printed for J. Wilford, . . . MDCCXXX.* [Later edns. 1731, 1743.]

An Epistle To His Excellency John Lord Carteret . . . To which is added, an Epistle upon an Epistle; . . . *Dublin: Printed, in the Year 1730.*

A Satire On Dr. D—ny. . . . To which is added, the Poem which occasion'd it. *Printed at Dublin: And Re-printed at London, for A. Moore, . . . M DCC XXX.*

A Libel On Dr. D—ny, . . . The Second Edition. *Printed at Dublin: And Re-printed at London, for A. Moore. M DCC XXX.* [Another edn., 1730, *Reprinted for Capt. Gulliver.*]

A Vindication of the Libel On Dr. Delany, . . . Together with A Panegyric On Dean Sw—t; . . . *Dublin: Printed, London: Re-printed for J. Wilford . . . M.DCC.XXX.*

Select Poems from Ireland: Part I. [Part II.] . . . *Printed at Dublin: London, Reprinted and Sold by T. Warner . . . M.DCC.XXX.*

The Hibernian Patriot: . . . To which are added, Poems and Songs . . . *Printed at Dublin. London: Reprinted and Sold by A. Moor . . . MDCCXXX.* [Reprinted from Fraud Detected, 1725, with alterations and additions.]

Poems On Several Occasions. . . . By Jonathan Smedley, Dean of Clogher. . . . *London: Printed in the Year M.DCC.XXX.*

1731 A Proposal Humbly offer'd to the P—t, . . . To which is added, The Humble Petition of the Weavers. . . . As also two Poems, viz. Helter Skelter, . . . and The Place of the Damn'd. *Dublin Printed. London, Re-printed for J. Roberts . . . MDCCXXXI.* [2nd edn. 1732.]

The Flower-Piece: A Collection Of Miscellany Poems. By Several Hands. . . . *London: Printed for J. Walthoe . . . and H. Walthoe, . . . M.DCC.XXXI.* [Republished 1733.]

1732 The Grand Question debated: Whether Hamilton's Bawn Should be turn'd into a Barrack, or a Malt-house. . . . *London Printed for A. Moore. And, Dublin Re-printed by George Faulkner . . . M,DCC,XXXII.*

The Lady's Dressing Room. To which is added, A Poem on Cutting down the Old Thorn at Market Hill. . . . *London, Printed for J. Roberts . . . MDCCXXXII.* [2nd edn. in the same year.]

An Elegy On Dicky and Dolly, . . . To which is Added The Narrative of D. S. when he was in the North of Ireland. *Dublin: Printed by James Hoey, . . . MDCCXXXII.*

Miscellanies. The Third Volume. *London: Printed for Benj. Motte, . . . and Lawton Gilliver . . . 1732.* [Variously re-printed. See under 1727–8.]

1733 The Drapier's Miscellany. . . . *Dublin: Printed by and for James Hoey, . . . 1733.* [At least three editions.]

The Presbyterians Plea of Merit; . . . To which is added, An Ode to Humphry French, Esq; . . . *London: Reprinted from the Dublin Edition, for G. F. and Sold by A. Dodd, . . .*

1734 Miscellanies. Consisting chiefly of Original Pieces in Prose and Verse. . . . *Dublin Printed. London: Reprinted for A. Moore . . . 1734.* [Two edns.]

An Epistle to a Lady, . . . Also A Poem, Occasion'd by Reading
Dr. Young's Satires, . . . *Dublin, Printed: And Reprinted at
London for J. Wilford, . . . M.DCC.XXXIV.*
A New Miscellany For the Year 1734. Part I.
An Account Of A Strange and Wonderful Apparition Lately
Seen in Trinity-College, Dublin. . . . *Printed in the Year
MDCCXXXIV.*
Mezentius on the Rack . . . *Printed in the Year MDCCXXXIV.*
A Beautiful Young Nymph Going to Bed. . . . To which are
added Strephon and Chloe. And Cassinus and Peter. *Dublin
printed: London reprinted for J. Roberts . . . MDCCXXXIV.*

1734 (?) The History of John Bull. And Poems on several Occa-
sions, . . . *Sold by D. Midwinter and A. Tonson in the Strand.*

1734–5 The Works of J. S, D. D, D. S. P. D. in Four Volumes.
Containing, I. The Author's Miscellanies in Prose. II. His
Poetical Writings. III. The Travels of Captain Lemuel
Gulliver. IV. His Papers relating to Ireland, . . . *Dublin:
Printed by and for George Faulkner, . . . M DCC XXXV.* [Issued
Nov. 1734–Jany. 1735. Another edn. of vol. ii in 1737. The
set increased to six volumes in 1738, with some additional
verse pieces in vol. vi. Gradually extended to twenty volumes,
1772. Vol. viii, 1746, contained more verse. The chief verse
addition thereafter was in 1762; reprinted in the London
edition of the *Works* in the same year.]

1735 Miscellanies, In Prose and Verse. Volume the Fifth. . . .
*London: Printed for Charles Davis, . . . MDCCXXXV.* [See under
1727–8. This volume is based on Faulkner.]
A Collection of Poems, &c. Omitted in the Fifth Volume of
Miscellanies in Prose and Verse. *London: Printed for Charles
Davis, . . . MDCCXXXV.*
Miscellaneous Poems on Several Occasions. By Mr. Dawson, . . .
And a Copy of Verses Spoke Extempore by Dean Swift upon
his Curate's Complaint of hard Duty. . . . *1735.*

1736 The Poetical Works, Of J. S. D. D. D. S. P. D. . . . Re-
printed from the Second Dublin Edition, with Notes and
Additions. . . . *Printed in the Year. MDCCXXXVI.*
S—t contra Omnes. An Irish Miscellany. . . . *London . . . Mrs. Dod . . .*
Miscellanies. . . . *London: Printed for Benjamin Motte, and Charles
Bathurst, . . . MDCCXXXVI.* [6 vols., 12mo, 1736, a trade
venture, with other printers' names in later volumes. Vols.
vii, viii, and ix added, *T. Cooper,* 1742. The first extension of
the Pope and Swift Miscellanies, 1727–8–32–35, into sets
which developed into Swift's works.]

1739 A Supplement to Dr. Swift's And Mr. Pope's Works. . . . *Dublin: Printed by S. Powell, For Edward Exshaw* . . . *MDCCXXXIX.*

1740 Poems on Various Subjects, . . . By Laurence Whyte. . . . *Dublin: Printed by S. Powell, And Sold by L. Dowling,* . . . *M DCC XL.*

1742 Miscellanies. In Four Volumes. . . . The Fourth Edition Corrected: . . . Vol. I. By Dr. Swift. *London: Printed for Charles Bathurst,* . . . *MDCCXLII.* [A further trade development of the Miscellanies. Other printers' names in subsequent volumes. Extended to eleven volumes, 1742–6; and followed by reprints of varying dates, 1747, 1749, 1750, 1751, 1753.]

A New Miscellany In Prose and Verse. Containing, Several Pieces never before made public. By the Reverend Dr. Swift, . . . And other Eminent Hands. *London: Printed for T. Read,* . . . *MDCCXLII.*

1744 The Muse in Good Humour. Or, a Collection of Comic Tales, &c. . . . *London: Printed for J. Noble,* . . . *1744.* [Other edns. 1745, 1751, 1766; a second volume, 1757.]

1746 The Story Of The Injured Lady. . . . With Letters and Poems. . . . *Printed for M. Cooper,* . . . *MDCCXLVI.*

1749 Poems on Several Occasions, from Genuine Manuscripts of Dean Swift, . . . *London: Printed for J. Bromage,* . . . *1749.*

1750 (?) The Poetical Works of Dr. Jonathan Swift, . . . In Two Volumes. . . . *London: Sold by A. Manson, R. Dilton, J. Thomson, H. Gray, T. Nelson, and P. Bland.* [A trade edition, not earlier than 1745.]

1750 A Supplement To The Works of The Most celebrated Minor Poets. . . . To which are added, Pieces omitted in the Works of . . . Dean Swift. *London: Printed for F. Cogan,* . . . *MDCCL.*

1751 The Works of Dr. Jonathan Swift, . . . Vol. I. . . . *London: Printed for C. Bathurst,* . . . *MDCCLI.* [Fourteen volumes, 12mo. The first four vols. and vols. vi, and viii, carry the name of Bathurst only; other names added, or differing names, in subsequent volumes.]

1752 A Supplement to the Works of Dr. Swift. *London: Printed for F. Cogan,* . . . *1752.*

Brett's Miscellany. Vol. II., *Dublin.*

1754 The Dreamer. . . . *London: Printed for W. Owen,* . . . *MDCCLIV.* [By Dr. William King. Contains the first printing of 'Paulus' and 'The Answer'.]

Poems on Various Subjects: Viz. The Legion Club, by D—n

S—t. . . . *Glasgow: Printed by Sawney McPherson. M.DCC.LIV.* [Another edn. 1756.]

1754–5. The Works of Jonathan Swift, D.D. . . . Accurately revised In Six Volumes, . . . *London, Printed for C. Bathurst, . . . MDCCLV.* [Edited by Hawkesworth, for the London trade, in opposition to Faulkner's Dublin edn. of the *Works.* The six volumes 4to also appeared as twelve volumes large and small 8vo. Gradually extended, 1755–79, to fourteen, twenty-five, and twenty-seven volumes respectively. Additions to the verse were made in 1762–4 by Bowyer, from Faulkner, 1762; by Deane Swift in 1765; and by Nichols in his *Supplement,* 1776 and 1779. This trade edn. was the basis of Sheridan's edn. of the *Works,* 1784, and Nichols, 1801. It was also used by Edinburgh, Glasgow, and Dublin publishers, whose edns. have no independent value, and are not here noted.]

1767 An Appendix To Dr. Swift's Works . . . *London, Printed for W. B. and sold by S. Bladon, . . . MDCCLXVII.*

1770 (?) The Trader's Garland, Composed of Five Excellent New Songs. . . . *Licensed and entered according tn* [*sic*] *order.*

1776 Additions to the Works of Alexander Pope, Esq. Together with Many Original Poems and Letters, Of Cotemporary Writers, Never Before Published. In Two Volumes. . . . *London: Printed for H. Baldwin, . . . 1776.*

1779 The Works of the English Poets. With Prefaces, . . . by Samuel Johnson. . . . [Vols. 39 and 40 contain Swift's Poems; but this trade edition has no textual or editorial value.]

1780–2. A Select Collection of Poems: With Notes Biographical and Historical. . . . *London: Printed By and For J. Nichols, . . .* [Eight volumes.]

1784 The Works of the Rev. Dr. Jonathan Swift, . . . Arranged, Revised, and Corrected, with Notes, By Thomas Sheridan, A.M. A New Edition, in Seventeen Volumes. *London: Printed for C. Bathurst, . . . M DCC LXXXIV.* [See under 1754–5.]

1789 Miscellaneous Pieces, In Prose and Verse. By the Rev. Dr. Jonathan Swift, . . . Not Inserted in Mr. Sheridan's Edition Of the Dean's Works. *London: Printed for C. Dilly, . . . MDCCLXXXIX.*

1801 The Works of the Rev. Jonathan Swift, D.D., Dean of St. Patrick's, Dublin. Arranged by Thomas Sheridan, . . . A New Edition, In Nineteen Volumes; Corrected and Revised By John Nichols, . . . *London: Printed for J. Johnson, J. Nichols, . . . 1801.* [See under 1784. Further edns., 1803, 24 vols., 1808, 19 vols.]

1804 Swiftiana. Vol. I. [Vol. II.] . . . *Printed for Richard Phillips, 71, St. Pauls Church Yard. 1804.*

1808 An Essay On The Earlier Part of the Life of Swift. By the Rev. John Barrett, D.D. . . . To Which are Subjoined Several Pieces Ascribed to Swift; . . . *London: Printed for J. Johnson; J. Nichols and Son; . . . 1808.*

1814 The Works of Jonathan Swift, D.D. Dean of St. Patrick's, Dublin; Containing Additional Letters, Tracts, and Poems, Not Hitherto Published; With Notes and A Life of the Author, By Walter Scott, Esq. . . . *Edinburgh: Printed for Archibald Constable and Co. . . . 1814.* [In nineteen volumes. A 2nd edn. in nineteen volumes, 1824, containing further additions. Reprinted in nineteen volumes, 1883.]

1833–4. The Poetical Works of Jonathan Swift. [Aldine Edition.] . . . *London William Pickering.* [In three volumes, based on Scott's 2nd edn., 1824. Further edns. 1853, 1866.]

1841 The Works of Jonathan Swift, . . . Containing Interesting and Valuable Papers, Not Hitherto Published. In Two Volumes. With Memoirs of the Author, by Thomas Roscoe; . . . *London: Henry Washbourne, . . . 1841.* [A number of later edns.]

1910 The Poems of Jonathan Swift, D.D. Edited by William Ernst Browning . . . *London G. Bell and Sons, Ltd. 1910.* [Two volumes.]

1929 Swift's Verse An Essay By F. Elrington Ball, Litt.D. . . . *London John Murray, Albemarle Street, W.*

1934 Swift Gulliver's Travels and Selected Writings in Prose & Verse. Ed. John Hayward. *Nonesuch Press, Bloomsbury, 1934.*

1935 The Letters of Jonathan Swift to Charles Ford. Ed. D. Nichol Smith . . . *Oxford At the Clarendon Press MCMXXXV.* [Prints six of Swift's poems from the Ford papers,—two from Swift's autograph.]

1935 The Drapier's Letters to the People of Ireland . . . Ed. Herbert Davis. *Oxford At the Clarendon Press MCMXXXV.* [Contains notes and bibliographical detail relative to verses connected with the Drapier.] Reprint, with revised Bibliography, 1965.

1937 The Poems of Jonathan Swift. Ed. Harold Williams. 3 vols. . . . *Oxford At the Clarendon Press MCMXXXVII*, second edition *MCMLVIII.*

1958 Collected Poems of Jonathan Swift. Ed. Joseph Horrell. 2 vols. *London Routledge and Kegan Paul Ltd.* [With Introduction, critical comments, and notes.]

# Swift's Advertisement to *Poems*, 1735

THE *first Collection of this Author's Writings were published near thirty Years ago, under the Title of Miscellanies in Verse and Prose. Several Years after, there appeared three Volumes of Miscellanies, with a Preface to the first, signed* J. Swift *and* A. Pope. *In these the Verses, with great Additions, were printed in a Volume by themselves. But in each Volume were mixed many Poems and Treatises, writ by the supposed Author's Friends, which we have laid aside; our Intention being only to publish the Works of one Writer. The following Poetical Volume is enlarged by above a third Part, which was never collected before, although some of them were occasionally printed in* London *in single Sheets. The rest were procured from the supposed Author's Friends, who at their earnest Request were permitted to take Copies.*

*The following Poems chiefly consist either of Humour or Satyr, and very often of both together. What Merit they may have, we confess ourselves to be no Judges of in the least; but out of due Regard to a Writer, from whose Works we hope to receive some Benefit, we cannot conceal what we have heard from several Persons of great Judgment; that the Author never was known either in Verse or Prose to borrow any Thought, Simile, Epithet, or particular Manner of Style; but whatever he writ, whether good, bad, or indifferent, is an Original in itself.*

*Although we are very sensible, that in some of the following Poems, the Ladies may resent certain satyrical Touches against the mistaken Conduct in some of the fair Sex: And that, some warm Persons on the prevailing Side, may censure this Author, whoever he be, for not thinking in publick Matters exactly like themselves: Yet we have been assured by several judicious and learned Gentlemen, that what the Author hath here writ, on either of those two Subjects, had no other Aim than to reform the Errors of both Sexes. If the Publick be right in its Conjectures of the Author, nothing is better known in* London, *than that while he had Credit at the Court of Queen* Anne, *he employed so much of it in favour of* Whigs *in both Kingdoms, that the Ministry used to railly him as the Advocate of that Party, for several of whom he got Employments, and preserved others from losing what they had: Of which some Instances remain even in this Kingdom. Besides, he then writ and declared against the* Pretender, *with equal Zeal, though not with equal Fury, as any of our modern Whigs; of which Party he always professed himself to be as to Politicks, as the Reader will find in many Parts of his Works.*

*Our Intentions were to print the Poems according to the Time they were writ in; but we could not do it so exactly as we desired, because we could never get the least Satisfaction in that or many other Circumstances from the supposed Author.*

# THE
# EARLY ODES
## 1690–1693

# ODE TO THE KING

## On his *Irish* Expedition

### AND

### *The Success of his Arms in general*

#### Written in the Year 1691

### I

SURE there's some Wondrous Joy in *Doing Good*;
Immortal Joy, that suffers no Allay from Fears,
   Nor dreads the Tyranny of Years,
By none but its Possessors to be understood:
   Else where's the Gain in being *Great*?
  Kings would indeed be Victims of the State;
  What can the Poet's humble Praise?
  What can the Poet's humble Bays?
  (We Poets oft our Bays allow,
  Transplanted to the Hero's Brow)        10
  Add to the Victor's Happiness?
  What do the Scepter, Crown and Ball,
Rattles for Infant Royalty to play withal,
  But serve t' adorn the Baby-dress
  Of one poor Coronation-day,
   To make the Pageant gay:
  A three Hours Scene of empty Pride,
  And then the Toys are thrown aside.

### II

  But the Delight of *Doing Good*
  Is fix't like Fate among the Stars,        20
   And Deifi'd in Verse;
  'Tis the best Gemm in Royalty,

Printed from *Vol. IV. of the Miscellanies Begun by Jonathan Swift, D.D. and Alexander Pope, Esq.* . . . Dublin, Printed by and for Samuel Fairbrother, . . . 1735, Verse section, pp. 1–6.

The Great Distinguisher of Blood,
Parent of Valour and of Fame,
Which makes a Godhead of a Name,
And is Contemporary to Eternity.
This made the Ancient Romans to afford
To *Valour* and to *Virtue* the *same Word*:
To shew the Paths of both must be together trod,
Before the *Hero* can commence *a God*.                  30

### III

These are the Ways
By which our happy Prince carves out his Bays;
Thus he has fix'd His Name
First, in the mighty List of Fame,
And thus He did the Airy Goddess Court,
He sought Her out in Fight,
And like a Bold Romantick Knight
Rescu'd Her from the Giant's Fort:
The Tyrant Death lay crouching down,
Waiting for Orders at his Feet,                  40
Spoil'd of his Leaden Crown;
He trampled on this Haughty *Bajazet*,
Made him his Footstool in the War,
And a Grim Slave to wait on his Triumphal Car.

### IV

And now I in the Spirit see
(The Spirit of Exalted Poetry)
I see the *Fatal Fight* begin;
And, lo! where a Destroying Angel stands,
(By all but Heaven and Me unseen,)
With Lightning in his Eyes, and Thunder in his Hands;
*In vain*, said He, *does* Utmost Thule *boast*                  51
*No poys'nous Beast will in Her breed,*
*Or no Infectious Weed,*
*When she sends forth such a malignant Birth,*
*When Man himself's the* Vermin *of Her Earth*;
*When* Treason *there in* Person *seems to stand,*
*And* Rebel *is the* growth *and* manufacture *of the Land.*

51. *Utmost Thule.* Ireland.

He spake, and a dark Cloud flung o're his light,
    And hid him from Poetick sight,
And (I believe) began himself the Fight,            60
    For strait I saw the Field maintain'd,
And what I us'd to laugh at in *Romance*,
And thought too great ev'n for effects of Chance,
The Battel almost by *Great William*'s single Valour gain'd;
    The *Angel* (doubtless) kept th' Eternal Gate,
        And stood 'twixt Him and every Fate;
And all those flying Deaths that aim'd him from the Field,
    (Th' impartial Deaths which come
    Like Love, wrapt up in Fire;
And like that too, make every breast their home)     70
    Broke on his everlasting Shield.

### V

    The *Giddy Brittish Populace*,
        That *Tyrant-Guard* on *Peace*,
        Who watch Her like a Prey,
    And keep Her for a Sacrifice,
And must be sung, like *Argus*, into *ease*
Before this *Milk-white Heifer* can be stole away,
    Our *Prince* has charm'd its many hundred Eyes;
        Has lull'd the Monster in a Deep
        And (I hope) an Eternal Sleep,            80
And has at last redeem'd the *Mighty Prize*[;]
The *Scots* themselves, that Discontented Brood,
Who always loudest for *Religion* bawl,
    (*As those still do wh'have none at all*)
Who claim so many Titles to be *Jews*,
(But, surely such whom God did never for *his People* chuse)
    Still murmuring in *their Wilderness* for *Food*,
    Who pine us like a *Chronical Disease*;
And one would think 'twere past Omnipotence to please;
Your Presence all their *Native Stubborness* controuls,    90
And for a while unbends their contradicting Souls:
    As in old Fabulous Hell,
When some *Patrician* God wou'd visit the Immortal Jayl,
    The very Brightness of His Face
    Suspended every Horror of the Place,

The Gyants under *Ætna* ceas'd to groan,
And *Sisiphus* lay sleeping on his Stone.
Thus has our Prince compleated every Victory,
        And glad *Iërne* now may see
Her Sister Isles are *Conquered* too as well as She.        100

### VI

How vainly (Sir) did Your fond *Enemy* try
Upon *a rubbish Heap of broken Laws*
        To climb at Victory
        Without the Footing of a *Cause*;
His Lawrel now must only be a Cypress Wreath,
        And His best Victory a Noble Death;
His scrap of Life is but a Heap of Miseries,
        The Remnant of a falling Snuff,
        Which hardly wants another puff,
And needs must *stink* when e're it dies;        110
Whilst at Your Victorious Light
        All lesser ones expire,
Consume, and perish from our sight,
        Just as the Sun puts out a Fire;
And every foolish *Flye* that dares to aim
        To buzz about the mighty Flame;
The wretched Insects singe their Wings, and fall,
        And humbly at the bottom crawl.

### VII

That *Restless Tyrant*, who of late
Is grown so impudently Great,        120
        That Tennis-Ball of Fate;
This Gilded Meteor which flyes
As if it meant to touch the Skies;
        For all its boasted height,
        For all its Plagiary Light,
        Took its first Growth and Birth
From the worst Excrements of Earth;
Stay but a little while and down again 'twill come,
And end as it began, in Vapour, Stink, and Scum.

127. *Excrements of Earth.* The French King suppos'd a Bastard.

Or has he like some fearful Star appear'd?     130
Long dreaded for his *Bloody Tail* and *Fiery Beard*,
  Transcending Nature's ordinary Laws,
    Sent by just Heaven to threaten Earth
    With War, and Pestilence, and Dearth,
Of which it is at once the Prophet and the Cause.
    Howe're it be, the Pride of *France*
    Has finish'd its short Race of Chance,
  And all Her boasted Influences are
  Rapt in the *Vortex* of the *Brittish* Star;
Her *Tyrant* too an unexpected Wound shall feel     140
  In the last wretched Remnant of his Days;
Our Prince has hit Him, like *Achilles*, in the *Heel*,
  The poys'nous Darts has made him reel,
  Giddy he grows, and down is hurl'd,
And as a Mortal to his *Vile Disease*,
Falls sick in the *Posteriors* of the World.


# ODE

## TO THE

# Athenian Society


## TO THE

## Athenian Society

### *Moor-Park*, Feb. 14, 1691

GENTLEMEN,

*SINCE* every Body *pretends to trouble you with their* Follies, *I thought I might claim the Priviledge of an* English-man, *and put in my share among the rest. Being last year in* Ireland, (*from*

145. *Vile Disease*. Fistula in Ano.

Printed from *The Supplement to the Fifth Volume of the Athenian Gazette*, London [published on 1 April 1692].

*whence I returned about half a year ago*) *I heard only a* loose talk of your Society, *and believed the design to be only some new* Folly *just suitable to the Age, which God knows, I little expected ever to produce any thing* extraordinary. *Since my being in* England, *having still continued in the Countrey, and much out of Company; I had but little advantage of knowing any more, till about two Months ago* passing through *Oxford,* a very learned Gentleman *there, first shew'd me two or three of your* Volumes, *and gave me his Account and Opinion of you; a while after, I came to this place, upon a Visit to* —— *where I have been ever since, and have seen all the* four Volumes with their Supplements, *which answering my Expectation. The perusal has produced, what you find inclosed.*

*As I have been somewhat inclined to this* Folly, *so I have seldom wanted some-body to flatter me in it. And for the* Ode *inclosed, I have sent it to a Person of very great* Learning and Honour, *and since to some others, the best of my Acquaintance,* (to which I thought very proper to inure it for a greater light) *and they have all been pleased to tell me, that they are sure it will not be unwelcome, and that I should* beg the Honour *of You to let it be Printed before Your* next Volume (*which I think, is soon to be published,*) *it being so usual before most Books of any great value among Poets, and before it's seeing the World, I submit it wholly to the* Correction of your Pens.

*I intreat therefore one of You would* descend *so far, as to write two or three lines to me of your Pleasure upon it. Which as I cannot but expect from Gentlemen, who have so well shewn upon so many occasions, that* greatest Character *of Scholars, in being favourable to the* Ignorant, *So I am sure nothing at present, can more highly oblige me, or make me happier.*

I am,

(Gentlemen)
Your ever most Humble,
and most
admiring Servant.
*Jonathan Swift.*

## I

AS when the *Deluge* first began to fall,
That *mighty Ebb* never to flow again,
(When this huge Bodies Moisture was so great
It quite o'recame the vital Heat,)
That Mountain which was highest first of all
Appear'd, above the Universal Main,
To bless the *Primitive Sailer's* weary sight,
And 'twas perhaps *Parnassus*, if in height
  It be as great as 'tis in Fame,
  And nigh to Heaven as is its Name.                    10
So after th' Inundation of a War
When *Learnings little Houshold* did embark
With her World's fruitful System in her sacred Ark,
  At the first Ebb of Noise and Fears,
  *Philosophy's* exalted head appears;
And the *Dove-muse,* will now no longer stay
But plumes her Silver Wings and flies away,
  And now a Laurel wreath she brings from far,
  To Crown the happy Conquerour,
  To shew the Flood begins to cease,                    20
  And brings the dear Reward of *Victory and Peace.*

## II

The eager *Muse* took wing upon the Waves decline,
  When War her cloudy aspect just withdrew,
  When the *Bright Sun* of Peace began to shine,
And for a while in heav'nly Contemplation sate
  On the high Top of peaceful *Ararat;*
And pluckt a *Laurel* branch (for Laurel was the first that grew,
The first of Plants after the Thunder, Storm, and Rain)
      And thence with joyful, nimble Wing
      Flew dutifully back again,                        30
      And made an *Humble Chaplet for the King.*
  And the *Dove-muse* is fled once more,
(Glad of the Victory, yet frighted at the War)
    And now discovers *from afar*
    A Peaceful and a Flourishing Shore:
      No sooner does she land
      On the delightful *Strand,*

31. *Humble Chaplet.* The Ode I writ to the King in Ireland.

When strait she sees the *Countrey all around*,
Where fatal *Neptune* rul'd e'rewhile,
Scatter'd with *flowry Vales*, with fruitful Gardens crown'd, 40
    And many a pleasant Wood,
      As if the Universal *Nile*
    Had rather water'd it, than drown'd:
It seems some floating piece of *Paradice*,
    Preserv'd by wonder from the Flood,
Long *wandring thrô the Deep*, as we are told
      Fam'd *Delos* did of old,
And the transported Muse imagin'd it
To be a fitter *Birth-place for the God of Wit*;
      Or the much-talkt Oracular Grove  50
    When with amazing Joy she hears,
    An *unknown Musick* all around,
      Charming her greedy Ears
      With many a heavenly Song
Of Nature and of Art, of deep *Philosophy and Love*,
*Whilst Angels tune the Voice, and God inspires the Tongue.*
    In vain she catches at the empty Sound,
In vain pursues the Musick with her longing Eye,
And *Courts* the wanton Echoes as they fly.

### III

Pardon 𝔜𝔢 𝔤𝔯𝔢𝔞𝔱 𝔘𝔫𝔨𝔫𝔬𝔴𝔫, and far-exalted Men,  60
The wild excursions of a youthful pen;
    Forgive a young and (almost) *Virgin-muse*,
    Whom blind and eager Curiosity
      (Yet Curiosity they say,
    Is in her Sex a Crime needs no excuse)
      Has forc't to grope her uncouth way
After a *mighty Light* that leads her wandring Eye;
No wonder then she quits the *narrow Path of Sense*
    For a dear Ramble thro' Impertinence,
    Impertinence, the *Scurvy* of Mankind,  70
And all we Fools, who are the greater part of it,
    Tho' we be of two different Factions still,
      Both the Good-natur'd and the Ill,
    Yet wheresoe're you look you'll always find
*We join like Flyes, and Wasps, in buzzing about Wit.*

In me, who am of the first Sect of these,
All Merit that transcends the humble Rules
   Of my own dazled, scanty Sense
Begets a kinder Folly and Impertinence
   Of Admiration and of Praise:             80
And our good Brethren of the *Surly Sect*
Must e'en all herd with us their *Kindred Fools*,
For tho' possess'd of present Vogue they've made
*Railing a Rule of Wit, and Obloquy a Trade,*
Yet the same want of Brains produces each effect;
  And you whom *Pluto*'s Helm does wisely shroud
     From us the Blind and thoughtless Croud,
  Like the fam'd Hero in his Mother's Cloud,
Who both our Follies and Impertinencies see,
*Do laugh* perhaps at theirs, and pity mine and me.    90


### IV

    But Censure's to be understood
    Th' *Authentick mark* of the Elect,
The publick Stamp Heav'n sets on all that's Great and Good,
  Our shallow Search and Judgment to direct.
        The War methinks has made
Our Wit and Learning, narrow as our Trade;
Instead of boldly sailing far to buy
*A Stock of Wisdom* and Philosophy,
    We fondly stay at home in fear
    *Of ev'ry censuring Privateer,*        100
Forcing a wretched Trade by beating down the sale,
    And selling *basely* by Retail,
*The Wits,* I mean the Atheists of the Age,
Who fain would rule the Pulpit, as they do the Stage,
  Wondrous *Refiners* of Philosophy,
      Of Morals and Divinity,
By the new *Modish System* of reducing all to sense,
  Against all Logick and concluding Laws,
    Do own th'Effects of Providence,
      And yet deny the Cause.     110

### V

This *hopeful Sect*, now it begins to see
How little, very little do prevail
   Their *first and chiefest force*
 To censure, to cry down, and rail,
*Not knowing What, or Where, or Who, You be,*
  Will quickly take another course
  And by their never-failing ways
Of Solving all Appearances they please,
We soon shall see them to their ancient Methods fall,
And straight deny you to be *Men, or any thing at all*;  120
 I laugh at the grave Answer they will make,
Which they have always ready, general and Cheap;
  'Tis but to say, that what we daily meet,
   And by a fond mistake
  Perhaps imagine to be *wondrous Wit*
  And think, alas, to be by mortals writ,
  Is but a *Crowd of Atoms* justling in a heap,
   Which from Eternal Seeds begun,
   Justling some thousand years till ripen'd by the Sun,
  They're now, just now, as naturally born,  130
  As from the *Womb of Earth* a field of Corn.

### VI

  But as for poor contented Me,
Who must my Weakness and my Ignorance confess,
That I believe in much, I ne're can hope to see;
  *Methinks I'm satisfied to guess*
 That this New, Noble, and Delightful Scene
Is wonderfully mov'd by some exalted Men,
 Who have well studied in the *Worlds Disease,*
(That Epidemick Error and Depravity
  Or in our Judgment or our Eye)  140
 That what *surprises us* can only please:
We often search contentedly the whole World round,
  To make some *great Discovery,*
   And scorn it when 'tis found.

Just so the Mighty *Nile* has suffer'd in it's Fame,
   Because 'tis said, (and perhaps only said)
We've found a little inconsiderable Head
       That feeds the huge unequal stream.
Consider *Humane Folly*, and you'll quickly own,
   That all the Praises it can give,        150
By which some fondly boast they shall for ever live,
   Won't pay th'*Impertinence* of being known;
     Else why should the fam'd *Lydian* King,
Whom all the *Charms* of an Usurped Wife and State,
With all that Power unfelt, courts Mankind to be Great,
   Did with new, unexperienc't Glories wait,
Still wear, still doat on his *Invisible Ring.*


## VII

   Were I to form a regular *Thought of Fame*,
   Which is perhaps as hard t'imagine right
     *As to paint Eccho to the Sight:*        160
I would not draw th'*Idea* from an empty Name;
     Because, alas, when we all dye
   Careless and Ignorant Posterity,
   Although they praise the Learning and the Wit,
     And tho' the Title seems to show
   The Name and Man, by whom the Book was writ,
     Yet how shall they be brought to know
Whether that very Name was *He, or You, or I?*
Less should I dawb it o're with transitory Praise,
     And *water-colours* of these Days,        170
*These Days!* where ev'n th'Extravagance of Poetry
   Is at a loss for Figures to express
   Men's Folly, Whimsyes, and Inconstancy,
   And by a faint Description make them less.
*Then tell us what is Fame?* where shall we search for it?
Look where exalted Vertue and Religion sit
     Enthron'd with Heav'nly Wit,
     Look where you see
   The greatest scorn of *Learned Vanity,*

(And then how much a nothing is Mankind!      180
Whose Reason is weigh'd down by Popular air,
Who by that, vainly talks of bafling Death,
And hopes to lengthen Life by a *Transfusion of Breath*,
   Which yet whoe're examines right will find
To be an Art as vain, as *Bottling up of Wind*:)
And when you find out these, believe true Fame is there.
Far above all Reward, yet to which all is due,
And this 𝕯𝖊 𝖌𝖗𝖊𝖆𝖙 𝖀𝖓𝖐𝖓𝖔𝖜𝖓, is only known in You.


## VIII

The *Jugling Sea-god* when by chance trepann'd
By some instructed *Querist* sleeping on the Sand,      190
   Impatient of all *Answers*, straight became
   A *Stealing Brook*, and strove to creep away
         Into his Native Sea,
   Vext at their Follies, murmur'd in his Stream;
   But disappointed of his fond Desire
   Would vanish in a *Pyramid of Fire*.
   This Surly, *Slipp'ry God*, when He design'd
         To furnish his Escapes,
   Ne'er borrow'd more *variety of Shapes*
   Than *You* to please and satisfie Mankind,      200
And seem (almost) transform'd to *Water, Flame, and Air*,
   *So well You answer all Phænomenaes there*;
Tho' Madmen and the Wits, Philosophers and Fools,
With all that Factious or Enthusiastick Dotards dream,
And all the incohærent Jargon of the Schools,
   Tho' all the Fumes of Fear, Hope, Love, and Shame,
*Contrive to shock your Minds, with many a sensless doubt*,
Doubts, where the *Delphick God* would grope in Ignorance
   and Night,
         The God of Learning and of Light
   *Would want a God Himself to help him out.*      210

210. *God Himself* . . . θεὸς ἀπὸ μηχανῆς.

## IX

Philosophy, as it before us lyes,
  Seems to have borrow'd some ungrateful tast
Of *Doubts,* Impertinence, and Niceties,
     From ev'ry Age through which it pass't,
But always with a stronger relish of the Last.
     This beauteous Queen by Heaven design'd
      To be the great Original
For Man to *dress and polish* his Uncourtly Mind,
In what *Mock-habits* have they put her, since the Fall!
  More oft in Fools and Mad-mens hands than Sages     220
    *She seems a Medly of all Ages,*
With a huge Fardingal to swell her Fustian Stuff,
A new Commode, a *Top-knot,* and a Ruff,
Her Face patch't o'er with *Modern Pedantry,*
     With a long sweeping Train
Of Comments and Disputes, ridiculous and vain,
*All of old Cut with a new Dye,*
How soon have You restor'd her Charms!
And rid her of her *Lumber and Her Books,*
  Drest her again Genteel and Neat,       230
    And rather Tite than Great,
How fond we are to court Her to our Arms!
*How much of Heav'n is in her naked looks.*

## X

Thus the *deluding Muse* oft blinds me to her Ways,
  And ev'n my very Thoughts transfers
And changes all to Beauty, and the Praise
    Of that proud Tyrant Sex of Hers.
    The *Rebel Muse,* alas, takes part
    But with my own Rebellious Heart,
And You with *fatal and Immortal Wit* conspire     240
    To fann th'unhappy Fire:
𝕮𝖗𝖚𝖊𝖑 𝖀𝖓𝖐𝖓𝖔𝖜𝖓! what is it You intend!
Ah, could You! could you hope *a Poet for your Friend!*
  Rather forgive what my first Transport said,
May all the Blood, which shall by *Womans scorn* be shed
  Lye on you, and on your Childrens Head,

For You (ah, did I think I e'er should live to see
   The fatal Time when that cou'd be)
   Have ev'n encreas't their *Pride and Cruelty.*
   Woman seems now above all Vanity grown,      250
     *Still boasting of Her Great Unknown;*
Platonick Champions, gain'd without one Female Wile,
    Or the vast 𝕮𝖍𝖆𝖗𝖌𝖊𝖘 𝖔𝖋 𝖆 𝕾𝖒𝖎𝖑𝖊;
   Which 'tis a shame to see how much of late
   You've taught the *Cov'tous* Wretches to o're-rate,
And which they've now the Conscience to way
   *In the same Ballance with our Tears,*
   And with such *Scanty* Wages pay
   The Bondage and the Slavery of Years.
Let the *vain sex* dream on, their Empire comes from Us,   260
   And had they *common* Generosity
    They would not use Us thus.
   Well—tho' you've rais'd Her to this high Degree,
    Our selves are rais'd as well as she,
   And 'spight of all that They or You can do,
   'Tis Pride and Happiness enough to Me
*Still to be of the same exalted Sex with You.*


# XI

   Alas, how fleeting, and how vain,
Is even the *nobler Man,* our Learning and our Wit,
   I sigh when e're I think of it      270
  As at the closing an unhappy Scene
   Of some *great King* and Conqu'rors Death,
   When the sad, melancholy Muse
   Stays but to catch his *utmost breath,*
I grieve, this Noble Work so happily begun,
So quickly, and so wonderfully carried on,
Must fall at last to Interest, Folly, and Abuse.
   There is a *Noon-tide* in our Lives
   Which still the sooner it arrives,
  Altho' we boast our *Winter-Sun looks bright,*   280
And foolishly are glad to see it at it's height

Yet so much sooner comes the long and gloomy Night.
    No Conquest ever yet begun
And by one mighty Hero carried to it's height
E'er flourish't under a Successor or a Son;
It lost some mighty Pieces thro' all hands it past
And vanisht to an *empty Title in the Last.*
  For when the animating Mind is fled,
    (Which Nature never can retain,
      Nor e'er call back again)        290
The Body, tho' Gigantick, lyes all *Cold and Dead.*

## XII

  And thus undoubtedly 'twill fare,
  With what unhappy Men shall dare,
*To be Successors to these Great Unknown,*
    On Learning's high-establish't Throne.
    Censure, and Pedantry, and Pride,
  Numberless Nations, stretching far and wide,
Shall (I foresee it) soon with *Gothick* Swarms come forth
    From Ignorance's Universal North,
And with blind Rage break all this peaceful Government;  300
Yet shall these *Traces of your Wit* remain
  Like a *just Map* to tell the vast Extent
  Of Conquest in your short and Happy Reign;
    And to all future Mankind shew
    How strange a *Paradox* is true,
*That Men, who liv'd and dy'd without a Name,*
*Are the chief Heroes in the sacred List of Fame.*

                           *Jonathan Swift*

# ODE

## *To the Hon^{ble} Sir* WILLIAM  TEMPLE

### I

VIRTUE, the greatest of all Monarchies,
   Till its first Emperor rebellious Man
     Depos'd from off his Seat
It fell, and broke with its own Weight
Into small States and Principalities,
   By many a petty Lord possess'd,
But ne'er since seated in one single Breast.
     'Tis you who must this Land subdue,
     The mighty Conquest's left for you,
     The Conquest and Discovery too:      10
     Search out this *Utopian* Ground,
     Virtue's *Terra Incognita*,
     Where none ever led the Way,
Nor ever since but in Descriptions found,
   Like the Philosopher's Stone,
With Rules to search it, yet obtain'd by none.

### II

   We have too long been led astray,
Too long have our misguided Souls been taught
   With Rules from musty Morals brought,
   'Tis you must put us in the Way;      20
   Let us (for shame) no more be fed
   With antique Reliques of the Dead,
   The Gleanings of Philosophy,
   Philosophy! the Lumber of the Schools,
   The Roguery of Alchymy,
     And we the bubbled Fools
Spend all our present Stock in hopes of golden Rules.

Printed from *Miscellanies. The Tenth Vol. By Dr. Swift.* London, 1745.

### III

But what does our proud Ign'rance Learning call,
   We odly *Plato*'s Paradox make good,
Our Knowledge is but mere Remembrance all,       30
   Remembrance is our Treasure and our Food;
Nature's fair Table-book our tender Souls
We scrawl all o'er with old and empty Rules,
   Stale Memorandums of the Schools;
   For Learning's mighty Treasures look
      In that deep Grave a Book,
   Think she there does all her Treasures hide,
And that her troubled Ghost still haunts there since she dy'd;
   Confine her Walks to Colleges and Schools,
   Her Priests, her Train and Followers show       40
   As if they all were Spectres too,
   They purchase Knowledge at the Expence
   Of common Breeding, common Sense,
   And at once grow Scholars and Fools;
   Affect ill-manner'd Pedantry,
Rudeness, Ill-nature, Incivility,
   And sick with Dregs of Knowledge grown,
   Which greedily they swallow down,
Still cast it up and nauseate Company.


### IV

Curst be the Wretch, nay doubly curst,       50
   (If it may lawful be
To curse our greatest Enemy)
Who learnt himself that Heresy first
   (Which since has seiz'd on all the rest)
That Knowledge forfeits all Humanity;
Taught us, like *Spaniards*, to be proud and poor,
   And fling our Scraps before our Door.
Thrice happy you have 'scap't this gen'ral Pest;
Those mighty Epithets, Learn'd, Good, and Great,
Which we ne'er join'd before, but in Romances meet,       60
   We find in you at last united grown.
     You cannot be compar'd to one,

I must, like him that painted *Venus'* Face,
    Borrow from every one a Grace;
*Virgil* and *Epicurus* will not do,
    Their courting a Retreat like you,
Unless I put in *Caesar*'s Learning too,
      Your happy Frame at once controuls
      This great triumvirate of Souls.


## V

Let not old *Rome* boast *Fabius*'s Fate,         70
    He sav'd his Country by Delays,
        But you by Peace,
    You bought it at a cheaper Rate;
Nor has it left the usual bloody Scar,
    To shew it cost its Price in War,
War! that mad Game, the World so loves to play,
    And for it does so dearly pay;
For though with Loss or Victory awhile
    Fortune the Gamesters does beguile,
Yet at the last the Box sweeps all away.        80


## VI

    Only the Laurel got by Peace
      No Thunder e'er can blast,
      Th' Artillery of the Skies
      Shoots to the Earth and dies;
Forever green and flourishing 'twill last,
Nor dipt in Blood, nor Widow's Tears, nor Orphan's Cries:
    About the Head crown'd with these Bays,
    Like Lambent Fire the Lightning plays;
Nor its triumphal Cavalcade to grace
    Make up its solemn Train with Death;      90
It melts the Sword of War, yet keeps it in the Sheath.


## VII

The wily Shafts of State, those Juggler's Tricks
Which we call deep Design and Politicks
(As in a Theatre the Ignorant Fry,
    Because the Cords escape their Eye
    Wonder to see the Motions fly)

Methinks, when you expose the Scene,
Down the ill-organ'd Engines fall;
Off fly the Vizards and discover all,
  How plain I see thro' the Deceit!        100
  How shallow! and how gross the Cheat!
  Look where the Pully's ty'd above!
  Great God! (said I) what have I seen!
    On what poor Engines move
The Thoughts of Monarchs, and Designs of States,
  What petty Motives rule their Fates!
How the Mouse makes the mighty Mountain shake!
The mighty Mountain labours with its birth,
  Away the frighted Peasants fly,
  Scar'd at th' unheard-of Prodigy,       110
Expect some great gigantick Son of Earth;
      Lo, it appears!
See, how they tremble! how they quake!
Out starts the little Beast, and mocks their idle Fears.

### VIII

  Then tell (dear fav'rite Muse)
What Serpent's that which still resorts,
Still lurks in Palaces and Courts,
    Take thy unwonted Flight,
    And on the Terras light.
      See where she lies!       120
    See how she rears her Head,
And rolls about her dreadful Eyes,
To drive all Virtue out, or look it dead!
'Twas sure this Basilisk sent *Temple* thence,
And tho' as some ('tis said) for their Defence
  Have worn a Casement o'er their Skin,
    So he wore his within,
Made up of Virtue and transparent Innocence:
  And tho' he oft renew'd the Fight,
And almost got priority of Sight,       130
  He ne'er could overcome her quite,
(In pieces cut, the Viper still did reunite)
  Till at last tir'd with loss of Time and Ease,
Resolv'd to give himself, as well as Country Peace.

## IX

Sing (belov'd Muse) the Pleasures of Retreat,
  And in some untouch'd Virgin Strain
Shew the Delights thy Sister Nature yields,
Sing of thy Vales, sing of thy Woods, sing of thy Fields;
    Go publish o'er the Plain
  How mighty a Proselyte you gain!                          140
How noble a Reprisal on the Great!
    How is the Muse luxuriant grown,
      Whene'er she takes this Flight
      She soars clear out of sight,
These are the Paradises of her own;
(The Pegasus, like an unruly Horse
    Tho' ne'er so gently led
To the lov'd Pasture where he us'd to feed,
Runs violently o'er his usual Course.)
      Wake from thy wanton Dreams,                          150
      Come from thy dear-lov'd Streams,
    The crooked Paths of wandering *Thames*.
    Fain the fair Nymph would stay,
    Oft she looks back in vain,
  Oft 'gainst her Fountain does complain,
And softly steals in many Windings down,
As loth to see the hated Court and Town,
    And murmurs as she glides away.


## X

    In this new happy Scene
  Are nobler Subjects for your learned Pen;                 160
    Here we expect from you
More than your Predecessor, *Adam*, knew;
Whatever moves our Wonder or our Sport,
Whatever serves for innocent Emblems of the Court;
    (How that which we a Kernel see,
Whose well-compacted Forms escape the Light,
    Unpierc'd by the blunt Rays of Sight)
    Shall e'er long grow into a Tree,
Whence takes it its Increase, and whence its Birth,
Or from the Sun, or from the Air, or from the Earth,       170

   Where all the fruitful Atoms lye,
    How some go downward to the Root,
  Some more ambitiously upwards fly,
And form the Leaves, the Branches, and the Fruit.
You strove to cultivate a barren Court in vain,
Your Garden's better worth your noble Pain,
Hence Mankind fell, and here must rise again.


### XI

Shall I believe a Spirit so divine
   Was cast in the same Mold with mine?
Why then does Nature so unjustly share          180
Among her Elder Sons the whole Estate[,]
   And all her Jewels and her Plate[?]
Poor we *Cadets* of Heav'n, not worth her Care,
Take up at best with Lumber and the Leavings of a Fate:
   Some she binds 'Prentice to the Spade,
   Some to the Drudgery of a Trade,
Some she does to *Egyptian* Bondage draw,
Bids us make Bricks, yet sends us to look out for Straw;
   Some she condemns for Life to try
To dig the leaden Mines of deep Philosophy:        190
Me she has to the Muse's Gallies ty'd,
In vain I strive to cross this spacious Main,
   In vain I tug and pull the Oar,
   And when I almost reach the Shore
Strait the Muse turns the Helm, and I launch out again;
     And yet to feed my Pride,
Whene'er I mourn, stops my complaining Breath,
With promise of a mad Reversion after Death.


### XII

Then (Sir,) accept this worthless Verse,
   The Tribute of an humble Muse,          200
'Tis all the Portion of my niggard Stars;
Nature the hidden Spark did at my Birth infuse,
And kindled first with Indolence and Ease,
   And since too oft debauch'd by Praise,
'Tis now grown an incurable Disease:

In vain to quench this foolish Fire I try
In Wisdom and Philosophy;
In vain all wholsome Herbs I sow,
Where nought but Weeds will grow.
Whate'er I plant (like Corn on barren Earth)     210
By an equivocal Birth
Seeds and runs up to Poetry.

# ODE

## *To Dr.* WILLIAM SANCROFT

### Late Lord Archbishop of CANTERBURY

### I

TRUTH is eternal, and the Son of Heav'n,
    Bright effluence of th' immortal ray,
Chief cherub, and chief lamp of that high sacred Seven,
Which guard the throne by night, and are its light by day:
    First of God's darling attributes,
        Thou daily seest Him face to face,
Nor does thy essence fix'd depend on giddy circumstance
        Of time or place,
Two foolish guides in ev'ry sublunary dance:
    How shall we find Thee then in dark disputes?     10
    How shall we search Thee in a battle gain'd,
    Or a weak argument by force maintain'd?
In dagger-contests, and th' artillery of words,
(For swords are madmen's tongues, and tongues are madmen's
        swords)
        Contriv'd to tire all patience out,
        And not to satisfy the doubt:

### II

    But where is ev'n thy Image on our earth?
        For of the person much I fear,
Since Heaven will claim its residence as well as birth,
And God himself has said, He shall not find it here.     20

Printed from *Miscellaneous Pieces*, 1789.

For this inferior world is but Heaven's dusky shade,
By dark reverted rays from its reflection made;
  Whence the weak shapes wild and imperfect pass,
Like sun-beams shot at too far distance from a glass;
    Which all the mimic forms express,
Tho' in strange uncouth postures, and uncomely dress;
      So when Cartesian artists try
      To solve appearances of sight
      In its reception to the eye,
And catch the living landscape thro' a scanty light,          30
      The figures all inverted shew,
      And colours of a faded hue;
Here a pale shape with upward footstep treads,
      And men seem walking on their heads;
      There whole herds suspended lie
  Ready to tumble down into the sky;
  Such are the ways ill-guided mortals go
  To judge of things above by things below.
Disjointing shapes as in the fairy-land of dreams,
      Or images that sink in streams;                         40
  No wonder, then, we talk amiss
  Of truth, and what, or where it is:
  Say Muse, for thou, if any, know'st
Since the bright essence fled, where haunts the reverend ghost?

### III

If all that our weak knowledge titles virtue, be
(High Truth) the best resemblance of exalted Thee,
  If a mind fix'd to combat fate
With those two pow'rful swords, Submission and Humility,
  Sounds truly good, or truly great;
Ill may I live, if the good SANCROFT in his holy rest,        50
      In the divin'ty of retreat,
  Be not the brightest pattern Earth can shew
      Of heav'n-born Truth below:
  But foolish Man still judges what is best
    In his own balance, false and light,
      Foll'wing Opinion, dark, and blind,
      That vagrant leader of the mind,
Till Honesty and Conscience are clear out of sight.

## IV

And some, to be large cyphers in a state,
Pleas'd with an empty swelling to be counted great;          60
Make their minds travel o'er infinity of space,
    Rapp'd through the wide expanse of thought,
  And oft in contradiction's vortex caught,
To keep that worthless clod, the body, in one place:
Errors like this did old Astronomers misguide,
Led blindly on by gross philosophy and pride,
    Who, like hard masters, taught the Sun
    Thro' many a needless sphere to run,
Many an eccentric and unthrifty motion make,
  And thousand incoherent journies take,          70
    Whilst all th' advantage by it got,
  Was but to light Earth's inconsiderable spot.
The herd beneath, who see the weathercock of state
  Hung loosely on the Church's pinnacle,
Believe it firm, because perhaps the day is mild and still;
But when they find it turn with the first blast of fate,
    By gazing upwards giddy grow,
    And think the Church itself does so;
    Thus fools, for being strong and num'rous known,
    Suppose the truth, like all the world, their own;          80
And holy SANCROFT's motion quite irregular appears,
    Because 'tis opposite to theirs.


## V

In vain then would the Muse the multitude advise,
  Whose peevish knowledge thus perversely lies
    In gath'ring follies from the wise;
  Rather put on thy anger and thy spight,
    And some kind pow'r for once dispense
  Thro' the dark mass, the dawn of so much sense,
To make them understand, and feel me when I write;
  The muse and I no more revenge desire,          90
Each line shall stab, shall blast, like daggers and like fire;
  Ah, BRITAIN, land of angels! which of all thy sins,
    (Say, hapless Isle, altho'
    It is a bloody list we know)

Has given thee up a dwelling-place to fiends?
　　Sin and the plague ever abound
In governments too easy, and too fruitful ground;
　　Evils which a too gentle king,
　　Too flourishing a spring,
　　And too warm summers bring:　　　　　　　　100
　　Our British soil is over-rank, and breeds
Among the noblest flow'rs a thousand pois'nous weeds,
　　And ev'ry stinking weed so lofty grows,
　　As if 'twould overshade the Royal Rose,
　　The Royal Rose the glory of our morn,
　　　　But, ah, too much without a thorn.


## VI

Forgive (Original Mildness) this ill-govern'd zeal,
　　'Tis all the angry slighted Muse can do
　　　In the pollution of these days;
No province now is left her but to rail,　　　　　110
And Poetry has lost the art to praise,
　　Alas, the occasions are so few:
　　None e'er but you,
　　And your Almighty Master, knew
　　With heavenly peace of mind to bear
(Free from our tyrant-passions, anger, scorn, or fear)
　　The giddy turns of pop'lar rage,
And all the contradictions of a poison'd age;
　　The Son of God pronounc'd by the same breath
　　Which strait pronounc'd his death;　　　　　120
　　And tho' I should but ill be understood
　　In wholly equalling our sin and theirs,
　　And measuring by the scanty thread of wit
　　What we call holy, and great, and just, and good,
(Methods in talk whereof our pride and ignorance make use)
　　And which our wild ambition foolishly compares
　　　With endless and with infinite;
　　Yet pardon, native ALBION, when I say
Among thy stubborn sons there haunts that spirit of Jews,
　　That those forsaken wretches who to-day　　130

Revile His great ambassador,
Seem to discover what they would have done
(Were his humanity on earth once more)
To his undoubted Master, Heaven's Almighty Son.

## VII

But zeal is weak and ignorant, tho' wond'rous proud,
    Though very turbulent and very loud;
        The crazy composition shews,
Like that fantastic medley in the idol's toes,
        Made up of iron mixt with clay,
        This, crumbles into dust,                    140
        That, moulders into rust,
        Or melts by the first show'r away.
Nothing is fix'd that mortals see or know,
Unless, perhaps, some stars above be so;
        And those, alas, do show
Like all transcendent excellence below;
    In both, false mediums cheat our sight,
And far exalted objects lessen by their height:
    Thus, primitive SANCROFT moves too high
    To be observ'd by vulgar eye,               150
        And rolls the silent year
        On his own secret regular sphere,
And sheds, tho' all unseen, his sacred influence here.

## VIII

Kind Star, still may'st thou shed thy sacred influence here,
    Or from thy private peaceful orb appear;
    For, sure, we want some guide from Heav'n to show
    The way which ev'ry wand'ring fool below
        Pretends so perfectly to know;
    And which for ought I see, and much I fear,
        The world has wholly miss'd;              160
    I mean, the way which leads to Christ:
Mistaken Ideots! see how giddily they run,
    Led blindly on by avarice and pride,
        What mighty numbers follow them;
        Each fond of erring with his guide:

Some whom ambition drives, seek Heaven's high Son
In Caesar's court, or in Jerusalem;
   Others, ignorantly wise,
Among proud Doctors and disputing Pharisees:
What could the Sages gain but unbelieving scorn;     170
   Their faith was so uncourtly when they said
That Heaven's high Son was in a village born;
     That the world's Saviour had been
     In a vile manger laid,
     And foster'd in a wretched inn.


### IX

Necessity, thou tyrant conscience of the great,
Say, why the Church is still led blindfold by the State?
   Why should the first be ruin'd and laid waste,
   To mend dilapidations in the last?
And yet the world, whose eyes are on our mighty Prince, 180
     Thinks Heav'n has cancel'd all our sins,
And that his subjects share his happy influence;
Follow the model close, for so I'm sure they should,
But wicked kings draw more examples than the good;
   And divine SANCROFT, weary with the weight
Of a declining Church, by Faction her worse foe opprest,
     Finding the Mitre almost grown
     A load as heavy as the Crown,
   Wisely retreated to his heavenly rest.


### X

   Ah, may no unkind earthquake of the State,     190
     Nor hurricano from the Crown,
Disturb the present Mitre, as that fearful storm of late,
   Which in its dusky march along the plain,
     Swept up whole churches as it list,
     Wrapp'd in a whirlwind and a mist;
Like that prophetic tempest in the virgin reign,
   And swallow'd them at last, or flung them down.
   Such were the storms good SANCROFT long has borne;
   The Mitre, which his sacred head has worn,
   Was, like his Master's Crown, inwreath'd with thorn. 200

Death's sting is swallow'd up in victory at last,
 The bitter cup is from him past:
 Fortune in both extremes,
 Tho' blasts from contrariety of winds,
 Yet to firm heavenly minds,
 Is but one thing under two different names;
And even the sharpest eye that has the prospect seen,
 Confesses ignorance to judge between;
And must, to human reasoning opposite, conclude
To point out which is moderation, which is fortitude.  210


# XI

Thus SANCROFT, in the exaltation of retreat,
 Shews lustre that was shaded in his seat;
 Short glimm'rings of the prelate glorify'd;
Which the disguise of greatness only served to hide;
 Why should the Sun, alas, be proud
 To lodge behind a golden cloud;
Tho' fring'd with ev'ning gold the cloud appears so gay,
'Tis but a low-born vapor kindled by a ray;
 At length 'tis over-blown and past,
 Puff'd by the people's spightful blast,  220
The daz'ling glory dimms their prostituted sight,
 No deflower'd eye can face the naked light:
 Yet does this high perfection well proceed
 From strength of its own native seed,
This wilderness the world, like that poetic wood of old,
 Bears one, and but one branch of gold,
 Where the bless'd spirit lodges like the dove,
And which (to heavenly soil transplanted) will improve,
To be, as 'twas below, the brightest plant above;
 For, whate'er theologic lev'llers dream,  230
  There are degrees above I know
  As well as here below,
(The goddess Muse herself has told me so)
Where high patrician souls dress'd heavenly gay,
Sit clad in lawn of purer woven day,

There some high spiritual throne to SANCROFT shall be given,
    In the metropolis of heaven;
Chief of the mitred saints, and from arch-prelate here,
    Translated to arch-angel there.


## XII

Since, happy Saint, since it has been of late        240
    Either our blindness or our fate,
    To lose the providence of thy cares,
Pity a miserable Church's tears,
That begs the pow'rful blessing of thy pray'rs.
Some angel say, what were the nation's crimes,
That sent these wild reformers to our times;
    Say what their senseless malice meant,
    To tear Religion's lovely face;
Strip her of ev'ry ornament and grace,
In striving to wash off th'imaginary paint:        250
    Religion now does on her death-bed lie,
Heart-sick of a high fever and consuming atrophy;
How the physicians swarm to shew their mortal skill,
And by their college-arts methodically kill:
Reformers and physicians differ but in name,
    One end in both, and the design the same;
    Cordials are in their talk, whilst all they mean
        Is but the patient's death, and gain—
        Check in thy satire, angry muse,
        Or a more worthy subject chuse:        260
    Let not the outcasts of this outcast age
    Provoke the honour of my Muse's rage,
        Nor be thy mighty spirit rais'd,
        Since Heaven and Cato both are pleas'd—

        [The rest of the poem is lost.]

# *To Mr.* CONGREVE

### Written November 1693

THRICE, with a prophet's voice and prophet's pow'r,
　The Muse was call'd in a poetic hour,
And insolently thrice, the slighted Maid
Dar'd to suspend her unregarded aid;
Then with that grief we form in spirits divine,
Pleads for her own neglect, and thus reproaches mine:
　Once highly honour'd! False is the pretence
You make to truth, retreat, and innocence;
Who, to pollute my shades, bring'st with thee down
The most ungen'rous vices of the town;　　　　　　10
Ne'er sprang a youth from out this isle before
I once esteem'd, and lov'd, and favour'd more,
Nor ever maid endur'd such court-like scorn,
So much in mode, so very city-born;
'Tis with a foul design the muse you send,
Like a cast mistress to your wicked friend;
But find some new address, some fresh deceit,
Nor practise such an antiquated cheat;
These are the beaten methods of the stews,
Stale forms of course, all mean deceivers use,　　　20
Who barbarously think to 'scape reproach,
By prostituting her they first debauch.
　Thus did the Muse severe unkindly blame
This off'ring long design'd to CONGREVE's fame;
First chid the zeal as unpoetic fire,
Which soon his merit forc'd her to inspire;
Then call this verse, that speaks her largest aid,
The greatest compliment she ever made,
And wisely judge, no pow'r beneath divine
Could leap the bounds which part your world and mine;　30

Printed from *Miscellaneous Pieces*, 1789.

For, youth, believe, to you unseen, is fix'd
A mighty gulph unpassable betwixt.
   Nor tax the goddess of a mean design
To praise your parts by publishing of mine;
That be my thought when some large bulky writ
Shews in the front the ambition of my wit;
There to surmount what bears me up, and sing
Like the victorious wren perch'd on the eagle's wing;
This could I do, and proudly o'er him tow'r,
Were my desires but heighten'd to my pow'r.            40
   Godlike the force of my young CONGREVE's bays,
Soft'ning the muse's thunder into praise;
Sent to assist an old unvanquish'd pride
That looks with scorn on half mankind beside;
*A pride that well suspends poor mortals fate,*
*Gets between them and my resentment's weight,*
*Stands in the gap 'twixt me and wretched men,*
*T'avert th'impending judgments of my pen.*
   Thus I look down with mercy on the age,
By hopes my CONGREVE will reform the stage;            50
For never did poetic mine before
Produce a richer vein or cleaner ore;
The bullion stampt in your refining mind
Serves by retail to furnish half mankind.
With indignation I behold your wit
Forc'd on me, crack'd, and clipp'd, and counterfeit,
By vile pretenders, who a stock maintain
From broken scraps and filings of your brain.
Through native dross your share is hardly known,
And by short views mistook for all their own;         60
So small the gain those from your wit do reap,
Who blend it into folly's larger heap,
Like the sun's scatter'd beams which loosely pass,
When some rough hand breaks the assembling-glass.
   Yet want your critics no just cause to rail,
Since knaves are ne'er oblig'd for what they steal.
These pad on wit's high road, and suits maintain
With those they rob, by what their trade does gain.
Thus censure seems that fiery froth which breeds
O'er the sun's face, and from his heat proceeds,       70

Crusts o'er the day, shadowing its parent beam
As antient nature's modern masters dream;
This bids some curious praters here below
Call Titan sick, because their sight is so;
And well, methinks, does this allusion fit
To scribblers, and the god of light and wit;
Those who by wild delusions entertain
A lust of rhiming for a poet's vein,
Raise envy's clouds to leave themselves in night,
But can no more obscure my CONGREVE's light          80
Than swarms of gnats, that wanton in a ray
Which gave them birth, can rob the world of day.
    What northern hive pour'd out these foes to wit?
Whence came these Goths to overrun the pit?
How would you blush the shameful birth to hear
Of those you so ignobly stoop to fear;
For, ill to them, long have I travell'd since
Round all the circles of impertinence,
Search'd in the nest where every worm did lie
Before it grew a city butterfly;          90
I'm sure I found them other kind of things
Than those with backs of silk and golden wings;
A search, no doubt, as curious and as wise
As virtuosoes' in dissecting flies;
For, could you think? the fiercest foes you dread,
And court in prologues, all are country-bred;
Bred in my scene, and for the poet's sins
Adjourn'd from tops and grammar to the inns;
Those beds of dung, where schoolboys sprout up beaus
Far sooner than the nobler mushroom grows:          100
These are the lords of the poetic schools,
Who preach the saucy pedantry of rules;
Those pow'rs the criticks, who may boast the odds
O'er Nile, with all its wilderness of gods;
Nor could the nations kneel to viler shapes,
Which worship'd cats, and sacrific'd to apes;
And can you think the wise forbear to laugh
At the warm zeal that breeds this golden calf?
    Haply you judge these lines severely writ
Against the proud usurpers of the pit;          110

Stay while I tell my story, short, and true;
To draw conclusions shall be left to you;
Nor need I ramble far to force a rule,
But lay the scene just here at Farnham school.
 Last year, a lad hence by his parents sent
With other cattle to the city went;
Where having cast his coat, and well pursu'd
The methods most in fashion to be lewd,
Return'd a finish'd spark this summer down,
Stock'd with the freshest gibberish of the town;     120
A jargon form'd from the lost language, wit,
Confounded in that Babel of the pit;
Form'd by diseas'd conceptions, weak, and wild,
Sick lust of souls, and an abortive child;
Born between whores and fops, by lewd compacts,
Before the play, or else between the acts:
Nor wonder, if from such polluted minds
Should spring such short and transitory kinds,
Or crazy rules to make us wits by rote
Last just as long as ev'ry cuckow's note:     130
What bungling, rusty tools, are us'd by fate!
'Twas in an evil hour to urge my hate,
*My hate, whose lash just heaven has long decreed*
*Shall on a day make sin and folly bleed;*
When man's ill genius to my presence sent
This wretch, to rouse my wrath, for ruin meant;
Who in his idiom vile, with Gray's-inn grace,
Squander'd his noisy talents to my face;
Nam'd ev'ry player on his fingers ends,
Swore all the wits were his peculiar friends;     140
Talk'd with that saucy and familiar ease
Of Wycherly, and you, and Mr. Bays;
Said, how a late report your friends had vex'd,
Who heard you meant to write heroics next;
For, tragedy, he knew, would lose you quite,
And told you so at Will's but t'other night.
 Thus are the lives of fools a sort of dreams,
Rend'ring shades, things, and substances of names;
Such high companions may delusion keep,
Lords are a footboy's cronies in his sleep.     150

CSPW

As a fresh miss, by fancy, face, and gown,
Render'd the topping beauty of the town,
Draws ev'ry rhyming, prating, dressing sot,
To boast of favours that he never got;
Of which, whoe'er lacks confidence to prate,
Brings his good parts and breeding in debate;
And not the meanest coxcomb you can find,
But thanks his stars, that Phyllis has been kind;
Thus prostitute my CONGREVE's name is grown
To ev'ry lew'd pretender of the town.                          160
'Troth I could pity you; but this is it,
You find, to be the fashionable wit;
These are the slaves whom reputation chains,
Whose maintenance requires no help from brains.
For, should the vilest scribbler to the pit,
Whom sin and want e'er furnish'd out a wit;
*Whose name must not within my lines be shewn,*
*Lest here it live, when perish'd with his own;*
Should such a wretch usurp my CONGREVE's place,
And chuse out wits who ne'er have seen his face;              170
I'll be[t] my life but the dull cheat would pass,
Nor need the lion's skin conceal the ass;
Yes, that beau's look, that voice, those critic ears,
Must needs be right, so well resembling theirs.

Perish the Muse's hour, thus vainly spent
In satire, to my CONGREVE's praises meant;
In how ill season her resentments rule,
What's that to her if mankind be a fool?
Happy beyond a private muse's fate,
In pleasing *all that's good among the great,*              180
Where tho' her elder sisters crowding throng,
She still is welcome with her inn'cent song;
Whom were my CONGREVE blest to see and know,
What poor regards would merit all below!
How proudly would he haste the joy to meet,
And drop his laurel at *Apollo*'s feet.

Here by a mountain's side, a reverend cave
Gives murmuring passage to a lasting wave;
'Tis the world's wat'ry hour-glass streaming fast,
Time is no more when th'utmost drop is past;              190

Here, on a better day, some druid dwelt,
And the young Muse's early favour felt;
Druid, a name she does with pride repeat,
Confessing Albion once her darling seat;
Far in this primitive cell might we pursue
Our predecessors foot-steps, still in view;
Here would we sing—But, ah! you think I dream,
And the bad world may well believe the same;
Yes; you are all malicious standers-by,
While two fond lovers prate, the Muse and I.     200
    Since thus I wander from my first intent,
Nor am that grave adviser which I meant;
Take this short lesson from the god of bayes,
And let my friend apply it as he please:

*Beat not the dirty paths where vulgar feet have trod,*
  *But give the vigorous fancy room.*
For when like stupid alchymists you try
    To fix this nimble god,
    This volatile mercury,
The subtil spirit all flies up in fume;     210
   Nor shall the bubbl'd virtuoso find
More than a fade insipid mixture left behind.

    Whilst thus I write, vast shoals of critics come,
And on my verse pronounce their saucy doom;
The Muse, like some bright country virgin, shows,
Fall'n by mishap amongst a knot of beaux;
They, in their lewd and fashionable prate,
Rally her dress, her language, and her gait;
Spend their base coin before the bashful maid,
Current like copper, and as often paid:     220
She, who on shady banks has joy'd to sleep
Near better animals, her father's sheep;
*Sham'd and amaz'd, beholds the chatt'ring throng,*
*To think what cattle she has got among;*
*But with the odious smell and sight annoy'd,*
*In haste she does th'offensive herd avoid.*
    'Tis time to bid my friend a long farewell,
The muse retreats far in yon chrystal cell;

Faint inspiration sickens as she flies,
Like distant echo spent, the spirit dies.     230
   In this descending sheet you'll haply find
Some short refreshment for your weary mind,
Nought it contains is common or unclean,
And once drawn up, is ne'er let down again.

# OCCASIONED BY
# SIR WILLIAM TEMPLE's LATE
# ILLNESS AND RECOVERY
## Written December 1693

STRANGE to conceive, how the same objects strike
   At distant hours the mind with forms so like!
Whether in time, deduction's broken chain
Meets, and salutes her sister link again;
Or hunted fancy, by a circling flight,
Comes back with joy to its own seat at night;
Or whether dead imagination's ghost
Oft hovers where alive it haunted most;
Or if thought's rolling globe her circle run,
Turns up old objects to the soul her sun;     10
Or loves the muse to walk with conscious pride
O'er the glad scene whence first she rose a bride:
   Be what it will; late near yon whisp'ring stream,
Where her own TEMPLE was her darling theme;
There first the visionary sound was heard,
When to poetic view the Muse appear'd.
Such seem'd her eyes, as when an evening ray
Gives glad farewell to a tempestuous day;
Weak is the beam to dry up nature's tears,
Still ev'ry tree the pendent sorrow wears;     20
*Such are the smiles where drops of chrystal show,*
*Approaching joy at strife with parting woe.*

Printed from *Miscellaneous Pieces*, 1789.

As when to scare th'ungrateful or the proud
Tempests long frown, and thunder threatens loud,
Till the blest sun to give kind dawn of grace
Darts weeping beams across heaven's wat'ry face;
When soon the peaceful bow unstring'd is shown,
A sign God's dart is shot, and wrath o'erblown;
Such to unhallowed sight the Muse divine
Might seem, when first she rais'd her eyes to mine.      30
What mortal change does in thy face appear,
Lost youth, she cry'd, since first I met thee here!
With how undecent clouds are overcast
Thy looks, when every cause of grief is past!
Unworthy the glad tidings which I bring,
Listen while the muse thus teaches thee to sing:
As parent earth, burst by imprison'd winds,
Scatters strange agues o'er men's sickly minds,
And shakes the atheist's knees; such ghastly fear
Late I beheld on every face appear;      40
Mild Dorothea, peaceful, wise and great,
Trembling beheld the doubtful hand of fate;
Mild Dorothea, whom we both have long
Not dar'd to injure with our lowly song;
Sprung from a better world, and chosen then
The best companion for the best of men:
As some fair pile, yet spar'd by zeal and rage,
Lives pious witness of a better age;
So men may see what once was womankind,
In the fair shrine of Dorothea's mind.      50
You that would grief describe, come here and trace
It's watery footsteps in Dorinda's face;
Grief from Dorinda's face does ne'er depart
Further than its own palace in her heart:
Ah, since our fears are fled, this insolent expel,
At least confine the tyrant to his cell.
And if so black the cloud, that heaven's bright queen
Shrouds her still beams; how should the stars be seen?
Thus, when Dorinda wept, joy ev'ry face forsook,
And grief flung sables on each menial look;      60
The humble tribe mourn'd for the quick'ning soul,
That furnish'd spirit and motion through the whole;

So would earth's face turn pale, and life decay,
Should heaven suspend to act but for a day;
So nature's craz'd convulsions make us dread
That time is sick, or the world's mind is dead.—
Take, youth, these thoughts, large matter to employ
The fancy furnish'd by returning joy;
And to mistaken man these truths rehearse,
Who dare revile the integrity of verse:                          70
Ah fav'rite youth, how happy is thy lot!—
But I'm deceiv'd, or thou regard'st me not;
Speak, for I wait thy answer, and expect
Thy just submission for this bold neglect.
   Unknown the forms we the high-priesthood use
At the divine appearance of the Muse,
Which to divulge might shake profane belief,
And tell the irreligion of my grief;
Grief that excus'd the tribute of my knees,
And shap'd my passion in such words as these.                     80
   Malignant goddess! bane to my repose,
Thou universal cause of all my woes;
Say, whence it comes that thou art grown of late
A poor amusement for my scorn and hate;
The malice thou inspir'st I never fail
On thee to wreak the tribute when I rail;
Fools common-place thou art, their weak ensconcing fort,
Th'appeal of dullness in the last resort:
Heaven with a parent's eye regarding earth,
Deals out to man the planet of his birth;                         90
But sees thy meteor blaze about me shine,
And passing o'er, mistakes thee still for mine:
Ah, should I tell a secret yet unknown,
That thou ne'er hadst a being of thy own,
But a wild form dependent on the brain,
Scatt'ring loose features o'er the optic vein;
Troubling the chrystal fountain of the sight,
Which darts on poets eyes a trembling light;
Kindled while reason sleeps, but quickly flies,
Like antic shapes in dreams, from waking eyes:                   100
In sum, a glitt'ring voice, a painted name,
A walking vapor, like thy sister fame.

But if thou be'st what thy mad vot'ries prate,
A female pow'r, loose-govern'd thoughts create;
Why near the dregs of youth perversely wilt thou stay,
So highly courted by the brisk and gay?
Wert thou right woman, thou shouldst scorn to look
On an abandon'd wretch by hopes forsook;
Forsook by hopes, ill fortune's last relief,
Assign'd for life to unremitting grief;                          110
For, let heaven's wrath enlarge these weary days,
If hope e'er dawns the smallest of its rays.
Time o'er the happy takes so swift a flight,
And treads so soft, so easy, and so light,
That we the wretched, creeping far behind,
Can scarce th'impression of his foot-steps find;
Smooth as that airy nymph so subtly borne
With inoffensive feet o'er standing corn;
Which bow'd by evening-breeze with bending stalks,
Salutes the weary trav'ller as he walks;                        120
But o'er th'afflicted with a heavy pace
Sweeps the broad scythe, and tramples on his face.
Down falls the summer's pride, and sadly shews
Nature's bare visage furrowed as he mows:
See Muse, what havock in these looks appear
These are the tyrant's trophies of a year;
Since hope his last and greatest foe is fled,
Despair and he lodge ever in its stead;
March o'er the ruin'd plain with motion slow,
Still scatt'ring desolation where they go.                      130
To thee I owe that fatal bent of mind,
Still to unhappy restless thoughts inclin'd;
To thee, what oft I vainly strive to hide,
That scorn of fools, by fools mistook for pride;
From thee whatever virtue takes its rise,
Grows a misfortune, or becomes a vice;
Such were thy rules to be poetically great,
"Stoop not to int'rest, flattery, or deceit;
"Nor with hir'd thoughts be thy devotion paid;
"Learn to disdain their mercenary aid;                          140
"Be this thy sure defence, thy brazen wall,
"Know no base action, at no guilt turn pale;

"And since unhappy distance thus denies
"T'expose thy soul, clad in this poor disguise;
"Since thy few ill-presented graces seem
"To breed contempt where thou hast hop'd esteem."—
    Madness like this no fancy ever seiz'd,
Still to be cheated, never to be pleas'd;
Since one false beam of joy in sickly minds
Is all the poor content delusion finds.—        150
There thy enchantment broke, and from this hour
I here renounce thy visionary pow'r;
And since thy essence on my breath depends,
Thus with a puff the whole delusion ends.

# POEMS
## 1698–1737

# VERSES

### wrote on a

## Lady's *Ivory Table-Book*

### *Anno* 1698

PERUSE my Leaves thro' ev'ry Part,
And think thou seest my owners Heart,
Scrawl'd o'er with Trifles thus; and quite
As hard, as sensless, and as light:
Expos'd to every Coxcomb's Eyes,
But hid with Caution from the Wise.
Here you may read (*Dear Charming Saint*)
Beneath (*A new Receipt for Paint*)
Here in Beau-spelling (*tru tel deth*)
There in her own (*far an el breth*)       10
Here (*lovely Nymph pronounce my doom*)
There (*A safe way to use Perfume*)
Here, a Page fill'd with Billet Doux;
On t'other side (*laid out for Shoes*)
(*Madam, I dye without your Grace*)
(Item, *for half a Yard of Lace.*)
Who that had Wit would place it here,
For every peeping Fop to jeer?
In power of Spittle and a Clout
When e're he please to blot it out;       20
And then to heighten the Disgrace
Clap his own Nonsense in the place.
Whoe're expects to hold his part
In such a Book and such a Heart,
If he be Wealthy and a Fool
Is in all Points the fittest Tool,
Of whom it may be justly said,
He's a Gold Pencil tipt with Lead.

Printed from *Miscellanies*, 1711, with corrections from *Works, Vol. II*, Dublin, 1735 (referred to hereafter as *Poems*, 1735).

# The Discovery

## An. 1699

WHEN wise L^d Berkeley first came here,
    We Irish Folks expected wonders,
Nor thought to find so great a Peer
E'er a week pas't committing Blunders:

Till on a Day cut out by Fate,
When Folks came thick to make their Court
Out slipp't a Mystery of State
To give the Town and Country Sport.

Now Enter Bush with new State-Airs,
His Lordship's premier Ministre,                    10
And who in all profound Affairs
Is held as needfull as His Glyster

With Head reclining on his Shoulder,
He deals, and Hears mysterious Chat;
While every ignorant Beholder
Asks of his Neighbor; Who is that?

With this He putt up to My Lord
The Courtiers kept their Distance due,
He twitcht his sleeve, and stole a word,
Then to a Corner both withdrew.                    20

Imagine now My Lord and Bush
Whisp'ring in Junto most profound,
Like good King Phys: and good King Ush:
While all the rest stood gaping round

Printed from Swift's Autograph, Fountaine MSS., Morgan Library.

9. *Bush.* My Lord's wise Secretary.
12. *Glyster.* Always taken before my Lord went to Council.

At length, a spark not too well bred
Of forward Face, and Ear acute,
Advanc't on tiptoe, lean'd his Head
To overheare the grand Dispute.

To learn what Northern Kings design,
Or from Whitehall some new Express,          30
Papists disarm'd, or Fall of Coin,
For sure (thought He) it can't be less.

My L<sup>d</sup>, s<sup>d</sup> Bush, a Friend and I
Disguis'd in two old thredbare Coats
Ere Mornings dawn stole out to spy
How markets went for Hey and Oats.

With that he draws two Handfulls out,
The one was Oats, the other Hay,
Putts This to's Excellency's Snout,
And begs, He would the other weigh.          40

My Lord seems pleas'd, but still directs
By all means to bring down the Rates,
Then with a Congee circumflex
Bush smiling round on all, retreats

Our Listner stood a while confus'd,
But gath'ring spirits, wisely ran for't,
Enrag'd to see the World abus'd
By two such whisp'ring Kings of Branford.


# The PROBLEM

DID ever Problem thus perplex,
    Or more employ the Female Sex?
So sweet a Passion who cou'd think,
Jove ever form'd to make a Stink?

Printed from Orrery Papers, Harvard Library.

The Ladys vow, and swear they'll try,
Whether it be a Truth, or Lye.
Love's Fire, it seems, like inward Heat,
Works in my Lord by Stool and Sweat,
Which brings a Stink from ev'ry Pore,
And from behind, and from before;                    10
Yet, what is wonderful to tell it,
None but the Fav'rite Nymph can smell it.
    But now, to solve the Nat'ral Cause
By sober, Philosophick Laws,
Whether all Passions, when in Ferment,
Work out, as Anger does in Vermin?
So, when a Weasel you torment,
You find his Passion by his Scent.
We read of Kings, who in a Fright,
Tho' on a Throne, wou'd fall to shite.                20
Beside all this, deep Scholars know,
That the main String of Cupid's Bow,
Once on a Time, was an Asses Gut,
Now to a nobler Office put,
By Favour, or Desert preferr'd
From giving Passage to a Turd.
But still, tho' fixt among the Stars,
Does sympathize with Human Arse.
Thus when you feel an hard-bound Breech
Conclude Love's Bow-String at full Stretch;           30
Till the kind Looseness comes, and then
Conclude the Bow relax'd again.
    And now the Ladys all are bent,
To try the great Experiment;
Ambitious of a Regent's Heart
Spread all their Charms to catch a Fart;
Watching the first unsav'ry Wind,
Some ply before, and some behind.
My Lord, on Fire amidst the Dames,
Farts like a Laurel in the Flames.                    40
The Fair approach the speaking Part,
To try the Back-way to his Heart;
For, as when we a Gun discharge,
Altho' the Bore be ne'er so large,

Before the Flame from Muzzle burst,
Just at the Breech it flashes first:
So from my Lord his Passion broke,
He farted first, and then he spoke.
   The Ladys vanish, in the Smother,
To confer Notes with one another;      50
And now they all agree, to name
Whom each one thought the happy Dame:
Quoth Neal, whate'er the rest may think,
I'm sure, 'twas I that smelt the Stink.
You smell the Stink? by God you lye,
Quoth Ross, for, I'll be sworn, 'twas I.
Ladys, quoth Levens, pray forbear,
Let's not fall out; We all had Share.
And, by the most we can discover,
My Lord's an universal Lover.      60


# TO THEIR

# EXCELLENCIES

## THE

## *Lords Justices of* Ireland

### *The Humble Petition of* Frances Harris,

### *Who must Starve, and Die a Maid if it miscarries*

#### *Anno* 1700

*Humbly Sheweth*

THAT I went to warm my self in Lady *Betty*'s Chamber,
because I was cold,
And I had in a Purse, seven Pound, four Shillings and six
Pence, besides Farthings, in Money, and Gold;

Printed from *Miscellanies*, 1711, with corrections from *Poems*, 1735.

*Title.* EXCELLENCIES. Earl of Berkeley, and the Earl of Galway.

So because I had been buying things for my *Lady* last Night,
I was resolved to tell my Money, to see if it was right:
Now you must know, because my Trunk has a very bad Lock,
Therefore all the Money, I have, which, *God* knows, is a very
    small Stock,
I keep in a Pocket ty'd about my Middle, next my Smock.
So when I went to put up my Purse, as *God* would have it, my
    Smock was unript,
And, instead of putting it into my Pocket, down it slipt:
Then the Bell rung, and I went down to put my *Lady* to Bed,  10
And, *God* knows, I thought my Money was as safe as my
    Maidenhead.
So when I came up again, I found my Pocket feel very light,
But when I search'd, and miss'd my Purse, *Lord!* I thought I
    should have sunk outright:
*Lord! Madam*, says *Mary*, how d'ye do? Indeed, said I, never
    worse;
But pray, *Mary*, can you tell what I have done with my Purse!
*Lord* help me, said *Mary*, I never stirr'd out of this Place!
Nay, said I, I had it in Lady *Betty*'s Chamber, that's a plain Case.
So *Mary* got me to Bed, and cover'd me up warm,
However, she stole away my Garters, that I might do my self
    no Harm:
So I tumbl'd and toss'd all Night, as you may very well think,  20
But hardly ever set my Eyes together, or slept a Wink.
So I was a-dream'd, methought, that we went and search'd
    the Folks round,
And in a Corner of Mrs. *Duke*'s Box, ty'd in a Rag, the Money
    was found.
So next Morning we told *Whittle*, and he fell a Swearing;
Then my Dame *Wadgar* came, and she, you know, is thick of
    Hearing;
*Dame*, said I, as loud as I could bawl, do you know what a
    Loss I have had?
Nay, said she, my Lord *Collway*'s Folks are all very sad,
For my Lord *Dromedary* comes a *Tuesday* without fail;

23. *Mrs. Dukes.* A servant, wife of one of the footmen.
24. *Whittle.* Earl of Berkeley's Valet.
25. *Dame Wadgar.* The old deaf housekeeper.
28. *Dromedary.* Drogheda and the Primate were to succeed the two Earls.

Pugh! said I, but that's not the Business that I ail.
Says *Cary*, says he, I have been a Servant this Five and Twenty
    Years, come Spring,                              30
And in all the Places I liv'd, I never heard of such a Thing.
Yes, says the *Steward*, I remember when I was at my Lady
    *Shrewsbury*'s,
Such a thing as this happen'd, just about the time of *Goosberries*.
So I went to the Party suspected, and I found her full of Grief;
(Now you must know, of all Things in the World, I hate a
    Thief.)
However, I was resolv'd to bring the Discourse slily about,
Mrs. *Dukes*, said I, here's an ugly Accident has happen'd out;
'Tis not that I value the Money three Skips of a Louse;
But the Thing I stand upon, is the Credit of the House;
'Tis true, seven Pound, four Shillings, and six Pence, makes a
    great Hole in my Wages,                          40
Besides, as they say, Service is no Inheritance in these Ages.
Now, Mrs. *Dukes*, you know, and every Body understands,
That tho' 'tis hard to judge, yet Money can't go without Hands.
The *Devil* take me, said she, (blessing her self,) if ever I saw't!
So she roar'd like a *Bedlam*, as tho' I had call'd her all to naught;
So you know, what could I say to her any more,
I e'en left her, and came away as wise as I was before.
Well: But then they would have had me gone to the Cunning
    Man;
No, said I, 'tis the same Thing, the *Chaplain* will be here anon.
So the *Chaplain* came in. Now the Servants say, he is my
    Sweet-heart,                                   50
Because he's always in my Chamber, and I always take his
    Part;
So, as the *Devil* would have it, before I was aware, out I
    blunder'd,
*Parson*, said I, can you cast a *Nativity*, when a Body's plunder'd?
(Now you must know, he hates to be call'd *Parson*, like the
    *Devil*.)
Truly, says he, Mrs. *Nab*, it might become you to be more civil:
If your Money be gone, as a Learned *Divine* says, d'ye see,
You are no *Text* for my Handling, so take that from me:

      30. *Cary*. Clerk of the Kitchen.
      38. *three Skips of a Louse*. An usual Saying of Hers.

I was never taken for a *Conjurer* before, I'd have you to know.
*Lord*, said I, don't be angry, I am sure I never thought you so;
You know, I honour the Cloth, I design to be a *Parson's*
 Wife,             60
I never took one in *Your Coat* for a *Conjurer* in all my Life.
With that, he twisted his Girdle at me like a Rope, as who
 should say,
Now you may go hang your self for me, and so went away.
Well; I thought I should have swoon'd: *Lord*, said I, what shall
 I do?
I have lost my *Money*, and I shall lose my *True-Love* too.
So, my *Lord* call'd me; *Harry*, said my *Lord*, don't cry,
I'll give something towards thy Loss; and says my *Lady*, so
 will I.
Oh but, said I, what if after all the Chaplain won't *come to?*
For that, he said, (an't please your *Excellencies*) I must Petition
 You.

The Premises tenderly consider'd, I desire your *Excellencies*
 Protection,         70
And that I may have a Share in next *Sunday's* Collection:
And over and above, that I may have your *Excellencies* Letter,
With an Order for the *Chaplain* aforesaid; or instead of Him,
 a Better:
And then your poor *Petitioner*, both Night and Day,
Or the *Chaplain*, (for 'tis his *Trade*) as in Duty bound, shall
 ever *pray*.

# A BALLAD

## *on the Game of* Traffick

M**Y** *Lord* to find out who must deal
 Delivers Cards about,
But the first Knave does seldom fail
 To find the *Doctor* out.

Printed from *Works, Vol. VIII*, Dublin, 1746.

66. *Harry.* A Cant Word of my Lord and Lady to Mrs. Harris.

But then his *Honour* cry'd, Godzooks!
  And seem'd to knit his Brow;
For on a Knave he never looks
  But H' thinks upon *Jack How*.

My *Lady* tho' she is no Player
  Some bungling Partner takes,                    10
And wedg'd in Corner of a Chair
  Takes Snuff, and holds the Stakes.

Dame *Floyd* looks out in grave Suspence
  For Pair-royals and Sequents;
But wisely cautious of her Pence,
  The Castle seldom frequents.

Quoth *Herries*, fairly putting Cases,
  I'd won it on my Word,
If I had but a Pair of Aces,
  And could pick up a Third.                      20

But *Weston* has a new-cast Gown
  On *Sundays* to be fine in,
And if she can but win a *Crown*,
  'Twill just new dye the Lining.

"With these is Parson *Swift*,
  "Not knowing how to spend his Time,
"Does make a wretched Shift,
  "To deafen 'em with Puns and Rhime."

25–28. Lady Berkeley finding this Ballad in the Author's Room unfinished, she
underwrit the last Stanza, and left the Paper where she had found it; which
occasioned the following Song, that the Author wrote in a counterfeit Hand, as
if a third Person had done it.

# *Lady* Betty Berkeley *finding in the Authors Room some Verses Unfinished, underwrit a* Stanza *of her own, with Railery upon him, which gave Occasion to this Ballade*

*August* 1702

*To the Tune of the Cutpurse*

### I

ONCE on a time, as old Stories reherse,
    A Fryer would needs show his Talent in *Latin*;
But was sorely put to't in the midst of a Verse,
    Because he could find no Word to come pat in.
        Then all in the Place
        He left a void Space,
And so went to Bed in a desperate Case.
When behold the next Morning, a wonderful Riddle,
He found it was strangely fill'd up in the Middle.

Cho. *Let Censuring Criticks then think what they list on't,*    10
    *Who would not Write Verses with such an assistant.*

### II

This put me the Fryar into an Amazement,
    For he wisely consider'd it must be a Sprite,
That came through the Key-Hole, or in at the Casement,
    And it needs must be one that could both Read and Write:
        Yet he did not know
        If it were Friend or Foe,
Or whether it came from Above or Below.
Howe'er it was civil in Angel or Elf,
For he ne're could have fill'd it so well of himself.    20

Cho. *Let Censuring,* &c.

Printed from *Miscellanies*, 1711, with corrections from *Poems*, 1735.

### III

Even so Master Doctor had Puzzled his Brains
   In making a Ballad, but was at a Stand,
He had mixt little Wit with a great deal of Pains,
   When he found a new Help from Invisible Hand.
      Then Good Dr. *Swift*
      Pay Thanks for the Gift,
For you freely must own you were at a Dead lift;
And tho' some Malicious Young Spirit did do't,
You may know by the Hand, it had no Cloven Foot.   30

Cho. *Let Censuring Criticks then think what they list on't,*
    *Who would not Write Verses with such an assistant.*


# Vanbrug's House

## An. 1703

### Built from the burnt Ruins of Whitehall

[p. 1]  IN times of old, when Time was young,
     And Poets their own Verses sung,
   A Song could draw a Stone or Beam,
   That now would overload a Team,
   Lead them a Dance of many a Mile,
   Then rear 'em to a goodly Pile,
   Each Number had it's diff'rent Power;
   Heroick Strains could build a Tower;
   Sonnets and Elegyes to Chloris
   Would raise a House about two Storyes;   10
   A Lyrick Ode would Slate; a Catch
   Would Tile; an Epigram would Thatch.
    Now Poets find this Art is lost,
   Both to their own and Landlord's Cost;
   Not one of all the tunefull Throng
   Can hire a Lodging for a Song;

Printed from Swift's autograph, Fountaine MSS., Morgan Library.

For Jove consider'd well the Case,
That Poets were a numerous Race,
And if they all had Power to build,
The Earth would very soon be filld:                    20

[p. 2]    Materials would be quickly spent,
And Houses would not give a Rent.
The God of Wealth was therefore made
Sole Patron of the building Trade,
Leaving to Wits the spatious Air,
With License to build Castles there;
And 'tis conceiv'd, their old Pretence
To lodge in Garrats comes from thence.

There is a Worm by Phœbus bred,
By Leaves of Mulberry is fed;                          30
Which unprovided where to dwell,
Consumes it self to weave a Cell.
Then curious Hands this Texture take,
And for themselves fine Garments make.
Mean time a Pair of awkward Things
Grew to his Back instead of Wings;
He flutters when he Thinks he flyes,
Then sheds about his Spaun, and dyes.

Just such an Insect of the Age
Is he that scribbles for the Stage;                    40
His Birth he does from Phœbus raise,
And feeds upon imagin'd Bays:

[p. 3]    Throws all his Witt and Hours away
In twisting up an ill-spun Play:
This gives him Lodging, and provides
A Stock of tawdry Stuff besides,
With the unravelld Shreds of which
The Under-wits adorn their Speech.
And now he spreads his little Fans,
(For all the Muses Geese are Swans)                    50
And borne on fancy's Pinions, thinks,
He soars sublimest when he Sinks:
But scatt'ring round his Fly-blows, dyes;
Whence Broods of insect Poets rise.

Premising thus in Modern way
The greater half I had to say,

Sing Muse the House of Poet Van
In higher Strain than we began.
    Van, (for 'tis fit the Reader know it)
Is both a Herald and a Poet;                          60
No wonder then, if nicely skill'd
In each Capacity to Build:
As Herald, he can in a Day
Repair a House gone to decay;
[p. 4]  Or by Atchievments, Arms, Device
Erect a new one in a Trice;
And Poets if they had their Due,
By antient Right are Builders too.
This made him to Apollo pray
For Leave to build the Poet's Way.                    70
His Pray'r was granted, for the God
Consented with the usuall Nod.
After hard Throws of many a Day
Van was deliver'd of a Play,
Which in due time brought forth a House;
Just as the Mountain did the Mouse;
One Story high, one postern Door,
And one small Chamber on a Floor.
Born like a Phœnix from the Flame,
But neither Bulk nor Shape the same:                  80
As Animals of largest Size
Corrupt to Maggots Worms and Flyes.
A Type of Modern Witt and Style,
The Rubbish of an antient Pile.
So Chymists boast they have a Power
From the dead Ashes of a Flow'r
[p. 5]  Some faint Resemblance to produce,
But not the Virtue Tast nor Juyce.
So, Modern Rhymers strive to blast
The Poetry of Ages past,                              90
Which having wisely overthrown,
They from it's Ruins build their own.

# THE DESCRIPTION

OF A

## Salamander

*Out of* Pliny *Nat. Hist.* L. 10 C. 67 *and* L. 29 C. 4

*Anno* 1705

AS Mastive Dogs in Modern Phrase are
Call'd *Pompey, Scipio* and *Cæsar*;
As *Pies* and *Daws* are often stil'd
With Christian Nick-names like a Child;
As we say, *Monsieur*, to an *Ape*
Without offence to Human Shape:
So men have got from Bird and Brute
Names that would best their Natures suit:
The *Lyon, Eagle, Fox* and *Boar*
Were Hero's Titles heretofore,                          10
Bestow'd as Hi'roglyphicks fit
To shew their Valor, Strength or Wit.
For, what is understood by *Fame*
Besides the getting of a Name?
But e're since Men invented Guns,
A different way their Fancy runs;
To paint a Hero, we enquire
For something that will conquer *Fire*.
Would you describe *Turenne* or *Trump*
Think of a Bucket or a Pump.                            20
Are these too low?—then find out grander,
Call my Lord *Cutts* a *Salamander*.
'Tis well.—But since we live among
Detractors with an evil Tongue,
Who may object against the Term,
*Pliny* shall prove what we affirm:
*Pliny* shall prove, and we'll apply,
And I'll be judg'd by standers-by.

Printed from *Miscellanies*, 1711, with corrections from *Poems*, 1735.

FIRST then, our Author has defin'd
This Reptil, of the Serpent kind,                    30
With gawdy Coat, and shining Train,
But loathsom Spots his Body stain:
Out from some Hole obscure he flies
When Rains descend, and Tempests rise,
Till the Sun clears the Air; and then
Crawls back neglected to his Den.

SO when the War has rais'd a Storm
I've seen a *Snake* in human Form,
All stain'd with Infamy and Vice,
Leap from the Dunghill in a trice,                   40
Burnish and make a gaudy show,
Become a General, Peer and Beau,
Till Peace hath made the Sky serene,
Then shrink into it's Hole again.

*All this we grant—why, then look yonder*
*Sure that must be a* Salamander!

FARTHER, we are by *Pliny* told
This *Serpent* is extreamly cold,
So cold, that put it in the Fire,
'Twill make the very Flames expire,                  50
Beside, it Spues a filthy Froth,
(Whether thro' Rage or Love, or both)
Of Matter purulent and white
Which happening on the Skin to light,
And there corrupting to a Wound
Spreads Leprosy and Baldness round.

SO have I seen a batter'd Beau
By Age and Claps grown cold as Snow,
Whose Breath or Touch, where e'er he came,
Blew out Love's Torch or chill'd the Flame:          60
And should some Nymph who ne'er was cruel,
Like *Carleton* cheap, or fam'd *Du-Ruel*,
Receive the Filth which he ejects,
She soon would find the same Effects,

Her tainted Carcase to pursue,
As from the *Salamander's* Spue;
A dismal shedding of her Locks
And, if no Leprosy, a Pox.

> *Then I'll appeal to each By-stander,*
> *If this be not a* Salamander?          70


# The History of Vanbrug's House

## 1706

[p. 1] WHEN Mother Clud had rise[n] from Play,
    And call'd to take the Cards away,
Van saw, but seemd not to regard,
How Miss pickt ev'ry painted Card,
And busy both with Hand and Eye
Soon reard a House two Storyes high;
Van's Genius without Thought or Lecture
Is hugely turnd to Architecture,
He saw the Edifice and smil'd,
Vow'd it was pretty for a Child;          10
It was so perfect in its kind,
He kept the Model in his Mind.
But when he found the Boys at play,
And saw them dabling in their Clay,
He stood behind a Stall to lurk,
And mark the Progress of their Work,
With true Delight observed them all
Raking up Mud to build a Wall;
The Plan he much admir'd, and took
The Model in his Table-book;          20
Thought himself now exactly skill'd,
And so resolv'd a House to build;
[p. 2] A reall House with Rooms and Stairs,
Five times at least as big as theirs,

Printed from Swift's autograph, Fountaine MSS., Morgan Library.

    Taller than Misse's by two yards,
    Not a sham Thing of Clay or Cards.
    And so he did; for in a while
    He built up such a monstrous Pile,
    That no two Chairmen could be found
    Able to lift it from the Ground;          30
    Still at Whitehall it stands in view,
    Just in the Place where first it grew,
    There all the little School-boys run
    Envying to see themselves outdone.
       From such deep Rudiments as these
    Van is become by due Degrees
    For Building fam'd, and justly reckond
    At Court, Vitruvius the second,
    No wonder, since wise Authors shew,
    That best Foundations must be low.        40
    And now the Duke has wisely ta'ne him
    To be his Architect at Blenheim.
[p. 3]    But Raillery, for once, apart,
    If this Rule holds in ev'ry Art,
    Or if his Grace were no more skilld in
    The Art of battring Walls, than building,
    We might expect to find next Year
    A Mousetrap-man chief Engineer.

# The Story of Baucis & Philemon

## Ov. Met. i. 8

[p. 1]  IN antient Time, as Story tells
     The Saints would often leave their Cells
    And strole about, but hide their Quality,
    To try the People's Hospitality.
       It happen'd on a Winter's night,
    As Authors of the Legend write

Printed from Swift's autograph, Fountaine MSS., Morgan Library.

Two Brother-Hermits, Saints by Trade
Taking their Tour in Masquerade
Came to a Village hard by Rixham
Ragged, and not a Groat betwixt 'em.                    10
It rain'd as hard as it could pour,
Yet they were forc't to walk an Hour
From House to House, wett to the Skin
Before one Soul would let 'em in.
They call'd at ev'ry Dore; Good People,
My Comrade's Blind, and I'm a Creeple
Here we ly starving in the Street
'Twould grieve a Body's Heart to see't:
No Christian would turn out a Beast
In such a dreadfull Night at least;                    20
Give us but Straw, and let us Ly
In yonder Barn to keep us dry.
Thus in the Strolers usuall Cant
They beg'd Relief which none would grant;
[p. 2]  No Creature valu'd what they se'd:
One Family was gone to bed;
The Master Bawl'd out half asleep
You Fellows, what a Noise you keep!
So many Beggers pass this way,
We can't be quiet Night nor day;                       30
We can not serve You every One,
Pray take your Answer and be gone.
One swore he'd send 'em to the Stocks,
A third could not forbear his Mocks,
But bawl'd as loud as he could roar,
You're on the wrong side of the Door.
One surly Clown lookt out, and said,
I'll fling the P— pot on your head;
You sha'n't come here nor get a Sous
You look like Rogues would rob a House                 40
Can't you go work, or serve the King?
You blind and lame! tis no such Thing
That's but a counterfeit sore Leg:
For shame! two sturdy Rascalls beg;
If I come down, I'll spoil your Trick
And cure You both with a good Stick.

[p. 3]     Our wand'ring Saints in wofull State,
           Treated at this ungodly Rate
           Having thro all the Village pass't,
           To a small Cottage came at last                    50
           Where dwelt a poor old honest Yeman
           Call'd thereabouts Goodman Philemon;
           Who kindlly did the Saints invite
           In his poor House to pass the Night;
           And then the hospitable Sire
           Bade Goody Baucis mend the Fire
           Whilst he from out the Chimny took
           A Flitch of Bacon off the Hook,
           And freely from the fattest Side
           Cutt off large Slices to be fry'd;                  60
           Which tosst up in a Pan with Batter,
           And serv'd up in an earthen Platter;
           Quoth Baucis, this is wholsom Fare,
           Eat, Honest Friends, and never spare,
           And if we find our Vittels fail
           We can but make it out in Ale.
               To a small Kilderkin of Beer
           Brew'd for the good time of the Year
           Philemon by his Wife's consent
           Step't with a Jug, and made a Vent;                 70
[p. 4]     And having fill'd it to the Brink,
           Invited both the Saints to Drink.
           When they had took a second Draught,
           Behold, a Miracle was wrought
           For, Baucis with Amazement found
           Although the Jug had twice gone round
           It still was full up to the Top
           As if they ne're had drunk a drop.
           You may be sure, so strange a Sight
           Put the old People in a Fright;                     80
           Philemon whisper'd to his Wife,
           These Men are Saints I'll lay my Life
           The Strangers overheard, and said,
           You're in the right, but be'n't afraid
           No hurt shall come to You or Yours;
           But for that Pack of churlish Boors

Not fitt to live on Christian Ground,
They and their Village shall be droun'd,
Whilst You shall see your Cottage rise,
And grow a Church before your Eyes.                    90
  Scarce had they spoke when fair and soft
The Roof began to mount aloft
[p. 5] Aloft rose ev'ry Beam and Rafter,
The heavy Wall went clamb'ring after.
The Chimny widen'd and grew high'r,
Became a Steeple with a Spire:
The Kettle to the Top was hoist
And there stood fastned to a Joyst,
But with the upside doun to shew
It's Inclination for below;                            100
In vain; for a superior Force
Apply'd at Bottom stops it's Course;
Doomd ever in suspense to dwell,
Tis now no Kettle but a Bell.
The groaning Chair began to crawll
Like a huge Insect up the Wall,
There stuck, and to a Pulpitt grew,
But kept it's Matter and it's Hue,
And mindfull of it's antient State,
Still Groans while tatling Gossips prate.              110
  The Mortar onely chang'd it's Name,
In it's old shape a Font became
  The Porrengers that in a Row
Hung high and made a glitt'ring Show
[p. 6] To a less noble Substance chang'd
Were now but leathern Buckets rang'd.
  The Ballads pasted round the Wall,
Of Chivy-chase, and English Mall,
Fair Rosamond, and Robin Hood,
The little Children in the Wood,                       120
Enlarg'd in Picture, Size and Letter
And painted, lookt abundance better
And now the Heraldry describe
Of a Churchwarden or a Tribe.
  The wooden Jack which had almost
Lost by Disuse the Art to roast

A sudden Alteration feels,
Encreas't by new intestin Wheels
But what adds to the Wonder more,
The Number made the Motion slower          130
The Fly'r, altho't had leaden Feet,
Would turn so quick you scarce could see't
But now stopt by some hidden Pow'rs
Moves round but twice in twice twelve Hours
While in the Station of a Jack
'Twas never known to turn its back
A Friend in Turns and Windings try'd
Nor ever left the Chimny side.
[p. 7] The Chimny to a Steeple grown,
The Jack would not be left alone           140
But up against the Steeple rear'd,
Became a Clock, and still adher'd,
And still it's Love to Houshold Cares
By a shrill Voice at noon declares,
Warning the Cook-maid not to burn
That Roast-meat which it cannot turn.
    A Bed-sted in the antique mode
Compos'd of Timber many a Load;
Such as our Grandfathers did use,
Was Metamorphos't into Pews;               150
Which yet their former Virtue keep,
By lodging Folks dispos'd to sleep.
    The Cottage with such Feats as these
Grown to a Church by just Degrees,
The holy Men desir'd their Host
To ask for what he fancy'd most.
Philemon having paus'd a while
Reply'd in complementall Style:
Your Goodness more than my Desert
Makes you take all things in good Part:    160
[p. 8] You've rais'd a Church here in a Minute,
And I would fain continue in it;
I'm good for little at my days;
Make me the Parson if you please.
He spoke, and presently he feels
His Grazier's Coat reach down his Heels,

The Sleeves new border'd with a List
Widn'd and gatherd at his Wrist;
But being old continued just
As threadbare, and as full of Dust.                    170
A shambling awkward Gate he took,
With a demure dejected Look.
Talkt of his Off'rings, Tyths, and Dues,
Could Smoak, and Drink, and read the News;
Or sell a Goose at the next Toun
Decently hid beneath his Goun.
Contrivd to preach his Sermon next
Chang'd in the Preface and the Text:
Carry'd it to his Equalls high'r,
But most obsequious to the Squire.                     180

&c

# VERSES

*said to be written on the*

# UNION

THE Queen has lately lost a Part
Of her entirely-*English* Heart,
For want of which by way of Botch,
She piec'd it up again with *Scotch*.
Blest Revolution, which creates
Divided Hearts, united States.
See how the double Nation lies;
Like a rich Coat with Skirts of Frize:
As if a Man in making Posies
Should bundle Thistles up with Roses                   10
Whoever yet a Union saw
Of Kingdoms, without Faith or Law.
Henceforward let no Statesman dare,
A Kingdom to a Ship compare;

Printed from *Works, Vol. VIII,* Dublin, 1746.

Lest he should call our Commonweal,
A Vessel with a double Keel:
Which just like ours, new rigg'd and man'd,
And got about a League from Land,
By Change of Wind to Leeward Side
The Pilot knew not how to guide.                    20
So tossing Faction will o'erwhelm
Our crazy double-bottom'd Realm.


# An ELEGY on

## Mr. *PATRIGE*, the Almanack-maker,

## who Died on the 29th of this Instant *March*, 1708

WELL, 'tis as *Bickerstaff* has guest,
Tho' we all took it for a Jest:
*Patrige* is Dead, nay more, he dy'd
E'er he could prove the good *Squire* ly'd.
Strange, an Astrologer should Die,
Without one Wonder in the Sky;
Not one of all his *Crony* Stars,
To pay their Duty at his Hearse?
No Meteor, no Eclipse appear'd?
No Comet with a Flaming Beard?                    10
The Sun has rose, and gone to Bed,
Just as if *Patrige* were not Dead;
Nor hid himself behind the Moon,
To make a dreadful Night at Noon:
He at fit Periods walks through *Aries*,
Howe'er our Earthly Motion varies,
And twice a Year he'll cut th' *Æquator*,
As if there had been no such Matter.
   Some Wits have wondred what Analogy
There is 'twixt *Cobling* and *Astrology*;                    20

Printed from the original Broadside, London, 1708, with corrections from
*Poems*, 1735.
20. Patrige was a Cobler.

How *Patrige* made his *Opticks* rise,
From a *Shoe Sole* to reach the Skies;
A *List* the Coblers Temples ties,
To keep the Hair out of their Eyes;
From whence 'tis plain the *Diadem*
That Princes wear, derives from them;
And therefore *Crowns* are now-a-days
Adorn'd with *Golden Stars* and *Rays*,
Which plainly shews the near Alliance
'Twixt *Cobling* and the *Planets Science*.                    30
    Besides, that slow-pac'd Sign *Bo-otes*
As 'tis miscall'd, we know not who 'tis;
But *Patrige* ended all Disputes,
He knew his Trade, and call'd it *Boots*.
The *Horned Moon* which heretofore
Upon their Shoes the *Romans* wore,
Whose Wideness kept their Toes from Corns,
And whence we claim our *shoeing horns*,
Shews how the Art of *Cobling* bears
A near Resemblance to the *Spheres*.                         40
    A Scrap of *Parchment* hung by *Geometry*,
A great Refinement in *Barometry*,
Can like the Stars foretel the Weather;
And what is *Parchment* else but *Leather*?
Which an Astrologer might use,
Either for *Almanacks* or *Shoes*.
    Thus *Patrige*, by his Wit and Parts,
At once did Practice both these Arts:
And as the Boding Owl, or rather
The Bat, because her Wings are *Leather*,                     50
Steals from her Private Cell by Night,
And flies about the Candle-Light;
So Learned *Patrige* could as well
Creep in the Dark from *Leathern* Cell,
And in his Fancy fly as far,
To peep upon a twinkling Star.
    Besides, he could confound the *Spheres*,
And set the *Planets* by the Ears:

---

34. *Boots*. See his Almanack.

To shew his Skill, he *Mars* would join
To *Venus* in *Aspect Mali'n*,                    60
Then call in *Mercury* for Aid,
And Cure the Wounds that *Venus* made.
 Great Scholars have in *Lucian* Read,
When *Philip* King of *Greece* was Dead,
His *Soul* and *Spirit* did divide,
And each Part took a diff'rent Side;
*One* rose a Star, the *other fell*
Beneath, and mended Shoes in Hell.
 Thus *Patrige* still shines in each Art,
The *Cobling* and *Star-gazing* Part,           70
And is *Install'd* as good a Star,
As any of the *Cæsars* are.
 *Triumphant* Star! Some Pity show
On *Coblers Militant* below,
Whom Roguish Boys in Stormy Nights
Torment, by pissing out their Lights;
Or thro' a Chink convey their Smoke,
Inclos'd *Artificers* to Choke.
 Thou, high-exalted in thy Sphere,
May'st follow still thy Calling there.          80
To thee the *Bull* will lend his *Hide*,
By *Phœbus* newly Tann'd and Dry'd.
For thee they *Argo*'s Hulk will Tax,
And scrape her Pitchy Sides for *Wax*.
Then *Ariadne* kindly Lends
Her Braided Hair to make thee *Ends*;
The Point of *Sagittarius* Dart,
Turns to an *Awl* by Heav'nly Art;
And *Vulcan* wheedled by his Wife,
Will Forge for thee a *Paring-Knife*,           90
For want of Room by *Virgo*'s Side,
She'll strain a Point, and sit astride,
To take thee kindly in *between*
And then the *Signs* will be *Thirteen*.

92–93. Tibi brachia contrahet Ingens Scorpius, &c. Virgil, *Georg*. i. 34–35.

## The EPITAPH

H ERE *Five Foot deep lyes on his Back*
*A* Cobler, Starmonger, *and* Quack,
*Who to the Stars in pure Good-will,*
*Does to his best look upward still.*
*Weep all you Customers that use*
*His* Pills, *his* Almanacks, *or* Shoes.          100
*And you that did your Fortunes seek,*
*Step to this Grave but once a Week,*
*This Earth which bears his Body's Print,*
*You'll find has so much Virtue in't,*
*That I durst Pawn my Ears, 'twill tell*
*Whate'er concerns you full as well,*
*In* Physick, Stolen Goods, *or* Love,
*As he himself could, when above.*

# A famous Prediction of *MERLIN*, the *British* Wizard; written above a Thousand Years ago, and relating to this present Year

## With Explanatory Notes. By *T. N.* Philomath

L AST Year was publish'd a Paper of Predictions pretended to be written by one *Isaac Bickerstaff*, Esq; but the true Design of it was to Ridicule the Art of Astrology, and Expose its Professors as ignorant, or Impostors. Against this Imputation, Dr. *Partridge* hath vindicated himself in his Almanack for the present Year.

For a further Vindication of this famous Art, I have thought fit to present the World with the following Prophecy. The Original is said to be of the famous *Merlin*, who lived about a

Printed from the original Half-sheet, London, 1709.

Thousand Years ago: And the following Translation is Two
Hundred Years old; for it seems to be written near the End of
*Henry* the Seventh's Reign. I found it in an Old Edition of
*Merlin*'s Prophecies; imprinted at *London* by *Johan Haukyns*, in
the Year 1530, *Pag.* 39. I set it down Word for Word in the
Old Orthography, and shall take Leave to subjoin a few
Explanatory Notes.

Seven and Ten addyd to nyne,
Of Fraunce hir woe thys is the sygne,
Tamys rivere twys y=frozen,
Walke sans wetynge Shoes ne hosen.
Then compth foorthe, Ich understonde,
From Toune of Stoffe to fattyn Londe
An herdie Chiftan, woe the morne
To Fraunce, that evere he was borne.
Than shall the Fyshe beweyle his Bosse;
Nor shall grin Berris make up the Losse.
Yonge Symnele shall agayne miscarrye:
And Norways pryd agayne shall marreye.
And from the Tree where Blosums fele,
Ripe fruit shall come, and all is wele.
Reaums shall daunce honde in honde,
And it shall be merye in olde Inglonde.
Then olde Inglonde shall be noe more,
And no Man shall be sorie therefore.
Geryon shall have three Hedes agayne
Till Hapsburge makyth them but twayne.

## Explanatory Notes

Seven and Ten. This Line describes the Year when these
Events shall happen. Seven and Ten makes Seventeen, which
I Explain Seventeen Hundred, and this Number added to
Nine, makes the Year we are now in; for it must be understood
of the Natural Year, which begins the First of *January*.

Tamys River twice, &c. The River *Thames* frozen twice
in one Year, so as Men to walk on it, is a very signal Accident;
which perhaps hath not fallen out for several Hundred Years
before, and is the Reason why some Astrologers have thought

that this Prophecy could never be fulfilled, because they imagined such a Thing would never happen in our Climate.

𝔉rom 𝔗oun of 𝔖tuff, &c. This is a plain designation of the Duke of *Marlborough*; One kind of Stuff used to fatten Land is called *Marle*, and every body knows that *Borough* is a Name for a Town; and this way of Expression is after the usual dark manner of Old Astrological Predictions.

𝔗hen shall the 𝔉ish, &c. By the *Fish* is understood the *Dolphin* of *France*, as their Kings Eldest Sons are called: 'Tis here said, He shall lament the Loss of the Duke of *Burgundy*, called the *Bosse*, which is an Old *English* Word from *Hump-Shoulder*, or *Crook-Back*, as that Duke is known to be; and the Prophecy seems to mean, that he shall be overcome or slain. By the *Green Berrys* in the next Line is meant the Young Duke of *Berry*, the *Dauphin*'s Third Son, who shall not have Valour or Fortune enough to supply the Loss of his Eldest Brother.

𝔜oung 𝔖ymnele, &c. By *Symnel* is meant the Pretended Prince of *Wales*, who if he offers to attempt any thing against *England*, shall miscarry as he did before. *Lambert Symnel* is the Name of a Young Man noted in our Histories for Personating the Son (as I remember) of *Edward* the Fourth.

𝔄nd 𝔑orways 𝔓ride, &c. I cannot guess who is meant by *Norway*'s *Pride*, perhaps the Reader may, as well as the Sense of the Two following Lines.

𝔑eaums shall, &c. *Reaums*, or, as the Word is now, *Realms*, is the old Name for *Kingdoms*: And this is a very plain Prediction of our Happy *Union*, with the Felicities that shall attend it. It is added, That *Old England* shall be no more, and yet no Man shall be sorry for it. And indeed, properly speaking, *England* is now no more; for the whole Island is one Kingdom, under the Name of *Britain*.

𝔊eryon shall, &c. This Prediction, though somewhat obscure, is wonderfully adapt. *Geryon* is said to have been a King of *Spain*, whom *Hercules* slew. It was a Fiction of the Poets, that he had Three Heads, which the Author says he shall have again. That is, *Spain* shall have Three Kings; which is now wonderfully verify'd: For besides the King of *Portugal*, which properly is Part of *Spain*, there are now Two Rivals for *Spain*; *Charles* and *Philip*. But *Charles* being descended from the Count of *Hapsburgh*, Founder of the *Austrian* Family, shall soon

make those Heads but Two; by Overcoming *Philip*, and Driving
him out of *Spain*.

Some of these Predictions are already fulfilled; and it is
highly probable the rest may be in due time: And, I think,
I have not forced the Words by my Explication, into any
other Sense than what they will naturally bear. If this be
granted, I am sure it may be also allow'd, that the Author,
whoever he were, was a Person of extraordinary Sagacity;
And that Astrology brought to such a Perfection as this, is
by no means an Art to be despis'd; whatever Mr. *Bickerstaff*,
or other Merry Gentlemen are pleased to think. As to the
Tradition, of these Lines having been writ in their Original
by *Merlin*; I confess, I lay not much Weight upon it: But it is
enough to justify their Authority, that the Book from whence
I have transcrib'd them, was printed 170 Years ago, as appears
by the Title-Page. For the Satisfaction of any Gentleman, who
may be either Doubtful of the Truth, or Curious to be inform'd;
I shall give Order to have the very Book sent to the Printer of
this Paper, with Directions to let any Body see it that pleases;
because, I believe, it is pretty scarce.

# *VANBRUG*'s HOUSE

## *Built from the Ruins of* White-Hall *that was Burnt*

IN Times of *Old*, when Time was *Young*,
And Poets their own Verses Sung,
A Verse could draw a Stone or Beam
That now would overload a Team;
Lead 'em a Dance of many a Mile,
Then rear 'em to a goodly Pile.
Each Number had it's diff'rent Pow'r;
Heroick Strains could build a Tow'r;

Printed from *Miscellanies*, 1711, with corrections from *Poems*, 1735.

Sonnets, or Elogies to *Chloris*
Might raise a House about two Stories;　　　　10
A Lyrick Ode would Slate; a Catch
Would Tile; an Epigram would Thatch.

BUT, to their own, or Landlord's Cost,
Now Poets feel this Art is lost:
Not one of all our tuneful Throng
Can raise a Lodging *for a Song*.
For, *Jove* consider'd well the Case,
Observ'd, they grew a num'rous Race.
And should they *Build* as fast as *Write*,
'Twould ruin Undertakers quite.　　　　20
This Evil, therefore to prevent,
He wisely chang'd their Element:
On Earth, the God of Wealth was made
Sole Patron of the Building Trade,
Leaving the Wits the Spacious Air
With Licence to *build Castles* there:
And 'tis conceiv'd, their old Pretence
To lodge in Garrats, comes from thence.

PREMISING thus in Modern way
The better Half we have to say;　　　　30
Sing Muse the House of Poet *Van*
In higher Strains than we began.

*VAN* (for 'tis fit the Reader know it)
Is both a Herald and a Poet,
No wonder then, if nicely skill'd
In both Capacities, to Build.
As Herald, he can in a Day
Repair a *House* gone to Decay,
Or by *Atchivement, Arms, Device,*
Erect a new one in a trice.　　　　40
And as a Poet, he has Skill
To build in Speculation still.
Great *Jove!* he cry'd, the Art restore
To build by Verse as heretofore,

And make my Muse the Architect;
What Palaces shall we erect!
No longer shall forsaken *Thames*
Lament his old *Whitehall* in Flames,
A Pile shall from its Ashes rise
Fit to Invade or prop the Skies.                    50

    *JOVE* Smil'd, and like a gentle God,
Consenting with his usual Nod,
Told *Van* he knew his Talent best,
And left the Choice to his own Breast.
So *Van* resolv'd to write a Farce,
But well perceiving Wit was scarce,
With Cunning that Defect supplies,
Takes a *French* Play as lawful Prize,
Steals thence his Plot, and ev'ry Joke,
Not once suspecting, *Jove* would *Smoak*,        60
And, (like a Wag) sat down to Write,
Would whisper to himself; *A Bite*,
Then, from this motly mingled Style
Proceeded to erect his Pile:
So, Men of old, to gain Renown, did
Build *Babel* with their Tongues confounded.
*Jove* saw the Cheat, but thought it best
To turn the Matter to a Jest;
Down from *Olympus* Top he Slides,
Laughing as if he'd burst his Sides:              70
Ay, thought the God, are these your Tricks?
Why then, *old Plays* deserve *old Bricks*,
And since you're sparing of your Stuff,
Your Building shall be small enough.
He spake, and grudging, lent his Ayd;
Th' experienc't Bricks that knew their Trade,
(As being Bricks at Second Hand,)
Now move, and now in Order Stand.

    THE Building, as the Poet Writ,
Rose in proportion to his Wit:                    80
And first the Prologue built a Wall
So wide as to encompass all.

The Scene, a Wood, produc'd no more
Than a few Scrubby Trees before.
The Plot as yet lay deep, and so
A Cellar next was dug below:
But this a Work so hard was found,
Two Acts it cost him under Ground.
Two other Acts we may presume
Were spent in Building each a Room;                90
Thus far advanc't, he made a shift
To raise a Roof with Act the Fift.
The Epilogue behind, did frame
A Place not decent here to name.

   NOW Poets from all Quarters ran
To see the House of Brother *Van*:
Lookt high and low, walkt often round,
But no such House was to be found;
One asks the Watermen hard by,
*Where may the Poets Palace ly?*                100
Another, of the *Thames* enquires,
If he has seen its gilded Spires?
At length they in the Rubbish spy
A Thing resembling a Goose Py,
Thither in haste the Poets throng,
And gaze in silent Wonder long,
Till one in Raptures thus began
To praise the Pile, and Builder *Van.*

   THRICE happy Poet, who may trail
Thy House about thee like a Snail;                110
Or Harness'd to a Nag, at ease
Take Journies in it like a Chaise;
Or in a Boat when e're thou wilt
Canst make it serve thee for a Tilt.
Capacious House! 'tis own'd by all
Thou'rt well contriv'd, tho' thou art small;
For ev'ry Wit in *Britain*'s Isle
May lodge within thy Spacious Pile.
Like *Bacchus* Thou, as Poets feign,
Thy Mother burnt, art Born again;                120

Born like a *Phœnix* from the Flame,
But neither *Bulk*, nor *Shape* the same:
As Animals of largest Size
Corrupt to Maggots, Worms and Flyes.
A Type of *Modern* Wit and Style,
*The Rubbish of an Antient Pile.*
So *Chymists* boast they have a Pow'r
From the dead Ashes of a Flow'r
Some faint Resemblance to produce,
But not the Virtue, Tast or Juice.       130
So *Modern* Rimers wisely *Blast*
The Poetry of Ages past,
Which after they have overthrown,
They from its Ruins build their own.


# *BAUCIS*

## AND

# *PHILEMON*

### *Imitated, From the Eighth Book of* OVID

IN antient Times, as Story tells,
The Saints would often leave their Cells,
And strole about, but hide their Quality,
To try good People's Hospitality.

    IT happen'd on a Winter Night,
(As Authors of the Legend write;)
Two Brother Hermits, Saints by Trade,
Taking their *Tour* in Masquerade;
Disguis'd in tatter'd Habits, went
To a small Village down in *Kent*;       10
Where, in the Strolers Canting Strain,
They beg'd from Door to Door in vain;
Try'd ev'ry Tone might Pity win,
But not a Soul would let them in.

Printed from *Miscellanies*, 1711, with corrections from *Poems*, 1735.

OUR wand'ring Saints in woful State,
Treated at this ungodly Rate,
Having thro' all the Village pass'd,
To a small Cottage came at last;
Where dwelt a good old honest Yeoman,
Call'd, in the Neighbourhood, *Philemon*.          20
Who kindly did the Saints invite
In his Poor Hut to pass the Night;
And then the Hospitable Sire
Bid *Goody Baucis* mend the Fire;
While He from out the Chimney took
A Flitch of Bacon off the Hook;
And freely from the fattest Side
Cut out large Slices to be fry'd:
Then stept aside to fetch 'em Drink,
Fill'd a large Jug up to the Brink;          30
And saw it fairly twice go round;
Yet (what was wonderful) they found,
'Twas still replenished to the Top,
As if they ne'er had toucht a Drop.
The good old Couple was amaz'd,
And often on each other gaz'd;
For both were frighted to the Heart,
And just began to cry;—What art!
Then softly turn'd aside to view,
Whether the Lights were burning blue.          40
The gentle *Pilgrims* soon aware on't,
Told 'em their Calling, and their Errant:
Good Folks, you need not be afraid,
We are but *Saints*, the Hermits said;
No Hurt shall come to You, or Yours;
But, for that Pack of churlish Boors,
Not fit to live on Christian Ground,
They and their Houses shall be drown'd:
Whilst you shall see your Cottage rise,
And grow a Church before your Eyes.          50

THEY scarce had Spoke; when, fair and soft,
The Roof began to mount aloft;

Aloft rose ev'ry Beam and Rafter,
The heavy Wall climb'd slowly after.

THE Chimney widen'd, and grew higher,
Became a Steeple with a Spire.

THE Kettle to the Top was hoist,
And there stood fast'ned to a Joist:
But with the Upside down, to shew
Its Inclination for below;     60
In vain; for some Superior Force
Apply'd at Bottom, stops its Course,
Doom'd ever in Suspence to dwell,
'Tis now no Kettle, but a Bell.

A wooden Jack, which had almost
Lost, by Disuse, the Art to Roast,
A sudden Alteration feels,
Increas'd by new Intestine Wheels:
And what exalts the Wonder more,
The Number made the Motion slow'r:     70
The Flyer, tho't had Leaden Feet,
Turn'd round so quick, you scarce cou'd see't;
Now slacken'd by some secret Power,
Can hardly move an Inch an Hour.
The Jack and Chimney near ally'd,
Had never left each other's Side;
The Chimney to a Steeple grown,
The Jack wou'd not be left alone,
But up against the Steeple rear'd,
Became a Clock, and still adher'd:     80
And still its Love to Houshold Cares
By a shrill Voice at Noon declares,
Warning the Cook-maid, not to burn
That Roast-meat which it cannot turn.

THE Groaning Chair was seen to crawl
Like an huge Snail half up the Wall;
There stuck aloft, in Publick View,
And with small Change, a Pulpit grew.

THE Porringers, that in a Row
Hung high, and made a glitt'ring Show,          90
To a less Noble Substance chang'd,
Were now but Leathern Buckets rang'd.

THE Ballads pasted on the Wall,
Of *Joan* of *France*, and *English Moll*,
Fair *Rosamond*, and *Robin Hood*,
The *Little Children in the Wood*:
Now seem'd to look abundance better,
Improv'd in Picture, Size, and Letter;
And high in Order plac'd, describe
The Heraldry of ev'ry Tribe.          100

A Bedstead of the Antique Mode,
Compact of Timber many a Load,
Such as our Grandsires wont to use,
Was Metamorphos'd into Pews;
Which still their antient Nature keep;
By lodging Folks dispos'd to Sleep.

THE Cottage by such Feats as these,
Grown to a Church by just Degrees,
The Hermits then desire their Host
To ask for what he fancy'd most:          110
*Philemon*, having paus'd a while,
Return'd 'em Thanks in homely Stile;
Then said; my House is grown so Fine,
Methinks, I still wou'd call it mine:
I'm Old, and fain wou'd live at Ease,
Make me the *Parson*, if you please.

HE spoke, and presently he feels,
His Grazier's Coat fall down his Heels;
He sees, yet hardly can believe,
About each Arm a Pudding-sleeve;          120
His Wastcoat to a Cassock grew,
And both assum'd a Sable Hue;
But being Old, continu'd just
As Thread-bare, and as full of Dust.

His Talk was now of *Tythes* and *Dues*,
Could smoak his Pipe, and read the News;
Knew how to preach old Sermons next,
Vampt in the Preface and the Text;
At Christnings well could act his Part,
And had the Service all by Heart;                     130
Wish'd Women might have Children fast,
And thought whose *Sow* had *farrow'd* last:
Against *Dissenters* would repine,
And stood up firm for *Right Divine*:
Found his Head fill'd with many a System,
But Classick Authors—he ne'er miss'd 'em.

THUS having furbish'd up a Parson,
Dame *Baucis* next, they play'd their Farce on:
Instead of Home-spun Coifs were seen,
Good Pinners edg'd with Colberteen:                   140
Her Petticoat transform'd apace,
Became Black Sattin, Flounc'd with Lace.
Plain *Goody* would no longer down,
'Twas *Madam*, in her Grogram Gown.
*Philemon* was in great Surprize,
And hardly could believe his Eyes,
Amaz'd to see Her look so Prim,
And she admir'd as much at Him.

THUS, happy in their Change of Life,
Were several Years the Man and Wife,                  150
When on a Day, which prov'd their last,
Discoursing o'er old Stories past,
They went by chance, amidst their Talk,
To the Church-yard, to fetch a walk;
When *Baucis* hastily cry'd out;
My Dear, I see your Forehead sprout:
Sprout, quoth the Man, What's this you tell us?
I hope you don't believe me Jealous:
But yet, methinks, I feel it true;
And really, Yours is budding too—                     160
Nay,—now I cannot stir my Foot:
It feels as if 'twere taking Root.

DESCRIPTION would but tire my Muse:
In short, they both were turn'd to *Yews.*
Old Good-man *Dobson* of the Green
Remembers he the Trees has seen;
He'll talk of them from Noon to Night,
And goes with Folks to shew the Sight:
On *Sundays,* after Ev'ning Prayer,
He gathers all the Parish there;                          170
Points out the Place of either *Yew*;
Here *Baucis,* there *Philemon* grew.
Till once, a Parson of our Town,
To mend his Barn, cut *Baucis* down;
At which, 'tis hard to be believ'd,
How much the other Tree was griev'd,
Grew Scrubby, dy'd a-top, was stunted:
So, the next Parson stub'd and burnt it.


# TO

# *Mrs.* BIDDY FLOYD

## *Anno* 1708

WHEN *Cupid* did his Grandsire *Jove* intreat,
    To form some Beauty by a new Receit,
*Jove* sent and found far in a Country Scene,
Truth, Innocence, Good Nature, Look serene;
From which Ingredients, first the dext'rous Boy
Pickt the Demure, the Aukward, and the Coy:
The *Graces* from the Court did next provide
Breeding, and Wit, and Air, and decent Pride.
These *Venus* cleans'd from ev'ry spurious Grain
Of Nice, Coquet, Affected, Pert, and Vain.          10
*Jove* mix'd up all, and his best Clay imploy'd;
Then call'd the happy Composition, *Floyd.*

Printed from *Miscellanies,* 1711, with corrections from *Poems,* 1735.

# *Apollo* Outwitted

### *To the Honourable Mrs.* Finch,

### *under her Name* of Ardelia,

#### Written 1709

P*HŒBUS* now shortning every Shade,
   Up to the Northern *Tropick* came,
And thence Beheld a Lovely Maid
   Attending on a Royal Dame.

THE God laid down his Feeble Rays,
   Then lighted from his Glitt'ring Coach,
But fenc'd his Head with his own Bays
   Before he durst the Nymph approach.

UNDER those Sacred Leaves, Secure
   From common Lightning of the Skies,     10
He fondly thought he might endure
   The Flashes of *Ardeliah*'s Eyes.

THE Nymph who oft had read in Books,
   Of that Bright God whom Bards invoke,
Soon knew *Apollo* by his looks,
   And Guest his Business e're he Spoke.

HE in the old Celestial Cant,
   Confest his Flame, and swore by *Styx*,
What e're she would desire, to Grant,
   But Wise *Ardelia* knew his Tricks.     20

*OVID* had warn'd her to beware,
   Of Stroling God's, whose usual Trade is,
Under pretence of Taking Air,
   To pick up Sublunary Ladies.

Printed from *Miscellanies*, 1711.

HOWE'ER she gave no flat Denial,
    As having Malice in her Heart,
And was resolv'd upon a Tryal,
    To Cheat the God in his own Art.


HEAR my Request the Virgin said
    Let which I please of all the Nine          30
Attend when e'er I want their Aid,
    Obey my Call, and only mine.


BY Vow Oblig'd, By Passion led,
    The God could not refuse her Prayer;
He wav'd his Wreath Thrice o'er her Head,
    Thrice mutter'd something to the Air.


AND now he thought to Seize his due,
    But she the Charm already try'd,
*Thalia* heard the Call and Flew
    To wait at Bright *Ardelia*'s Side.          40


ON Sight of this Celestial *Prude*,
    *Apollo* thought it vain to stay,
Nor in her Presence durst be Rude,
    But made his Leg and went away.


HE hop'd to find some lucky Hour,
    When on their Queen the Muses wait;
But *Pallas* owns *Ardelia*'s Power,
    For Vows Divine are kept by Fate.


THEN full of Rage *Apollo* Spoke,
    Deceitful Nymph I see thy Art,          50
And tho' I can't my gift revoke,
    I'll disappoint its Nobler Part.


LET Stubborn Pride Possess thee long,
    And be thou Negligent of Fame,
With ev'ry Muse to Grace thy Song,
    May'st thou despise a Poets Name.

OF Modest Poets thou be first,
  To silent Shades repeat thy Verse,   .
Till *Fame* and *Eccho* almost burst,
  Yet hardly dare one Line Rehearse.                    60

AND last, my Vengeance to Compleat,
  May you Descend to take Renown,
Prevail'd on by the Thing you hate,
  A Whig and one that wears a Gown.


## 'In pity to the empty'ng Town'

[p. 1]    IN pity to the empty'ng Town
      Some God May-Fair invented,
  When Nature would invite us down,
      To be by Art prevented.

  What a corrupted Tast is ours
      When Milk-maids in mock-state
  Instead of Garlands made of Flowrs
      Adorn their Pails with Plate.

  So are the Joys which Nature yields
      Inverted in May-Fair                              10
  In painted Cloth we look for Fields,
      And step in Booths for Air.

  Here a Dog dancing on his Hamms
      And Puppets mov'd by Wire
  Do far exceed your frisking Lambs
      Or Song of feather'd Quire.

  Howe'er such Verse as yours, I grant
      Would be but too inviting
  Were fair Ardelia not my Aunt,
      Or were it Worsly's writing.                      20

Printed from Swift's autograph, Fountaine MSS., Morgan Library.

[p. 2]    Then pray think this a lucky Hitt,
    Nor e'er expect another
For honest Harry is no Witt,
    Tho' he's a younger Brother.


# A DESCRIPTION

## OF THE

# MORNING

*The Tatler, Numb. 9. From Thursday April 28. to Saturday April 30. 1709*

NOW hardly here and there a Hackney-Coach
   Appearing, show'd the Ruddy Morns Approach.
Now *Betty* from her Masters Bed had flown,
And softly stole to discompose her own.
The Slipshod Prentice from his Masters Door,
Had par'd the Dirt, and Sprinkled round the Floor.
Now *Moll* had whirl'd her Mop with dext'rous Airs,
Prepar'd to Scrub the Entry and the Stairs.
The Youth with Broomy Stumps began to trace
The Kennel-Edge, where Wheels had worn the Place.    10
The Smallcoal-Man was heard with Cadence deep,
'Till drown'd in Shriller Notes of *Chimney-Sweep*.
Duns at his Lordships Gate began to meet,
And Brickdust *Moll* had Scream'd through half a Street.
The Turnkey now his Flock returning sees,
Duly let out a Nights to Steal for Fees.
The watchful Bailiffs take their silent Stands,
And School-Boys lag with Satchels in their Hands.

Printed from *Miscellanies*, 1711, with corrections from *Poems*, 1735.

9–10. To find old Nails.

## On the Little House by the Church Yard of Castleknock

WHOEVER pleaseth to enquire,
Why yonder Steeple wants a Spire,
The gray old Fellow Poet *Joe*
The Philosophic Cause will shew.
Once, on a Time a Western Blast,
At least twelve Inches overcast,
Reckoning Roof, Weather Cock and all,
Which came with a prodigious Fall;
And tumbling topsi-turvy round
Light with its Bottom on the Ground.                    10
     For by the Laws of Gravitation,
It fell into its proper Station.
     This is the little strutting Pile,
You see just by the Church-yard Stile;
The Walls in tumbling gave a Knock;
And thus the Steeple got a Shock;
From whence the neighbouring Farmer calls
The Steeple, Knock, the Vicar, *Walls*.
     The Vicar once a Week creeps in,
Sits with his Knees up to his Chin;                     20
Here conns his Notes, and takes a Whet,
Till the small ragged Flock is met.
     A Traveller, who by did pass,
Observ'd the Roof behind the Grass;
On Tiptoe stood and rear'd his Snout,
And saw the Parson creeping out;
Was much surpriz'd to see a Crow
Venture to build his Nest so low.
     A School-boy ran unto't and thought,
The Crib was down, the Blackbird caught.                30
A Third, who lost his Way by Night,
Was forc'd, for Safety, to alight,

Printed from *Works*, *Vol. VIII*, Dublin, 1746.

And stepping o'er the Fabrick-roof,
His Horse had like to spoil his Hoof.
   *Warburton* took it in his Noddle,
This Building was designed a Model,
Or of a Pigeon-house, or Oven,
To bake one Loaf, and keep one Dove in.
   Then Mrs. *Johnson* gave her Verdict,
And every one was pleas'd, that heard it:        40
All that you make this Stir about,
Is but a Still which wants a Spout.
The Rev'rend Dr. *Raymond* guess'd,
More probably than all the rest;
He said, but that it wanted Room,
It might have been a Pigmy's Tomb.
   The Doctor's Family came by,
And little Miss began to cry;
Give me that House in my own Hand;
Then Madam bid the Chariot stand,        50
Call'd to the Clerk in manner mild,
Pray reach that Thing here to the Child,
That Thing, I mean, among the Kale,
And here's to buy a Pot of Ale.
   The Clerk said to her in a Heat,
What? sell my Master's Country Seat?
Where he comes ev'ry Week from Town;
He wou'd not sell it for a Crown.
Poh! Fellow keep not such a Pother
In half an Hour thou'lt make another.        60
   Says *Nancy*, I can make for Miss,
A finer House ten times than this,
The Dean will give me Willow-Sticks,
And *Joe* my Apron full of Bricks.

# THE

# VIRTUES

### OF

## *SID HAMET* the MAGICIAN's

## ROD

THE *Rod* was but a harmless Wand,
While *Moses* held it in his Hand,
But soon as e'er he *lay'd it down*,
'Twas a devouring Serpent grown.

OUR great Magician, *Hamet Sid*,
Reverses what the Prophet did;
His *Rod* was honest *English* Wood,
That, senseless, in a Corner stood,
Till Metamorphos'd by his Grasp,
It grew an all-devouring Asp;         10
Would hiss, and sting, and roll, and twist,
By the meer Virtue of his Fist:
But when he *lay'd it down*, as quick
Resum'd the Figure of a Stick.

SO to Her Midnight Feasts the Hag,
Rides on a Broomstick for a Nag,
That, rais'd by Magick of her Breech,
O'er Sea and Land conveys the Witch;
But, with the Morning-Dawn, resumes
The Peaceful State of common Brooms.    20

THEY tell us something strange and odd,
About a certain Magick *Rod*,
That, bending down it's Top, divines
When e'er the Soil has Golden Mines:
Where there are none, it stands erect,
Scorning to show the least Respect.

Printed from the original Half-sheet, London, 1710.

As ready was the *Wand* of *Sid*
To *bend* where *Golden Mines* were hid;
In *Scottish* Hills found precious Ore,
Where none e'er look'd for it before;                    30
And, by a *gentle Bow*, divin'd
How well a *Cully*'s Purse was lin'd:
To a forlorn and broken *Rake*,
Stood without Motion, like a Stake.

THE *Rod* of *Hermes* was renown'd
For Charms above and under Ground;
To sleep could Mortal Eye-lids fix
And drive departed Souls to *Styx*.
That *Rod* was just a Type of *Sid*'s,
Which, o'er a *British* Senate's Lids,                   40
Could *scatter Opium* full as well,
And drive as many *Souls to Hell*.

*SID*'s Rod was slender, white, and tall,
Which oft he us'd to *fish* withal:
A *PLACE* was fastned to the Hook,
And many Score of *Gudgeons* took;
Yet, still so happy was his Fate,
He caught his *Fish*, and sav'd his *Bait*.

*SID*'s Brethren of the conj'ring Tribe
A Circle with their *Rod* describe,                      50
Which proves a Magical Redoubt
To keep *mischievous Spirits* out:
*Sid*'s *Rod* was of a larger Stride,
And made a Circle thrice as wide,
Where *Spirits* throng'd with hideous Din,
And he stood there to *take them in*.
But, when th' enchanted *Rod* was *broke*,
They vanish'd in a stinking Smoak.

*ACHILLES*'s Scepter was of Wood,
Like *Sid*'s, but nothing near so good;                  60
Tho' down from Ancestors Divine
Transmitted to the Heroes Line,

Thence, thro' a long Descent of Kings,
Came an 𝕳eir=loom, as *Homer* sings,
Tho' this Description looks so big,
That *Scepter* was a sapless Twig:
Which, from the fatal Day when first
It left the Forest where 'twas nurst,
As *Homer* tells us o'er and o'er,
Nor Leaf, nor Fruit, nor Blossom bore.     70
*Sid*'s Scepter, full of Juice, did shoot
In Golden Boughs, and Golden Fruit,
And He, the *Dragon* never sleeping,
Guarded each fair *Hesperian* Pippin.
No *Hobby-horse*, with gorgeous Top,
The dearest in *Charles Mather*'s Shop,
Or glitt'ring Tinsel of *May-Fair*,
Could with this *Rod* of *Sid* compare.

DEAR *Sid*, then why wer't thou so mad
To break thy *Rod* like naughty Lad?     80
You should have kiss'd it in your Distress,
And then return'd it to *your Mistress*,
Or made it a *Newmarket* Switch,
And not a *Rod* for thy own Breech.
For since old *Sid* has broken this,
His next will be a *Rod in Piss*.

# A DESCRIPTION
## OF A
# *CITY SHOWER*

*The Tatler, Numb. 238. From Saturday October 14. to Tuesday October 17. 1710.*

CAREFUL Observers may fortel the Hour
  (By sure Prognosticks) when to dread a Show'r:
While Rain depends, the pensive Cat gives o'er
Her Frolicks, and pursues her Tail no more.

Printed from *Miscellanies*, 1711, with corrections from *Poems*, 1735.

Returning Home at Night, you'll find the Sink
Strike your offended Sense with double Stink.
If you be wise, then go not far to Dine,
You spend in Coach-hire more than save in Wine.
A coming Show'r your shooting Corns presage,
Old Aches throb, your hollow Tooth will rage.          10
Sauntring in Coffee-house is *Dulman* seen;
He damns the Climate, and complains of Spleen.

MEAN while the South rising with dabbled Wings,
A Sable Cloud a-thwart the Welkin flings,
That swill'd more Liquor than it could contain,
And like a Drunkard gives it up again.
Brisk *Susan* whips her Linen from the Rope,
While the first drizzling Show'r is born aslope,
Such is that Sprinkling which some careless Quean
Flirts on you from her Mop, but not so clean.          20
You fly, invoke the Gods; then turning, stop
To rail; she singing, still whirls on her Mop.
Not yet, the Dust had shun'd th' unequal Strife,
But aided by the Wind, fought still for Life;
And wafted with its Foe by violent Gust,
'Twas doubtful which was Rain, and which was Dust.
Ah! where must needy Poet seek for Aid,
When Dust and Rain at once his Coat invade;
Sole Coat, where Dust cemented by the Rain,
Erects the Nap, and leaves a cloudy Stain.          30

NOW in contiguous Drops the Flood comes down,
Threat'ning with Deluge this *Devoted* Town.
To Shops in Crouds the dagled Females fly,
Pretend to cheapen Goods, but nothing buy.
The Templer spruce, while ev'ry Spout's a-broach,
Stays till 'tis fair, yet seems to call a Coach.
The tuck'd-up Sempstress walks with hasty Strides,
While Streams run down her oil'd Umbrella's Sides.
Here various Kinds by various Fortunes led,
Commence Acquaintance underneath a Shed.          40

26. ''Tis doubtful which is Sea, and which is Sky.' Garth's *Dispensary* (Canto v, 176).

Triumphant Tories, and desponding Whigs,
Forget their Fewds, and join to save their Wigs.
Box'd in a Chair the Beau impatient sits,
While Spouts run clatt'ring o'er the Roof by Fits;
And ever and anon with frightful Din
The Leather sounds, he trembles from within.
So when *Troy* Chair-men bore the Wooden Steed,
Pregnant with *Greeks*, impatient to be freed,
(Those Bully *Greeks*, who, as the Moderns do,
Instead of paying Chair-men, run them thro'.)                    50
*Laoco'n* struck the Outside with his Spear,
And each imprison'd Hero quak'd for Fear.


NOW from all Parts the swelling Kennels flow,
And bear their Trophies with them as they go:
Filth of all Hues and Odours seem to tell
What Streets they sail'd from, by the Sight and Smell.
They, as each Torrent drives, with rapid Force
From *Smithfield*, or St. *Pulchre*'s shape their Course,
And in huge Confluent join at *Snow-Hill* Ridge,
Fall from the *Conduit* prone to *Holborn-Bridge*.               60
Sweepings from Butchers Stalls, Dung, Guts, and Blood, ⎫
Drown'd Puppies, stinking Sprats, all drench'd in Mud, ⎬
Dead Cats and Turnip-Tops come tumbling down the ⎭
    Flood.

41. N.B. This was the first Year of the Earl of Oxford's Ministry.

61–63. These three last lines were intended against that licentious Manner of
modern Poets, in making three Rhimes together, which they call *Triplets*; and
the last of the three, was two or sometimes more Syllables longer, called an
*Alexandrian*. These *Triplets* and *Alexandrians* were brought in by Dryden, and other
Poets in the Reign of Charles II. They were the mere Effect of Haste, Idleness,
and want of Money; and have been wholly avoided by the best Poets, since these
Verses were written.

# To M^r Harlyes Surgeon

On Britain Europes safety lyes
And Britain's lost if Harly dyes
Harly depends upon your skill,
Think what you save or what you kill

J

Printed from Swift's autograph, Portland Papers at Longleat.

## AN

# EXCELLENT NEW SONG,

### BEING THE

### *Intended SPEECH of a famous Orator against Peace*

AN Orator *dismal* of *Nottinghamshire*,
Who has forty Years let out his Conscience to hire,
Out of Zeal for his Country, and *want of a Place*,
Is come up, *vi & armis*, to *break the Queen's Peace*.
He has vamp't an old Speech, and the Court to their sorrow,
Shall hear Him harangue against PRIOR to Morrow.
When once he begins, he never will flinch,
But repeats the same Note a whole Day, like a *Finch*.
I have heard all the Speech repeated by *Hoppy*.
And, *mistakes to prevent*, I *have obtain'd a Copy*.          10

## The SPEECH

WHEREAS, *Notwithstanding*, I am in great Pain,
To hear we are making a Peace without *Spain*;
But, *most noble Senators*, 'tis a great Shame
There should be a Peace, while I'm *Not in game*.

Printed from the original Half-sheet, London, 1711.

The Duke shew'd me all his fine House; and the Duchess
From her Closet brought out a full Purse in her Clutches
I talk'd of a *Peace*, and they both gave a start,
His Grace swore by God, and her Grace let a Fart:
My *long old-fashion'd Pocket*, was presently cramm'd;
And sooner than Vote for a Peace I'll be damnd.     20
But, some will cry, *Turn-Coat*, and rip up old Stories,
How I always pretended to be for the *Tories*:
I answer; the Tories were in my good Graces,
Till all my *Relations* were put into *Places*.
But still I'm in Principle ever the same,
And will quit my best Friends, while I'm *Not in game*.
    When I and some others subscribed our Names
To a Plot for expelling my Master K. *James*;
I withdrew my Subscription by help of a *Blot*,
And so might discover, or gain by the Plot:     30
I had my Advantage, and stood at Defiance,
For *Daniel* was got from the Den of the Lions:
I *came in* without Danger; and was I to blame?
For rather than *hang*, I would be *Not in game*.
    I swore to the *Queen* that the *Prince* of *Hanover*
During Her Sacred Life, should never come over:
I made use of a *Trope*; that *an Heir to invite*,
*Was like keeping her Monument always in sight.*
But when I thought proper, I alter'd my Note;
And in Her own hearing I boldly did Vote,     40
That Her *Majesty* stood in great need of a *Tutor*,
And must have an *old*, or a *young Coadjutor*:
For why; I would fain have put all in a Flame,
Because, for some Reasons, I was *Not in game*.
    Now my new *Benefactors* have *brought me about*,
And I'll Vote against Peace, *with Spain*, or *without*:
Tho' the *Court* gives my *Nephews*, and *Brothers*, and *Cousins*,
And all my whole Family, Places by Dozens;
Yet since I know where a *full Purse* may be found,
And hardly pay Eighteenpence Tax in the Pound:     50
Since the *Tories* have thus disappointed my Hopes,
And will neither regard my *Figures* nor *Tropes*;
I'll *Speech* against *Peace* while *Dismal's* my Name,
And be a *true Whig*, while I am *Not in game*.

# The Windsor Prophecy

ABOUT three Months ago at *Windsor*, a poor Knight's Widow was buried in the Cloysters. In digging the Grave, the Sexton struck against a small Leaden Coffer, about half a Foot in length, and four Inches wide. The poor Man expecting he had discovered a Treasure, opened it with some difficulty; but found only a small Parchment, rolled up very fast, put into a Leather Case; which Case was tied at the top, and sealed with a St. *George*, the Impression on black Wax, very rude and *Gothick*. The Parchment was carried to a Gentleman of Learning, who found in it the following Lines, written in a black Old *English* Letter, and in the Orthography of the Age, which seems to be about Two hundred Years ago. I made a shift to obtain a Copy of it; but the Transcriber, I find, hath in many Parts alter'd the Spelling to the Modern way. The Original, as I am informed, is now in the Hands of the Ingenious Dr. *W*[oodward], F.R.S. where, I suppose, the Curious will not be refused the Satisfaction of seeing it.

The Lines seem to be a sort of Prophesie, and written in Verse, as old Prophesies usually are, but in a very Hobling kind of Measure. Their Meaning is very dark, if it be any at all; of which the Learned Reader can judge better than I: However it be, several Persons were of Opinion, that they deserved to be Published, both as they discover somewhat of the Genius of a former Age, and may be an Amusement to the present.

When a holy black Suede, the Son of Bob,
With a Saint at his Chin, and a Seal in his Fob;
Shall not see one New Years-day in that Year,
Then let old Englond make good Chear:
Windsor and Bristow then shall be
Joyned together in the Low-Countree.
Then shall the tall black Daventry Bird
Speak against Peace right many a Word;

Printed from one of the black-letter Broadsides, London, 1711.

And some shall admire his conyng Witt,
For many good Groats his Tongue shall slitt:    10
But spight of the Harpy that crawls on all four,
There shall be Peace, pardie, and War no more.
But Englond must cry alack and well a day,
If the Stick be taken from the dead Sea.
And dear Englond, if ought I understond,
Beware of Carrots from Northumberlond.
Carrots sown Thyn a deep root may get,
If so be they are in Sommer set:
Their Conyngs mark thou, for I have been told,
They Assassine when young, and Poison when old.    20
Root out these Carrots, O Thou, whose Name
Is backwards and forwards always the same;
And keep close to Thee always that Name,
Which backwards and forwards is allmost the same.
And Englond wouldst thou be happy still,
Bury those Carrots under a Hill.


# CORINNA

THIS Day, (the Year I dare not tell,)
    *Apollo* play'd the Midwife's Part,
Into the World *Corinna* fell,
    And he endow'd her with his Art.

But *Cupid* with a *Satyr* comes;
    Both softly to the Cradle creep:
Both stroke her Hands, and rub her Gums,
    While the poor Child lay fast asleep.

Then *Cupid* thus: This little Maid
    Of Love shall always speak and write;    10
And I pronounce, (the *Satyr* said)
    The World shall feel her scratch and bite.

Printed from *Miscellanies*, 1727, with corrections from *Poems*, 1735.

Her Talent she display'd betimes;
　　For in twice twelve revolving Moons,
She seem'd to laugh and squawl in Rhimes,
　　And all her Gestures were Lampoons.

At six Years old, the subtle Jade
　　Stole to the Pantry-Door, and found
The Butler with my Lady's Maid;
　　And you may swear the Tale went round.　　20

She made a Song, how little Miss
　　Was kiss'd and slobber'd by a Lad:
And how, when Master went to piss,
　　Miss came, and peep'd at all he had.

At twelve, a Poet, and Coquette;
　　Marries for Love, half Whore, half Wife;
Cuckolds, elopes, and runs in Debt;
　　Turns Auth'ress, and is *Curll*'s for Life.

# A FABLE

## OF THE

## Widow and her Cat

### I

A WIDOW kept a Favourite Cat,
　　At first a gentle Creature;
But when he was grown Sleek and Fat,
With many a Mouse, and many a Rat,
　　He soon disclos'd his Nature.

Printed from the original Half-sheet, London, 1712.

*Title.* The Widow is Queen Anne; the Cat, Marlborough. (H.W.)

## II

The *Fox* and He were Friends of old,
  Nor cou'd they now be parted;
They Nightly slunk to rob the Fold,
Devour'd the Lambs, the Fleeces sold,
  And Puss grew Lion-hearted.         10

## III

He scratch'd her Maid, he stole the Cream,
  He tore her best lac'd Pinner;
Nor Chanticleer upon the Beam,
Nor Chick, nor Duckling 'scapes, when *Grim*
  Invites the *Fox* to Dinner.

## IV

The Dame full wisely did Decree,
  For fear He shou'd dispatch more,
That the false Wretch shou'd worry'd be:
But in a sawcy manner He
  Thus Speech'd it like a *Lechmere*.        20

## V

"Must I, against all Right and Law,
  "Like Pole-Cat vile be treated?
"I! who so long with Tooth and Claw
"Have kept Domestick Mice in awe,
  "And Foreign Foes defeated!

## VI

"Your Golden Pippins, and your Pies,
  "How oft have I defended?
"'Tis true, the Pinner which you prize
"I tore in Frolick; to your Eyes
  "I never Harm intended.         30

6. *The Fox.* The Earl of Godolphin. (H.W.)

### VII

"I am a Cat of Honour"——Stay,
  Quo' She, no longer parly;
Whate'er you did in Battle slay,
By Law of Arms became your Prey,
  I hope you won it fairly.

### VIII

Of this, we'll grant you stand acquit,
  But not of your Outrages:
Tell me, Perfidious! Was it fit
To make my Cream a PERQUISITE,
  And Steal to mend your Wages?     40

### IX

So flagrant is Thy Insolence,
  So vile Thy Breach of Trust is;
That longer with Thee to Dispense,
Were want of Pow'r, or want of Sense:
  Here, *Towzer!*—Do Him Justice.

# The Fable of Midas

*MIDAS*, we are in Story told,
  Turn'd ev'ry thing he touch't to *Gold*:
He *chip't* his *Bread*, the Pieces round
Glitter'd like Spangles on the Ground:
A Codling e'er it went his Lip in,
Would strait become a *Golden* Pippin:
He call'd for Drink, you saw him Sup
*Potable Gold* in *Golden Cup*.
His empty Paunch that he might fill,
He suck't his Vittels thro' a Quill;     10
Untouch't it pass't between his Grinders,
Or't had been happy for *Gold-finders*.

Printed from the original Half-sheet, London, 1712.

45. *Towzer*. The watch-dog, Parliament. (H.W.)

He cock't his Hat, you would have said
*Mambrino*'s Helm adorn'd his Head.
Whene'er he chanc'd his Hands to lay,
On Magazines of *Corn* or *Hay*,
*Gold* ready Coin'd appear'd, instead
Of paultry *Provender* and *Bread*:
Hence we are by wise Farmers told,
*Old* Hay *is equal to old* Gold;     20
And hence a Critick deep maintains,
We learn't to weigh our *Gold* by *Grains*.
    This *Fool* had got a *lucky Hit*,
And People fancy'd he had *Wit*:
Two Gods their Skill in Musick try'd,
And both chose *Midas* to decide;
He against *Phebus* Harp decreed,
And gave it for *Pan*'s oaten Reed:
The God of Wit to shew his Grudge,
Clap't *Asses* Ears upon the Judge,     30
A goodly pair, erect and wide,
Which he could neither *Gild* nor hide.
    And now the Virtue of his *Hands*,
Was lost among *Pactolus* Sands,
Against whose Torrent while he Swims,
The *Golden* Scurf peels off his Limbs:
Fame spreads the News, and People travel
From far, to gather *golden* Gravel;
*Midas*, expos'd to all their Jears,
Had lost his *Art*, and kept his *Ears*.     40


THIS Tale inclines the gentle Reader,
    To think upon a certain *Leader*,
To whom from *Midas* down, descends
That Virtue in the Fingers ends:
What else by *Perquisites* are meant,
By *Pensions*, *Bribes*, and *three per Cent*?
By *Places* and *Commissions* sold,
And turning *Dung* it self to *Gold*?
By starving in the midst of Store,
As t'other *Midas* did before?     50

None e'er did modern *Midas* chuse,
Subject or Patron of his Muse,
But found him thus their Merit Scan,
That *Phebus* must give Place to *Pan*:
He values not the Poet's Praise,
Nor will exchange His *Plumbs* for *Bays*:
To *Pan* alone rich Misers call,
And there's the Jest, for *Pan* is *ALL*:
Here *English* Wits will be to seek,
Howe'er, *'tis all one in the* Greek.                        60

Besides, it plainly now appears,
Our *Midas* too has *Asses* Ears;
Where every Fool his Mouth applies,
And whispers in a thousand Lies;
Such gross Delusions could not pass,
Thro' any Ears but of an *Ass*.

But *Gold* defiles with frequent Touch,
There's nothing *fouls* the Hands so much:
And Scholars give it for the Cause,
Of *British Midas* dirty Paws;                               70
Which while the *Senate* strove to scower,
They washt away the *Chymick* Power.
While He his utmost Strength apply'd,
To Swim against this *Pop'lar Tide*,
The *Golden* Spoils flew off apace,
Here fell a *Pension*, there a *Place*:
The *Torrent*, merciless, imbibes
*Commissions, Perquisites,* and *Bribes,*
By their own Weight sunk to the Bottom;
*Much good may do 'em that have caught 'um.*                 80
And *Midas* now neglected stands,
With *Asses Ears,* and *dirty Hands.*

# ATLAS

## writt. 1712

### TO THE

## EARL OF OXFORD

ATLAS we read in antient Song
  Was so exceeding tall and Strong,
He bore the Skyes upon his Back
Just as a Porter does his Pack
But, as a Porter overpresst
Unloads upon a Stall to rest
Or when he can no longer stand
Desires some Friend to lend a Hand
So Atlas, lest the pondrous Sphears
Should sink and fall about his Ears          10
Got Hercules to bear the Pile
That he might take his Rest awhile,
Yet Hercules was not so strong,
Nor could have borne it half so long.
  All Statesmen are in this Condition,
  And Atlas is a Politician
  A Premier Minister of State
  Alcides, one of second Rate.
  Suppose then Atlas ne'er so wise,
  Yet when the Weight of Kingdoms lyes          20
  Too long upon his single Shoulders
  He must sink down, or find Up-holders.

Printed from Swift's autograph. The Rothschild Library, No. 2260.

# *Toland*'s Invitation to *DISMAL,* to Dine with the CALVES-HEAD Club

*Imitated from* Horace, *Epist. 5, Lib. 1*

IF, dearest 𝔇𝔦𝔰𝔪𝔞𝔩, you for once can Dine
Upon a single Dish, and Tavern Wine,
*Toland* to you this Invitation sends,
To eat the *CALVES-HEAD* with your trusty Friends.
Suspend a while your vain ambitious Hopes,
Leave hunting after Bribes, forget your Tropes:
To morrow We our *Mystick Feast* prepare,
Where Thou, our latest *Proselyte,* shalt share:
When We, by proper Signs and Symbols tell,
How, by *Brave Hands,* the *Royal TRAYTOR* fell;          10
The Meat shall represent the *TYRANT*'s Head,
The Wine, his Blood, *our Predecessors* shed:
Whilst an *alluding* Hymn some Artist sings,
We toast Confusion to the Race of Kings:

> SI potes archiacis conviva recumbere lectis,
> Nec modica cœnare times olus omne patella:
> Supremo te sole domi, Torquate, manebo.
>
> \*     \*     \*     \*     \*     \*     \*     \*
>
> Mitte leves spes, & certamina divitiarum,
> Et Moschi causam: Cras nato Cæsare festus
> Dat veniam somnumque dies: impune licebit
> Æstivam sermone benigno tendere noctem.
>
> \*     \*     \*     \*     \*     \*     \*     \*

At Monarchy we nobly shew our Spight,
And talk *what Fools call Treason* all the Night.
   Who, by Disgraces or ill Fortune sunk,
Feels not his Soul enliven'd when he's Drunk?
Wine can clear up *Godolphin*'s cloudy Face,
And fill *Jack Smith* with Hopes to keep his Place;          20
By Force of Wine ev'n *Scarborow* is Brave,
*Hal* grows more Pert, and *Sommers* not so Grave:

Printed from the original Broadside, London, 1712.

Quid non ebrietas designat? operta recludit;
Spes jubet esse ratas; in prælia trudit inermem:

Wine can give *Portland* Wit, and *Cleveland* Sense,
*Montague* Learning, *Bolton* Eloquence:
*Cholmondely*, when Drunk, can never lose his *Wand*,
And *Lincoln* then imagines he has Land.

Sollicitis animis onus eximit; addocet artes.
Fœcundi calices quem non fecere disertum?
Contracta quem non in paupertate solutum?

My Province is, to see that all be right,
Glasses and Linnen clean, and Pewter bright;
From our *Mysterious Club* to keep out Spies,
And *Tories* (dress'd like Waiters) in Disguise.                   30
You shall be coupled as you best approve,
Seated at Table next the Men you love.
*Sunderland, Orford, Boyle,* and *Richmond*'s Grace
Will come; and *Hampden* shall have *Walpool*'s Place.

Hæc ego procurare & idoneus imperor, & non
Invitus; ne turpe toral, ne sordida mappa
Corruget nares, ne non & cantharus & lanx
Ostendat tibi te; ne fidos inter amicos
Sit qui dicta foras eliminet: ut coeat par
Jungaturque pari, Brutum tibi Septimiumque,

*Wharton*, unless prevented by a Whore,
Will hardly fail, and there is room for more:
But I love Elbow-room when're I drink,
And honest *Harry* is too apt to stink.
    Let no pretence of Bus'ness make you stay,
Yet take one Word of Counsel by the way:                           40
If *Guernsey* calls, send word you're gone abroad;
He'll teaze you with King *Charles* and Bishop *Laud*,
Or make you Fast, and carry you to Prayers:
But if he will break in, and walk up Stairs,
Steal by the Back-door out, and leave him there;
Then order *Squash* to call a Hackney Chair.   *January* 29.

Et nisi cœna prior potiorque puella Sabinum
Detinet, assumam, locus est & pluribus umbris:
Sed nimis arcta premunt olidæ convivia capræ.
Tu quotus esse velis rescribe: & rebus omissis,
Atria servantem postico falle clientem.

# Peace and Dunkirk;

## BEING AN

## *Excellent New Song upon the Surrender of* Dunkirk *to General* Hill

To the Tune of, *The King shall enjoy his own again*

### I

SPIGHT of *Dutch* Friends and *English* Foes,
  Poor *Britain* shall have Peace at last;
*Holland* got Towns, and we got Blows,
    But *Dunkirk*'s ours, we'll hold it fast:
      We have got it in a String,
      And the 𝕎𝕙𝕚𝕘𝕤 may all go Swing,
For among good Friends, I love to be plain;
      All their false deluded Hopes,
      Will, or ought to end in Ropes;
*But the* QUEEN *shall enjoy Her own again.*          10

### II

*Sunderland*'s run out of his Wits,
  And 𝕯𝖎𝖘𝖒𝖆𝖑 double-𝕯𝖎𝖘𝖒𝖆𝖑 looks;
*Wharton* can only Swear by Fits,
  And strutting *Hal* is off the Hooks;
    Old *Godolphin* full of Spleen,
    Made *false Moves*, and lost his QUEEN;
*Harry* look'd fierce, and shook his ragged Mane:
    But a Prince of high Renown,
    Swore he'd rather lose a *Crown*,
*Than the* QUEEN *should enjoy Her own again.*          20

Printed from the original Broadside, London, 1712.

### III

Our Merchant Ships may cut the Line,
　　And not be snapt by Privateers,
And Commoners who love good Wine,
　　Will drink it now as well as Peers:
　　　　Landed-Men shall have their Rent,
　　　　Yet our Stocks rise *Cent. per Cent,*
The *Dutch* from hence shall no more Millions drain;
　　　　We'll bring on us no more Debts,
　　　　Nor with Bankrupts fill *Gazetts,*
*And the* QUEEN *shall enjoy Her own again.*          30

### IV

The Towns we took ne'er did us good,
　　What signify'd the *French* to beat?
We spent our Mony and our Blood,
　　To make the *Dutch*-men proud and great:
　　　　But the Lord of *Oxford* Swears,
　　　　*Dunkirk* never shall be theirs,
The *Dutch*-hearted 𝔚𝔥𝔦𝔤𝔰 may rail and complain;
　　　　But true *English* Men will fill,
　　　　A good Health to Gen'ral *Hill,*
*For the* QUEEN *now enjoys Her own again.*          40


## Part of the SEVENTH EPISTLE

## of the FIRST BOOK of

## *HORACE*

### IMITATED

HARLEY, the Nation's great Support,
　　Returning home one Day from Court,
　　(His Mind with Publick Cares possest,
All *Europe*'s Bus'ness in his Breast)

Printed from the first edition, London, 1713, with corrections from *Poems,* 1735.

Observ'd a *Parson* near *Whitehall*,
Cheapning old Authors on a Stall.
The Priest was pretty well in case,
And shew'd some Humour in his Face;
Look'd with an easie, careless Mien,
A perfect Stranger to the Spleen;                    10
Of Size that might a Pulpit fill,
But more inclining to sit still.
MY LORD, who (if a Man may say't)
Loves Mischief better than his Meat,
Was now dispos'd to crack a Jest;
And bid Friend *Lewis* go in quest
(This *Lewis* is a Cunning Shaver,
And very much in *HARLEY*'s Favour)
In quest, who might this *Parson* be,
What was his Name, of what Degree;                   20
If possible, to learn his Story,
And whether he were *Whig* or *Tory*?
    *Lewis* his Patron's Humour knows;
Away upon his Errand goes,
And quickly did the Matter sift,
Found out that it was Dr. *Swift*:
A Clergyman of special Note,
For shunning those of his own Coat;
Which made his Brethren of the Gown
Take care betimes to run him down:                   30
No Libertine, nor Over-nice,
Addicted to no sort of Vice;
Went where he pleas'd, said what he thought,
Not Rich, but ow'd no Man a Groat;
In State-Opinions *a-la Mode*,
He hated *Wharton* like a Toad;
Had giv'n the *Faction* many a Wound,
And Libell'd all the Junta round;
Kept Company with Men of Wit,
Who often father'd what he writ;                     40
His Works were hawk'd in ev'ry Street,
But seldom rose above a Sheet:
Of late indeed the Paper-*Stamp*
Did very much his Genius cramp;

And, since he could not spend his Fire,
He now intended to Retire.
   Said *HARLEY*, I desire to know
From his own Mouth, if this be so?
Step to the Doctor straight, and say,
I'd have him Dine with me to Day.     50
*Swift* seem'd to wonder what he meant,
Nor wou'd believe MY LORD had sent;
So never offer'd once to stir,
But coldly said, *Your Servant, Sir.*
Does he refuse me? *HARLEY* cry'd:
He does, with Insolence and Pride.
Some few Days after *HARLEY* spies
The Doctor fasten'd by the Eyes,
At *Charing-Cross*, among the Rout,
Where painted Monsters are hung out.     60
He pull'd the String, and stopt his Coach,
Beck'ning the Doctor to approach.
   *Swift*, who could neither fly nor hide,
Came sneaking to the Chariot-side,
And offer'd many a lame Excuse;
He never meant the least Abuse—
*My Lord—The Honour you design'd—*
*Extremely proud—but I had din'd—*
*I'm sure I never shou'd neglect—*
*No Man alive has more Respect—*     70
Well, I shall think of that no more,
If you'll be sure to come at *Four.*
   The Doctor now obeys the Summons,
Likes both his Company and Commons;
Displays his Talent, sits till Ten,
Next Day invited, comes agen;
Soon grows Domestick, seldom fails
Either at Morning, or at Meals;
Comes early, and departeth late:
In short, the Gudgeon took the Bait:     80
MY LORD wou'd carry on the Jest,
And down to *Windsor* takes his Guest.
*Swift* much admires the Place and Air,
And longs to be a *Canon* there;

In Summer round the Park to ride,
In Winter—never to reside.
A *Canon!* that's a Place too mean:
No, Doctor, you shall be a *Dean*;
Two Dozen *Canons* round your Stall,
And you the Tyrant o'er them all:                90
You need but cross the *Irish* Seas,
To live in Plenty, Power and Ease.

Poor *Swift* departs, and, what is worse,
With borrow'd Money in his Purse;
Travels at least a Hundred Leagues,
And suffers numberless Fatigues.

Suppose him, now, a *Dean* compleat,
Demurely lolling in his Seat;
The Silver Virge, with decent Pride,
Stuck underneath his Cushion-side:                100
Suppose him gone through all Vexations,
Patents, Instalments, Abjurations,
First-Fruits and Tenths, and Chapter-Treats,
Dues, Payments, Fees, Demands and Cheats,
(The wicked Laity's contriving,
To hinder Clergymen from thriving);
Now all the Doctor's Money's spent,
His Tenants wrong him in his Rent;
The Farmers, spightfully combin'd,
Force him to take his Tythes in kind;             110
And *Parvisol* discounts Arrears,
By Bills for Taxes and Repairs.

Poor *Swift*, with all his Losses vext,
Not knowing where to turn him next;
Above a Thousand Pounds in Debt,
Takes Horse, and in a mighty Fret
Rides Day and Night at such a Rate,
He soon arrives at *HARLEY*'s Gate;
But was so dirty, pale and thin,
Old *Read* would hardly let him in.               120

Said *HARLEY*, Welcome Rev'rend Dean!
What makes your Worship look so lean?

111. *Parvisol.* The Dean's Agent, a Frenchman.
120. *Read.* The Lord Treasurer's Porter.

Why sure you won't appear in Town,
In that old Wig and rusty Gown!
I doubt your Heart is set on Pelf
So much, that you neglect your Self.
What! I suppose now Stocks are high,
You've some good Purchase in your Eye;
Or is your Money out at use?—

   Truce, good MY LORD, I beg a Truce!    130
The Doctor in a Passion cry'd;
Your Raillery is misapply'd:
Experience I have dearly bought,
You know I am not worth a Groat:
But it's a folly to contest,
When you resolve to have your Jest;
And since you now have done your worst,
Pray leave me where you found me first.


# *To* LORD HARLEY,

## since Earl of OXFORD, on his
## MARRIAGE

### Written in the Year M DCC XIII

AMONG the numbers who employ
   Their tongues and pens to give you joy,
Dear Harley, gen'rous Youth, admit
What friendship dictates more than wit.

   Forgive me, when I fondly thought
(By frequent observation taught)
A spirit so inform'd as yours
Could never prosper in amours.
The God of Wit, and Light, and Arts,
With all acquir'd and nat'ral parts,    10

Printed from the *Works*, *4to, Vol. VIII* (2), London, 1765.

Whose harp could savage beasts enchant,
Was an unfortunate gallant.
Had Bacchus after Daphne reel'd,
The Nymph had soon been brought to yield;
Or, had Embroider'd Mars pursu'd,
The Nymph would ne'er have been a prude.
Ten thousand footsteps, full in view,
Mark out the way where Daphne flew.
For such is all the sex's flight,
They fly from learning, wit, and light:        20
They fly, and none can overtake
But some gay coxcomb, or a rake.


How then, dear Harley, could I guess
That you should meet, in love, success?
For, if those antient Tales be true,
Phœbus was beautiful as you:
Yet Daphne never slack'd her pace,
For wit and learning spoil'd his face.
And, since the same resemblance held
In gifts, wherein you both excell'd,        30
I fancy'd ev'ry nymph would run
From you, as from Latona's son.


Then where, said I, shall Harley find
A virgin of superior mind,
With wit and virtue to discover,
And pay the merit of her Lover?


This character shall Ca'ndish claim,
Born to retrieve her sex's fame.
The chief among that glitt'ring crowd,
Of titles, birth, and fortune proud,        40
(As fools are insolent and vain)
Madly aspir'd to wear her chain:
But Pallas, guardian of the Maid,
Descending to her Charge's aid,
Held out Medusa's snaky locks,
Which stupify'd them all to stocks.

The Nymph, with indignation, view'd
The dull, the noisy, and the lewd:
For Pallas, with celestial light,
Had purify'd her mortal sight;     50
Shew'd her the Virtues all combin'd,
Fresh blooming, in young Harley's mind.

    Terrestrial nymphs, by formal arts,
Display their various nets for hearts:
Their looks are all by method set,
When to be prude, and when coquette;
Yet, wanting skill and pow'r to chuse,
Their only pride is to refuse.
But, when a Goddess would bestow
Her love on some bright youth below,     60
Round all the earth she casts her eyes;
And then, descending from the skies,
Makes choice of him she fancies best,
And bids the ravish'd youth be bless'd.

    Thus the bright Empress of the Morn
Chose, for her spouse, a mortal born:
The Goddess made advances first,
Else what aspiring hero durst?
Tho', like a virgin of fifteen,
She blushes when by mortals seen;     70
Still blushes, and with speed retires,
When Sol pursues her with his fires.

    Diana thus, Heav'n's chastest queen,
Struck with Endymion's graceful mien,
Down from her silver chariot came,
And to the Shepherd own'd her flame.

    Thus Ca'ndish, as Aurora bright,
And chaster than the Queen of Night,
Descended from her sphere to find
A Mortal of superior kind.     80

# CADENUS

## AND

# VANESSA

THE *Shepherds* and the *Nymphs* were seen
Pleading before the *Cyprian* Queen.
The Council for the Fair began,
Accusing that false Creature, *Man*.

The Brief with weighty Crimes was charg'd,
On which the Pleader much enlarg'd;
That *Cupid* now has lost his Art,
Or blunts the Point of ev'ry Dart;
His Altar now no longer smokes,
His Mother's Aid no Youth invokes:            10
This tempts Free-thinkers to refine,
And bring in doubt their Pow'r divine;
Now Love is dwindled to Intrigue,
And Marriage grown a Money-League.
Which Crimes aforesaid (*with her Leave*)
Were (*as he humbly did conceive*)
Against our Sov'reign Lady's Peace,
Against the Statute in that Case,
Against her Dignity and Crown:
Then pray'd an Answer, and sat down.            20

The *Nymphs* with Scorn beheld their Foes:
When the Defendant's Council rose,
And, what no Lawyer ever lack'd,
With Impudence own'd all the Fact.
But, what the gentlest Heart would vex,
Laid all the Fault on t'other Sex.
That modern Love is no such Thing
As what those antient Poets sing;

Printed from *Miscellanies. The Last Volume*, 1727, with corrections from *Poems*, 1735.

A Fire celestial, chaste, refin'd,
Conceiv'd and kindled in the Mind,     30
Which having found an equal Flame,
Unites, and both become the same,
In different Breasts together burn,
Together both to Ashes turn.
But Women now feel no such Fire,
And only know the gross Desire;
Their Passions move in lower Spheres,
Where-e'er Caprice or Folly steers.
A Dog, a Parrot, or an Ape,
Or some worse Brute in human Shape,     40
Engross the Fancies of the Fair,
The few soft Moments they can spare,
From Visits to receive and pay,
From Scandal, Politicks, and Play,
From Fans, and Flounces, and Brocades,
From Equipage and Park-Parades,
From all the thousand Female Toys,
From every Trifle that employs
The out or inside of their Heads,
Between their Toylets and their Beds.     50

In a dull Stream, which moving slow
You hardly see the Current flow,
If a small Breeze obstructs the Course,
It whirls about for Want of Force,
And in its narrow Circle gathers
Nothing but Chaff, and Straws, and Feathers:
The Current of a Female Mind
Stops thus, and turns with ev'ry Wind;
Thus whirling round, together draws
Fools, Fops, and Rakes, for Chaff and Straws.     60
Hence we conclude, no Women's Hearts
Are won by Virtue, Wit, and Parts;
Nor are the Men of Sense to blame,
For Breasts incapable of Flame;
The Fault must on the *Nymphs* be plac'd,
Grown so corrupted in their Taste.

The Pleader having spoke his best,
Had Witness ready to attest,
Who fairly could on Oath depose,
When Questions on the Fact arose,                    70
That ev'ry Article was true;
*Nor further those Deponents knew:*
Therefore he humbly would insist,
The Bill might be with Costs dismist.


The Cause appear'd of so much Weight,
That *Venus*, from her Judgment-Seat,
Desir'd them not to talk so loud,
Else she must interpose a Cloud:
For if the Heav'nly Folk should know
These Pleadings in the Courts below,                 80
That Mortals here disdain to love;
She ne'er could shew her Face above.
For Gods, their Betters, are too wise
To value that which Men despise.
And then, said she, my Son and I
Must strole in Air 'twixt Land and Sky;
Or else, shut out from Heaven and Earth,
Fly to the Sea, my Place of Birth;
There live with daggl'd *Mermaids* pent,
And keep on Fish perpetual *Lent*.                   90


But since the Case appear'd so nice,
She thought it best to take Advice.
The *Muses*, by their King's Permission,
Tho' Foes to Love, attend the Session,
And on the Right Hand took their Places
In Order; on the Left, the *Graces*:
To whom she might her Doubts propose
On all Emergencies that rose.
The *Muses* oft were seen to frown;
The *Graces* half asham'd look'd down;               100
And 'twas observ'd, there were but few ⎫
Of either Sex, among the Crew,       ⎬
Whom she or her Assessors knew.      ⎭

The Goddess soon began to see
Things were not ripe for a Decree,
And said she must consult her Books,
The Lovers *Fleta's, Bractons, Cokes.*
First to a dapper Clerk she beckon'd,
To turn to *Ovid,* Book the Second;
She then referr'd them to a Place 110
In *Virgil* (*vide Dido*'s Case:)
As for *Tibullus*'s Reports,
They never pass'd for Law in Courts;
For *Cowley*'s Briefs, and Pleas of *Waller,*
Still their Authority was smaller.

There was on both Sides much to say:
She'd hear the Cause another Day,
And so she did, and then a Third,
She heard it—there she kept her Word;
But with Rejoinders and Replies, 120
Long Bills, and Answers, stuff'd with Lies,
Demur, Imparlance, and Essoign,
The Parties ne'er could Issue join:
For Sixteen Years the Cause was spun,
And then stood where it first begun.

Now, gentle *Clio,* sing or say,
What *Venus* meant by this Delay.
The Goddess much perplex'd in Mind,
To see her Empire thus declin'd,
When first this grand Debate arose 130
Above her Wisdom to compose,
Conceiv'd a Project in her Head,
To work her Ends; which if it sped,
Wou'd shew the Merits of the Cause,
Far better than consulting Laws.

In a glad Hour *Lucina*'s Aid
Produc'd on Earth a wond'rous Maid,
On whom the Queen of Love was bent
To try a new Experiment:
She threw her Law-books on the Shelf, 140
And thus debated with herself.

Since Men alledge they ne'er can find
Those Beauties in a Female Mind,
Which raise a Flame that will endure
For ever, uncorrupt and pure;
If 'tis with Reason they complain,
This Infant shall restore my Reign.
I'll search where ev'ry Virtue dwells,
From Courts inclusive, down to Cells,
What Preachers talk, or Sages write,                    150
These I will gather and unite,
And represent them to Mankind
Collected in that Infant's Mind.

This said, she plucks in Heav'ns high Bow'rs
A Sprig of *Amaranthine* Flow'rs,
In Nectar thrice infuses Bays,
Three times refin'd in *Titan*'s Rays:
Then calls the *Graces* to her Aid,
And sprinkles thrice the new-born Maid.
From whence the tender Skin assumes                    160
A Sweetness above all Perfumes;
From whence a Cleanliness remains,
Incapable of outward Stains;
From whence that Decency of Mind,
So lovely in the Female Kind,
Where not one careless Thought intrudes,
Less modest than the Speech of Prudes;
Where never Blush was call'd in Aid,
That spurious Virtue in a Maid,
A Virtue but at second-hand;                    170
They blush because they understand.

The *Graces* next wou'd act their Part,
And shew'd but little of their Art;
Their Work was half already done,
The Child with native Beauty shone,
The outward Form no Help requir'd:
Each breathing on her thrice, inspir'd
That gentle, soft, engaging Air,
Which in old Times adorn'd the Fair;

And said, "*Vanessa* be the Name,       180
"By which thou shalt be known to Fame:
"*Vanessa*, by the Gods enroll'd:
"Her Name on Earth —— shall not be told."

    But still the Work was not compleat,
When *Venus* thought on a Deceit:
Drawn by her Doves, away she flies,
And finds out *Pallas* in the Skies:
Dear *Pallas*, I have been this Morn
To see a lovely Infant born:
A Boy in yonder Isle below,       190
So like my own, without his Bow,
By Beauty cou'd your Heart be won,
You'd swear it is *Apollo*'s Son;
But it shall ne'er be said, a Child
So hopeful, has by me been spoil'd;
I have enough besides to spare,
And give him wholly to your Care.

    *Wisdom*'s above suspecting Wiles:
The Queen of Learning gravely smiles,
Down from *Olympus* comes with Joy,       200
Mistakes *Vanessa* for a Boy;
Then sows within her tender Mind
Seeds long unknown to Womankind,
For manly Bosoms chiefly fit,
The Seeds of Knowledge, Judgment, Wit.
Her Soul was suddenly endu'd
With Justice, Truth and Fortitude;
With Honour, which no Breath can Stain,
Which Malice must attack in vain;
With open Heart and bounteous Hand:       210
But *Pallas* here was at a Stand;
She knew in our degen'rate Days
Bare Virtue could not live on Praise,
That Meat must be with Money bought;
She therefore, upon second Thought,
Infus'd, yet as it were by Stealth,
Some small Regard for State and Wealth:

Of which, as she grew up, there stay'd
A Tincture in the prudent Maid:
She manag'd her Estate with Care,      220
Yet lik'd three Footmen to her Chair.
But lest he shou'd neglect his Studies
Like a young Heir, the thrifty Goddess
(For fear young Master shou'd be spoil'd,)
Wou'd use him like a younger Child;
And, after long computing, found
'Twou'd come to just Five Thousand Pound.

    The Queen of Love was pleas'd, and proud,
To see *Vanessa* thus endow'd;
She doubted not but such a Dame      230
Thro' ev'ry Breast wou'd dart a Flame;
That ev'ry rich and lordly Swain
With Pride wou'd drag about her Chain;
That Scholars wou'd forsake their Books
To study bright *Vanessa*'s Looks:
As she advanc'd, that Womankind
Wou'd by her Model form their Mind,
And all their Conduct wou'd be try'd
By her, as an unerring Guide.
Offending Daughters oft wou'd hear      240
*Vanessa*'s Praise rung in their Ear:
Miss *Betty*, when she does a Fault,
Lets fall her Knife, or spills the Salt,
Will thus be by her Mother chid,
"'Tis what *Vanessa* never did."
Thus by the Nymphs and Swains ador'd,
My Pow'r shall be again restor'd,
And happy Lovers bless my Reign ——
So *Venus* hop'd, but hop'd in vain.

    For when in time the *Martial Maid*      250
Found out the Trick that *Venus* play'd,
She shakes her Helm, she knits her Brows,
And fir'd with Indignation vows,
To-morrow, ere the setting Sun,
She'd all undo, that she had done.

But in the Poets we may find,
A wholesome Law, Time out of mind,
Had been confirm'd by Fate's Decree;
That Gods, of whatso'er Degree,
Resume not what themselves have giv'n,                    260
Or any Brother-God in Heav'n:
Which keeps the Peace among the Gods,
Or they must always be at Odds.
And *Pallas*, if she broke the Laws,
Must yield her Foe the stronger Cause;
A Shame to one so much ador'd
For Wisdom, at *Jove*'s Council-Board.
Besides, she fear'd the Queen of Love
Wou'd meet with better Friends above.
And tho' she must with Grief reflect,                     270
To see a Mortal Virgin deck'd
With Graces, hitherto unknown
To Female Breasts, except her own;
Yet she wou'd act as best became
A Goddess of unspotted Fame:
She knew, by Augury Divine,
*Venus* wou'd fail in her Design:
She study'd well the Point, and found
Her Foe's Conclusions were not sound,
From Premisses erroneous brought,                         280
And therefore the Deductions nought,
And must have contrary Effects
To what her treach'rous Foe expects.

In proper Season *Pallas* meets
The Queen of Love, whom thus she greets,
(For Gods, we are by *Homer* told,
Can in Celestial Language scold)
Perfidious Goddess! but in vain
You form'd this Project in your Brain,
A Project for thy Talents fit,                            290
With much Deceit and little Wit;
Thou hast, as thou shalt quickly see,
Deceiv'd thy self, instead of me;

For how can Heav'nly Wisdom prove
An Instrument to earthly Love?
Know'st thou not yet that Men commence
Thy Votaries, for Want of Sense?
Nor shall *Vanessa* be the Theme
To manage thy abortive Scheme;
She'll prove the greatest of thy Foes: 300
And yet I scorn to interpose,
But using neither Skill, nor Force,
Leave all Things to their Nat'ral Course.

 The Goddess thus pronounc'd her Doom:
When, lo! *Vanessa* in her Bloom,
Advanc'd like *Atalanta*'s Star,
But rarely seen, and seen from far:
In a new World with Caution stept,
Watch'd all the Company she kept,
Well knowing from the Books she read 310
What dangerous Paths young Virgins tread;
Wou'd seldom at the Park appear,
Nor saw the Play-House twice a Year;
Yet not incurious, was inclin'd
To know the Converse of Mankind.

 First issu'd from Perfumers Shops
A Croud of fashionable Fops;
They ask'd her, how she lik'd the Play,
Then told the Tattle of the Day,
A Duel fought last Night at Two, 320
About a Lady —— You know who;
Mention'd a new *Italian*, come
Either from *Muscovy* or *Rome*;
Gave Hints of who and who's together;
Then fell to talking of the Weather:
Last Night was so extremely fine,
The Ladies walk'd till after Nine.
Then in soft Voice and Speech absurd,
With Nonsense ev'ry second Word,
With Fustian from exploded Plays, 330
They celebrate her Beauty's Praise,

Run o'er their Cant of stupid Lies,
And tell the Murders of her Eyes.

   With silent Scorn *Vanessa* sat,
Scarce list'ning to their idle Chat;
Further than sometimes by a Frown,
When they grew pert, to pull them down.
At last she spitefully was bent
To try their Wisdom's full Extent;
And said, she valu'd nothing less       340
Than Titles, Figure, Shape, and Dress;
That, Merit should be chiefly plac'd
In Judgment, Knowledge, Wit, and Taste;
And these, she offer'd to dispute,
Alone distinguish'd Man from Brute:
That, present Times have no Pretence
To Virtue, in the Noblest Sense,
By *Greeks* and *Romans* understood,
To perish for our Country's Good.
She nam'd the antient Heroes round,       350
Explain'd for what they were renown'd;
Then spoke with Censure, or Applause,
Of foreign Customs, Rites, and Laws;
Thro' Nature, and thro' Art she rang'd,
And gracefully her Subject chang'd:
In vain: her Hearers had no Share
In all she spoke, except to stare.
Their Judgment was upon the Whole,
—That Lady is the dullest Soul—
Then tipt their Forehead in a Jeer,       360
As who should say—she wants it here;
She may be handsome, young and rich,
But none will burn her for a Witch.

   A Party next of glitt'ring Dames,
From round the Purlieus of *St. James*,
Came early, out of pure Good-will,
To see the Girl in Deshabille.
Their Clamour 'lighting from their Chairs,
Grew louder, all the Way up Stairs;

At Entrance loudest, where they found          370
The Room with Volumes litter'd round
*Vanessa* held *Montaigne*, and read,
Whilst Mrs. *Susan* comb'd her Head:
They call'd for Tea and Chocolate,
And fell into their usual Chat,
Discoursing with important Face,
On Ribbons, Fans, and Gloves and Lace;
Shew'd Patterns just from *India* brought,
And gravely ask'd her what she thought,
Whether the Red or Green were best,          380
And what they cost? *Vanessa* guess'd,
As came into her Fancy first,
Nam'd half the Rates, and lik'd the worst.
To Scandal next —— What aukward Thing
Was that, last *Sunday* in the Ring?
—— I'm sorry *Mopsa* breaks so fast;
I said her Face would never last.
*Corinna* with that youthful Air,
Is thirty, and a Bit to spare.
Her Fondness for a certain Earl          390
Began, when I was but a Girl.
*Phyllis*, who but a Month ago
Was marry'd to the *Tunbridge* Beau,
I saw coquetting t'other Night
In publick with that odious Knight.

    They railly'd next *Vanessa*'s Dress;
That Gown was made for Old Queen *Bess*.
Dear Madam, Let me set your Head:
Don't you intend to put on Red?
A Pettycoat without a Hoop!          400
Sure, you are not asham'd to stoop;
With handsome Garters at your Knees,
No matter what a Fellow sees.

    Fill'd with Disdain, with Rage inflam'd,
Both of her self and Sex asham'd,
The Nymph stood silent out of spight,
Nor wou'd vouchsafe to set them right.

Away the fair Detractors went,
And gave, by turns, their Censures Vent.
She's not so handsome, in my Eyes:                    410
For Wit, I wonder where it lies.
She's fair and clean, and that's the most;
But why proclaim her for a Toast?
A Baby Face, no Life, no Airs,
But what she learnt at Country Fairs;
Scarce knows what Diff'rence is between
Rich *Flanders* Lace, and Colberteen.
I'll undertake my little *Nancy*
In Flounces has a better Fancy.
With all her Wit, I wou'd not ask                     420
Her Judgment, how to buy a Mask.
We begg'd her but to patch her Face,
She never hit one proper Place;
Which every Girl at five Years old
Can do as soon as she is told.
I own, that out-of-fashion Stuff
Becomes the *Creature* well enough.
The Girl might pass, if we cou'd get her
To know the World a little better.
(*To know the World!* a modern Phrase,                430
For Visits, Ombre, Balls and Plays.)

    Thus, to the World's perpetual Shame,
The *Queen of Beauty* lost her Aim.
Too late with Grief she understood,
*Pallas* had done more Harm than Good;
For great Examples are but vain,
Where Ignorance begets Disdain.
Both Sexes, arm'd with Guilt and Spite,
Against *Vanessa*'s Pow'r unite;
To copy her, few Nymphs aspir'd;                      440
Her Virtues fewer Swains admir'd:
So Stars beyond a certain Height
Give Mortals neither Heat nor Light.

    Yet some of either Sex, endow'd
With Gifts superior to the Crowd,

With Virtue, Knowledge, Taste and Wit,
She condescended to admit:
With pleasing Arts she could reduce
Mens Talents to their proper Use;
And with Address each Genius held                    450
To that wherein it most excell'd;
Thus making others Wisdom known,
Cou'd please them, and improve her own.
A modest Youth said something new,
She plac'd it in the strongest View.
All humble Worth she strove to raise;
Would not be prais'd, yet lov'd to praise.
The Learned met with free Approach,
Although they came not in a Coach.
Some Clergy too she wou'd allow,                     460
Nor quarrell'd at their aukward Bow.
But this was for *Cadenus*' sake;
A Gownman of a diff'rent Make;
Whom *Pallas*, once *Vanessa*'s Tutor,
Had fix'd on for her Coadjutor.

But *Cupid*, full of Mischief, longs
To vindicate his Mother's Wrongs.
On *Pallas* all Attempts are vain;
One way he knows to give her Pain:
Vows, on *Vanessa*'s Heart to take                   470
Due Vengeance, for her Patron's sake.
Those early Seeds by *Venus* sown,
In spight of *Pallas*, now were grown;
And *Cupid* hop'd they wou'd improve
By Time, and ripen into Love.
The Boy made use of all his Craft,
In vain discharging many a Shaft,
Pointed at Col'nels, Lords, and Beaux;
*Cadenus* warded off the Blows:
For placing still some Book betwixt,                 480
The Darts were in the Cover fix'd,
Or often blunted and recoil'd,
On *Plutarch*'s Morals struck, were spoil'd.

The Queen of Wisdom cou'd foresee,
But not prevent the Fates decree;
And human Caution tries in vain
To break that Adamantine Chain.
*Vanessa*, tho' by *Pallas* taught,
By *Love* invulnerable thought,
Searching in Books for Wisdom's Aid,     490
Was, in the very Search, betray'd.

*Cupid*, tho' all his Darts were lost,
Yet still resolv'd to spare no Cost;
He could not answer to his Fame
The Triumphs of that stubborn Dame,
A Nymph so hard to be subdu'd,
Who neither was Coquette nor Prude.
I find, says he, she wants a Doctor,
Both to adore her and instruct her;
I'll give her what she most admires,     500
Among those venerable Sires.
*Cadenus* is a Subject fit,
Grown old in Politicks and Wit;
Caress'd by Ministers of State,
Of half Mankind the Dread and Hate.
Whate'er Vexations Love attend,
She need no Rivals apprehend.
Her Sex, with universal Voice,
Must laugh at her capricious Choice.

*Cadenus* many things had writ;     510
*Vanessa* much esteem'd his Wit,
And call'd for his Poetick Works;
Mean time the Boy in secret lurks,
And while the Book was in her Hand,
The Urchin from his private Stand
Took Aim, and shot with all his Strength
A Dart of such prodigious Length,
It pierc'd the feeble Volume thro',
And deep transfix'd her Bosom too.
Some Lines, more moving than the rest,     520
Stuck to the Point that pierc'd her Breast;

And, born directly to the Heart,
With Pains unknown increas'd her Smart.

    *Vanessa*, not in Years a Score,
Dreams of a Gown of forty-four;
Imaginary Charms can find,
In Eyes with Reading almost blind;
*Cadenus* now no more appears
Declin'd in Health, advanc'd in Years.
She fancies Musick in his Tongue,        530
Nor further looks, but thinks him young.
What Mariner is not afraid,
To venture in a Ship decay'd?
What Planter will attempt to yoke
A Sapling with a falling Oak?
As Years increase, she brighter shines,
*Cadenus* with each Day declines,
And he must fall a Prey to Time,
While she continues in her Prime.

    *Cadenus*, common Forms apart,        540
In every Scene had kept his Heart;
Had sigh'd and languish'd, vow'd, and writ,
For Pastime, or to shew his Wit;
But Time, and Books, and State Affairs
Had spoil'd his fashionable Airs;
He now cou'd praise, esteem, approve,
But understood not what was Love.
His Conduct might have made him styl'd
A Father, and the Nymph his Child.
That innocent Delight he took        550
To see the Virgin mind her Book,
Was but the Master's secret Joy
In School to hear the finest Boy.
Her Knowledge with her Fancy grew;
She hourly press'd for something new;
*Ideas* came into her Mind
So fast, his Lessons lagg'd behind:
She reason'd, without plodding long,
Nor ever gave her Judgment wrong.

But now a sudden Change was wrought,      560
She minds no longer what he taught.
*Cadenus* was amaz'd to find
Such Marks of a distracted Mind;
For tho' she seem'd to listen more
To all he spoke, than e'er before;
He found her Thoughts would absent range,
Yet guess'd not whence could spring the Change.
And first he modestly conjectures
His Pupil might be tir'd with Lectures;
Which help'd to mortify his Pride,      570
Yet gave him not the Heart to chide;
But in a mild dejected Strain,
At last he ventur'd to complain:
Said, she shou'd be no longer teiz'd;
Might have her Freedom when she pleas'd:
Was now convinc'd he acted wrong,
To hide her from the World so long;
And in dull Studies to engage
One of her tender Sex and Age.
That ev'ry Nymph with Envy own'd,      580
How she might shine in the *Grand-Monde*,
And ev'ry Shepherd was undone
To see her cloister'd like a Nun.
This was a visionary Scheme,
He wak'd, and found it but a Dream;
A Project far above his Skill,
For Nature must be Nature still.
If he was bolder than became
A Scholar to a Courtly Dame,
She might excuse a Man of Letters;      590
Thus Tutors often treat their Betters.
And since his Talk offensive grew,
He came to take his last Adieu.

    *Vanessa*, fill'd with just Disdain,
Wou'd still her Dignity maintain,
Instructed from her early Years
To scorn the Art of Female Tears.

Had he employ'd his Time so long,
To teach her what was Right or Wrong,
Yet cou'd such Notions entertain,                    600
That all his Lectures were in vain?
She own'd the wand'ring of her Thoughts,
But he must answer for her Faults.
She well remember'd to her Cost,
That all his Lessons were not lost.
Two Maxims she could still produce,
And sad Experience taught their Use:
That Virtue, pleas'd by being shown,
Knows nothing which it dare not own;
Can make us without Fear disclose                    610
Our inmost Secrets to our Foes:
That common Forms were not design'd
Directors to a noble Mind.
Now, said the Nymph, I'll let you see
My Actions with your Rules agree,
That I can vulgar Forms despise,
And have no Secrets to disguise.
I knew by what you said and writ,
How dang'rous Things were Men of Wit,
You caution'd me against their Charms,               620
But never gave me equal Arms:
Your Lessons found the weakest Part,
Aim'd at the Head, but reach'd the Heart.

   *Cadenus* felt within him rise
Shame, Disappointment, Guilt, Surprize.
He knew not how to reconcile
Such Language, with her usual Style:
And yet her Words were so exprest,
He cou'd not hope she spoke in Jest.
His Thoughts had wholly been confin'd                630
To form and cultivate her Mind.
He hardly knew, 'till he was told,
Whether the Nymph were Young or Old;
Had met her in a publick Place,
Without distinguishing her Face.

Much less could his declining Age
*Vanessa*'s earliest Thoughts engage.
And if her Youth Indifference met,
His Person must Contempt beget.
Or grant her Passion be sincere,       640
How shall his Innocence be clear?
Appearances were all so strong,
The World must think him in the Wrong;
Wou'd say, He made a treach'rous Use
Of Wit, to flatter and seduce:
The Town wou'd swear he had betray'd,
By Magick Spells, the harmless Maid;
And ev'ry Beau wou'd have his Jokes,
That Scholars were like other Folks:
That when Platonick Flights were over,       650
The Tutor turn'd a mortal Lover.
So tender of the Young and Fair?
It shew'd a true Paternal Care—
Five thousand Guineas in her Purse?
The Doctor might have fancy'd worse.—

    Hardly at length he Silence broke,
And faulter'd ev'ry Word he spoke;
Interpreting her Complaisance,
Just as a Man *sans Consequence.*
She railly'd well, he always knew,       660
Her Manner now was something new;
And what she spoke was in an Air,
As serious as a Tragick Play'r.
But those who aim at Ridicule
Shou'd fix upon some certain Rule,
Which fairly hints they are in jest,
Else he must enter his Protest:
For, let a Man be ne'er so wise,
He may be caught with sober Lies;
A Science which he never taught,       670
And, to be free, was dearly bought:
For, take it in its proper Light,
'Tis just what Coxcombs call, *a Bite.*

But not to dwell on Things minute,
*Vanessa* finish'd the Dispute,
Brought weighty Arguments to prove
That Reason was her Guide in Love.
She thought he had himself describ'd,
His Doctrines when she first imbib'd;
What he had planted, now was grown;          680
His Virtues she might call her own;
As he approves, as he dislikes,
Love or Contempt, her Fancy strikes.
Self-Love, in Nature rooted fast,
Attends us first, and leaves us last:
Why she likes him, admire not at her,
She loves herself, and that's the Matter.
How was her Tutor wont to praise
The Genius's of ancient Days!
(Those Authors he so oft had nam'd          690
For Learning, Wit, and Wisdom fam'd;)
Was struck with Love, Esteem, and Awe,
For Persons whom he never saw.
Suppose *Cadenus* flourish'd then,
He must adore such God-like Men.
If one short Volume cou'd comprise
All that was witty, learn'd, and wise,
How wou'd it be esteem'd, and read,
Altho' the Writer long were dead?
If such an Author were alive,          700
How all wou'd for his Friendship strive;
And come in Crowds to see his Face:
And this she takes to be her Case.
*Cadenus* answers every End,
The Book, the Author, and the Friend.
The utmost her Desires will reach,
Is but to learn what he can teach;
His Converse is a System, fit
Alone to fill up all her Wit;
While ev'ry Passion of her Mind          710
In him is center'd and confin'd.

Love can with Speech inspire a Mute,
And taught *Vanessa* to dispute.
This Topick, never touch'd before,
Display'd her Eloquence the more:
Her Knowledge, with such Pains acquir'd,
By this new Passion grew inspir'd.
Thro' this she made all Objects pass,
Which gave a Tincture o'er the Mass:
As Rivers, tho' they bend and twine,                720
Still to the Sea their Course incline;
Or, as Philosophers, who find
Some fav'rite System to their Mind,
In ev'ry Point to make it fit,
Will force all Nature to submit.

*Cadenus*, who cou'd ne'er suspect
His Lessons wou'd have such Effect,
Or be so artfully apply'd,
Insensibly came on her Side;
It was an unforeseen Event,                          730
Things took a Turn he never meant.
Whoe'er excels in what we prize,
Appears a Hero to our Eyes;
Each Girl when pleas'd with what is taught,
Will have the Teacher in her Thought.
When Miss delights in her Spinnet,
A Fidler may a Fortune get;
A Blockhead with melodious Voice
In Boarding-Schools can have his Choice;
And oft' the Dancing-Master's Art                    740
Climbs from the Toe to touch the Heart.
In Learning let a Nymph delight,
The Pedant gets a Mistress by't.
*Cadenus*, to his Grief and Shame,
Cou'd scarce oppose *Vanessa*'s Flame;
But tho' her Arguments were strong,
At least, cou'd hardly wish them wrong.
Howe'er it came, he cou'd not tell,
But, sure, she never talk'd so well.

His Pride began to interpose,                    750
Preferr'd before a Crowd of Beaux,
So bright a Nymph to come unsought,
Such Wonder by his Merit wrought;
'Tis Merit must with her prevail,
He never knew her Judgment fail,
She noted all she ever read,
And had a most discerning Head.

    'Tis an old Maxim in the Schools,
That Vanity's the Food of Fools;
Yet now and then your Men of Wit          760
Will condescend to take a Bit.

    So when *Cadenus* could not hide,
He chose to justify his Pride;
Constr'ing the Passion she had shown,
Much to her Praise, more to his Own.
Nature in him had Merit plac'd,
In her, a most judicious Taste.
Love, hitherto a transient Guest,
Ne'er held Possession of his Breast;
So, long attending at the Gate,          770
Disdain'd to enter in so late.
*Love*, why do we one Passion call?
When 'tis a Compound of them all;
Where hot and cold, where sharp and sweet,
In all their Equipages meet;
Where Pleasures mix'd with Pains appear,
Sorrow with Joy, and Hope with Fear;
Wherein his Dignity and Age
Forbid *Cadenus* to engage.
But Friendship in its greatest Height,          780
A constant, rational Delight,
On Virtue's Basis fix'd to last,
When Love's Allurements long are past;
Which gently warms, but cannot burn;
He gladly offers in return:
His Want of Passion will redeem,
With Gratitude, Respect, Esteem:

With that Devotion we bestow,
When Goddesses appear below.

 While thus *Cadenus* entertains   790
*Vanessa* in exalted Strains,
The Nymph in sober Words intreats
A Truce with all sublime Conceits.
For why such Raptures, Flights, and Fancies,
To her, who durst not read Romances;
In lofty Style to make Replies,
Which he had taught her to despise.
But when her Tutor will affect
Devotion, Duty, and Respect,
He fairly abdicates his Throne,   800
The Government is now her own;
He has a Forfeiture incurr'd,
She vows to take him at his Word,
And hopes he will not think it strange
If both shou'd now their Stations change.
The Nymph will have her Turn, to be
The Tutor; and the Pupil, he:
Tho' she already can discern,
Her Scholar is not apt to learn;
Or wants Capacity to reach   810
The Science she designs to teach:
Wherein his Genius was below
The Skill of ev'ry common Beau;
Who, tho' he cannot spell, is wise
Enough to read a Lady's Eyes;
And will each accidental Glance
Interpret for a kind Advance.

 But what Success *Vanessa* met,
Is to the World a Secret yet:
Whether the Nymph, to please her Swain,   820
Talks in a high Romantick Strain;
Or whether he at last descends
To like with less Seraphick Ends;
Or, to compound the Business, whether
They temper Love and Books together;

Must never to Mankind be told,
Nor shall the conscious Muse unfold.

Mean time the mournful *Queen of Love*
Led but a weary Life above.
She ventures now to leave the Skies,                    830
Grown by *Vanessa*'s Conduct wise.
For tho' by one perverse Event
*Pallas* had cross'd her first Intent,
Tho' her Design was not obtain'd,
Yet had she much Experience gain'd;
And, by the Project vainly try'd,
Cou'd better now the *Cause* decide.

She gave due Notice, that both Parties,
*Coram Regina prox' die Martis*,
Should at their Peril without fail                      840
Come and appear, and save their Bail.
All met, and Silence thrice proclaim'd,
One Lawyer to each Side was nam'd.
The Judge discover'd in her Face
Resentments for her late Disgrace;
And, full of Anger, Shame, and Grief,
Directed them to mind their Brief;
Nor spend their Time to shew their Reading;
She'd have a summary Proceeding.
She gather'd, under ev'ry Head,                         850
The Sum of what each Lawyer said;
Gave her own Reasons last; and then
Decreed the Cause against the *Men*.

But, in a weighty Case like this,
To shew she did not judge amiss,
Which evil Tongues might else report,
She made a Speech in open Court;
Wherein she grievously complains,
"How she was cheated by the Swains:
On whose Petition (humbly shewing                       860
That Women were not worth the wooing,

839. Before the Queen on Tuesday next.

And that unless the Sex would mend,
The Race of Lovers soon must end:)
"She was at Lord knows what Expence,
"To form a Nymph of Wit and Sense;
"A Model for her Sex design'd,
"Who never cou'd one Lover find.
"She saw her Favour was misplac'd;
"The Fellows had a wretched Taste;
"She needs must tell them to their Face,     870
"They were a stupid, senseless Race:
"And were she to begin agen,
"She'd study to reform the *Men*;
"Or add some Grains of Folly more
"To *Women* than they had before,
"To put them on an equal Foot;
"And this, or nothing else, wou'd do't.
"This might their mutual Fancy strike,
"Since ev'ry Being loves its *Like*.


   "But now, repenting what was done,     880
"She left all Business to her Son:
"She puts the World in his Possession,
"And let him use it at Discretion."


   The Cry'r was order'd to dismiss
The Court, so made his last *O yes!*
The Goddess wou'd no longer wait;
But rising from her Chair of State,
Left all below at Six and Sev'n,
Harness'd her Doves, and flew to Heav'n.

# A REBUS

Written by a LADY, On

## The Rev. *Dean Swift*

### WITH HIS

### ANSWER

CUTT the Name of the MAN who his *Mistress* deny'd, ⎫ *Jo—seph,*
And let the *first* of it, be only apply'd ⎬
To join with the *Prophet* who DAVID did Chide. ⎭ *Nathan.*
Then say what a *Horse* is that runs very *fast*,
And that which deserves to be *first* put the *last*;
Spell all then, and put them together, to find
The NAME and the VERTUES of *Him* I design'd.
Like the *Patriarch* in *Egypt*, he's vers'd in the *State*.
Like the *Prophet* in *Jury*, he's free with the *Great*.
Like a *Racer* he *flys* to Succour with speed,       10
When his *Friends* want his Aid, or *Desert* is in need.


## *The Answer*

THE NYMPH who wrote this in an Amorous Fit,
I cannot but Envy the Pride of her *Wit*.
Which thus she will Venture profusely to throw,
On so mean a *Design*, and a *Subject* so low.
For mean's her *Design*, and her *Subject* as mean,
The *First* but a REBUS, the *Last* but a DEAN.
A *Dean*'s but a *Parson*, and what is a *Rebus*?
A Thing never known to the *Muses* or *Phœbus*:
The Corruption of Verse, for when all is done,
It is but a *Paraphrase* made on a *Punn*;      10
But a Genius like her's no Subject can stifle,
It shews and discovers it self through a *Trifle*.

Printed from the original Fo. Half-sheet (n.d or p.).
*Title*. Written by a LADY. By Vanessa.—Curll.

By reading this *Trifle*, I quickly began
To find her a great *Witt*, but the *Dean* a small Man.
Rich Ladies will furnish their Garrets with Stuff,
Which others for Mantuas wou'd think fine enough;
So the *Wit* that is lavishly thrown away here,
Might furnish a Second Rate *Poet* a Year:
Thus much for the *Verse*, we proceed to the next,
Where the NYMPH has entirely forsaken her *Text*:        20
Her fine Panegyricks are quite out of Season,
And what *She* describes to be *Merit* is *Treason*:
The Changes which Faction has made in the State,
Have put the *Dean*'s Politicks quite out of Date;
Now no one regards what he Utters with freedom,
And shou'd he write *Pamphlets*, no Great Man wou'd read 'em:
And shou'd *Want* or *Desert* stand in need of his Aid,
This *Racer* wou'd prove but a dull founder'd *Jade*.


# THE

# FIRST *ODE*

## OF THE

# SECOND BOOK

## OF

# HORACE

## PARAPHRAS'D:

### And Address'd to *Richard Steele*, Esq;

D*ICK*, thou'rt resolv'd, as I am told,
    Some strange *Arcana* to unfold,
And with the help of *Buckley*'s Pen
To vamp the *good Old Cause* again,
Which thou (such *Burnet*'s shrewd Advice is)
Must furbish up and Nickname *CRISIS*.

Printed from the first edition, London, 1714.

Thou pompously wilt let us know
What all the World knew long ago,
(Ere since Sir *William Gore* was May'r,
And *HARLEY* fill'd the *Commons* Chair)          10
That we a *German* Prince must own
When *ANN* for Heav'n resigns Her Throne.
But more than that, thou'lt keep a rout
With—who is *in*—and who is *out*,
Thou'lt rail devoutly at the *Peace*,
And all its secret *Causes* trace,
The *Bucket-play* 'twixt Whigs and Tories,
Their ups and downs, with fifty Stories
Of *Tricks*, the Lord of *Oxford* knows,
And *Errors* of our *Plenipoes*.          20
Thou'lt tell of *Leagues* among the Great
Portending ruin to our State,
And of that dreadful *coup d'eclat*,
Which has afforded thee much Chat,
The Queen (*forsooth, Despotick*) gave
Twelve *Coronets*, without *thy* leave!
A Breach of Liberty, 'tis own'd,
For which no Heads have *yet* atton'd!
Believe me, what thou'st undertaken
May bring in Jeopardy thy Bacon,          30
For Madmen, Children, Wits and Fools
Shou'd never meddle with Edg'd Tools.
But since thou'rt got into the Fire,
And canst not easily retire,
Thou must no longer deal in *Farce*,
Nor pump to cobble wicked Verse;
Untill thou shalt have eas'd thy Conscience,
Of Spleen, of Politicks and Nonsense,
And when thou'st bid adieu to Cares,
And settled *Europe*'s *Grand* Affairs,          40
'Twill then, perhaps, be worth thy while
For *Drury-lane* to shape thy Stile:
"To make a pair of Jolly Fellows,
"The Son and Father, join to tell us,

23. *Vide* Englishman, No. 36.

"How Sons may safely disobey,
"And Fathers never shou'd say nay,
"By which wise Conduct they grow Friends
"At last—and so the Story ends."

When first I knew thee, *Dick*, thou wert
Renown'd for Skill in *Faustus* Art,                    50
Which made thy Closet much frequented
By buxom Lasses—Some repented
Their luckless Choice of Husbands—others,
Impatient to be like their Mothers,
Receiv'd from thee profound Directions
How best to settle their Affections;
Thus thou, a Friend to the Distress'd,
Didst in thy calling do thy best.

But now the *Senate* (if things *hit*
And thou at *Stockbridge* wert not *bit*)                60
Must feel thy Eloquence and Fire,
Approve thy Schemes, thy Wit admire,
Thee with *Immortal Honours* crown,
Whilst *Patr'ot-like* thou'lt strut and frown.

What, tho' by Enemies 'tis said,
The *Lawrel*, which adorns thy Head;
Must one Day come in competition,
By vertue of some sly *Petition*:
Yet *Mum* for that, hope still the best,
Nor let such Cares disturb thy Rest.                     70

Methinks I hear thee loud, as Trumpet,
As Bagpipe shrill, or Oyster-Strumpet,
Methinks I see thee, spruce and fine,
With Coat embroider'd richly shine,
And dazzle all the *Idol-Faces*
As thro' the *HALL* thy Worship paces:
(Tho' this I speak but at a venture,
Supposing thou hast *Tick* with *Hunter*)

43–48. This is said to be the Plot of a Comedy with which Mr. Steele has long
threatned the Town.
49. *Vide* Tatlers.

Methinks I see a *black-guard Rout*
Attend thy Coach, and hear them shout        80
In Approbation of thy Tongue,
Which (in their Stile) is *purely hung*.
Now, now you carry all before ye,
Nor dares one *Jacobite* or *Tory*
Pretend to answer one Syl — lable,
Except the Matchless Hero *Abel*.
What tho' her *Highness* and her *Spouse*
In *Antwerp* keep a frugal House,
Yet not forgetful of a Friend
They'll soon enable thee to spend,        90
If to *Maccartney* thou wilt toast,
And to his *Pious Patron*'s *Ghost*.
Now manfully thou'lt run a Tilt
"On *Popes*, for all the Blood they've spilt,
"For Massacres, and Racks, and Flames,
"For Lands enrich'd by crimson Streams,
"For Inquisitions taught by *Spain*,
"Of which the Christian World complain."

*Dick*, we agree—all's true, thou'st said,
As that my Muse is yet a Maid,        100
But, if I may with freedom talk,
All this is foreign to thy Walk:
Thy *Genius* has perhaps a knack
At trudging in a beaten Track,
But is for *State-Affairs* as fit,
As mine for Politicks and Wit.
Then let us both in time grow wise,
Nor higher, than our Talents, rise,
To some snug Cellar let's repair
From Dunns and Debts, and drown our Care;        110
Now quaff of honest Ale a Quart,
Now venture at a Pint of Port,
With which inspir'd we'll club each Night
Some tender Sonnet to indite,
And with *Tom D'urfey*, *Phillips*, *Dennis*,
Immortalize our *Dolls* and *Jenneys*.

# JEUX D'ESPRIT

## OF THE

# SCRIBLERUS CLUB

### I

THE Doctor and Dean, Pope, Parnell and Gay
In manner submissive most humbly do pray,
That your Lordship would once let your Cares all alone
And Climb the dark Stairs to your Friends who have
none:
To your Friends who at least have no Cares but to please
you
To a good honest Junta that never will teaze you.

From the Doctor's Chamber
past eight.

### II

April 14, 1714. Back Stairs, past Eight.
IN a summons so large, which all clergy contains,
I must turn *Dismal*'s convert, or part with my brains,
Should I scruple to quit the back stairs for your blind ones,
Or refuse your true juncto for one of—

### III

The following is their answer to his lordship, chiefly written by the Dean.

LET not the whigs our tory club rebuke;
Give us our earl, the devil take their duke.
*Ouædam quæ attinent ad Scriblerum,*
Want your assistance now to clear 'em.
One day it will be no disgrace,
In *Scribler* to have had a place.
Come then, my lord, and take your part in
The important history of *Martin*.

Printed from the Longleat transcript, Portland Papers.

## IV

A Pox of all Senders
For any Pretenders
Who tell us these troublesome stories,
In their dull hum-drum key
Of Arma Virumque
Hannoniae qui primus ab oris.


A fig too for Hanmer
Who prates like his Grand mere
And all his old Friends would rebuke
In spite of the Carle                              10
Give us but our Earle,
And the Devil may take their Duke.


Then come and take part in
The Memoirs of Martin,
Lay by your White Staff & gray Habit,
For trust us, friend Mortimer
Should you live years forty more
Haec olim meminisse juvabit.
                    by order of yᵉ Club
                              A. Pope
                              J. Gay
                              J. Swift
                              J. Arbuthnot
                              T. Parnel


## V

More Lines of Humour, by Lord TREASURER.

                              April 14, 1714.
I HONOUR the men, Sir,
Who are ready to answer,
When I ask them to stand by the queen;
In spite of orâtors,
And blood-thirsty praters,
Whose hatred I highly esteem.

Let our faith's defender
Keep out ev'ry pretender,
And long enjoy her own;
Thus you four, five,                                    10
May merrily live,
Till faction is dead as a stone.

### VI

My Lord, forsake your Politick Utopians,
To sup, like Jove, with blameless Ethiopians.
Pope

In other Words, You with the Staff,
Leave John of Bucks, come here and laugh.
Dean

For Frolick Mirth give ore affairs of State,
To night be happy, be to morrow great.
Parnell

Give Clans your money, us your smile
your Scorn to Townshend & Argile
Doctor

Leave Courts, and hye to simple Swains,
Who feed *no* Flock Upon *no* Plains
Gay

# THE
# FAGGOT

*Written in the Year 1713, when the* QUEEN's *Ministers were
quarrelling among themselves*

OBSERVE the dying Father speak:
Try Lads, can you this Bundle break;
Then, bids the youngest of the Six,
Take up a well-bound Heap of Sticks.
Printed from Poems, 1735.

They thought it was an old Man's Maggot;
And strove by Turns to break the Faggot:
In vain: The complicated Wands
Were much too strong for all their Hands.
See, said the Sire, how soon 'tis done:
Then, took and broke them one by one.          10
So strong you'll be, in Friendship ty'd;
So quickly broke if you divide.
Keep close then Boys, and never quarrel.
Here ends the Fable and the Moral.

THIS Tale may be apply'd in few Words
To Treasurers, Controllers, Stewards,
And others, who in solemn Sort
Appear with slender Wands at Court:
Not firmly join'd to keep their Ground,
But lashing one another round:          20
While, wise Men think they ought to fight
With *Quarter*-staffs instead of *White*;
Or Constable with *Staff* of Peace,
Should come and make the Clatt'ring cease;
Which now disturbs the Queen and Court,
And gives the *Whigs* and Rabble Sport.

IN History we never found
The Consul's Fasces were unbound;
Those *Romans* were too wise to think on't,
Except to lash some grand Delinquent.          30
How would they blush to hear it said,
The Prætor broke the Consul's Head;
Or, Consul in his Purple Gown,
Came up, and knock't the Prætor down.

COME Courtiers: Every Man his Stick:
Lord-Treasurer; for once be quick:
And, that they may the closer cling,
Take your blue Ribbin for a String.
Come trimming *Harcourt*; bring your Mace;
And squeeze it in, or quit your Place:          40

Dispatch; or else that Rascal *Northey*,
Will undertake to do it for thee:
And, be assur'd, the Court will find him
Prepar'd to *leap o'er Sticks*, or bind 'em.


   To make the Bundle strong and safe,
Great *Ormonde* lend thy Gen'ral's Staff:
And, if the *Crosier* could be cramm'd in,
A Fig for *Lechmere*, *King*, and *Hambden*.
You'll then defy the strongest *Whig*,
With both his Hands to bend a Twig;     50
Though with united Strength they all pull,
From *Sommers* down to *Craigs* and *Walpole*.


# THE
# Author upon Himself

*A few of the first Lines were wanting in the Copy
sent us by a Friend of the Author's from* London

\*   \*   \*   \*   \*   \*   \*   \*
  \*   \*   \*   \*   \*   \*   \*
  \*   \*   \*   \*   \*   \*   \*
\*   \*   \*   \*   \*   \*   \*   \*

B Y an old red-Pate, murd'ring Hag pursu'd,
  A Crazy Prelate, and a Royal Prude.
By dull Divines, who look with envious Eyes,
On ev'ry Genius that attempts to rise;
And pausing o'er a Pipe, with doubtful Nod,
Give Hints, that Poets ne'er believe in God.
So, Clowns on Scholars as on Wizards look,
And take a Folio for a conj'ring Book.

Printed from *Poems*, 1735 (uncancelled state).

  1. *Hag.* The late Duchess of Somerset.
  2. *Crazy Prelate.* Dr. Sharpe, Archbishop of York.   *Royal Prude.* Her late
Majesty.

*Swift* had the Sin of Wit no venial Crime;
Nay, 'twas affirm'd, he sometimes dealt in Rhime:        10
Humour, and Mirth, had Place in all he writ:
He reconcil'd Divinity and Wit.
He mov'd, and bow'd, and talk't with too much Grace;
Nor shew'd the Parson in his Gait or Face;
Despis'd luxurious Wines, and costly Meat;
Yet, still was at the Tables of the Great.
Frequented Lords; *saw those that saw the Queen*;
At *Child*'s or *Truby*'s never once had been;
Where Town and Country Vicars flock in Tribes,
Secur'd by Numbers from the Lay-men's Gibes;        20
And deal in Vices of the graver Sort,
Tobacco, Censure, Coffee, Pride, and Port.

BUT, after sage Monitions from his Friends,
His Talents to employ for nobler Ends;
To better Judgments willing to submit,
He turns to Pol[it]icks his dang'rous Wit,

AND now, the publick Int'rest to support,
By *Harley Swift* invited comes to Court.
In Favour grows with Ministers of State;
Admitted private, when Superiors wait:        30
And, *Harley*, not asham'd his Choice to own,
Takes him to *Windsor* in his Coach, alone.
At *Windsor Swift* no sooner can appear,
But, *St. John* comes and whispers in his Ear;
The Waiters stand in Ranks; the Yeomen cry,
*Make Room*; as if a Duke were passing by.

Now *Finch* alarms the Lords; he hears for certain,
This dang'rous Priest is got behind the Curtain:
*Finch*, fam'd for tedious Elocution, proves
That *Swift* oils many a Spring which *Harley* moves.        40

18. *At Child's or Truby's* . . . A Coffee-house and Tavern near St. Paul's, much
frequented by the Clergy.

34. *St. John*. Then Secretary of State, now Lord Bolingbroke, the most universal
Genius in Europe.

37. *Finch*. Late Earl of Nottingham, who made a Speech in the House of Lords
against the Author.

*Walpole* and *Ayslaby*, to clear the Doubt,
Inform the Commons, that the Secret's out:
"A *certain* Doctor is observ'd of late,
"To haunt a *certain* Minister of State:
"From whence, with half an Eye we may discover,
"The Peace is made, and *Perkin* must come over."
*York* is from *Lambeth* sent, to shew the Queen
A dang'rous Treatise writ against the Spleen;
Which by the Style, the Matter, and the Drift,
'Tis thought could be the Work of none but *Swift*.     50
Poor *York*! the harmless Tool of others Hate;
He sues for Pardon, and repents too late.

    Now, Madam *Coningsmark* her Vengeance vows
On *Swift*'s Reproaches for her murder'd Spouse:
From her red Locks her Mouth with Venom fills:
And thence into the Royal Ear instills.
The Queen incens'd, his Services forgot,
Leaves him a Victim to the vengeful *Scot*;
Now, through the Realm a Proclamation spread,
To fix a Price on his devoted Head.     60
While innocent, he scorns ignoble Flight;
His watchful Friends preserve him by a Sleight.

    By *Harley*'s Favour once again he shines;
Is now caress't by Candidate Divines;
Who change Opinions with the changing Scene:
Lord! how were they mistaken in the Dean!
Now, *Delawere* again familiar grows;

41. *Walpole and Ayslaby.* Those two made Speeches in the House of Commons against the Author, although the latter professed much Friendship for him.

52. *He sues for Pardon.* It is known that his Grace sent a Message to the Author, to desire his Pardon, and that he was very sorry for what he had said and done.

53–54. The Lady hinted at before. There was a short severe Satyr writ against her, which she charged on the Author, and did him ill Offices by her great Credit with the Queen.

58. . . . *the vengeful Scot.* The Proclamation was against the Author of a Pamphlet, called, *The publick Spirit of the Whigs*, against which the Scotch Lords complained.

67. *Delaware.* Lord Delawere, then Treasurer of the Household, always caressing the Author at Court. But during the Tryal of the Printers before the House of Lords, and while the Proclamation hung over the Author, his Lordship would not seem to know him, till the Danger was past.

And, in *Swift*'s Ear thrusts half his powder'd Nose.
The *Scottish* Nation, whom he durst offend,
Again apply that *Swift* would be their Friend.          70

BY Faction tir'd, with Grief he waits a while,
His great contending Friends to reconcile.
Performs what Friendship, Justice, Truth require:
What could he more, but decently retire?

# HORACE, *Lib. 2. Sat. 6*

### PART of it imitated

I Often wish'd, that I had clear
For Life, six hundred Pounds a Year,
A handsome House to lodge a Friend,
A River at my Garden's End,
A Terras Walk, and half a Rood
Of Land set out to plant a Wood.

Well, now I have all this and more,
I ask not to increase my Store,
And should be perfectly content,
Could I but live on this side *Trent*;          10
Nor cross the *Channel* twice a Year,
To spend six Months with *Statesmen* here.

I must by all means come to Town,
'Tis for the Service of the Crown.
"*Lewis*; the *Dean* will be of Use,
"Send for him up, take no Excuse."
The Toil, the Danger of the Seas;
Great Ministers ne'er think of these;

Printed from *Poems*, 1735.

69, 70. The Scotch Lords treated and visited the Author more after the Proclamation than before, except the Duke of Argyle, who could never be reconciled.

74. The Author retired to a Friend in Berkshire, ten Weeks before the Queen died; and never saw the Ministry after.

Or let it cost Five hundred Pound,
No matter where the Money's found;     20
It is but so much more in Debt,
And that they ne'er consider'd yet.


   "Good Mr. *Dean* go change your Gown,
"Let my Lord know you're come to Town."
I hurry me in haste away,
Not thinking it is Levee-Day;
And find his Honour in a Pound,
Hemm'd by a triple Circle round,
Chequer'd with Ribbons blew and green;
How should I thrust my self between?     30
Some Wag observes me thus perplext,
And smiling, whispers to the next,
"I thought the *Dean* had been too proud,
"To justle here among a Crowd."
Another in a surly Fit,
Tells me I have more Zeal than Wit,
"So eager to express your Love,
"You ne'er consider whom you shove,
"But rudely press before a Duke."
I own, I'm pleas'd with this Rebuke,     40
And take it kindly meant to show
What I desire the World should know.


   I get a Whisper, and withdraw,
When twenty Fools I never saw
Come with Petitions fairly pen'd,
Desiring I would stand their Friend.


   This, humbly offers me his Case:
That, begs my Interest for a Place.
A hundred other Men's Affairs
Like Bees, are humming in my Ears.     50
"To morrow my Appeal comes on,
"Without your Help the Cause is gone———"
The Duke expects my Lord and you,
About some great Affair, at Two———

"Put my Lord *Bolingbroke* in Mind,
"To get my Warrant quickly signed:
"Consider, 'tis my first Request.———"
Be satisfy'd, I'll do my best:———
Then presently he falls to teize,
"You may for certain, if you please;                    60
"I doubt not, if his Lordship knew——
"And Mr. *Dean*, one Word from you——"

    'Tis (let me see) three Years and more,
(*October* next, it will be four)
Since HARLEY bid me first attend,
And chose me for an humble Friend;
Would take me in his Coach to chat,
And question me of this and that;
As, "What's a-Clock?" And, "How's the Wind?
"Whose Chariot's that we left behind?"                   70
Or gravely try to read the Lines
Writ underneath the Country *Signs*;
Or, "Have you nothing new to day
"From *Pope*, from *Parnel*, or from *Gay*?"
Such Tattle often entertains
My Lord and me as far as *Stains*,
As once a week we travel down
To *Windsor*, and again to Town,
Where all that passes, *inter nos*,
Might be proclaim'd at *Charing-Cross*.                  80

    Yet some I know with Envy swell,
Because they see me us'd so well:
"How think you of our Friend the *Dean*?
"I wonder what some People mean;
"My Lord and he are grown so great,
"Always together, *tête à tête*:
"What, they admire him for his Jokes——
"See but the Fortune of some Folks!"
There flies about a strange Report
Of some Express arriv'd at Court;                        90
I'm stopt by all the Fools I meet,
And catechis'd in ev'ry Street.

"You, Mr. *Dean* frequent the Great;
"Inform us, will the Emp'ror treat?
"Or do the Prints and Papers lye?"
Faith Sir, you know as much as I.
"Ah Doctor, how you love to jest?
"'Tis now no Secret"—I protest
'Tis one to me.—"Then, tell us, pray
"When are the Troops to have their Pay?"    100
And, though I solemnly declare
I know no more than my *Lord Mayor*,
They stand amaz'd, and think me grown
The closest Mortal ever known.

   Thus in a Sea of Folly tost,
My choicest Hours of Life are lost:
Yet always wishing to retreat;
Oh, could I see my Country Seat.
There leaning near a gentle Brook,
Sleep, or peruse some antient Book;    110
And there in sweet Oblivion drown
Those Cares that haunt a Court and Town.

# In SICKNESS

*Written soon after the Author's coming to live in* Ireland, *upon the* Queen's Death, *October* 1714

'TIS true,—then why should I repine,
   To see my Life so fast decline?
But, why obscurely here alone?
Where I am neither lov'd nor known.
My State of Health none care to learn;
My Life is here no Soul's Concern.
And, those with whom I now converse,
Without a Tear will tend my Herse.
Remov'd from kind *Arbuthnot*'s Aid,
Who knows his Art but not the Trade;    10

Printed from *Poems*, 1735.

Preferring his Regard for me
Before his Credit or his Fee.
Some formal Visits, Looks, and Words,
What meer Humanity affords,
I meet perhaps from three or four,
From whom I once expected more;
Which those who tend the Sick for pay
Can act as decently as they.
But, no obliging, tender Friend
To help at my approaching End,                    20
My Life is now a Burthen grown
To others, e'er it be my own.

    YE formal Weepers for the Sick,
In your last Offices be quick:
And spare my absent Friends the Grief
To hear, yet give me no Relief;
Expir'd To-day, entomb'd To-morrow,
When known, will save a double Sorrow.


# The FABLE of the BITCHES

### Wrote in the Year 1715, on an attempt to repeal the Test Act

A BITCH that was full pregnant grown,
   By all the Dogs and Curs in Town;
Finding her ripen'd Time was come,
Her Litter teeming from her Womb,
Went here and there, and ev'ry where,
To find an easy Place to lay-her.

    AT length to *Musick*'s House she came,
And begg'd like one both blind and lame;

Printed from *Works, Vol. X,* Dublin, 1762.

7. *Musick's House.* The Church of England.

"My only Friend, my Dear," said she,
"You see 'tis meer Necessity, 10
"Hath sent me to your House to whelp,
"I'll dye, if you deny your Help."

WITH fawning Whine, and rueful Tone,
With artful Sigh and feigned Groan,
With couchant Cringe, and flattering Tale,
Smooth *Bawty* did so far prevail;
That *Musick* gave her Leave to litter,
But mark what follow'd,—Faith she bit her.

WHOLE Baskets full of Bits and Scraps,
And Broth enough to fill her Paps, 20
For well she knew her num'rus Brood,
For want of Milk, wou'd suck her Blood.

BUT when she thought her Pains were done,
And now 'twas high Time to be gone;
In civil Terms,—"My Friend," says she,
"My House you've had on Courtesy;
"And now I earnestly desire,
"That you wou'd with your Cubbs retire:
"For shou'd you stay but one Week longer,
"I shall be starv'd with Cold and Hunger." 30

THE Guest reply'd,—"My Friend, your Leave,
"I must a little longer crave;
"Stay till my tender Cubs can find,
"Their Way—for now you see they're blind;
"But when we've gather'd Strength, I swear,
"We'll to our Barn again repair."

THE Time pass'd on, and *Musick* came,
Her Kennel once again to claim;
But, *Bawty*, lost to Shame and Honour,
Set all her Cubs at once upon her; 40
Made her retire, and quit her Right,
And loudly cry'd—a Bite, a Bite.

16. Bawty, (the Name of a Bitch in Scotch,) alludes to the Kirk.

## The MORAL

THUS did the *Grecian* Wooden Horse,
Conceal a fatal armed Force;
No sooner brought within the Walls,
But *Illium*'s lost, and *Priam* falls.


## TO

# The Earl of *OXFORD*, Late Lord Treasurer. Sent to him when he was in the Tower, before his Tryal

### *Out of HORACE*

#### Written in the Year 1716

HOW blest is he, who for his Country dies;
Since Death pursues the Coward as he flies.
The Youth, in vain, would fly from Fate's Attack,
With trembling Knees, and Terror at his Back;
Though Fear should lend him Pinions like the Wind,
Yet swifter Fate will seize him from behind.

VIRTUE repuls't, yet knows not to repine;
But shall with unattainted Honour shine;
Nor stoops to take the *Staff*, nor lays it down,
Just as the Rabble please to smile or frown.          10

VIRTUE, to crown her Fav'rites, loves to try
Some new unbeaten Passage to the Sky;
Where *Jove* a Seat among the Gods will give
To those who die, for meriting to live.

NEXT, faithful Silence hath a sure Reward:
Within our Breast be ev'ry Secret barr'd:
He who betrays his Friend, shall never be
Under one Roof, or in one Ship with me.

Printed from *Poems*, 1735.

For, who with Traytors would his Safety trust,
Lest with the Wicked, Heaven involve the Just?    20
And, though the Villain 'scape a while, he feels
Slow Vengeance, like a Blood-hound at his Heels.


Ad Amicum Eruditum

## THOMAM SHERIDAN

Scripsit *Oct. Ann. Dom.* 1717

DELICIÆ *Sheridan* Musarum, dulcis amice,
  Sic tibi propitius Permessi ad flumen *Apollo*
Occurrat, seu te mimum convivia rident;
Æquivocosve sales spargis, seu ludere versu
Malles; dic, *Sheridan*, quisnam fuit ille Deorum,
Quæ melior natura orto tibi tradidit artem
Rimandi genium puerorum, atq; ima cerebri
Scrutandi? Tibi nascenti ad cunabula *Pallas*
Astitit; & dixit, mentis præsaga futuræ,
Heu puer infelix! nostro sub sydere natus;     10
Nam tu pectus eris sine corpore, corporis umbra;
Sed levitate umbram superabis, voce cicadam:
Musca femur, palmas tibi Mus dedit, ardea crura.
Corpore sed tenui tibi quod natura negavit;
Hoc animi dotes supplebunt; teq; docente,
Nec longum Tempus, surget tibi docta juventus,
Artibus egregiis animas instructa novellas.
Grex hinc Pœonius venit, ecce, *salutifer* orbi.
Ast, illi causas orant; his infula visa est
Divinam capiti nodo constringere mitram.     20

    NATALIS te horæ non fallunt signa; sed usq;
Conscius, expedias puero seu lætus *Apollo*
Nascenti arrisit; sive illum frigidus horror
Saturni premit, aut septem inflavere triones.

Printed from *Poems*, 1735.

Quin tu altè penitusq; latentia semina cernis,
Quæq; diu obtundendo olim sub luminis auras
Erumpent, promis; quo ritu saepè puella
Sub cinere hesterno sopitos suscitat ignes.

Te Dominum agnoscit quocunq; sub aere natus;
Quos indulgentis nimium custodia matris          30
Pessundat: Nam sæpè vides in stipite matrem.

Aureus at ramus venerandæ dona Sibyllæ,
Æneæ sedes tantùm patefecit Avernas:
Sæpè puer, tua quem tetigit semel aurea virga,
Cœlumq; terrasq; videt, noctemq; profundam.


# *To Mr.* DELANY

[p. 1]  TO You, whose Virtues I must own
        With shame, I have too lately known;
To you, by Art and Nature taught
To be the Man I long have sought,
Had not ill Fate, perverse and blind,
Plac'd you in Life too far behind;
Or what I should repine at more,
Plac'd me in Life too far before;
To you the Muse this Verse bestows,
Which might as well have been in Prose;          10
No Thought, no Fancy, no Sublime,
But simple Topicks told in Rime.
    Three Gifts for Conversation fit
Are Humor, Raillery and Witt:
The last, as boundless as the Wind;
Is well conceiv'd thô not defin'd;
For, sure, by Wit is onely meant
Applying what we first Invent:
What Humor is, not all the Tribe
Of Logick-mongers can describe;          20

Printed from Swift's autograph, Forster Collection.

Here, onely Nature acts her Part,
Unhelpt by Practice, Books, or Art.
For Wit and Humor differ quite,
That gives Surprise, and this Delight:
Humor is odd, grotesque, and wild,
Onely by Affectation spoild,
Tis never by Invention got,
Men have it when they know it not.
   Our Conversation to refine
True Humor must with Wit combine:    30
From both, we learn to Railly well;
Wherein French Writers most excell:

[p. 2]   Voiture in various Lights displays
That Irony which turns to Praise,
His Genius first found out the Rule
For an obliging Ridicule:
He flatters with peculiar Air
The Brave, the Witty, and the Fair;
And Fools would fancy he intends
A Satyr where he most commends.    40
   But as a poor pretending Beau
Because he fain would make a Show,
Nor can afford to buy gold Lace,
Takes up with Copper in the Place;
So, the pert Dunces of Mankind
Whene're they would be thought refin'd,
Because the Diff'rence lyes abstruse
'Twixt Raillery and gross Abuse,
To show their Parts, will scold and rail,
Like Porters o'er a Pot of Ale.    50
   Such is that Clan of boist'rous Bears
Always together by the Ears;
Shrewd Fellows, and arch Wags, a Tribe
That meet for nothing but to gibe;
Who first Run one another down,
And then fall foul on all the Town;
Skilld in the Horse-laugh and dry Rub,
And calld by Excellence, *the Club*:
I mean your Butler, Dawson, Car,
All special Friends, and allways jarr.    60

The mettled and the vicious Steed
Do not more differ in their Breed,
Nay, Voiture is as like Tom Lee,
As Rudeness is to Repartee.

[p. 3]   If what You said, I wish unspoke,
'Twill not suffice, it was a Joke.
Reproach not tho in jest, a Friend
For those Defects he cannot mend;
His Lineage, Calling, Shape or Sense
If nam'd with Scorn, gives just Offence.    70

What Use in Life, to make Men frett?
Part in worse humor than they met?
Thus all Society is lost,
Men laugh at one another's Cost;
And half the Company is teazd
That came together to be pleasd:
For all Buffoons have most in View
To please themselves by vexing You

When Jests are carryd on too far,
And the loud Laugh proclaims the War;    80
You keep Your Countenance for shame
Yet still you think your Friend to blame.
And thô men cry, they love a Jest,
Tis but when others stand the Test,
For would you have their Meaning known?
They love a Jest—when 'tis their own.

[p. 4]   You wonder now to see me write
So gravely, where the Subject's light.
Some part of what I here design
Regards a Friend of yours and mine,    90
Who full of Humor, Fire and Wit,
Not allways judges what is fit;
But loves to take prodigious Rounds,
And sometimes walks beyond his Bounds.
You must, although the Point be nice,
Venture to give him some Advice.
Few Hints from you will set him right,
And teach him how to be polite.
Let him, like you, observe with Care
Whom to be hard on, whom to spare:    100

Nor indiscreetly to suppose
All Subjects like Dan Jackson's Nose.
To study the obliging Jest,
By reading those who teach it best.
For Prose, I recommend Voiture's,
For Verse, (I speak my Judgment) Yours:
He'll find the Secret out from thence
To Rime all day without Offence;
And I no more shall then Accuse
The Flirts of his ill-mannerd Muse.                    110
    If he be Guilty, you must mend him,
If he be innocent, defend him.


# SHERIDAN, A GOOSE

TOM, for a goose you keep but base quills,
   They're fit for nothing else but pasquils.
I've often heard it from the wise,
That inflammations in the eyes
Will quickly fall upon the tongue,
And thence, as fam'd John Bunyan sung,
From out the pen will presently
On paper dribble daintily.
Suppose I call'd you goose, it is hard
One word shou'd stick thus in your gizzard.             10
You're my goose, and no other man's;
And you know all my geese are swans:
Only one scurvy thing I find,
Swans sing when dying, geese when blind.
But now I smoak where lies the slander,—
I call'd you goose instead of gander;
For that, dear Tom, ne'er fret and vex,
I'm sure you cackle like the sex.
I know the gander always goes
With a quill stuck across his nose.                      20

Printed from *The Whimsical Medley.*

So your eternal pen is still,
Or in your claw, or in your bill.
But whether you can tread or hatch,
I've something else to do than watch.
As for you're writing I am dead,
I leave it for the second head.

Dean'ry house
    Oct<sup>br</sup> 27<sup>th</sup> 1718.


# THE REPLY

## BY SHERIDAN

A HIGHLANDER once fought a Frenchman at Margate,
    The weapons a rapier, a backsword and target;
Brisk Monsieur advanc'd as fast as he could,
But all his fine pushes were caught in the wood;
While Sawny with backsword did slash him and nick him,
While t'other, enraged that he could not once prick him,
Cry'd, "Sirrah, you rascal, you son of a whore,
Me'll fight you, begar, if you'll come from your door!"
    Our case is the same; if you'll fight like a man,
Don't fly from my weapon, and sculk behind Dan;
For he's not to be pierc'd; his leather's so tough,
The Devil himself can't get through his bluff.
Besides, I cannot but say that it is hard,
Not only to make him your shield, but your vizard;
And, like a tragedian, you rant and you roar,
Thro' the horrible grin of your *larva*'s wide bore.
Nay further, which makes me complain much, and frump it,
You make his long nose your loud speaking-trumpet;
With the din of which tube my head you so bother,
That I scarce can distinguish my right ear from t'other.

        You made me in your last a goose;
            I lay my life on't you are wrong,
        To raise me by such foul abuse;
            My quill you'll find's a woman's tongue;

And slit, just like a bird, will chatter,
    And like a bird do something more;
When I let fly, 'twill so bespatter,
    I'll change you to a black-a-moor.

I'll write while I have half an eye in my head;
I'll write while I live, and I'll write when you're dead.    30
Tho' you call me a goose, you pitiful slave,
I'll feed on the grass that grows on your grave.


# *Mary* the Cook-Maid's

# LETTER

## TO

## Dr. *SHERIDAN*

WELL; if ever I saw such another Man since my Mother
    bound my Head,
You a Gentleman! marry come up, I wonder where you were
    bred?
I am sure such Words does not become a Man of your Cloth,
I would not give such Language to a Dog, faith and troth.
Yes; you call'd my Master a Knave: Fie Mr. *Sheridan*, 'tis a
    Shame
For a Parson, who shou'd know better Things, to come out
    with such a Name.
Knave in your Teeth, Mr. *Sheridan*, 'tis both a Shame and a
    Sin,
And the Dean my Master is an honester Man than you and all
    your kin:
He has more Goodness in his little Finger, than you have in
    your whole Body,
My Master is a parsonable Man, and not a spindle-shank'd
    hoddy doddy.    10

Printed from *Miscellanies*. *The Third Volume*, 1732, with corrections from *Poems*, 1735.
Gspw

And now whereby I find you would fain make an Excuse,
Because my Master one Day in anger call'd you Goose.
Which, and I am sure I have been his Servant four Years since
    *October*,
And he never call'd me worse than Sweet-heart drunk or
    sober:
Not that I know his Reverence was ever concern'd to my
    knowledge,
Tho' you and your Come-rogues keep him out so late in your
    wicked Colledge.

   You say you will eat Grass on his Grave: a Christian eat
    Grass!
Whereby you now confess your self to be a Goose or an Ass:
But that's as much as to say, that my Master should die before
    ye,
Well, well, that's as God pleases, and I don't believe that's a
    true Story,                           20
And so say I told you so, and you may go tell my Master; what
    care I?
And I don't care who knows it, 'tis all one to *Mary*.
Every body knows, that I love to tell Truth and shame the
    Devil,
I am but a poor Servant, but I think Gentle folks should be
    civil.
Besides, you found fault with our Vittles one Day that you was
    here,
I remember it was upon a *Tuesday*, of all Days in the Year.
And *Saunders* the Man says, you are always jesting and mocking,
*Mary* said he, (one Day, as I was mending my Master's
    Stocking,)
My Master is so fond of that Minister that keeps the School;
I thought my Master a wise Man, but that Man makes him a
    Fool.                                       30
*Saunders* said I, I would rather than a Quart of Ale,
He would come into our Kitchin, and I would pin a Dishclout
    to his Tail.
And now I must go, and get *Saunders* to direct this Letter,
For I write but a sad Scrawl, but my Sister *Marget* she writes
    better.

Well, but I must run and make the Bed before my Master
    comes from Pray'rs,
And see now, it strikes ten, and I hear him coming up Stairs:
Whereof I cou'd say more to your Verses, if I could write
    written hand,
And so I remain in a civil way, your Servant to command,
Mary.

# A LETTER

## TO THE

## Reverend Dr. *SHERIDAN*

### Written in the Year 1718

WHATE'ER your Predecessors taught us,
    I have a great Esteem for *Plautus*;
And think your Boys may gather there-hence
More Wit and Humour than from *Terence*.
But as to Comic *Aristophanes*,
The Rogue's too Bawdy and too Prophane is.
I went in vain to look for *Eupolis*,
Down in the *Strand* just where the new Pole is,
For I can tell you one Thing, that I can,
You will not find it in the *Vatican*.        10
He and *Cratinus* used, as *Horace* says,
To take his greatest Grandees for Asses.
Poets, in those Days, us'd to venture high,
But these are lost full many a Century.

    THUS you may see, dear Friend, *ex pede* hence
My Judgment of the old Comedians.

Printed from Works, Vol. VI, Dublin, 1738.

8. N.B. The Strand in London. The Fact may be false, but the Rhyme cost
me some Trouble.

PROCEED to Tragicks, first *Euripides*
(An Author, where I sometimes dip a Days)
Is rightly censur'd by the Stagirite,
Who says, his Numbers do not fadge a-right.          20
A Friend of mine, that Author despises ⎫
So much, he swears the very best Piece is ⎬
For ought he knows, as bad as *Thespis*'s. ⎭
And that a Woman, in those Tragedies
Commonly speaking, but a sad Jade is.
At least, I'm well assured, that no Folk lays
The Weight on him, they do on *Sophocles*.
But above all I prefer *Æschylus*,
Whose moving Touches, when they please, kill us.

AND now I find my Muse but ill able          30
To hold out longer in Trysyllable.
I chose these Rhymes out, for their Difficulty.
Will you return as hard ones, if I call t'ye?

# THE ANSWER

## BY DR. SHERIDAN

SIR,
I THANK you for your comedies.
I'll stay and read 'em now at home a-days,
Because Pareus wrote but sorrily
Thy notes, I'll read Lambinus thoroughly;
And then I shall be stoutly set a-gog
To challenge every Irish Pedagogue.
I like your nice epistle critical,
Which does in threefold rhymes so witty fall;
Upon the comic dram' and tragedy
Your notion's right, but verses maggotty;          10
'Tis but an hour since I heard a man swear it,
The Devil himself could hardly answer it.
As for your friend the sage Euripides,
I believe you give him now the slip o'days;

14. N.B. You told me you forgot your Greek.

But mum for that—pray come a Saturday
And dine with me, you can't a better day:
I'll give you nothing but a mutton chop,
Some nappy mellow'd ale with rotten hop,
A pint of wine as good as Falern',
Which we poor masters, God knows, all earn;      20
We'll have a friend or two, sir, at table,
Right honest men, for few're comeatable;
Then when our liquor makes us talkative,
We'll to the fields, and take a walk at eve.
    Because I'm troubled much with laziness,
    These rhymes I've chosen for their easiness.


# On Stella's Birth-day

## Written AD. 1718-[19]

STELLA this Day is thirty four,
   (We shan't dispute a Year or more)
However Stella, be not troubled,
Although thy Size and Years are doubled,
Since first I saw Thee at Sixteen
The brightest Virgin on the Green,
So little is thy Form declin'd
Made up so largly in thy Mind.
Oh, would it please the Gods to split
Thy Beauty, Size, and Years, and Wit,      10
No Age could furnish out a Pair
Of Nymphs so gracefull, Wise and fair
With half the Lustre of Your Eyes,
With half your Wit, your Years and Size:
And then before it grew too late,
How should I beg of gentle Fate,
(That either Nymph might have her Swain,)
To split my Worship too in twain.

Printed from Stella's transcript, with corrections from *Poems*, 1735.

# A quiet Life, and a good Name

## To &c. Writ A.D. 1719

NELL scolded in so loud a Din  
   That Will durst hardly venture in;  
He mark't the Conjugall Dispute,  
Nell roar'd incessant, Dick sate mute:  
But when He saw his Friend appear  
Cry'd bravely, Patience, good my Dear.  
At sight of Will she bawl'd no more,  
But hurry'd out, and clapp't the Dore.  
  Why Dick! the Devil's in thy Nell  
Quoth Will; thy House is worse than Hell:     10  
Why, what a Peal the Jade has rung,  
Damn her, why don't you Slit her Tongue?  
For nothing else will make it cease,—  
Dear Will, I suffer this for Peace;  
I never quarrell with my Wife,  
I bear it for a quiet Life  
Scripture you know exhorts us to it,  
Bids us to seek Peace and ensue it.  
  Will went again to visit Dick  
And entring in the very nick,     20  
He saw Virago Nell belabor  
With Dick's own Staff his Peacefull Neighbor,  
Poor Will, who needs must interpose,  
Receiv'd a brace or two of Blows.  
  But now, to make my Story Short  
Will drew out Dick to take a Quart,  
Why Dick, thy Wife has dev'lish Whims:  
Ods buds, why don't you break her Limbs:  
If she were Mine, and had such Tricks,  
I'd teach her how to handle Sticks:     30  
Zounds I would ship her for Jamaica  
And truck the Carrion for Tobacca,

Printed from Stella's transcript.

I'd send her far enough away—
Dear Will, but, what would People say?
Lord! I should get so ill a Name,
The Neighbors round would cry out Shame.
   Dick suffer'd for his Peace and Credit,
But who believ'd him when he said it:
Can he who makes himself a Slave
Consult his Peace, or Credit save?        40
Dick found it by his ill Success
His Quiet small, his Credit less;
Nell serv'd him at the usu'll Rate
She stun'd, and then she broke his Pate.
And what he thought the hardest Case,
The Parish jear'd him to his Face:
Those Men who wore the Breeches least
Call'd him a Cuckold, Fool, and Beast,
At home, he was pursu'd with Noise,
Abroad, was pester'd by the Boys,       50
Within, his wife would break his Bones,
Without, they pelted him with Stones,
The Prentices procur'd a Riding
To act his Patience, and her chiding.
   False Patience, and mistaken Pride!
There are ten thousand Dicks beside;
Slaves to their Quiet and good Name,
Are us'd like Dick, and bear the Blame.


# PHILLIS,

## Or, the Progress of Love

### Written A.D. 1719

DESPONDING Phillis was endu'd
    With ev'ry Talent of a Prude,
She trembled when a Man drew near;
Salute her, and she turn'd her Ear:

Printed from Stella's transcript, with corrections from *Poems*, 1735.

If o'er against her you were plac't
She durst not look above your Wast;
She'd rather take you to her Bed
Than let you see her dress her Head;
In Church you heard her thrô the Crowd
Repeat the Absolution loud;                    10
In Church, secure behind her Fan
She durst behold that Monster, Man:
There practic'd how to place her Head,
And bit her Lips to make them red:
Or on the Matt devoutly kneeling
Would lift her Eyes up to the Ceeling,
And heave her Bosom unaware
For neighb'ring Beaux to see it bare.
　　At length a lucky Lover came,
And found Admittance to the Dame.        20
Suppose all Partyes now agreed,
The Writings drawn, the Lawyer fee'd,
The Vicar and the Ring bespoke:
Guess how could such a Match be broke.
See then what Mortals place their Bliss in!
Next morn betimes the Bride was missing,
The Mother scream'd, the Father chid,
Where can this idle Wench be hid?
No news of Phil. The Bridegroom came,
And thought his Bride had sculk't for shame,  30
Because her Father us'd to say
The Girl had such a Bashfull way.
　　Now John the Butler must be sent
To learn the Road that Phillis went;
The Groom was wisht to saddle Crop,
For John must neither light nor stop;
But find her where so'er she fled,
And bring her back, alive or dead.
See here again the Dev'l to do;
For truly John was missing too:                40
The Horse and Pillion both were gone
Phillis, it seems, was fled with John.
Old Madam who went up to find
What Papers Phil had left behind,

35. *wisht.* A trades-men's Phrase. [Swift's MS. note, 1727.]

A Letter on the Toylet sees
To my much honor'd Father; These:
('Tis always done, Romances tell us,
When Daughters run away with Fellows)
Fill'd with the choicest common-places,
By others us'd in the like Cases.                    50
That, long ago a Fortune-teller
Exactly said what now befell her,
And in a Glass had made her see
A serving-Man of low Degree:
It was her Fate; must be forgiven;
For Marriages were made in Heaven:
His Pardon begg'd, but to be plain,
She'd do't if 'twere to do again.
Thank God, 'twas neither Shame nor Sin,
For John was come of honest Kin:                     60
Love never thinks of Rich and Poor,
She'd beg with John from Door to Door:
Forgive her, if it be a Crime,
She'll never do't another Time,
She ne'r before in all her Life
Once disobey'd him, Maid nor Wife.
One Argument she summ'd up all in,
The Thing was done and past recalling:
And therefore hop'd she should recover
His Favor, when his Passion's over.                  70
She valued not what others thought her;
And was—His most obedient Daughter.
   Fair Maidens all attend the Muse
Who now the wandring Pair pursues:
Away they rode in homely Sort
Their Journy long, their Money Short;
The loving Couple well bemir'd,
The Horse and both the Riders tir'd:
Their Vittells bad, their Lodging worse,
Phil cry'd, and John began to curse;                 80
Phil wish't, that she had strained a Limb
When first she ventur'd out with him.
John wish't, that he had broke a Leg
When first for her he quitted Peg.

But what Adventures more befell 'em
The Muse hath now no time to tell 'em.
How Jonny wheadled, threatned, fawnd,
Till Phillis all her Trinkets pawn'd:
How oft she broke her marriage Vows
In kindness to maintain her Spouse;                    90
Till Swains unwholsome spoyld the Trade,
For now the Surgeon must be paid;
To whom those Perquisites are gone
In Christian Justice due to John.
    When Food and Rayment now grew scarce
Fate put a Period to the Farce;
And with exact Poetick Justice:
For John is Landlord, Phillis Hostess;
They keep at Stains the old blue Boar,
Are Cat and Dog, and Rogue and Whore.                 100


# THE

# PROGRESS of BEAUTY

### Written A.D. 1719

WHEN first Diana leaves her Bed
    Vapors and Steams her Looks disgrace,
A frouzy dirty colour'd red
Sits on her cloudy wrinckled Face.

But by degrees when mounted high
Her artificiall Face appears
Down from her Window in the Sky,
Her Spots are gone, her Visage clears.

'Twixt earthly Femals and the Moon
All Parallells exactly run;                            10
If Celia should appear too soon
Alas, the Nymph would be undone.

Printed from Stella's transcript, with corrections from *Poems*, 1735.

To see her from her Pillow rise
All reeking in a cloudy Steam,
Crackt Lips, foul Teeth, and gummy Eyes,
Poor Strephon, how would he blaspheme!

Three Colours, Black, and Red, and White,
So gracefull in their proper Place,
Remove them to a diff'rent Light
They form a frightfull hideous Face,     20

For instance; when the Lilly skips
Into the Precincts of the Rose,
And takes Possession of the Lips,
Leaving the Purple to the Nose.

So Celia went entire to bed,
All her Complexions safe and sound,
But when she rose, White, Black, and Red
Though still in Sight, had chang'd their Ground.

The Black, which would not be confin'd
A more inferior Station seeks     30
Leaving the fiery red behind,
And mingles in her muddy Cheeks.

But Celia can with ease reduce
By help of Pencil, Paint and Brush
Each Colour to it's Place and Use,
And teach her Cheeks again to blush.

She knows her Early self no more,
But fill'd with Admiration, stands,
As Other Painters oft adore
The Workmanship of their own Hands.     40

Thus after four important Hours
Celia's the Wonder of her Sex;
Say, which among the Heav'nly Pow'rs
Could cause such marvellous Effects?

Venus, indulgent to her Kind
Gave Women all their Hearts could wish
When first she taught them where to find
White Lead, and Lusitanian Dish.

Love with White lead cements his Wings,
White lead was sent us to repair                    50
Two brightest, brittlest earthly Things
A Lady's Face, and China ware.

She ventures now to lift the Sash,
The Window is her proper Sphear;
Ah Lovely Nymph be not too rash,
Nor let the Beaux approach too near.

Take Pattern by your Sister Star,
Delude at once and Bless our Sight,
When you are seen, be seen from far,
And chiefly chuse to shine by Night.                    60

But, Art no longer can prevayl
When the Materialls all are gone,
The best Mechanick Hand must fayl
Where Nothing's left to work upon.

Matter, as wise Logicians say,
Cannot without a Form subsist,
And Form, say I, as well as They,
Must fayl if Matter brings no Grist.

And this is fair Diana's Case
For, all Astrologers maintain                    70
Each Night a Bit drops off her Face
When Mortals say she's in her Wain.

While Partridge wisely shews the Cause
Efficient of the Moon's Decay,
That Cancer with his pois'nous Claws
Attacks her in the milky Way:

48. *Lusitanian*. Portugal.

But Gadbury in Art profound
From her pale Cheeks pretends to show
That Swain Endymion is not sound,
Or else, that Mercury's her Foe.     80


But, let the Cause be what it will,
In half a Month she looks so thin
That Flamstead can with all his Skill
See but her Forehead and her Chin.


Yet as she wasts, she grows discreet,
Till Midnight never shows her Head;
So rotting Celia stroles the Street
When sober Folks are all a-bed.


For sure if this be Luna's Fate,
Poor Celia, but of mortall Race     90
In vain expects a longer Date
To the Materialls of Her Face.


When Mercury her Tresses mows
To think of Black-head Combs is vain,
No Painting can restore a Nose,
Nor will her Teeth return again.


Ye Pow'rs who over Love preside,
Since mortal Beautyes drop so soon,
If you would have us well supply'd,
Send us new Nymphs with each new Moon.     100

# From Dr. Swift to Dr. Sheridan

SIR,                                    *Dec.* 14, 1719, 9 *at Night.*

IT is impossible to know by your Letter whether the Wine is to be bottled To-morrow, or no.

If it be, or be not, why did not you in plain *English* tell us so?

For my part, it was by meer Chance I came back to sit with the Ladies this Night.

And, if they had not told me there was a Letter from you, and your Man *Alexander* had not gone, and come back from the Deanry, and the Boy here had not been sent to let *Alexander* know I was here, I should have missed the Letter outright.

Truly I don't know who's bound to be sending for Corks to stop your Bottles, with a Vengeance.

Make a Page of your own Age, and send your Man *Alexander* to buy Corks, for *Saunders* already hath got above ten Jaunts.

Mrs. *Dingley* and Mrs. *Johnson* say, truly they don't care for your Wife's Company, although they like your Wine; but they had rather have it at their own House, to drink in quiet.

However, they own it is very civil in Mr. *Sheridan*, to make the Offer; and they cannot deny it.

I wish *Alexander* safe at St. *Catherine*'s To-night, with all my Heart and Soul, upon my Word and Honour.

Printed from *Works, Vol, VIII.* Dublin, 1746, with the following note:

Dr. *Sheridan* was an eminent School-master, whom the Dean is supposed thus to describe under the Character of *Lilly.*

*Lilly* is a Person very excellent in his Art; perfectly skilled in the Writings and Languages of ancient *Greece* and *Rome.* He hath much Invention; often writes humorous Verses that are diverting enough, but is defective in Judgment. He is honest, generous, friendly, and good-natured, but without one Grain of Discretion: And, with all, so heedless, unattentive, shattered and absent, that you cannot depend a Minute on his Promise or Engagement. He is somewhat too careless in Expences. How subject he was to be deceived, appears from the following Certificate under the Doctor's own Hand, dated *Oct.* 22, 1731.

'Dr. Sheridan, *forced to premise and allowed, that he hath been thirty Times deceived in affirming his Servants and Agents to be honest; does now, the one and thirtieth Time, positively assert, that his present Agent at* Quilca, Wooly *by Name, is the most honest, diligent, and skilful Fellow in* Ireland.

Signed at Dr *Grattan*'s House.
THOMAS SHERIDAN.'

But I think it base in you to send a poor Fellow out so late at this Time of Year, when one would not turn out a Dog that one valued; I appeal to your Friend Mr. *Conna*.                    10

I would present my humble Service to my Lady *Mountcashell*: but, truly, I thought she would have made Advances to have been acquainted with me, as she pretended.

But now I can write no more, for you see plainly my Paper is ended.

P.S.    *I wish when you prated,*
        *Your Letter you'd dated,*
        *Much Plague it created,*
        *I scolded and rated;*
        *My Soul it much grated,*
        *For your Man, I long waited.*
        *I think you are fated,*
        *Like a Bear to be baited:*                    20
        *Your Man is belated,*
        *The Case, I have stated,*
        *And me you have cheated.*
        *My Stable's unslated,*
        *Come back t'us well freighted;*
        *I remember my late-head*
        *And wish you Translated,*
                    *For teazing me.*


2 P.S.    *Mrs.* Dingley
          *Desires me singly*                    30
          *Her Service to present you,*
          *Hopes that will content you;*
          *But* Johnson *Madam*
          *Is grown a Sad Dame,*
          *For want of your Converse,*
          *And cannot send one Verse.*


3 P.S.    *You keep such a twattling*          [Vida,
          *With you and your bottling,*          [Rule 34
          *But I see the Sum Total,*
          *We shall ne'er have one Bottle;*                    40

*The long and the short,*
*We shall not have a Quart.*
*I wish you would sign't,*
*That we may have a Pint.*
*For all your colloguing,*
*I'd be glad of a Knogging:*
*But I doubt 'tis a Sham,*
*You won't give us a Dram.*
*'Tis of Shine, a Mouth Moon-full,*
*You won't part with a Spoon-full,*                    50
*And I must be nimble,*
*If I can fill my Thimble,*
*You see I won't stop,*
*Till I come to a Drop;*
*But I doubt the Oraculum,*
*Is a poor Supernaculum;*
*Tho' perhaps you may tell it*
*For a Grace, if we smell it.*          STELLA.

# THE

# PROGRESS

## OF

# POETRY

THE Farmer's Goose, who in the Stubble,
   Has fed without Restraint, or Trouble;
Grown fat with Corn and Sitting still,
Can scarce get o'er the Barn-Door Sill:
And hardly waddles forth, to cool
Her Belly in the neighb'ring Pool:
Nor loudly cackles at the Door;
For Cackling shews the Goose is poor.

Printed from *Miscellanies. The Last Volume,* 1727.

But when she must be turn'd to graze,
And round the barren Common strays,　　10
Hard Exercise, and harder Fare
Soon make my Dame grow lank and spare:
Her Body light, she tries her Wings,
And scorns the Ground, and upward springs,
While all the Parish, as she flies,
Hear Sounds harmonious from the Skies.

Such is the Poet, fresh in Pay,
(The third Night's Profits of his Play;)
His Morning-Draughts 'till Noon can swill,
Among his Brethren of the Quill:　　20
With good Roast Beef his Belly full,
Grown lazy, foggy, fat, and dull:
Deep sunk in Plenty, and Delight,
What Poet e'er could take his Flight?
Or stuff'd with Phlegm up to the Throat,
What Poet e'er could sing a Note?
Nor *Pegasus* could bear the Load,
Along the high celestial Road;
The Steed, oppress'd, would break his Girth,
To raise the Lumber from the Earth.　　30

But, view him in another Scene,
When all his Drink is *Hippocrene*,
His Money spent, his Patrons fail,
His Credit out for Cheese and Ale;
His Two-Year's Coat so smooth and bare,
Through ev'ry Thread it lets in Air;
With hungry Meals his Body pin'd,
His Guts and Belly full of Wind;
And, like a Jockey for a Race,
His Flesh brought down to Flying-Case:　　40
Now his exalted Spirit loaths
Incumbrances of Food and Cloaths;
And up he rises like a Vapour,
Supported high on Wings of Paper;
He singing flies, and flying sings,
While from below all *Grub-street* rings.

# TO
# *STELLA,*
## Visiting me in my Sickness

$P$*ALLAS* observing *Stella*'s Wit
  Shine more than for her Sex was fit;
And that her Beauty, soon or late,
Might breed Confusion in the State,
In high Concern for human Kind,
Fixt *Honour* in her Infant Mind.

  But, (not in Wranglings to engage
With such a stupid vicious Age,)
If Honour I would here define,
It answers Faith in Things divine.                    10
As nat'ral Life the Body warms,
And, Scholars teach, the Soul informs;
So Honour animates the Whole,
And is the Spirit of the Soul.

  Those num'rous Virtues which the Tribe
Of tedious Moralists describe,
And by such various Titles call,
True Honour comprehends them all.
Let Melancholy rule supreme,
Choler preside, or Blood, or Phlegm,                  20
It makes no Diff'rence in the Case,
Nor is Complexion Honour's Place.

  But, lest we should for Honour take
The drunken Quarrels of a Rake,
Or think it seated in a Scar,
Or on a proud triumphal Car,
Or in the Payment of a Debt
We lose with Sharpers at Piquet;

Printed from *Miscellanies, The Last Volume,* 1727, with corrections from *Poems,*
1735.

Or, when a Whore in her Vocation,
Keeps punctual to an Assignation;                    30
Or that on which his Lordship swears,
When vulgar Knaves would lose their Ears:
Let *Stella*'s fair Example preach
A Lesson she alone can teach.


   In Points of Honour to be try'd,
All Passions must be laid aside:
Ask no Advice, but think alone,
Suppose the Question not your own:
How shall I act? is not the Case,
But how would *Brutus* in my Place?                  40
In such a Cause would *Cato* bleed?
And how would *Socrates* proceed?


   Drive all Objections from your Mind,
Else you relapse to Human Kind:
Ambition, Avarice, and Lust,
And factious Rage, and Breach of Trust,
And Flatt'ry tipt with nauseous Fleer,
And guilty Shame, and servile Fear,
Envy, and Cruelty, and Pride,
Will in your tainted Heart preside.                  50


   Heroes and Heroins of old,
By Honour only were enroll'd
Among their Brethren of the Skies,
To which (though late) shall *Stella* rise.
Ten thousand Oaths upon Record,
Are not so sacred as her Word:
The World shall in its Atoms end,
E'er *Stella* can deceive a Friend.
By Honour seated in her Breast,
She still determines what is best:                   60
What Indignation in her Mind
Against Enslavers of Mankind!
Base Kings and Ministers of State,
Eternal Objects of her Hate.

She thinks that Nature ne'er design'd
Courage to Man alone confin'd:
Can Cowardice her Sex adorn,
Which most exposes ours to Scorn?
She wonders where the Charm appears
In *Florimel*'s affected Fears:      70
For *Stella* never learn'd the Art,
At proper Times to scream and start;
Nor calls up all the House at Night,
And swears she saw a Thing in White.
*Doll* never flies to cut her Lace,
Or throw cold Water in her Face,
Because she heard a sudden Drum,
Or found an Earwig in a Plum.

Her Hearers are amaz'd from whence
Proceeds that Fund of Wit and Sense;      80
Which though her Modesty would shroud,
Breaks like the Sun behind a Cloud,
While Gracefulness its Art conceals,
And yet through ev'ry Motion steals.

Say, *Stella*, was *Prometheus* blind,
And forming you, mistook your Kind?
No: 'Twas for you alone he stole
The Fire that forms a manly Soul;
Then to compleat it ev'ry way,
He molded it with Female Clay:      90
To that you owe the nobler Flame,
To this, the Beauty of your Frame.

How would Ingratitude delight?
And, how would Censure glut her Spight?
If I should *Stella*'s Kindness hide
In Silence, or forget with Pride.
When on my sickly Couch I lay,
Impatient both of Night and Day,
Lamenting in unmanly Strains,
Call'd ev'ry Pow'r to ease my Pains,      100
Then *Stella* ran to my Relief
With chearful Face, and inward Grief;

And, though by Heaven's severe Decree
She suffers hourly more than me,
No cruel Master could require
From Slaves employ'd for daily Hire
What *Stella* by her Friendship warm'd,
With Vigour and Delight perform'd.
My sinking Spirits now supplies
With Cordials in her Hands, and Eyes.                    110
Now, with a soft and silent Tread,
Unheard she moves about my Bed.
I see her taste each nauseous Draught,
And so obligingly am caught:
I bless the Hand from whence they came,
Nor dare distort my Face for shame.

    Best Pattern of true Friends, beware;
You pay too dearly for your Care;
If, while your Tenderness secures
My Life, it must endanger yours.                    120
For such a Fool was never found,
Who pull'd a Palace to the Ground,
Only to have the Ruins made
Materials for an House decay'd.

# TO

# *STELLA*,

## Who Collected and Transcribed his

## POEMS

AS when a lofty Pile is rais'd,
We never hear the Workmen prais'd,
Who bring the Lime, or place the Stones;
But all admire *Inigo Jones*:

Printed from *Miscellanies. The Last Volume*, 1727, with corrections from *Poems*, 1735.

So if this Pile of scatter'd Rhymes
Should be approv'd in After-times,
If it both pleases and endures,
The Merit and the Praise are yours.


Thou *Stella*, wert no longer young,
When first for thee my Harp I strung:          10
Without one Word of *Cupid*'s Darts,
Of killing Eyes, or bleeding Hearts:
With Friendship and Esteem possesst,
I ne'er admitted Love a Guest.


In all the Habitudes of Life,
The Friend, the Mistress, and the Wife,
Variety we still Pursue,
In Pleasure seek for something new:
Or else, comparing with the rest,
Take Comfort, that our own is best:          20
(The best we value by the worst,
As Tradesmen shew their Trash at first:)
But his Pursuits are at an End,
Whom *Stella* chuses for a *Friend*.


A Poet, starving in a Garret,
Conning old Topicks like a Parrot,
Invokes his Mistress and his Muse,
And stays at home for want of Shoes:
Should but his Muse descending drop
A Slice of Bread, and Mutton-Chop,          30
Or kindly when his Credit's out,
Surprize him with a Pint of Stout,
Or patch his broken Stocking Soals,
Or send him in a Peck of Coals;
Exalted in his mighty Mind
He flies, and leaves the Stars behind,
Counts all his Labours amply paid,
Adores her for the timely Aid.

32. *Stout*. A Cant Word for Strong-Beer.

Or should a Porter make Enquiries
For *Chloe, Sylvia, Phillis, Iris*;                    40
Be told the Lodging, Lane, and Sign,
The Bow'rs that hold those Nymphs divine;
Fair *Chloe* would perhaps be found
With Footmen tippling under Ground,
The charming *Silvia* beating Flax,
Her Shoulders mark'd with bloody Tracks;
Bright *Phillis* mending ragged Smocks,
And radiant *Iris* in the Pox.

These are the Goddesses enroll'd
In *Curll*'s Collections, new and old,                 50
Whose Scoundrel Fathers would not know 'em,
If they should meet 'em in a Poem.

True Poets can depress and raise;
Are Lords of Infamy and Praise:
They are not scurrilous in Satire,
Nor will in Panygyrick flatter.
Unjustly Poets we asperse;
Truth shines the brighter, clad in Verse;
And all the Fictions they pursue
Do but insinuate what is true.                         60

Now should my Praises owe their Truth
To Beauty, Dress, or Paint, or Youth,
What Stoicks call *without our Power*,
They could not be insur'd an Hour;
'Twere grafting on an annual Stock
That must our Expectation mock,
And making one luxuriant Shoot
Die the next Year for want of Root:
Before I could my Verses bring,
Perhaps you're quite another Thing.                    70

So *Mævius*, when he drain'd his Skull
To celebrate some Suburb Trull;
His Similes in Order set,
And ev'ry Crambo he could get;

Had gone through all the Common-Places
Worn out by Wits who rhyme on Faces;
Before he could his Poem close,
The lovely Nymph had lost her Nose.

Your Virtues safely I commend,
They on no Accidents depend: 80
Let Malice look with all her Eyes,
She dares not say the Poet lyes.

*Stella*, when you these Lines transcribe,
Lest you should take them for a Bribe,
Resolv'd to mortify your Pride,
I'll here expose your weaker Side.

Your Spirits kindle to a Flame,
Mov'd with the lightest Touch of Blame,
And when a Friend in Kindness tries
To shew you where your Error lies, 90
Conviction does but more incense;
Perverseness is your whole Defence:
Truth, Judgment, Wit, give Place to Spite,
Regardless both of Wrong and Right.
Your Virtues, all suspended, wait
Till Time hath open'd Reason's Gate:
And what is worse, your Passion bends
Its Force against your nearest Friends;
Which Manners, Decency, and Pride,
Have taught you from the World to hide: 100
In vain; for see, your Friend hath brought
To publick Light your only Fau't;
And yet a Fault we often find
Mix'd in a noble generous Mind;
And may compare to *Ætna's* Fire,
Which, tho' with Trembling, all admire;
The Heat that makes the Summit glow,
Enriching all the Vales below.
Those who in warmer Climes complain
From *Phœbus* Rays they suffer Pain, 110
Must own, that Pain is largely paid
By gen'rous Wines beneath a Shade.

Yet when I find your Passions rise,
And Anger sparkling in your Eyes,
I grieve those Spirits should be spent,
For nobler Ends by Nature meant.
One Passion, with a diff'rent Turn,
Makes Wit inflame, or Anger burn;
So the Sun's Heat, by different Powers,
Ripens the Grape, the Liquor sours.      120
Thus *Ajax*, when with Rage possesst
By *Pallas* breath'd into his Breast,
His Valour would no more employ;
Which might alone have conquer'd *Troy*;
But blinded by Resentment, seeks
For Vengeance on his Friends the *Greeks*.

You think this Turbulence of Blood
From stagnating preserves the Flood;
Which thus fermenting, by Degrees
Exalts the Spirits, sinks the Lees.      130

*Stella*, for once you reason wrong;
For should this Ferment last too long,
By Time subsiding, you may find
Nothing but Acid left behind.
From Passion you may then be freed,
When Peevishness and Spleen succeed.

Say, *Stella*, when you copy next,
Will you keep strictly to the Text?
Dare you let these Reproaches stand,
And to your Failing set your Hand?      140
Or if these Lines your Anger fire,
Shall they in baser Flames expire?
Whene'er they burn, if burn they must,
They'll prove my Accusation just.

# AN ELEGY

On the much lamented Death of Mr. *Demar*, the
Famous rich Man, who died the *6th* of this Inst.

*July*, 1720

*K N O W all Men by these Presents,* Death the Tamer
By *Mortgage* hath secur'd the *Corps* of *Demar*;
Nor can *four hundred thousand sterling Pound*
Redeem him from his *Prison* under Ground.
His Heirs might well of all his Wealth possest,
Bestow to bury him one Iron Chest.
*Pluto* the god of Wealth, will joy to know
His faithful Steward, in the Shades below.
He walk'd the Streets, and wore a Thread-bare Cloak;
He Din'd and Sup'd at Charge of other Folk,               10
And by his Looks, had he held out his Palms,
He might be thought an Object fit for Alms.
So to the Poor if he refus'd his Pelf,
He us'd 'em full as kindly as himself.
    Where'er he went he never saw his *Betters*,
*Lords*, *Knights* and *Squires* were all his humble Debtors.
And under *Hand* and *Seal* the *Irish* Nation
Were forc'd to own to him their *Obligation*.
    He that cou'd once have half a Kingdom bought,
In half a Minute is not worth a Groat;                    20
His *Coffers* from the *Coffin* could not save,
Nor all his Int'rest keep him from the Grave.
A golden Monument would not be Right,
Because we wish the Earth upon him Light,
    Oh *London Tavern*! Thou hast lost a Friend,
Tho' in thy Walls he ne'er did Farthing spend,
He *touch'd* the *Pence* when others *touch'd the Pot*;
The Hand that sign'd the Mortgage paid the Shot.

Printed from the Fo. Broadside, Dublin, 1720, with corrections from *Poems*, 1735.
    25. A Tavern in Dublin where Mr. Demar kept his Office. [fn. 1737.]

Old as he was, no vulgar known Disease
On him could ever boast a Pow'r to seize;                    30
But as his Gold he weigh'd, grim Death in spight,
Cast in his Dart which made three Moydores Light.
And as he saw his darling *Money* fail,
Blew his last Breath to sink the lighter Scale.

He who so long was *Currant* 'twould be strange
If he shou'd now be *cry'd down* since his *Change*.

The *Sexton* shall green Sods on thee bestow.
Alas the *Sexton* is thy *Banker* now!
A dismal *Banker* must that *Banker* be,
Who gives no *Bills*, but of *Mortality*.                    40

## The EPITAPH

BENEATH this verdant *Hillock* lies
*Demar* the *Wealthy*, and the *Wise*.
His *Heirs* that he might safely rest,
Have put his *Carcass* in a *Chest*.
The very *Chest*, in which they say
His *other Self*, his *Money* lay.
And if his *Heirs* continue kind,
To that dear *Self* he left behind;
I dare believe that Four in Five
Will think his *better Self* alive.                          50

## VERSES *to* VANESSA

[p. 1]  NYMPH, would you learn the onely Art
To keep a worthy Lover's heart
First, to adorn your Person well,
In utmost Cleanlyness excell

Printed from Swift's autograph, B.M. Add. MS. 39839.
31–34. [These four lines were written by Stella.]

And thô you must the Fashions take,
Observe them but for fashion sake.
  The strongest Reason will submit
To Virtue,—Honor, Sense, and Wit.
To such a Nymph the Wise and Good
Cannot be faithless if they wou'd:          10
For Vices all have diff'rent Ends,
But Virtue still to Virtue tends.
[p. 2]    And when your Lover is not true,
Tis Virtue fails in Him or You:
And either he deserves Disdain,
Or You without a Cause complain.
But here Vanessa cannot err,
Nor are these Rules applyd to Her:
For who could such a Nymph forsake
Except a Blockhead or a Rake          20
Or how could she her Heart bestow
Except where Wit and Virtue grow

———

Dorinda dreams of Dress a bed
  'Tis all her Thought and Art,
Her Lace hath got within her Head
  Her Stays stick to her Heart.

———

A Fig for Partridges and Quails
Ye Daintyes, I know nothing of ye,
But on the highest mount in Wales
Would chuse in Peace to drink my Coffee.

# An Excellent new SONG on a seditious Pamphlet

### *To the Tune of* Packington's Pound

#### Written in the Year 1720

The Author having writ a Treatise, advising the People of Ireland to wear their own Manufactures; that infamous Wretch Whitshed prosecuted Waters the

Printed from *Poems*, 1735 (uncancelled state).

Printer with so much Violence and Injustice, that he kept the Jury Nine Hours, and sent them away Eleven Times, till out of meer Weariness they were forced to give a special Verdict.

## I

BROCADO'S, and Damasks, and Tabbies, and Gawses,
   Are by *Robert Ballentine* lately brought over;
With Forty Things more: Now hear what the Law says,
   Whoe'er will not wear them, is not the King's Lover.
            Tho' a Printer and Dean
            Seditiously mean
   Our true *Irish* Hearts from old *England* to wean;
We'll buy *English* Silks for our Wives and our Daughters,
In Spight of his Deanship and Journeyman *Waters*.

## II

In *England* the Dead in Woollen are clad,                10
   The Dean and his Printer then let us cry Fye on;
To be cloath'd like a Carcass would make a Teague mad,
   Since a living Dog better is than a dead Lyon,
            Our Wives they grow sullen
            At wearing of Woollen,
   And all we poor Shopkeepers must our Horns pull in.
Then we'll buy *English* Silks, *&c.*

## III

Whoever our Trading with *England* would hinder,
   To *inflame* both the Nations do plainly conspire;
Because *Irish* Linen will soon turn to Tinder;          20
   And Wool it is greasy, and quickly takes Fire.
            Therefore I assure ye,
            Our noble Grand Jury,
   When they saw the Dean's Book they were in a great Fury:
They would buy *English* Silks for their Wives, *&c.*

## IV

This wicked Rogue *Waters*, who always is sinning,
  And before *Corum Nobus* so oft has been call'd,
Henceforward shall print neither Pamphlets nor Linnen,
  And, if Swearing can do't, shall be swingingly mawl'd:
        And as for the Dean,        30
        You know whom I mean,
If the Printer will peach him, he'll scarce come off clean.
Then we'll buy *English* Silks for our Wives and our Daughters,
In Spight of his Deanship and Journeyman *Waters*.


# The Run upon the Bankers

### Written A.D. 1720

THE bold Encroachers on the Deep,
  Gain by Degrees huge Tracts of Land,
'Till Neptune with a Gen'ral Sweep
Turns all again to barren Strand.


  The Multitude's Capricious Pranks
Are said to represent the Seas,
Breaking the Bankers and the Banks,
Resume their own when e'er they please.


  Money, the Life-blood of the Nation,
Corrupts and stagnates in the Veins,      10
Unless a proper Circulation
Its Motion and its Heat maintains.


  Because 'tis Lordly not to pay,
Quakers and Aldermen, in State,
Like Peers, have Levees ev'ry Day
Of Duns, attending at their Gate.

Printed from Stella's transcript, with corrections from *Poems*, 1735.

We want our Money on the Nail;
The Banker's ruin'd if he pays;
They seem to act an Ancient Tale,
The Birds are met to strip the Jays.                    20

Riches, the Wisest Monarch sings,
Make Pinions for themselves to fly,
They fly like Bats, on Parchment Wings,
And Geese their silver Plumes supply.

No Money left for squandring Heirs!
Bills turn the Lenders into Debters,
The Wish of Nero now is Theirs,
That, they had never known their Letters.

Conceive the Works of Midnight Hags,
Tormenting Fools behind their Backs;                    30
Thus Bankers o'er their Bills and Bags
Sit squeezing Images of Wax.

Conceive the whole Enchantment broke,
The Witches left in open Air,
With Pow'r no more than other Folk,
Expos'd with all their Magick Ware.

So Pow'rful are a Banker's Bills
Where Creditors demand their Due;
They break up Counter, Doors, and Tills,
And leave his empty Chests in View.                    40

Thus when an Earthquake lets in Light
Upon the god of Gold and Hell,
Unable to endure the Sight,
He hides within his darkest Cell.

As when a Conj'rer takes a Lease
From Satan for a Term of Years,
The Tenant's in a Dismal Case
When e'er the bloody Bond appears.

A baited Banker thus desponds,
From his own Hand foresees his Fall,                    50
They have his Soul who have his Bonds,
'Tis like the Writing on the Wall.

How will the Caitiff Wretch be scar'd
When first he finds himself awake
At the last Trumpet, unprepar'd,
And all his Grand Account to make?

For in that Universall Call
Few Bankers will to Heav'n be Mounters:
They'll cry, Ye Shops, upon us fall
Conceal, and cover us, Ye Counters.                    60

When Other Hands the Scales shall hold,
And They in Men and Angels Sight
Produc'd with all their Bills and Gold,
Weigh'd in the Ballance, and found Light.

# *Part of the* 9th Ode *of the* 4th Book *of* Horace, *address'd to Doctor* William King, *late Lord Arch-Bishop of* Dublin

VIRTUE conceal'd within our Breast
    Is Inactivity at best:
But, never shall the Muse endure
To let your Virtues lye obscure,
Or suffer Envy to conceal
Your Labours for the Publick Weal.
Within your Breast all Wisdom lyes,
Either to govern or advise;
Your steady Soul preserves her Frame
In good and evil Times the same.                    10

Printed from *Works, Vol. VIII*, Dublin, 1746.

Pale Avarice and lurking Fraud
Stand in your sacred Presence aw'd;
Your Hand alone from Gold abstains,
Which drags the slavish World in Chains.

  Him for an happy Man I own,
Whose Fortune is not overgrown;
And, happy he, who wisely knows
To use the Gifts, that Heav'n bestows;
Or, if it please the Powers Divine,
Can suffer Want, and not repine.    20
The Man, who Infamy to shun,
Into the Arms of Death would run,
That Man is ready to defend
With Life his Country, or his Friend.

# The Description of an *Irish-Feast*, translated almost literally out of the Original *Irish*

### Translated in the Year 1720

O *ROURK*'s noble Fare
  Will ne'er be forgot,
By those who were there,
  Or those who were not.
His Revels to keep,
  We sup and we dine,
On seven Score Sheep,
  Fat Bullocks and Swine.
*Usquebagh* to our Feast
  In Pails was brought up,    10
An Hundred at least,
  And a Madder our Cup.

Printed from *Poems*, 1735.

12. *Madder*. Wooden Vessel.

HSPW

O there is the Sport,
   We rise with the Light,
In disorderly Sort,
   From snoring all Night.
O how was I trick't,
   My Pipe it was broke,
My Pocket was pick't,
   I lost my new Cloak.          20
I'm rifled, quoth *Nell*,
   Of Mantle and Kercher,
Why then fare them well,
   The De'el take the Searcher.
Come, Harper, strike up,
   But first by your Favour,
Boy, give us a Cup;
   Ay, this has some Savour:
O *Rourk*'s jolly Boys
   Ne'er dream't of the Matter,      30
Till rowz'd by the Noise,
   And musical Clatter,
They bounce from their Nest,
   No longer will tarry,
They rise ready drest,
   Without one *Ave Mary*.
They dance in a Round,
   Cutting Capers and Ramping,
A Mercy the Ground
   Did not burst with their stamping.     40
The Floor is all wet
   With Leaps and with Jumps,
While the Water and Sweat,
   Splish, splash in their Pumps.
Bless you late and early,
   *Laughlin O Enagin,*
By my Hand, you dance rarely,
   *Margery Grinagin.*
Bring Straw for our Bed,
   Shake it down to the Feet,       50
Then over us spread,
   The winnowing Sheet.

To show, I don't flinch,
  Fill the Bowl up again,
Then give us a Pinch
  Of your Sneezing; *a Yean.*
Good Lord, what a Sight,
  After all their good Cheer,
For People to fight
  In the Midst of their Beer:                60
They rise from their Feast,
  And hot are their Brains,
A Cubit at least
  The Length of their Skeans.
What Stabs and what Cuts,
  What clatt'ring of Sticks,
What Strokes on the Guts,
  What Bastings and Kicks!
With Cudgels of Oak,
  Well harden'd in Flame,                     70
An hundred Heads broke,
  An hundred struck lame.
You Churle, I'll maintain
  My Father built *Lusk,*
The Castle of *Slain,*
  And *Carrickdrumrusk*:
The Earl of *Kildare,*
  And *Moynalta,* his Brother,
As great as they are,
  I was nurs'd by their Mother.               80
Ask that of old *Madam,*
  She'll tell you who's who,
As far up as *Adam,*
  She knows it is true,
Come down with that Beam,
  If Cudgels are scarce,
A Blow on the Weam,
  Or a Kick on the Arse.

56. *a Yean.* Another Irish Name for a Woman.
64. *Skeans.* Daggers, or short Swords.

# *The* BUBBLE

[p.1]     Y E wise Philosophers explain
      What Magick makes our Money rise
   When dropt into the Southern Main,
   Or do these Juglers cheat our Eyes?

     Put in Your Money fairly told;
   Presto be gone—Tis here ag'en,
   Ladyes, and Gentlemen, behold,
   Here's ev'ry Piece as big as ten.

     Thus in a Basin drop a Shilling,
   Then fill the Vessel to the Brim,          10
   You shall observe as you are filling
   The pond'rous Metal seems to swim;

     It rises both in Bulk and Height,
   Behold it swelling like a Sop!
   The liquid Medium cheats your Sight,
   Behold it mounted to the Top!

     In Stock three hundred thousand Pounds;
   I have in view a Lord's Estate,
   My Mannors all contig'ous round,
   A Coach and Six, and serv'd in Plate:      20

     Thus the deluded Bankrupt raves,
   Puts all upon a desp'rate Bett,
   Then plunges in the *Southern* Waves,
   Dipt over head and Ears—in Debt.

     So, by a Calenture misled,
   The Mariner with Rapture sees
   On the smooth Ocean's azure Bed
   Enamell'd Fields, and verdant Trees;

Printed from Swift's autograph. The Rothschild Library, No. 2265, with corrections from *Poems*, 1735.

With eager Hast he longs to rove
In that fantastick Scene, and thinks                    30
It must be some enchanted Grove,
And in he leaps, and down he sinks.

Five hundred Chariots just bespoke
Are sunk in these devouring Waves,
The Horses drown'd, the Harness broke,
And here the Owners find their Graves.

Like *Pharaoh*, by *Directors* led,
They with their *Spoils* went safe before;
His Chariots tumbling out the Dead
Lay shatter'd on the *Red-Sea* Shore.                    40

Rais'd up on Hope's aspiring Plumes,
The young Advent'rer o'er the Deep
An Eagle's Flight and State assumes,
And scorns the middle Way to keep:

On *Paper* Wings he takes his Flight,
With *Wax* the *Father* bound them fast,
The *Wax* is melted by the Height,
And down the towring Boy is cast:

A Moralist might here explain
The Rashness of the *Cretan* Youth,                    50
Describe his Fall into the Main,
And from a Fable form a Truth:

[col. 2]    His *Wings* are his *Paternall Rent*,
He melts his *Wax* at ev'ry Flame,
His Credit sunk, his Money spent,
*In* Southern *Seas he leaves his Name.*

Inform us, You that best can tell,
Why in yon dang'rous Gulph profound
Where hundreds and where thousands fell,
*Fools* chiefly float, the *Wise* are drown'd.            60

So have I seen from *Severn's* Brink
A Flock of *Geese* jump down together,
Swim where the Bir[d] of Jove would sink,
And swimming ne[ver] wet a Feather.

One Fool may f[r]om another win,
And then get off with Money stor'd,
But if a *Sharper* once comes in,
He throws at all, and sweeps the Board.

As Fishes on each other prey
The great ones swall'wing up the small          70
So fares it in the *Southern* Sea
But Whale *Directors* eat up all.

When *Stock* is high they come between,
Making by second hand their Offers,
Then cunningly retire unseen,
With each a Million in his Coffers.

So when upon a Moon-shine Night
An Ass was drinking at a Stream,
A Cloud arose and stopt the Light,
By intercepting e[v]'ry Beam;          80

The Day of Judgment will be soon,
Cryes out a Sage among the Croud,
An Ass hath swallow'd up the Moon,
The Moon lay safe behind the Cloud.

Each poor *Subscriber* to the Sea
Sinks down at once, and there he lyes,
*Directors* fall as well as they,
Their Fall is but a Trick to rise:

So Fishes rising from the Main
Can soar with moistned Wings on high,          90
The Moysture dry'd they sink again,
And dip their Fins again to fly.

[p. 2]      Undone at Play, the Femal Troops
Come here their Losses to retrieve,
Ride o'er the Waves in spacious Hoops,
Like *Lapland* Witches in a Sieve:

Thus *Venus* to the Sea descends
As Poets feign; but where's the Moral?
It shews the Queen of Love intends
To search the Deep for Pearl and Coral.      100

The Sea is richer than the Land,
I heard it from my Grannam's Mouth,
Which now I clearly understand,
For by the Sea she meant the *South*.

Thus by *Directors* we are told,
Pray Gentlemen, believe your Eyes,
Our Ocean's cover[d o]'er with Gold,
Look round about [h]ow thick it lyes:

Oh! would those Patriots be so kind
Here in the Deep to *wash their Hands*,      110
Then like *Pactolus* we should find
The Sea indeed had *golden Sands*.

A Shilling in the *Bath* You fling,
The Silver takes a nobler Hue,
By Magick Virtue in the Spring,
And seems a Guinnea to your View:

But as a Guinnea will not pass
At Market for a Farthing more
Shewn through a multiplying Glass
Than what it allways did before;      120

So cast it in the *Southern* Seas,
And view it through a *Jobber*'s Bill,
Put on what Spectacles You please,
Your Guinnea's but a Guinnea still.

One Night a Fool into a Brook
Thus from a Hillock looking down,
The *Golden* Stars for Guinneas took,
And *Silver Cynthia* for a Crown;

The Point he could no longer doubt,
He ran, he leapt into the Flood,                    130
There sprawl'd a while, and scarce got out,
All cover'd o'er with Slime and Mud.

[col. 2]     Upon the Water cast thy Bread
And after many Days thou'lt find it,
But Gold upon this Ocean spred
Shall sink, and leave no mark behind it.

There is a Gulph where thousands fell,
Here all the bold Advent'rers came,
A narrow Sound, though deep as Hell,
*'Change-Alley* is the dreadfull Name;               140

Nine times a day it ebbs and flows,
Yet He that on the Surface lyes
Without a Pilot seldom knows
The Time it falls, or when 'twill rise.

Subscribers here by thousands float,
And justle one another down,
Each padling in his leaky Boat,
And here they fish for Gold and drown:

*Now bury'd in the Depth below,*
*Now mounted up to Heav'n again,*                     150
*They reel and stagger too and fro,*
*At their Wits end like drunken Men.*

Mean time secure on GARR'WAY Clifts
A savage Race by Shipwrecks fed,
Ly waiting for the foundred Skiffs,
And strip the Bodyes of the Dead.

149. Psalm 107.          153. A Coffee House in Change-Alley.

But these, you say, are factious Lyes
From some malicious Tory's Brain,
For, where Directors get a Prize,
The *Swiss* and *Dutch* whole Millions drain.          160

Thus when by Rooks a Lord is ply'd,
Some Cully often wins a Bett
By vent'ring on the cheating Side,
Tho not into the Secret let.

While some build Castles in the Air,
*Directors* build 'em in the Seas;
*Subscribers* plainly see 'em there,
For Fools will see as Wise men please.

Thus oft by Mariners are shown,
Unless the Men of *Kent* are Ly'rs,          170
*Earl Godwin*'s Castles overflown,
And Palace-Roofs, and Steeple Spires.

Mark where the Sly *Directors* creep,
Nor to the Shore approach too nigh,
The Monsters nestle in the Deep
To seise you in your passing by:

[p. 3]          Then, like the Dogs of *Nile* be wise,
Who taught by Instinct how to shun
The Crocodile that lurking lyes,
Run as they drink and drink and run.          180

*Antæus* could by Magick Charms
Recover Strength whene'er he fell,
*Alcides* held him in his Arms,
And sent him *up in Air* to Hell.

*Directors* thrown into the Sea
Recover Strength and Vigor there,
But may be tam'd another way,
*Suspended for a while in Air.*

*Directors*; for tis you I warn,
By long Experience we have found                    190
What Planet rul'd when you were born;
We see you never can be drown'd:

Beware, nor over-bulky grow,
Nor come within your Cullyes Reach,
For if the Sea should sink so low
To leave you dry upon the Beach,

You'll ow Your Ruin to your Bulk;
Your Foes already waiting stand
To tear you like a foundred Hulk
While you ly helpless on the Sand:                   200

[col. 2]     Thus when a Whale hath lost the Tide
The Coasters crowd to seise the Spoyl,
The Monster into Parts divide,
And strip the Bone, and melt the Oyl.

Oh, may some *Western* Tempest sweep
These *Locusts* whom our Fruits have fed,
That Plague, *Directors*, to the Deep,
Driv'n from the *South*-Sea to the *Red*.

May He whom Nature's Laws obey,
Who *lifts* the Poor, and *sinks* the Proud,          210
*Quiet the Raging of the Sea*,
And *Still the Madness of the Crowd*.

But never sh[all our is]le have Rest
Till those devour[ing] *Swine* run down,
(*The Devils leavi[ng] the Possess't*)
And *headlong i[n] the Waters drown.*

The Nation t[oo] too late will find
Computing all th[eir] Cost and Trouble,
*Directors* Promi[ses] but Wind,
South-Sea at best [a m]ighty BUBBLE.                  220

Verses on

# THE DEANERY WINDOW

## By DELANY

ARE the Guests of this House still doom'd to be cheated?
Sure, the Fates have decreed, they by Halves should be treated.
In the Days of good *John*, if you came here to dine,
You had Choice of good Meat, but no Choice of good Wine.
In *Jonathan*'s Reign, if you come here to eat,
You have Choice of good Wine, but no Choice of good Meat.
O *Jove*, then how fully might all Sides be bless'd,
Would'st Thou but agree to this humble Request;
Put both Deans in one, or if that's too much Trouble,
Instead of the Dean, make the Dean'ry double.                    10

# ANOTHER

## By the SAME

A Bard, on whom *Phœbus* his Spirit bestow'd,
Resolv'd to acknowledge the Bounty he ow'd;
Found out a new Method at once of confessing,
And making the most of so mighty a Blessing:
To the God he'd be grateful, but Mortals he'd chouse.
By making his Patron preside in his House;
And wisely foresaw this Advantage from thence,
That the God must in Honour bear most of th' Expence:
So the Bard he finds Drink, and leaves *Phœbus* to treat
With the Thoughts he inspires, regardless of Meat:              10
Hence they that come hither, expecting to dine,
Are always fob'd off, with Sheer-Wit, and Sheer-Wine.

Printed from *Miscellaneous Poems ... Published by Mr. Concanen*. London, 1724.

# APOLLO

## TO

## Dean *SWIFT*

### By Himself

RIGHT Trusty, and so forth; We let you to know,
   We are very ill us'd by you Mortals below;
For, first, I have often by Chymists been told,
Tho' I know nothing on't, it is I that makes Gold;
Which when you have got, you so carefully hide it,
That since I was born, I hardly have spy'd it;
Then, it must be allow'd, whenever I shine,
I forward the Grass, and I ripen the Vine:
To me the good Fellows apply for Relief,
Without whom they could get neither Claret nor Beef;   10
Yet their Wine and the Victuals, these curmudgeon Lubbards
Lock up from my Sight in Cellars and Cupboards:
That I have an ill Eye, they wickedly think,
And taint all their Meat, and sour all their Drink.
But thirdly and lastly, it must be allow'd,
I alone can inspire the poetical Crowd;
This is gratefully own'd by each Boy in the College,
Whom if I inspire, it is not to my Knowledge;
This every Pretender to Rhyme will admit,
Without troubling his Head about Judgment or Wit:   20
These Gentlemen use me with Kindness and Freedom,
And as for their Works, when I please I may read 'em;
They lie open on Purpose, on Counters and Stalls,
And the Titles I view, when I shine on the Walls:
But a Comrade of yours, that Traytor *Delany*,
Whom I, for your Sake, love better than any;
And of my meer Motion, and special good Grace,
Intended in Time to succeed in your Place;

Printed from Swift's autograph, Morgan Library, with corrections from *Poems*, 1735.

On *Tuesday* the Ninth, seditiously came,
With a certain false Traitress, one *Stella* by Name,    30
To the Dean'ry House, and on the *North* Glass,
Where for fear of the Cold, I never can pass;
Then and there, *Vi & Armis*, with a certain Utensil,
Of Value five Shillings, in *English* a Pencil;
Did maliciously, falsly, and traiterously write,
Whilst *Stella* aforesaid stood by with the Light;
My Sister has lately depos'd upon Oath,
That she stopt in her Course to look at them both;
That *Stella* was helping, abetting and aiding,
And still as he writ, stood smiling and reading;    40
That her Eyes were as bright as our self at Noon-Day;
But her graceful black Locks, were all mingled with Grey,
And by the Description I certainly know,
'Tis the Nymph that I courted some ten Years ago;
Who, when I with the best of my Talents endu'd,
On her Promise of yielding, she acted the Prude;
That some Verses were writ with felonious Intent,
Direct to the *North*, where I never went;
That the letters appear'd revers'd thro' the Pane,
But in *Stella*'s bright Eyes they were plac'd right again;    50
Wherein she distinctly could read ev'ry Line,
And presently guess'd the Fancy was mine;
Now you see why his Verses so seldom are shown,
The Reason is plain, they are none of his own;
And observe while you live, that no Man is shy
To discover the Goods he came honestly by:
If I light on a Thought, he will certainly steal it,
And when he has got it, find Ways to conceal it;
Of all the fine Things he keeps in the Dark,
There's scarce one in ten, but what has my Mark;    60
And let them be seen by the World if he dare,
I'll make it appear they are all stol'n Ware:
But as for the Poem he writ on your Sash,
I think I have now got him under my Lash;
My Sister transcrib'd it last Night, to his Sorrow,
And the Publick shall see't, if I live 'till to Morrow;
Thro' the *Zodiack* around, it shall quickly be spread,
In all Parts of the Globe, where your Language is read;

He knows very well I ne'er gave a Refusal,
When he ask'd for my Aid, in the Forms that are usual:    70
But the Secret is this; I did lately intend
To write a few Verses on you as my Friend;
I study'd a Fortnight, before I could find,
As I rode in my Chariot, a Thought to my Mind;
And resolv'd the next Winter, for that is my Time,
When the Days are at shortest, to get it in Rhyme;
Till then it was lock'd in my Box at *Parnassus*;
When that subtle Companion, in hopes to surpass us,
Conveys out my Paper of Hints by a Trick,
For I think in my Conscience he deals with *Old Nick*;    80
And from my own Stock, provided with Topicks,
He gets to a Window beyond both the *Tropicks*;
There out of my Sight, just against the *North-Zone*,
Writes down my Conceits, and then calls them his own:
And you like a Cully, the *Bubble* can swallow;
Now who but *Delany* that writes like *Apollo*?
High Treason by Statute! But here you object,
He only stole Hints; the Verse is correct;
Tho' the Thought be *Apollo*'s, 'tis finely express'd;
So a Thief steals my Horse, and has him well drest;    90
Now, whereas the said Criminal seems past Repentance,
We *Phœbus* think fit to proceed to the Sentence;
Since *Delany* has dar'd, like *Prometheus* his Sire,
To climb to our Region, and thence to steal Fire;
We order a Vulture, in Shape of the *Spleen*,
To prey on his Liver, but not to be seen:
And we order our Subjects, of every Degree,
To believe all his Verses were written by me;
And under the Pain of our highest Displeasure,
To call nothing his, but the Rhyme and the Measure.    100
And lastly for *Stella*, just out of her Prime,
I am too much reveng'd already by Time;
In return to her Scorn, I sent her Diseases,
But will now be her Friend whenever she pleases;
And the Gifts I bestow'd her, will find her a Lover,
Tho' she lives to be Grey as a Badger all over.

# *NEWS from* Parnassus

## By DELANY

P*ARNASSUS, February* the twenty-seventh,
  The *Poets* assembled here on the Eleventh;
Conven'd by *Apollo*, who gave them to know,
He'd have a *Vicegerent* in his Empire below;
But declar'd that no *Bard* shou'd this Honour inherit,
'Till the rest had agreed he surpass'd them in Merit:
Now this you'll allow was a difficult Case,
For each *Bard* believ'd he had a Right to the Place;
So finding the Assembly grow warm in Debate,
He put 'em in Mind of his *Phaeton*'s Fate:          10
'Twas urged to no Purpose, the Dispute higher rose,
Scarce *Phœbus* himself cou'd their Quarrels compose.
'Till at length he determin'd that every *Bard*
Shou'd (each in their Turn) be patiently heard.

   *First*, one who believ'd he excell'd in Translation,
Founds his Claim on the Doctrine of *Transmigration*:
"Since the Soul of great *Milton* was given to me,
"I hope the Convention will quickly agree—"
Agree, quoth *Apollo*, from whence is this Fool?
Is he just come from reading *Pythagoras* at School?    20
Begone, Sir, you've got your Subscriptions in Time,
And giv'n in Return neither Reason nor Rhyme.

   To the *next*, says the God, tho' now I won't chuse you,
I'll tell you the Reason for which I refuse you;
*Love*'s Goddess has oft to her Parent complain'd,
Of my fav'ring a *Bard* who her Empire disdain'd,
That at my Instigation a Poem you writ,
Which to Beauty and Youth prefer'd Judgment and Wit;
That to make you a Laureat I gave the first Voice,
Inspiring the *Britons* t'approve of my Choice.      30
*Jove* sent her to me her Power to try;
The Goddess of *Beauty* what God can deny?
She forbids your Preferment, I grant her Desire,
Appease the fair Goddess, you then may rise higher.

Printed from *Miscellaneous Poems , , , Published by Mr. Concanen.* London, 1724.

The *next* that appear'd, had good Hopes of succeeding,
For he merited much for his Wit and his Breeding.
'Twas wise in the *Britons* no favour to shew him,
He else might expect they shou'd pay what they owe him.
And therefore they prudently chose to discard
The Patriot, whose Merits they wou'd not reward:        40
The God with a Smile bid his Fav'rite advance,
You were sent by *Astrea* her Envoy to *France*.
You bent your Ambition to rise in the *State*,
I refuse you, because you cou'd stoop to be great.


Then a *Bard*, who had been a successful Translator,
"The Convention allows me a Versificator."


Says *Apollo*, you mention the least of your Merit,
By your Works it appears you have much of my Spirit;
I esteem you so well, that to tell you the Truth,
The greatest Objection against you's your Youth;        50
Then be not concerned you are now laid aside,
If you live you shall certainly one Day preside.


Another, low bending, *Apollo* thus greets,
"'Twas I taught your Subjects to walk thro' the Streets."
You taught 'em to walk, why they knew it before,
But give me the *Bard* that can teach them to soar;
Whenever he claims his Right, I'll confess
Who lately attempted my Style with Success;
Who writes like *Apollo*, has most of his Spirit,
And therefore 'tis just I distinguish his Merit;       60
Who makes it appear by all he has writ,
His Judgment alone can set Bounds to his Wit;
Like *Virgil* correct, with his own Native Ease,
But excels ev'n *Virgil* in elegant Praise;
Who admires the Ancients, and knows 'tis their due,
Yet writes in a Manner entirely new;
Tho' none with more Ease their Depths can explore,
Yet whatever he wants he takes from my Store;
Tho' I'm fond of his Virtues, his Pride I can see,
In scorning to borrow from any but me;                 70
'Tis owing to this, that like *Cynthia*, his Lays
Enlighten the World by reflecting my Rays.
This said, the whole Audience soon found out his Drift,
The Convention was summon'd in Favour of *Swift*.

# *Apollo*'s Edict

## [By Mrs. Barber?]¹

*IRELAND* is now our royal Care,
We lately fix'd our *Viceroy* there:
How near was she to be undone,
Till pious Love inspir'd her Son?
What cannot our *Vicegerent* do,
As *Poet* and as *Patriot* too?
Let his Success our Subjects sway
Our Inspirations to obey,
And follow where *he* leads the Way:
Then study to correct your Taste,          10
Nor *beaten* Paths be longer trac'd.

   No Simile shall be begun,
With *rising* or with *setting* Sun:
And let the *secret Head of* Nile
Be ever banish'd from your Isle.
   When wretched Lovers live on Air,
I beg you'll the *Camelion* spare.
And when you'd make an Heroe grander,
Forget he's like a *Salamander*.
   No Son of mine shall dare to say, ⎫          20
*Aurora usher'd in the Day,*          ⎬
Or ever name the *milky Way*.          ⎭
   You all agree, I make no doubt,
*Elijah's Mantle*'s worn out.
   The *Bird of Jove* shall toil no more,
To teach the humble *Wren* to soar.
   Your tragick Heroes shall not rant,
Nor Shepherds use *poetick Cant*:
Simplicity alone can grace,
The Manners of the rural Race,          30
*Theocritus* and *Philips* be,
Your guides to *true* Simplicity.

Printed from the original 4to (n.d. or p.).

¹ See article by Oliver Ferguson, *PMLA*, LXX. 433–40, June 1955. Whether
Swift had a hand in this poem or not, he allowed Mary Barber to print it in her
*Poems on Several Occasions*, 1734, in a slightly altered version.

When *Damon's Soul shall take its Flight,*&#125;
Tho' Poets have the second Sight,&#125;
They shall not see a *Trail of Light*:&#125;
Nor shall the *Vapour upwards rise,*
Nor a *new Star* adorn the Skies:
For who can hope to place one there,
As glorious as *Belinda's Hair?*
Yet if his Name you'd eternize                40
And must exalt him to the Skies:
Without a *Star* this may be done,
So *TICKELL* mourn'd his *ADDISON.*

If *ANNA's* happy Reign you praise,
Pray not a word of *Halcyon Days.*
Nor let my Votaries show their Skill
In apeing Lines from *Cooper's Hill;*
For know I cannot bear to hear,
The Mimickry of *deep yet clear.*

When e'er my *Viceroy* is address'd,         50
Against the *Phœnix* I protest.

When Poets soar in youthful Strains,
No *Phaeton* to *hold the Reins.*

When you describe a lovely Girl,
No Lips of *Coral* Teeth of *Pearl.*

*Cupid* shall ne'er mistake another
However beauteous for his Mother:
Nor shall his Darts at random fly
From Magazeen in *Cælia's* Eye.

With Women Compounds I am cloy'd,            60
Which only pleased in *Biddy Floyd:*
For foreign Aid what need they roam,
Whom Fate has amply bless'd at home?
Unerring Heav'n, with bounteous Hand,
Has form'd a Model for your Land;
Whom *Jove* endow'd with ev'ry Grace,
The Glory of the *Granard* Race;
Now destin'd, by the Powers divine,
The Blessing of *another Line*:
Then wou'd you paint a *matchless* Dame,      70
Whom you'd consigne to endless Fame?
Invoke not *Citherea's* Aid,
Nor borrow from the *Blew-ey'd* Maid,
Nor need you on the *Graces* call,
Take Qualities from *DONEGAL.*

# Stella's Birth-day

### Written A.D. 1720–21

ALL Travellers at first incline
  Where'e'er they see the fairest Sign,
And if they find the Chambers neat,
And like the Liquor and the Meat
Will call again and recommend
The Angel-Inn to ev'ry Friend:
What though the Painting grows decayd
The House will never loose it's Trade;
Nay, though the treach'rous Tapster Thomas
Hangs a new Angel two doors from us       10
As fine as Dawbers Hands can make it
In hopes that Strangers may mistake it,
We think it both a Shame and Sin
To quit the true old Angel-Inn.
  Now, this is Stella's Case in Fact;
And Angel's Face, a little crack't;
(Could Poets or could Painters fix
How Angels look at thirty six)
This drew us in at first to find
In such a Form an Angel's Mind       20
And ev'ry Virtue now supplyes
The fainting Rays of Stella's Eyes:
See, at her Levee crowding Swains
Whom Stella freely entertains
With Breeding, Humor, Wit, and Sense,
And puts them to so small Expence,
Their Minds so plentifully fills,
And makes such reasonable Bills
So little gets for what she gives
We really wonder how she lives;       30
And, had her Stock been less, no doubt
She must have long ago run out.

Printed from Stella's transcript, with corrections from *Poems*, 1735.

Then, who can think we'll quit the Place
When Doll hangs out a newer Face
Or stop and light at Cloe's Head
With Scraps and Leavings to be fed.
    Then Cloe, still go on to prate
Of thirty six, and thirty eight;
Pursue thy Trade of Scandall picking,
Your Hints that Stella is no Chickin,                    40
Your Innuendo's when you tell us
That Stella loves to talk with Fellows
But let me warn you to believe
A Truth for which your Soul should grieve,
That, should you live to see the Day
When Stella's Locks must all be grey
When Age must print a furrow'd Trace
On ev'ry Feature of her Face;
Though you and all your senceless Tribe
Could Art or Time or Nature bribe                    50
To make you look like Beauty's Queen
And hold for ever at fifteen:
No Bloom of Youth can ever blind
The Cracks and Wrinckles of your Mind,
All Men of Sense will pass your Dore
And crowd to Stella's at fourscore.

# AN EPILOGUE,

To be spoke at the

## THEATRE-ROYAL

This present Saturday being *April* the 1st. In the Behalf
of the Distressed *WEAVERS*

WHO dares affirm this is no pious age,
    When Charity begins to tread the Stage?
When Actors who at best are hardly Savers,
Will give a Night of Benefit to Weavers?

Printed from the Fo. Broadside, Dublin [1721], with corrections from *Poems*, 1735.

Stay—let me see how finely will it Sound,
Imprimis: From his Grace an Hundred pound.
Peers, Clergy, Gentry, all are Benefactors;
And then Comes in the Item of the Actors.
Item the Actors, freely gave a Day,
The Poet had no more who made the Play.                    10
   But whence this Wonderous Charity, in Play'rs?
They learnt it not at Sermons or at pray'rs.
Under the Rose since here are none but friends;
To own the truth we have some private Ends.
Since Waiting Women like Exacting Jades,
Hold up the prices of their Old *Brocades*;
We'll dress in *Manufactures*, made at home;
Equip our *KINGS*, and *Generalls* at the Comb.
We'll Rigg in Meath-Street, *Egypt*'s hauty *Queen*,
And *Anthony* shall Court her in *Ratteen*.             20
In *blew shalloon*, shall *Hanniball* be Clad,
And *Scipio*, trail an *Irish purple Plad*.
In Drugget drest of Thirteen Pence a Yard,
See *Philip*'s Son amidst his *Persian* Guard;
And proud *Roxana* fir'd with jealous Rage,
With fifty Yards of Crape, shall sweep the Stage.
In short our Kings and Princesses within,
Are all resolv'd the Project to begin;
And you, our Subjects, when you here resort,
Must Imitate the Fashion of the Court.                  30

   O! Cou'd I see this Audience Clad in *Stuff*,
Tho' Moneys scarce we shou'd have Trade enough;
But *Chints*, *Brocades*, and *Lace* take all away,
And scarce a Crown is left to see a Play:
Perhaps you wonder whence this Friendship Springs,
Between the *Weavers* and us Play-House Kings.
But Wit and Weaving had the same beginning,
*Pallas* first taugh[t] us Poetry and Spinning;
And next Observe how this Alliance fits,
For *Weavers* now are just as poor as Wits;             40
Their Brother Quill-Men Workers for the Stage,
For sorry *Stuff*, can get a Crown a Page;

18. *at the Comb*. A Street in Dublin famous for Woollen Manufactures.

But *Weavers* will be Kinder to the *Players*,
And Sell for Twenty Pence a Yard [of] theirs;
And to your knowledge there is often less in,
The *Poets* Wit, than in the *Players* Dressing.


# THE JOURNAL

*T*HALIA, tell in sober Lays,
   How *George, Nim, Dan, Dean* pass their Days;
Begin, my Muse, first from our Bowers,
We issue forth at different Hours;
At Seven, the *Dean* in Night-gown drest,
Goes round the House to wake the rest:
At Nine, grave *Nim* and *George* Facetious,
Go to the *Dean* to read *Lucretius*.
At Ten, my Lady comes and Hectors,
And kisses *George*, and ends our Lectures:        10
And when she has him by the Neck fast,
Hawls him, and scolds us down to Breakfast.
We squander there an Hour or more,
And then all hands, Boys, to the Oar
All, Heteroclite *Dan* except,
Who never time nor order kept.
But by peculiar Whimseys drawn,
Peeps in the Ponds to look for Spawn:
O'er sees the Work, or *Dragon* rowes,
Or mars a Text, or mends his Hose.        20
Or—but proceed we in our *Journal*,—
At Two or after we return all,
From the four Elements assembling,
Warn'd by the Bell, all Folks come trembling,
From Airy Garrets some descend,
Some from the Lakes remotest end.
My Lord and *Dean*, the Fire forsake;
*Dan* leaves the Earthly Spade and Rake,

Printed from the Broadside, with corrections from *Poems*, 1735.

19. *Dragon.* My Lord Chief Baron's smaller Boat.

The Loyt'rers quake, no Corner hides them,
And Lady *Betty* soundly chides them.                    30
Now Water's brought, and Dinner's done,
With Church and King, the Lady's gone;
Not reckoning half an hour we pass,
In talking ore a moderate Glass.
*Dan* growing drowsy like a Thief,
Steals off to dose away his Beef,
And this must pass for reading *Hammond*:
While *George*, and *Dean*, go to Back-Gammon.
*George*, *Nim* and *Dean*, set out at Four,
And then again, Boys, to the Oar.                        40
But when the Sun goes to the Deep,
Not to disturb him in his Sleep;
Or make a rumbling o'er his Head,
His Candle out, and he a Bed.
We watch his Motions to a Minute,
And leave the Flood when he goes in it:
Now stinted in the short'ning Day,
We go to Pray'rs, and then to play
Till Supper comes, and after that,
We sit an hour to drink and chat.                        50
'Tis late, the old and younger Pairs,
By *Adam* lighted walk up stairs:
The weary *Dean* goes to his Chamber,
And *Nim* and *Dan* to Garret clamber:
So when this Circle we have run,
The Curtain falls, and all is done.
I might have mention'd several facts,
Like *Episodes* between the Acts;
And tell who loses, and who wins,
Who gets a Cold, who breaks his Shins.                   60
How *Dan* caught nothing in his Net,
And how the Boat was over set,
For brevity I have retrench'd,
How in the Lake the *Dean* was drench'd:
It would be an Exploit to brag on,
How Valiant *George* rode o'er the *Dragon*;
How steady in the Storm he sat,
And sav'd his Oar, but lost his Hat.

How *Nim*, no Hunter 'ere could match him,
Still brings us Hares when he can catch them:        70
How skilfully *Dan* mends his Nets,
How Fortune fails him when he sets:
Or how the *Dean* delights to vex
The Ladys, and Lampoon the Sex.
Or how our Neighbour lifts his Nose,
To tell what ev'ry School Boy knows:
And with his Finger on his Thumb,
Explaining strikes opposers Dumb;
Or how his Wife that Female Pedant,
But now there need no more be said on't,        80
Shews all her Secrets of House keeping,
For Candles, how she trucks her Driping;
Was forc'd to send three Miles for Yest,
To brew her Ale, and raise her Paste:
Tells ev'ry thing that you can think of,
How she cur'd *Tommy* of the Chincough;
What gave her Brats and Pigs the Meazles,
And how her Doves were kill'd by Weezles:
How Jowler howl'd, and what a fright
She had with Dreams the other Night.        90
But now, since I have gone so far on,
A word or two of Lord Chief *Baron*;
And tell how little weight he sets,
On all Whig Papers, and Gazets:
But for the Politicks of Pue,
Thinks ev'ry Syllable is true;
And since he owns the King of *Sweden*
Is dead at last without evading;
Now all his hopes are in the *Czar*;
"Why *Muscovy* is not so far,        100
Down the black Sea, and up the Streights,
And in a Month he's at your Gates:
Perhaps from what the Packet brings,
By *Christmas* we shall see strange things."
Why shou'd I tell of Ponds and Drains,
What Carps we met with for our pains:

92. Mr. Rochfort's Father.        95. *Pue.* A Tory News-Writer.

Of Sparrows tam'd, and Nuts innumerable,
To Choak the Girls, and to consume a Rabble?
But you, who are a Scholar, know
How transient all things are below:     110
How prone to change is human life,
Last Night arriv'd *Clem* and his Wife.
This Grand Event hath broke our Measures,
Their Reign began with cruel Seizures;
The *Dean* must with his Quilt supply,
The Bed in which these Tyrants lie:
*Nim* lost his Wig-block, *Dan* his Jordan,
My Lady says she can't afford one;
*George* is half scar'd out of his Wits,
For *Clem* gets all the tiny bits.     120
Henceforth expect a different survey,
This House will soon turn topsy turvey;
They talk of further Alterations,
Which causes many Speculations.

> 112. *Clem.* Mr. Clement Barry.

# A quibbling ELEGY on the Worshipful Judge *BOAT*

TO mournful Ditties, *Clio*, change thy Note,
Since cruel Fate hath *sunk* our Justice *Boat*;
Why should he *sink* where nothing seem'd to press?
His *Lading* little, and his *Ballast* less.
*Tost* in the *Waves* of this *tempestuous* World,
At length, his *Anchor* fixt, and *Canvas* furl'd,
To *Lazy-Hill* retiring from his Court,
At his *Ring*'s-*End* he *founders* in the *Port*.
With *Water* fill'd he could no longer *float*,
The common Death of many a stronger *Boat*.     10

> Printed from *Poems*, 1735.
>
> 7, 8. *Lazy-Hill . . . Ring's-End.* Two Villages near the Sea, where Boatmen and Seamen live.
> 9. *With Water fill'd . . .* It was said he dy'd of a Dropsy.

A Post so fill'd, on Nature's Laws entrenches;
*Benches* on *Boats* are plac't, not *Boats* on *Benches.*
And yet our *Boat,* how shall I reconcile it?
Was both a *Boat,* and in one Sense a *Pilat.*
With ev'ry *Wind* he *sail'd,* and well could *tack:*
Had many *Pendents,* but abhor'd a *Jack.*
He's gone, although his Friends began to hope
That he might yet be lifted by a *Rope.*

Behold the awful *Bench* on which he sat,
He was as *hard,* and pond'rous *Wood* as that:        20
Yet, when his *Sand* was out, we find at last,
That, Death has *overset* him with a *Blast.*
Our *Boat* is now *sail'd* to the *Stygian* Ferry,
There to supply old *Charon's* leaky Wherry:
*Charon* in him will ferry Souls to Hell;
A Trade, our *Boat* had practic'd here so well.
And, *Cerberus* hath ready in his Paws,
Both *Pitch* and *Brimstone* to fill up his *Flaws;*
Yet, spight of Death and Fate, I here maintain
We may place *Boat* in his old *Post* again.        30
The Way is thus; and well deserves your Thanks:
Take the three strongest of his broken Planks,
Fix them on high, conspicuous to be seen,
Form'd like the Triple-Tree near *Stephen's*-Green;
And, when we view it thus, with Thief at End on't,
We'll cry; look, here's our *Boat,* and there's the *Pendent.*

## The EPITAPH

*HERE lies Judge* Boat *within a Coffin.*
*Pray gentle-Folks forbear your Scoffing.*
*A* Boat *a Judge! yes, where's the Blunder?*
*A wooden Judge is no such Wonder.*        40
*And in his Robes, you must agree,*
*No* Boat *was better* deckt *than He.*
*'Tis needless to describe him fuller.*
*In short, he was an able* Sculler.

16. *Jack.* A Cant Word for a Jacobite.    26. *A Trade.* In hanging People as a Judge.    34. *Stephen's-Green.* Where the Dublin Gallows stands.
44. *Sculler.* Query, Whether the Author meant *Scholar,* and wilfully mistook?

# The BANK thrown down

### To an Excellent New TUNE

PRAY, what is this BANK of which the Town Rings?
  The BANKS of a River I know are good Things,
But a Pox o' those BANKS that choak up the SPRINGS.
    Some Mischief is Brewing, the Project smells Rank,
    To shut out the *River* by raising the BANK.


The DAMS and the WEIRS must all be your own,
You get all the FISH, and others get none,
We look for a SALMON, you leave us a *Stone*.
    But Thanks to the HOUSE, the Projectors look blank,
    And Thanks to the MEMBERS that Kickt down the BANK.   10


This BANK is to make us a New Paper Mill,
This Paper they say, by the Help of a Quill,
The whole Nations Pockets with Money will fill.
    But we doubt that our Purses will quickly grow lank,
    If nothing but Paper comes out of this BANK.


'Tis happy to see the whole Kingdom in *Rags*,
For *Rags* will make *Paper*, and Pa-ba-ba-brags,
This Paper will soon make us richer than *Crags*.
    From a bo-bo-bo-Boy he pursues his old Hank,
    And now he runs mad for a ba-ba-ba-BANK.     20


Oh! then but to see how the *Beggars* will Vapour,
For Beggars have *Rags* and Rags will make Paper,
And Paper makes Money, and what can be cheaper?
    Methinks I now see them so jovial and crank,
    All riding on Horseback to *Hell* and the BANK.

Printed from the Fo. Half-sheet.

But the *Cobler* was angry, and swore he had rather
As they did in old Times, make Money of *Leather*,
For then he could *Coyn* and could *Cobble* together;
   And then he could pay for the Liquor he drank
   With the Scrap of a *Sole*, and a Fig for the BANK.   30


By a Parliament Man when the *Farmer* was told,
That *Paper* would quickly be dearer than *Gold*,
He wonder'd for how much an Inch 'twould be Sold:
   Then Plodding, he thought on a whimsical Prank
   To turn to small Money a Bill on the BANK.


For nicely computing the Price by Retail,
He found he could purchase Two Tankards of Ale
With a Scrap of Bank Paper the Breadth of his Nail;
   But the *Tapster* well Cudgell'd him both Side and Flank,
   And made him to Curse the poor innocent BANK.   40


The Ghost of old *Demar*, who left not his Betters,
When it heard of a BANK appear'd to his Debtors,
And lent them for Money the *Backs* of his Letters:
   His Debtors they wonder'd to find him so frank,
   For *old Nick* gave the Papers the *Mark* of the BANK.


In a *Chancery* Bill your Attorney engages,
For so many Six-pences, so many *Pages*,
But Six-pence a *Letter* is monstrous high Wages:
   Those that dropt in the *South-Sea* discover'd this *Plank*,
   By which they might Swimmingly *land* on a BANK.   50


But the *Squire* he was cunning and found what they meant,
That a Pack of sly Knaves should get fifty per Cent,
While his Tenants in *Paper* must pay him his Rent:
   So for their *Quack-Bills* he knows whom to thank,
   For those are but *Quacks*, who *mount* on a BANK.

# The Progress of Marriage. Jan^y. 1721–2

[p. 1]   ÆTATIS suæ fifty two
A rich Divine began to woo
A handsome young imperious *Girl*
Nearly related to an Earl.
Her Parents and her Friends consent,
The Couple to the Temple went:
They first invite the Cyprian Queen,
'Twas answered, she would not be seen.
The Graces next, and all the Muses
Were bid in form, but sent Excuses:          10
Juno attended at the Porch
With farthing Candle for a Torch,
While Mistress Iris held her Train,
The faded Bow distilling Rain.
Then Hebe came and took her Place
But showed no more than half her Face
Whate'er these dire fore-bodings meant,
In Mirth the wedding-day was spent.
The *Wedding-day*, you take me right,
I promise nothing for the Night:          20
The Bridegroom dresst, to make a Figure,
Assumes an artificiall Vigor;
[p. 2]   A flourisht Night-cap on, to grace
His ruddy, wrinckled, smirking Face,
Like the faint red upon a Pippin
Half wither'd by a Winters keeping . .
     And, thus set out this happy Pair,
The Swain is rich, the Nymph is fair;
But, which I gladly would forget,
The Swain is old, the Nymph Coquette.          30
Both from the Goal together start;
Scarce run a Step before they part;
No common Ligament that binds
The various Textures of their Minds,

Printed from Swift's autograph MS., Forster Coll.

Their Thoughts, and Actions, Hopes, and Fears,
Less corresponding than their Years.
Her Spouse desires his Coffee soon,
She rises to her Tea at noon.
While He goes out to cheapen Books,
She at the Glass consults her Looks          40
While Betty's buzzing at her Ear,
Lord, what a Dress these Parsons wear,
So odd a Choice, how could she make,
Wish't him a Coll'nell for her Sake.
[p. 3] Then on her fingers Ends she counts
Exact to what his Age amounts,
The Dean, she heard her Uncle say
Is fifty, if he be a Day;
His ruddy Cheeks are no Disguise;
You see the Crows feet round his Eyes.       50
At one she rambles to the Shops
To cheapen Tea, and talk with Fops.
Or calls a Councel of her Maids
And Tradesmen, to compare Brocades.
Her weighty Morning Bus'ness o'er
Sits down to Dinner just at four;
Minds nothing that is done or said,
Her ev'ning *Work* so fills her Head;
The *Dean*, who us'd to dine at one,
Is maukish, and his Stomach gone;            60
In threed-bare Goun, would scarce a louse hold,
Looks like the Chaplain of the Houshold,
Beholds her from the Chaplain's Place
In French brocades and Flanders Lace;
[p. 4] He wonders what employs her Brain;
But never asks, or asks in vain;
His Mind is full of other Cares,
And in the sneaking Parsons Airs
Computes, that half a Parish Dues
Will hardly find his Wife in Shoes.          70
Canst thou imagine, dull Divine,
'Twill gain her Love to make her fine?
Hath she no other wants beside?
You raise Desire as well as Pride,

Enticing Coxcombs to adore,
And teach her to despise thee more
If in her Coach she'll condescend
To place him at the hinder End
Her Hoop is hoist above his Nose,
His odious Goun would soil her Cloaths,               80
And drops him at the Church, to pray
While she drives on to see the Play.
He like an orderly Divine
Comes home a quarter after nine,
And meets her hasting to the Ball,
Her Chairmen push him from the Wall:
He enters in, and walks up Stairs,
And calls the Family to Prayrs,
[p. 5] Then goes alone to take his Rest
In bed, where he can spare her best.                   90
At five the Footmen make a Din,
Her Ladyship is just come in,
The Masquerade began at two,
She stole away with much ado,
And shall be chid this afternoon
For leaving company so soon;
She'll say, and she may truly say't
She can't abide to stay out late.


But now, though scarce a twelvemonth marry'd,
His Lady has twelve times miscarry'd,                 100
The Cause, alas, is quickly guesst,
The Town has whisper'd round the Jest:
Think on some Remedy in time
You find His Rev'rence past his Prime,
Already dwindled to a Lath;
No other way but try the Bath:
For Venus rising from the Ocean
Infus'd a strong prolifick Potion,
That mixt with Achelous Spring,
The *horned* Floud, as Poets sing:                    110
[p. 6] Who with an English Beauty smitten
Ran under Ground from Greece to Brittain,

The genial Virtue with him brought,
And gave the Nymph a plenteous Draught;
Then fled, and left his Horn behind
For Husbands past their Youth to find;
The Nymph who still with Passion burnd,
Was to a boiling Fountain turn'd,
Where Childless wives crowd ev'ry morn
To drink in Achilous' Horn.                    120
And here the Father often gains
That Title by anothers Pains.

 Hither, though much against his Grain,
The *Dean* has carry'd Lady Jane
He for a while would not consent,
But vow'd his Money all was spent;
His Money spent! a clownish Reason?
And, must my Lady slip her Season?
The Doctor with a double Fee
Was *brib'd* to make the *Dean* agree          130
 Here, all Diversions of the Place
Are *proper* in my Lady's Case
[p. 7] With which she patiently complyes,
Merely because her Friends advise;
His Money and her Time employs
In musick, Raffling-rooms, and Toys,
Or in the *cross-bath* seeks an Heir
Since others oft have found one there;
Where if the Dean by chance appears
It shames his Cassock and his Years            140
He keeps his Distance in the Gallery
*Till* banisht by some Coxcombs Raillery;
For, it would his Character Expose
To bath among the Belles and Beaux.

 So have I seen within a Pen
Young Ducklings, fostered by a Hen;
But when let out, they run and muddle
As Instinct leads them, in a Puddle;
The sober Hen not born to swim
With mournful Note clocks round the Brim.      150

The Dean with all his best Endeavour
Gets not an Heir, but gets a Feaver;
A Victim to the last Essays
Of Vigor in declining Days.
He dyes, and leaves his mourning Mate
(What could he less,) his whole Estate.

[p. 8]    The Widow goes through all her Forms;
New Lovers now will come in Swarms.
Oh, may I see her soon dispensing
Her Favors to some broken Ensign          160
Him let her Marry for his Face,
And only Coat of tarnish't Lace;
To turn her Naked out of Doors,
And spend her Joynture on his Whores:
But for a parting Present leave her
A rooted Pox to last for ever.


# To Stella on her Birth-day

### Written A.D. 1721–2

WHILE, Stella to your lasting Praise
     The Muse her ann'all Tribute pays,
While I assign my self a Task
Which you expect, but scorn to ask;
If I perform this Task with Pain
Let me of partiall Fate complain;
You, every Year the Debt enlarge,
I grow less equall to the Charge:
In you, each Virtue brighter shines,
But my Poetick Vein declines.          10
My Harp will soon in vain be strung,
And all Your Virtues left unsung:
For, none among the upstart Race
Of Poets dare assume my Place;

Printed from Stella's transcript.

Ispw

Your Worth will be to them unknown,
They must have Stella's of their own;
And thus, my Stock of Wit decay'd;
I dying leave the Debt unpay'd,
Unless Delany as my Heir,
Will answer for the whole Arrear.                    20

# A SATIRICAL ELEGY

### On the DEATH of a late

## FAMOUS GENERAL

HIS Grace! impossible! what dead!
   Of old age too, and in his bed!
And could that Mighty Warrior fall?
And so inglorious, after all!
Well, since he's gone, no matter how,
The last loud trump must wake him now:
And, trust me, as the noise grows stronger,
He'd wish to sleep a little longer.
And could he be indeed so old
As by the news-papers we're told?              10
Threescore, I think, is pretty high;
'Twas time in conscience he should die.
This world he cumber'd long enough;
He burnt his candle to the snuff;
And that's the reason, some folks think,
He left behind *so great a stink*.
Behold his funeral appears,
Nor widow's sighs, nor orphan's tears,
Wont at such times each heart to pierce,
Attend the progress of his herse.              20
But what of that, his friends may say,
He had those honours in his day.
True to his profit and his pride,
He made them weep before he dy'd.

Printed from *Works, 4to, Vol. VIII* (2), London, 1765.

Come hither, all ye empty things,
Ye bubbles rais'd by breath of Kings;
Who float upon the tide of state,
Come hither, and behold your fate.
Let pride be taught by this rebuke,
How very mean a thing's a Duke;                    30
From all his ill-got honours flung,
Turn'd to that dirt from whence he sprung.

# Upon the horrid *Plot* discovered by *Harlequin* the Bishop of *Rochester*'s *French* Dog

## In a Dialogue between a *Whig* and a *Tory*

### Written in the Year 1722

I ASK'D a *Whig* the other Night,
How came this wicked Plot to Light:
He answer'd, that a *Dog* of late
Inform'd a Minister of State.
Said I, from thence I nothing know;
For, are not all Informers so?
A Villain, who his Friend betrays,
We style him by no other Phrase;
And so a perjur'd *Dog* denotes
*Porter,* and *Prendergast,* and *Oates.*          10
And forty others I could name—
    *Whig.* But you must know this Dog was lame.
    *Tory.* A Weighty Argument indeed;
Your *Evidence* was *lame.* Proceed:
Come, help your *lame Dog o'er the Style.*
    *Whig.* Sir, you mistake me all this while:
I mean a *Dog,* without a Joke,
Can howl, and bark, but never spoke.

Printed from *Poems,* 1735.

*Tory.* I'm still to seek which *Dog* you mean;
Whether Curr *Plunket*, or Whelp *Skean*,                    20
An *English* or an *Irish* Hound;
Or t'other *Puppy* that was drown'd,
Or *Mason* that abandon'd Bitch:
Then pray be free, and tell me which:
For, ev'ry Stander-by was marking
That all the Noise they made was *barking*:
You pay them well; the *Dogs* have got
Their *Dogs-heads in a Porridge-pot*:
And 'twas but just; for, wise Men say,
That, *every Dog must have his Day.*                         30
*Dog Walpole* laid a Quart of *Nog* on't,
He'd either *make a Hog or Dog on't*,
And look't since he has got his Wish,
As if he had *thrown down a Dish*.
Yet, this I dare foretel you from it,
He'll soon *return to his own Vomit*.
      *Whig.* Besides, this horrid Plot was found
By *Neno* after he was drown'd.
      *Tory.* Why then the Proverb is not right,
Since you can teach *dead Dogs to bite*.                     40
      *Whig.* I prov'd my Proposition full:
But, *Jacobites* are strangely dull.
Now, let me tell you plainly, Sir,
Our Witness is a real *Curr*,
A *Dog* of Spirit for his Years,
Has twice two Legs, two hanging Ears;
His Name is *Harlequin*, I wot,
And that's a Name in ev'ry *Plot*:
Resolv'd to save the *British* Nation,
Though *French* by Birth and Education:                      50
His Correspondence plainly dated,
Was all *decypher'd*, and *translated*.
His Answers were exceeding pretty
Before the secret wise Committee;
Confess't as plain as he could bark;
Then with his Fore-foot set his *Mark*.
      *Tory.* Then all this while have I been bubbled;
I thought it was a *Dog in Doublet*:

The Matter now no longer sticks;
For Statesmen never want *Dog-tricks*.                    60
But, since it was a real *Curr*,
And not a *Dog* in Metaphor,
I give you Joy of the Report,
That he's to have a Place at Court.
   *Whig.* Yes, and a Place he will grow rich in;
A Turn-spit in the Royal Kitchen.
Sir, to be plain, I tell you what;
We had Occasion for a Plot;
And, when we found the *Dog* begin it,
We guess't the *Bishop*'s *Foot was in it*.                70
   *Tory.* I own it was a dang'rous Project;
And you have prov'd it by *Dog-Logick*.
Sure such Intelligence between
A *Dog* and *Bishop* ne'er was seen,
Till you began to change the Breed;
Your *Bishops* all are *Dogs* indeed.


# THE STORM;

## Minerva's Petition

PALLAS, a Goddess chaste and wise,
   Descending lately from the Skies,
To *Neptune* went, and begg'd in Form
He'd give his Orders for a Storm;
A Storm, to drown that Rascal Hort,
And she wou'd kindly thank him for't.
A Wretch! whom *English* Rogues to spite her,
Had lately honour'd with a Mitre.

   The God, who favour'd her Request,
Assur'd her he wou'd do his best:                          10
But *Venus* had been there before
Pleaded the Bishop lov'd a Whore,

Printed from *Works, Vol. X,* Dublin, 1762.

And had enlarg'd her Empire wide,
He own'd no Deity beside.
At Sea, or Land, if e'er you found him,
Without a Mistress, hang or drown him.
Since *Burnet*'s Death, the Bishop's Bench,
'Till Hort arriv'd ne'er kept a Wench;
If Hort must sink, she grieves to tell it,
She'll not have left one single Prelate:     20
For to say Truth, she did intend him,
Elect of *Cyprus* in *commendam*.
And since her Birth the Ocean gave her,
She could not doubt her Uncle's Favour.


THEN *Proteus* urg'd the same Request,
But half in Earnest, half in Jest;
Said he—"Great Sovereign of the Main,
"To drown him all Attempts are vain,
"Hort can assume more Forms than I,
"A Rake, a Bully, Pimp, or Spy.     30
"Can creep, or run, can fly or swim,
"All Motions are alike to him:
"Turn him adrift, and you shall find
"He knows to sail with ev'ry Wind;
"Or, throw him overboard, he'll ride
"As well against, as with the Tide,
"But, *Pallas*, you've apply'd too late,
"For 'tis decreed by *Jove* and Fate,
"That *Ireland* must be soon destroy'd,
"And who but Hort can be employ'd?     40
"You need not then have been so pert,
"In sending *Bolton* to *Clonfert*.
"I found you did it by your Grinning;
"Your Business is to mind your Spinning.
"But how you came to interpose,
"In making Bishops, no one knows.
"And if you must have your Petition,
"There's *Berkeley* in the same Condition;

42. *Bolton*. Afterwards Archbishop of Cashell.
48. Dr. George Berkeley, Dean of Derry and afterwards Bishop of Cloyne.

"Look, there he stands, and 'tis but just
"If one must drown, the other must;                    50
"But, if you'll leave us Bishop *Judas*,
"We'll give you *Berkeley* for *Bermudas*.
"Now, if 'twill gratify your Spight,
"To put him in a plaguy Fright,
"Although 'tis hardly worth the Cost,
"You soon shall see him soundly tost.
"You'll find him swear, blaspheme, and damn,
"And ev'ry Moment take a Dram,
"His ghostly Visage with an Air
"Of Reprobation and Despair:                           60
"Or, else some hiding Hole he seeks,
"For Fear the rest shou'd say he squeeks;
"Or, as *Fitzpatrick* did before,
"Resolve to perish with his Whore;
"Or, else he raves, and roars, and swears,
"And, but for Shame, wou'd say his Pray'rs.
"Or, wou'd you see his Spirits sink,
"Relaxing downwards in a Stink?
"If such a Sight as this can please ye,
"Good Madam *Pallas*, pray be easy,                    70
"To *Neptune* speak, and he'll consent;
"But he'll come back the Knave he went."


THE Goddess, who conceiv'd an Hope,
That Hort was destin'd to a Rope,
Believ'd it best to condescend
To spare a Foe, to save a Friend:
But fearing *Berkeley* might be scar'd
She left him Virtue for a Guard.

52. *Bermudas.* See his Scheme in his Miscellanies for erecting an University at Bermudas.

64. Brigadier Fitzpatrick was drowned in one of the packet-boats in the Bay of Dublin, in a great storm.

# BILLET

## to the

### COMPANY of PLAYERS

THE inclosed Prologue is formed upon the story of the Secretary's not suffering you to act, unless you would pay him 300*l. per annum*, upon which you got a licence from the Lord Mayor to act as strollers.

The Prologue supposes, that, upon your being forbidden to act, a company of country-strollers came and hired the Play-house, and your cloaths, *&c.* to act in.

## The PROLOGUE

OUR set of strollers, wand'ring up and down,
Hearing the House was empty, came to town;
And, with a licence from our good Lord May'r,
Went to one Griffith, formerly a play'r:
Him we persuaded with a mod'rate bribe,
To speak to Elrington, and all the tribe,
To let our company supply their places,
And hire us out their scenes, and cloaths, and faces.
Is not the truth the truth? Look full on me;
I am not Elrington, nor Griffith he.          10
When we perform, look sharp among our crew,
There's not a creature here you ever knew.
The former folks were servants to the king,
We, humble strollers, always on the wing.
Now, for my part, I think upon the whole,
Rather than starve, a better man would strole.

Stay, let me see—Three hundred pounds a year,
For leave to act in town? 'Tis plaguy dear.
Now, here's a warrant; Gallants please to mark,
For three thirteens and sixpence to the clerk.          20

Printed from *Works, 4to, Vol. VIII* (2), London, 1765.

Three hundred pounds! Were I the price to fix,
The public should bestow the actors six.
A score of guineas, given under-hand,
For a good word or so, we understand.
To help an honest lad that's out of place,
May cost a crown or so; a common case:
And, in a crew, 'tis no injustice thought
To ship a rogue, and pay him not a groat.
But, in the chronicles of former ages,
Who ever heard of servants paying wages?                    30

    I pity Elrington with all my heart;
Would he were here this night to act my part.
I told him what it was to be a stroller,
How free we acted, and had no controller:
In ev'ry town we wait on Mr. May'r,
First get a licence, then produce our ware:
We sound a trumpet, or we beat a drum;
Huzza! the school-boys roar, the play'rs are come!
And then we cry, to spur the bumkins on,
Gallants, by Tuesday next we must be gone.                  40
I told him, in the smoothest way I could,
All this and more, yet it would do no good.
But Elrington, tears falling from his cheeks,
He that has shone with Betterton and Weeks,
To whom our country has been always dear,
Who chose to leave his dearest pledges here,
Owns all your favours; here intends to stay,
And, as a stroller, act in ev'ry play:
And the whole crew this resolution takes,
To live and die all strollers for your sakes;              50
Not frighted with an ignominious name,
For your displeasure is their only shame.

    A pox on Elrington's majestic tone!
Now to a word of bus'ness in our own.

    Gallants, next Thursday night will be our last,
Then, without fail, we pack up for Belfast.
Lose not your time, nor our diversion miss,
The next we act shall be as good as this.

## To Charles Ford Esq<sup>r</sup>. on his Birth-day
## Jan<sup>ry.</sup> 31<sup>st</sup> for the Year 1722–3

[p. 1]     COME, be content, since out it must,
              For, Stella has betray'd her Trust,
And, whisp'ring, charg'd me not to say
That M<sup>r</sup> Ford was born to day:
Or if at last, I needs must blab it,
According to my usuall habit,
She bid me with a serious Face
Be sure conceal the Time and Place,
And not my Compliment to spoyl
By calling This your native Soyl;                    10
Or vex the Ladyes, when they knew
That you are turning fourty two.
But if these Topicks should appear
Strong Arguments to keep You here,
We think, though You judge hardly of it,
Good Manners must give Place to Profit.
    The Nymphs with whom You first began
Are each become a Harridan;
And Mountague so far decayd,
That now her Lovers must be payd;                    20
And ev'ry Belle that since arose
Has her Cotemporary Beaux.
Your former Comrades, once so bright,
With whom you toasted half the Night,
Of Rheumatism and Pox complain,
And bid adieu to dear Champain:
Your great Protectors, once in Power,
Are now in Exil, or the Tower,
Your Foes, triumphant o'er the Laws,
Who hate Your Person, and Your Cause,                30
[p. 2]     If once they get you on the Spot
You must be guilty of the Plot,

Printed from Swift's autograph, Ford Papers, The Rothschild Library, No. 2287.

For, true or false, they'll ne'r enquire,
But use You ten times worse than Pri'r.
In London! what would You do there?
Can You, my Friend, with Patience bear,
Nay would it not Your Passion raise
Worse than a Pun, or Irish Phrase,
To see a Scoundrel Strut and hector,
A Foot-boy to some Rogue Director?                    40
To look on Vice triumphant round,
And Virtue trampled on the Ground:
Observe where bloody Townshend stands
With Informations in his Hands,
Hear him Blaspheme; and Swear, and Rayl,
Threatning the Pillory and Jayl.
If this you think a pleasing Scene
To London strait return again,
Where you have told us from Experience,
Are swarms of Bugs and Hanoverians.                   50
I thought my very Spleen would burst
When Fortune hither drove me first;
Was full as hard to please as You,
Nor Persons Names, nor Places knew;
But now I act as other Folk,
Like Pris'ners when their Gall is broke.
If you have London still at heart
We'll make a small one here by Art:
The Diff'rence is not much between
St. James's Park and Stephen's Green;                 60
And, Dawson street will serve as well
To lead you thither, as Pell-mell,
(Without your passing thro the Palace
To choque your Sight, and raise your Malice)
[p. 3]     The Deanry-house may well be match't
(Under Correction)with the thatcht,
Nor shall I, when you hither come,
Demand a Croun a Quart for Stumm.
Then, for a middle-aged Charmer,
Stella may vye with your Mountharmar:                 70
She's Now as handsom ev'ry bit,
And has a thousand times her Wit.

The Dean and Sheridan, I hope,
Will half supply a Gay and Pope,
Corbet, though yet I know his Worth not,
No doubt, will prove a good Arbuthnot:
I throw into the Bargain, Jim:
In London can you equall Him?
    What think you of my fav'rite Clan,
Robin, and Jack, and Jack, and Dan?                    80
Fellows of modest Worth and Parts,
With chearfull Looks, and honest Hearts.
    Can you on Dublin look with Scorn?
Yet here were You and Ormonde born
Oh, were but You and I so wise
To look with Robin Grattan's Eyes:
Robin adores that Spot of Earth,
That litt'rall Spot which gave him Birth,
And swears, Cushogue is to his Tast,
As fine as Hampton-court at least.                     90
    When to your Friends you would enhance
The Praise of Italy or France
For Grandeur, Elegance and Wit,
We gladly hear you, and submit:
But then, to come and keep a Clutter
For this, or that Side of a Gutter,
To live in this or t'other Isle,
We cannot think it worth your while.
For, take it kindly, or amiss,
The Diff'rence but amounts to this,                    100
[p. 4]  You bury on our Side the Channell
In Linnen, and on Yours, in Flannell.
You, for the News are ne'r to seek,
While We perhaps must wait a Week:
You, happy Folks, are sure to meet
A hundred Whores in ev'ry Street,
While We may search all Dublin o'er
And hardly hear of half a Score.
    You see, my Arguments are Strong;
I wonder you held out so long,                         110

89. *Cushogue.* The true Name of Belcamp.

But since you are convinc't at last
We'll pardon you for what is past.
   So—let us now for Whisk prepare;
Twelvepence a Corner, if you dare.

## *STELLA*'s Birth-day

### A great Bottle of Wine, long buried, being that Day dug up

[Written 1722–3]

RESOLV'D my annual Verse to pay
   By Duty bound, on *Stella*'s Day;
Furnish'd with Paper, Pens, and Ink,
I gravely sat me down to think:
I bit my Nails, and scratch'd my Head,
But found my Wit and Fancy fled:
Or, if with more than usual Pain,
A Thought came slowly from my Brain,
It cost me Lord knows how much Time
To shape it into Sense and Rhyme;       10
And, what was yet a greater Curse,
Long-thinking made my Fancy worse.

   Forsaken by th'inspiring Nine,
I waited at *Apollo*'s Shrine;
I told him what the World would say
If *Stella* were unsung to Day;
How I should hide my Head for Shame,
When both the *Jacks* and *Robin* came;
How *Ford* would frown, how *Jim* would leer,
How *Sheridan* the Rogue would sneer,       20
And swear it does not always follow,
That *Semel'n anno ridet Apollo*.
I have assur'd them twenty times,
That *Phœbus* help'd me in my Rhymes,

Printed from *Miscellanies. The Last Volume*, 1727, with corrections from *Poems*, 1735.

*Phœbus* inspir'd me from above,
And he and I were Hand in Glove.
But finding me so dull and dry since,
They'll call it all poetick Licence:
And when I brag of Aid divine,
Think *Eusden*'s Right as good as mine.          30

Nor do I ask for *Stella*'s sake;
'Tis my own Credit lies at Stake.
And *Stella* will be sung, while I
Can only be a Stander-by.

*Apollo* having thought a little,
Return'd this Answer to a Tittle.

Though you should live like old *Methusalem*,
I furnish Hints, and you should use all 'em,
You yearly sing as she grows old,
You'd leave her Virtues half untold.          40
But to say truth, such Dulness reigns
Through the whole set of *Irish* Deans;
I'm daily stunn'd with such a Medley,
Dean *Wood*, Dean *Daniel*, and Dean *Smedley*;
That, let what Dean soever come,
My Orders are, I'm not at Home;
And if your Voice had not been loud,
You must have pass'd among the Crowd.

But, now, your Danger to prevent,
You must apply to Mrs. *Brent*,          50
For she, as Priestess, knows the Rites
Wherein the God of *Earth* delights.
First, nine Ways looking, let her stand
With an old Poker in her Hand;
Let her describe a Circle round
In *Saunder*'s Cellar on the Ground:
A Spade let prudent *Archy* hold,
And with Discretion dig the Mould:

50. *Mrs. Brent*. The House-Keeper.     56. *Saunders*. The Butler.
57. *Archy*. The Footman.

Let *Stella* look with watchful Eye,
*Rebecca, Ford,* and *Grattans* by.                          60

 Behold the BOTTLE, where it lies
With Neck elated tow'rds the Skies!
The God of Winds and God of Fire
Did to it's wond'rous Birth conspire;
And *Bacchus* for the Poet's Use
Pour'd in a strong inspiring Juice:
See! as you raise it from its Tomb,
It drags behind a spacious Womb,
And in the spacious Womb contains
A Sov'reign Medicine for the Brains.                         70

 You'll find it soon if Fate consents;
If not, a thousand Mrs. *Brents,*
Ten thousand *Archy*'s arm'd with Spades
May dig in vain in *Pluto*'s Shades.

 From thence a plenteous Draught infuse,
And boldly then invoke the Muse:
(But first let *Robert* on his Knees
With Caution drain it from the Lees)
The Muse will at your Call appear,
With *Stella*'s Praise to crown the Year.                     80

# *Carberiæ Rupes in Comitatu* Corgagensi *apud* Hybernicos

### Scripsit *Jun. Ann. Dom.* 1723

ECCE ingens fragmen scopuli quod vertice summo
 Desuper impendet, nullo fundamine nixum
Decidit in fluctus: maria undiq; & undiq; saxa
Horisono Stridore tonant, & ad æthera murmur
Erigitur; trepidatq; suis *Neptunus* in undis.
Nam, longâ venti rabie, atq; aspergine crebrâ

Printed from *Poems,* 1735.

60. *Rebecca.* A Lady, friend to Stella. *Ford and Grattans.* Gentlemen, Friends to the Author.   77. *Robert.* The Valet.

Æquorei laticis, specus imâ rupe cavatur:
Jam fultura ruit, jam summa cacumina nutant;
Jam cadit in præceps moles, & verberat undas.
Attonitus credas, hinc dejecisse Tonantem                10
Montibus impositos montes, & *Pelion* altum
In capita anguipedum cœlo jaculâsse gigantum.

S&#x00C6;pe etiam spelunca immani aperitur hiatu
Exesa è scopulis, & utrinq; foramina pandit,
Hinc atq; hinc a ponto ad pontum pervia Phœbo:
Cautibus enormè junctis laquearia tecti
Formantur; moles olim ruitura supernè.
Fornice sublimi nidos posuere palumbes,
Inq; imo stagni posuere cubilia phocæ.

Sed, cum sævit hyems, & venti carcere rupto          20
Immensos volvunt fluctus ad culmina montis;
Non obsessæ arces, non fulmina vindice dextrâ
Missa Jovis, quoties inimicas sævit in urbes,
Exæquant sonitum undarum, veniente procellâ:
Littora littoribus reboant; vicinia latè,
Gens assueta mari, & pedibus percurrere rupes,
Terretur tamen, & longè fugit, arva relinquens.

Gramina dum carpunt pendentes rupe capellæ
Vi salientis aquæ de summo præcipitantur,
Et dulces animas imo sub gurgite linquunt.          30

Piscator terrâ non audet vellere funem;
Sed latet in portu tremebundus, & aera sudum
Haud sperans, Nereum precibus votisq; fatigat.

## A Translation by William Dunkin

Faulkner introduced this translation with the following note:
*We have added a Translation of the preceding Poem, for the Benefit
of our* English *Readers. It is done by Mr.* W. Dunkin, *M.A. for whom
our supposed Author hath expressed a great Regard, on Account of his
ingenious Performances, although unacquainted with him.*

# Carbery *Rocks in the County of* Cork, Ireland

L O! from the Top of yonder Cliff, that shrouds
　　Its airy Head amidst the azure Clouds,
Hangs a huge Fragment; destitute of props
Prone on the Waves the rocky Ruin drops.
With hoarse Rebuff the swelling Seas rebound,
From Shore to Shore the Rocks return the Sound:
The dreadful Murmur Heav'n's high Convex cleaves,
And *Neptune* shrinks beneath his Subject Waves;
For, long the whirling Winds and beating Tides
Had scoop'd a Vault into its nether Sides.          10
Now yields the Base, the Summits nod, now urge
Their headlong Course, and lash the sounding Surge.
Not louder Noise could shake the guilty World,
When *Jove* heap'd Mountains upon Mountains hurl'd,
Retorting *Pelion* from his dread abode,
To crush Earth's rebel Sons beneath the Load.

　OFT too with hideous yawn the Cavern wide
Presents an Orifice on either Side,
A dismal Orifice from Sea to Sea
Extended, pervious to the God of Day:          20
Uncouthly joyn'd, the Rocks stupendous form
An Arch, the Ruin of a future Storm:
High on the Cliff their Nests the *Woodquests* make,
And Sea calves stable in the oozy Lake.

　BUT when bleak Winter with her sullen Train
Awakes the Winds, to vex the watry Plain;
When o'er the craggy Steep without Controul,
Big with the Blast, the raging Billows rowl;
Not Towns beleaguer'd, not the flaming Brand
Darted from Heav'n by *Jove*'s avenging Hand,          30
Oft as on impious Men his Wrath he pours,
Humbles their Pride, and blasts their gilded Tow'rs,
Equal the Tumult of this wild Uproar:
Waves rush o'er Waves, rebellows Shore to Shore.
The neighb'ring Race, tho' wont to brave the Shocks,
Of angry Seas, and run along the Rocks,
Now pale with Terror, while the Ocean foams,
Fly far and wide, nor trust their native Homes.

THE Goats, while pendent from the Mountain top
The wither'd Herb improvident they crop,                    40
Wash'd down the Precipice with sudden Sweep,
Leave their sweet Lives beneath th' unfathom'd Deep.

THE frighted Fisher with desponding Eyes,
Tho' safe, yet trembling in the Harbour lies,
Nor hoping to behold the Skies serene,
Wearies with Vows the Monarch of the Main.

# Stella's Distress

## on the 3ᵈ fatal day of Octobʳ 1723

[p. 1]    THE Winter now begins to frown;
          Poor Stella must pack off to Town.
From purling Streams & Fountains bubbling
To Liffy's filthy side in Dublin;
From wholesom Exercise and Air
To sossing in an elbow chair:
From stomach sharp, and hearty feeding
To piddle like a Lady breeding.
From ruling there the Household singly
To be directed here by Dingley.                              10
From ev'ry day a Lordly Banquet
To half a Joynt, & God be thanked:
From every Meal Pontack in plenty
To a sour Pint one day in twenty.
From growing richer with good Cheer,
And yet run out by starving here:
From Ford who thinks of nothing mean
To the poor Doings of the Dean:
From Ford attending at her Call
To Visits of Archdeacon Wall.                                20
Say, Stella, which you most repent
You e're return'd, or ever went?

---

Printed from Ford's original transcript, The Rothschild Library, No. 2268,
which gives the two draft poems (separated by a double rule) from which *Stella at
Wood-Park* (p. 247) was constructed. Heavily indented lines have been transferred
from the margin, and variant readings are excluded from the line-count.

——— Cuicunque nocere volebat
Vestimenta dabat pretiosa.

Don Carlos in a merry Spight
Did Stella to his House invite,
He entertain'd her half a year
With richest Wines and costly Cheer:
Surpriz'd with ev'ry day a hot meal
She thought that all the world was Oatmeal:
That she might o're the Servants hector
Don Carlos made her sole Director.
    Don Carlos made her chief Director
    She now can or'e the servants hector.
In half a week the Dame grew nice,
Got all things at the highest Price.      10
Now at the Table head she sits
Presented with the choicest Bits:
[p. 2] She look'd on Partridges with scorn
Except they tasted of the Corn:
A Haunch of Ven'son made her sweat
Unless it had the right Fumette:
Don Carlos earnestly would beg,
Dear Madam try this Pigeon's leg:
Was happy when he could prevail
To make Her only touch a Quail:      20
Thrô candle-light she view'd the Wine
To see that ev'ry Glass was fine.
    At last grown prouder than the Devil
With feeding high, & Treatment civil,
Too soon arrives the dismal Day,
She must return to Ormond-Key.
    As the Coach stopp'd, she look'd & swore
The Rascal had mistook the Door:
At entring you might see her stoop
Nor would the Door admit her Hoop.      30
    Don Carlos now began to find
    His Med'cine work as he design'd
    As the Coach stopp'd, she look'd & swore
    The Rascal had mistook the Door
    At going in you saw her stoop
    The narrow Entry crushd her Hoop

She curs'd the dark & winding Stairs
And still encreasing in her Airs
Began a thousand faults to spy
The Cieling hardly six foot high
The smoaky Wainscot full of cracks
And half the Chairs with broken backs.
The Cubbard fasten'd with a Peg
The rusty Tongs have lost a Leg        40
Her Quarter's out at Lady Day
She'll have 'em know she scorns to stay
(While there are Houses to be let)
In Lodgings like a poor Grisette.
Howe're to keep her Spirits up
                Mean time to keep
She sent for Company to sup,
                She sends
When all the while you might remark
                Where all
She did her best to ape Woodpark.
                She strove in vain to ape
Two Bottles call'd for, (half her Store,
The Cellar could contain but four)        50
A Supper worthy of her self,
Five Nothings in five Plates of Delf.
And thus the Farce a fortnight went
When all her little Money spent,
      Thus for a week the Farce went on
      When the whole month's Allowance gone
She fell into her former Scene,
Small Beer, a Herring, and the Dean.
      Since I must laugh, or cannot live,
      Good-natur'd Stella will forgive:
      We Poets when a Hint is new
      Regard not what is false or true,      60
      No Raillery gives just Offence
      Where Truth has not the least Pretence;
      Nor can be more securely plac't
      Than on a Nymph of Stella's Tast.
        I must confess your Wine and Vittle
      I was too hard upon—a little.

And you must know in what I writ
I had some Anger in my Wit.
For when you sigh to leave Woodpark,
The Place, the Welcome, and the Spark,  70
To languish in this odious Town,
And pull your haughty Stomach down,
You shew Don Carlos where to dwell,
And grieve he ever left Pell-mell.
 Yet granting all I said were true,
A Cottage is Woodpark with You.


# *STELLA*

## AT

# *WOOD-PARK,*

### A House of *Charles Ford*, Esq; eight

### Miles from *Dublin*

——— *Cuicunuqe; nocere volebat*
*Vestimenta dabat pretiosa.*

### Written in the Year 1723

DON *Carlos* in a merry Spight,
 Did *Stella* to his House invite:
He entertain'd her half a Year
With gen'rous Wines and costly Chear.
Don *Carlos* made her chief Director,
That she might o'er the Servants hector.
In half a Week the Dame grew nice,
Got all things at the highest Price.
Now at the Table-Head she sits,
Presented with the nicest Bits:   10
She look'd on Partridges with scorn,
Except they tasted of the Corn:

Printed from *Poems*, 1735.

A Haunch of Ven'son made her sweat,
Unless it had the right *Fumette*.
Don *Carlos* earnestly would beg,
Dear Madam, try this Pigeon's Leg;
Was happy when he could prevail
To make her only touch a Quail.
Through Candle-Light she view'd the Wine,
To see that ev'ry Glass was fine.                    20
At last grown prouder than the Devil,
With feeding high, and Treatment civil,
Don *Carlos* now began to find
His Malice work as he design'd:
The Winter-Sky began to frown,
Poor *Stella* must pack off to Town.
From purling Streams and Fountains bubbling,
To *Liffy*'s stinking Tide in *Dublin*:
From wholsome Exercise and Air
To sossing in an easy Chair;                         30
From Stomach sharp and hearty feeding,
To piddle like a Lady breeding:
From ruling there the Houshold singly,
To be directed here by *Dingly*:
From ev'ry Day a lordly Banquet,
To half a Joint, and God be thank it:
From ev'ry Meal *Pontack* in plenty,
To half a Pint one Day in twenty.
From *Ford* attending at her Call,
To visits of Archdeacon Wall[,]                      40
From *Ford*, who thinks of nothing mean,
To the poor Doings of the Dean.
From growing Riche[r] with good Chear,
To running out by starving here.


   BUT now arrives the dismal Day:
She must return to *Ormond Key*:
The Coachman stopt, she lookt, and swore
The Rascal had mistook the Door:

   34. *Dingly*. A Lady. The two Ladies lodged together.
   46. *Ormond Key*. Where both the Ladies lodged.

At coming in you saw her stoop;
The Entry brusht against her Hoop:            50
Each Moment rising in her Airs,
She curst the narrow winding Stairs:
Began a Thousand Faults to spy;
The Ceiling hardly six Foot high;
The smutty Wainscot full of Cracks,
And half the Chairs with broken Backs:
Her Quarter's out at *Lady-Day*,
She vows she will no longer stay,
In Lodgings, like a poor *Grizette*,
While there are Lodgings to be lett.           60


    Howe'er, to keep her Spirits up,
She sent for Company to sup;
When all the while you might remark,
She strove in vain to ape *Wood-Park*.
Two Bottles call'd for, (half her Store;
The Cupboard could contain but four;)
A Supper worthy of her self,
Five *Nothings* in five Plates of *Delph*.


    Thus, for a Week the Farce went on;
When all her Count[r]y-Savings gone,          70
She fell into her former Scene.
Small Beer, a Herring, and the Dean.


    Thus, far in jest. Though now I fear
You think my jesting too severe:
But Poets when a Hint is new
Regard not whether false or true:
Yet Raillery gives no Offence,
Where Truth has not the least Pretence;
Nor can be more securely plac't
Than on a Nymph of *Stella*'s Taste.          80
I must confess, your Wine and Vittle
I was too hard upon *a little*;
Your Table neat, your Linnen fine;
And, though in Miniature, you shine,

Yet, when you sigh to leave *Wood-Park*,
The Scene, the Welcome, and the Spark,
To languish in this odious Town,
And pull your haughty Stomach down;
We think you quite mistake the Case;
The Virtue lies not in the Place:                    90
For though my Raillery were true,
A Cottage is *Wood-Park* with you.

# The First of April:

## A POEM

Inscrib'd to Mrs. *E. Cope*

THIS morn the *God of Wit* and Joke,
Thus to his *Choir of Muses* spoke;

"Go, Sisters Nine, into that Cabbin,
"Where most true Sons of *Phœbus* ha' bin.
"Each take a Child into her Care,
"There's one for each and one to spare:
"Tho' there's a Boy whom a Lord chuses,
"Who is as good as all the Muses;
"And beauteous *Bess* a diff'rent case is,
"For she belongs to all the Graces;                  10
"Divide the rest, but then take care,
"Ye don't fall out about the Heir."

They dropp'd low Court'sies, One and All,
And took their Progress tow'rds *Loughall*.
*Apollo* laugh'd till he was sick,
That he had serv'd the Prudes a Trick.

"With due Submission to the God,
"*Thalia* said, 'tis somewhat odd,
"We all shou'd march on this Occasion,
"And not leave one for Invocation.                   20

Printed from the Fo. Half-sheet (n.d. or p.).
7. *a Lord.* Anglesey.

"Poets till they grow hoarse may bawl,
"And not a Muse will hear their Call:
"Besides, to me this seems a Bubble,
" 'Tis all to save their Mother trouble;
"I'll warrant she's some flaunting Dame,
"Regardless of her House and Fame;
"When we come there we'll stand unseen,
"T' observe her Management within."

They peep'd, and saw a Lady there
Pinning on Coifs and combing Hair;     30
Soft'ning with Songs to Son or Daughter,
The persecution of cold Water.
Still pleas'd with the *good-natur'd Noise*,
And *harmless Frolicks* of her *Boys*;
*Equal* to all in *Care* and *Love*,
Which all *deserve* and all *improve*.
To *Kitchin, Parlour, Nurs'ry* flies,
And seems all *Feet*, and *Hands*, and *Eyes*.
No Thought of her's does ever *roam*,
But for her 'Squire when he's *from home*;     40
And scarce a *Day*, can spare a *Minute*
From *Husband, Children, Wheel*, or *Spinnet*.
The Muses when they saw *her* care,
Wonder'd the God had sent them there.
And said, "His Worship might ha' told us,
"This House don't *want*, nor will it *hold* us.
"We govern here! where she presides
"With *Virtue, Prudence, Wit* besides;
"A Wife as good as Heart cou'd wish one,
"What need we open our Commission,     50
"There's no occasion here for us,
"Can *we* do more than what *she* does."

*Thalia* now began to smoke,
That all this Bus'ness was a Joke.

"Sisters, said she, my Life I'll lay,
"Ye have forgot this *Month* and *Day*.—
" 'Tis a *fair Trick*, by *ancient* Rules—
"The God has made us *April-Fools*."

# *PETHOX*
# the Great

FROM *Venus* born, thy Beauty shows,
　But who thy Father, no Man knows,
Nor can the skilful Herald trace
The Founder of thy antient Race.
Whether thy Temper, full of Fire,
Discovers *Vulcan* for thy Sire,
The God who made *Scamander* boil,
And round his Margin sing'd the Soil,
(From whence Philosophers agree,
An equal Pow'r descends to thee.)            10
Whether from dreadful *Mars* you claim
The high Descent from whence you came,
And, as a Proof, shew num'rous Scars
By fierce Encounters made in Wars;
(Those honourable Wound[s] you bore
From Head to Foot, and all before;)
And still the bloody Field frequent,
Familiar in each Leader's Tent.
Or whether, as the Learn'd contend,
You from the Neighb'ring *Gaul* descend;      20
Or from *Parthenope* the proud,
Where numberless thy Vot'ries crowd:
Whether thy Great Forefathers came
From Realms that bear *Vesputio*'s Name:
For so Conjectors would obtrude,
And from thy painted Skin conclude.
Whether, as *Epicurus* shows
The World from justling Seeds arose,
Which mingling with prolifick Strife
In Chaos, kindled into Life;                   30
So your Production was the same,
And from contending Atoms came.

Printed from *Miscellanies. The Last Volume*, 1727, with corrections from *Poems*, 1735.

21. *Parthenope.* The ancient name of Naples.

Thy fair indulgent Mother crown'd
Thy Head with sparkling Rubies round;
Beneath thy decent Steps, the Road
Is all with precious Jewels strow'd.
The Bird of *Pallas* knows his Post,
Thee to attend where-e'er thou go'st.

*Byzantians* boast, that on the Clod
Where once their *Sultan*'s Horse hath trod,    40
Grows neither Grass, nor Shrub, nor Tree;
The same thy Subjects boast of Thee.

The greatest Lord, when you appear,
Will deign your Livery to wear,
In all thy various Colours seen,
Of Red, and Yellow, Blue, and Green.

With half a Word, when you require,
The Man of Bus'ness must retire.

The haughty Minister of State
With Trembling must thy Leisure wait;    50
And while his Fate is in thy Hands,
The Bus'ness of the Nation stands.

Thou dar'st the greatest Prince attack,
Can'st hourly set him on the Rack,
And, as an Instance of thy Pow'r,
Inclose him in a wooden Tow'r,
With pungent Pains on ev'ry Side:
So *Regulus* in Torments dy'd.

From thee our Youth all Virtues learn,
Dangers with Prudence to discern;    60
And well thy Scholars are endu'd
With Temp'rance, and with Fortitude;
With Patience, which all Ills supports,
And Secrecy, the Art of Courts.

37. *The Bird of Pallas*. Bubo, the Owl.

The glitt'ring Beau could hardly tell,
Without your Aid, to read or spell;
But, having long convers'd with you,
Knows how to scrawl a Billet-doux.

With what Delight, methinks, I trace
Thy Blood in ev'ry Noble Race!                        70
In whom thy Features, Shape, and Mien,
Are to the Life distinctly seen.

The *Britons*, once a savage Kind,
By you were brighten'd and refin'd,
Descendents of the barbarous *Huns*,
With Limbs robust, and Voice that stuns;
But you have molded them afresh,
Remov'd the tough superfluous Flesh,
Taught them to modulate their Tongues,
And speak without the Help of Lungs.                  80

*Proteus* on you bestow'd the Boon
To change your Visage like the Moon,
You sometimes half a Face produce,
Keep t'other Half for private Use.

How fam'd thy Conduct in the Fight,
With *Hermes*, Son of *Pleias* bright.
Out-number'd, half encompass'd round,
You strove for ev'ry Inch of Ground;
Then, by a Soldierly Retreat,
Retir'd to your Imperial Seat.                        90
The Victor, when your Steps he trac'd,
Found all the Realms before him waste;
You, o'er the high Triumphal Arch
Pontifick, made your glorious March;
The wond'rous Arch behind you fell,
And left a Chasm profound as Hell:
You, in your Capitol secur'd,
A Siege as long as *Troy* endur'd.

86. *Hermes*. Mercury.

# EPIGRAMS

AS Thomas was cudgelld one day by his Wife,
He took to the Street, and fled for his Life,
Tom's three dearest Friends came by in the Squabble,
And sav'd him at once from the Shrew and the Rabble;
Then ventur'd to give him some sober Advice,
But Tom is a Person of Honor so nice,
Too wise to take Council, too proud to take Warning,
That he sent to all three a Challenge next morning.
Three Duels he fought, thrice ventur'd his Life
Went home, and was cudgell'd again by his Wife.      10


WHEN Margery chastises Ned
She calls it combing of his Head,
A Kinder Wife was never born,
She combs his Head, and finds him Horn.


JOAN cudgell's Ned, yet Ned's a Bully
Will cudgell's Bess, yet Will's a Cully
Dye Ned and Bess; give Will to Joan,
She dares not say her Life's her own.
Dye Joan and Will; give Bess to Ned,
And ev'ry day she combs his Head.

Printed from Stella's transcript.

# A

# NEW-YEAR'S-GIFT for BEC

### Written in the Year M DCC XXIII–IV

RETURNING Janus now prepares,
For Bec, a new supply of cares,
Sent in a bag to Doctor Swift,
Who thus displays the New-year's-gift.

   First, this large parcel brings you tidings
Of our good Dean's eternal chidings;
Of Nelly's pertness, Robin's leasings,
And Sheridan's perpetual teazings.
This box is cramm'd on ev'ry side
With Stella's magisterial pride.          10
Behold a cage with sparrows fill'd,
First to be fondled, then be kill'd.
Now to this hamper I invite you,
With six imagin'd cares to fright you.
Here in this bundle Janus sends
Concerns by thousands for your friends:
And here's a pair of leathern pokes,
To hold your cares for other folks.
Here from a barrel you may broach
A peck of troubles for a coach.          20
This ball of wax your ears will darken,
Still to be curious, never hearken.
Lest you the town may have less trouble in,
Bring all your Quilca cares to Dublin,
For which he sends this empty sack;
And so take all upon your back.

Printed from *Works*, *4to*, *Vol. VIII* (2), London, 1765.

# To the Dean of St Patricks

## [By Dr. Thomas Sheridan]

How few can be of Grandeur sure!
The high may fall, the rich be poor.
The only Fav'rite at Court
To morrow may be Fortune's Sport;
For all her Pleasure & her Aim
Is to destroy both Pow'r & Fame.
　　Of this the Dean is an Example
No instance is more plain & ample
The World did never yet produce
For Courts a Man of greater Use.　　　　　　10
Nor has the World, supply'd us yet
With more vivacity & Wit;
Merry alternatly & wise,
To please the Statesman & advise.
Thro' all the last & glorious Reign
Was nothing done without the Dean;
The Courtiers Prop, the Nation's Pride,
But now alass he's thrown aside!
He's quite forgot & so's the Queen,
As if they both had never been.　　　　　　20
　　To see him now a Mountaineer!
O w$^t$ a mighty fall is here!
From set'ling Governments & Thrones
To splitting Rocks & piling Stones
Instead of Bolinbroke & Anna,
Shane Tunelly & Bryan Granna,
Oxford & Ormond he supplies
In ev'ry Irish Teague he spies;
So far forgetting his old Station
He seems to like their Conversation.　　　　30
Conforming to the tatter'd Rabble
He learns their Irish Tongue to gabble,
And w$^t$ our Anger more provokes
He's pleas'd with their insipid jokes.
Then turns & asks them who does lack a
Good Plug, or Pipe full of tobacca,

Printed from Sheridan's autograph, Huntington Library, HM 14369.

All cry they want, to ev'ry Man
He gives extravagant a Span.
Thus are they grown more fond than ever,
And he is highly in their Favour.        40
     Bright Stella Quilcah's greatest Pride
For them he scorns, & lays aside;
And Sheridan is left alone
All day to gape & stretch and groan,
While grumbling poor complaining Dingly
Is left to Care & Trouble singly.
     All o'er the Mountains spreads the Rumor
Both of his Bounty, & good Humor,
So that each Sheperdess & Swain
Comes flocking here to see the Dean.        50
All spread around the Land, you'd swear
That ev'ry day we kept a Fair.
My Fields are brought to such a pass
I have not left one blade of Grass,
That all my Weathers & my Beeves
Are slighted by the very Thieves.
     At Night, right loath to quit the Park,
His work just ended by the Dark
With all his Pioneers he comes,
To make more Work for Whisks & Brooms.        60
Then, seated in an elbow-chair,
To take a Nap he does prepare,
While two fair Damsells from the Lawns
Lull him asleep with soft Cronawns.
     Thus are his Days in Delving spent,
His Nights in Musick & Content.
He seems to gain by his Distress
His Friends are more, his Honours Less.

MS. endorsed by Sheridan "A new Year's-Gift for the Dean of St Patricks given him at Quilcah 1723/4."

# A True and Faithful Inventory of the Goods belonging to Dr. SWIFT, Vicar of *Lara Cor*; upon lending his House to the Bishop of *Meath,* until his own was built

[By Sheridan]

AN Oaken, broken, Elbow-Chair;
  A Cawdle-Cup, without an Ear;
A batter'd, shatter'd Ash Bedstead;
A Box of Deal, without a Lid;
A Pair of Tongs, but out of Joint;
A Back-Sword Poker, without Point;
A Pot that's crack'd a-cross, around,
With an old knotted Garter bound;
An Iron Lock, without a Key;
A Wig, with hanging, quite grown grey;      10
A Curtain worn to Half a Stripe;
A Pair of Bellows, without Pipe;
A Dish, which might good Meat afford once;
An *Ovid*, and an old *Concordance*;
A Bottle Bottom, Wooden Platter,
One is for Meal, and one for Water:
There likewise is a Copper Skillet,
Which runs as fast out as you fill it;
A Candlestick, Snuff dish, and Save-all,
And thus his Houshold Goods you have all.      20
These, to your Lordship, as a Friend,
Till you have built, I freely lend:
They'll save your Lordship for a Shift;
Why not, as well as Doctor *Swift?*

Printed from *Works, Vol. VIII*, Dublin, 1762.

# To STELLA

MARCH 13, M DCC XXIII–IV
[Written on the Day of her Birth, but not on the Subject,
when I was sick in bed.]

TORMENTED with incessant pains,
Can I devise poetic strains?
Time was, when I could yearly pay
My verse on Stella's native day:
But now, unable grown to write,
I grieve she ever saw the light.
Ungrateful; since to her I owe
That I these pains can undergo.
She tends me, like an humble slave;
And, when indecently I rave,                               10
When out my brutish passions break,
With gall in ev'ry word I speak,
She, with soft speech, my anguish chears,
Or melts my passions down with tears:
Although 'tis easy to descry
She wants assistance more than I;
Yet seems to feel my pains alone,
And is a Stoic in her own.
When, among scholars, can we find
So soft, and yet so firm a mind?                           20
All accidents of life conspire
To raise up Stella's virtue higher;
Or else, to introduce the rest
Which had been latent in her breast.
Her firmness who could e'er have known,
Had she not evils of her own?
Her kindness who could ever guess,
Had not her friends been in distress?
Whatever base returns you find
From me, Dear Stella, still be kind.                       30

Printed from *Works*, *4to*, *Vol. VIII* (2), London, 1765.

In your own heart you'll reap the fruit,
Tho' I continue still a brute.
But when I once am out of pain,
I promise to be good again:
Meantime your other juster friends
Shall for my follies make amends:
So may we long continue thus,
Admiring you, you pitying us.

# DINGLEY, and BRENT

## A SONG

To the Tune of *Ye Commons and Peers*

DINGLEY and Brent
      Wherever they went,
Ne'er minded a word that was spoken;
      Whatever was said,
      They ne'er troubled their head,
But laugh'd at their own silly joking.

      Should Solomon wise
      In majesty rise,
And shew them his wit and his learning;
      They never would hear,                          10
      But turn the deaf ear,
As a matter they had no concern in.

      You tell a good jest,
      And please all the rest,
Comes Dingley, and asks you, What was it?
      And curious to know,
      Away she will go
To seek an old rag in the closet.

Printed from *Works, 4to, Vol. VIII* (2), London, 1765.

## An EPISTLE to his Grace the Duke of GRAFTON, *Lord Lieutenant of* Ireland.

### [By Jonathan Smedley]

*Non Domus & Fundus*——Hor.

IT was my Lord, the dextrous Shift,
Of t'other *Jonathan*, viz. *Swift*,
But now, St. *Patrick*'s sawcy Dean,
With Silver Verge, and Surplice clean,
Of *Oxford*, or of *Ormond*'s Grace,
In looser Rhyme, to beg a Place:
A Place he got, yclyp'd a *Stall*,
And eke a Thousand Pounds withal;
And, were he a less *witty Writer*,
He might, as well, have got a *Mitre*.                    10

Thus I, *The Jonathan of Clogher*,
In humble Lays, my Thanks to offer,
Approach your Grace, with grateful Heart;
My Thanks and Verse both void of Art:
Content with what your Bounty gave;
No larger Income do I crave:
Rejoicing, that, in *better Times*,
GRAFTON requires my *Loyal Rhimes*.
Proud! while my *Patron* is *Polite*,
*I likewise to the Patriot write:*                          20
Proud! that, at once, I can commend,
*King George*'s and the *Muse*'s Friend.
Endear'd to *Britain*: And to *Thee*
(Disjoin'd, *Hibernia*, by the Sea)
Endear'd by twice three anxious Years;
Endear'd by Guardian Toils and Cares!

But where shall *SMEDLEY* make his Nest,
And lay his wandring Head to Rest?
Where shall he find a decent House,
To treat his Friends, and chear his Spouse?                30
Oh! *Tack*, my Lord, some pretty Cure,
In wholesome Soil, and Æther pure.
The Garden stor'd with artless Flowers,

In every Angle, shady Bowers.
No gay Parterre, with costly Green,
Within the ambient Hedge be seen;
Let Nature, freely, take her Course,
Nor fear from me ungrateful Force:
No Shears shall check her sprouting Vigour:
Nor shape the Yews to antick Figure.                           40
A limpid Brook shall *Trouts* supply
In *May*, to take the mimick Fly;
Round a small Orchard may it run,
Whose *Apples* redden to the Sun:
Let all be snug and warm and neat,
For *Fifty-turn'd*, a fit Retreat:
A little *Euston* may it be:
*Euston* I'll carve on every Tree:
But then, to keep it in Repair,
My Lord——*Twice Fifty Pounds a Year*                           50
Will barely do: But if your Grace      ⎫
Could make them *Hundreds*—Charming Place! ⎬
Thou then would'st shew another Face.  ⎭

　　*Clogher!* far North, my Lord, it lies,
Beneath *High Hills*, and *Angry Skies*.
One shivers with the *Artick* Wind,
One hears the *Polar Axis* grind.
Good *John*, indeed, with Beef and Claret,
Makes the Place warm, that one may bear it;
He has a Purse to keep a Table,                                60
And eke a Soul as hospitable:
My Heart is good, but Assets fail
To fight with Storms of Snow and Hail;
Besides, the Country's thin of People,
Who seldom meet, but at the Steeple:
The *Strapping Dean*, that's gone to *Down*,
Ne'er named the Thing without a Frown.
When much fatigued with Sermon-Study,
He felt his Brain grow dull and muddy,
No fit Companion could be found,                               70
To push the lazy Bottle round:
Sure then, for want of better Folks,
To pledge his *Clerk* was Orthodox.

　　Ah! how unlike to *Gerard-street*,
Where *Beaus* and *Belles*, in Parties meet;

Where gilded Chairs and Coaches throng,
And jostle, as they trowl along;
Where Tea and Coffee, hourly, flow;
And *Gape-seed* does, in Plenty, grow;
And *Griz* (no Clock more certain) cries,                    80
Exact at Seven, *Hot Mutton Pyes*:
There Lady *Luna*, in her Sphere,
Once shone, when *Paunceforth* was not near;
But now she *wains*, and as 'tis said,
Keeps sober Hours, and goes to Bed.
There——But 'tis endless to write down,
All the Amusements of the Town:
And Spouse will think herself quite undone;
To trudge to *Clogher*, from sweet *London*;
And Care we must our Wives to please,                    90
Or else—we shall be ill at Ease.

You see, my Lord, what 'tis I lack,
'Tis only some convenient TACK,
Some Parsonage House, with Garden sweet,
To be my late, my last Retreat;
A decent Church, close by its Side,
There preaching, praying, to Reside,
And, as my Time securely rolls,
*To save my own, and others Souls.*

# His Grace's ANSWER

## TO

# JONATHAN

DEAR *Smed* I read thy Brilliant Lines,
       Where Wit in all its Glory shines;
Where Compliments with all their Pride
Are by thy Numbers dignify'd.
I hope to make you yet as clean,
As that same VIZ. St. *Patrick*'s *Dean*.
I'll give thee *Surplice, Verge* and *Stall*,
And may be something else withall.

Printed from the original Broadside, Dublin, 1724.

And were you not so good a Writer
I should present you with a *Mitre*.          10
Write worse then if you can —— be wise ——
Believe me 'tis *the Way to Rise*.
Talk not of *making of thy Nest*,
*Ah never lay thy Head to Rest!*
*That Head so well by Wisdom fraught!*
*That writes without the Toil of Thought.*
While others wrack their busy Brains,
You are not in the least at Pains.
Down to your *Deanery* repair
And build *a Castle in the Air*.          20
I'm sure a Man of your fine Sense
Can do it with a Small Expence.
There your *Dear Spouse* and you together
May breath your Bellies full of *Æther*.
When *Lady Luna* is your Neighbour
She'll help your *Wife* when she's in Labour.
Well skill'd in Mid-wife Artifices;
For she her self oft *falls in Pieces*.
There you shall see a *Rary-Show*
Will make you scorn this *World below*.          30
When you behold *the milky Way*
As White as Snow, as bright as Day;
The Glitt'ring Constellations Roll,
About the grinding artick Pole;
The lovely tingling in your Ears,
Wrought by the Musick of the Spheres ——
Your Spouse shall there no longer hector
You need not fear a Curtain-Lecture.
Nor shall she think that she is *un-done*
For quitting her beloved *London*.          40
When she's exalted in the Skies,
She'll never think of *Mutton Pies*.
When you're advanc'd above Dean VIZ.
You'll never think of Goody GRIZ.
But ever ever live at Ease,
And strive, and strive, *your Wife to please*.
In her you'll center all your Joys,
*And get Ten thousand Girls and Boys.*

Ten thousand *Girls* and *Boys* you'll get
And they like *Stars* shall *Rise* and *Set*.          50
While *you and Spouse* transform'd, shall soon
Be *a New Sun*, and *a New Moon*.
Nor shall you strive your *Horns to hide*,
For then your *Horns* will be your *Pride*.


# ON DREAMS

AN

Imitation of PETRONIUS

*Somnia quæ mentes ludunt volitantibus umbris*, &c.


THOSE Dreams that on the silent Night intrude,
And with false flitting Shades our Minds delude,
*Jove* never sends us downward from the Skies,
Nor can they from infernal Mansions rise;
But all are meer Productions of the Brain,
And Fools consult Interpreters in vain.

For, when in Bed we rest our weary Limbs,
The Mind unburthen'd sports in various Whims,
The busy Head with mimick Art runs o'er
The Scenes and Actions of the Day before.          10

The drowsy Tyrant, by his Minions led,
To regal Rage devotes some Patriot's Head.
With equal Terrors, not with equal Guilt,
The Murd'rer dreams of all the Blood he spilt.

The Soldier smiling hears the Widows Cries,
And stabs the Son before the Mother's Eyes.
With like Remorse his Brother of the Trade,
The Butcher, feels the Lamb beneath his blade.

Printed from *Miscellanies. The Last Volume*, 1727, with corrections from *Poems*, 1735.

The Statesman rakes the Town to find a Plot,
And dreams of Forfeitures by Treason got.                    20
Nor less Tom-Turd-Man of true Statesman mold,
Collects the City Filth in search of Gold.

Orphans around his Bed the Lawyer sees,
And takes the Plaintiff's and Defendant's Fees.
His Fellow Pick-Purse, watching for a Job,
Fancies his Fingers in the Cully's Fob.

The kind Physician grants the Husband's Prayers,
Or gives Relief to long-expecting Heirs.
The sleeping Hangman ties the fatal Noose,
Nor unsuccessful waits for dead Mens Shoes.                    30

The grave Divine with knotty Points perplext,
As if he were awake, nods o'er his Text:
While the sly Mountebank attends his Trade,
Harangues the Rabble, and is better paid.

The hireling Senator of modern Days,
Bedaubs the guilty Great with nauseous Praise:
And *Dick* the Scavenger with equal Grace,
Flirts from his Cart the Mud in *Walpole*'s Face.

# Sent by Dr. *Delany* to Dr. *Swift*, in order to be admitted to speak to him

### Written about the YEAR 1724

DEAR Sir, I think 'tis doubly hard
    Your Ears and Doors shou'd both be barr'd.
Can any thing be more unkind?
Must I not see, 'cause you are blind?
Methinks, a Friend at Night shou'd cheer you,
A Friend that loves to see and hear you:

Printed from *Poems*, 1735.

Why am I robb'd of that Delight?
When you can be no Loser by't.
Nay, when 'tis plain, for what is plainer?
That, if you heard you'd be no Gainer.        10
For sure you are not yet to learn,
That Hearing is not your Concern.
Then be your Doors no longer barr'd,
Your Business, Sir, is to be heard.


# The ANSWER

THE Wise pretend to make it clear,
'Tis no great Loss to lose an Ear;
Why are we then so fond of two?
When by Experience one will do.

'TIS true, say they, cut off the Head,
And there's an End; the Man is dead;
Because, among all human Race,
None e'er was known to have a Brace.
But confidently they maintain,
That, where we find the Members twain,        10
The Loss of one is no such Trouble,
Since t'other will in Strength be double;
The Limb surviving, you may swear,
Becomes his Brother's lawful Heir:
Thus, for a Tryal, let me beg of
Your Rev'rence, but to cut one Leg off,
And you shall find by this Device,
The t'other will be stronger twice;
For, ev'ry Day you shall be gaining
New Vigour to the Leg remaining.        20
So, when an Eye hath lost it's Brother,
You see the better with the other:
Cut off your Hand, and you may do
With t'other Hand the Work of two:
Because, the Soul her Power contracts,
And on the Brother Limb *re-acts*.

But, yet the Point is not so clear in
Another Case; the Sense of Hearing:
For tho' the Place of either Ear,
Be distant as one Head can bear;                    30
Yet *Galen* most acutely shews you,
(Consult his Book *de Partium usu*)
That from each Ear, as he observes,
There creeps two Auditory Nerves,
(Not to be seen without a Glass)
Which near the *Os Petrosum* pass;
Thence to the Neck; and moving thorow there;
One goes to this, and one to t'other Ear.
Which made my Grand-Dame always stuff-her-Ears,
Both Right and Left, as Fellow-sufferers.           40
You see my Learning; but to shorten it,
When my Left Ear was deaf a Fortnight,
To t'other Ear I felt it coming on,
And thus I solve this hard Phænomenon.

'Tis true, a Glass will bring supplies
To weak, or old, or clouded Eyes.
Your Arms, tho' both your Eyes were lost,
Would guard your Nose against a Post.
Without your Legs, two Legs of Wood
Are stronger, and almost as good.                   50
And, as for Hands, there have been those,
Who, wanting both, have us'd their Toes.
But no Contrivance yet appears,
To furnish artificial Ears.

# POLITICAL POEMS
## RELATING TO
## WOOD'S HALFPENCE
### (pp. 270–87)

# A SERIOUS POEM
## UPON
## WILLIAM WOOD

*Brasier, Tinker, Hard-Ware-Man, Coiner,*
*Counterfeiter, Founder* and *Esquire*

WHEN Foes are o'ercome, we preserve them from
    Slaughter,
To be *Hewers* of WOOD and *Drawers* of *Water*,
Now, although to *Draw Water* is not very good,
Yet we all should Rejoyce to be *Hewers* of WOOD.
I own it hath often provok'd me to Mutter,
That, a Rogue so *Obscure* should make such a Clutter,
But antient *Philosophers* wisely Remark,
That old rotten WOOD will *Shine* in the *Dark*.
The *Heathens*, we Read, had *Gods* made of WOOD,
Who could do them no Harm, if they did them no Good:   10
But this Idol WOOD may do us great Evil,
Their Gods were of WOOD, but our WOOD is the DEVIL:
To cut down fine WOOD is a very bad Thing,
And yet we all know much *Gold* it will bring,
Then if cutting down WOOD brings Money good Store,
Our Money to keep, let us *Cut down ONE more.*

   Now hear an old Tale. There antiently stood
(I forget in what Church) an Image of *Wood*;

*Printed from the original Half-sheet, Dublin [1724].*

Concerning this Image there went a Prediction,
It would Burn a whole *Forest*; nor was it a Fiction; 20
'Twas cut into Faggots, and put to the Flame,
To burn an old Fryer, one *Forrest* by Name.
My Tale is a wise one if well understood,
Find you but the *Fryer*, and I'll find the WOOD.

I hear among Scholars there is a great Doubt
From what Kind of Tree this WOOD was Hewn out.
*Teague* made a good PUN by a *Brogue* in his Speech,
And said: *By my Shoul he's the Son of a* BEECH:
Some call him a *Thorn*, the Curse of a Nation,
As *Thorns* were design'd to be from the Creation. 30
Some think him cut out from the Poisonous *Yew*,
Beneath whose ill Shade no Plant ever grew.
Some say he's a *Birch*, a Thought very odd,
For none but a *Dunce* would come under his *Rod*.
But I'll tell you the Secret, and pray do not Blab,
He is an old *Stump* cut out of a *Crab*,
And *England* has put this *Crab* to hard Use,
To Cudgel our Bones, and for Drink give us *Verjuice*;
And therefore his *Witnesses* justly may boast
That none are more properly Knights of the POST. 40

But here Mr. *Wood* complains that we Mock,
Though he may be a *Block*-head, he is no real *Block*.
He can Eat, Drink and Sleep; now and then for a Friend
He'll not be too proud an old Kettle to mend;
He can *Lye* like a *Courtier*, and think it no Scorn,
When *Gold*'s to be got, to FORSWEAR and SUBORN.
He can RAP his own RAPs, and has the true Sapience
To turn a *Good* Penny to Twenty *Bad* Ha'pence.
Then in Spight of your Sophistry, Honest WILL. WOOD
Is a Man of this World all true Flesh and Blood; 50
So you are but in Jest, and you will not I hope
*Un-man* the poor Knave for sake of a *Trope*.
'Tis a *Metaphor* known to ev'ry plain Thinker.
Just as when we say, *the Devil's a Tinker*
Which cannot in Literal Sense be made Good,
Unless by the *Devil* we mean Mr. WOOD.

But some will object, that the *Devil* oft spoke
In *Heathenish* Times from the *Trunk* of an *Oak*:
And, since we must grant, there never were known
More *Heathenish* Times than those of our own;        60
Perhaps you will say, 'tis the *Devil* that puts
The Words in wood's Mouth, or speaks from his Guts:
And then your old Argument still will return:
Howe'er let us try him and see how he'll burn.
You'll pardon me Sir, your Cunning I smoak,
But wood I assure you is no *Heart of* oak;
And instead of the *Devil*, this Son of Perdition
Hath joyn'd with himself two hags in Commission:

.  I ne'er could endure my Talent to smother,
I told you one Tale, I will tell you another.        70
A *Joyner* to fasten a *Saint* in a *Nitch*,
Bor'd a large *Augre-hole* in the Image's Breech;
But finding the *Statue* to make no Complaint,
He would ne'er be convinc'd it was a *True Saint*:
When the *True* wood arrives, as he soon will no doubt,
(For that's but a Sham wood they carry about)
What *Stuff* he is made on you quickly may find,
If you make the same Tryal, and *Bore* him *Behind*;
I'll hold you a Groat, when you *wimble* his Bumm,
He'll Bellow as loud as the *Dee'l in a Drum*:        80
From me I declare you shall have no Denial,
And there can be no Harm in making a Tryal;
And when to the Joy of your Hearts he has Roar'd,
You may shew him about for a new *Groaning Board*.

Now ask me a Question. How came it to pass
Wood got so much Copper? He got it by brass;
This brass was a Dragon (observe what I tell ye)
This *Dragon* had gotten two *Sows* in it's Belly;
I know you will say, this is all *Heathen Greek*;
I own it, and therefore I leave you to seek.        90

I often have seen two Plays very Good,
Call'd, love in a tub, and love in a wood.

These Comedies twain Friend *Wood* will contrive
On the *Scene* of this *Land* very soon to *revive.*
First, LOVE IN A TUB: 'Squire *Wood* has in Store
Strong *Tubs* for his *Raps,* Two thousand and more;
These *Raps* he will honestly dig out with Shovels,
And sell them for Gold, or he can't shew his Love else,
WOOD swears he will do it for *Ireland*'s Good,
Then can you deny it is *Love in a* WOOD?     100
However, if Criticks find Fault with the Phrase,
I hope you will own it is *Love in a Maze*;
For when you express a Friend's Love we are willing,
We never say more than, your *Love is a Million*;
But with honest WOOD's *Love* there is no contending,
'Tis Fifty round *Millions* of *Love,* and a *Mending.*
Then in his First *Love* why should he be crost?
I hope he will find that *no Love is lost.*

    Hear one Story more and then I will stop.
I dream't WOOD was told he should Dye by a *Drop*     110
So methought, he resolv'd no Liquor to taste,
For fear the *First Drop* might as well be his *Last*:
But *Dreams* are like *Oracles,* hard to explain 'em,
For it prov'd that he dy'd of a DROP at *Killmainham*:
I wak'd with Delight, and not without Hope,
Very soon to see WOOD *Drop* down from *a Rope.*
How he and how we at each other should grin!
'Tis Kindness to hold a Friend up by the Chin;
But soft says the Herald, I cannot agree;
For *Metal on Metal is false Heraldry*:     120
Why that may be true, yet WOOD upon WOOD,
I'll maintain with my Life, is *Heraldry* Good.

114. *Killmainham.* A Gallows in the County of Dublin, near the City [fn. 1763].

## *An* EPIGRAM

### ON

### *WOODS*'s BRASS-MONEY

CART'RET was welcom'd to the Shore
First with the brazen Cannons Roar.
To meet him next, the Soldier comes,
With brazen Trumps and brazen Drums.
Approaching near the Town, he hears
The brazen Bells salute his Ears:
But when *Wood*'s Brass began to sound,
Guns, Trumpets, Drums, and Bells were drown'd.

Printed from *Works, Vol. VIII*, Dublin, 1746.

## To his Grace the Arch-Bishop of DUBLIN,

### A POEM

*Serus in cœlum redeas diuq;*
*Lætus intersis Populo*——Hor.

GREAT, GOOD and JUST was once apply'd
To *One* who for his Country died,
To *One* who lives in its Defence,
We speak it in a Happier Sense.
O may the *Fates* thy Life prolong!
Our Country then can dread no Wrong:
In thy great Care we place our Trust,
Because thou'rt GREAT, and GOOD, and JUST.
Thy *Breast unshaken* can oppose
Our Private and our *Publick Foes*,                10
The Latent Wiles, and *Tricks of State*,
Your *Wisdom* can with Ease Defeat.

Printed from the Dublin Broadside.

When Pow'r in all its Pomp appears,
It falls before thy Rev'rend Years,
And willingly resigns its Place
To something Nobler in thy Face.
When once the fierce pursuing *Gaul*
Had drawn his Sword for *Marius'* Fall,
The Godlike Hero with one frown
Struck all his Rage and Malice down;                20
Then how can we dread *William Wood*,
If by *thy Presence* he's withstood?
Where Wisdom stands to keep the Field,
In Vain he brings his *Brazen Shield*.
Tho' like the *Cybel's* Priest he comes,
With furious Din of *Brazen Drums*,
The Force of thy superior Voice
Shall strike him dumb, and quell their Noise.


An Excellent

# NEW SONG

Upon His GRACE

## Our good Lord Archbishop of

# DUBLIN

By honest JO. one of HIS GRACE's Farmers in FINGAL
*To the Tune of . . .*

I Sing not of the *Draper's* Praise, nor yet of *William Wood*;
But I sing of a *Famous Lord*, who seeks his *Country's* Good.
Lord WILLIAM's Grace of *Dublin* Town, 'tis he that first appears,
Whose Wisdom and whose Piety, do far exceed his Years.
In ev'ry *Council* and *Debate* he stands for what is *Right*;
And still the *Truth* he will *Maintain*, whate'er he loses by't.

Printed from the original Broadside, Dublin, 1724.

And though some think him in the Wrong, yet still there comes
    a Season
When ev'ry one turns round about, and owns His Grace had
    Reason.
His *Firmness* to the *publick Good*, as one that knows it Swore,
Has lost His Grace for Ten Years past Ten thousand Pounds
    and more:           10
Then come the Poor and strip him so, they leave him not a Cross,
For he regards Ten thousand Pounds no more than *Woods*'s
    Dross.
To beg his Favour is the Way new Favours still to win,
He makes no more to give ten Pounds than I to give a Pin.
Why, there's my Landlord now the *'Squire*, who all in Money
    wallows,
He would not give a Groat to save his Father from the Gallows.
A *Bishop* says the noble *'Squire*, I hate the very Name,
To have two thousand Pounds a Year, O 'tis a burning Shame!
Two thousand Pounds a Year, Good Lord! and I to have but
    Five.
And under him no Tenant yet was ever known to thrive.    20
Now from his Lordship's Grace I hold a little Piece of Ground,
And all the Rent I pay is scarce five Shillings in the Pound.
Then Master *Steward* takes my Rent, and tells me, honest *Jo*.
Come, you must take a Cup of Sack or two before you go.
He bids me then to hold my Tongue, and up the Money locks,
For fear my Lord should send it all into the poor Man's Box.
And once I was so bold to beg that I might see His Grace,
Good Lord! I wondred how I dar'd to look him in the Face.
Then down I went upon my Knees, his Blessing to obtain,
He gave it me, and ever since I find I thrive amain.    30
Then said my Lord, I'm very glad to see thee honest Friend,
I know the Times are something hard, but hope they soon will
    mend,
Pray never press your self for Rent, but pay me when you can,
I find you bear a good Report, and are an honest Man.
Then said his Lordship with a Smile, I must have LAWFUL *Cash*,
I hope you will not pay my Rent in that same *Woods*'s Trash.
God Bless your Grace I then reply'd, I'd see him hanging
    high'r,
Before I'd touch his filthy Dross, than is *Clandalkin* Spire.

To every Farmer twice a Week all round about the *Yoke*,
Our *Parsons* Read the *Draper*'s Books, and make us honest
   *Foke*.                                             40
And then I went to pay the *'Squire* and in the Way I found,
His *Baily* Driving all my Cows into the Parish Pound.
Why Sirrah said the Noble *'Squire*, how dare you see my Face,
Your Rent is due almost a Week beside the Days of Grace.
And Yet the Land I from him hold is set so on the Rack,
That only for the *Bishop*'s Lease 'twould quickly break my
   Back.
   Then God Preserve his Lordship's Grace, and make him live
     as long
   As did *Methusalem* of old, and so I end my SONG.


# PROMETHEUS,

## A POEM

WHEN first the *'Squire*, and *Tinker Wood*
      Gravely consulting *Ireland*'s Good,
Together mingl'd in a Mass
Smith's *Dust*, and *Copper*, *Lead* and *Brass*,
The Mixture thus by Chymick Art,
United close in ev'ry Part.
In Fillets roll'd, or cut in Pieces,
Appear'd like one continu'd Spec'es,
And by the forming Engine struck,
On all the same IMPRESSION stuck.          10

   So to confound, this *hated Coin*
All *Parties* and *Religions* joyn;
*Whigs*, *Tories*, *Trimmers*, *Hannoverians*,
*Quakers*, *Conformists*, *Presbyterians*,
*Scotch*, *Irish*, *English*, *French* unite
With *equal Int'rest*, *equal Spight*,

Printed from the Broadside, Dublin, 1724.

Together mingled in a Lump,
Do all in *One Opinion* jump;
And ev'ry one begins to find,
The same IMPRESSION on his Mind;        20
A strange Event! whom *Gold* incites,
To Blood and Quarrels, *Brass* unites:
So Goldsmiths say, the coursest Stuff,
Will serve for *Sodder* well enuff.
So, by the *Kettles* loud Allarm,
The *Bees* are gather'd to a *Swarm*:
So by the *Brazen* Trumpets Bluster,
Troops of all Tongues and Nations Muster:
And so the *Harp* of *Ireland* brings,
Whole Crouds about its *Brazen* Strings.        30

There is a *Chain* let down from *Jove*,
But fasten'd to his Throne above;
So strong, that from the lower End,
They say, all human Things depend:
This *Chain*, as Antient Poets hold,
When *Jove* was Young, was made of *Gold*.
*Prometheus* once this *Chain* purloin'd,
Dissolv'd, and into *Money* Coin'd;
Then whips me on a *Chain* of *Brass*,
(*Venus* was Brib'd to let it pass.)        40

Now while this *Brazen Chain* prevail'd,
*Jove* saw that all *Devotion* fail'd;
No *Temple*, to his *Godship* rais'd,
No *Sacrifice* on *Altars* blaz'd;
In short such *dire Confusions* follow'd,
*Earth* must have been in *Chaos* swallow'd.
*Jove* stood amaz'd, but looking round,
With much ado, the *Cheat* he found;
'Twas plain he cou'd no longer hold
The *World* in any *Chain* but *Gold*;        50
And to the *God of Wealth* his *Brother*,
Sent *Mercury* to get another.

40. *Venus.* A great Lady was reported to have been bribed by Wood [fn. 1735].

> *Prometheus* on a Rock is laid,
>
> Ty'd with the *Chain* himself had made;
>
> On Icy *Caucasus* to shiver,
>
> While *Vultures* eat his growing Liver:

    Ye Pow'rs of *Grub-street* make me able,
Discreetly to apply this *Fable.*
Say, who is to be understood,
By that old Thief *Prometheus?* WOOD         60
For *Jove*, it is not hard to guess him,
I mean *His Majesty, God bless him.*
This *Thief* and *Black-Smith* was so bold,
He strove to steal that *Chain* of *Gold*,
Which links the *Subject* to the *King*:
And change it for a *Brazen String.*
But sure if nothing else must pass,
Between the *King* and US but *Brass,*
Altho' the *Chain* will never crack,
Yet *Our Devotion* may *Grow Slack.*         70

    But *Jove* will soon convert I hope,
This *Brazen Chain* into a *Rope*;
With which *Prometheus* shall be ty'd,
And high in Air for ever ride;
Where, if we find his *Liver* grows,
For want of *Vultures*, we have *Crows.*

# *WHITSHED*'s MOTTO ON HIS COACH

*Libertas & natale Solum*

Liberty and my native Country

Written in the Year 1724

*LIBERTAS & natale Solum*;
Fine Words; I wonder where you stole 'um.
Could nothing but thy chief Reproach,
Serve for a Motto on thy Coach?
But, let me now the Words translate:
*Natale Solum*: My Estate:
My dear Estate, how well I love it;
My Tenants, if you doubt, will prove it:
They swear I am so kind and good,
I hug them till I squeeze their Blood.        10


*LIBERTAS* bears a large Import;
First; how to swagger in a Court;
And, secondly, to shew my Fury
Against an uncomplying Jury:
And, Thirdly; 'tis a new Invention
To favour *Wood* and keep my Pension:
And, Fourthly; 'tis to play an odd Trick,
Get the Great Seal, and turn out *Brod'rick*.
And, Fifthly; you know whom I mean,
To humble that vexatious Dean.        20
And, Sixthly; for my Soul, to barter it
For Fifty Times its Worth, to *Carteret*.

Printed from *Poems*, 1735.

*Title. WHITSHED*'s. That noted Chief Justice, who twice prosecuted the Drapier, and dissolved the Grand Jury for not finding the Bill against him.

Now, since your Motto thus you construe,
I must confess you've spoken once true.
*Libertas & natale Solum*;
You had good Reason when you stole 'um.


# Verses on the upright *Judge, who condemned the* Drapier's *Printer*

## Written in the Year 1724

THE Church I hate, and have good Reason:
For, there my Grandsire cut his Weazon:
He cut his Weazon at the Altar;
I keep my Gullet for the Halter.


## On the same

IN Church your Grandsire cut his Throat;
To do the Jobb too long he tarry'd,
He should have had my hearty Vote,
 To cut his Throat before he marry'd.


## On the same

### *The Judge speaks*

I'M not the Grandson of that Ass *Quin*;
Nor can you prove it, Mr. *Pasquin*.
My Grand-dame had Gallants by Twenties,
And bore my Mother by a Prentice.
This, when my Grandsire knew; they tell us he,
In *Christ-Church* cut his Throat for Jealousy.
And, since the Alderman was mad you say,
Then, I must be so too, *ex traduce*.

Printed from *Poems*, 1735.

[III] 1. *Quin*. An Alderman.

# *HORACE*

## BOOK I ODE XIV

*O navis, referent,* &c.

Paraphrased and inscribed to *Ireland*

## The INSCRIPTION

*Poor floating Isle, tost on ill Fortune's Waves,*
*Ordain'd by* Fate *to be the Land of Slaves:*
*Shall moving* Delos *now deep-rooted stand,*
*Thou, fixt of old, be now the moving Land?*
*Altho' the Metaphor be worn and stale*
*Betwixt a State, and Vessel under Sail;*
*Let me suppose thee for a Ship a-while,*
*And thus address thee in the Sailor Stile.*

UNHAPPY Ship, thou art return'd in Vain:
    New Waves shall drive thee to the Deep again.          10
Look to thy Self, and be no more the Sport
Of giddy Winds, but make some friendly Port.
Lost are thy Oars that us'd thy Course to guide,
Like faithful Counsellors on either Side.
Thy Mast, which like some aged Patriot stood
The single Pillar for his Country's Good,
To lead thee, as a Staff directs the Blind,
Behold, it cracks by yon rough *Eastern* Wind.
Your Cable's burst, and you must quickly feel
The Waves impetuous entring at your Keel.               20
Thus, Commonwealths receive a foreign Yoke,
When the strong Cords of Union once are Broke.
Torn by a sudden Tempest is thy Sail,
Expanded to invite a milder Gale.
    As when some Writer in a public Cause,
His Pen to save a sinking Nation draws,

Printed from first ed., [Dublin] 1730.

While all is Calm, his Arguments prevail,
The People's Voice expand[s] his Paper Sail;
'Till Pow'r, discharging all her stormy Bags,
Flutters the feeble Pamphlet into Rags.                    30
The Nation scar'd, the Author doom'd to Death,
Who fondly put his Trust in pop'lar Breath.

   A larger Sacrifice in Vain you vow;
There's not a Pow'r above will help you now:
A Nation thus, who oft Heav'ns Call neglects,
In Vain from injur'd Heav'n Relief expects.
'Twill not avail, when thy strong Sides are broke,
That thy Descent is from the *British* Oak:
Or when your Name and Family you boast,
From Fleets triumphant o'er the *Gallick* Coast.          40
Such was *Ierne*'s Claim, as just as thine,
Her Sons descended from the *British* Line;
Her matchless Sons; whose Valour still remains
On *French* Records for twenty long Campains;
Yet from an Empress, now a Captive grown,
She saved *Britannia*'s Right, and lost her own.

   In Ships decay'd no Mariner confides,
Lur'd by the gilded Stern, and painted Sides.
So, at a Ball, unthinking Fools delight
In the gay Trappings of a Birth-Day Night:                50
They on the Gold Brocades and Satins rav'd,
And quite forgot their Country was enslav'd.

   Dear Vessel, still be to thy Steerage just,
Nor, change thy Course with ev'ry sudden Gust:
Like supple Patriots of the modern Sort,
Who turn with ev'ry Gale that blows from Court.

   Weary and Sea-sick when in thee confin'd,
Now, for thy Safety Cares distract my Mind,
As those who long have stood the Storms of State,
Retire, yet still bemoan their Country's Fate.            60
Beware, and when you hear the Surges roar,
Avoid the Rocks on *Britain*'s angry Shore:
They lye, alas, too easy to be found,
For thee alone they lye the Island round.

# *WOOD*, an Insect

## Written in the Year 1725

BY long Observation I have understood,
   That three little Vermin are kin to *Will. Wood*:
The first is an Insect they call a *Wood*-Louse,
That folds up itself in itself for a House:
As round as a Ball, without Head without Tail,
Inclos'd *Cap-a-pee* in a strong Coat of Mail.
And thus *William Wood* to my Fancy appears
In Fillets of Brass roll'd up to his Ears:
And, over these Fillets he wisely has thrown,
To keep out of Danger, a Doublet of Stone.          10

   THE Louse of the *Wood* for a Med'cine is us'd,
Or swallow'd alive, or skilfully bruis'd.
And, let but our Mother *Hibernia* contrive
To swallow *Will. Wood* either bruis'd or alive.
She need be no more with the *Jaundice* possess't;
Or sick of *Obstructions*, and *Pains in her Chest*.

   THE Third is an Insect we call a *Wood*-Worm,
That lies in old *Wood* like a Hare in her Form;
With Teeth or with Claws it will bite or will scratch,
And Chambermaids christen this Worm a Death-Watch:   20
Because like a Watch it always cries *Click*:
Then Woe be to those in the House who are sick:
For, as sure as a Gun they will give up the Ghost
If the Maggot cries *Click* when it scratches the Post.
But a Kettle of scalding hot Water injected,
Infallibly cures the Timber affected;
The Omen is broke, the Danger is over;
The Maggot will dye, and the Sick will recover.
Such a Worm was *Will. Wood* when he scratcht at the Door
Of a governing Statesman, or favorite Whore:          30

Printed from *Poems*, 1735.

10. *a Doublet of Stone.* He was in Jayl for Debt.

The Death of our Nation it seem'd to foretell,
And the Sound of his Brass we took for our Knell.
But now, since the *Drapier* hath heartilly maul'd him,
I think the best Thing we can do is to scald him.
For which Operation there's nothing more proper
Than the Liquor he deals in, his own melted Copper;
Unless, like the *Dutch*, you rather would boyl
This Coyner of *Raps* in a Cauldron of Oyl.
Then chuse which you please, and let each bring a Faggot,
For our Fear's at an End with the Death of the Maggot.    40

# ON

# *WOOD* the Iron-monger

## Written in the Year 1725

SALMONEUS, as the *Grecian* Tale is,
Was a mad Copper-Smith of *Elis*:
Up at his Forge by Morning-peep,
No Creature in the Lane could sleep.
Among a Crew of royst'ring Fellows
Would sit whole Ev'nings at the Ale-house:
His Wife and Children wanted Bread,
While he went always drunk to Bed.
This vap'ring Scab must needs devise
To ape the Thunder of the Skies;          10
With *Brass* two fiery Steeds he shod,
To make a Clatt'ring as they trod.
Of polish't *Brass*, his flaming Car,
Like Light'ning dazzled from a-far:
And up he mounts into the Box,
And HE must thunder, with a Pox.
Then, furious he begins his March;
Drives rattling o'er a brazen Arch:
With Squibs and Crackers arm'd, to throw
Among the trembling Croud below.          20

Printed from *Poems*, 1735.

38. *Raps*. A Cant Word in Ireland for a counterfeit Half-penny.

All ran to Pray'rs, both Priests and Laity,
To pacify this angry Deity;
When *Jove*, in pity to the Town,
With real Thunder knock't him down.
Then what a huge Delight were all in,
To see the wicked Varlet sprawling;
They search't his Pockets on the Place,
And found his Copper all was base;
They laught at such an *Irish* Blunder,
To take the Noise of Brass for Thunder!        30

    THE Moral of this Tale is proper,
Apply'd to *Wood*'s adult'rate Copper;
Which, as he scatter'd, we like Dolts,
Mistook at first for Thunder-Bolts;
Before the *Drapier* shot a Letter,
(Nor *Jove* himself could do it better)
Which lighting on th' Impostor's Crown,
Like real Thunder knock't him down.


# A SIMILE

## ON

## Our Want of Silver, and the only Way to remedy it

### Written in the Year 1725

AS when of old, some Sorc'ress threw
  O'er the Moon's Face a sable Hue,
To drive unseen her magick Chair,
At Midnight, through the dark'ned Air;
Wise People, who believ'd with Reason
That this Eclipse was out of Season,
Affirm'd the Moon was sick, and fell
To cure her by a Counter-spell:

Printed from *Poems*, 1735.

Ten Thousand Cymbals now begin
To rend the Skies with brazen Din;
The Cymbals rattling Sounds dispell
The Cloud, and drive the Hag to Hell:
The Moon, deliver'd from her Pain,
Displays her *Silver* Face again.
(Note here, that in the Chymick Style,
The Moon is *Silver* all this while.)

So, (if my Simile you minded,
Which, I confess, is too long winded)
When late a Feminine Magician,
Join'd with a *brazen* Politician,          20
Expos'd, to blind the Nation's Eyes,
A Parchment of prodigious Size;
Conceal'd behind that ample Screen,
There was no Silver to be seen.
But, to this Parchment let the *Draper*
Oppose his Counter-Charm of Paper,
And ring *Wood*'s Copper in our Ears
So loud, till all the Nation hears;
That Sound will make the Parchment shrivel,
And drive the Conj'rers to the Devil:       30
And when the Sky is grown serene,
Our Silver will appear again.

# VERSES LEFT IN A WINDOW
## OF DUBLIN CASTLE

M Y very good Lord, it's a very hard task
  To wait so long and have nothing to ask.

Carteret's reply, written by Sir William Fownes:

M Y very good Dean, there's few come here
  But have something to ask or something to fear.

Printed from *H.M.C.; Various Collections*, viii. 386 [1725?].

22. *A Parchment.* A Patent to W. Wood, for coining Half-pence.

# A SATYR

[by Dean Smedley]

*Canit, ante Victoriam Triumphum*

MOST Reverend *Dean*, pray cease to Write;
Nor longer dwell on Things so Trite;
Teize not unto thy Feeble Aid,
Each *Grace* and *Heliconian* Maid;
*Apollo*'s tir'd, *Minerva* Swears,
She never more will hear thy Prayers;
And, to speak Truth, I think it odd is,
To Nauseate, thus, The God and Goddess;
To *Ditto* it, daily, through the Town,
And Write, and Write our Spirits down.                    10

 *Great Sir*, its own'd, you well behav'd;
Your Skin is whole, your Country's sav'd;
The Grand Dispute! you've made an End on't:
*Our State and Church are Independent.*
The Weather's good, and *Phœbus* Smiles,
On This, just, as on other Isles;
In Gold we wallow; But, nor Brass,
Thank God, or Silver current pass;
Priests bent, and People are, on Gains,
No Politicks disturb our Brains.                    20
No Popish Plot, nor Wars Alarms
Our Warlike Genius wakes to Arms.
Long since, the *Muses* Nine were seen,
To take their leave of *College-Green*;
The *Graces* too, are either Dead,
Or, Opiated, are gone to Bed,
And (unless Fame does much bely 'em,)
Dos'd, sleeps *Præpos. Cum sociis*, by 'em;
No Midnight Hours consume the Taper;
Cheaply are sold Pen, Ink and Paper.                    30
Science and Arts are at a Stand;
Were't not for *Helsham*'s *Slight of Hand*,

Printed from the original Broadside, [Dublin] 1725.

For *Sherry*'s Quibles, and thy Quill,
The Dusty Press wou'd stand, quite, still;
A Stop to Literature be put,
And the *Musæum*' Gates be shut:
And, as it happen'd, once at *Paris*,
(Not fetch'd, the Simile, too far is,)
With Milk, the Maids, so *jeune et Tendre*,
Wou'd cry about, *Latin A vendre*.                    40

But pray, *Great Sir*, (our Isle's *Apollo*,)
From what dull Logic, does it follow,
That, 'cause, in Writing you have Skill,
Can joke off Hand, have Wit at Will,
That *a whole People* you must cully,
And feed with nought but *Chapon Bouilli*:
And make us all for Idiots pass
With Foreign Nations: *Wood and Brass*
Being all the Subjects, that you write on,
And squander Wit, and vent your Spite on:            50
Unless that, now and then, you deign
*To praise your self*, in humble Strain.

Stop then thy Hand, my dear *Dean Bluff*;
Believe me Sir, you've done enuff:
Ay, and much more, a deal, than any
Poet before; wrote against Money.

Then let us chaw, no more, your *Crambe*;
No such disgustful Thing there can be;
*Thy Saint* ordain'd not such Lent-Diet:
His Broad-fac'd Mob's Mouth's shut and quiet:        60
*Snarlerus* does, no longer press
In fervent Pray'r, for thy Success:
No longer frown, no longer flatter;
The Saint, again, is turn'd The Satyr.
Ev'n *Præcox*, who did, once, abhor thee,
Has ceas'd, at length, to stutter for thee.
And I must say (what e'er be ment)
Thy Works are no great Complement,
For Learned *Carteret* to lay before him,
*Et spes et Ratio Studiorum*.                          70
Nor do I see the wondrous Glory,
You're like to get, by all this Story;
You Print, just as you Preach and Pray,
No mortal ever yet said, *Nay*.

You write, a while; and then write on;
*Sole Arbiter of Pro & Con.*
No Knight attempting to oppose,
*The Olive Dean and Black-guard Foes.*
And you'll be, fully, answer'd, when,
For want of *Brass*, your *Huzza-Men*,                        80
Find *Butter-Milk* nor Bought, nor sold here,
Which happen may, e're, you're much Older.
                    *And so* ADIEU.


# A LETTER

## FROM

### Dean Swift to Dean Smedley

*Quid de quoque Viro, cui dicas sepe caveto*

DEAR Dean, if e're again you Write,
    Beware of Subjects you call *Trite*,
For *Satyr* now's so common grown
That ev'ry S——th, and Type in Town
Have teiz'd, by calling to their Aid
The *Graces* and the other *Maid*;
That, Faith, I think, there scarce is Room
For you or I to crave a *Boon*;
But, Yet, you'll find by what will follow,
That I'm Befriended by *APPOLLO*,                        10
And that by all I e're did hear
*Minerva* ne'er an Oath did Swear
Unless by you she was Entreated
When first of *Griz*, you *Grafton* reated
*But as to* DITTO'T *thro the Town,*
*You never did, for 'twould not down.*
    My *Country's* sav'd, as you have shown,
And *Skin's* yet whole, I needs must own,
But if by Chance I should deny it
I'm sure Old *Jour*—— you'd not stand by it;                        20
And if you should, we'd ne'er have end on't,
Both Church and State, being still dependent.

Printed from the original Broadside, [Dublin] 1725.

The Weather's Fair, nay, that is true,
But what is it to me or you?
Or if 'tis true, Great *Phabus* smiles
On this, as upon other Isles,
I know no Reason at this Time
We should them Quote, unless for Rhime.
In Gold, Perhaps, my Friend you Wallow
And W[hitshe]d's ditto Pills do Swallow,                    30
Being possitive there is no P[rie]st
So bent on Gains, Ju—ro by C—est
As you Dr. Smedley are, being sure
The Coyn's Currant and Mettal Pure.
If Wood's Coin should 'mongst Us pass
Tho' now I'm poor I them might pass
As well as you, for a *Midas*:
Then as to War's Alarms I pray
What is't that you or I've to say,
(Who ought for Peace and Plenty Pray.)                    40
Science and Art you say at stand are,
How that can be, when you at hand are,
I can't Conjecture, for Dr. Dean
You hate to see ought that seems Clean
Since *Cindercola*, first you Courted
And with the youthful Damsel sported.
*Helsham* does truly Wit command
And surely Writes with slight of Hand
For *Sherry*'s Quibbles, and thy Skill
They are as once, and *Idem* still.                    50
Since I'm *Apollo* stil'd by you,
When e're I 'gin, you should pursue
And boldly Force the winged Quill
Unto the utmost Bounds of Skill,
And never turn upon thy Master
Who sav'd thee from a great Disaster.
What's meant by *Chapoon* I can't guess
And making — some for Ideots pass
Unless i'th' Answer, of his Grace,
Which if right ta'en, and but good Luck-hold                    60
By the horned Sun, he sure meant Cuckold,

Not saying, lest I go too far,
That you an *Actæon* was, or are.
  Now let's no more caress thy *French*,
Nor *Cindercola*, c[h]arming Wench!
Lest my *Mobb's* Mouth, being seldom quiet
Should them Ordain for *Lenten* Diet
*Snarlerus* next, I'm sure has need
Of Prayers, that he might well succeed,
And bravely *Precox* might oppose    &#125;      70
*Cum Multis aliis* (all his Foes)    &#125;
When they're to pull him by the Nose,  &#125;
And by the Orders of his Betters
Have him confin'd in Iron Fetters;
Now you've done right, *No Knight attempting*
To oppose the Dean your-self Exempting
Because no —— But B[lac]k Gown'd Foe,
As when Time serves, you more shall know.

# *STELLA*'s BIRTH-DAY, 1725

AS when a beauteous Nymph decays
  We say, she's past her Dancing Days;
So, Poets lose their Feet by Time,
And can no longer dance in Rhyme.
Your Annual Bard had rather chose
To celebrate your Birth in Prose;
Yet, merry Folks who want by chance
A Pair to make a Country Dance,
Call the Old Housekeeper, and get her
To fill a Place, for want of better;      10
While *Sheridan* is off the hooks,
And Friend *Delany* at his Books,
That *Stella* may avoid Disgrace
Once more the Dean supplies their Place.

  Beauty and Wit, too sad a Truth,
Have always been confin'd to Youth;
The God of Wit, and Beauty's Queen,
He Twenty one, and She Fifteen:

Printed from *Miscellanies. The Last Volume*, 1727.

No Poet ever sweetly sung,
Unless he were like *Phœbus*, young;      20
Nor ever Nymph inspir'd to Rhyme,
Unless, like *Venus*, in her Prime.
At Fifty six, if this be true,
Am I a Poet fit for you?
Or at the Age of Forty three,
Are you a Subject fit for me?
Adieu bright Wit, and radiant Eyes;
You must be grave, and I be wise.
Our Fate in vain we would oppose,
But I'll be still your Friend in Prose:      30
Esteem and Friendship to express,
Will not require Poetick Dress;
And if the Muse deny her Aid
To have them *sung*, they may be *said*.

But, *Stella* say, what evil Tongue
Reports you are no longer young?
That *Time* sits with his Scythe to mow
Where erst sate *Cupid* with his Bow;
That half your Locks are turn'd to Grey;
I'll ne'er believe a Word they say.      40
'Tis true, but let it not be known,
My Eyes are somewhat dimmish grown;
For Nature, always in the Right,
To your Decays adapts my Sight,
And Wrinkles undistinguish'd pass,
For I'm asham'd to use a Glass;
And till I see them with these Eyes,
Whoever says you have them, lyes.

No Length of Time can make you quit
Honour and Virtue, Sense and Wit,      50
Thus you may still be young to me,
While I can better *hear* than *see*;
Oh, ne'er may Fortune shew her Spight,
To make me *deaf*, and mend my *Sight*.

54. Swift underlined the word '*deaf*' in his copy of the *Miscellanies*, and wrote in the margin 'now deaf 1740'.

# A
# RECEIPT
## TO
### Restore STELLA's Youth
#### Written in the Year 1724-5

THE *Scottish* Hinds too poor to house
In frosty Nights their starving Cows,
While not a Blade of Grass, or Hay,
Appears from *Michaelmas* to *May*;
Must let their Cattle range in vain
For Food, along the barren Plain;
Meager and lank with fasting grown,
And nothing left but Skin and Bone;
Expos'd to Want, and Wind, and Weather,
They just keep Life and Soul together,          10
'Till Summer Show'rs and Ev'ning Dew,
Again the verdant Glebe renew;
And as the Vegetables rise,
The famish't Cow her Want supplies;
Without an Ounce of last Year's Flesh,
Whate'er she gains is young and fresh;
Grows plump and round, and full of Mettle,
As rising from *Medea*'s Kettle;
With Youth and Beauty to enchant
*Europa*'s counterfeit Gallant.          20
    WHY, *Stella*, should you knit your Brow,
If I compare you to the Cow?
'Tis just the Case: For you have fasted
So long till all your Flesh is wasted,
And must against the warmer Days
Be sent to *Quilca* down to graze;
Where Mirth, and Exercise, and Air,
Will soon your Appetite repair.

Printed from *Poems*, 1735.

26. *Quilca*. A Friend's House [forty-] seven or eight miles from Dublin.

The Nutriment will from within
Round all your Body plump your Skin;                    30
Will agitate the lazy Flood,
And fill your Veins with sprightly Blood:
Nor Flesh nor Blood will be the same,
Nor ought of *Stella*, but the Name;
For, what was ever understood
By human Kind, but Flesh and Blood?
And if your Flesh and Blood be new,
You'll be no more your former *You*;
But for a blooming Nymph will pass,
Just Fifteen, coming Summer's Grass:                    40
Your jetty Locks with Garlands crown'd,
While all the Squires from nine Miles round,
Attended by a Brace of Curs,
With Jocky Boots, and Silver Spurs;
No less than Justices o' *Quorum*,
Their Cow-boys bearing Cloaks before 'um,
Shall leave deciding broken Pates,
To kiss your Steps at *Quilca* Gates;
But, lest you should my Skill disgrace,
Come back before you're out of Case;                    50
For if to *Michaelmas* you stay,
The new-born Flesh will melt away;
The Squires in Scorn will fly the House
For better Game, and look for Grouse:
But here, before the Frost can marr it,
We'll make it firm with Beef and Claret.


*To* Quilca, *a Country House in no very good Repair, where the supposed Author, and some of his Friends, spent a Summer, in the Year* 1725

LET me my Properties explain,
   A rotten Cabbin, dropping Rain;

Printed from *Poems*, 1735.

Chimnies with Scorn rejecting Smoak;
Stools, Tables, Chairs, and Bed-steds broke:
Here Elements have lost their Uses,
Air ripens not, nor Earth produces:
In vain we make poor *Sheelah* toil,
Fire will not roast, nor Water boil.
Thro' all the Vallies, Hills, and Plains,
The Goddess *Want* in Triumph reigns;                10
And her chief Officers of State,
*Sloth, Dirt,* and *Theft* around her wait.


# AN APOLOGY

## TO THE

# LADY CARTERET

On Her Inviting Dean SWIFT To Dinner; He
came accordingly, but, Her Ladyship being Abroad,
went away: At Her Return, She enquired for him;
and not hearing of him, sent the next Day to invite
him again: When he came, he went to make an
*APOLOGY*, for his going away, but my Lady wou'd
accept of none but in Verse.

A LADY, Wise as well Fair,
  Whose Conscience always was her care,
Thoughtful upon a Point of Moment:
Wou'd have the Text as well as Comment;
So hearing of a grave Divine,
She sent to bid him come and dine.
But you must know he was not quite
So grave, as to be unpolite;
Thought human Learning wou'd not lessen
The Dignity of his Profession;                10

Printed from the octavo pamphlet of 1730.

And if you had heard the Man discourse,
Or preach, you'd like him scarce the worse.
He long had bid the Court farewel,
Retreating silent to his Cell;
Suspected for the Love he bore
To one who sway'd some time before;
Which made it more surprising how
He should be sent for thither now.
  The Message told, he gapes—and stares,
And scar[c]e believes his Eyes, or Ears;                    20
Could not conceive what it should mean,
And fain wou'd hear it told again;
But then the 'Squire so trim and nice,
'Twere rude to make him tell it twice;
So bow'd, was thankful for the Honour:
And wou'd not fail to wait upon her.
His Beaver brush'd, his Shoes, and Gown,
Away he trudges into Town;
Passes the Lower Castle Yard,
And now advancing to the Guard,                             30
He trembles at the Thoughts of State;
For, conscious of his Sheepish Gait,
His Spirits of a sudden fail'd him,
He stop'd, and cou'd not tell what ail'd him.
  What was the Message I receiv'd;
Why certainly the Captain rav'd?
To dine with Her! and come at Three!
Inpossible! it can't be me.
Or may be I mistook the Word;
My Lady—it must be my Lord.                                 40
  My Lord's Abroad; my Lady too;
What must the unhappy Doctor do?
*Is Capt.* Crach'rode *here, pray?—No.*
*Nay then 'tis time for me to go.*
Am I awake, or do I dream?
I'm sure he call'd me by my Name;
Nam'd me as plain as he cou'd speak:
And yet there must be some Mistake.
Why what a Jest shou'd I have been,
Had now my Lady been within.                                50

What cou'd I've said? I'm mighty glad
She went Abroad —— She'd thought me mad.
The Hour of Dining now is past;
Well then, I'll e'en go home, and fast;
And since I 'scap'd being made a Scoff,
I think I'm very fairly off.
My Lady now returning home
Calls, *Crach'rode, is the Doctor come?*
He had not heard of him—*Pray see,*
*'Tis now a Quarter after three*                         60
The Captain walks about, and searches
Thro' all the Rooms, and Courts, and Arches;
Examines all the Servants round,
In vain —— no Doctor's to be found[.]
My Lady could not chuse but wonder:
*Captain, I fear you've made some Blunder;*
*But pray. To morrow go at Ten,*
*I'll Try his Manners once again;*
*If Rudeness be the Effect of Knowledge,*
*My Son shall never see a College.*                      70
   The Captain was a Man of Reading,
And much good Sense, as well as Breeding:
Who, loth to blame, or to incense,
Said little in his own Defence:
Next Day another Message brought;
The Doctor frighten'd at his Fault,
Is dress'd, and stealing thro' the Crowd,
Now pale as Death, then blush'd and bow'd;
Panting —— and faultring —— Humm'd and Ha'd,
*Her Ladyship was gone Abroad;*                          80
*The Captain too —— he did not know*
*Whether he ought to stay or go.*
Beg'd she'd forgive him; in Conclusion,
My Lady, pittying his Confussion,
Call'd her good Nature to relieve him;
Told him, she thought she might believe him;
And wou'd not only grant his Suit[,]
But visit him, and eat some Fruit;
Provided, at a proper Time;
He told the real Truth in Rhime.                         90

'Twas to no purpose to oppose,
She'd hear of no Excuse in Prose.
The Doctor stood not to debate,
Glad to compound at any Rate;
So, bowing, seemingly comply'd;
Tho' if he durst, he had denied.
But first resolv'd, to shew his Taste
Was too refin'd to give a Feast,
He'd treat with nothing that was Rare,
But winding Walks and purer Air;                    100
Wou'd entertain without Expence,
Or Pride, or vain Magnificence;
For well he knew, to such a Guest,
The plainest M[ea]ls must be the best:
To Stomachs clog'd with costly Fare,
Simplicity alone is rare;
Whilst high, and nice, and curious Meats,
Are really but Vulgar Treats:
Instead of Spoils of *Persian* Looms,
The costly Boast of Regal Rooms,                    110
Thought it more courtly and discreet,
To scatter Roses at her Feet;
Roses of richest Dye, that shone
With native Lustre like her own;
Beauty that needs no Aid of Art,
Thro' ev'ry Sense to reach the Heart.
The gracious Dame, tho' well she knew
All this was much beneath her Due,
Like'd ev'ry Thing —— at least thought fit
To praise it, *par maniere d'acquit*;               120
But yet, tho' seeming pleas'd, can't bear
The scorching Sun, or chilling Air;
Frighted alike at both Extremes,
If he displays, or hides his Beams;
Tho' seeming pleas'd at all she sees,
Starts at the Rust'ling of the Trees;
Can scarsely speak for want of Breath,
In half a Walk fatigu'd to Death.
The Doctor takes his hint from hence,
To vindicate his late Offence:                      130

'Madam, the mighty Pow'r of Use
'Now strangely pleads in my Excuse:
'If you, unus'd, have scarsely Strength
'To move this Walk's untoward Length[;]
'If startled at a Scene so rude,
'Thro' long Disuse of Solitude;
'If long confin'd to Fires and Screens,
'You dread the waving of these Greens;
'If you, who long have breath'd the Fumes
'Of City Fogs and crowded Rooms,                    140
'Do now solicitously shun
'The cooler Air, and dazzling Sun;
'If his Majestick Eye you flee,
'Learn hence t'excuse and pity me.
'Consider what it is to bear
'The powder'd Courtier's witty Sneer;
'To see th' important Men of Dress,
'Scoffing my College Aukwardness.
'To be the strutting Cornet's Sport,
'To run the Gauntlet of the Court;                  150
'Winning my Way by slow Approaches,
'Thro' Crowds of Coxcombs & of Coaches;
'From the first fierce cockaded Centry,
'Quite thro' the Tribe of waiting Gentry;
'To pass to many crowded Stages,
'And stand the Staring of your Pages;
'And after all, to crown my Spleen,
'Be told——*You are not to be seen*:
'Or, if you are, be forc'd to bear
'The Awe of your Majestick Air?                     160
'And can I then be faulty found
'In dreading this vexatious Round?
'Can it be strange if I eschew
'A Scene so glorious and so new?
'Or is he criminal that flies
'The living Lusture of your Eyes?'

# THE

# BIRTH

OF

# *MANLY VIRTUE*

FROM

# CALLIMACHUS

## The PREFACE

'TIS to be hope'd the courteous Reader will not be displeas'd with any Remain of so fame'd an Author as *Callimachus*, even in a Translation. His particular Turn was Panegyric, and 'tis evident *Propertius* believ'd he excell'd in it, when he wish'd to attain no higher Honour in Poetry than the Glory of imitating our Author's Manner with Success: as appears from one of the Lemmas prefixt to this Translation, which I shall beg leave to explain in the following Manner, for the Benefit of my fair Readers.

> Great Bard, of matchless Art and Ease,
> Polite Artificer of Praise,
> My vainest Wish were but to shine
> In courtly Lays resembling thine.

Printed from the Folio, Dublin [1725]. Not included in Swift's *Works* in his life-time, this poem is possibly by Dr. Delany.

# THE
# BIRTH
## OF
# *MANLY VIRTUE*
## FROM
# CALLIMACHUS

*Inter Callimachi sat erit placuisse Libellos,*
*Et cecinisse modis, pure Poeta, tuis.* Propert.

*Gratior & pulchro veniens in corpore virtus.* Virg. Æn. V.

O NCE on a Time, a righteous Sage,
   Griev'd at the Vices of the Age,
Apply'd to *Jove* with fervent Prayer;
"O *Jove*, if Virtue be so fair
"As it was deem'd in former Days
"By *Plato*, and by *Socrates*,
"(Whose Beauties mortal Eyes escape,
"Only for want of outward Shape)
"Make thou its real Excellence
"For once the Theme of human Sense.      10
"So shall the Eye, by Form confin'd,
"Direct, and fix the wandring Mind,
"And long-deluded Mortals see,
"With Rapture, what they wont to flee."

  JOVE grants the Prayer, gives Virtue Birth,
And bids him bless, and mend the Earth;
Behold him blooming, fresh, and fair,
Now made—ye Gods!—a Son and Heir,
An Heir? and Stranger yet to hear,
An Heir, and Orphan of a Peer;      20
But Prodigies are wrought to prove
Nothing impossible to *Jove*.

VIRTUE was of this Sex design'd,
In mild Reproof to Woman-kind;
In manly Form to let them see
The Loveliness of Modesty,
The thousand Decencies, that shone
With lessen'd Lustre in their own;
Which few had learnt enough to prize,
And some thought modish to despise. 30

To make his Merit more discern'd,
He goes to School! he reads! is learn'd!
Rais'd high above his Birth by Knowledge,
He shines distinguish'd in a College;
Resolv'd, nor Honour, nor Estate,
Himself alone shou'd make him great.
Here, soon for every Art renown'd,
His Influence is diffus'd around;
Th' inferiour Youth, to Learning led
Less to be fam'd, than to be fed, 40
Behold the Glory he has won,
And blush to be so far out-done:
And now, inflame'd with rival Rage,
In scientific Strife engage;
Engage, and in the glorious Strife,
The Arts new kindle into Life.

HERE would our Hero ever dwell,
Fix'd in a lonely, learned Cell,
Contented to be truly great,
In Virtue's best-belov'd Retreat; 50
Contented he, but Fate ordains
He now shall shine in nobler Scenes:
(Rais'd high like some celestial Fire
To shine the more still rising higher)
Compleatly form'd in every Part,
To win the Soul, and glad the Heart;
The powerful Voice, the graceful Mien,
Lovely alike, or heard or seen;
His outward Form, and Inward, vie,
His Soul bright-beaming from his Eye, 60

Ennobling every Act, and Air,
With Just, and Generous, and Sincere.


ACCOMPLISH'D thus, his next Resort
Is to the Council, and the Court;
Where Virtue is in least Repute,
And Interest the one Pursuit,
Where Right, and Wrong, are bought and sold,
Barter'd for Beauty, and for Gold;
Yet Manly Virtue even here
Pleas'd in the Person of a Peer;                    70
A Peer, a scarcely bearded Youth,
Who talk'd of Justice, and of Truth,
Of Innocence, the surest Guard,
Tales here forgot, or yet unheard;
That he alone deserv'd Esteem,
Who was the Man, he wish'd to seem;
Call'd it unmanly and unwise
To lurk behind a mean Disguise;
(Give fraudful Vice the Mask and Screen,
'Tis Virtue's Int'rest to be seen:)                 80
Call'd want of Shame, a want of Sense,
And found in Blushes, Eloquence.


THUS, acting what he taught so well,
He drew dumb Merit from her Cell,
Led with amazing Art along
The bashful Dame, and loose'd her Tongue;
And whilst he made her Value known,
Yet more display'd, and rais'd his own.


THUS young, thus proof to all Temptations,
He rises to the highest Stations;                   90
(For, where high Honour is the Prize,
True Virtue has a Right to rise.)
Let courtly Slaves low bend the Knee
To Wealth and Vice, in high Degree,
Exalted Worth disdains to owe
Its Grandeur to its greatest Foe.

Now rais'd on high, see, Virtue shews
The Godlike Ends for which he rose;
From him let proud Ambition know,
The Height of Glory here below,                          100
Grandeur, by Goodness made compleat!
To bless, is truly to be great!
He taught, how Men to Honours rise,
Like gilded Vapours to the Skies,
Which, howsoever they display
Their Glory from the God of Day,
Their noblest Use is to abate
His dangerous Excess of Heat,
To shield the infant Fruits and Flowers,
And bless the Earth with genial Showers.                 110


Now change the Scene; a nobler Care
Demands him in an higher Sphere;
Distress of Nations calls him hence,
Permitted so by Providence:
For Models, made to mend our Kind,
To no one Clime shou'd be confin'd;
And Manly Virtue, like the Sun,
His Course of glorious Toil shou'd run,
Alike diffusing in his Flight
Congenial Joy, and Life, and Light.                      120
Pale Envy sickens—Errour flies—
And Discord, in his Presence, dies—
Oppression hides, with guilty Dread,
And Merit rears her drooping Head;
The Arts revive, the Vallies sing,
And Winter softens into Spring:
The wondring World, where'er he moves,
With new Delight looks up and loves;
One Sex consenting to admire,
Nor less the other to desire;                            130
Whilst he, tho' seated on a Throne,
Confines his Faith to one alone;
The rest condemn'd, with rival Voice,
Repining, to applaud his Choice.

FAME now reports, the western Isle
Is made his Mansion for a while;
Whose anxious Natives, Night and Day,
(Happy beneath his righteous Sway)
Weary the Gods with ceaseless Prayer,
To bless him and to keep him there;                    140
And claim it as a Debt from Fate,
Too lately found! to lose him late!


# VERSES ON THE REVIVAL OF
# THE ORDER OF THE BATH

About 1726 The Order of the Bath was instituted or revived,
under the ministry of S$^r$ Rob$^t$. Walpole.

QUOTH King Robin, our Ribbands I see are too few
Of S$^t$ Andrew's the Green, and S$^t$ George's the Blue
I must have another of Colour more gay
That will make all my Subjects with pride to obey.
Tho the Exchequer be drained by prodigal Donours
Our King ne'er exhausted his fountain of Honours.
Men of more Wit than Money, our Pensions will fit
And this will suit Men of more Money than Wit.
Thus my Subjects with pleasure will obey my Commands
Tho as empty as Younge and as saucy as Sandes          10
And he who will leap over a Stick for the King
Is qualified best for a Dog in a String.

T.C.D. (Misc. MSS.), Barrett to Provost, 18 May 1813.

# ON READING
# Dr. YOUNG's *SATIRES*,
## CALLED THE
## UNIVERSAL PASSION

IF there be Truth in what you sing,
Such Godlike Virtues in the *King*,
A *Minister* so filled with Zeal,
And Wisdom for the Common-Weal.
If *he*, who in the Chair presides,
So steadily the *Senate* guides:
If Others, whom you make your Theme,
Are Seconds in this glorious Scheme;
If ev'ry *Peer* whom you commend,
To Worth and Learning be a Friend.          10
If this be Truth, as you attest,
What *Land* was ever *half* so *blest?*
No Falshood now among the *Great*,
And *Tradesmen* now no longer cheat;
Now, on the Bench fair *Justice* shines,
Her Scale to neither Side inclines;
Now *Pride* and *Cruelty* are flown,
And *Mercy* here exalts her Throne;
For, such is good Example's Pow'r,
It does its Office ev'ry Hour,              20
Where *Governors* are good and wise;
Or else the truest Maxim lyes:
For, so we find, all antient Sages
Decree, that *ad exemplum Regis*,
Thro' all the Realm his *Virtues* run,
Rip'ning, and kindling like the Sun.
If this be true, then how much more,
When you have nam'd at least a *Score*

Printed from the folio, London, 1734, with corrections from *Poems*, 1735.

3. *Minister*. Walpole.          5. *Chair*. Compton, the Speaker.

Of *Courtiers*, each in their Degree
If possible, as good as He.                              30

   Or take it in a diff'rent View;
I ask, if what you say be *true*,
If you affirm, the present Age
Deserves your *Satire's* keenest Rage;
If that same *Universal Passion*
With ev'ry *Vice* hath fill'd the Nation;
If *Virtue* dares not venture down,
But just a *Step* below the *Crown*:
If *Clergymen*, to shew their Wit,
Prize *Classicks* more than *Holy Writ*:          40
If Bankrupts, when they are undone,
Into the *Senate-House* can run,
And sell their Votes at such a Rate,
As will retrieve a lost Estate:
If *Law* be such a partial Whore,
To spare the Rich, and plague the Poor;
If these be of all Crimes the worst,
What *Land* was ever *half* so *curst*?


# A COPY OF VERSES

## *Upon two celebrated Modern Poets*

BEHOLD those Monarch-Oaks that rise,
With lofty Branches to the Skies,
Have large proportion'd Roots that grow
With equal Longitude below:
Two Bards that now in fashion reign,
Most aptly this Device explain:
If This to Clouds and Stars will venture,
That creeps as far to reach the Centre;
Or more to show the Thing I mean,
Have you not o'er a Sawpit seen,                   10

Printed from Moore's *Miscellanies*, Dublin, 1734.

A skill'd Mechanick that has stood,
High on a Length of prostrate Wood,
Who hir'd a subterraneous Friend,
To take his Iron by the End;
But which excell'd was never found,
The Man above, or under Ground.

   The Moral is so plain to hit,
That had I been the God of Wit,
Then in a Sawpit and wet Weather,
Shou'd *Young* and *Phillips* drudge together.     20

# ADVICE
## TO THE
## Grub-street *Verse-Writers*
### Written in the Year 1726

Y E Poets ragged and forlorn,
   Down from your Garrets haste,
Ye Rhimers, dead as soon as born,
   Not yet consign'd to Paste;

I KNOW a Trick to make you thrive;
   O, 'tis a quaint Device:
Your still-born Poems shall revive,
   And scorn to wrap up Spice.

GET all your Verses printed fair,
   Then, let them well be dry'd;     10
And, *Curl* must have a special Care
   To leave the Margin wide.

LEND these to Paper-sparing *Pope*;
   And, when he sits to write,
No Letter with an *Envelope*
   Could give him more Delight.

Printed from *Poems*, 1735.

WHEN *Pope* has fill'd the Margins round,
   Why, then recal your Loan;
Sell them to *Curl* for Fifty Pound,
   And swear they are your own.          20


# THE
# *DOG* and *THIEF*

### Written in the Year 1726

QUOTH the Thief to the Dog; let me into your Door,
   And I'll give you these delicate Bits:
Quoth the Dog, I should then be more Villain than you're,
   And besides must be out of my Wits:

Your delicate Bits will not serve me a Meal,
   But my Master each Day gives me Bread;
You'll fly when you get what you come here to steal,
   And I must be hang'd in your Stead.

The Stock-jobber thus, from *Change-Alley* goes down,
   And tips you the Freeman a Wink;          10
Let me have but your Vote to serve for the Town,
   And here is a Guinea to drink.

Said the Freeman, your Guinea To-night would be spent,
   Your Offers of Bribery cease;
I'll vote for my Landlord to whom I pay Rent,
   Or else I may forfeit my Lease.

From *London* they come, silly People to chouse,
   Their Lands and their Faces unknown;
Who'd vote a Rogue into the Parliament-house,
   That would turn a Man out of his own?          20

Printed from *Poems*, 1735.

# To the Earl of *Peterborow*

### Written in the Year 1726

MORDANTO fills the Trump of Fame,
The Christian World his Deeds proclaim,
And Prints are crowded with his Name.

In Journeys he out-rides the Post,
Sits up till Midnight with his Host,
Talks Politicks, and gives the Toast.

Knows ev'ry Prince in *Europe*'s Face,
Flies like a Squib from Place to Place,
And travels not, but runs a Race.

From *Paris* Gazette *A-la-main*,                    10
This Day arriv'd without his Train,
*Mordanto* in a Week from *Spain*.

A Messenger comes all a-reek,
*Mordanto* at *Madrid* to seek:
He left the Town above a Week.

Next Day the Post-boy winds his Horn,
And rides through *Dover* in the Morn:
*Mordanto*'s landed from *Leghorn*.

MORDANTO gallops on alone,
The Roads are with his Foll'wers strown,              20
This breaks a Girth, and that a Bone.

His Body active as his Mind,
Returning sound in Limb and Wind,
Except some Leather lost behind.

Printed from *Poems*, 1735.

A SKELETON in outward Figure,
His meagre Corps, though full of Vigour,
Would halt behind him, were it bigger.

So wonderful his Expedition,
When you have not the least Suspicion,
He's with you like an Apparition.          30

SHINES in all Climates like a Star;
In Senates bold, and fierce in War,
A Land-Commander, and a Tarr.

HEROICK Actions early bred in,
Ne'er to be match't in modern Reading,
But by his Name-sake *Charles* of *Sweden.*

## *Clever* Tom Clinch *going to be hanged*

### Written in the Year 1726

AS clever *Tom Clinch*, while the Rabble was bawling,
Rode stately through *Holbourn*, to die in his Calling;
He stopt at the *George* for a Bottle of Sack,
And promis'd to pay for it when he'd come back.
His Waistcoat and Stockings, and Breeches were white,
His Cap had a new Cherry Ribbon to ty't.
The Maids to the Doors and the Balconies ran,
And said, lack-a-day! he's a proper young Man.
But, as from the Windows the Ladies he spy'd,
Like a Beau in the Box, he bow'd low on each Side;          10
And when his last Speech the loud Hawkers did cry,
He swore from his Cart, it was all a damn'd Lye.
The Hangman for Pardon fell down on his Knee;
*Tom* gave him a Kick in the Guts for his Fee.
Then said, I must speak to the People a little,
But I'll see you all damn'd before I will *whittle.*

Printed from *Poems*, 1735.

16. *whittle.* A Cant Word for confessing at the Gallows.

My honest Friend *Wild*, may he long hold his Place,
He lengthen'd my Life with a whole Year of Grace.
Take Courage, dear Comrades, and be not afraid,
Nor slip this Occasion to follow your Trade.                    20
My Conscience is clear, and my Spirits are calm,
And thus I go off without Pray'r-Book or Psalm.
Then follow the Practice of clever *Tom Clinch*,
Who hung like a Hero, and never would flinch.

# *On seeing Verses written upon Windows in Inns*

## I

THE Sage, who said he should be proud
    Of Windows in his Breast;
Because he ne'er one Thought allow'd
    That might not be confess't;
His Window scrawl'd by ev'ry Rake,
    His Breast again would cover;
And fairly bid the Devil take
    The Di'mond and the Lover.

## II

BY *Satan* taught, all Conj'rers know
Your Mistress in a Glass to show,
    And, you can do as much:
In this the Dev'l and you agree;
None e'er made Verses worse than he,
    And thine I swear are such.

## III

THAT Love is the Devil, I'll prove when requir'd:
    These Rhimers abundantly show it:
They swear that they all by Love are inspir'd,
    And, the Devil's a damnable Poet.

I–IV printed from *Poems*, 1735.
17. *Wild.* The noted Thief-Catcher.

### IV

THE Church and Clergy here, no doubt,
  Are very near a-kin;
Both, weather-beaten are without;
  And empty both within.

### V

## Written upon a Window in an Inn

WE fly from luxury and wealth,
  To hardships in pursuit of health;
From gen'rous wines and costly fare,
And doting in an easy chair;
Pursue the Goddess Health in vain,
To find her in a country scene,
And ev'ry where her footsteps trace,
And see her marks in ev'ry face;
And still her favourites we meet,
Crouding the roads with naked feet.      10
But oh! so faintly we pursue,
We ne'er can have her full in view.

### VI

## Written upon Windows at Inns, in
## ENGLAND

THE glass, by lovers nonsense blurr'd,
  Dims and obscures our sight:
So when our passions Love hath stirr'd,
  It darkens Reason's light.

### VII

## Another, written upon a Window where
## there was no Writing before

THANKS to my Stars, I once can see
  A window here from scribbling free:
Here no conceited coxcombs pass,
To scratch their paultry drabs on glass;
No party-fool is calling names,
Or dealing crowns to *George* and *James.*

V–X printed from *Works, 4to, VIII,* London, 1765.

## VIII
## Another at CHESTER

M Y landlord is civil,
    But dear as the Devil:
Your pockets grow empty,
With nothing to tempt ye:
The wine is so sour,
    'Twill give you a scour:
The beer and the ale
Are mingled with stale.
The veal is such carrion,
A dog would be weary on.        10
All this I have felt,
For I live on a smelt.

## IX
## Another, in CHESTER

T H E walls of this Town
    Are full of renown,
And strangers delight to walk round 'em:
    But, as for the dwellers,
    Both buyers and sellers,
For me, you may hang 'em, or drown 'em.

## X
## Another, at HOLYHEAD

O NEPTUNE! Neptune! must I still
    Be here detained against my will?
Is this your justice, when I'm come
Above two hundred miles from home?
O'er mountains steep, o'er dusty plains,
Half choak'd with dust, half down'd with rains;
Only your Godship to implore,
To let me kiss your other shore?
A boon so small! But I may weep,
Whilst you're, like Baal, fast asleep.        10

## XI

# At the Sign of the FOUR CROSSES

### To the Landlord

THERE hang three crosses at thy door:
Hang up thy wife, and she'll make four.

## XII

'J. S. D. S. P. D. hospes ignotus,
Patriæ (ut nunc est) plusquam vellet notus,
Tempestate pulsus,
Hic pernoctavit,
A.D. 17—'

XI *Swiftiana*, 1804; XII Scott (ed.), *Works*, 1814.

# BEC's BIRTH-DAY

### November 8th, M DCC XXVI

THIS day, dear Bec, is thy nativity,
  Had fate a lucky'r one, she'd give it ye:
She chose a thread of greatest length
And doubly twisted it for strength;
Nor will be able with her shears
To cut it off these forty years.
Then, who says care will kill a cat?
Rebecca shews they're out in that.
For she, tho' over-run with care,
Continues healthy, fat, and fair.         10

  As, if the gout should seize the head,
Doctors pronounce the patient dead;
But, if they can, by all their arts,
Eject it to th'extreamest parts,
They give the sick man joy, and praise
The gout that will prolong his days:

Printed from *Works, 4to, VIII* (2), London, 1765.

Rebecca thus I gladly greet,
Who drives her cares to hands and feet:
For, tho' philosophers maintain
The limbs are guided by the brain,      20
Quite contrary Rebecca's led,
Her hands and feet conduct her head,
By arbitrary pow'r convey her
She ne'er considers why, or where:
Her hands may meddle, feet may wander,
Her head is but a mere by-stander:
And all her bustling but supplies
The part of wholesome exercise:
Thus, nature hath resolved to pay her
The cat's nine lives and eke the care.      30

Long may she live, and help her friends
Whene'er it suits her private ends;
Domestic business never mind
'Till coffee has her stomach lin'd;
But, when her breakfast gives her courage,
Then, think on Stella's chicken porridge;
I mean when Tyger has been serv'd,
Or else poor Stella may be starv'd.

May Bec have many an evening nap
With Tyger slabb'ring in her lap;      40
But always take a special care
She does not overset the chair;
Still be she curious, never hearken
To any speech but Tyger's barking.

And, when she's in another scene,
Stella long dead, but first the Dean,
May fortune and her coffee get her
Companions that will please her better;
Whole afternoons will sit beside her,
Nor for neglects or blunders chide her;      50
A goodly set as can be found
Of hearty gossips prating round;

37. *Tyger*. Mrs. Dingley's favourite lap-dog.

Fresh from a wedding, or a christ'ning,
To teach her ears the art of list'ning,
And please her more to hear them tattle
Than the Dean storm, or Stella rattle.

Late be her death, one gentle nod,
When Hermes, waiting with his rod,
Shall to Elysian fields invite her,
Where there will be no cares to fright her.          60

# On the Collar of Mrs. DINGLEY's Lap-Dog

PRAY steal me not, I'm Mrs. *Dingley's*
Whose Heart in this Four-footed Thing lies.

Printed from *Works, Vol. VIII*, Dublin, 1762.

# *STELLA*'s BIRTH-DAY

*March 13, 172$\frac{6}{7}$*

THIS Day, whate'er the Fates decree,
Shall still be kept with Joy by me:
This Day then, let us not be told,
That you are sick, and I grown old,
Nor think on our approaching Ills,
And talk of Spectacles and Pills;
To morrow will be Time enough
To hear such mortifying Stuff.
Yet, since from Reason may be brought
A better and more pleasing Thought,          10

Printed from *Miscellanies. The Last Volume*, 1727, with corrections from *Poems*, 1735.

Which can in spite of all Decays,
Support a few remaining Days:
From not the gravest of Divines,
Accept for once some serious Lines.

Although we now can form no more
Long Schemes of Life, as heretofore;
Yet you, while Time is running fast,
Can look with Joy on what is past.

Were future Happiness and Pain,
A mere Contrivance of the Brain,                    20
As Atheists argue, to entice,
And fit their Proselytes for Vice;
(The only Comfort they propose,
To have Companions in their Woes.)
Grant this the Case, yet sure 'tis hard,
That Virtue, stil'd its own Reward,
And by all Sages understood
To be the chief of human Good,
Should acting, die, nor leave behind
Some lasting Pleasure in the Mind,                   30
Which by Remembrance will assuage,
Grief, Sickness, Poverty, and Age;
And strongly shoot a radiant Dart,
To shine through Life's declining Part.

Say, *Stella*, feel you no Content,
Reflecting on a Life well spent?
Your skilful Hand employ'd to save
Despairing Wretches from the Grave;
And then supporting with your Store,
Those whom you dragg'd from Death before:            40
(So Providence on Mortals waits,
Preserving what it first creates)
Your gen'rous Boldness to defend
An innocent and absent Friend;
That Courage which can make you just,
To Merit humbled in the Dust:

The Detestation you express
For Vice in all its glitt'ring Dress:
That Patience under tort'ring Pain,
Where stubborn Stoicks would complain.        50


    Shall these like empty Shadows pass,
Or Forms reflected from a Glass?
Or mere Chimæra's in the Mind,
That fly and leave no Marks behind?
Does not the Body thrive and grow
By Food of twenty Years ago?
And, had it not been still supply'd,
It must a thousand Times have dy'd.
Then, who with Reason can maintain,
That no Effects of Food remain?        60
And, is not Virtue in Mankind
The Nutriment that feeds the Mind?
Upheld by each good Action past,
And still continued by the last:
Then, who with Reason can pretend,
That all Effects of Virtue end?


    Believe me *Stella*, when you show
That true Contempt for Things below,
Nor prize your Life for other Ends
Than merely to oblige your Friends;        70
Your former Actions claim their Part,
And join to fortify your Heart.
For Virtue in her daily Race,
Like *Janus*, bears a double Face;
Looks back with Joy where she has gone,
And therefore goes with Courage on.
She at your sickly Couch will wait,
And guide you to a better State.


    O then, whatever Heav'n intends,
Take Pity on your pitying Friends;        80
Nor let your Ills affect your Mind,
To fancy they can be unkind.

Me, surely me, you ought to spare,
Who gladly would your Suff'rings share;
Or give my Scrap of Life to you,
And think it far beneath your Due;
You, to whose Care so oft I owe,
That I'm alive to tell you so.

# Dr. Swift to Mr. Pope,

## While he was writing the Dunciad

POPE has the Talent well to speak,
But not to reach the Ear;
His loudest Voice is low and weak,
The *Dean* too deaf to hear.

A while they on each other look,
Then diff'rent Studies chuse,
The *Dean* sits plodding on a Book,
*Pope* walks, and courts the Muse.

Now Backs of Letters, though design'd
For those who more will need 'em,                    10
Are fill'd with Hints, and interlin'd,
Himself can hardly read 'em.

Each Atom by some other struck,
All Turns and Motions tries;
Till in a Lump together stuck,
Behold a *Poem* rise!

Yet to the *Dean* his Share allot;
He claims it by a Canon;
*That, without which a Thing is not*
Is, *causa sine quâ non*.                             20

Printed from *Miscellanies. The Third Volume*, 1732, with corrections from *Poems*, 1735.

Thus, *Pope*, in vain you boast your Wit;
    For, had our deaf Divine
Been for your Conversation fit,
    You had not writ a Line.

Of Sherlock thus, for preaching fam'd,
    The Sexton reason'd well,
And justly half the Merit claim'd
    Because he *rang the Bell*.

# A PASTORAL DIALOGUE

## BETWEEN

## *Richmond-Lodge* and *Marble-Hill*

*Written June 1727, just after the News of the King's Death*

'Richmond-*Lodge is a House with a small Park belonging to the Crown: It was usually granted by the Crown for a Lease of Years; the Duke of* Ormonde *was the last who had it. After his Exile, it was given to the Prince of* Wales, *by the King. The Prince and Princess usually passed their* Summer *there. It is within a Mile of* Richmond.

    Marble-Hill *is a House built by Mrs.* Howard, *then of the Bed-chamber, now Countess of* Suffolk, *and Groom of the Stole to the Queen. It is on the* Middlesex *Side, near* Twickenham, *where Mr.* Pope *lives, and about two Miles from* Richmond-Lodge. *Mr.* Pope *was the Contriver of the Gardens, Lord* Herbert *the Architect, and the Dean of St.* Patrick's *chief Butler, and Keeper of the* Ice House. *Upon King* George's *Death, these two Houses met, and had the following Dialogue.*'

IN Spight of *Pope*, in Spight of *Gay*,
  And all that He or They can say;
Sing on I must, and sing I will
Of *Richmond*-Lodge, and *Marble*-Hill.

    LAST *Friday* Night, as Neighbours use,
This Couple met to talk of News.
For by old Proverbs it appears,
That Walls have Tongues, and Hedges, Ears.

Printed from *Poems*, 1735, with the note: *This Poem was carried to Court, and read to the K. and Q.*

25. *Sherlock.* N.B. Not the present Bishop of Bangor, but his Father, who was Dean of St. Paul's; the Son being only famous for his enslaving Speech in the House of Lords.

## MARBLE-HILL

Quoth *Marble-Hill*, right well I ween,
Your Mistress now is grown a Queen;          10
You'll find it soon by woful Proof,
She'll come no more beneath your Roof.

## RICHMOND-LODGE

The kingly Prophet well evinces,
That we should put no Trust in Princes;
My Royal Master promis'd me
To raise me to a high Degree:
But now He's grown a King, God wot,
I fear I shall be soon forgot.
You see, when Folks have got their Ends,
How quickly they neglect their Friends;       20
Yet I may say 'twixt me and you,
Pray God they now may find as true.


*Marble-H.* My House was built but for a Show,
My Lady's empty Pockets know:
And now she will not have a Shilling
To raise the Stairs, or build the Cieling;
For, all the Courtly Madams round,
Now pay four Shillings in the Pound.
'Tis come to what I always thought;
My Dame is hardly worth a Groat.              30
Had You and I been Courtiers born,
We should not thus have layn forlorn;
For, those we dext'rous Courtiers call,
Can *rise* upon their Master's *Fall*.
But, we unlucky and unwise,
Must *fall*, because our Masters *rise*.
  *Richmond-L.* My Master scarce a Fortnight since,
Was grown as wealthy as a Prince;
But now it will be no such thing,
For he'll be poor as any *King*:              40
And, by his Crown will nothing get;
But, like a King, to run in Debt.

MSPW

*Marble-H.* No more the Dean, that grave **Divine**,
Shall keep the Key of my (no) Wine;
My Ice-house rob as heretofore,
And steal my Artichokes no more;
Poor *Patty Blount* no more be seen
Bedraggled in my Walks so green:
Plump *Johnny Gay* will now elope;
And here no more will dangle *Pope*.                     50
   *Richmond-L.* Here wont the *Dean* when he's to seek,
To spunge a Breakfast once a Week;
To cry the Bread was stale, and mutter
Complaints against the Royal Butter.
But, now I fear it will be said,
No Butter sticks upon his Bread.
We soon shall find him full of Spleen,
For want of tattling to the Queen;
Stunning her Royal Ears with talking;
His *Rev'rence* and her *Highness* walking:                60
Whilst Lady *Charlotte*, like a Stroller,
Sits mounted on the Garden Roller.
A goodly Sight to see her ride,
With antient *Mirmont* at her Side.
In Velvet Cap his Head lies warm;
His Hat for Show, beneath his Arm.
   *Marble-H.* Some *South Sea* Broker from the City,
Will purchase me, the more's the Pity,
Lay all my fine Plantations waste,
To fit them to his Vulgar Taste;                         70
Chang'd for the worse in ev'ry Part,
My Master *Pope* will break his Heart.
   *Richmond-L.* In my own *Thames* may I be drownded,
If e'er I stoop beneath a crown'd Head:
Except her Majesty prevails
To place me with the Prince of *Wales*.
And then I shall be free from Fears,
For, he'll be Prince these fifty Years.
I then will turn a Courtier too,
And serve the Times as others do.                        80

61. *Lady Charlotte.* Lady Charlotte de Roussy, a French Lady.
64. *Mirmont.* Marquis de Mirmont, a French Man of Quality.

Plain Loyalty not built on Hope,
I leave to your Contriver, *Pope*:
None loves his King and Country better,
Yet none was ever less their Debtor.
   *Marble-H.* Then, let him come and take a Nap,
In *Summer*, on my verdant Lap:
Prefer our *Villaes* where the *Thames* is,
To *Kensington*, or hot St. *James*'s;
Nor shall I dull in Silence sit;
For, 'tis to me he owes his Wit;          90
My Groves, my Ecchoes, and my Birds,
Have taught him his poetick Words.
We Gardens, and you Wildernesses,
Assist all Poets in Distresses,
Him twice a Week I here expect,
To rattle *Moody* for Neglect;
An idle Rogue, who spends his Quartridge
In tipling at the *Dog* and *Partridge*;
And I can hardly get him down
Three times a Week to brush my Gown.     100
   *Richmond-Lodge.* I pity you, dear *Marble-Hill*;
But, hope to see you flourish still.
All Happiness—and so adieu.
   *Marble-Hill.* Kind *Richmond-Lodge*; the same to you.


# *Desire* and *Possession*

## Written in the Year 1727

'TIS strange, what diff'rent Thoughts inspire
  In Man, *Possession*, and *Desire*;
Think what they wish so great a Blessing,
So disappointed when possessing.

Printed from *Poems*, 1735.

96. *Moody*. The Gardener.

A MORALIST profoundly sage,
I know not in what Book or Page,
Or, whether o'er a Pot of Ale,
Related thus the following Tale.

*Possession*, and *Desire*, his Brother,
But, still at Variance with each other,     10
Were seen contending in a Race;
And, kept at first an equal Pace:
'Tis said, their Course continu'd long;
For, This was active, That was strong:
Till Envy, Slander, Sloth, and Doubt,
Misled them many a League about.
Seduc'd by some deceiving Light,
They take the wrong Way for the right.
Through slipp'ry By-roads dark and deep,
They often climb, and oftner creep.     20

*Desire*, the swifter of the two,
Along the plain like Lightning flew:
Till entring on a broad High-way,
Where *Power* and *Titles* scatter'd lay,
He strove to pick up all he found,
And by Excursions lost his Ground:
No sooner got, than with Disdain
He threw them on the Ground again;
And hasted forward to pursue
Fresh Objects fairer to his View;     30
In hope to spring some nobler Game:
But, all he took was just the same:
Too scornful now to stop his Pace,
He spurn'd them in his Rival's Face.

*Possession* kept the beaten Road;
And, gather'd all his Brother strow'd;
But overcharg'd, and out of Wind,
Though strong in Limbs, he lagg'd behind.

*Desire* had now the Goal in Sight:
It was a Tow'r of monstrous Height,     40

Where, on the Summit *Fortune* stands:
A Crown and Scepter in her Hands;
Beneath, a Chasm as deep as Hell,
Where many a bold Advent'rer fell.
*Desire*, in Rapture gaz'd a while,
And saw the treach'rous Goddess smile;
But, as he climb'd to grasp the Crown,
She knock't him with the Scepter down.
He tumbled in the Gulph profound;
There doom'd to whirl an endless Round.                    50

    *Possessions*'s Load was grown so great,
He sunk beneath the cumbrous Weight:
And, as he now expiring lay,
Flocks ev'ry ominous Bird of Prey;
The Raven, Vulture, Owl, and Kite,
At once upon his Carcase light;
And strip his Hyde, and pick his Bones,
Regardless of his dying Groans.

# *On* Censure

## Written in the Year 1727

YE Wise, instruct me to endure
  An Evil, which admits no Cure:
Or, how this Evil can be born,
Which breeds at once both Hate and Scorn.
Bare Innocence is no Support,
When you are try'd in Scandal's Court.
Stand high in Honour, Wealth, or Wit;
All others who inferior sit,
Conceive themselves in Conscience bound
To join, and drag you to the Ground.                    10
Your Altitude offends the Eyes,
Of those who want the Pow'r to rise.

Printed from *Poems*, 1735.

The World, a willing Stander-by,
Inclines to aid a specious Lye:
Alas; they would not do you wrong;
But, all Appearances are strong.

YET, whence proceeds this Weight we lay
On what detracting People say?
For, let Mankind discharge their Tongues
In Venom, till they burst their Lungs,          20
Their utmost Malice cannot make
Your Head, or Tooth, or Finger ake:
Nor spoil your Shape, distort your Face,
Or put one Feature out of Place;
Nor, will you find your Fortune sink,
By what they speak, or what they think.
Nor can ten Hundred Thousand Lyes,
Make you less virtuous, learn'd, or wise.

THE most effectual Way to baulk
Their Malice, is—to let them talk.          30


# THE
# Furniture of a Woman's
# MIND

### Written in the Year 1727

A SET of Phrases learn't by Rote;
A Passion for a Scarlet-Coat;
When at a Play to laugh, or cry,
Yet cannot tell the Reason why:
Never to hold her Tongue a Minute;
While all she prates has nothing in it.
Whole Hours can with a Coxcomb sit,
And take his Nonsense all for Wit:
Her Learning mounts to read a Song,
But, half the Words pronouncing wrong;          10

Printed from *Poems*, 1735.

Has ev'ry Repartee in Store,
She spoke ten Thousand Times before.
Can ready Compliments supply
On all Occasions, cut and dry.
Such Hatred to a Parson's Gown,
The Sight will put her in a Swown.
For Conversation well endu'd;
She calls it witty to be rude;
And, placing Raillery in Railing,
Will tell aloud your greatest Failing;          20
Nor makes a Scruple to expose
Your bandy Leg, or crooked Nose.
Can, at her Morning Tea, run o'er
The Scandal of the Day before.
Improving hourly in her Skill,
To cheat and wrangle at Quadrille.

    In chusing Lace a Critick nice,
Knows to a Groat the lowest Price;
Can in her Female Clubs dispute
What Lining best the Silk will suit;            30
What Colours each Complexion match:
And where with Art to place a Patch.

    If chance a Mouse creeps in her Sight,
Can finely counterfeit a Fright;
So, sweetly screams if it comes near her,
She ravishes all Hearts to hear her.
Can dext'rously her Husband teize,
By taking Fits whene'er she please:
By frequent Practice learns the Trick
At proper Seasons to be sick;                   40
Thinks nothing gives one Airs so pretty;
At once creating Love and Pity.
If *Molly* happens to be careless,
And but neglects to warm her Hair-Lace,
She gets a Cold as sure as Death;
And vows she scarce can fetch her Breath.
Admires how modest Women can
Be so *robustious* like a Man.

In Party, furious to her Power;
A bitter Whig, or Tory sow'r;                    50
Her Arguments directly tend
Against the Side she would defend:
Will prove herself a Tory plain,
From Principles the Whigs maintain;
And, to defend the Whiggish Cause,
Her Topicks from the Tories draws.

O YES! If any Man can find
More virtues in a Woman's Mind,
Let them be sent to Mrs. *Harding*;
She'll pay the Charges to a Farthing:            60
Take Notice, she has my Commission
To add them in the next Edition;
They may out-sell a better Thing;
So, Holla Boys; God save the King.


# POEMS

## FROM THE

## HOLYHEAD JOURNAL, 1727


# Shall I repine

IF neither brass nor marble can withstand
The mortal force of Time's dystructive hand
If mountains sink to vales, if cityes dye
And lessening rivers mourn their fountains dry
When my old cassock says a Welch divine
Is out at elbows why should I repine?

Printed from Swift's autograph, Forster Collection (519). Reprinted in 1735
with the title *The Power of Time*, and a note: 'Scarron hath a larger Poem on the
same Subject.'

59. *Mrs. Harding.* A Printer.

# Holyhead. Sept. 25, 1727

[p. 1]    LO here I sit at holy head
      With muddy ale and mouldy bread
All Christian vittals stink of fish
I'm where my enemyes would wish
Convict of lyes is every sign,
The Inn has not one drop of wine
I'm fasnd both by wind and tide
I see the ship at anchor ride
The Captain swears the sea's too rough
He has not passengers enough.          10
And thus the Dean is forc't to stay
Till others come to help the pay
In Dublin they'd be glad to see
A packet though it brings in me.
[p. 2]    They cannot say the winds are cross
Your Politicians at a loss
For want of matter swears and fretts,
Are forced to read the old gazettes.
I never was in hast before
To reach that slavish hateful shore      20
Before, I always found the wind
To me was most malicious kind
But now, the danger of a friend
On whom my fears and hopes depend
Absent from whom all Clymes are curst
With whom I'm happy in the worst
With rage impatient makes me wait
A passage to the land I hate.
Else, rather on this bleaky shore
Where loudest winds incessant roar      30
Where neither herb nor tree will thrive,
Where nature hardly seems alive,
I'd go in freedom to my grave,
Than Rule yon Isle and be a Slave.

# Ireland

[p. 1] REMOVE me from this land of slaves
    Where all are fools, and all are knaves
Where every knave & fool is bought
Yet kindly sells himself for nought
Where Whig and Tory fiercely fight
Who's in the wrong, who in the right
And when their country lyse at stake
They only fight for fighting sake,
While English sharpers take the pay,
And then stand by to see fair play,        10
Mean time the whig is always winner
And for his courage gets—a dinner.
His Excellency too perhaps
Spits in his mouth and stroaks his Chaps
The humble whelp gives ev'ry vote.
To put the question strains his throat.
His Excellency's condescension
Will serve instead of place or pension
When to the window he's trepan'd
When my L^d shakes him by the hand    20
Or in the presence of beholders,
His arms upon the booby's shoulders
[p. 2] You quickly see the gudgeon bite,
He tells his broth^r fools at night
How well the Governor's inclind.
So just, so gentle and so kind
He heard I kept a pack of hounds,
And longd to hunt upon my grounds
He sd our Ladyes were so fair
The Court had nothing to compair.    30
But that indeed which pleasd me most
He calld my Dol a perfect toast.
He whisprd publick things at last,
Askt me how our elections past.
Some augmentation S^r You know
Would make at least a handsom show

New Kings a compliment expect
I shall not offer to direct
There are some prating folks in town,
But S<sup>r</sup> we must support the Crown.            40
Our Letters say a Jesuite boasts
Of some Invasion on your coasts
The King is ready when you will
To pass another Pop-ry bill
And for dissenters he intends
To use them as his truest friends
[p. 3] I think they justly ought to share
In all employm<sup>ts</sup> we can spare.
Next for encouragem<sup>t</sup> of spinning,
A duty might be layd on linnen               50
An act for laying down the Plough,
England will send you corn enough.
Anoth<sup>r</sup> act that absentees
For licences shall pay no fees.
If Englands friendship you would keep
Feed nothing in your lands but sheep
But make an act secure and full
To hang up all who smuggle wool.
And then he kindly give[s] me hints
That all our wives should go in Chints.       60
To morrow I shall tell you more,
For I'm to dine with him at four
    This was the Speech, and here's the jest
His arguments convinc't the rest.
Away he runs with zealous hotness
Exceeding all the fools of Totness.
To move that all the Nation round
Should pay a guinea in the pound
Yet should this Blockhead beg a Place
Either from Excellence or grace              70
Tis pre eng[a]ged and in his room
Townshends cast Page or Walpole's groom[.]

# On L^d Carterets Arms given as the custom is, at every Inn where the L^d Lt. dines or lyes, with all the titles in a long Parchment

TIS fourty to one
When Carteret is gone
These praises we blot out
The truth will be got out
And then we'll be smart on
His L^d ship as Wharton

[*Inserted in the margin:*

Or Shrewsbury's Duke
with many rebuke.
Or Bolton the wise
With his Spanish flyes
Or Grafton the deep
Either drunk or asleep.]

These Titles and Arms
Will then lose their charms
For If somebody's grace
Should come in his place                    10
And thus it goes round
We praise and confound
They can do no good
Nor would if they could,
To injure the nation
Is recommendation
And why should they save her
By losing their favor
Poor Kingdom thou wouldst be that Governor's debtor,
Who kindly would leave thee no worse nor no better.   20

*From the diary, under Sept. 27th:*

When M^rs Welch's Chimny smoks,
'Tis a sign she'll keep her folks,
But, when of smoak the room is clear,
It is a sign we shan't stay here.

# On the five Ladies at *Sots*-Hole, with the Doctor at their Head

*The Ladies treated the Doctor*
*Sent as from an Officer in the Army*

Written in the Year 1728

FAIR Ladies, Number five,
  Who in your merry Freaks,
With little *Tom* contrive
  To feast on Ales and Steaks.
While he sits by a grinning,
  To see you safe in *Sots-Hole*,
Set up with greasy Linnen,
  And neither Muggs nor Pots whole.
Alas! I never thought
  A Priest would please your Palate; 10
Besides, I'll hold a Groat,
  He'll put you in a Ballad:
Where I shall see your Faces
  On Paper daub'd so foul,
They'll be no more like Graces,
  Than *Venus* like an Owl.
And we shall take you rather
  To be a Midnight Pack
Of Witches met together,
  With *Belzebub* in Black 20
It fills my Heart with Woe,
  To think such Ladies fine,
Should be reduc'd so low,
  To treat a dull Divine:
Be by a Parson cheated!
  Had you been cunning Stagers,
You might yourselves be treated

Printed from *Poems*, 1735.

6. *Sots-Hole.* A famous Ale-house in Dublin for Beef-stakes.

By Captains and by Majors.
See how Corruption grows,
  While Mothers, Daughters, Aunts,          30
Instead of powder'd Beaus,
  From Pulpits chuse Gallants.
If we who wear our Wigs
  With Fan-Tail and with Snake,
Are bubbled thus by Prigs;
  Zounds who wou'd be a Rake?
Had I a Heart to fight,
  I'd knock the Doctor down;
Or could I read and write,
  I'gad I'd wear a Gown.          40
Then leave him to his Birch;
  And at the *Rose* on *Sunday*,
The Parson safe at Church,
  I'll treat you with *Burgundy*.

# The five Ladies Answer to the Beau With the Wig and Wings at his head

### [by Thomas Sheridan]

Y O U Little scribbling Beau
    What Demon made you write?
Because to write you know
    As much as you can fight.

For Complement so scurvy,
    I wish we had you here,
We'd turn you topsie Turvy
    Into a Mug of Beer.

You thought to make a farce on
    The man, and place we Chose,          10
We're sure a single parson
    Is worth a hundred Beaux.

Printed from Sheridan's MS., Huntington Library, HM 14335.

And you wou'd Make us Vassals
　　Good M^r Wig and Wings,
To silver Clocks and Tassels
　　You wou'd you thing of things.

Because around your Cane
　　A ring of diamonds is set,
And you in some by Lane
　　Have gain'd a paltry Grisset.　　　20

Shall we of sence refin'd
　　Your Trifling Nonsense bear,
As Noisy as the wind,
　　As empty as the Air?

We hate your empty prattle,
　　And vow and swear, 'tis true
There's more in one child's Rattle,
　　Than twenty Fops like you—

# The Beau's reply to the five Ladyes answer

WHY, how now dapper black
　　I smell your gown and cassock
As strong upon your back
As Tisdel smells of a sock:

　　To write such scurvy stuff!
Fine Ladyes never do't
I know you well enough,
And eke your cloven foot.

　　Fine Ladyes when they write,
Nor scold, nor keep a splutter.　　　10
Their verses give delight
Are soft and sweet as butter.

　　But, Satan never saw
Such haggard lines as these
They stick athwart my maw
As bad as Suffolk cheese.

Printed from Swift's autograph, Huntington Library, HM 14335.

# AN *ELEGY*

## ON

## *Dicky* and *Dolly*

UNDER this Stone, lies *Dicky* and *Dolly*,
  *Doll* dying first, *Dick* grew Melancholly,
For *Dick* without *Doll* thought Living a Folly.

*Dick* lost in *Doll*, *a* Wife Tender and Dear,
But *Dick* lost by *Doll*, twelve hundred a Year,
A Loss that *Dick* thought, no Mortal cou'd bear.

*Dick* Sigh'd for his *Doll* and his mournfull Arms Cross'd,
Thought much of his *Doll*, and the Jointure he lost,
The first vex'd him much, but the other vex'd most.

Thus loaded with Grief, *Dick* Sigh'd and he cry'd,            10
To live without both full three Months he try'd,
But lik'd neither loss and so quietly dy'd.

One Bed while alive held both *Doll* and *Dick*
One Coach oft' carried them when they were quick,
One Grave now contains them both *Hæc et Hic.*

*Dick* left a Pattern few will copy after,
Then Reader pray shed some tears of Salt Water,
For so sad a Tale is no Subject of Laughter.

*Meath* Smiles for the Joynture, though gotten, so late,
The Son laughs that got, the hard gotten Estate,            20
And *Cuffe* grins for getting, the *Alicant* Plate.

Here quiet they Lie, in hopes to rise one Day,
Both Solemnly put, in this hole on a *Sunday*,
And here rest, *Sic transit Gloria Mundi.*

Printed from 8vo pamphlet, Dublin, 1732.

# MAD MULLINIX

## AND

# TIMOTHY

*M.* I Own 'tis not my Bread and Butter,
But prithee *Tim*, why all this Clutter?
Why ever in these raging Fits,
Damning to Hell the *Jacobits*?
When, if you search the Kingdom round,
There's hardly twenty to be found;
No, not among the *Priests* and *Fryers*.
   *T.* 'Twixt you and me God Damn the Lyers.
   *M.* The *Tories* are gone ev'ry Man over
To our Illustrious House of *Hanover*.                    10
From all their Conduct this is plain,
And then— *T.* God Damn the Lyars again.
Did not an Earl but lately Vote
To bring in (I could Cut his Throat)
Our whole Account of publick Debts.
   *M.* Lord how this Frothy Coxcomb frets! (aside)
   *T.* Did not an able Statesman Bishop
This dang'rous horrid motion Dish up?
As *Popish* Craft? Did he not rail on't?
Shew Fire and Faggot in the Tail on't?                   20
Proving the *Earl* a grand Offender,
And in a Plot for the *Pretender*?
Whose Fleet, in all our Friends Opinion,
Was then embarking at *Avignion*.
   *M.* These brangling jars of *Whig* and *Tory*,
Are Stale, and Worn as *Troy-Town Story*.
The Wrong 'tis certain you were both in,
And now you find you fought for nothing.

Printed from *The Intelligencer*, *No. VIII*, *Dublin*, 1728, with corrections from
*Poems*, 1735 (uncancelled state).

13. *an Earl*. Earl of Barrymore.
24. *Avignon*. A mid-land City in France.

Your Faction, when their Game was new,
Might want such noisy Fools as you;                    30
But you when all the Show is past
Resolve to stand it out the last;
Like *Martin Marrall*, gaping on,
Not minding when the Song was done.
When all the *Bees* are gone to settle,
You Clutter still your Brazen Kettle.
The Leaders whom you listed under,
Have dropt their Arms, and seiz'd the Plunder.
And when the War is past you come
To rattle in their Ears your Drum.                    40
And, as that hateful hideous *Grecian
Thersites* (he was your Relation)
Was more abhor'd, and scorn'd by those
With whom he serv'd, than by his Foes,
So thou art grown the Detestation
Of all thy Party through the Nation.
Thy peevish, and perpetual teizing,
With Plots; and *Jacobites* and Treason;
Thy busy never-meaning Face;
Thy Screw'd up front; thy State Grimace;               50
Thy formal Nods; important Sneres;
Thy Whisp'rings foisted in all Ears;
(Which are, whatever you may think,
But Nonsence wrapt up in a Stink)
Have made thy Presence in a true Sence,
To thy own Side so Damn'd a Nuisance,
That when they have you in their Eye,
As if the *Devil* drove, they fly.
      *T.* My good Friend *Mullinix* forbear.
I vow to God you're too severe.                        60
If it could ever yet be known
I took Advice except my own,
It shou'd be yours. But Damn my Blood
I must pursue the publick Good.
The Faction, (is it not Notorious?)
Keck at the Memory of *Glorious.*
'Tis true, nor need I to be told,

33. *Martin Marrall.* A Play of Dryden's, called Sir Martin Marrall.

My quondam Friends are grown so Cold,
That scarce a Creature can be found,
To Prance with me his Statue round.          70
The publick Safety I foresee,
Henceforth depends alone on me.
And while this Vital Breath I blow,
Or from above, or from below,
I'll Sputter, Swagger, Curse and Rail,
The *Tories* Terror, Scourge and Flail.
   *M. Tim*, you mistake the matter quite,
The Tories! you are their Delight.
And should you act, a diff'rent Part,
Be grave and wise, 'twou'd break their Heart.          80
Why, *Tim*, you have a Taste I know,
And often see a Puppet-show.
Observe, the Audience is in Pain,
While *Punch* is hid behind the Scene,
But when they hear his rusty Voice,
With what Impatience they rejoice.
And then they value not two Straws,
How *Solomon* decides the Cause,
Which the true Mother, which *Pretender*,
Nor listen to the Witch of *Endor*;          90
Shou'd *Faustus*, with the Devil behind him,
Enter the Stage they never mind him;
If Punch, to spur their fancy, shews
In at the door his monstrous Nose,
Then sudden draws it back again,
O what a pleasure mixt with pain!
You e'ry moment think an Age,
Till he appears upon the Stage.
And first his Bum you see him Clap,
Upon the Queen of *Sheba's* lap.          100
The Duke of *Lorrain* drew his Sword,
Punch roaring ran, and running roar'd.
Reviles all People in his Jargon,
And sells the *King of Spain* a Bargain.

70. *his Statue.* A Statue of King William in College Green, Dublin, round which
his Adorers, every Year of his Birth, go on Foot, or in their Coaches: But the
Number is much lessened.

*St. George* himself he plays the wag on,
And mounts astride upon the *Dragon*.
He gets a thousand Thumps and Kicks
Yet cannot leave his roguish Tricks;
In every Action thrusts his Nose
The reason why no Mortal knows.                    110
In doleful Scenes, that breaks our heart,
Punch comes, like you, and lets a Fart.
There's not a Puppet made of Wood,
But what wou'd hang him if they cou'd.
While teizing all, by all he's teiz'd,
How well are the Spectators pleas'd!
Who in the motion have no share;
But purely come to hear, and stare;
Have no concern for *Sabra*'s sake,
Which gets the better, Saint, or Snake.             120
Provided *Punch* (for there's the Jest)
Be soundly mawl'd, and plagues the rest.
    Thus *Tim*, Philosophers suppose,
*The World consists of Puppet-shows;*
Where petulant, conceited Fellows
Perform the part of *Punchinelloes*;
So at this Booth, which we call *Dublin*,
*Tim* thou'rt the *Punch* to stir up trouble in;
You Wrigle, Fidge, and make a Rout
Put all your Brother Puppets out,                   130
Run on in one perpetual Round,
To Teize, Perplex, Disturb, Confound,
Intrude with Monkey grin, and clatter
To interrupt all serious Matter,
Are grown the Nuissance of your *Clan*,
Who hate and scorn you, to a Man;
But then the Lookers on, the *Tories*
You still divert with merry Stories;
They wou'd Consent, that all the Crew
Were hanged, before they'd part with you.            140
    But tell me, *Tim*, upon the spot,
By all this Coyl what hast thou got?
If *Tories* must have all the sport,
I feel you'll be disgrac'd at *Court*.

*T.* Got? Damn my Blood *I frank my Letters,*
Walk by my place, before my Betters,
And simple as I now stand here,
Expect in time, to be a Peer[;]
Got? Damn me, why I got my will!
Ne're hold my peace, and ne'er stand still.          150
I Fart with twenty Ladies by;
They call me Beast, and what Care I?
I bravely call the Tories Jacks,
And Sons of Whores—behind their Backs.
But cou'd you bring me once to think,
That when I strut, and stair, and stink,
Revile and slander, fume and storm,
Betray, make Oath, impeach, inform,
With such a constant, Loyal Zeal,
To serve my self and Common-weal,          160
And fret the *Tories* Souls to Death,
I did but lose my precious Breath,
And when I damn my Soul to plague 'em,
Am, as you tell me, but their may-game,
Consume my Vitals! they shall know,
I am not to be treated so,
I'd rather hang my self by half,
Then give those Rascals cause to laugh.
   But how, my Friend, can I endure
Once so renown'd to Live obscure?          170
No little Boys and Girls to cry
*There's Nimble Tim a passing by.*
No more my dear Delightful way tread,
Of keeping up *a party hatred.*
Will none the *Tory Dogs* pursue,
When thro' the streets I cry *holloo?*
Must all my Dammee's, Bloods and Wounds
Pass only now for empty sounds?
Shall *Tory* Rascals be Elected,
Although I swear them Disaffected?          180
And when I roar *a Plot, a Plot,*

153. *Jacks.* A Cant Word for Jacobites, or those who continued in the Interest
of King James II, after King William got the Crown, and now are for his Son,
commonly called the Pretender.

Will our own Party mind me not?
So qualify'd to Swear and Lye,
Will they not trust me for a Spy?
Dear *Mullinix*, your good Advice
I beg, you see the Case is Nice,
O, were I equal in Renown,
Like thee, to please this thankless Town!
Or blest with such engaging Parts,
To win the Truant School-Boys Hearts!                190
Thy Vertues meet their just Reward,
Attended by the *Sable-guard*,
Charm'd by thy voice the 'Prentice drops
The Snow-ball destin'd at thy Chops;
Thy graceful Steps, and Coll'nell's Air
Allure the Cinder-picking Fair.
    *M.* No more—In mark of true Affection
I take thee under my Protection.
Thy Parts are good, 'tis not deny'd,
I wish they had been well apply'd.                  200
But now observe my Counsel (*viz*)
Adapt your Habit to your Phiz.
You must no longer thus equip 'ye
As *Horace* says, *Optat ephippia.*
(There's *Latin* too that you may see
How I improv'd by Dr. Lee)
I have a Coat at home, that you may try,
'Tis just like this, which hangs by Geometry.
My Hat has much the nicer air,
Your Block will fit it to a hair.                   210
That Wig, I wou'd not for the world
Have it so formal, and so Curl'd,
'Twill be so oyly, and so sleek
When I have lain in it a Week!
You'll find it well prepar'd to take
The figure of *Toopee* or *Snake.*
Thus drest alike from Top to Toe,
That which is which, 'tis hard to know.
When first in publick we appear,
I'll lead the Van, keep you the Rear.               220

206. *Dr. Lee.* A deceased Clergyman, whose Footman he was.

Be careful, as you walk behind,
Use all the Talents of your mind.
Be studious well to imitate
My portly Motion, Mien, and Gate.
Mark my Address, and learn my Style,
When to look Scornful, when to Smile,
Nor sputter out your Oaths so fast,
But keep your Swearing to the last.
Then at our leisure we'll be witty,
And in the Streets divert the City                          230
The Ladies from the Windows gaping:
The Children all our motions Aping.
Your Conversation to refine,
I'll take you to some Friends of mine;
*Choice Spirits*, who employ their Parts,
To mend the World by useful Arts.
Some cleansing hollow Tubes, to spy
Direct the *Zenith* of the Sky;
Some have the City in their Care,
From noxious Steams to purge the Air;                       240
Some teach us in these dang'rous Days,
How to walk upright in our ways;
Some whose reforming Hands engage,
To lash the Lewdness of the Age;
Some for the publick Service go,
Perpetual Envoys too and fro;
Whose able Heads support the Weight,
Of twenty Ministers of State.
We scorn, for want of talk, to jabber
Of Parties o're our *Bonny-Clabber*.                        250
Nor are we studious to enquire,
Who votes for Manners, who for Hire.
Our Care is to improve the mind,
With what concerns all human kind,
The various Scenes of mortal Life,
Who beats her Husband, who his Wife;

237. *cleansing*. Chimney-Sweepers.      239. *Some*. Scavengers.      241. *Some*.
Coblers.      243. *Some*. Keeper of Bridewell.      245. *Some*. Porters.      249. *We
scorn*.—Non de domibus rebusve alienis, &c. Hor.      253. *Our Care*.—Sed, quod
magis ad nos, Et nescire malum est, agitamus &c. Id.

Or how the Bulley at a stroke
Knockt down the Boy, the Lanthorn broke;
One tells the Rise of Cheese, and Oat-meal,
Another when he got a hot Meal;        260
One gives Advice in Proverbs Old,
Instructs us how to tame a Scold;
Or how by *Almanacks* 'tis clear,
That Herrings will be cheap this Year.
    *T*. Dear *Mullinix*, I now lament
My precious Time, so long mispent,
By nature meant for nobler Ends,
O, introduce me to your Friends!
For whom, by Birth, I was design'd,
'Till Politicks debas'd my mind.        270
I give my self intire to you,
God damn the *Whigs* and *Tories* too.


# *Tim* and the *Fables*

M Y *meaning will be best unravell'd,*
  *When I premise, that* Tim *has Travell'd.*

In *Lucass*'s by chance there lay
The *Fables* writ by Mr. *Gay*,
*Tim* set the Volume on a Table,
Read over here and there a *Fable*,
And found, as he the pages twirl'd,
The *Monkey*, who had seen the World.
(For *Tonson* had, to help the Sale,
Prefixt a Cut to ev'ry Tale.)        10
The *Monkey* was compleatly drest,
The *Beau* in all his Ayrs exprest.
*Tim* with surprize and pleasure staring,
Ran to the Glass, and then comparing
His own sweet Figure with the Print,
Distinguish'd ev'ry Feature in't;
The Twist, the Squeeze, the Rump, the Fidge an'all,

Printed from *The Intelligencer, No. X, Dublin,* 1728.

Just as they lookt in the Original.
By God says *Tim* (and let a Fart)
This Graver understood his Art.                              20
'Tis a true Copy, I'll say that for't,
I well remember when I sat for[']t.
My very Face, at first I knew it,
Just in this Dress the Painter drew it.
*Tim*, with his likeness deeply smitten,
Wou'd read what underneath was written,
The merry Tale with moral Grave.
He now began to storm and rave;
*The cursed Villain! now I see*
*This was a Libel meant at me;*                              30
*These Scriblers grow so bold of late,*
*Against us Ministers of State!*
*Such Jacobites as he deserve,—*
*Dammee, I say, they ought to starve.*
Dear *Tim*, no more such angry Speeches,
Unbutton and let down your Breeches,
Tare out the Tale, and wipe your Arse
I know you love to act a *Farce*.


# TOM MULLINEX

## AND

# DICK

TOM and *Dick* had equal Fame,
   And both had equal Knowledge;
*Tom* cou'd write and spell his Name,
   But *Dick* had seen a College.

*Dick* a Coxcomb, *Tom* was mad,
   And both alike diverting,
*Tom* was held the merrier Lad,
   But *Dick* the best at farting.

Printed from *Miscellanies. The Tenth Volume. London*, 1745.

*Dick* would cock his Nose in scorn,
     But *Tom* was kind and loving;          10
*Tom* a Foot-Boy bred and born,
     But *Dick* was from an Oven.

*Dick* could neatly dance a Jig,
     But *Tom* was best at Borees;
*Tom* would pray for ev'ry Whig,
     And *Dick* curse all the Tories.

*Dick* would make a woful Noise,
     And scold at an Election;
*Tom* huzza'd the black-guard Boys,
     And held them in subjection.          20

*Tom* could move with lordly Grace,
     *Dick* nimbly skip the Gutter;
*Tom* could talk with solemn Face,
     But *Dick* could better sputter.

*Dick* was come to high Renown
     Since he commenc'd Physician;
*Tom* was held by all the Town
     The deeper Politician.

*Tom* had the genteeler Swing,
     His Hat could nicely put on;          30
*Dick* knew better how to swing
     His Cane upon a Button.

*Dick* for Repartee was fit,
     And *Tom* for deep discerning;
*Dick* was thought the brighter Wit,
     But *Tom* had better Learning.

*Dick* with zealous No's and Ay's,
     Could roar as loud as *Stenter*,
In the House 'tis all he says;
     But *Tom* is eloquenter.          40

# DICK, *A Maggot*

AS when rooting in a Bin,
  All powder'd o'er from Tail to Chin;
A lively Maggot sallies out,
You know him by his hazel Snout:
So, when the Grandson of his Grandsire,
Forth issues wriggling *Dick Drawcensir*,
With powder'd Rump, and Back and Side,
You cannot blanch his tawny Hide;
For 'tis beyond the Pow'r of Meal,
The Gypsey Visage to conceal:                    10
For, as he shakes his Wainscot Chops,
Down ev'ry mealy Atom drops
And leaves the Tartar Phiz, in show
Like a fresh Turd just dropt on Snow.

Printed from *Miscellanies. The Tenth Volume*. London, 1745.

# *Clad all in Brown*

## Imitated from COWLEY

### *To* DICK

FOULEST Brute that stinks below,
  Why in this Brown dost thou appear?
For, would'st thou make a fouler Show,
  Thou must go naked all the Year.
Fresh from the Mud a wallowing Sow
Would then be not so brown as thou.

'Tis not the Coat that looks so dun,
  His Hide emits a Foulness out,
Not one Jot better looks the Sun
  Seen from behind a dirty Clout:                10
So Turds within a Glass inclose,
The Glass will seem as brown as those.

Printed from *Miscellanies. The Tenth Volume*. London, 1745.

Thou now one Heap of Foulness art,
　All outward and within is foul;
Condensed Filth in e'ry Part,
　Thy Body's cloathed like thy Soul.
Thy Soul, which through thy Hide of Buff,
Scarce glimmers, like a dying Snuff.

Old carted Bawds such Garments wear,
　When pelted all with Dirt they shine;　　　　20
Such their *exalted* Bodies are,
　As shrivelled and as black as thine.
If thou wer't in a Cart, I fear
Thou would'st be pelted worse than they're.

Yet when we see thee thus array'd,
　The Neighbours think it is but just
That thou shouldst take an honest Trade,
　And weekly carry out our Dust.
Of cleanly Houses who will doubt,
When *Dick* cries, *Dust to carry out*?　　　　30

# DICK's *Variety*

D ULL Uniformity in Fools
　I hate, who gape and sneer by Rules.
You, *Mullinex*, and slobb'ring *Carr*
Who ev'ry Day and Hour the same are;
That vulgar Talent I despise
Of pissing in the Rabble's Eyes.
And when I listen to the Noise,
Of Ideots roaring to the Boys.
To better Judgments still submitting,
I own I see but little Wit in:　　　　10
Such Pastimes, when our Taste is nice,
Can please at most but once or twice.

Printed from *Miscellanies. The Tenth Volume.* London, 1745.

But then, consider *Dick*, you'l find
His Genius of superior Kind;
He never muddles in the Dirt,
Nor scow'rs the Streets without a Shirt;
Though *Dick*, I dare presume to say,
Could do such Feats as well as they.
*Dick* I could venture every where,
Let the Boys pelt him if they dare;                    20
He'd have 'em try'd at the Assizes
For Priests and Jesuits in Disguises;
Swear they were with the *Swedes* at *Bender*,
And listing Troops for the Pretender.
   But *Dick* can fart, and dance and frisk,
No other Monkey half so brisk;
Now has the Speaker by the Ears,
Next Moment in the House of Peers,
Now scolding at my Lady *Eustace*,
Or thrashing *Babby* in her new Stays.                 30
*Presto* be gone; with t'other Hop
He's powd'ring in a Barber's Shop;
Now at the Anti-Chamber thrusting
His Nose to get the Circle just in,
And damns his Blood that in the Rear
He sees one single Tory there:
Then, wo be to my Lord Lieutenant,
Again he'll tell him, and again on't.

.

# PAULUS,

## By Mr. LINDSAY

DUBLIN, Sept. 7th, 1728.

A Slave to crouds, scorch'd with the summer's heats,
   In court the wretched lawyer toils, and sweats:
While smiling nature, in her best attire,
Doth sooth each sense, and joy and love inspire.

Printed from *The Dreamer*, London, 1754.

Can he, who knows, that real good should please,
Barter for gold his liberty and ease?
Thus PAULUS preach'd: when entring at the door
Upon his board a client pours the ore:
He grasps the shining gift, pores o'er the cause,
Forgets the sun, and dozes on the laws.          10

## The ANSWER by Dr. SWIFT

LYNDSAY mistakes the matter quite,
    And honest PAULUS judges right.
Then, why these quarrels to the sun,
Without whose aid you're all undone?
Did PAULUS e'er complain of sweat?
Did PAULUS e'er the sun forget?
The influence of whose golden beams
Soon licks up all unsav'ry steams;
The sun, you say, his face has kist:
It has; but then it greas'd his fist.          10
True lawyers, for the wisest ends,
Have always been APOLLO's friends;
Not for his superficial powers
Of rip'ning fruits, and gilding flow'rs;
Not for inspiring poets brains
With pennyless and starv'ling strains;
Not for his boasted healing art;
Not for his skill to shoot the dart;
Nor yet, because he sweetly fiddles;
Nor for his prophecies in riddles:          20
But for a more substantial cause:
APOLLO's patron of the laws;
Whom PAULUS ever must adore,
As parent of the golden ore,
By PHOEBUS (an incestuous birth)
Begot upon his grandame Earth;
By PHOEBUS first produc'd to light:
By VULCAN form'd so round and bright:
Then offer'd at the throne of justice,
By clients to her priests and trustees.          30
Nor when we see ASTRÆA stand
With equal balance in her hand,

Must we suppose she has in view,
How to give ev'ry man his due:
Her scales you only see her hold
To weigh her priests, the lawyers, gold.
Now, should I own your case was grievous,
Poor sweaty PAULUS, who'd believe us?
'Tis very true, and none denies,
At least, that such complaints are wise:                    40
'Tis wise, no doubt, as clients fat ye more,
To cry, like statesmen, *quanta patimur*!
But, since the truth must needs be stretched
To prove, that lawyers are so wretched;
This paradox I'll undertake
For PAULUS' and for LYNDSAY's sake
By topicks, which tho' I abomine 'em,
May serve, as arguments *ad hominem*.
Yet I disdain to offer those,
Made use of by detracting foes.                             50

   I own, the curses of mankind
Sit light upon a lawyer's mind:
The clamours of ten thousand tongues
Break not his rest, nor hurt his lungs:
I own his conscience always free,
(Provided he has got his fee.)
Secure of constant peace within,
He knows no guilt, who knows no sin.

   Yet well they merit to be pitied,
By clients always overwitted.                               60
And, though the gospel seems to say,
What heavy burthens lawyers lay
Upon the shoulders of their neighbour,
Nor lend a finger to the labour,
Always for saving their own bacon:
No doubt the text is here mistaken:
The copy's false, and sense is rack'd:
To prove it I appeal to fact;
And thus by demonstration show,
What burthens lawyers undergo.                              70

With early clients at his door,
Though he were drunk the night before,
And crop-sick with unclub'd for wine,
The wretch must be at court by nine:
Half sunk beneath his brief and bag,
As ridden by a midnight hag:
Then, from the bar, harangues the bench
In *English* vile, and viler *French*,
And *Latin*, vilest of the three:
And all for ten poor moidores fee!          80
Of paper how is he profuse,
With periods long, in terms abstruse!
What pains he takes to be prolix!
A thousand words to stand for six!
Of common sense without a word in!
And is not this a grievous burden?

The lawyer is a common drudge,
To fight our cause before the judge:
And, what is yet a greater curse,
Condemn'd to bear his client's purse;          90
While he, at ease, secure and light,
Walks boldly home at dead of night;
When term is ended, leaves the town,
Trots to his country mansion down;
And, disencumbred of his load,
No danger dreads upon the road;
Despises rapparees, and rides
Safe through the NEWRY mountains sides.

LYNDSAY, 'tis you have set me on
To state the question *pro* and *con*:          100
My satire may offend, 'tis true:
However, it concerns not you.
I own, there may in ev'ry clan
Perhaps be found one honest man:
Yet link them close; in this they jump,
To be but rascals in the lump.
Imagine LYNDSAY at the bar:
He's just the same, his brethren are;

106. rascals] Sharpers. [1762].

Well taught by practice to imbibe
The fundamentals of his tribe;      110
And, in his client's just defence,
Must deviate oft from common sense,
And make his ignorance discerned,
To get the name of council learned;
(As *lucus* comes *à non lucendo*)
And wisely do as other men do.
But, shift him to a better scene,
Got from his crew of rogues in grain;
Surrounded with companions, fit
To taste his humour, and his wit;      120
You'd swear, he never took a fee,
Nor knew in law his *A, B, C*.

   'Tis hard, where dulness over-rules,
To keep good sense in crouds of fools;
And, we admire the man, who saves
His honesty in crouds of knaves;
Nor yields up virtue, at discretion,
To villains of his own profession.
LYNDSAY, you know, what pains you take
In both, yet hardly save your stake.      130
And will you venture both a-new?
To sit among that scoundrel crew,
That pack of mimick legislators,
Abandon'd, stupid, slavish praters!
For, as the rabble daub, and rifle
The fool, who scrambles for a trifle;
Who for his pains is cuff'd, and kick'd,
Drawn through the dirt, his pockets pick'd;
You must expect the like disgrace,
Scrambling with rogues to get a place:      140
Must lose the honour, you have gain'd,
Your num'rous virtues foully stain'd;
Disclaim for ever all pretence
To common honesty and sense;
And join in friendship, with a strict tye,
To MARSHALL, CONOLLY, and DICK TIGHE.

# BALLYSPELLIN

## By Dr. SHERIDAN

ALL you that wou'd refine your Blood,
  As pure as fam'd *Llewellyn,*
By Waters clear, come ev'ry Year
  To drink at *Ballyspellin.*

Tho' Pox or Itch, your Skins enrich
  With Rubies past the telling,
'Twill clear your Skin before you've been
  A Month at *Ballyspellin.*

If Ladies cheek be green as Leek
  When she comes from her Dwelling,          10
The kindling Rose within it glows
  When she's at *Ballyspellin.*

The sooty Brown, who comes from Town,
  Grows here as fair as *Helen,*
Then back she goes to kill the Beaux
  By Dint of *Ballyspellin.*

Our Ladies are as fresh and fair
  As *Ross,* or bright *Dunkelling*:
And *Mars* might make a fair Mistake,
  Were he at *Ballyspellin.*          20

We Men submit as they think fit,
  And here is no rebelling;
The Reason's plain, the Ladies reign,
  They're Queens at *Ballyspellin.*

By matchless Charms, unconquer'd Arms,
  They have the Pow'r of quelling
Such desperate Foes as dare oppose
  Their Power at *Ballyspellin.*

Printed from *Works, Vol. VIII*, Dublin, 1762.

Cold Water turns to Fire, and burns,
 I know, because I fell in                                  30
A Stream which came from one bright Dame
 Who drank at *Ballyspellin*.

Fine Beaux advance, equipt for Dance,
 And bring their *Anne* or *Nell* in
With so much Grace, I'm sure no Place
 Can vie with *Ballyspellin*.

No Politicks, no subtle Tricks,
 No Man his Country selling,
We eat, we drink, we never think
 Of these at *Ballyspellin*.                                40

The troubled Mind, the puft with Wind,
 Do all come here *Pell Mell* in;
And, they are sure, to work their Cure
 By drinking *Ballyspellin*.

If dropsy fills you to the Gills,
 From Chin to Toe tho' swelling,
Pour in, pour out, you cannot doubt
 A Cure at *Ballyspellin*.

Death throws no Darts through all these Parts,
 No Sextons here are knelling;                              50
Come, judge and try, you'll never *die*,
 But *live* at *Ballyspellin*:

Except you feel Darts tipt with Steel,
 Which here are ev'ry Belle in;
When from their Eyes sweet Ruin flies,
 We die at *Ballyspellin*.

Good Chear, sweet Air, much Joy, no Care,
 Your Sight, your Taste, your Smelling,
Your Ears, your Touch, transporteth much
 Each Day at *Ballyspellin*.                                60

Within this Ground we all sleep sound,
 No noisy Dogs a yelling;
Except you wake, for *Cælia's* Sake,
 All Night at *Ballyspellin*.

Here all you see, both he and she,
  No Lady keeps her Cell in;
But all partake the Mirth we make
  Who drink at *Ballyspellin*.

My Rhimes are gone, I think I've none,
  Unless I should bring Hell in;                    70
But since I am here to Heav'n so near,
  I can't at *Ballyspellin*.


# AN ANSWER

## to the Ballyspellin Ballad

D ARE you dispute,
    You sawcy Brute,
And think there's no rebelling
Your scurvey Lays,
And senseless praise
You give to Ballyspellin.
  Howe'er you bounce,
I here pronounce
Your Med'cine is repelling,
Your Water's mud,                                    10
And sowrs the blood
When drank at Ballyspellin
  Those pocky Drabs
To cure their Scabs
You thither are compelling
Will back be sent
Worse than they went
From nasty Ballyspellin
  Lewellin! why?
As well may I                                        20
Name honest Doctor Pelling;
So hard sometimes
You tug for Rimes
To bring in Ballyspellin.

Printed from Swift's MS. (B.M. Add MSS. 4805, f. 181), corrected from the
original folio printed sheet, Dublin, 1728, recently found.

No Subject fit
To try your Wit
When you went Colonelling
But dull Intrigues
'Twixt Jades and Teagues
That met at Ballyspellin?                    30
   Our Lasses fair
Say what you dare,
Who Sowins make with Shelling
At Market-hill
More Beaus can kill
Than yours at Ballyspellin
   Would I was whipt
When Sheelah strip't
To wash her self our Well in
A Bum so white                               40
Ne'r came in sight
At paltry Ballyspellin
   Your Maukins there
Smocks hempen wear;
For Holland, not an Ell in
No, not a rag,
Whate'er you brag,
Is found at Ballyspellin
   But, Tom will prate
At any rate,                                 50
All other Nymphs expelling
Because he gets
A few Grisetts
At lowsy Ballyspellin.
   There's bony Jane
In yonder lane
Just o'er against the Bell Inn
Where can you meet
A Lass so sweet
Round all your Ballyspellin?                 60

---

33. *Sowins*. A Food much used in Scotland, the North of Ireland and other
Parts: It is made of Oatmeal, and sometimes of the Shellings of Oats, and known
by the Names of Sowings or Flummery. [1762.]

We have a Girl
Deserves an Earl,
She came from Eniskellin
So fair so young,
No such among
The Belles of Ballyspellin
  How would you stare
To see her there
The foggy mists dispelling
That cloud the Brows                    70
Of ev'ry Blowse
Who lives at Ballyspellin
  Now, as I live,
I would not give
A Stiver or a Skellin
To towse and kiss
The fairest Miss
That leaks at Ballyspellin.
  Whoe'er will raise
Such Lyes as these                       80
Deserves a good Cud-gelling
Who falsly boasts
Of Belles and Toasts
At dirty Ballyspellin
  My Rhimes are gone
To all but one,
Which is, Our Trees are felling;
As proper quite
As those you write
To force in Ballyspellin.                90

# On Cutting down the

# OLD THORN

## AT

## *MARKET HILL*

AT *Market Hill*, as well appears
　　By Chronicle of antient Date,
There stood for many a hundred Years
　　A spacious Thorn before the Gate.

Hither came every Village Maid
　　And on the Boughs her Garland hung,
And here, beneath the spreading Shade,
　　Secure from Satyrs sat and sung.

Sir *Archibald* that val'rous Knight,
　　Then Lord of all the fruitful Plain,　　　　10
Would come to listen with Delight,
　　For he was fond of rural Strain.

(Sir *Archibald* whose fav'rite Name
　　Shall stand for Ages on Record,
By *Scotish* Bards of highest Fame,
　　Wise *Hawthornden* and *Sterline*'s Lord.)

But Time with Iron Teeth I ween
　　Has canker'd all its Branches round;
No Fruit or Blossom to be seen,
　　Its Head reclining tow'rds the Ground.　　20

Printed from first edition, London, 1732, with corrections from *Poems*, 1735.

9. *Sir Archibald*. Sir Archibald Acheson, Secretary of State for Scotland.
16. *Wise Hawthornden and Sterline's Lord*. Drummond of Hawthornden, and Sir William Alexander, E. of Sterling, both famous for their Poetry, who were Friends to Sir Archibald.

This aged, sickly, sapless Thorn
   Which must alas no longer stand;
Behold! the cruel Dean in Scorn
   Cuts down with sacrilegious Hand.

Dame Nature, when she saw the Blow,
   Astonish'd gave a dreadful Shriek;
And Mother *Tellus* trembled so
   She scarce recover'd in a Week.

The *Silvan* Pow'rs with Fear perplex'd
   In Prudence and Compassion sent         30
(For none could tell whose Turn was next)
   Sad Omens of the dire Event.

The Magpye, lighting on the Stock,
   Stood chatt'ring with incessant Din;
And with her Beak gave many a Knock
   To rouse and warn the Nymph within.

The Owl foresaw in pensive Mood
   The Ruin of her antient Seat;
And fled in Haste with all her Brood
   To seek a more secure Retreat.         40

Last trotted forth the gentle Swine
   To ease her Itch against the Stump,
And dismally was heard to whine
   All as she scrubb'd her meazly Rump.

The Nymph who dwells in every Tree,
   (If all be true that Poets chant)
Condemn'd by Fate's supreme Decree,
   Must die with her expiring Plant.

Thus, when the gentle *Spina* found
   The Thorn committed to her Care,         50
Receive its last and deadly Wound,
   She fled and vanish'd into Air.

But from the Root a dismal Groan
 First issuing, struck the Murd'rer's Ears;
And in a shrill revengeful Tone,
 This Prophecy he trembling hears.

"Thou chief Contriver of my Fall,
 "Relentless Dean! to Mischief born,
"My Kindred oft' thine Hide shall gall;
 "Thy Gown and Cassock oft be torn:   60

"And thy confed'rate Dame, who brags
 "That she condemn'd me to the Fire,
"Shall rent her Petticoats to Rags,
 "And wound her Legs with ev'ry Bry'r.

"Nor thou, Lord *Arthur*, shalt escape:
 "To thee I often call'd in vain,
"Against that Assassin in Crape,
 "Yet thou could'st tamely see me slain.

"Nor, when I felt the dreadful Blow,
 "Or chid the Dean, or pinch'd thy Spouse. 70
"Since you could see me treated so,
 "An old Retainer to your House,

"May that fell Dean, by whose Command
 "Was formed this *Machi'villian* Plot,
"Not leave a Thistle on thy Land;
 "Then who will own thee for a *Scot*?

"Pigs and Fanaticks, Cows, and Teagues
 "Through all thy Empire I foresee,
"To tear thy Hedges join in Leagues,
 "Sworn to revenge my Thorn and me.  80

"And thou, the Wretch ordain'd by Fate,
 "*Neal Gahagan*, *Hibernian* Clown,
"With Hatchet blunter than thy Pate
 "To hack my hallow'd Timber down;

65. Lord Arthur. Sir Arthur Acheson.

"When thou, suspended high in Air,
 "Dy'st on a more ignoble Tree,
 "(For thou shalt steal thy Landlord's Mare)
 "Then bloody *Caitiff* think on me."

# MY LADY's

## LAMENTATION and COMPLAINT

### against the DEAN

JULY 28, 1728

SURE never did man see
 A wretch like poor Nancy,
So teaz'd day and night
By a Dean and a Knight;
To punish my sins,
Sir Arthur begins,
And gives me a wipe
With Skinny and Snipe:
His malice is plain,
Hallooing the Dean.                                    10
The Dean never stops,
When he opens his chops;
I'm quite over-run
With rebus and pun.


    Before he came here
    To spunge for good cheer,
    I sat with delight,
    From morning till night,
    With two bony thumbs
    Could rub my own gums,                             20

Printed from *Works*, *4to*, *Vol. VIII* (2), London, 1765.

8. *Skinny and Snipe.* The Dean used to call [Lady Acheson] by those names.

Or scratching my nose,
And jogging my toes;
But at present, forsooth,
I must not rub a tooth:
When my elbows he sees
Held up by my knees,
My arms, like two props,
Supporting my chops,
And just as I handle 'em
Moving all like a pendulum;                    30
He trips up my props,
And down my chin drops,
From my head to my heels,
Like a clock without wheels;
I sink in the spleen,
An useless machine.

If he had his will,
I should never sit still:
He comes with his whims,
I must move my limbs;                           40
I cannot be sweet
Without using my feet;
To lengthen my breath
He tires me to death.
By the worst of all Squires,
Thro' bogs and thro' briers,
Where a cow would be startled,
I'm in spite of my heart led:
And, say what I will,
Haul'd up every hill;                           50
'Till, daggled and tatter'd,
My spirit's quite shatter'd,
I return home at night,
And fast out of spite:
For I'd rather be dead,
Than it e'er should be said
I was better for him,
In stomach or limb.

But, now to my diet,
No eating in quiet,                                60
He's still finding fault,
Too sour or too salt:
The wing of a chick
I hardly can pick,
But trash without measure
I swallow with pleasure.

Next, for his diversion,
He rails at my person:
What court-breeding this is?
He takes me to pieces.                             70
From shoulder to flank
I'm lean and am lank;
My nose, long and thin,
Grows down to my chin;
My chin will not stay,
But meets it half way;
My fingers, prolix,
Are ten crooked sticks:
He swears my el——bows
Are two iron crows,                                80
Or sharp pointed rocks,
And wear out my smocks:
To 'scape them, Sir Arthur
Is forc'd to lie farther,
Or his sides they would gore
Like the tusk of a boar.

Now, changing the scene,
But still to the Dean:
He loves to be bitter at
A lady illiterate;                                 90
If he sees her but once,
He'll swear she's a dunce;
Can tell by her looks
A hater of books:
Thro' each line of her face
Her folly can trace;

1728 MY LADY'S LAMENTATION 367

Which spoils ev'ry feature
Bestow'd her by nature,
But sense gives a grace
To the homeliest face:              100
Wise books and reflection
Will mend the complexion.
(A civil Divine!
I suppose meaning mine.)
No Lady who wants them
Can ever be handsome.


    I guess well enough
What he means by this stuff:
He haws and he hums,
At last out it comes.              110


    What, Madam? No walking,
No reading, nor talking?
You're now in your prime,
Make use of your time.
Consider, before
You come to threescore,
How the hussies will fleer
Where'er you appear:
That silly old puss
Would fain be like us,              120
What a figure she made
In her tarnish'd brocade?


    And then he grows mild;
Come, be a good child:
If you are inclin'd
To polish your mind,
Be ador'd by the men
'Till threescore and ten,
And kill with the spleen
The jades of sixteen,              130
I'll shew you the way:
Read six hours a-day.

The wits will frequent ye,
And think you but twenty.

Thus was I drawn in,
Forgive me my sin.
At breakfast he'll ask
An account of my task.
Put a word out of joint,
Or miss but a point,                             140
He rages and frets,
His manners forgets;
And, as I am serious,
Is very imperious.
No book for delight
Must come in my sight;
But, instead of new plays,
Dull Bacon's Essays,
And pore ev'ry day on
That nasty Pantheon.                             150
If I be not a drudge,
Let all the world judge.
'Twere better be blind,
Than thus be confin'd.

But, while in an ill tone,
I murder poor Milton,
The Dean, you will swear,
Is at study or pray'r.
He's all the day saunt'ring,
With labourers bant'ring,                        160
Among his colleagues,
A parcel of Teagues,
(Whom he brings in among us
And bribes with mundungus.)

134. Scott, *Works*, 2nd edn., 1824, xv. 215, here inserts four lines:
'To make you learn faster,
I'll be your schoolmaster
And leave you to choose
The books you peruse.'
as 'Added from the Dean's manuscript'. This manuscript has not been traced.

Hail fellow, well met,
All dirty and wet:
Find out, if you can,
Who's master, who's man;
Who makes the best figure,
The Dean or the digger;                    170
And which is the best
At cracking a jest.
How proudly he talks
Of zigzacks and walks;
And all the day raves
Of cradles and caves;
And boasts of his feats,
His grottos and seats;
Shews all his gew-gaws,
And gapes for applause?                     180
A fine occupation
For one of his station!
A hole where a rabbit
Would scorn to inhabit,
Dug out in an hour,
He calls it a bow'r.


But, Oh, how we laugh,
To see a wild calf
Come, driven by heat,
And foul the green seat;                     190
Or run helter-skelter
To his arbor for shelter,
Where all goes to ruin
The Dean has been doing.
The girls of the village
Come flocking for pillage,
Pull down the fine briers,
And thorns, to make fires;
But yet are so kind
To leave something behind:                   200
No more need be said on't,
I smell when I tread on't.

Dear friend, Doctor Jenny,
If I could but win ye,
Or Walmsley or Whaley,
To come hither daily,
Since Fortune, my foe,
Will needs have it so,
That I'm, by her frowns,
Condemn'd to black gowns;          210
No 'Squire to be found
The neighbourhood round,
(For, under the rose,
I would rather chuse those:)
If your wives will permit ye,
Come here out of pity,
To ease a poor Lady,
And beg her a play-day.
So may you be seen
No more in the spleen:          220
May Walmsley give wine,
Like a hearty divine;
May Whaley disgrace
Dull Daniel's whey-face;
And may your three spouses
Let you lie at friends houses.

# LADY ACHESON
## Weary of the
# DEAN

### I

THE Dean wou'd visit Market-hill,
  Our Invitation was but slight
I said—why—Let him if he will,
  And so I bid Sir *Arthur* write.

Printed from the Folio Broadside, 1730.

## II

His Manners would not let him wait,
   Least we should think ourselves neglected,
And so we saw him at our Gate
   Three Days before he was expected.

## III

After a Week, a Month, a Quarter,
   And Day succeeding after Day,         10
Says not a Word of his Departure
   Tho' not a Soul would have him stay.

## [IV]

I've said enough to make him blush
   Methinks, or else the Devil's in't,
But he cares not for it a Rush,
   Nor for my Life will take the Hint.

## V

But you, my Life, may let him know,
   In civil Language, if he stays
How deep and foul the Roads may grow,
   And that he may command the Chaise.    20

## VI

Or you may say—my Wife intends,
   Tho' I should be exceeding proud,
This Winter to invite some Friends,
   And Sir I know you hate a Crowd.

## VII

Or, Mr. Dean—I should with Joy
   Beg you would here continue still,
But we must go to *Aghnacloy*;
   Or Mr. *Moor* will take it ill.

## VIII

The House Accounts are daily rising
   So much his Stay do's swell the Bills;    30
My dearest Life it is surprizing,
   How much he eats, how much he swills[.]

### IX

His Brace of Puppies how they stuff,
  And they must have three Meals a Day,
Yet never think they get enough;
  His Horses too eat all our Hay.

### X

Oh! if I could, how I would maul
  His Tallow Face and Wainscot Paws,
His Beetle-brows and Eyes of Wall,
  And make him soon give up the Cause.        40

### XI

Must I be every Moment chid
  With skinny, boney, snip and lean,
Oh! that I could but once be rid
  Of that insulting Tyrant Dean.

# ON A
# VERY OLD GLASS

*The following Lines were wrote upon a very
old Glass of Sir* Arthur Acheson's

FRAIL Glass, thou Mortal art, as well as I,
  Tho' none can tell, which of us first shall dye.

*Answered extempore by Dr.* SWIFT

WE both are Mortal; but thou, frailer Creature,
  May'st dye like me by Chance; but not by Nature.

Printed from *Works, Vol. VIII*, Dublin, 1746.

# TO JANUS

## ON NEW YEAR'S DAY

### Written in the Year 1729

TWO-fac'd *Janus*, God of Time,
Be my *Phœbus* while I rhime.
To oblige your Crony *Swift*,
Bring our Dame a New-Year's Gift:
She has got but half a Face;
*Janus*, since thou hast a Brace,
To my Lady once be kind;
Give her half thy Face behind.

GOD of Time, if you be wise,
Look not with your future Eyes:                    10
What imports thy forward Sight?
Well, if you could lose it quite.
Can you take Delight in viewing
This poor Isle's approaching Ruin?
When thy Retrospection vast
Sees the glorious Ages past.

HAPPY Nation were we blind,
Or, had only Eyes behind.—

DROWN your Morals, Madam cryes;
I'll have none but forward Eyes:                   20
Prudes decay'd about may tack,
Strain their Necks with looking back:
Give me *Time* when coming on:
Who regards him when he's gone?
By the Dean though gravely told,
New Years help to make me old;
Yet I find, a New-Years Lace
Burnishes an old Year's Face.
Give me Velvet and Quadrille,
*I'll have Youth and Beauty still.*                30

Printed from *Poems,* 1735.

.

# THE JOURNAL
## OF A
### *Modern Lady*

IT was a most unfriendly Part
In you, who ought to know my Heart,
Are well acquainted with my Zeal
For all the Female Commonweal:
How cou'd it come into your Mind,
To pitch on me, of all Mankind,
Against the Sex to write a Satyre,
And brand me for a Woman-Hater?
On me, who think them all so fair,
They rival *Venus* to a Hair;                    10
Their Virtues never ceased to sing,
Since first I learn'd to tune a String.
Methinks I hear the Ladies cry,
Will he his Character belye?
Must never our Misfortunes end?
And have we lost our only Friend?
Ah lovely Nymphs, remove your Fears,
No more let fall those precious Tears.
Sooner shall, *&c.*
          [*Here several Verses are omitted.*]
The Hound be hunted by the Hare,                    20
Than I turn Rebel to the Fair.


'Twas you engag'd me first to write,
Then gave the Subject out of Spite:
The *Journal of a Modern Dame*,
Is by my Promise what you claim;
My Word is past, I must submit,
And yet perhaps you may be bit.

Printed from *Miscellanies. The Third Volume*, 1732, with corrections from *Poems*, 1735.

I but transcribe, for not a Line
Of all the Satyre shall be mine.
Compell'd by you to tag in Rhimes                    30
The common Slanders of the Times,
Of modern Times, the Guilt is yours,
And me my Innocence secures.
Unwilling Muse begin thy Lay,
The Annals of a Female Day.


   By Nature turn'd to play the Rake-well,
(As we shall shew you in the Sequel)
The modern Dame is wak'd by Noon,
Some Authors say not quite so soon,
Because, though sore against her Will,                40
She sat all Night up at *Quadrill*.
She stretches, gapes, unglues her Eyes,
And asks if it be time to rise;
Of Head-ach, and the Spleen complains;
And then to cool her heated Brains,
Her Night-gown and her Slippers brought her,
Takes a large Dram of Citron Water.
Then to her Glass; and "*Betty*, pray
"Don't I look frightfully to Day?
"But, was it not confounded hard?                     50
"Well, if I ever touch a Card:
"Four *Mattadores*, and lose *Codill*!
"Depend upon't, I never will.
"But run to *Tom*, and bid him fix
"The Ladies here to Night by Six."
Madam, the Goldsmith waits below,
He says, his Business is to know
If you'll redeem the Silver Cup
He keeps in Pawn?—"Why, shew him up."
Your Dressing-Plate, he'll be content                 60
To take, for Interest *Cent. per Cent.*
And, Madam, there's my Lady *Spade*
Hath sent this Letter by her Maid.
"Well, I remember what she won;
"And hath she sent so soon to dun?

"Here, carry down those ten Pistoles
"My husband left to pay for Coals:
"I thank my Stars they all are light;
"And I may have Revenge to Night."
Now, loit'ring o'er her Tea and Cream,                70
She enters on her usual Theme;
Her last Night's ill Success repeats,
Calls Lady *Spade* a hundred Cheats:
She slipt Spadillo in her Breast,
Then thought to turn it to a Jest.
There's Mrs. *Cut* and she combine,
And to each other give the Sign.
Through ev'ry Game pursues her Tale,
Like Hunters o'er their Evening Ale.

Now to another Scene give Place,                80
Enter the Folks with Silks and Lace:
Fresh Matter for a World of Chat,
Right *Indian* this, right *Macklin* that;
Observe this Pattern; there's a Stuff,
I can have Customers enough.
Dear Madam, you are grown so hard,
This Lace is worth twelve Pounds a Yard:
Madam, if there be Truth in Man,
I never sold so cheap a Fan.

This Business of Importance o'er,                90
And Madam almost dress'd by Four;
The Footman in his usual Phrase,
Comes up with, "Madam, Dinner stays;"
She answers in her usual Style,
"The Cook must keep it back a while;
"I never can have Time to Dress,
"No Woman breathing takes up less;
"I'm hurry'd so, it makes me sick,
"I wish the Dinner at *Old Nick*."
At Table now she acts her Part,                100
Has all the Dinner-Cant by Heart:
"I thought we were to Dine alone,
"My Dear, for sure if I had known

"This Company would come to Day—
"But really 'tis my Spouse's Way;
"He's so unkind, he never sends
"To tell, when he invites his Friends:
"I wish you may but have enuff."
And while, with all this paultry Stuff,
She sits tormenting every Guest,                    110
Nor gives her Tongue one Moment's Rest,
In Phrases battered, stale, and trite,
Which modern Ladies call polite;
You see the Booby Husband sit
In Admiration at her Wit!

    But let me now a while survey
Our Madam o'er her Ev'ning Tea;
Surrounded with her Noisy Clans
Of Prudes, Coquets, and Harridans;
When frighted at the clam'rous Crew,                120
Away the God of *Silence* flew,
And fair *Discretion* left the Place,
And *Modesty* with blushing Face;
Now enters over-weening *Pride*,
And *Scandal* ever gaping wide,
*Hypocrisy* with Frown severe,
*Scurrility* with gibing Air;
Rude *Laughter* seeming like to burst;
And *Malice* always judging worst;
And *Vanity* with Pocket-Glass;                     130
And *Impudence* with Front of Brass;
And studied *Affectation* came,
Each Limb, and Feature out of Frame;
While *Ignorance*, with Brain of Lead,
Flew hov'ring o'er each Female Head.

    Why should I ask of thee, my Muse,
An Hundred Tongues, as Poets use,
When, to give ev'ry Dame her due,
An Hundred Thousand were too few!

119. *Harridans*. A cant word.

Or how should I, alas! relate,                    140
The Sum of all their senseless Prate,
Their Inuendo's, Hints, and Slanders,
Their Meanings lewd, and double 'Entendres.
Now comes the gen'ral Scandal-Charge,
What some invent, the rest enlarge;
And, "Madam, if it be a Lye,
"You have the Tale as cheap as I:
"I must conceal my Author's Name,
"But now 'tis known to common Fame."

Say, foolish Females, Bold and Blind,             150
Say, by what fatal Turn of Mind,
Are you on Vices most severe
Wherein yourselves have greatest Share?
Thus every Fool her self deludes;
The Prude condemns the absent Prudes;
*Mopsa*, who stinks her Spouse to Death,
Accuses *Chloe*'s tainted Breath;
*Hircina* rank with Sweat, presumes
To censure *Phillis* for Perfumes;
While crooked *Cynthia* snearing says,           160
That *Florimel* wears Iron Stays:
*Chloe* of ev'ry Coxcomb jealous,
Admires how Girls can talk with Fellows,
And full of Indignation frets
That Women should be such Coquets:
*Iris*, for Scandal most notorious,
Cries, "Lord, the World is so censorious!"
And *Rufa* with her Combs of Lead,
Whispers that *Sappho*'s Hair is Red:
*Aura*, whose Tongue you hear a Mile hence,      170
Talks half a Day in Praise of Silence;
And *Silvia* full of inward Guilt,
Calls *Amoret* an arrant Jilt.

Now Voices over Voices rise;
While each to be the loudest vies,
They contradict, affirm, dispute,
No single Tongue one Moment mute;

All mad to speak, and none to hearken,
They set the very Lap-Dog barking;
Their Chattering makes a louder Din        180
Than Fish-Wives o'er a Cup of Gin:
Not School-boys at a Barring-out,
Rais'd ever such incessant Rout:
The Jumbling Particles of Matter
In Chaos made not such a Clatter:
Far less the Rabble roar and rail,
When drunk with sour Election Ale.


 Nor do they trust their Tongue alone,
But speak a Language of their own;
Can read a Nod, a Shrug, a Look,        190
Far better than a printed Book;
Convey a Libel in a Frown,
And wink a Reputation down;
Or by the tossing of the Fan,
Describe the Lady and the Man.


 But see, the Female Club disbands,
Each twenty visits on her Hands.
Now all alone poor Madam sits,
In Vapours and Hysterick Fits:
"And was not *Tom* this Morning sent?        200
"I'd lay my Life he never went:
"Past Six, and not a living Soul!
"I might by this have won a Vole."
A dreadful Interval of Spleen!
How shall we pass the Time between?
"Here *Betty*, let me take my Drops,
"And feel my Pulse, I know it stops:
"This Head of mine, Lord, how it Swims!
"And such a Pain in all my Limbs!"
Dear Madam, try to take a Nap—        210
But now they hear a Foot-Man's Rap:
"Go run, and light the Ladies up:
"It must be One before we Sup."

The Table, Cards, and Counters set,
And all the Gamester Ladies met,
Her Spleen and Fits recover'd quite,
Our Madam can sit up all Night;
"Whoever comes, I'm not within—
*Quadrill*'s the Word, and so begin."


How can the Muse her Aid impart,          220
Unskill'd in all the Terms of Art?
Or in harmonious Numbers put
The Deal, the Shuffle, and the Cut?
The superstitious Whims relate,
That fill a Female Gamester's Pate?
What Agony of Soul she feels
To see a Knave's inverted Heels:
She draws up Card by Card, to find
Good Fortune peeping from behind;
With panting Heart, and earnest Eyes,          230
In hope to see *Spadillo* rise;
In vain, alas! her Hope is fed;
She draws an Ace, and sees it red.
In ready Counters never pays,
But pawns her Snuff-Box, Rings, and Keys.
Ever with some new Fancy struck,
Tries twenty Charms to mend her Luck.
"This Morning when the *Parson* came,
"I said I should not win a Game.
"This odious Chair how came I stuck in't,          240
"I think I never had good Luck in't.
"I'm so uneasy in my Stays;
"Your Fan, a Moment, if you please.
"Stand further Girl, or get you gone,
"I always lose when you look on."
Lord, Madam, you have lost Codill;
I never saw you play so ill.
"Nay, Madam, give me leave to say
"'Twas you that threw the Game away;
"When Lady *Tricksy* play'd a Four,          250
"You took it with a Matadore;

"I saw you touch your Wedding-Ring
"Before my Lady call'd a King.
"You spoke a Word began with H,
"And I know whom you mean to teach,
"Because you held the King of Hearts:
"Fie, Madam, leave these little Arts."
That's not so bad as one that rubs
Her Chair to call the King of Clubs,
And makes her Part'ner understand                260
A Matadore is in her Hand.
"Madam, you have no Cause to flounce,
"I swear I saw you thrice renounce."
And truly, Madam, I know when
Instead of Five you scor'd me Ten.
*Spadillo* here has got a Mark,
A Child may know it in the Dark:
I guess the Hand, it seldom fails,
I wish some Folks would pare their Nails.

While thus they rail, and scold, and storm,       270
It passes but for common Form;
And conscious that they all speak true,
They give each other but their Due;
It never interrupts the Game,
Or makes 'em sensible of Shame.

The Time too precious now to waste,
And Supper gobbled up in haste,
Again a-fresh to Cards they run,
As if they had but just begun.
But I shall not again repeat                      280
How oft they squabble, snarl and Cheat:
At last they hear the Watchman knock,
*A frosty Morn—Past Four a-Clock.*
The Chair-Men are not to be found,
"Come, let us play the t'other Round."

Now, all in haste they huddle on
Their Hoods, and Cloaks, and get them gone:
But first, the Winner must invite
The Company to-morrow Night.

Unlucky Madam left in Tears,          290
(Who now again *Quadrill* forswears,)
With empty Purse, and aching Head,
Steals to her sleeping Spouse to Bed.


# DEAN SMEDLEY

## Gone to seek his

## FORTUNE

*Per varios casus, per tot discrimina rerum.* Virg. *Æn.* i. 204

R*EVERENDUS Decanus, Jonathan Smedley*
　'*Theologia instructus; in Poesi exercita-*
'*tus; Politioribus excultus Literis: Parce*
'*Pius; Impius minime: Veritatis In-*
'*dagator; Libertatis Assertor: Subsanna-*
'*tus multis; Fastiditus Quibusdam; Ex-*
'*optatus plurimis; Omnibus Amicus;*
'*Author hujus Sententiae,*
　'PATRES SUNT VETULÆ.
'*Domata Invidia; Superato Odio; per Lau-*
'*dem et Vituperium; per Famam atq;*
'*Infamiam: Utramque Fortunam, Variosq;*
'*expertus Casus; Mente Sana; Sano*
'*Corpore; Volens, Lætusq; Lustris plus*
'*quam* XI *numeratis; ad Rem Familia-*
'*rem Restaurandam, augendamq; et ad*
'*Evangelium, Indos inter Orientales, præ-*
'*dicandum; Grevæ, Idibus Februarii,*
'*Navem ascendens, Arcemq; Sancti petens*
'*Georgii, Vernale per Æquinoxium; Anno*
'* Æræ Christianæ, Millesimo Septingen-*
'*tesimo Vicesimo Octa*[v]*o* TRANSFRE-
'*TAVIT.*
　—Fata vocant—Revocentq; precamur.

Printed from *The Intelligencer, No. XX, Dublin,* 1729.

## Thus translated

THE very Reverend *Dean Smedley*,
Of *Dullness, Pride, Conceit,* a medley,
Was equally allowed to shine,
As *Poet, Scholar* and *Divine.*
With *Godliness* cou'd well dispense,
Wou'd be a *Rake*, but wanted Sense.
Wou'd strictly after *Truth* enquire
Because he dreaded to come nigh'r.
For *Liberty* no Champion bolder,
He hated *Bailiffs* at his shoulder.                    10
To half the world a standing jest,
A perfect *Nuissance* to the rest.
From many (and we may believe him)
Had the best wishes they cou'd give him.
To all mankind a constant friend,
Provided they had *Cash* to lend.
One thing he did before he went hence,
He left us a *Laconick* Sentence,
By cutting of his Phrase, and trimming,
To prove that *Bishops* were old Women.              20
Poor Envy durst not shew her Phiz,
She was so terrify'd at his.
He waded without any shame,
Thro' thick and thin, to get a name.
Try'd ev'ry sharping Trick for Bread,
And after all he seldom Sped.
When *fortune* favour'd, he was nice,
He never once wou'd cog the *Dice*,
But if she turn'd against his play,
He knew to stop *a quater trois.*                      30
Now sound in mind, and sound in *corpus*,
(Says he) tho' swell'd like any *porpus.*
He heys from hence at forty four,
(*But by his Leave he sinks a Score,*)
To the *East Indies*, there to cheat,
'Till he can purchase an Estate;

Where after he has fill'd his chest,
He'll mount his *Tub*, and preach his best,
And plainly prove by dint of Text,
This World is his, and theirs the next.          40

    Lest that the reader shou'd not know,
The Bank where last he set his Toe,
'Twas *Greenwich*. There he took a Ship,
And gave his Creditors the Slip.
But lest *Chronology* should vary,
Upon the *Ides* of *February*,
*In seventeen hundred eight and twenty*,
To *Fort St. George* a *Pedlar* went he.
Ye *Fates*, when all he gets is Spent,
RETURN HIM BEGGAR AS HE WENT.          50


# On *PADDY*'s Character of the
# INTELLIGENCER

AS a *Thorn-bush*, or *Oaken-bough*,
  *Stuck* in an *Irish* Cabbin's *Brow*,
*Above* the *Door*, at *Country-fair*,
Betokens *Entertainment there*,
So, *Bays* on Poets *Brows* have bin
*Sett*, for a *Sign* of *Wit Within*.
And as *ill Neighbours* in the Night,
*Pull down* an Ale-house-Bush, *for Spite*,
The *Lawrel* so, by Poets worn,
Is by the Teeth of *Envy* torn,          10
*Envy*, a Canker-worm which *tears*
Those *Sacred Leaves* that *Lightning spares*.
And now to' *exemplifie* this *Moral*,
Tom having *earn'd* a *Twig* of Lawrel,
(Which measur'd on his *Head*, was found
Not *long enough* to reach *half round*,

Printed from the Broadside (n.d. or p.).

But like a Girl's *Cockade*, was ty'd
A Trophy, on his *Temple-side*.)
PADDY *repin'd* to see him *wear*
This *Badge of Honour* in his *Hair*,                   20
And thinking this *Cockade of Wit*
Wou'd his *own Temples* better fit,
Forming his Muse by SMEDLEY's *Modell*,
Lets drive at TOM's *devoted* Noddle,
Pelts him by *Turns* with *Verse* and *Prose*,
*Humms*, like a *Hornet* at his Nose,
At length, presumes to vent his Satyr on
The DEAN, TOM's *honour'd Friend and Patron*.
The EAGLE in the Tale, ye know,
*Teaz'd* by a *Buzzing Wasp*, *Below*,                   30
Took Wing to JOVE, and hop'd to *rest*
*Securely*, in the *Thunderer's* Breast,
In vain; *even there* to spoil his Nod
The SPITEFUL INSECT *stung* the *God*.

# Verses occasioned by the sudden drying up of ST. PATRICK'S WELL near Trinity College, *Dublin*, in 1726 [1729?]

B Y holy Zeal inspir'd, and led by Fame (*a*),
To thee, once fav'rite Isle, with Joy I came;
What Time the *Goth*, the *Vandal*, and the *Hun*,
Had my own native (*b*) *Italy* o'er-run.

Printed from *Works*, *Vol. X*, Dublin, 1762.

(*a*) *Festus Avienus* flourished in 370. See his Poem *De oris Maritimis*, where he uses this expression concerning Ireland, *Insula sacra et sic Insulam dixere Prisci; eamque late Gens Hibernorum colit*.

(*b*) *Italy* was not properly the native Place of St. Patrick, but the Place of his Education, and whence he received his Mission; and because he had his new Birth there, hence, by poetical Licence, and by Scripture-Figure, our Author calls that Country his native Italy.

*Ierne*, to the World's remotest Parts,
Renown'd for Valour, (c) Policy and Arts.
HITHER from (d) *Colchos*, with the fleecy Ore,
*Jason* arriv'd two thousand Years before.
(e) Thee, happy Island, *Pallas* call'd her own,
When haughty *Britain* was a Land unknown.        10
From thee, with Pride, the (f) *Caledonians* trace
The glorious Founder of their kingly Race:

(c) *Julius Solinus*, who lived about the Time of Tacitus, in the Year 80, Chap. 21, speaking of the Irish as a warlike Nation, says, that the Wives in Ireland, when delivered of a Son, give the Child its first Food off the Point of their Husband's Sword. *Puerpera, si quando marem edidit, primos Cibos Gladio imponit mariti, inque os Parvuli summo mucrone auspicium alimentorum leviter infert et Gentilibus votis optat, non aliter quam in Bello et inter Arma mortem oppetat.* Again, *Praecipua viris Gloria est in Armorum tutela.*

*Polydore Virgil* says, they were distinguished for their Skill in Musick. *Hiberni sunt Musicae peritissimi.* So *Giraldus Cambrensis*, who was Preceptor to King John, in his *Topographia Hiberniae*, Chap. 11. *In Musicis solum prae omni Natione, quam vidimus incomparabiliter est instructa Gens haec.*

(d) *Orpheus*, or the antient Author of the Greek Poem on the Argonautic Expedition, whoever he be, says, that Jason, who manned the Ship *Argos* at Thessaly, sailed to Ireland. And *Adrianus Junius* says the same Thing in these Lines

> *Illa ego sum Graiis, olim glacialis Ierne*
> *Dicta, et Jasoniae Puppis bene cognita Nautis.*

(e) *Tacitus*, in the Life of Julius Agricola says, that the Harbours of Ireland, on account of their Commerce, were better known to the trading Part of the World, than those of Britain. *Solum, caelumque, & ingenia, cultusque Hominum, haud multum a Britannia differunt; melius aditus, Portusque per Commercia et Negociatores cogniti.*

(f) *Fordon*, in his *Scoti-Chronicon*, Hector Boethius, Buchanan, and all the Scotch Historians agree, that Fergus, Son of Ferquard King of Ireland, was first King of Scotland, which Country he subdued. That he began to reign 330 Years before the Christian Æra, and in returning to visit his native Country, was shipwrecked on those Rocks in the County of Antrim, which from that Accident have been since named Carrickfergus. His Descendants reigned after him in Scotland; for the Crown was settled on him and his lineal Successors. See the List of the Kings of Scotland in Hector Boethius and George Buchanan, which begins thus: 1. *Fergusius Primus Scotorum Rex, filius Ferquardi Regis Hiberniae, regnare incepit anno ante Christi Servatoris in carnem adventem trecentesimo trigesimo. Regnavit annis* xxv. *et naufragio periit ad Scopulum Fergusis (Cragfergus vernacule) in mari Hiberniae.*

The Irish Language and Habit are still retained in the Northern Parts of Scotland, where the Highlanders speak the Irish Tongue, and use their antient Dress. As to the Name Scotland, Camden de Hibernia mentions it from the Authority of Isidore and Beda, that they called Ireland, *Scotia*, and that Scotland was termed *Scotia a Scotis Incolis, et inde Scotiae nomen cum Scotis in Britanniam nostram commigrasse.* Bede, Lib. 1. cap. 1, says, *Hibernia propria Scotorum Patria.*

Thy martial Sons, whom now they dare despise,
Did once their Land subdue and civilize:
Their Dress, their Language, and the *Scottish* Name,
Confess the Soil from whence the Victors came.
Well may they boast that antient Blood, which runs
Within their Veins, who are thy younger Sons,
A Conquest and a Colony from thee,
The Mother-Kingdom left her Children free;      20
From thee no Mark of Slavery they felt,
Not so with thee thy base Invaders dealt;
Invited here to 'vengeful *Morrough*'s Aid (*g*),
Those whom they could not conquer, they betray'd.
*Britain*, by thee we fell, ungrateful Isle!
Not by thy Valour, but superior Guile:
*Britain*, with Shame confess, this Land of mine (*h*)
First taught thee human Knowledge and divine;

(*g*) In the Reign of King Henry II. Dermot M'Morough, King of Leinster, being deprived of his Kingdom by Roderick O'Connor, King of Connaught, he invited the English over as Auxiliaries, and promised Richard Strangbow, Earl of Pembroke, his Daughter, and all his Dominions as a Portion. By this Assistance M'Morough recovered his Crown, and Strangbow became possessed of all Leinster. After this, more Forces being sent into Ireland, the English became powerful here; and when Henry II. arrived, the Irish Princes submitted to his Government, and began to use the English Laws.

(*h*) St. Patrick arrived in Ireland in the Year 431, and compleated the Conversion of the Natives, which had been begun by Palladius and others. And as Bishop Nicholson observes, (who was better acquainted with the Contents of all the antient Histories of both Kingdoms than any Man of the Age) Ireland soon became the Fountain of Learning, to which all the Western Christians, as well as English, had Recourse, not only for Instruction in the Principles of Religion, but in all Sorts of Literature; *viz. Legendi & Scholasticæ Eruditionis gratia.* For within a Century after the Death of St. Patrick, the Irish Seminaries of Learning increased to such a Degree, that most Parts of Europe sent hither their Children to be educated, and had from hence both their Bishops and Doctors. See venerable Bede, an English Historian of undoubted Credit, *Hist. Eccles.* Lib. 3, cap. 4, 7, 10, 11, 27. Among other Irish Apostles, he says, Saint Columb converted all the Picts, and many other Britons; and that Saint Aidan was the Instructer of King Oswald's Saxon Subjects in Christianity. Camden de Hibernia writes; *Subsequente ætate Scoticis Monarchis nihil Sanctius, nihil Eruditius fuerit, et in universam Europam sanctissimorum virorum Examina emiserint.* He says farther, that they not only repaired to Ireland, as to the Mart of Learning, but also brought from thence even the Form of their Letters: *Anglosaxones etiam nostri illa ætate in Hiberniam tanquam ad bonarum Literarum Mercaturam undique confluxerunt; unde de Viris Sanctis sæpissime in nostris Scriptoribus legitur; Amandatus est ad disciplinam in Hibernia. Indeque nostrates Saxones rationem formandi Literas accepisse videantur, quum eodem plene Charactere usi fuerint, qui hodie Hibernicis est in usu.*

OSPW

My Prelates and my Students, sent from hence,
Made your Sons Converts both to God and Sense:        30
Not like the Pastors of thy rav'nous Breed,
Who come to fleece the Flocks, and not to feed.
　WRETCHED *Ierne*! with what Grief I see
The fatal Changes Time hath made in thee.
The Christian Rites I introduc'd in vain:
Lo! Infidelity return'd again.
Freedom and Virtue in thy Sons I found,
Who now in Vice and Slavery are drown'd.
　BY Faith and Prayer, this Crosier in my Hand,
I drove the venom'd Serpent from thy Land;        40
The Shepherd in his Bower might sleep or sing (*i*),
Nor dread the Adder's Tooth, nor Scorpion's Sting.
　WITH Omens oft I strove to warn thy Swains,
Omens, the Types of thy impending Chains.
I sent the Magpye from the *British* Soil,
With restless Beak thy blooming Fruit to spoil,
To din thine Ears with unharmonious Clack,
And haunt thy holy Walls in white and black.
What else are those thou seest in Bishop's Geer
Who crop the Nurseries of Learning here?        50
Aspiring, greedy, full of senseless Prate,
Devour the Church, and chatter to the State.
　As you grew more degenerate and base,
I sent you Millions of the croaking Race;
Emblems of Insects vile, who spread their Spawn
Through all thy Land, in Armour, Fur and Lawn.
A nauseous Brood, that fills your Senate Walls,
And in the Chambers of your Viceroy crawls.
　SEE, where the new-devouring Vermin runs,
Sent in my Anger from the Land of *Huns*;        60
With harpy Claws it undermines the Ground,
And sudden spreads a numerous Offspring round;
Th' amphibious Tyrant, with his rav'nous Band,
Drains all thy Lakes of Fish, of Fruits thy Land.

---

(*i*) There are no Snakes, Vipers or Toads in Ireland; and even Frogs were not known here until about the Year 1700. The Magpyes came a short Time before, and the Norway Rats since.

WHERE is the sacred Well, that bore my Name?
Fled to the Fountain back, from whence it came!
Fair Freedom's Emblem once, which smoothly flows,
And Blessings equally on all bestows.
Here, from the neighbouring (k) Nursery of Arts,
The Students drinking, rais'd their Wit and Parts;          70
Here, for an Age and more, improv'd their Vein,
Their *Phœbus* I, my Spring their *Hippocrene*.
Discourag'd Youths, now all their Hopes must fail,
Condemn'd to Country Cottages and Ale;
To foreign Prelates make a slavish Court,
And by their Sweat procure a mean Support;
Or, for the Classicks read th'Attorney's Guide;
Collect Excise, or wait upon the Tide.
O! had I been Apostle to the *Swiss*,
Or hardy *Scot*, or any Land but this;                     80
Combin'd in Arms, they had their Foes defy'd,
And kept their Liberty, or bravely dy'd.
Thou still with Tyrants in Succession curst,
The last Invaders trampling on the first:
Nor fondly hope for some Reverse of Fate,
Virtue herself would now return too late.
Not half thy Course of Misery is run,
Thy greatest Evils yet are scarce begun.
Soon shall thy Sons, the Time is just at Hand,
Be all made Captives in their native Land;                 90
When, for the Use of no *Hibernian* born,
Shall rise one Blade of Grass, one Ear of Corn;
When Shells and Leather shall for Money pass,
Nor thy oppressing Lords (l) afford thee Brass.
But all turn Leasers to that (m) Mongril Breed,
Who from thee sprung, yet on thy Vitals feed;
Who to yon rav'nous Isle thy Treasures bear,
And waste in Luxury thy Harvests there;

(k) The University of Dublin, called Trinity College, was founded by Queen Elizabeth in 1591.

(l) Wood's ruinous Project against the People of Ireland, was supported by Sir Robert Walpole in 1724.

(m) The Absentees, who spend the Income of their Irish Estates, Places and Pensions in England.

For Pride and Ignorance a Proverb grown,
The Jest of Wits, and to the Court unknown.          100

I SCORN thy spurious and degenerate Line,
And from this Hour my Patronage resign.


# DRAPIER's HILL

WE give the World to understand,
    Our thriving Dean has purchas'd Land;
A Purchase which will bring him clear,
Above his Rent four Pounds a Year;
Provided, to improve the Ground,
He will but add two Hundred Pound,
And from his endless hoarded Store,
To build a House five Hundred more.
Sir *Arthur* too shall have his Will,
And call the Mansion *Drapier*'s Hill;          10
That when a Nation long enslav'd,
Forgets by whom it once was sav'd;
When none the DRAPIER's Praise shall sing;
His Signs aloft no longer swing;
His Medals and his Prints forgotten,
And all his Handkerchiefs are rotten;
His famous LETTERS made waste Paper;
This Hill may keep the Name of DRAPIER:
In Spight of Envy flourish still,
And DRAPIER's vye with COOPER's Hill.          20

Printed from *Poems*, 1735.

9. *Sir Arthur*. The Gentleman of whom the Purchase was made.
16. *Handkerchiefs*. Medals were cast; many Signs hung up; and Handkerchiefs made with Devices in honour of the Author, under the Name of M. B. Drapier.

# TO

# DEAN SWIFT

## By Sir ARTHUR ACHESON

GOOD cause have I to sing and vapour,
　For I am landlord to the Drapier:
He, that of ev'ry ear's the charmer,
Now condescends to be my farmer,
And grace my villa with his strains;
Lives such a Bard on British plains?
No; not in all the British Court;
For none but witlings there resort,
Whose names and works (tho' dead) are made
Immortal by the Dunciad;       10
And sure, as monument of brass,
Their fame to future times shall pass,
How, with a weakly warbling tongue,
Of Brazen Knight they vainly sung:
A subject for their genius fit;
He dares defy both sense and wit.
What dares he not? He can, we know it,
A laureat make that is no poet;
A judge, without the least pretence
To common law, or common sense;       20
A bishop that is no divine;
And coxcombs in red ribbons shine:
Nay, he can make what's greater far,
A middle-state 'twixt peace and war;
And say, there shall, for years together,
Be peace and war, and both, and neither.
Happy, O Market-Hill! at least,
That court and courtiers have no taste:
You never else had known the Dean,
But, as of old, obscurely lain;       30

Printed from *Works*, *4to*, *Vol. VIII* (2), London, 1765, ed. Deane Swift, who
first attributes the verses to Swift.

All things gone on the same dull track,
And Drapier's-hill been still Drumlack;
But now your name with Penshurst vies,
And wing'd with fame shall reach the skies.


# Robin and Harry

[p. 1] ROBIN, to beggars, with a curse
Throws the last shilling in his purse,
And, when the Coach-man comes for pay,
The Rogue must call another day.
    Grave Harry, when the poor are pressing
Gives them a peny, and God's blessing
But, always carefull of the main,
With two pence left, walks home in rain.
    Robin from noon to night will prate,
Runs out in tongue, as in estate;                    10
And e'er a twelvemonth and a day
Will not have one new thing to say.
Much talking is not Harry's vice,
He need not tell a Story twice,
And, if he always be so thrifty,
His fund may last to five and fifty.
    It so fell out, that cautious Harry
As Soldiers use, for love must marry,
And with his Dame the ocean crosst,
All for Love, or the World well lost.                20
[p. 2] Repairs a cabin gone to ruin,
Just big enough to shelter two in;
And, in his house, if any body come,
Will make them welcome to his modicum:
Where Goody Julia milks the Cows,
And boyls Potatoes for her Spouse,
Or darns his hose, or mends his Breeches,
While Harry's fencing up his ditches.

Printed from Swift's autograph, Forster Collection, No. 521.

    Robin, who ne'r his mind could fix
To live without a coach and six,      30
To patch his broken fortunes, found
A Mistress worth five thousand pound;
Swears, he could get her in an hour
If Gaffer Harry would endow her;
And sell, to pacify his wrath,
A Birth-right for a mess of broth.
    Young Harry, as all Europe knows,
Was long the quintessence of Beaux;
But, when espous'd, he ran the fate
That must attend the marry'd state;      40
From gold brocade and shining armour,
Was metamorphos'd to a farmer;
[p. 3] His Grazier's coat with dirt besmear'd,
Nor, twice a week will shave his beard.
    Old Robin, all his youth a sloven,
At fifty two, when he grew loving,
Clad in a coat of Podesway,
A flaxen wig, and wast-coat gay,
Powder'd from shoulder down to flank,
In courtly style addresses Franck;      50
Twice ten years older than his wife
Is doom'd to be a Beau for life:
Supplying those defects by dress
Which I must leave the world to guess.

# A PASTORAL DIALOGUE

### DERMOT, SHEELAH

A NYMPH and Swain, *Sheelah* and *Dermot* hight,
Who wont to weed the Court of *Gosford Knight*,
While each with stubbed Knife remov'd the Roots
That rais'd between the Stones their daily Shoots;

Printed from *Miscellanies. The Third Volume*, 1732, with notes from *Poems*, 1735.

2. *Gosford Knight.* Sir Arthur Acheson, whose Great Grand-Father was Sir Archibald of Gosford in Scotland.

As at their Work they sate in counterview,
With mutual Beauty smit, their Passion grew.
Sing heavenly Muse in sweetly flowing Strain,
The soft Endearments of the Nymph and Swain.

### DERMOT

My Love to *Sheelah* is more firmly fixt
Than strongest Weeds that grow these Stones betwixt:     10
My Spud these Nettles from the Stones can part,
No Knife so keen to weed thee from my Heart.

### SHEELAH

My Love for gentle *Dermot* faster grows
Than yon tall Dock that rises to thy Nose.
Cut down the Dock, 'twill sprout again: but O!
Love rooted out, again will never grow.

### DERMOT

No more that Bry'r thy tender Leg shall rake:
(I spare the Thistle for Sir *Arthur*'s sake.)
Sharp are the Stones, take thou this rushy Matt;
The hardest Bum will bruise with sitting squat.          20

### SHEELAH

Thy Breeches torn behind, stand gaping wide;
This Petticoat shall save thy dear Back-side;
Nor need I blush, although you feel it wet;
*Dermot*, I vow, 'tis nothing else but Sweat.

### DERMOT

At an old stubborn Root I chanc'd to tug,
When the Dean threw me this Tobacco-plug:
A longer half-p'orth never did I see;
This, dearest *Sheelah*, thou shalt share with me.

### SHEELAH

In at the Pantry-door this Morn I slipt,
And from the Shelf a charming Crust I whipt:              30
*Dennis* was out, and I got hither safe;
And thou, my dear, shalt have the bigger half.

18. *Sir Arthur*, who is a great Lover of Scotland.
31. *Dennis*. Sir Arthur's Butler.

### DERMOT

When you saw *Tady* at long-bullets play,
You sat and lows'd him all the Sun-shine Day.
How could you, *Sheelah*, listen to his Tales,
Or crack such Lice as his betwixt your Nails?

### SHEELAH

When you with *Oonah* stood behind a Ditch,
I peept, and saw you kiss the dirty Bitch.
*Dermot*, how could you touch those nasty Sluts!
I almost wisht this Spud were in your Guts.     40

### DERMOT

If *Oonah* once I kiss'd, forbear to chide:
Her Aunt's my Gossip by my Father's Side:
But, if I ever touch her Lips again,
May I be doom'd for Life to weed in Rain.

### SHEELAH

*Dermot*, I swear, tho' *Tady*'s Locks could hold
Ten thousand Lice, and ev'ry Louse was gold,
Him on my Lap you never more should see;
Or may I loose my Weeding-knife—and Thee.

### DERMOT

O, could I earn for thee, my lovely Lass,
A pair of Brogues to bear thee dry to Mass!     50
But see, where *Norah* with the Sowins comes—
Then let us rise, and rest our weary Bums.

# The Grand Question debated

### WHETHER

### *Hamilton's Bawn* should be turned into a *Barrack* or a *Malt House*

*THE Author of the following Poem, is said to be Dr J. S. D. S. P. D. who writ it, as well as several other Copies of Verses of the like Kind, by Way of Amusement, in the Family of an honourable Gentleman in the North of Ireland, where he spent a Summer about two or three Years ago.*

*A certain very great Person, then in that Kingdom, having heard much of this Poem, obtained a Copy from the Gentleman, or, as some say, the Lady, in whose House it was written, from whence, I know not by what Accident, several other Copies were transcribed, full of Errors. As I have a great Respect for the supposed Author, I have procured a true Copy of the Poem, the Publication whereof can do him less Injury than printing any of those incorrect ones which run about in Manuscript, and would infallibly be soon in the Press, if not thus prevented.*

*Some Expressions being peculiar to Ireland, I have prevailed on a Gentleman of that Kingdom to explain them, and I have put the several Explanations in their proper Places.*

THUS spoke to my Lady, the Knight full of Care;
Let me have your Advice in a weighty Affair.
This HAMILTON's *Bawn*, while it sticks on my Hand,
I lose by the House what I get by the Land;
But how to dispose of it to the best Bidder,
For a *Barrack* or *Malt-House*, we must now consider.

FIRST, let me suppose I make it a *Malt-House*:
Here I have computed the Profit will fall t'us.

Printed from *Poems*, 1735.

Title: *Bawn*. A Bawn was a place near the House enclosed with Mud or Stone Walls, to keep Cattle from being stolen in the Night. They are now little used.

3. 'A large old house two miles from Sr A A's Seat.' [Swift's MS. note.]

There's nine Hundred Pounds for Labour and Grain,
I increase it to Twelve, so three Hundred remain:          10
A handsome Addition for Wine and good Chear,
Three Dishes a Day, and three Hogsheads a Year.
With a Dozen large Vessels my Vault shall be stor'd,
No little scrub Joint shall come on my Board:
And you and the *Dean* no more shall combine,
To stint me at Night to one Bottle of Wine;
Nor shall I for his Humour, permit you to purloin
A Stone and a quarter of Beef from my Sirloin.
If I make it a *Barrack*, the Crown is my Tenant.
My Dear, I have ponder'd again and again on't:          20
In Poundage and Drawbacks, I lose half my Rent,
Whatever they give me I must be content,
Or join with the Court in ev'ry Debate,
And rather than that, I would lose my Estate.


THUS ended the Knight: Thus began his *meek* Wife:
It *must*, and it *shall* be a *Barrack*, my Life.
I'm grown a meer Mopus; no Company comes;
But a Rabble of Tenants, and rusty dull Rumms;
With *Parsons*, what Lady can keep herself clean?
I'm all over dawb'd when I sit by the *Dean*.          30
But, if you will give us a *Barrack*, my Dear,
The *Captain*, I'm sure, will always come here;
I then shall not value his Deanship a Straw,
For the *Captain*, I warrant, will keep him in Awe;
Or should he pretend to be brisk and alert,
Will tell him that Chaplains should not be so pert;
That Men of his Coat should be minding their Prayers,
And not among Ladies to give themselves Airs.


THUS argu'd my Lady, but argu'd in vain;
The Knight his Opinion resolv'd to maintain.          40
BUT *Hannah*, who listen'd to all that was past,
And could not endure so vulgar a Taste,

28. *Rumms*. 'A cant Word in Ireland for a poor Country Clergyman.'
41. *Hannah*. 'My Lady's Waiting woman.'

As soon as her Ladyship call'd to be drest,
Cry'd, Madam, why surely my Master's possest;
Sir *Arthur* the Malster! how fine it will sound?
I'd rather the BAWN were sunk under Ground.
But Madam, I guest there wou'd never come Good,
When I saw him so often with *Darby* and *Wood*.
And now my Dream's out: For I was a-dream'd
That I saw a huge Rat: O dear, how I scream'd!    50
And after, me thought, I had lost my new Shoes;
And, *Molly*, she said, I should near some ill News.

DEAR Madam, had you but the Spirit to teaze,
You might have a *Barrack* whenever you please:
And, Madam, I always believ'd you so stout,
That for twenty Denials you would not give out.
If I had a Husband like him, I *purtest*,
'Till he gave me my Will, I wou'd give him no Rest:
And rather than come in the same Pair of Sheets
With such a cross Man, I wou'd lye in the Streets.    60
But, Madam, I beg you contrive and invent,
And worry him out, 'till he gives his Consent.

DEAR Madam, whene'er of a *Barrack* I think,
An I were to be hang'd, I can't sleep a Wink:
For, if a new Crotchet comes into my Brain,
I can't get it out, tho' I'd never so fain.
I fancy already a *Barrack* contriv'd
At HAMILTON's *Bawn*, and the Troop is arriv'd.
Of this, to be sure, Sir *Arthur* has Warning,
And waits on the *Captain* betimes the next Morning.    70

Now, see, when they meet, how their Honour's behave;
Noble *Captain*, your Servant—Sir *Arthur* your Slave;
You honour me much—the Honour is mine,—
'Twas a sad rainy Night—but the Morning is fine—
Pray, how does my Lady?—My Wife's at your Service.—
I think I have seen her Picture by *Jervis*.—
Good Morrow, good *Captain*,—I'll wait on you down,—
You shan't stir a Foot—You'll think me a Clown—

48. *Darby and Wood*. 'Two of Sir Arthur's Managers.'

For all the World, *Captain*, not half an Inch farther—
You must be obey'd—your Servant, Sir *Arthur*; 80
My humble Respects to my Lady unknown.—
I hope you will use my House as your own.

  "Go, bring me my Smock, and leave off your Prate,
"Thou hast certainly gotten a Cup in thy Pate."
Pray, Madam, be quiet; what was it I said?—
You had like to have put it quite out of my Head.

  NEXT Day, to be sure, the *Captain* will come,
At the Head of his Troop, with Trumpet and Drum:
Now, Madam, observe, how he marches in State:
The Man with the Kettle-drum enters the Gate; 90
*Dub, dub, a-dub, dub.* The Trumpeters follow,
*Tantara, tantara,* while all the Boys hollow.
See, now comes the *Captain* all dawb'd with gold Lace:
O law! the sweet Gentleman! look in his Face;
And see how he rides like a Lord of the Land,
With the fine flaming Sword that he holds in his Hand;
And his Horse, the dear *Creter*, it prances and rears,
With Ribbins in Knots, at its Tail and its Ears:
At last comes the Troop, by the Word of Command
Drawn up in our Court; when the *Captain* cries, STAND. 100
Your *Ladyship* lifts up the Sash to be seen,
(For sure, I had *dizen'd* you out like a *Queen*:)
The *Captain*, to shew he is proud of the Favour,
Looks up to your Window, and cocks up his Beaver.
(His Beaver is cock'd; pray, Madam, mark that,
For, a *Captain* of Horse never takes off his Hat;
Because he has never a Hand that is idle;
For, the Right holds the Sword, and the Left holds the Bridle,)
Then flourishes thrice his Sword in the Air,
As a Compliment due to a Lady so fair; 110
How I tremble to think of the Blood it hath spilt!
Then he low'rs down the Point, and kisses the Hilt.
Your *Ladyship* smiles, and thus you begin;
Pray, *Captain*, be pleas'd to light, and walk in:
The *Captain* salutes you with Congee profound;
And your *Ladyship* curchyes half way to the Ground!

*KIT*, run to your Master, and bid him come to us.
I'm sure he'll be proud of the Honour you do us;
And, *Captain*, you'll do us the Favour to stay,
And take a short Dinner here with us to-Day:          120
You're heartily welcome: But as for good Chear,
You come in the very worst Time of the Year;
If I had expected so worthy a Guest:—
Lord! Madam! your Ladyship sure is in jest;
You *banter* me, Madam, the Kingdom must grant—
You Officers, *Captain*, are so complaisant.


"Hist, Huzzy, I think I hear some Body coming—"
No, Madam; 'tis only Sir *Arthur* a humming.


To shorten my Tale, (for I hate a long Story,)
The *Captain* at Dinner appears in his Glory;          130
The *Dean* and the *Doctor* have humbled their Pride,
For the *Captain*'s entreated to sit by your Side;
And, because he's their Betters, you carve for him first,
The *Parsons*, for Envy, are ready to burst:
The Servants amaz'd, are scarce ever able,
To keep off their Eyes, as they wait at the Table;
And, *Molly* and I have t[h]rust in our Nose,
To peep at the *Captain*, in all his fine *Clo'es*:
Dear Madam, be sure he's a fine spoken Man,
Do but hear on the Clergy how glib his Tongue ran;          140
"And Madam, says he, if such Dinners you give,
"You'll never want *Parsons* as long as you live;
"I ne'er knew a *Parson* without a good Nose,
"But the Devil's as welcome wherever he goes:
"God damn me, they bid us reform and repent,
"But, Zounds, by their Looks, they never keep Lent:
"Mister *Curate*, for all your grave Looks, I'm afraid,
"You cast a Sheep's Eye on her Ladyship's Maid;
"I wish she wou'd lend you her pretty white Hand,
"In mending your Cassock, and smoothing your Band:          150
(For the *Dean* was so shabby and look'd like a *Ninny*,
That the *Captain* suppos'd he was *Curate* to *Jenny*.)

131. 'Doctor Jenny, a Clergyman at Armagh.'

"Whenever you see a Cassock and Gown,
"A Hundred to One, but it covers a Clown;
"Observe how a *Parson* comes into a Room,
"God damn me, he hobbles as bad as my Groom;
"A *Scholard*, when just from his College broke loose,
"Can hardly tell how to cry *Bo* to a Goose;
"Your *Noveds*, and *Blutraks*, and *Omurs* and Stuff,
"By God they don't signify this Pinch of Snuff.    160
"To give a young Gentleman right Education,
"The Army's the only good School in the Nation;
"My School-Master call'd me a Dunce and a Fool,
"But at Cuffs I was always the Cock of the School;
"I never cou'd take to my Book for the Blood o'me,
"And the Puppy confess'd, he expected no Good o'me.
"He caught me one Morning coquetting his Wife,
"But he maul'd me, I ne'er was so maul'd in my Life;
"So, I took to the Road, and what's very odd,
"The first Man I robb'd was a Parson by God.    170
"Now Madam, you'll think it a strange Thing to say,
"But, the Sight of a Book makes me sick to this Day."

NEVER since I was born did I hear so much Wit,
And, Madam, I laugh'd till I thought I shou'd split.
So, then you look'd scornful, and snift at the Dean,
As, who shou'd say, *Now, am I Skinny and Lean?*
But, he durst not so much as once open his Lips,
And, the *Doctor* was plaguily down in the Hips.

THUS merciless *Hannah* ran on in her Talk,
Till she heard the *Dean* call, *Will your Ladyship walk?*    180
Her *Ladyship* answers, *I'm just coming down;*
Then, turning to *Hannah*, and forcing a Frown,
Altho' it was plain, in her Heart she was glad,
Cry'd, Huzzy, why sure the *Wench* is gone mad:
How cou'd these *Chimeraes* get into your Brains?—
Come hither, and take this old Gown for your Pains.
But the *Dean*, if this Secret shou'd come to his Ears,
Will never have done with his Gibes and his Jeers:
For your Life, not a Word of the Matter, I charge ye:
Give me but a *Barrack*, a Fig for the *Clergy*.    190

159. Ovids, Plutarchs, Homers.    176. *Skinny and Lean?* 'Nick-names for my Lady.'

# Directions for a Birth-day Song

## Oct. 30, 1729

TO form a just and finish'd piece,
Take twenty Gods of Rome or Greece,
Whose Godships are in chief request,
And fit your present Subject best.
And should it be your Hero's case
To have both male & female Race,
Your bus'ness must be to provide
A score of Goddesses beside.
   Some call their Monarchs Sons of Saturn,
For which they bring a modern Pattern,          10
Because they might have heard of one
Who often long'd to eat his Son:
But this I think will not go down,
For here the Father kept his Crown.
   Why then appoint him Son of Jove,
Who met his Mother in a grove;
To this we freely shall consent,
Well knowing what the Poets meant:
And in their Sense, 'twixt me and you,
It may be literally true.          20
   Next, as the Laws of Song require,
He must be greater than his Sire:
For Jove, as every School-boy knows,
Was able Saturn to depose;
And sure no Christian Poet breathing
Should be more scrup'lous than a Heathen.
Or if to Blasphemy it tends,
That's but a trifle among Friends.
   Your Hero now another Mars is,
Makes mighty Armys turn their Arses.          30
[p. 2] Behold his glitt'ring Faulchion mow
Whole Squadrons with a single blow:

Printed from Ford's transcript, The Rothschild Library, No. 2272.

While Victory, with Wings outspread,
Flyes like an Eagle or'e his head;
His milk-white Steed upon it's haunches,
Or pawing into dead mens paunches.
As Overton has drawn his Sire
Still seen o'r'e many an Alehouse fire.
Then from his Arm hoarse thunder rolls
As loud as fifty mustard bowls;                    40
For thunder still his arm supplyes,
And lightning always in his Eyes:
They both are cheap enough in Conscience,
And serve to eccho ratling Nonsence;
The rumbling words march fierce along,
Made trebly dreadfull in your Song.
   Sweet Poet, hir'd for birth-day Rimes,
To sing of Wars choose peaceful times.
What tho for fifteen years and more
Janus hath lock'd his Temple-door?                 50
Tho not a Coffee-house we read in
Hath mention'd arms on this side Sweden;
Nor London Journals, nor the Post-men,
Tho fond of warlike Lyes as most men;
Thou still with Battles stuff thy head full
For must a Hero not be dreadfull?
   Dismissing Mars, it next must follow
Your Conqu'rer is become Apollo:
That he's Apollo, is as plain, as
That Robin Walpole is Mecaenas:                    60
But that he struts, and that he squints,
You'd know him by Apollo's Prints
aliter  But that he squints, and that he struts,
   You'd know him by Apollo's Cuts.
[p. 3] Old Phœbus is but half as bright,
For yours can shine both day and night,
The first perhaps may once an Age
Inspire you with poetick Rage;
Your Phœbus royal, every day
Not only can inspire, but pay.                     70
   Then make this new Apollo sit
Sole Patron, Judge, and God of Wit.

"How from his Altitude he stoops,
"To raise up Virtue when she droops,
"On Learning how his Bounty flows,
"And with what Justice he bestows.
"Fair Isis, and ye Banks of Cam,
"Be witness if I tell a Flam:
"What Prodigys in Arts we drain
"From both your Streams in George's Reign!        80
"As from the flowry Bed of Nile—"
But here's enough to shew your Style.
    Broad Innuendos, such as this,
If well apply'd, can hardly miss:
For when you bring your Song in print,
He'll get it read, and take the hint,
(It must be read before 'tis warbled
The paper gilt, & Cover marbled)
And will be so much more your Debter
Because he never knew a letter.        90
And as he hears his Wit and Sence,
To which he never made pretence,
Set out in Hyperbolick Strains,
A Guinea shall reward your pains.
For Patrons never pay so well,
As when they scarce have learn'd to spell.
[p. 4]    Next call him Neptune with his Trident,
He rules the Sea, you see him ride in't;
And if provok'd, he soundly ferks his
Rebellious Waves with rods like Xerxes.        100
He would have seiz'd the Spanish Plate,
Had not the Fleet gone out too late,
And in their very Ports besiege,
But that he would not disoblige,
And made the Rascals pay him dearly
For those affronts they give him yearly.
    'Tis not deny'd that when we write,
Our Ink is black, our Paper white;
And when we scrawl our Paper o'r'e,
We blacken what was white before.        110
I think this Practice only fit
For dealers in Satyrick Wit:

But you some white-lead ink must get,
And write on paper black as Jet:
Your Int'rest lyes to learn the knack
Of whitening what before was black.
  Thus your Encomiums, to be strong,
Must be apply'd directly wrong:
A Tyrant for his Mercy praise,
And crown a Royal Dunce with Bays:          120
A squinting Monkey load with charms;
And paint a Coward fierce in arms.
Is he to Avarice inclin'd?
Extol him for his generous mind:
And when we starve for want of Corn,
Come out with Amalthea's Horn.
For Princes love you should descant
On Virtues which they know they want.
  One Compliment I had forgot,
But Songsters must omit it not.              130
[p. 5] (I freely grant the Thought is old)
Why then, your Hero must be told,
In him such Virtues lye inherent,
To qualify him God's Vicegerent,
That with no Title to inherit,
He must have been a King by Merit.
Yet be the Fancy old or new,
'Tis partly false, and partly true,
And take it right, it means no more
Than George and William claim'd before.     140
  Should some obscure inferior fellow
As Julius, or the Youth of Pella,
When all your list of Gods is out,
Presume to shew his mortal snout,
And as a Deity intrude,
Because he had the world subdu'd:
Oh! let him not debase your Thoughts,
Or name him, but to tell his Faults.
  Of Gods I only quote the best,
But you may hook in all the rest.            150
  Now Birth-day Bard, with joy proceed
To praise your Empress, and her Breed.

First, of the first. To vouch your Lyes
Bring all the Females of the Skyes:
The Graces and their Mistress Venus
Must venture down to entertain us.
With bended knees when they adore her
What Dowdys they appear before her!
Nor shall we think you talk at random,
For Venus might be her great Grandam.          160
Six thousand years hath liv'd the Goddess,
Your Heroine hardly fifty odd is.
[p. 6] Besides you Songsters oft have shewn,
That she hath Graces of her own:
Three Graces by Lucina brought her,
Just three; and every Grace a Daughter.
Here many a King his heart and Crown
Shall at their snowy feet lay down:
In Royal Robes they come by dozens
To court their English German Cousins,          170
Besides a pair of princely Babyes,
That five years hence will both be Hebes.
    Now see her seated on her Throne
With genuin lustre all her own.
Poor Cynthia never shone so bright,
Her Splendor is but borrow'd light;
And only with her Brother linkt
Can shine, without him is extinct.
But Carolina shines the clearer
With neither Spouse nor Brother near her,          180
And darts her Beams or'e both our Isles,
Tho George is gone a thousand miles.
Thus Berecynthia takes her place,
Attended by her heavenly Race,
And sees a Son in every God
Unaw'd by Jove's all-shaking Nod.
    Now sing his little Highness Freddy,
Who struts like any King already.
With so much beauty, shew me any maid
That could refuse this charming Ganymede,          190
Where Majesty with Sweetness vyes,
And like his Father early wise.

Then cut him out a world of work,
To conquer Spain, and quell the Turk.
Foretell his Empire crown'd with Bays,
And golden Times, and Halcyon days,
[p. 7] But swear his Line shall rule the Nation
For ever—till the Conflagration.
    But now it comes into my mind,
We left a little Duke behind;              200
A Cupid in his face and size,
And only wants to want his eyes.
Make some provision for the Yonker,
Find him a Kingdom out to conquer;
Prepare a Fleet to waft him o'r'e,
Make Gulliver his Commodore,
Into whose pocket valiant Willy put,
Will soon subdue the Realm of Lilliput.
    A skilfull Critick justly blames
Hard, tough, cramp, gutt'rall, harsh, stiff Names.
The Sense can ne're be too jejune,        211
But smooth your words to fit the tune,
Hanover may do well enough;
But George, and Brunswick are too rough.
Hesse Darmstedt makes too rough a sound,
And Guelph the strongest ear will wound.
In vain are all attempts from Germany
To find out proper words for Harmony:
And yet I must except the Rhine,
Because it clinks to Caroline.        220
Hail Queen of Britain, Queen of Rhymes,
Be sung ten hundred thousand times.
Too happy were the Poets Crew,
If their own happyness they knew.
Three Syllables did never meet
So soft, so sliding, and so sweet.
Nine other tuneful words like that
Would prove ev'n Homer's Numbers flat.
Behold three beauteous Vowels stand
With Bridegroom liquids hand in hand,    230
[p. 8] In Concord here for ever fixt,
No jarring consonant betwixt.

May Caroline continue long,
For ever fair and young—in Song.
What tho the royal Carcase must
Squeez'd in a Coffin turn to dust;
Those Elements her name compose,
Like Atoms are exempt from blows.
   Tho Caroline may fill your gaps
Yet still you must consult the Maps,          240
Find Rivers with harmonious names,
Sabrina, Medway, and the Thames.
Britannia long will wear like Steel
But Albion's cliffs are out at heel,
And Patience can endure no more
To hear the Belgick Lyon roar.
Give up the phrase of haughty Gaul,
But proud Iberia soundly maul,
Restore the Ships by Philip taken,
And make him crouch to save his bacon.    250
   Nassau, who got the name of glorious
Because he never was victorious,
A hanger on has always been,
For old acquantance bring him in.
   To Walpole you might lend a Line,
But much I fear he's in decline;
And if you chance to come too late
When he goes out, you share his fate,
And bear the new Successor's frown;
Or whom you once sung up, sing down.    260
   Reject with scorn that stupid Notion
To praise your Hero for Devotion:
Nor entertain a thought so odd,
That Princes should believe in God:
[p. 9] But follow the securest rule,
And turn it all to ridicule:
'Tis grown the choicest Wit at Court,
And gives the Maids of Honor Sport.
For since they talk'd with Doctor Clark,
They now can venture in the dark.    270
That sound Divine the Truth has spoke all
And pawn'd his word Hell is not local.

This will not give them half the trouble
Of Bargains sold, or meanings double.
    Supposing now your Song is done,
To Minheer Hendel next you run,
Who artfully will pare and prune
Your words to some Italian Tune.
Then print it in the largest letter,
With Capitals, the more the better.                    280
    Present it boldly on your knee,
And take a Guinea for your Fee.

# On burning a dull Poem

### Written in the Year 1729

AN Ass's Hoof alone can hold
    That pois'nous Juice which kills by Cold.
Methought, when I this Poem read,
No Vessel but an Ass's Head,
Such frigid Fustian could contain;
I mean the Head without the Brain.
The cold Conceits, the chilling Thoughts,
Went down like stupifying Draughts:
I found my Head began to swim,
A Numbness crept through ev'ry Limb:                   10
In Haste, with Imprecations dire,
I threw the Volume in the Fire:
When, who could think, tho' cold as Ice,
It burnt to Ashes in a Trice.

    How could I more enhaunce it's Fame?
Though born in Snow, it dy'd in Flame.

Printed from *Poems*, 1735.

# AN EPISTLE

## To His Excellency

# John *Lord* Carteret, &c.

[by Delany]

*Credis ob hoc, me, Pastor, opes fortasse rogare,*
  *Propter quod, vulgus, crassaq; turba rogat:* Mart. Epig. lib. 9

THOU wise, and learned Ruler of our Ile,
  Whose Guardian Care can all her Griefs beguile;
When next your generous Soul shall condescend,
T'Instruct, or entertain your humble Friend,
Whether retiring from your weighty Charge,
On some high Theme you learnedly enlarge;
Of all the Ways of Wisdom reason well,
How RICHLEU rose, and how SEJANUS fell:
Or when your Brow less thoughtfully unbends,
Circled with SWIFT, and some delighted Friends;          10
When mixing Mirth and Wisdom with your Wine,
Like that your Wit shall flow, your Genius shine,
Nor with less Praise the Conversation guide,
Than in the publick Councils you decide:
Or when the *Dean*, long privileg'd to rail,
Asserts his Friend with more impetuous Zeal;
You hear, (whilst I sit by abash'd and mute)
With soft Concessions shortning the Dispute;
Then close with kind Enquiries of my State,
'How are your Tythes, and have they rose of late?          20
'Why *Christ-Church* is a pretty Situation,
'There are not many better in the Nation!
'This, with your other *Things*, must yield you clear
'Some six—at least five hundred Pounds a Year.'

SUPPOSE at such a Time, I took the Freedom
To speak these Truths, as plainly as you read 'em,
(You shall rejoin, my Lord, when I've replied,
And, if you please, my Lady shall decide.)

Printed from the original 8vo pamphlet, Dublin, 1730.

My Lord, I'm satisfied you meant me well,
And that I'm thankful, all the World can tell,          30
But you'll forgive me, if I own th' Event
Is short, is very short of your Intent;
At least I feel some Ills, unfelt before,
My Income less, and my Expences more.

How Doctor! double Vicar! double Rector!
A Dignitary! with a City Lecture—
What Glebes—what Dues—what Tythes—
        what Fines—what Rent!
Why Doctor——will you never be content?

Would my good Lord but cast up the Account,
And see to what my Revenues amount,          40
My Titles ample! but my Gains so small,
That one good Vicarage is worth 'em all—
And very wretched, sure, is he, that's double,
In nothing, but his Titles, and his Trouble.

Add to this crying Grievance if you please,
My Horses founder'd on FERMANAGH Ways;
Ways of well-polish'd, and well-pointed Stone,
Where every Step endangers every Bone;
And more to raise your Pity, and your Wonder,
Two Churches——twelve HIBERNIAN Miles asunder!          50
With complicated *Cures*, I labour hard in,
Besides whole Summers absent from my Garden!
But that the World would think I plaid the Fool,
I'd Change with CHARLY GRATTAN for his School—
What fine Cascades, what Vistos might I make,
Fixt in Centre of th' IERNIAN Lake!
There might I sail delighted, smooth, and safe,
Beneath the Conduct of my good Sir RALPH:
There's not a better Steerer in the Realm;
I hope, my Lord, you'll call him to the *Helm*—          60

Doctor—a glorious Scheme to ease your Grief!
When *Cures* are cross, a School's a sure Relief.
You cannot fail of being happy there,
The Lake will be the *Lethe* of your Care:
The Scheme is for your Honour and your Ease!
And Doctor, I'll promote it when you please.

58. *Sir Ralph.* Sir Ralph Gore, who has a Villa in the Lake of Erin.

Mean while, allowing Things—below your Merit,
Yet Doctor, you've a philosophick Spirit;
Your Wants are few, and, like your Income, small,
And you've enough to gratify 'em all:        70
You've Trees, and Fruits, and Roots enough in store,
And what would a Philosopher have more?
You cannot wish for Coaches, Kitchens, Cooks—

—My Lord, I've not enough to buy me Books—
Or pray, suppose my Wants were all supplied,
Are there no Wants I should regard beside?
Who's Breast is so unman'd, as not to grieve,
Compass'd with Miseries he can't relieve?
Who can be happy—who would wish to live,
And want the Godlike Happiness to give?        80
(That I'm a Judge of this you must allow,
I had it once—and I'm debarr'd it now.)
Ask your own Heart, my Lord, if this be true—
Then how unblest am I! how blest are you!

'Tis true—but, Doctor, let us wave all that—
Say, if you had your Wish what you'd be at:

Excuse me, good my Lord—I won't be sounded,
Nor shall your Favour by my Wants be bounded.
My Lord, I challenge nothing as my Due,
Nor is it fit I should prescribe to You.        90
Yet this might symmachus himself avow,
(Whose rigid Rules are antiquated now)
'My Lord, I'd wish—to *pay the Debts I owe,*—
'I'd wish besides—to *build,* and to *bestow.*'

91. *Symmachus*. Symmachus, Bishop of Rome A.D. 499 made a Decree, that
no Man should sollicit for Ecclesiastical Preferment, before the Death of the
Incumbent.

# AN EPISTLE

## UPON AN

## EPISTLE From a certain DOCTOR

## To a certain great LORD:

### BEING A

### *Christmas-Box* for D. *Delany*

—— *Palatinæ Cultor facunde Minervæ,*
*Ingenio frueris qui propriore Dei.*
*Nam tibi nascentes* DOMINI *cognoscere Curas,*
*Et secreta* DUCIS *Pectora nôsse licet.*

Mart. Lib. 5, Ep. 5

AS *Jove* will not attend on less,
　　When Things of more Importance press:
You can't, grave Sir, believe it hard,
That you, a low *Hibernian* Bard,
Shou'd cool your Heels a while, and wait
Unanswer'd at your *Patron*'s Gate;
And wou'd my Lord vouchsafe to grant
This one, poor, humble Boon I want,
Free Leave to play his *Secretary*,
As *Falstaff* acted old King *Harry*:　　　　　10
I'd tell of yours in Rhyme and Print:
Folks shrug, and cry, *There's nothing in't.*
And after several Readings over,
It shines most in the Marble Cover.

　How cou'd so fine a Taste dispense
With mean Degrees of Wit and Sense?
Nor will my Lord so far *Beguile*
The *Wise* and *Learned* of our *Isle*;
To make it pass upon the Nation,
By Dint of his sole Approbation.　　　　　20
The Task is Arduous, Patrons find,
To warp the Sense of all Mankind:

Printed from the original pamphlet, Dublin, 1730.

Who think your Muse must first aspire;
E're he advance the Doctor higher[.]

   You've Cause to say he *meant you well*:
That you *are thankful* who *can tell*?
For still you're short (which grieves your Spirit)
Of his Intent, you mean, your Merit.

   Ah! *Quanto rectiùs, Tu Adepte,*
*Qui nil moliris tam ineptè?*                          30
*Smedley*, thou *Jonathan* of *Clogher*,
"When thou thy humble Lays do'st offer
"To *Grafton*'s Grace, with grateful Heart;
"Thy Thanks and Verse, devoid of Art:
"Content with what his Bounty gave,
"No larger Income dost thou Crave."

   But you must have Cascades, and all
*Ierna*'s Lake, for your Canal,
Your Vistos, Barges, and (A Pox on
All Pride) our *Speaker* for your Coxon:         40
It's Pity that he can't bestow you
Twelve Commoners in Caps to Row you.
Thus *Edgar* proud, in Days of Yore,
Held Monarchs labouring at the Oar;
And as he pass'd, so swell'd the *Dee*
Inrag'd, as *Ern* would do at thee.

   How different is this from *Smedley*?
(His Name is up, he may in Bed lye)
"Who only asks some pretty Cure,
"In wholesome Soil and Æther Pure;                50
"The Garden stor'd with artless Flowers,
"In either Angle shady Bowers:
"No gay Parterre with costly Green,
"Must in the Ambient Hedge be seen;
"But Nature freely takes her Course,
"Nor fears from him ungrateful Force:
"No Sheers to check her sprouting Vigour,
"Or shape the *Yews* to Antick Figure."

But you forsooth, your *All* must squander,
On that poor Spot, call'd *Del-Ville*, yonder:                    60
And when you've been at vast Expences
In Whims, Parterres, Canals and Fences:
Your Assets fail, and Cash is wanting
For farther Buildings, farther Planting.
No wonder when you raise and level,
Think this Wall low, and that Wall bevel.
Here a convenient Box you found,
Which you demolish'd to the Ground:
Then Built, then took up with your Arbour,
And set the House to *Rupert Barber*.                    70
You sprung an Arch, which in a Scurvy
Humour, you tumbled Topsy Turvy.
You change a Circle to a Square,
Then to a Circle, as you were:
Who can imagine whence the Fund is,
That you *Quadrata* change *Rotundis*?

To *Fame* a Temple you Erect,
A *Flora* does the Dome protect;
Mounts, Walks, on high; and in a Hollow
You place the *Muses* and *Apollo*;                    80
There shining 'midst his Train, to Grace
Your Whimsical Poetick Place.

These Stories were, of old, design'd
As Fables: But you have refin'd
The Poets Mythologick Dreams,
To real Muses, Gods, and Streams.
Who wou'd not swear, when you contrive thus,
That you're *Don Quixote Redivivus*?

Beneath a dry Canal there lies,
Which only *Winter*'s Rain supplies.                    90
Oh! cou'd'st thou, by some Magick Spell,
Hither convey St. *Patrick*'s *Well*;
Here may it re-assume its Stream,
And take a Greater *Patrick*'s Name.

If your Expences rise so high;
What Income can your Wants supply?
Yet still you fancy you inherit
A Fund of such Superior Merit,
That you can't fail of more Provision,
All by my *Lady*'s kind Decision.                    100
For the more Livings you can fish up,
You think you'll sooner be a Bishop:
That cou'd not be *my Lord*'s *Intent*,
Nor can it *answer in the Event*.
Most think what has been heap'd on You,
To other sort of Folk was due:
Rewards too great for your Flim-Flams,
*Epistles, Riddles, Epigrams.*

Tho' now your Depth must not be Sounded,
The Time was, when you'd have compounded     110
For less than CHARLY GRATTAN's School:
Five hundred Pound a Year's no Fool.

Take this Advice then from your Friend,
To Your Ambition put an End.
Be frugal, *Patt*: pay what you owe,
Before you *Build* and You *Bestow*[;]
Be Modest: nor Address your Betters
With Begging, Vain, Familiar Letters.

A Passage may be found, I've heard,
In some old *Greek* or *Latian* Bard,              120
Which says, wou'd Crows in Silence eat
Their Offals, or their better Meat,
Their generous Feeders not provoking
By loud and unharmonious Croaking:
They might, unhurt by Envy's Claws,
Live on, and Stuff, to Boot, their Maws.

# A LIBEL

# On DOCTOR DELANY

### AND A

## Certain Great Lord

DELUDED Mortals, whom the *Great*
Chuse for Companions *tete à tete*,
Who at their Dinners, *en famille*
Get Leave to sit whene'er you will;
Then, boasting tell us where you din'd,
And, how his *Lordship* was so kind;
How many pleasant Things he spoke,
And, how you *laugh'd* at every *Joke*:
Swear, he's a most facetious Man,
That you and he are *Cup* and *Cann*.                    10
You Travel with a heavy Load,
And quite mistake *Preferment*'s Road.
  Suppose my *Lord* and you alone;
Hint the least Int'rest of your own;
His Visage drops, he knits his Brow,
He cannot talk of Bus'ness now:
Or, mention but a vacant *Post*,
He'll turn it off with; *Name your Toast.*
Nor could the nicest Artist Paint,
A Countenance with more Constraint.                     20
  For, as their Appetites to quench,
Lords keep a Pimp to bring a Wench;
So, Men of Wit are but a kind
Of Pandars to a vicious Mind,
Who proper Objects must provide
To gratify their Lust of Pride,
When weary'd with Intrigues of State,
They find an idle Hour to Prate.
Then, shou'd you dare to ask a *Place*,

Printed from the original pamphlet, Dublin, 1730, with corrections from *Poems*,
1735.

You Forfeit all your *Patron*'s Grace,                    30
And disappoint the sole Design,
For which he summon'd you to *Dine*.
   Thus, *Congreve* spent, in writing Plays,
And one poor Office, half his Days;
While *Montague*, who claim'd the Station
To be *Mæcenas* of the Nation,
For *Poets* open Table kept,
But ne'er consider'd where they Slept.
Himself, as rich as fifty *Jews*,
Was easy, though they wanted Shoes;                    40
And, crazy *Congreve* scarce cou'd spare
A Shilling to discharge his Chair,
Till Prudence taught him to appeal
From *Pæan*'s Fire to *Party* Zeal;
Not owing to his happy Vein
The Fortunes of his latter Scene,
Took proper *Principles* to thrive;
And so might ev'ry *Dunce* alive.
   Thus, *Steel* who own'd what others writ,
And flourish'd by imputed Wit,                    50
From Perils of a hundred Jayls,
Withdrew to starve, and dye in *Wales*.
   Thus *Gay*, the *Hare* with many Friends,
Twice sev'n long Years the *Court* attends,
Who, under Tales conveying Truth,
To Virtue form'd a *Princely* Youth,
Who pay'd his Courtship with the Croud,
As far as *Modest Pride* allow'd,
Rejects a servile *Usher*'s Place,
And leaves *St. James*'s in Disgrace.                    60
   Thus *Addison* by Lords Carest,
Was left in Foreign Lands distrest,
Forgot at Home, became for Hire,
A trav'lling Tutor to a *Squire*;
But, wisely left the *Muses* Hill,
To Bus'ness shap'd the *Poet*'s Quil,
Let all his barren Lawrel's fade
Took up himself the *Courtier*'s Trade,

53. *Gay*. See his Fables.

And grown a *Minister of State*,
Saw Poets at his Levee wait.                70
   Hail! happy *Pope*, whose gen'rous Mind,
Detesting all the Statesmen kind,
Contemning *Courts*, at *Courts* unseen,
Refus'd the Visits of a Queen;
A Soul with ev'ry Virtue fraught
By *Sages*, *Priests*, or *Poets* taught;
Whose filial Piety excels
Whatever *Grecian* Story tells:
A Genius for all Stations fit,
Whose *meanest Talent* is his *Wit*:          80
His Heart too Great, though Fortune little,
To lick a *Rascal Statesman*'s Spittle.
Appealing to the Nation's Taste,
Above the Reach of Want is plac't:
By *Homer* dead was taught to thrive,
Which *Homer* never cou'd alive.
And, sits aloft on *Pindus* Head,
Despising *Slaves* that *cringe* for Bread.
   True *Politicians* only Pay
For solid Work, but not for Play;          90
Nor ever chuse to Work with Tools
Forg'd up in *Colleges* and *Schools*.
Consider how much more is due
To all their *Journey-Men*, than you,
At Table you can *Horace* quote;
They at a Pinch can bribe a Vote:
You shew your Skill in *Grecian* Story,
But, they can manage *Whig* and *Tory*:
You, as a *Critick*, are so curious
To find a Verse in *Virgil* Spurious;      100
But, they can *smoak* the deep Designs,
When *Bolingbroke* with *Pult'ney* Dines.
   Besides; your Patron may upbraid ye,
That you have got a Place already,
An Office for your Talents fit,
To Flatter, Carve, and shew your Wit;
To snuff the Lights, and stir the Fire,
And get a *Dinner* for your Hire,

PSPW

What Claim have you to *Place*, or *Pension*?
He overpays in Condescension.                                   110
    But, Rev'rend *Doctor*, you, we know,
Cou'd never Condescend so low;
The *Vice-Roy*, whom you now attend,
Wou'd, if he durst, be more your Friend;
Nor will in you those Gifts despise,
By which himself was taught to rise:
When he has Virtue to retire,
He'll Grieve he did not raise you higher,
And place you in a better Station,
Although it might have pleas'd the Nation.                      120
    This may be true—submitting still
To Walpole's more than Royal Will.
And what Condition can be worse?
He comes to *drain* a *Beggar*'s *Purse*:
He comes to tye our Chains on faster,
And shew us, *England* is our Master:
Caressing Knaves and Dunces wooing,
To make them work their own undoing.
What has he else to bait his Traps,
Or bring his *Vermin* in, but *Scraps*?                         130
The Offals of a *Church* distress't,
A hungry *Vicarage* at best;
Or, some remote inferior *Post*,
With forty Pounds a Year at most.
    But, here again you interpose;
Your favourite *Lord* is none of those,
Who owe their Virtues to their Stations,
And Characters to Dedications:
For keep him in, or turn him out,
His *Learning* none will call in doubt;                         140
His *Learning*, though a *Poet* said it,
Before a Play, wou'd lose no Credit:
Nor POPE wou'd dare deny him Wit,
Although to Praise it PHILIPS Writ.
I own, he hates an Action base,
His *Virtues* battling with his *Place*;
Nor wants a nice discerning Spirit,
Betwixt a true and spurious Merit;

Can sometimes drop a *Voter*'s Claim,
And give up Party to his Fame.                    150
I do the most that *Friendship* can;
I hate the *Vice-Roy*, love the Man.
    But, You, who till your Fortune's made
Must be a Sweet'ner by your Trade,
Shou'd swear he never meant us ill;
We suffer sore against his Will;
That, if we could but see his Heart,
He wou'd have chose a milder part;
We rather should Lament his Case
Who must Obey, or lose his *Place*.                160
    Since this Reflection slipt your Pen,
Insert it when you write agen:
And, to Illustrate it, produce
This *Simile* for his Excuse.
    "So, to destroy a guilty Land,
"An *Angel* sent by *Heav'n*'s Command,
"While he obeys *Almighty* Will,
"Perhaps, may feel *Compassion* still,
"And wish the Task had been assign'd
"To *Spirits* of less gentle kind."                170
    But I, in *Politicks* grown old,
Whose Thoughts are of a diff'rent Mold,
Who, from my Soul, sincerely hate
Both *Kings* and *Ministers* of *State*,
Who look on *Courts* with stricter Eyes,
To see the Seeds of *Vice* arise,
Can lend you an Allusion fitter,
Though *flatt'ring Knaves* may call it *bitter*.
Which, if you durst but give it place,
Would shew you many a *Statesman*'s Face.          180
Fresh from the *Tripod* of Apollo,
I had it in the Words that follow.
(Take Notice, to avoid Offence
I here except *His Excellence*.)
    So, to effect his *Monarch*'s ends,
From *Hell* a *Viceroy* DEV'L ascends,
His *Budget* with *Corruptions* cramm'd,
The Contributions of the *damn'd*;

Which with unsparing Hand, he strows
Through *Courts* and *Senates* as he goes;          190
And then at *Beelzebub*'s *Black-Hall*,
Complains his *Budget* was too small.
      Your *Simile* may better shine
In Verse; but there is *Truth* in mine.
For, no imaginable things
Can differ more than GOD and *Kings*
And, *Statesmen* by ten thousand odds
Are ANGELS, just as *Kings* are GODS.

# TRAULUS

## The first PART

## IN A

## DIALOGUE

### BETWEEN

## TOM and ROBIN

### TOM

SAY, *Robin*, what can *Traulus* mean
    By bell'wing thus against the Dean?
Why does he call him paultry Scribler,
*Papist*, and *Jacobite*, and *Lib'ller*?
Yet cannot prove a single Fact.

### ROBIN

Forgive him, *Tom*, his Head is crackt.

### TOM

What Mischief can the Dean have done him,
That *Traulus* calls for Vengeance on him?

Printed from the first ed., [Dublin] 1730, with corrections from *Poems*, 1735
(uncancelled state).

Title: 'Traulus is my Ld. Allen' (Marmaduke Coghill, 1730).

Why must he sputter, spaul and slaver it
In vain, against the People's Fav'rite?      10
Revile that Nation-saving Paper,
Which gave the Dean the Name of *Draper*?


### ROBIN

Why *Tom*, I think the Case is plain,
Party and Spleen have turn'd his Brain.


### TOM

Such Friendship never Man profest,
The Dean was never so carest:
For *Traulus* long his Rancour nurst,
Till, God knows why, at last it burst.
That clumsy outside of a Porter,
How could it thus conceal a Courtier?      20


### ROBIN

I own, Appearances are bad;
But still insist the Man is mad.


### TOM

Yet many a Wretch in *Bedlam*, knows,
How to distinguish Friends from Foes;
And tho' perhaps among the Rout,
He wildly flings his Filth about,
He still has Gratitude and Sap'ence,
To spare the Folks that gave him Ha'pence
Nor, in their Eyes at Random pisses,
But turns aside like mad *Ulysses*:      30
While *Traulus* all his Ordure scatters[,]
To foul the Man he chiefly flatters.
Whence come these inconsistent Fits?


### ROBIN

Why *Tom*, the Man has lost his Wits!

## TOM

Agreed. And yet, when *Towzer* snaps
At People's Heels with frothy Chaps;
Hang's down his Head, and drops his Tail,
To say he's mad will not avail:
The Neighbours all cry, *Shoot him dead,*
*Hang, Drown, or knock him on the Head.*          40
So, *Traulus* when he first harangu'd,
I wonder why he was not hang'd:
For of the two, without Dispute,
*Towzer*'s the less offensive Brute.

## ROBIN

*Tom*, you mistake the Matter quite;
Your barking Curs will seldom bite:
And, though you hear him Stut-tut-tut-ter,
He barks as fast as he can utter.
He prates in Spight of all Impediment
While none believes that what he said he meant:          50
Puts in his Finger and his Thumb,
To grope for Words, and out they come.
He calls you Rogue; There's nothing in it,
He fawns upon you in a Minute.
Begs leave to rail, but damn his Blood,
He only meant it for your Good.
His Friendship was exactly tim'd,
He shot before your Foes were prim'd:
By this Contrivance Mr. Dean
By God I'll bring you off as clean.—          60
Then let him use you e'er so rough,
'Twas all for Love, and that's enough.
For let him sputter thro' a Session,
It never makes the least Impression.
What e'er he speaks for Madness goes,
With no Effect on Friends or Foes.

55-60. This is the usual Excuse of Traulus when he abuses you to others without Provocation.

## TOM

The scrubest Cur in all the Pack
Can set the Mastiffs on your Back.
I own, his Madness is a Jest,
If that were all. But he's possess't:                70
Incarnate with a thousand Imps,
To work whose Ends, his Madness pimps.
Who o'er each String and Wire preside,
Fill ev'ry Pipe, each Motion guide.
Directing ev'ry Vice we find
In Scripture, to the Dev'l assign'd:
Sent from the Dark infernal Region
In him they lodge, and make him *Legion*.
Of *Brethren* he's *a false Accuser*,
A Sland'rer, Traytor and Seducer;                80
A fawning, base, trepaning Lyar,
The Marks peculiar of his Sire.
    Or, grant him but a Drone at best:
A Drone can raise a Hornet's Nest:
The Dean hath felt their Stings before;
And, must their Malice ne'er give o'er?
Still swarm and buzz about his Nose?
But *Ireland*'s Friends ne'er wanted Foes.
A Patriot is a dang'rous Post
When wanted by his Country most;                90
Perversely comes in evil Times,
Where Virtues are imputed Crimes,
His Guilt is clear the Proofs are pregnant,
A Traytor to the Vices regnant.
    What Spirit since the World began,
Could *always* bear to *Strive with Man*?
Which God pronounc'd he never wou'd,
And soon convinc'd them by a Floud.
Yet still the Dean on Freedom raves,
His Spirit always strives with Slaves.                100
'Tis Time at last to spare his Ink,
And let them rot, or hang, or sink.

# TRAULUS

### The Second PART

TRAULUS of amphibious Breed,
Motly Fruit of Mungril Seed:
By the *Dam* from Lordlings sprung,
By the *Sire* exhal'd from Dung:
Think on ev'ry Vice in both,
Look on him and see their Growth.

VIEW him on the Mother's Side,
Fill'd with Falshood, Spleen and Pride;
Positive and over-bearing,
Changing still, and still adhering,                    10
Spightful, peevish, rude, untoward;
Fierce in Tongue, in Heart a Coward:
When his Friends he most is hard on,
Cringing comes to beg their Pardon;
Reputation ever tearing,
Ever dearest Friendship swearing;
Judgement weak, and Passion strong,
Always various, always wrong:
Provocation never waits,
Where he loves, or where he hates.                    20
Talks whate'er comes in his Head,
Wishes it were all unsaid.

LET me now the Vices trace,
From his *Father*'s scoundrel Race,
Who cou'd give the Looby such Airs?
Were they Masons, were they Butchers?
Herald lend the Muse an answer;
From his *Atavus* and Grandsire;
This was dext'rous at his Trowel,
That was bred to kill a Cow well:                    30

Printed from the first ed., [Dublin] 1730, with corrections from *Poems*, 1735
(uncancelled state).

Hence the greazy clumsy Mien,
In his Dress and Figure seen:
Hence the mean and sordid Soul,
Like his Body, rank and foul:
Hence that wild suspicious Peep,
Like a Rogue that steals a Sheep:
Hence he learnt the Butcher's Guile,
How to cut a Throat and smile:
Like a Butcher doom'd for Life,
In his Mouth to wear his Knife.          40
Hence he draws his daily Food,
From his Tenants vital Blood.

LASTLY, let his Gifts be try'd,
Borrow'd from the Mason Side:
Some perhaps may think him able
In the State to build a *Babel*:
Cou'd we place him in a Station,
To destroy the old *Foundation*,
True indeed, I should be gladder,
Cou'd he learn to mount a Ladder.          50

MAY he at his latter End
Mount alive, and dead descend.

IN him, tell me which prevail,
Female Vices most, or Male,
What produc'd him, can you tell?
Human Race, or *Imps* of *Hell*.

# ON THE
# IRISH-CLUB

YE paultry underlings of state,
Ye senators, who love to prate;
Ye rascals of inferior note,
Who, for a dinner, sell a vote;

Printed from *Works, 4to, Vol. VIII* (2), London, 1765.

Ye pack of pensionary Peers,
Whose fingers itch for poets ears;
Ye bishops far remov'd from saints;
Why all this rage? Why these complaints?
Why against Printers all this noise?
This summoning of blackguard boys?          10
Why so sagacious in your guesses?
Your *effs* and *tees*, and *arrs*, and *esses*?
Take my advice; to make you safe,
I know a shorter way by half.
The point is plain: Remove the cause;
Defend your liberties and laws.
Be sometimes to your country true,
Have once the public good in view:
Bravely despise Champagne at Court,
And chuse to dine at home with Port:          20
Let Prelates, by their good behaviour,
Convince us they believe a Saviour;
Nor sell what they so dearly bought,
This country, now their own, for nought.
Ne'er did a true satyric muse
Virtue or innocence abuse;
And 'tis against poetic rules
To rail at men by nature fools:
But * * * * * * * *
* * * * * * * * * * *          30

# A Dialogue between an eminent Lawyer and DR. SWIFT Dean of ST. PATRICK'S, being an allusion to the first Satire of the second book of HORACE

*Sunt quibus in satyra, &c.*

SINCE there are persons who complain
There's too much satire in my vein,
That I am often found exceeding
The rules of raillery and breeding,
With too much freedom treat my betters,
Not sparing even men of letters,
You, who are skill'd in lawyer's lore,
What's your advice? shall I give o're,
Nor ever fools or knaves expose
Either in verse or hum'rous prose,                    10
And, to avoid all future ill,
In my 'scritore lock up my quill?
   SINCE you are pleas'd to condescend
To ask the judgment of a friend,
Your case consider'd, I must think
You shou'd withdraw from pen and ink,
Forbear your poetry and jokes,
And live like other christian fokes;
Or, if the MUSES must inspire
Your fancy with their pleasing fire,                    20
Take subjects safer for your wit
Than those on which you lately writ,
Commend the times, your thoughts correct
And follow the prevailing sect,
Assert that HYDE in writing story
Shews all the malice of a TORY,

Printed from *An Essay . . . by Deane Swift*, 1755.

While BURNET in his deathless page
Discovers freedom without rage;
To WOOLSTON recommend our youth
For learning, probity and truth,                    30
That noble genius, who unbinds
The chains which fetter free-born minds,
Redeems us from the slavish fears
Which lasted near two thousand years,
He can alone the priesthood humble,
Make gilded spires and altars tumble.
    MUST I commend against my conscience
Such stupid blasphemy and nonsense?
To such a subject tune my lyre
And sing like one of MILTON's choir,                40
Where DEVILS to a vale retreat
And call the laws of wisdom fate,
Lament upon their hapless fall
That force free virtue shou'd enthrall?
Or, shall the charms of wealth and power
Make me pollute the MUSES' bower?
    As from the tripod of APOLLO
Hear from my desk the words that follow;
Some by philosophers misled,
Must honour you alive and dead,                     50
And such as know what *Greece* has writ
Must taste your irony and wit,
While most that are or would be great,
Must dread your pen, your person hate,
And you on DRAPIER's *Hill* must lye,
And there without a mitre dye.

# A PANEGYRIC

## ON THE

# Reverend Dean *Swift*

### IN ANSWER TO THE LIBEL

### ON

## Dr. *Delany*, and a certain Great Lord

COULD all we little Folks that wait,
  And dance Attendance on the *Great*,
Obtain such Privilege as you,
To rail, and go unpunish'd too;
To treat our *Betters* like our *Slaves*,
And all Mankind as *Fools*, or *Knaves*;
The Pleasure of so large a Grant
Would much compensate all we want.
*Mitres*, and *Glebes* could scarce do more
To *scratch* our endless *Itch* of Pow'r.         10
For next to being Great our selves
It is to think all great Ones *Elves*,
And when we can't be *tete à tete*
Their Fellows, turn their *Dread and Hate*.
How amply then does Pow'r provide
For you to gratify your Pride?
Where'er the Wind of *Favour* sits,
It still your Constitution hits.
If fair, it brings you safe to Port,
And when 'tis foul, affords you Sport.       20
A *Deanery* you got, when in,
And now you're *out*, enjoy your *Grin*.
  But hark'ee, is it truly so,
(And you of all Mankind should know)
That Men of *Wit* can be no more
Than *Pimps* to Wickedness in *Pow'r*?

Printed from the original pamphlet, Dublin, 1729–30.

Then pray, dear Doctor, condescend
To teach the Science to your Friend.
For long enur'd to musty Rules,
And idle Morals in the Schools                    30
My highest Progress in the Myst'ry
Is of *short Sessions a long Hist'ry*;
Lampoons on *Whigs*, when in Disgrace;
Or vile *Submissions*, when in Place;
Poems address'd to great Men's *Whores*;
Or other *Lap-Dog* Cures for *Sores*.
But form'd more perfect *Gamester*, you
The deepest *Tricks* of *Courtiers* knew.
Your *Horace* not content to quote,
You at a Pinch could *forge* a Plot;               40
The fatal *Box* it self display'd,
Where *Whigs* their cursed *Trains* had laid;
Nor ceas'd the *Faction* to pursue,
Till you had got them in a *Screw*.
Oh, wond'rous *Box*! my Lyre unstrung
Shall be, when thou art left unsung;
More precious far than ev'n the Gift
Of our *Metropolis* to *Swift*;
The Gift (good Heav'ns preserve't from Thieves)
Of *Lord-May'r*, *Aldermen*, and *Shrieves*,       50
Where, if the curious List to read 'em,
They'll find his Life, and Acts, and *Freedom*,
And the great Name engrav'd most fairly,
Of him that *Ireland* sav'd, and *Harley*;
With quaint *Inscription*, which contains,
Laid out with no less Art than Pains,
Most of his Virtues, all *my* Brains.
   No Wonder you should think it *little*
To *lick a Rascal Statesman's Spittle*,
Who have, to shew your great Devotion,             60
Oft' swallow'd down a stronger Potion,
A Composition more absurd,
*Bob*'s *Spittle* mix'd with *Harry*'s Turd.
Oh, could'st thou teach us how to *zest*
Such Draughts as this, and then *digest*,

Then we might also have in Time
More beneficial Ways than *Rhime*;
Refuse our Patron's Call to dine;
*Pish* at his Cook'ry, *damn* his Wine;
Assume a *Dignitary*'s Airs,                    70
And go to *Church*, and say our Prayers.
   Rightly you shew, that *Wit* alone
Advances few, enriches none,
And 'tis as true, or Story lies,
Men seldom by their *Good Deeds* rise:
From whence the Consequence is plain,
You never had commenc'd a *Dean*,
Unless you other Ways had trod
Than those of *Wit*, or Trust in GOD.
'Twas therefore cruel, hard, by *Jove*,          80
Your Industry no better throve,
Nor could atchieve the promis'd *Lawn*,
Though *Robin*'s Honour was in Pawn;
Because it chanc'd, an old grave *Don*
Believ'd in GOD, and you in *none*.
Be this however your Relief,
Whene'er your Pride recals your Grief,
That all the Loss your Purse sustain'd
By that rebuff your *Virtue* gain'd.
For must you not have often *ly'd*,               90
And griev'd your *righteous Soul* beside,
Th' *Almighty*'s *Orders* to *perform*,
Not to *direct* a *Plague*, or *Storm*,
But 'gainst the Dictates of your Mind,
To *bless*, as now you *curse* Mankind?
   You tell me, till my *Fortune*'s *made*,
I must take up the *sweet'ning Trade*.
I own, the Counsel were not wrong,
Did *Congreve*'s Wit inspire my Song:
Or could my Muse exert the Rage                  100
Of *Addison*'s immortal Page,
When rapt in Heav'nly Airs, he sings
The Acts of GODS, and god-like Kings.
But form'd by You, how should their Model
E'er enter any Mortal's Noddle.

Our Thoughts, to hit your nicer Taste,
Must in a diff'rent Mold be cast;
The Language *Billingsgate* excel,
The Sentiments resemble *Hell*.

Thus, should I give your Humour place,                110
And draw like you my *Patron*'s Face;
To pay him Honour due, in Course
I must compare him to a *Horse*;
Then shew, how *Statesmen* oft are stung
By Gnats, and draw the Nation's *Dung*,
The *stinking* Load of all the Crimes,
And *Nastiness* of modern Times,
Not only what themselves have shit,
For that were not unjust a Bit,
But all the *Filth* both *Spiss*, and *Sparse*        120
Of e'ery Rogue that wears an arse.

To add more Dignity and Light
To an Allusion so polite,
The Devil ready stands, my *Swift*,
To help our Fancy at a Lift;
Yet envy not, that I repeat
The damnable the dear Conceit.

"So when poor *Irish Rapparee*,
"Is sentenc'd to the fatal *Tree*,
"Or naughty Boy elopes from School,                  130
"Or pretty Miss has play'd the Fool,
"And crack'd her tender *Maidenhead*
"With lying on too hard a Bed;
"Their Loads they all on *Satan* lay:
"The Devil did the Deed, not they!"

The Simile would better *jump*,
Were you but plac'd on *Satan*'s Rump;
For if bestrode by you, *Old Nick*,
Himself could scarce forbear to kick,
And curse his wicked Burthen more                    140
Than all the Sins he ever bore.

Is this the Art, good Doctor, say,
The true, the genuine sweet'ning Lay?
Then must it truly be confest;
Our *Ministers* are void of Taste,

When such *Adepts* as you, and I
So long *unbishoprick*'d lie by,
While *Dunces* of the coarsest Clay,
That only know to *preach* and *pray*,
Devour the *Church's tiddest Bits*,                    150
The Perquisites of *Pimps* and *Wits*.
And leave us nought but *Guts* and *Garbage*,
Or dirty *Offals* cook'd with *Herbage*.
   No less than Reasons of such Weight, ⎫
Could make you so *sincerely hate* ⎬
Both *Kings* and *Ministers* of *State*. ⎭
For once there was a Time, God wot,
Before our Friends were gone to *Pot*,
When *Jonathan* was great at *Court*,
The *Ruin'd Party* made his Sport,                    160
Despis'd the *Beast* with *many Heads*,
And damn'd the *Mob*, whom now he leads.
But Things are strangely chang'd since then,
And *Kings* are now no more than *Men*;
From whence 'tis plain, they quite have lost
God's *Image*, which was once their Boast.
For *Gulliver* divinely shews,
That *Humankind* are all *Yahoos*.
Both Envy then and Malice must
Allow your hatred strictly just;                    170
Since you alone of all the Race
Disclaim the *Human Name*, and Face,
And with the *Virtues* pant to wear
(May Heav'n Indulgent hear your Pray'r!)
The *Proof* of your high *Origine*,
The *Horse's Countenance Divine*.
While *Grattan*, *Sheridan*, and I,
Who after you *adoring* fly,
An humbler Prospect only wait,
To be your *Asses Colts* of *State*,                    180
The *Angels* of your awful *Nods*,
Resembling you as *Angel Gods*.

# TO

# Doctor *DELANY*,

## ON THE

# LIBELS

## Writ against him

——*Tanti tibi not sit opaci
Omnis arena Tagi.* Juv.

AS some raw Youth in Country bred,
To Arms by Thirst of Honour led,
When at a Skirmish first he hears
The Bullets whistling round his Ears,
Will duck his Head, aside will start,
And feel a trembling at his Heart:
Till, scaping oft without a Wound,
Lessens the Terror of the Sound:
Fly Bullets now as thick as Hops,
He runs into a Cannon's Chops.                           10
An Author thus who pants for Fame
Begins the World with Fear and Shame,
When first in Print, you see him dread
Each Pot-gun levell'd at his Head:
The Lead yon Critick's Quill contains,
Is destin'd to beat out his Brains.
As if he heard Loud Thunders roul,
Cryes, Lord have Mercy on his Soul,
Concluding, that another Shot
Will strike him dead upon the Spot:                      20
But, when with squibbing, flashing, popping,
He cannot see one Creature dropping:

Printed from the original pamphlet, London, 1730, with corrections from
*Poems*, 1735.

That, missing Fire, or missing Aim
His Life is safe, I mean his Fame,
The Danger past, takes Heart of Grace,
And looks a Critick in the Face.

   Though Splendor gives the fairest Mark
To poison'd Arrows from the Dark,
Yet, *in Your self when smooth and round*,
They glance aside without a Wound.      30

   'Tis said, the Gods try'd all their Art,
How, *Pain* they might from *Pleasure* part:
But, little could their Strength avail,
Both still are fastned by the Tayl.
Thus, Fame and Censure with a Tether
By Fate are always link'd together.

   Why will you aim to be preferr'd
In wit before the common Herd?
And yet, grow mortify'd and vext
To pay the Penalty annext.      40

   'Tis Eminence makes Envy rise,
As fairest Fruits attract the Flyes.
Shou'd stupid Libels grieve your Mind,
You soon a Remedy may find;
Lye down obscure like other Folks
Below the Lash of Snarlers Jokes.
Their Faction is five hundred Odds,
For, ev'ry Coxcomb lends them Rods;
Can sneer as learnedly as they,
Like Females o'er their Morning Tea.      50

You say, the Muse will not contain,
And write you must, or break a Vein:
Then, if you find the Terms too hard,
No longer my Advice regard:

      29. In seipso totus teres atque rotundus. *Hor.*

But raise your Fancy on the Wing;
The *Irish Senate*'s Praises sing:
How jealous of the Nation's Freedom,
And, for Corruptions, how they weed 'em.
How each the Public Good pursues,
How far their Hearts from private Views,          60
Make all true Patriots up to Shoe-boys
Huzza their Brethren at the *Blue-boys*.
Thus grown a Member of the Club,
No longer dread the Rage of *Grub*.

How oft' am I for Rime to seek?
To dress a Thought, may toyl a Week;
And then, how thankful to the Town,
If all my Pains will earn a Crown.
Whilst, ev'ry Critick can devour
My Work and me in half an Hour.          70
Would Men of Genius cease to write,
The Rogues must dye for Want and Spight,
Must dye for Want of Food and Rayment,
If Scandal did not find them Payment.
How chearfully the Hawkers cry
A Satyr, and the Gentry buy!
While my hard-labour'd Poem pines
Unsold upon the Printer's Lines.

A Genius in the Rev'rend Gown,
Must ever keep it's Owner down:          80
'Tis an unnatural Conjunction,
And spoils the Credit of the Function.
Round all your Brethren cast your Eyes,
Point out the surest Men to rise,
That Club of Candidates in Black,
The least deserving of the Pack;
Aspiring, factious, fierce and loud
With Grace and Learning unendow'd,
Can turn their Hands to ev'ry Jobb,
The fittest Tools to work for *Bobb*.          90

62. *Blue-boys*. The Irish Parliament met at the Blue-Boys Hospital, while the new
Parliament house was building.

Will sooner coyn a Thousand Lyes
Than suffer Men of Parts to rise:
They croud about Preferment's Gate,
And press you down with all their Weight.
For, as of old, Mathematicians
Were by the Vulgar thought Magicians;
So Academick dull Ale-drinkers
Pronounce all Men of Wit, Free-thinkers.

Wit, as the chief of Virtue's Friends,
Disdains to serve ignoble Ends.                    100
Observe what Loads of stupid Rimes
Oppress us in corrupted Times:
What Pamphlets in a Court's Defence
Shew Reason, Grammer, Truth, or Sense?
For, though the Muse delights in Fiction,
She ne'er inspires against Conviction:
Then keep your Virtue still unmixt,
And let not Faction come betwixt.
By Party-steps no Grandeur climb at,
Tho' it would make you *England*'s Primate:          110
First learn the Science to be dull,
You then may soon your Conscience lull;
If not, however seated high,
Your Genius in your Face will fly.

When *Jove* was, from his teeming Head,
Of Wit's fair Goddess brought to Bed,
There follow'd at his lying-in
For after-birth a *Sooterkin*;
Which, as the Nurse pursu'd to kill,
Attain'd by Flight the Muses Hill;                  120
There in the Soil began to root,
And litter'd at *Parnassus'* Foot.
From hence the Critick Vermin sprung
With Harpy Claws, and Pois'nous Tongue,
Who fatten on poetick Scraps;
Too cunning to be caught in Trapps.
Dame Nature as the Learned show,
Provides each Animal it's Foe:

Hounds hunt the Hare, the wily Fox
Devours your Geese, the Wolf your Flocks:          130
Thus, Envy pleads a nat'ral Claim
To persecute the Muses Fame;
On Poets in all times abusive,
From *Homer* down to *Pope* inclusive.

  Yet, what avails it to complain:
You try to take Revenge in vain.
A Rat your utmost Rage defyes
That safe behind the Wainscoat lyes.
Say, did you ever know by Sight
In Cheese an individual Mite?          140
Shew me the same numerick Flea,
That bit your Neck but Yesterday,
You then may boldly go in Quest
To find the Grub-Street Poet's Nest,
What Spunging-House in dread of Jayl
Receives them while they wait for Bayl?
What Ally are they nestled in,
To flourish o'er a Cup of Ginn?
Find the last Garrat where they lay,
Or Cellar, where they starve to Day.          150
Suppose you had them all trepann'd
With each a Libel in his Hand,
What Punishment would you inflict?
Or call 'em Rogues, or get 'em kickt:
These they have often try'd before;
You but oblige 'em so much more:
Themselves would be the first to tell,
To make their Trash the better sell.

  You have been Libell'd—Let us know
What fool officious told you so,          160
Will you regard the Hawker's Cryes
Who in his Titles always lyes?
Whate'er the noisy Scoundrel says
It might be something in your Praise:
And, Praise bestow'd in Grub-Street Rimes,
Would vex one more a thousand Times.

'Till *Criticks* blame, and *Judges* praise,
The Poet cannot claim his Bays;
On me, when Dunces are satyrick,
I take it for a Panegyrick.      170
*Hated by Fools*, and *Fools to hate*,
Be that my Motto, and my Fate.

## To a Friend who had been much abused in many inveterate Libels

THE greatest monarch may be stabb'd by night,
And fortune help the murd'rer in his flight;
The vilest Ruffian may commit a rape,
Yet safe from injured innocence escape:
And calumny, by working under ground,
Can, unreveng'd, the greatest merit wound.

What's to be done? shall wit and learning chuse,
To live obscure, and have no fame to lose?
By censure frighted out of honour's road,
Nor dare to use the gifts by heav'n bestow'd;      10
Or fearless enter in thro' virtue's gate,
And buy distinction at the dearest rate.

Printed from Delany's *Observations upon Lord Orrery's Remarks* . . ., 1754.

# THE
# PHEASANT
## AND THE
# LARK &c.

[by Delany]

IN antient Times, as Bards indite,
  (If Clerks have con'd the Record right)
A PEACOCK reign'd, whose glorious Sway
His Subjects with delight obey;
His Tail was beauteous to behold,
Replete with goodly Eyes and Gold,
(Fair Emblem of that Monarch's Guise,
Whose *Train* at once is Rich and Wise)
And princely rul'd he many Regions,
By Statesman Wise, and valiant Legions.          10

    A *Pheasant* Lord, above the rest,
With ev'ry Grace and Talent bless't,
Was sent to sway with all his Skill,
The Sceptre of a neighb'ring Hill;
No Science was to him unknown,
For all the Arts were all his own;
In all the living Learned read,
Tho' more delighted with the Dead:
(For Birds, if antient Tales say true,
Had then their *Popes* and *Homers* too          20
Cou'd Read and Write in Prose and Verse,
And speak like — and build like *Pearce*)
He knew their Voices and their Wings,
Who smoothest Soars, who sweetest Sings:
Who toils with ill-fledg'd Penns to climb,
And who attain'd the true Sublime:
Their Merits he cou'd well descry,
He had so exquisite an Eye;
And where that fail'd to shew them clear,
He had as exquisite an Ear.          30

    Printed from the 8vo pamphlet, Dublin, 1730.

It chanc'd, as on a Day he stray'd,
Beneath an *Academick* Shade,
He lik'd amid'st a thousand Throats,
The wildness of a *Woodlark*'s Notes,
And search'd, and spy'd, and seiz'd his Game,
And took him Home, and made him Tame;
Found him, on Tryal, true, and able,
So chear'd, and fed him at his Table.

Here some shrewd Critick finds I'm caught,
And Crys out, *better fed than taught*—          40
Then jests on *Game,* and *Tame,* and reads,
And Jests, and so my Tale proceeds.

Long had he study'd in the Wood,
Conversing with the Wise and Good;
His Soul with Harmony inspir'd,
With love of Truth and Virtue fir'd:
His Brother's Good, and Maker's Praise,
Were all the Study of his Lays:
Were all his Study in Retreat,
And now employ'd him with the Great.          50
His Friendship was the sure Resort,
Of all the wretched at the Court,
But chiefly Merit in Distress
His greatest *blessing* was to *Bless*—

This fixt him in his Patron's Breast,
But fir'd with Envy all the rest:
I mean, that noisy craving Crew,
Who round the Court incessant flew,
And prey'd like *Rooks,* by Pairs, and Dozens,
To fill the Maws of *Sons* and *Cousins!*          60
*Unmov'd their Heart, and chill their Blood,*
*To ev'ry thought of common good,*
*Confining ev'ry Hope and Care,*
*To their own low contracted Sphere.*

These run him down with ceaseless Cry,
But found it hard to tell you why,
Till his own Wit and Worth supply'd
Sufficient Matter to deride:
*'Tis* Envy's *safest, surest rule,*
*To hide her Rage in Ridicule:*          70

*The vulgar Eye she best beguiles,*
*When all her Snakes are deck't in Smiles:*
SARDONIC Smiles, by Rancour rais'd!
*Tormented most, when* seeming pleas'd!
Their Spight had more than half expir'd,
Had he not wrote, what all admir'd;
What morsels had their malice wanted,
But that he *built,* and *plann'd,* and *planted*!
How had his Sense and learning griev'd 'em,
But that his *Charity* reliev'd 'em!                    80

*At highest worth dull malice reaches*
*As Slugs pollute the fairest peaches:*
*Envy defames, as Harpyes vile*
*Devour the food, they first defile.*

Now ask the fruit of all his Favour—
*He was not hitherto, a Saver—*
What then cou'd make their rage run mad?
*Why what he* hop'd, *not what he had—*

*What Tyrants e're invented ropes,*
*Or racks, or rods to punish hopes?*                    90
*Th' inheritance of hope and fame,*
*Is seldom earthly wisdoms aim,*
*Or if it were, is not so small*
*But there is Room enough for all.*

If he but chanc'd to breathe a Song
(He seldom Sung, and never long)
The noisy, rude, malignant Croud,
Where it was *high* pronounc'd it *loud,*
*Plain Truth* was *pride,* and what was Sillyer
*Easy* and *Friendly* was *Familiar.*                    100

Or if he tun'd his lofty lays,
With solemn air, to virtue's praise,
Alike, abusive, and erroneous,
They call'd it *hoarse* and *unharmonious*:
Yet so it was to Souls like theirs,
Tuneless as ABEL to the *bears*!

A *Rook* with harsh malignant caw,
Began, was follow'd by a *Daw*;

(Tho' some who wou'd be thought to know,
Are positive it was a *Crow*.)                              110
*Jack-Daw* was seconded by *Tit*
Tom-*tit* cou'd write, and so he *writ*.
A Tribe of tuneless praters follow,
The *Jay*, the *Magpye*, and the *Swallow*,
And twenty more, their Throats let loose,
Down to the *witless, wadling, Goose*.

    Some thought they meant to show their wit,
Might think so still—*but that they writ*—
Cou'd it be Spight or Envy?—*No*—
*Who did no ill, coud have no Foe*—                         120
So *wise Simplicity* esteem'd,
Quite otherwise *true wisdom* deem'd;
This question rightly understood,
*What more Provokes*, than doing good?
*A Soul enobled, and refin'd,*
*Reproaches ev'ry* baser *mind:*
*As Strains exalted, and melodious,*
*Make ev'ry meaner musick, odious*—

    At length the *Nightingale* was heard,
For *voice* and *wisdom* long rever'd,                      130
Esteem'd of all the wise, and good,
The *Guardian Genius* of the Wood:
He long in Discontent retir'd,
Yet not *obscur'd* but more *admir'd*;
His Brethren's Servile Souls disdaining,
He liv'd indignant, and complaining:
They now afresh provok'd his choler,
It seems the *Lark* had been his Scholar,
A fav'rite Scholar always near him,
And oft had wak'd whole Nights to hear him:                 140
Enrag'd he canvasses the matter,
Exposes all their Senseless chatter,
Shews Him, and them in such a light,
As more enflames, yet quells their Spight,
They hear his voice, and frighted fly,
For rage had rais'd it very high,
Sham'd by the wisdom of his Notes,
They hide their Heads, and hush their Throats.

# AN ANSWER

## TO

### Dr. *Delany's* FABLE

#### OF THE

### PHEASANT and the LARK

*The Reader is desired to compare the Doctor's* Fable
*with the following Answer*

IN antient Times the Wise were able,
    In proper Terms to write a Fable:
Their Tales wou'd always justly suit
The Characters of ev'ry Brute:
The Ass was dull, the Lyon brave,
The Stagg was swift, the Fox a Knave:
The Daw a Thief, the Ape a Drole,
The Hound wou'd scent, the Wolf would prole:
A Pigeon wou'd, if shown by *Æsop*,
Fly from the Hawk, or pick his Pease up.          10
Far otherwise a great Divine,
Has learnt his Fables to refine;
He jumbles Men and Birds together,
As if they all were of a Feather:
You see him first the Peacock bring,
Against all Rules to be a King:
That in his Tail he wore his Eyes,
By which he grew both rich and wise.
Now pray observe the Doctor's Choice,
A Peacock chose for Flight and Voice:          20
Did ever mortal see a Peacock
Attempt a Flight above a Haycock?
And for his singing, Doctor, you know,
Himself complain'd of it to *Juno*.

Printed from the 8vo pamphlet, Dublin, 1730.

He squals in such a hellish Noise
It frightens all the Village Boys.
This Peacock kept a standing Force,
In Regiments of Foot and Horse;
Had Statesmen too of ev'ry Kind,
Who waited on his Eyes behind.                    30
(And this was thought the highest Post;
For, rule the Rump, you rule the Roast.)
The Doctor names but one at present,
And he of all Birds was a Pheasant.
This Pheasant was a Man of Wit,
Cou'd read all Books were ever writ;
And when among Companions privy,
Cou'd quote you *Cicero* and *Livy*.
Birds, as he says, and I allow,
Were Scholars then, as we are now;               40
Could read all Volumes up to Folio's,
And feed on Fricassees and Olio's.
This Pheasant by the Peacock's Will,
Was Viceroy of a neighbouring Hill:
And as he wandred in his Park,
He chanc't to spy a Clergy Lark;
Was taken with his Person outward,
So prettily he pickt a Cow-turd:
Then in a Net the Pheasant caught him,
And in his Palace fed and taught him.            50
The Moral of the Tale is pleasant,
Himself the Lark, my Lord the Pheasant:
A Lark he is, and such a Lark
As never came from *Noah*'s Ark:
And though he had no other Notion,
But Building, Planning, and Devotion;
Tho' tis a Maxim you must know,
Who does no Ill, can have no Foe,
Yet how shall I express in Words,
The strange Stupidity of Birds.                  60
This Lark was hated in the Wood,
Because he did his Brethren good.
At last the Nightingal comes in,
To hold the Doctor by the Chin:

We all can find out whom he means,
The Worst of disaffected Deans:
Whose Wit at best was next to none,
And now that little next is gone.
Against the Court is always blabbing,
And calls the Senate-House a Cabbin;                    70
So dull, that but for Spleen and Spite,
We ne'er shou'd know that he could write:
Who thinks the Nation always err'd,
Because himself is not preferr'd;
His Heart is through his Libel seen,
Nor cou'd his Malice spare the Queen;
Who, had she known his vile Behaviour,
Would ne'er have shown him so much Favour;
A noble LORD hath told his Pranks,
And well deserves the Nation's Thanks.                  80
O, wou'd the Senate deign to show
Resentment on this publick Foe;
Our Nightingal might fit a Cage,
There let him starve, and vent his Rage.
Or wou'd they but in Fetters bind,
This Enemy of human Kind.
Harmonious *Coffee* show thy Zeal,
Thou Champion for the Common-weal:
Nor on a Theme like this repine,
For once to wet thy Pen Divine:                         90
Bestow that Libeller a Lash,
Who daily vends seditious Trash:
Who dares revile the Nation's Wisdom,
But in the Praise of Virtue is dumb:
That Scribbler lash, who neither knows,
The Turn of Verse, nor Stile of Prose;
Whose Malice, for the Worst of Ends,
Wou'd have us lose our ENGLISH Friends.
Who never had one publick Thought,
Nor ever gave the Poor a Groat.                        100
One Clincher more, and I have done,
I end my Labours with a Pun.

87. *Harmonious Coffee.* A Dublin Gazetteer [fn. 1765].

*Jove* send, this Nightingal may fall,
Who spends his Day and *Night in gall.*
So Nightingal and Lark adieu, ⎱
I see the greatest Owls in you, ⎰
That ever screecht or ever *flew.* ⎰


# THE

# Revolution at *Market-Hill*

### Written in the Year 1730

FROM distant Regions, Fortune sends
  An odd Triumvirate of Friends;
Where *Phœbus* pays a scanty Stipend,
Where never yet a Codling ripen'd:
Hither the frantick Goddess draws
Three Suff'rers in a ruin'd Cause.
By Faction banish't here unite,
A Dean, a *Spaniard*, and a Knight.
Unite; but on Conditions cruel;
The Dean and *Spaniard* find it too well;      10
Condemn'd to live in Service hard;
On either Side his Honour's Guard:
The Dean, to guard his Honour's Back,
Must build a Castle at *Drumlack*:
The *Spaniard*, sore against his Will,
Must raise a Fort at *Market-Hill.*
And thus, the Pair of humble Gentry,
At *North* and *South* are posted Centry;
While in his lordly Castle fixt,
The Knight triumphant reigns betwixt:      20
And, what the Wretches most resent,
To be his Slaves must pay him Rent;

Printed from *Poems*, 1735.

8. *Spaniard.* Col. Harry Leslie, who served and lived long in Spain.

14. *Drumlack.* The Irish Name of a Farm the Dean took, and was to build on,
but changed his Mind. He called it Drapier's-Hill. Vide that Poem.

Attend him daily as their *Chief*,
Decant his Wine, and carve his Beef.

O Fortune, 'tis a Scandal for thee
To smile on those who are least worthy.
Weigh but the Merits of the three,
His Slaves have ten Times more than he.

Proud Baronet of *Nova Scotia*,
The Dean and *Spaniard* must reproach ye;          30
Of *their* two Fames the World enough rings;
Where are *thy* Services and Suff'rings?
What, if for nothing once you kiss't,
Against the Grain, a Monarch's Fist?
What, if among the courtly Tribe,
You lost a Place, and sav'd a Bribe?
And, then in surly Mode come here
To Fifteen Hundred Pounds a Year,
And fierce against the Whigs harangu'd?
You never ventur'd to be hang'd.          40
How dare you treat your Betters thus?
Are you to be compar'd to Us?

Come *Spaniard*, let us from our Farms
Call forth our Cottagers to Arms;
Our Forces let us both unite,
Attack the Foe at Left and Right;
From *Market-Hill*'s exalted Head,
Full Northward, let your Troops be led:
While I from *Drapier's-Mount* descend,
And to the *South* my Squadrons bend:          50
*New-River-walk* with friendly Shade,
Shall keep my Host in Ambuscade;
While you, from where the Basin stands,
Shall scale the Rampart with your Bands.
Nor need we doubt the Fort to win;
I hold Intelligence within.
True, Lady *Anne* no Danger fears,
Brave as the *Upton* Fan she wears:

47. *Market-Hill.* A Village near Sir Arthur Acheson's Seat.

Then, least upon our first Attack
Her valiant Arm should force us back,                    60
And we of all our Hopes depriv'd;
I have a Stratagem contriv'd;
By these embroider'd high Heel Shoes,
She shall be caught as in a Noose:
So well contriv'd her Toes to pinch,
She'll not have Pow'r to stir an Inch;
These gaudy Shoes must *Hannah* place
Direct before her Lady's Face.
The Shoes put on; our faithful Portress
Admits us in, to storm the Fortress;                     70
While tortur'd Madam bound remains,
Like *Montezume* in golden Chains:
Or, like a Cat with Walnuts shod,
Stumbling at ev'ry Step she trod.
Sly Hunters thus, in *Borneo*'s Isle,
To catch a Monkey by a Wile;
The mimick Animal amuse;
They place before him Gloves and Shoes;
Which when the Brute puts awkward on,
All his Agility is gone;                                  80
In vain to frisk or climb he tries;
The Huntsmen seize the grinning Prize.

  But, let us on our first Assault
Secure the Larder, and the Vault.
The valiant *Dennis* you must fix on,
And, I'll engage with *Peggy Dixon*:
Then if we once can seize the Key,
And Chest, that keeps my Lady's Tea,
They must surrender at Discretion:
And soon as we have got Possession,                      90
We'll act as *other* Conqu'rors do;
Divide the Realm between us two.
Then, (let me see) we'll make the Knight
Our Clerk, for he can read and write;

67. *Hannah.* My Lady's Waiting-Maid.
85. *Dennis.* The Butler.
86. *Peggy Dixon.* The House-Keeper.

But, must not think, I tell him that,
Like *Lorimer*, to wear his Hat.
Yet, when we dine without a Friend,
We'll place him at the lower End.
Madam, whose Skill does all in Dress lye,
May serve to wait on Mrs. *Leslie*:                    100
But, lest it might not be so proper,
That her own Maid should overtop her;
To mortify the *Creature* more,
We'll take her Heels five Inches lower.

FOR *Hannah*; when we have no need of her,
'Twill be our Int'rest to get rid of her:
And when we execute our Plot,
'Tis best to hang her on the Spot;
As all your Politicians wise
Dispatch the Rogues by whom they Rise.                 110

# A PANEGYRICK
## ON THE DEAN
### in the Person of a Lady in the *North*

#### Written in the Year 1730

RESOLV'D my Gratitude to show,
Thrice Rev'rend Dean for all I owe;
Too long I have my Thanks delay'd;
Your Favours left too long unpay'd;
But now in all our Sexes Name,
My artless Muse shall sing your Fame.

INDULGENT you to Female Kind,
To all their weaker Sides are blind;
Nine more such Champions as the Dean,
Would soon restore our antient Reign.                  10

Printed from *Poems*, 1735.
96. *Lorimer*. The Agent.

How well to win the Ladies Hearts,
You celebrate their Wit and Parts!
How have I felt my Spirits rais'd,
By you so oft, so highly prais'd!
Transform'd by your convincing Tongue
To witty, beautiful, and young.
I hope to quit that awkward Shame
Affected by each vulgar Dame;
To Modesty a weak Pretence;
And soon grow pert on Men of Sense;                    20
To show my Face with scornful Air;
Let others match it if they dare.

    IMPATIENT to be out of Debt,
O, may I never once forget
The Bard, who humbly deigns to chuse
Me for the Subject of his Muse.
Behind my Back, before my Nose,
He sounds my Praise in Verse and Prose.

    MY Heart with Emulation burns
To make you suitable Returns;                          30
My Gratitude the World shall know:
And, see, the Printer's Boy below:
Ye Hawkers all, your Voices lift;
A Panegyrick on Dean *Swift*.
And then, to mend the Matter still;
By Lady *Anne* of *Market-Hill*.

    I THUS begin. My grateful Muse
Salutes the Dean in diff'rent Views;
Dean, Butler, Usher, Jester, Tutor;
*Robert* and *Darby*'s Coadjutor:                      40
And, as you in Commission sit,
To rule the Dairy next to *Kit*.

    IN each Capacity I mean
To sing your Praise. And, first as Dean:

36. *Market-Hill*. A Village near Sir Arthur Acheson's House, where the Author
passed two Summers.
    40. *Robert and Darby's Coadjutor*. The Names of two Overseers.
    42. *Kit*. My Lady's Footman.

Envy must own, you understand your
Precedence, and support your Grandeur:
Nor, of your Rank will bate an Ace,
Except to give Dean *Daniel* place.
In you such Dignity appears;
So suited to your State, and Years!                    50
With Ladies what a strict Decorum!
With what Devotion you adore 'um!
Treat me with so much Complaisance,
As fits a Princess in Romance.
By your Example and Assistance,
The *Fellows* learn to know their Distance.
Sir *Arthur*, since you set the Pattern,
No longer calls me *Snipe* and *Slattern*;
Nor dares he, though he were a Duke,
Offend me with the least Rebuke.                       60


    PROCEED we to your preaching next:
How nice you split the hardest Text!
How your superior Learning shines
Above our neighb'ring dull Divines!
At *Beggar*'s-*Op'ra* not so full Pit
Is seen, as when you mount our Pulpit.


    CONSIDER now your Conversation;
Regardful of your Age and Station,
You ne'er was known, by Passion stir'd,
To give the least offensive Word;                      70
But still, whene'er you Silence break,
Watch ev'ry Syllable you speak:
Your style so clear, and so concise,
We never ask to hear you twice.
But then, a Parson so genteel,
So nicely clad from Head to Heel;
So fine a Gown, a Band so clean,
As well become St. *Patrick*'s Dean;
Such reverential Awe express,
That Cow-boys know you by your Dress!                  80

---

61. *Proceed we to your preaching.* The Author preached but once while he was there.

Then, if our neighb'ring Friends come here,
How proud are we when you appear!
With such Address, and graceful Port,                    •
As clearly shows you bred at Court!

Now raise your Spirits, Mr. Dean:
I lead you to a nobler Scene;
When to the Vault you walk in State,
In Quality of Butler's Mate;
You, next to *Dennis* bear the Sway:
To you we often trust the Key:                          90
Nor, can he judge with all his Art
So well, what Bottle holds a Quart:
What Pints may best for Bottles pass,
Just to give ev'ry Man his Glass:
When proper to produce the best;
And, what may serve a common Guest.
With *Dennis* you did ne'er combine,
Not you, to steal your Master's Wine;
Except a Bottle now and then,
To welcome *Brother* Serving-men;                       100
But, that is with a good Design,
To drink Sir *Arthur*'s Health and mine:
Your Master's Honour to maintain;
And get the like Returns again.

Your Usher's Post must next be handled:
How bles't am I by such a Man led!
Under whose wise and careful Guardship,
I now despise Fatigue and Hardship:
Familiar grown to Dirt and Wet,
Though daggled round, I scorn to fret:                  110
From you my Chamber-Damsels learn
My broken Hose to patch and dearn.

Now, as a Jester, I accost you;
Which never yet one Friend has lost you.
You judge so nicely to a Hair,
How far to go, and when to spare:

88. *Butler's Mate.* He sometimes used to direct the Butler.   89. *Dennis.* The Butler.
105. *Usher's Post.* He sometimes used to walk with the Lady.

By long Experience grown so wise,
Of ev'ry Taste to know the Size;
•  There's none so ignorant or weak
To take Offence at what you speak.          120
Whene'er you joke, 'tis all a Case;
Whether with *Dermot*, or *His Grace*;
With *Teague O'Murphy*, or an Earl;
A Dutchess or a Kitchen Girl.
With such Dexterity you fit
Their sev'ral Talents to your Wit,
That *Moll* the Chamber-maid can smoak,
And *Gaghagan* take ev'ry Joke.

I NOW become your humble Suitor,
To let me praise you as my Tutor.          130
Poor I, a Savage bred and born,
By you instructed ev'ry Morn,
Already have improv'd so well,
That I have almost learn't to spell:
The Neighbours who come here to dine,
Admire to hear me speak so *fine*.
How enviously the Ladies look,
When they surprize me at my Book!
And, sure as they're alive, at Night;
As soon as gone, will show their Spight:          140
Good Lord! what can my Lady mean,
Conversing with that rusty Dean!
She's grown so nice, and so *penurious*,
With *Socratus* and *Epicurius*.
How could she sit the live-long Day,
Yet never ask us once to play?

BUT, I admire your Patience most;
That, when I'm duller than a Post,
Nor can the plainest Word pronounce,
You neither fume, nor fret, nor flounce;          150

120. *To take Offence.* The neighbouring Ladies were no great Understanders of Raillery.

130. *Tutor.* In bad Weather the Author used to direct my Lady in her Reading.

143. *penurious.* Ignorant Ladies often mistake the Word *Penurious* for *nice* and *dainty.*

Are so indulgent, and so mild,
As if I were a darling Child.
So gentle in your whole Proceeding,
That I could spend my Life in reading.

   You merit new Employments daily:
Our Thatcher, Ditcher, Gard'ner, Baily.
And, to a Genius so extensive,
No Work is grievous or offensive.
Whether, your fruitful Fancy lies
To make for Pigs convenient Styes:          160
Or, ponder long with anxious Thought,
To banish Rats that haunt our Vault.
Nor have you grumbled, Rev'rend Dean,
To keep our Poultry sweet and clean;
To sweep the Mansion-house they dwell in;
And cure the Rank unsav'ry Smelling.

   Now, enter as the Dairy Hand-maid:
Such charming Butter never Man made.
Let others with Fanatick Face,
Talk of their *Milk* for *Babes of Grace*;    170
From *Tubs* their snuffling Nonsense utter:
Thy *Milk* shall make us *Tubs* of Butter.
The Bishop with his *Foot* may burn it;
But, with his *Hand*, the Dean can churn it.
How are the Servants overjoy'd
To see thy Deanship thus employ'd!
Instead of poring on a Book,
Providing Butter for the Cook.
Three Morning-Hours you toss and shake
The Bottle, till your Fingers ake:           180
Hard is the Toil, nor small the Art,
The Butter from the Whey to part:
Behold; a frothy Substance rise;
Be cautious, or your Bottle flies.
The Butter comes; our Fears are ceas't;
And, out you squeeze an Ounce at least.

   168. *Butter*. A Way of making Butter for Breakfast, by filling a Bottle with
Cream, and shaking it till the Butter comes.

Your Rev'rence thus, with like Success,
Nor is your Skill, or Labour less,
When bent upon some smart Lampoon,
You toss and turn your Brain till Noon;            190
Which, in its Jumblings round the Skull,
Dilates, and makes the Vessel full:
While nothing comes but Froth at first,
You think your giddy Head will burst:
But, squeezing out four Lines in Rhime,
Are largely paid for all your time.

But, you have rais'd your gen'rous Mind
To Works of more exalted Kind.
*Palladio* was not half so skill'd in
The Grandeur or the Art of Building.              200
Two Temples of magnifick Size,
Attract the curious Trav'llers Eyes,
That might be envy'd by the *Greeks*;
Rais'd up by you in twenty Weeks:
Here, gentle Goddess *Cloacine*
Receives all Off'rings at her Shrine.
In sep'rate Cells the He's and She's
Here pay their Vows with *bended Knees*:
(For, 'tis prophane when Sexes mingle;
And ev'ry Nymph must enter single;                210
And when she feels an *inward Motion*,
Comes fill'd with *Rev'rence* and Devotion.)
The bashful Maid, to hide her Blush,
Shall creep no more behind a Bush;
Here unobserv'd, she boldly goes,
As who should say, to *pluck a Rose*.

Ye who frequent this hallow'd Scene,
Be not ungrateful to the Dean;
But, duly e'er you leave your Station,
Offer to him a pure Libation;                     220
Or, of his own, or *Smedley*'s Lay,
Or Billet-doux, or Lock of Hay:
And, O! may all who hither come,
Return with unpolluted Thumb.

221. *Smedley*. See his Character hereafter.

YET, when your lofty Domes I praise,
I sigh to think of antient Days.
Permit me then to raise my Style,
And sweetly moralize a while.


THEE bounteous Goddess *Cloacine*,
To Temples why do we confine?                230
Forbid in open Air to breath;
Why are thine Altars fix't beneath?


WHEN *Saturn* rul'd the Skies alone,
That *golden* Age, to *Gold* unknown;
This earthly Globe to thee assign'd,
Receiv'd the Gifts of all Mankind.
Ten Thousand Altars *smoaking* round
Were built to thee, with Off'rings crown'd:
And here thy daily Vot'ries plac't
Their Sacrifice with Zeal and Haste:         240
The Margin of a purling Stream,
Sent up to thee a grateful Steam[:]
(Though sometimes thou wer't pleas'd to wink,
If *Nayads* swept them from the Brink)
Or, where appointing Lovers rove,
The Shelter of a shady Grove:
Or, offer'd in some flow'ry Vale,
Were wafted by a gentle Gale.
There, many a Flow'r abstersive grew,
Thy fav'rite Flow'rs of yellow Hue           250
The Crocus and the Daffodil,
The Cowslip soft, and sweet Jonquil.


BUT, when at last usurping *Jove*
Old *Saturn* from his Empire drove;
Then *Gluttony* with greasy Paws,
Her Napkin pinn'd up to her Jaws,
With watry Chaps, and wagging Chin,
Brac'd like a Drum her oily Skin;
Wedg'd in a spacious Elbow-Chair,
And on her Plate a treble Share,             260

As if she ne'er could have enuff;
Taught harmless Man to cram and stuff.
She sent her Priests in Wooden Shoes
From haughty *Gaul* to make Ragous.
Instead of wholsome Bread and Cheese,
To dress their Soupes and Fricassyes;
And, for our home-bred *British* Chear,
Botargo, Catsup, and Caveer.

THIS bloated Harpy sprung from Hell,
Confin'd Thee Goddess to a Cell:                    270
Sprung from her Womb that impious Line,
Contemners of thy Rites divine.
First, lolling *Sloth* in Woollen Cap,
Taking her After-dinner Nap:
Pale *Dropsy* with a sallow Face,
Her Belly burst, and slow her Pace:
And, lordly *Gout* wrapt up in Furr:
And, wheezing *Asthma*, loth to stir:
Voluptuous *Ease*, the Child of *Wealth*,
Infecting thus our Hearts by Stealth;               280
None seek thee now in open Air;
To thee no verdant Altars rear;
But, in their Cells and Vaults obscene
Present a Sacrifice unclean;
From whence unsav'ry Vapours rose,
Offensive to thy nicer Nose.
Ah! who in our degen'rate Days
As Nature prompts, his Off'ring pays?
Here, Nature never Diff'rence made
Between the Scepter and the Spade.                  290

YE Great ones, why will ye disdain
To pay your Tribute on the Plain?
Why will you place in lazy Pride
Your Altars near your Couches Side?
When from the homeliest Earthen Ware
Are sent up Off'rings more sincere
Than where the haughty Dutchess Locks,
Her Silver Vase in Cedar-Box.

295. *Earthen Ware.* Vide Virgil and Lucretius.

YET, some Devotion still remains
Among our harmless Northern Swains;     300
Whose Off'rings plac't in golden Ranks,
Adorn our chrystal River's Banks:
Nor seldom grace the flow'ry downs,
With spiral Tops, and Copple-Crowns:
Or gilding in a sunny Morn
The humble Branches of a Thorn.
(So Poets sing, with golden Bough
The *Trojan* Heroe paid his Vow.)

HITHER by luckless Error led,
The crude Consistence oft I tread.     310
Here, when my Shoes are out of case,
Unweeting gild the tarnish'd Lace:
Here, by the sacred Bramble ting'd,
My Petticoat is doubly fring'd.

BE Witness for me, Nymph divine,
I never robb'd thee with Design:
Nor, will the zealous *Hannah* pout
To wash thy injur'd Off'rings out.

BUT, stop ambitious Muse, in time;
Nor dwell on Subjects too sublime.     320
In vain on lofty Heels I tread,
Aspiring to exalt my Head:
With Hoop expanded wide and light,
In vain I tempt too high a Flight.

ME *Phœbus* in a midnight Dream
Accosting; said, *Go shake your Cream.*
Be humbly minded; know your Post;
Sweeten your Tea, and watch your Toast.
Thee best befits a lowly Style:
Teach *Dennis* how to stir the Guile:     330

307. *golden Bough.* Virg. lib. 6.
325. *Phœbus.* Cynthius aurem vellis. Hor.    *Dream.* Cum somnia vera. Hor.
326. *Go shake.* In the Bottle to make Butter.

With *Peggy Dixon* thoughtful sit,
Contriving for the Pot and Spit.
Take down thy proudly swelling Sails,
And rub thy Teeth, and pair thy Nails.
At nicely carving show thy Wit;
But ne'er presume to eat a Bit:
Turn ev'ry Way thy watchful Eye;
And ev'ry Guest be sure to ply:
Let never at your Board be known
An empty Plate except your own.                      340
Be these thy Arts; nor higher Aim
Than what befits a rural Dame.

But, *Cloacina* Goddess bright,
Sleek —— claims her as his Right:
And *Smedley*, Flow'r of all Divines,
Shall sing the Dean in *Smedley*'s Lines.


# THE

# DEAN's REASONS

## For not Building at

## DRAPIER'S HILL

I WILL not build on yonder mount:
And, should you call me to account,
Consulting with myself, I find,
It was no levity of mind.
Whate'er I promised or intended,
No fault of mine, the scheme is ended:

Printed from *Works, 4to, Vol. VIII* (2), London, 1765.

331. *Peggy Dixon.* Mrs. Dixon the Housekeeper.
341. *Be these thy Arts.* Haec tibi erunt artes. Virg.
345. *Smedley.* A very stupid, insolent, factious, deformed, conceited Parson; a vile Pretender to Poetry, preferred by the D. of Grafton for his Wit.

Nor can you tax me as unsteady,
I have a hundred causes ready:
All risen since that flatt'ring time,
When Drapier's-hill appear'd in rhyme.          10

    I am, as now too late I find,
The greatest cully of mankind:
The lowest boy in Martin's school
May turn and wind me like a fool.
How could I form so wild a vision,
To seek, in deserts, Fields Elysian?
To live in fear, suspicion, variance,
With Thieves, Fanatics, and Barbarians?

    But here my Lady will object;
Your Deanship ought to recollect,          20
That, near the Knight of Gosford plac't,
Whom you allow a man of taste,
Your intervals of time to spend
With so conversible a friend,
It would not signify a pin
Whatever climate you were in.

    'Tis true, but what advantage comes
To me from all a us'rer's plumbs;
Though I should see him twice a day,
And am his neighbour cross the way;          30
If all my rhetoric must fail
To strike him for a pot of ale?

    Thus, when the learned and the wise
Conceal their talents from our eyes,
And, from deserving friends, with-hold
Their gifts, as misers do their gold;
Their knowledge, to themselves confin'd,
Is the same avarice of mind:
Nor makes their conversation better,
Than if they never knew a letter.          40
Such is the fate of Gosford's Knight,
Who keeps his wisdom out of sight;

Whose uncommunicative heart,
Will scarce one precious word impart:
Still rapt in speculations deep,
His outward senses fast asleep;
Who, while I talk, a song will hum,
Or, with his fingers, beat the drum;
Beyond the skies transports his mind,
And leaves a lifeless corpse behind.            50

But, as for me, who ne'er could clamber high,
To understand Malebranche or Cambray;
Who send my mind (as I believe) less
Than others do, on errands sleeveless;
Can listen to a tale humdrum,
And, with attention, read Tom Thumb;
My spirits with my body progging,
Both hand in hand together jogging;
Sunk over head and ears in matter,
Nor can of metaphysics smatter;                60
Am more diverted with a quibble
Than dreams of worlds intelligible;
And think all notions too abstracted
Are like the ravings of a crackt head;
What intercourse of minds can be
Betwixt the Knight sublime and me?
If when I talk, as talk I must,
It is but prating to a bust.

Where friendship is by Fate design'd,
It forms an union in the mind:                70
But, here I differ from the Knight
In every point, like black and white:
For, none can say that ever yet
We both in one opinion met:
Not in philosophy, or ale,
In state affairs, or planting cale;
In rhetoric, or picking straws;
In roasting larks, or making laws:
In public schemes, or catching flies,
In parliaments, or pudding-pies.              80

The neighbours wonder why the Knight
Should in a country life delight,
Who not one pleasure entertains
To chear the solitary scenes:
His guests are few, his visits rare,
Nor uses time, nor time will spare;
Nor rides, nor walks, nor hunts, nor fowls,
Nor plays at cards, or dice, or bowls;
But, seated in an easy chair,
Despises exercise and air.                          90
His rural walks he ne'er adorns;
Here poor Pomona sits on thorns:
And there neglected Flora settles
Her bum upon a bed of nettles.


        Those thankless and officious cares
I use to take in friends affairs,
From which I never could refrain,
And have been often chid in vain:
From these I am recover'd quite,
At least in what regards the Knight.                100
Preserve his health, his store increase;
May nothing interrupt his peace.
But now, let all his tenants round
First milk his cows, and after, pound:
Let ev'ry cottager conspire
To cut his hedges down for fire;
The naughty boys about the village
His crabs and sloes may freely pillage:
He still may keep a pack of knaves
To spoil his work, and work by halves:              110
His meadows may be dug by swine,
It shall be no concern of mine.
For, why should I continue still
To serve a friend against his will?

# DEATH and DAPHNE

To an agreeable young Lady, but
extremely lean

Written in the Year 1730

DEATH went upon a solemn Day,
  At *Pluto*'s Hall, his Court to pay:
The Phantom, having humbly kiss't
His griesly Monarch's sooty Fist,
Presented him the weekly Bills
Of Doctors, Fevers, Plagues, and Pills.
*Pluto* observing, since the Peace,
The Burial Article decrease;
And, vext to see Affairs miscarry,
Declar'd in Council, *Death* must marry:     10
Vow'd, he no longer could support
Old Batchelors about his Court:
The Int'rest of his Realm had need
That *Death* should get a num'rous Breed;
Young *Deathlings*, who, by Practice made
Proficients in their Father's Trade,
With Colonies might stock around
His large Dominions under Ground.

  A CONSULT of Coquets below
Was call'd, to rig him out a Beau:     20
From her own Head, *Megæra* takes
A Perriwig of twisted Snakes;
Which in the nicest Fashion curl'd,
Like *Toupets* of this upper World;
(With Flow'r of Sulphur powder'd well,
That graceful on his Shoulders fell)
An Adder of the sable Kind,
In Line direct, hung down behind.

Printed from Poems, 1735.

24. *Toupets*. The Perriwigs now in Fashion are so called.

The Owl, the Raven, and the Bat,
Club'd for a Feather to his Hat;     30
His Coat, an Us'rer's Velvet Pall,
Bequeathed to *Pluto*, Corps and all.
But, loth his Person to expose
Bare, like a Carcase pick't by Crows,
A Lawyer o'er his Hands and Face,
Stuck artfully a Parchment Case.
No new-flux't Rake shew'd fairer Skin;
Not *Phyllis* after lying-in.
With Snuff was fill'd his Ebon Box,
Of Shin-Bones rotted by the Pox.     40
Nine Spirits of blaspheming Fops,
With Aconite anoint his Chops:
And give him Words of dreadful Sounds,
God damn his Blood, and Bloods and Wounds.

     THUS furnish't out, he sent his Train
To take a House in *Warwick* Lane:
The *Faculty*, his humble Friends,
A complimental Message sends:
Their President, in Scarlet Gown,
Harangu'd, and welcom'd him to Town.     50

     BUT, *Death* had Bus'ness to dispatch:
His Mind was running on his Match.
And, hearing much of *Daphne*'s Fame,
His *Majesty of Terrors* came,
Fine as a Col'nel of the Guards,
To visit where she sat at Cards:
She, as he came into the Room,
Thought him *Adonis* in his Bloom.
And now her Heart with Pleasure jumps,
She scarce remembers what is Trumps.     60
For, such a Shape of Skin and Bone
Was never seen, except her own:
Charm'd with his Eyes and Chin and Snout,
Her Pocket-Glass drew slily out;
And, grew enamour'd with her Phiz,
As just the Counterpart of his.

She darted many a private Glance,
And freely made the first Advance:
Was of her Beauty grown so vain,
She doubted not to win the *Swain*.                    70
Nothing she thought could sooner gain him,
Than with her Wit to entertain him.
She ask't about her Friends below;
This meagre Fop, that batter'd Beau:
Whether some late departed Toasts
Had got Gallants among the Ghosts?
If *Chloe* were a Sharper still,
As great as ever, at Quadrille?
(The Ladies there must needs be Rooks,
For, Cards we know, are *Pluto*'s Books)        80
If *Florimel* had found her Love
For whom she hang'd herself above?
How oft a Week was kept a Ball
By *Proserpine*, at *Pluto*'s Hall?
She fancy'd, those *Elysian* Shades
The sweetest Place for Masquerades:
How pleasant on the Banks of Styx,
To troll it in a Coach and Six!


    WHAT Pride a Female Heart enflames!
How endless are Ambition's Aims!                90
Cease haughty Nymph; the Fates decree
*Death* must not be a Spouse for thee:
For, when by chance the meagre Shade
Upon thy Hand his Finger laid;
Thy Hand as dry and cold as Lead,
His matrimonial Spirit fled;
He felt about his Heart a Damp,
That quite extinguish't *Cupid*'s Lamp:
Away the frighted Spectre scuds,
And leaves my Lady in the Suds.                  100

# DAPHNE

DAPHNE knows, with equal ease,
How to vex and how to please;
But, the folly of her sex
Makes her sole delight to vex.
Never woman more devis'd
Surer ways to be despis'd:
Paradoxes weakly wielding,
Always conquer'd, never yielding.
To dispute, her chief delight,
With not one opinion right:　　　　　　　　10
Thick her arguments she lays on,
And with cavils combats reason:
Answers in decisive way,
Never hears what you can say:
Still her odd perverseness shows
Chiefly where she nothing knows.
And where she is most familiar,
Always peevisher and sillier:
All her spirits in a flame
When she knows she's most to blame.　　　　20


Send me hence ten thousand miles,
From a face that always smiles:
None could ever act that part,
But a Fury in her heart.
Ye who hate such inconsistence,
To be easy keep your distance;
Or in folly still befriend her,
But have no concern to mend her.
Lose not time to contradict her,
Nor endeavour to convict her.　　　　　　30
Never take it in your thought,
That she'll own, or cure a fault.

Printed from *Works, 4to, Vol. VIII* (2), London, 1765.

Into contradiction warm her,
Then, perhaps, you may reform her:
Only take this rule along,
Always to advise her wrong;
And reprove her when she's right;
She may then grow wise for spight.

No—that scheme will ne'er succeed,
She has better learnt her creed:                    40
She's too cunning, and too skilful,
When to yield, and when be willful.
Nature holds her forth two mirrors,
One for truth, and one for errors:
That looks hideous, fierce, and frightful;
This is flatt'ring, and delightful;
That she throws away as foul;
Sits by this, to dress her soul.

Thus you have the case in view,
Daphne, 'twixt the Dean and you,                    50
Heav'n forbid he should despise thee;
But will never more advise thee.

### Twelve Articles

1. Lest it may more quarrels breed
   I will never hear you read.
2. By disputing I will never
   To convince you, once endeavour.
3. When a paradox you stick to,
   I will never contradict you.
4. When I talk, and you are heedless,
   I will shew no anger needless.                    60
5. When your speeches are absurd,
   I will ne'er object a word.
6. When you furious argue wrong,
   I will grieve, and hold my tongue.
7. Not a jest, or hum'rous story,
   Will I ever tell before ye:
   To be chidden for explaining
   When you quite mistake the meaning.

DAPHNE
1730
471



8. Never more will I suppose
   You can taste my verse or prose:    70
9. You no more at me shall fret,
   While I teach, and you forget;
10. You shall never hear me thunder,
    When you blunder on, and blunder.
11. Shew your poverty of spirit,
    And in dress place all your merit;
    Give yourself ten thousand airs
    That with me shall break no squares.
12. Never will I give advice
    Till you please to ask me thrice;    80
    Which, if you in scorn reject,
    'Twill be just as I expect.

Thus we both shall have our ends,
And continue special friends.

# An Excellent New

# BALLAD:

## OR

## The true *English* Dean to be hang'd for a Rape

### I

OUR Brethren of *England* who love us so dear,
 And in all they do for us so kindly do mean,
A Blessing upon them, have sent us this Year,
For the Good of our Church a true *English* Dean.
 A holier Priest ne'er was wrapt up in Crape,
The worst you can say, he committed a Rape.

Printed from the original Broadside, with corrections from *Poems*, 1735.

Title: *English Dean.* Sawbridge, Dean of Ferns, lately deceased.

## II

In his Journey to *Dublin*, he lighted at *Chester*,
And there he grew fond of another Man's Wife,
Burst into her Chamber, and wou'd have Carest her,
But she valu'd her Honour much more than her Life.     10
   She bustled and strugled, and made her Escape,
To a Room full of Guests for fear of a Rape.

## III

The *Dean* he pursu'd to recover his Game,
And now to attack her again he prepares,
But the Company stood in Defence of the Dame,
They Cudgell'd, and Cuft him, and kickt him down Stairs.
   His Deanship was now in a damnable Scrape,
And this was no Time for committing a Rape.

## IV

To *Dublin* he comes, to the *Bagnio* he goes,
And orders the Landlord to bring him a Whore;     20
No Scruple came on him his Gown to expose,
'Twas what all his Life he had practis'd before.
   He had made himself Drunk with the Juice of the Grape,
And got a good *Clap*, but committed no Rape.

## V

The Dean, and his Landlord, a jolly Comrade,
Resolv'd for a Fortnight to Swim in Delight,
For why, they had both been brought up to the Trade
Of drinking all Day, and of whoring all Night.
   His Landlord was ready his Deanship to Ape
In ev'ry Debauch, but committing a Rape.     30

## VI

This *Protestant* Zealot, this *English* Divine
In Church and in State was of Principles sound,
Was truer than *Steele* to the *Hanover* Line,
And griev'd that a *Tory* should live above Ground.
   Shall a Subject so Loyal be hang'd by the Nape,
For no other Crime but committing a Rape.

## VII

By old *Popish* Cannons, as wise Men have Penn'd 'em,
Each Priest had a Concubine, *jure Ecclesiæ*;
Who'd be Dean of *Ferns* without a *Commendam*?
And Precedents we can produce, if it please ye,     40
    Then, why should the Dean, when Whores are so cheap,
Be put to the Peril, and Toyl of a Rape?

## VIII

If Fortune should please but to take such a Crotchet,
(To thee I apply great *Smedley*'s Successor)
To give thee *Lawn-Sleeves* a *Mitre* and *Rotchet*,
Whom would'st thou resemble? I leave thee a Guesser;
    But I only behold thee in *Atherton*'s Shape,
For *Sodomy* hang'd, as thou for a Rape.

## IX

Ah! dost thou not Envy the brave Colonel *Chartres*,
Condemn'd for thy Crime, at three score and ten?     50
To Hang him all *England* would lend him their Garters;
Yet he lives, and is ready to ravish agen,
    Then Throttle thy self with an Ell of strong Tape,
For thou hast not a Groat to Attone for a Rape.

## X

The Dean he was vext that his Whores were so willing,
He long'd for a Girl that would struggle and squal,
He ravish'd her fairly, and sav'd a good Shilling;
But, here was to pay the Devil and all.
    His Trouble and Sorrows now come in a Heap,
And hang'd he must be for committing a Rape.     60

## XI

If Maidens are ravish't, it is their own Choice,
Why are they so willful to struggle with Men?
If they would but lye quiet, and stifle their Voice,
No Devil nor Dean could Ravish 'em then,
    Nor would there be need of a strong Hempen Cape,
Ty'd round the Dean's Neck, for committing a Rape.

47. *Atherton.* A Bishop of Waterford, sent from England a Hundred Years ago.

### XII

Our Church and our State dear *England* maintains,
For which all true Protestant Hearts should be glad;
She sends us our Bishops and Judges and Deans,
And better would give us, if better she had;                    70
 But, Lord how the Rabble will stare and will gape,
When the good *English* Dean is hang'd up for a Rape.

## On *Stephen Duck*, the Thresher, and favourite Poet,

### A *QUIBBLING EPIGRAM*

Written in the Year 1730

THE Thresher *Duck*, could o'er the *Queen* prevail.
 The Proverb says; *No Fence against a Flayl.*
From *threshing* Corn, he turns to *thresh* his Brains;
For which Her *Majesty* allows him *Grains.*
Though 'tis confess't that those who ever saw
His Poems, think them all not worth a *Straw.*
Thrice happy *Duck*, employ'd in threshing *Stubble*!
Thy Toil is lessen'd, and thy Profits double.

Printed from *Poems*, 1735.

## The Dean to himself

on

## St. Cecilia's day

GRAVE D. of S^t Patrick's ho[w] comes it to pass
 That y[ou] who know musick no more than an ass
That you [who] was found writing of Drapiers
Should lend your cathedrall to players and scrapers

Printed from Swift's autograph, Forster Collection, No. 533.

To act such an opera once in a year
Is offensive to every true Protestant ear
With trumpets and fiddles and organs and singing
Will sure the Pretend$^r$ and Popery bring in.
No Protestant Prelate, His L$^d$shp or Grace
Durst there show his right or most rev$^{nd}$ face            10
How would it pollute their Crosiers and Rochets
To listen to minimms and quavers and Crochets


# TO

## *BETTY* the Grizette

### Written in the Year 1730

QUEEN of Wit and Beauty, *Betty*,
   Never may the Muse forget ye:
How thy Face charms ev'ry Shepherd,
Spotted over like a Le'pard!
And, thy freckled Neck display'd,
Envy breeds in ev'ry Maid.
Like a fly blown Cake of Tallow,
Or, on Parchment, Ink turn'd yellow:
Or, a tawny speckled Pippin,
Shrivel'd with a Winter's keeping.                            10

AND, thy Beauty thus dispatcht;
Let me praise thy Wit unmatcht.

SETS of Phrases, cut and dry,
Evermore thy Tongue supply.
And, thy Memory is loaded
With old Scraps from Plays exploded.
Stock't with Repartees and Jokes,
Suited to all Christian Fokes:
Shreds of Wit, and senseless Rhimes,
Blunder'd out a Thousand Times.                               20

Printed from *Poems*, 1735.

Nor, wilt thou of Gifts be sparing,
Which can ne'er be worse for wearing.
Picking Wit among Collegions,
In the Play-House upper Regions;
Where, in Eighteen-penny Gall'ry,
*Irish* Nymphs learn *Irish* Raillery:
But, thy Merit is thy Failing,
And, thy Raillery is Railing.

   THUS, with Talents well endu'd
To be scurrilous, and rude;      30
When you pertly raise your Snout,
Fleer, and gibe, and laugh, and flout;
This, among *Hibernian* Asses,
For sheer Wit, and Humour passes!
Thus, indulgent *Chloe* bit,
Swears you have a World of Wit.

# THE
# LADY's DRESSING ROOM

FIVE Hours, (and who can do it less in?)
  By haughty *Celia* spent in Dressing;
The Goddess from her Chamber issues,
Array'd in Lace, Brocade and Tissues.
*Strephon*, who found the Room was void,
And *Betty* otherwise employ'd;
Stole in, and took a strict Survey,
Of all the Litter as it lay;
Whereof, to make the Matter clear,
An Inventory follows here.     10

   And first a dirty Smock appear'd,
Beneath the Arm-pits well besmear'd.
*Strephon*, the Rogue, display'd it wide,
And turn'd it round on every Side.

Printed from original 4to, London, 1732, with corrections from *Poems*, 1735.

In such a Case few Words are best,
And *Strephon* bids us guess the rest;
But swears how damnably the Men lie,
In calling *Celia* sweet and cleanly.

    Now listen while he next produces,
The various Combs for various Uses,     20
Fill'd up with Dirt so closely fixt,
No Brush could force a way betwixt.
A Paste of Composition rare,
Sweat, Dandriff, Powder, Lead and Hair;
A Forehead Cloth with Oyl upon't
To smooth the Wrinkles on her Front;
Here Allum Flower to stop the Steams,
Exhal'd from sour unsavoury Streams,
There Night-gloves made of *Tripsy*'s Hide,
Bequeath'd by *Tripsy* when she dy'd,     30
With Puppy Water, Beauty's Help
Distill'd from *Tripsy*'s darling Whelp;
Here Gallypots and Vials plac'd,
Some fill'd with Washes, some with Paste,
Some with Pomatum, Paints and Slops,
And Ointments good for scabby Chops.
Hard by a filthy Bason stands,
Fowl'd with the Scouring of her Hands;
The Bason takes whatever comes
The Scrapings of her Teeth and Gums,     40
A nasty Compound of all Hues,
For here she spits, and here she spues.

    But oh! it turn'd poor *Strephon*'s Bowels,
When he beheld and smelt the Towels,
Begumm'd, bematter'd, and beslim'd
With Dirt, and Sweat, and Ear-Wax grim'd.
No Object *Strephon*'s Eye escapes,
Here Pettycoats in frowzy Heaps;
Nor be the Handkerchiefs forgot
All varnish'd o'er with Snuff and Snot.     50
The Stockings, why shou'd I expose,
Stain'd with the Marks of stinking Toes;

Or greasy Coifs and Pinners reeking,
Which *Celia* slept at least a Week in?
A Pair of Tweezers next he found
To pluck her Brows in Arches round,
Or Hairs that sink the Forehead low,
Or on her Chin like Bristles grow.

    The Virtues we must not let pass,
Of *Celia*'s magnifying Glass.          60
When frighted *Strephon* cast his Eye on't
It shew'd the Visage of a Gyant.
A Glass that can to Sight disclose,
The smallest Worm in *Celia*'s Nose,
And faithfully direct her Nail
To squeeze it out from Head to Tail;
For catch it nicely by the Head,
It must come out alive or dead.

    Why *Strephon* will you tell the rest?
And must you needs describe the Chest?          70
That careless Wench! no Creature warn her
To move it out from yonder Corner;
But leave it standing full in Sight
For you to exercise your Spight.
In vain, the Workman shew'd his Wit
With Rings and Hinges counterfeit
To make it seem in this Disguise,
A Cabinet to vulgar Eyes;
Which *Strephon* ventur'd to look in,
Resolv'd to go thro' thick and thin;          80
He lifts the Lid, there need no more,
He smelt it all the Time before.
As from within *Pandora*'s Box,
When *Epimetheus* op'd the Locks,
A sudden universal Crew
Of humane Evils upward flew;
He still was comforted to find
That *Hope* at last remain'd behind;
So *Strephon* lifting up the Lid,
To view what in the Chest was hid,          90

The Vapours flew from out the Vent,
But *Strephon* cautious never meant
The Bottom of the Pan to grope,
And fowl his Hands in Search of *Hope*.
O ne'er may such a vile Machine
Be once in *Celia*'s Chamber seen!
O may she better learn to keep
"Those Secrets of the hoary deep!"

     As Mutton Cutlets, Prime of Meat,
Which tho' with Art you salt and beat,       100
As Laws of Cookery require,
And roast them at the clearest Fire;
If from adown the hopeful Chops
The Fat upon a Cinder drops,
To stinking Smoak it turns the Flame
Pois'ning the Flesh from whence it came;
And up exhales a greasy Stench,
For which you curse the careless Wench;
So Things, which must not be exprest,
When plumpt into the reeking Chest;       110
Send up an excremental Smell
To taint the Parts from whence they fell.
The Pettycoats and Gown perfume,
And waft a Stink round every Room.

     Thus finishing his grand Survey,
The Swain disgusted slunk away.

     But Vengeance, Goddess never sleeping
Soon punish'd *Strephon* for his Peeping;
His foul Imagination links
Each Dame he sees with all her Stinks:       120
And, if unsav'ry Odours fly,
Conceives a Lady standing by:
All Women his Description fits,
And both Idea's jump like Wits:

98. '*Those Secrets . . .*' [Milton *Paradise Lost*, ii. 890–1].
99. *Prime of Meat.* Prima Virorum.
103. *adown.* Vide Dean Daniel's *Works*, and Namby Pamby's.

By vicious Fancy coupled fast,
And still appearing in Contrast.
I pity wretched *Strephon* blind
To all the Charms of Woman Kind;
Should I the Queen of Love refuse,
Because she rose from stinking Ooze?        130
To him that looks behind the Scene,
*Satira*'s but some pocky Quean.

When *Celia* in her Glory shows,
If *Strephon* would but stop his Nose;
(Who now so impiously blasphemes
Her Ointments, Daubs, and Paints and Creams,
Her Washes, Slops, and every Clout,
With which he makes so foul a Rout;)
He soon would learn to think like me,
And bless his ravisht Eyes to see        140
Such Order from Confusion sprung,
Such gaudy Tulips rais'd from Dung.

# *To Mr.* Gay

## *on his being Steward to the Duke of* Queensberry

HOW could you, *Gay*, disgrace the Muses Train,
To serve a tastless Court twelve Years in vain?
Fain would I think, our *Female Friend* sincere,
Till *Bob*, the Poet's Foe, possess't her Ear.
Did Female Virtue e'er so high ascend,
To lose an Inch of Favour for a Friend?

SAY, had the Court no better place to chuse
For thee, than make a dry Nurse of thy Muse?
How cheaply had thy Liberty been sold,
To squire a Royal Girl of two Years old!        10

Printed from *Poems*, 1735 (uncancelled state).

3. *Female Friend*. Mrs. Howard, now Countess of Suffolk.
8. *dry Nurse*. He was offered to be Gentleman-Usher to a young Princess, then of that Age, but made his Excuses.

In Leading strings her Infant-Steps to guide;
Or, with her Go-Cart amble Side by Side.


   But princely *Douglas*, and his glorious Dame,
Advanc'd thy Fortune, and preserv'd thy Fame.
Nor, will your nobler Gifts be misapply'd,
When o'er your Patron's Treasure you preside,
The World shall own, his Choice was wise and just,
For, Sons of *Phœbus* never break their Trust.


   Not Love of Beauty less the Heart inflames
Of Guardian Eunuchs to the *Sultan*-Dames,         20
Their Passions not more impotent and cold,
Than those of Poets to the *Lust* of Gold.
With *Pœan*'s purest Fire his Favourites glow;
The Dregs will serve to ripen Ore below;
His meanest Work: For, had he thought it fit,
That, Wealth should be the Appenage of Wit,
The God of *Light* could ne'er have been so *blind*,
To deal it to the worst of Human-kind.


   But let me now, for I can do it well,
Your Conduct in this new Employ foretell.         30


   And first: To make my Observation right,
I place a STATESMAN full before my Sight.
A bloated *Minister* in all his Geer,
With shameless Visage, and perfidious Leer,
Two Rows of Teeth arm each devouring Jaw;
And, *Ostrich*-like, his all-digesting Maw.
My Fancy drags this *Monster* to my View,
To show the World his chief Reverse in you.
Of loud un-meaning Sounds, a rapid Flood
Rolls from his Mouth in plenteous Streams of Mud;    40
With these, the Court and Senate-house he plies,
Made up of Noise, and Impudence, and Lies.

---

  13. *princely Douglas.* The Duke of Queensberry, and his excellent Duchess; so renowned for her Behaviour upon her Banishment from Court on her patronizing Mr. Gay.

Now, let me show how *Bob* and you agree.
You serve a *potent Prince*, as well as He.
The *Ducal* Coffers, trusted to your Charge,
Your honest Care may fill; perhaps enlarge.
His Vassals easy, and the Owner blest;
They pay a Trifle, and enjoy the rest.
Not so a Nation's Revenues are paid:
The Servants Faults are on the Master laid.          50
The People with a Sigh their Taxes bring;
And cursing *Bob*, forget to bless the King.

NEXT, hearken GAY, to what thy Charge requires,
With *Servants*, *Tenants*, and the neighb'ring *Squires*.
Let all Domesticks feel your gentle Sway;
Nor bribe, insult, nor flatter, nor betray.
Let due Reward to Merit be allow'd;
Nor, with your *KINDRED half the Palace crowd*.
Nor, think your self secure in doing wrong,
By *telling Noses with a Party strong*.          60

BE rich; but of your Wealth make no Parade;
At least, *before your Master's Debts are paid*.
Nor, *in a Palace built with Charge immense*,
*Presume to treat him at his own Expence*.
Each Farmer in the Neighbourhood can count
To what your lawful Perquisites amount.
The Tenants poor, the Hardness of the Times,
Are ill excuses for a Servant's Crimes:
With Int'rest, and a *Præmium* paid beside,
The Master's pressing Wants must be supply'd;          70
With hasty Zeal, behold, the Steward come,
By his own Credit to advance the Sum;
Who, while *th' unrighteous Mammon* is his Friend,
May well conclude his Pow'r will never end.
A faithful Treas'rer! What could he do more?
*He lends my Lord, what was my Lord's before.*

44. *potent Prince*. A Title given to every Duke by the Heralds.
54. *Servants, Tenants, Squires*. It is thought there is an Allusion here, to Ministers, to Subjects in general, and to Princes in Alliance.
60. *By telling Noses*. This seems to allude to the Arts of procuring a Majority.
62. *your Master's Debts*. The Author seems to mean the Nation's Debts.

THE Law so strictly guards the Monarch's Health,
That no Physician dares prescribe by Stealth:
The Council sit; approve the Doctor's Skill;
And give Advice before he gives the Pill.                    80
But, the *State-Emp'ric* acts a safer Part;
And while he *poisons, wins* the Royal Heart.

BUT, how can I describe the rav'nous Breed?
Then, let me now by Negatives proceed.

SUPPOSE your Lord a trusty Servant send,
On weighty Bus'ness, to some neighb'ring Friend:
Presume not, *Gay,* unless you serve a Drone,
To countermand his Orders by your own.

SHOULD some *imperious Neighbour* sink the Boats,
And drain the *Fish-ponds*; while your *Master* doats;      90
Shall he upon the *Ducal* Rights intrench,
Because he brib'd you with a Brace of Tench?

NOR, from your Lord his bad Condition hide;
To feed his Luxury, or sooth his Pride.
Nor, at an under Rate his *Timber* sell;
And, with an Oath, assure him; *all is well.*
Or *swear it rotten; and with humble Airs,*
*Request it of him to compleat your Stairs.*
Nor, when a Mortgage lies on half his Lands,
Come with a Purse of Guineas in your Hands.                 100

HAVE *Peter Waters* always in your Mind;
That Rogue of *genuine ministerial* Kind
Can half the Peerage by his Arts bewitch;
Starve twenty Lords to make one Scoundrel rich:

86. *neighb'ring Friend.* Meaning, I suppose, some foreign Prince.

89. *imperious Neighbour.* Perhaps a hint of Injuries and Affronts received at Sea, &c.

97, 98. These Lines are thought to allude to some Story concerning a great Quantity of Mahoganny, declared rotten, and then applied by some Body to Wainscots, Stairs, Door-Cases, &c.

101. *Peter Waters.* He hath practiced this Trade for many Years, and still continues it with Success; and after he hath ruined one Lord, is earnestly sollicited to take another.

RSPW

And, when he gravely has undone a Score,
Is humbly pray'd to ruin Twenty more.

A DEXT'ROUS Steward, when his Tricks are found,
*Hush-money* sends to all the Neighbours round:
His Master, unsuspicious of his Pranks,
Pays all the Cost, and gives the Villain Thanks.          110
And, should a Friend attempt to set him right,
His Lordship would impute it all to Spight:
Would love his Fav'rite better than before;
And trust his Honesty just so much more.
Thus Realms, and Families, with equal Fate,
Are sunk by *premier Ministers of State.*

SOME, when an Heir succeeds; go boldly on,
And, as they robb'd the *Father*, rob the *Son.*
A Knave, who deep embroils his Lord's Affairs,
Will soon grow *necessary* to his Heirs.          120
His Policy consists in *setting Traps*,
In finding *Ways and Means*, and *stopping Gaps*:
He knows a Thousand Tricks, whene'er he please,
Though not to cure, yet palliate each Disease.
In either Case, an equal Chance is run:
For, keep, or turn him out, my Lord's undone.
You want a Hand to clear a filthy Sink;
No cleanly Workman can endure the Stink.
A strong Dilemma in a desp'rate Case!
To act with Infamy, or quit the Place.          130

A BUNGLER thus, who scarce the Nail can hit,
With driving wrong, will make the Pannel split:
Nor, dares an abler Workman undertake
To drive a second, lest the whole should break.

IN ev'ry Court the Parallel will hold;
And Kings, like private Folks, are bought and sold:
The ruling Rogue, who dreads to be cashier'd;
Contrives, as he is *hated*, to be *fear'd*:
*Confounds Accounts, perplexes all Affairs;*
For, *Vengeance* more *embroils*, than *Skill repairs.*          140

So, Robbers (and their Ends are just the same)
To 'scape Enquiries, *leave the House in Flame.*

I KNEW a *brazen* Minister of State,
Who bore for twice ten Years the publick Hate.
In every Mouth the Question most in Vogue
Was, *When will* THEY *turn out this odious Rogue?*
A Juncture happen'd in his highest Pride:
While HE went robbing on; *old Master* dy'd.
We thought, there now remain'd no room to doubt:
*His Work is done, the Minister must out.*          150
The Court *invited* more than One, or Two;
Will you, Sir *Spencer?* or, will *you,* or *you?*
But, not a Soul his Office durst accept:
The subtle Knave had all the Plunder swept.
And, such was then the Temper of the Times,
He ow'd his Preservation to his Crimes.
The Candidates observ'd his dirty Paws,
Nor found it difficult to guess the Cause:
But when they smelt such foul Corruptions round him;
Away they fled, and left him as they found him.          160

THUS, when a greedy Sloven once has thrown
His *Snot* into the *Mess*; *'tis all his own.*


# ON

# Mr. *Pulteney* being put out of the Council

## Written in the Year 1731

SIR *Robert* weary'd by *Will. Pulteney's* Teazings,
Who interrupted him in all his Leasings;
Resolved that *Will.* and he should meet no more;
Full in his Face *Bob* shuts the Council Door:

Printed from *Poems,* 1735.

Nor lets him sit as Justice on the Bench,
To punish Thieves, or lash a Suburb Wench.
Yet still St. *Stephen*'s Chappel open lies
For *Will.* to enter.—What shall I advise?
E'en quit the HOUSE, for thou too long hast sat in't,
Produce at last thy dormant Ducal Patent:                    10
There, near thy Master's Throne in Shelter plac't,
Let *Will.* unheard by thee, his Thunder waste.
Yet still I fear your Work is done but Half;
For while he keeps his Pen, you are not safe.


     HEAR an old Fable, and a dull one too;
Yet bears a Moral when apply'd to you.


     A HARE had long escap'd pursuing Hounds,
By often shifting into distant Grounds;
Till, finding all his Artifices vain;
To save his Life he leapt into the Main.                     20
But there, alas! he could no Safety find;
A Pack of *Dog-fish* had him in the Wind:
He scours away; and to avoid the Foe,
Descends for Shelter to the Shades below.
There *Cerberus* lay watching in his Den,
(He had not seen a Hare the Lord knows when)
Out bounc't the Mastiff of the triple Head;
Away the Hare with double Swiftness fled.
Hunted from Earth, and Sea, and Hell, he flies
(Fear lent him Wings) for Safety to the Skies.              30
How was the fearful Animal distress't!
Behold a Foe more fierce than all the rest:
*Syrius*, the swiftest of the heavn'ly Pack,
Fail'd but an Inch to seize him by the Back.
He fled to Earth, but first it cost him dear;
He left his Scut behind, and Half an Ear.


     THUS was the Hare pursu'd, tho' free from Guilt;
Thus *Bob* shal't thou be mawl'd, fly where thou wil't:
Then, honest *Robin*, of thy Corps beware:
Thou art not half so nimble as a Hare:                       40

Too pond'rous is thy Bulk to mount the Sky;
Nor can you go to *Hell* before you dye.
So keen thy *Hunters,* and thy *Scent* so strong;
Thy *Turns* and *Doublings* cannot save thee long.

# The Character of

# SIR ROBERT WALPOLE

[In Imitation of the following lampoon on Cardinal Fleury.

> *Confondant du passé le leger souvenir,*
> *Ebloüi du present, sans percer l'avenir;*
> *Dans l'art de gouverner decrepit, & Novice,*
> *Punissant la Vertu, recompensant le Vice.*
> *Malgré sa Tête altiere accablé de son rang,*
> *Fourbe dans le Petit, & Dupe dans le Grand.*
> *On connoit à ces traits, même sans qu'on le nomme,*
> *Le* MAITRE *de la* France, *& le* VALET *de* Rome.]

WITH favour & fortune fastidiously blest
he's loud in his laugh & he's coarse in his Jest
of favour & fortune unmerited vain
a sharper in trifles a dupe in the main
atchieving of nothing Still promising wonders
by dint of experience improving in Blunders
oppressing true merit exalting the base
and selling his Country to purchase his peace
a Jobber of Stocks by retailing false news
a prater at Court in the Stile of the Stews          10
of Virtue & worth by profession a giber
of Juries & senates the bully & briber
Tho I name not the wretch you know who I mean
T'is the Cur dog of Brittain & spaniel of Spain.

Printed from MS. copy, B.M. Add. MSS. 22625. f. 26.

44. This hunting ended in the promotion both of Will and Bob. Bob was no longer first minister, but earl of Orford, and Will was no longer his opponent, but earl of Bath. [Hawkesworth, 1755.]

# THE
# LIFE

AND

## GENUINE CHARACTER

OF

Doctor *SWIFT*

Written by Himself

### To the READER

THIS Poetical Account *of the* Life *and* Character *of the
Reverend* Dean SWIFT, *so celebrated through the World for his
many* Ingenious Writings, *was occasioned by a* Maxim *of* Roche-
foucault: *and is now published from the* Author's last corrected
Copy, *being Dedicated by the* Publisher, *To* ALEXANDER POPE, *of*
Twickenham, *Esq*;

### TO

Alexander Pope, *Esq*;

OF

*Twickenham* in the County of *Middlesex*

AS You have been long an *intimate Friend* of the *Author* of
the following *Poem*, I thought you would not be displeased
with being informed of some Particulars, how *he* came to write
it, and how *I*, very innocently, procured a *Copy*.

It seems the Dean, in conversation with some *Friends*, said,
he could guess the discourse of the World concerning his
*Character* after his Death, and thought it might be no improper
*Subject* for a *Poem*. This happened above a Year before he

Printed from the Folio, London, 1733.

finished it; for it was written by small pieces, just as *Leisure* or *Humour* allowed Him.

He shewed some Parts of it to *several Friends*, and when it was compleated, he seldom refused the sight of it to any *Visiter*: So that, probably, it has been perused by *fifty Persons*; which, being against his *usual Practice*, many People judged, likely enough, that he had a desire to make the People of *Dublin* impatient to see it *published*, and at the same time resolved to *disappoint* them; For, he never would be prevailed on to grant a *Copy*, and yet several Lines were *retained* by *Memory*, and are often repeated in *Dublin*.

It is thought, that one of his *Servants* in whom he had great *confidence*, and who had access to his *Closet*, took an opportunity, while his *Master* was riding some miles out of town, to *transcribe* the whole *Poem*: and it is probable, that the *Servant* lent it to *others*, who were not *trusty* (as it is generally the case). By this accident, I, having got a very *correct Copy* from a *Friend* in *Dublin*, lye under no obligation to conceal it.

I have shewn it to very *good Judges*, and *Friends* of the *Dean*, (if I may venture to say so to You, who are such a *Superior Judge* and *Poet*), who are well acquainted with the *Author*'s Stile, and Manner, and they all allow it to be *Genuine*, as well as perfectly *finished* and *correct*; his particular *Genius* appearing in every Line, together with his *peculiar* way of *thinking* and *writing*.

I should be very sorry to offend the *Dean*, altho' I am a perfect Stranger to his *Person*: But since the *Poem* will infallibly be soon printed, either *here*, or in *Dublin*, I take my self to have the best *title* to send it to the *Press*; and I shall direct the *Printer* to commit as few *errors* as possible.

> *I am*, SIR, *with the greatest respect,*
> *Your most Obedient and*
> *most Humble Servant,*
>                                       L. M.

*From my Chambers*
*in the* Inner Temple,
*Lond.* Apr. 1. 1733.

# THE
# LIFE and CHARACTER
## OF
# Dean *SWIFT*

Upon a *Maxim* in *Rochefoucault*

WISE *Rochefoucault* a *Maxim* writ,
  Made up of *Malice*, *Truth*, and *Wit*:
If, what he says be not a *Joke*,
We *Mortals* are strange kind of *Folk*.
  But hold—: before we farther go,
'Tis fit the *Maxim* we should know.

  He says, "Whenever *Fortune* sends
"*Disasters*, to our *Dearest Friends*,
"Although, we *outwardly* may Grieve,
"We oft, are *Laughing in our Sleeve*."                    10
And, when I think upon't, this minute,
I fancy, there is something in it.

  We see a *Comrade* get a fall,
Yet *laugh* our hearts out, *one* and *all*.

  *Tom* for a *wealthy Wife* looks round,
A *Nymph*, that brings *ten thousand* Pound:
He no where could have better pick'd;
A *Rival* comes, and *Tom*—is nick'd—.
See, how behave his *Friends* profest,
They turn the *Matter* to a *Jest*;                    20
*Loll* out their Tongues, and thus they talk,
*Poor Tom has got a plaguy baulk—!*

  I could give Instances Enough,
That *Human Friendship* is but *Stuff*.
Whene'er a *flatt'ring Puppy* cries
*You* are his *Dearest Friend*—; he *lyes*—:

To lose a *Guinea* at *Picquet*,
Wou'd make him *rage*, and *storm*, and *fret*,
Bring from his Heart *sincerer* Groans,
Than if he heard you *broke your Bones*.                30

    Come, tell me truly, wou'd you take well,
Suppose your *Friend* and *You*, were *Equal*,
To see him always *foremost* stand,
Affect to take the *upper hand*,
And strive to pass, in *publick* view,
For much a *better Man* than *You*?
*Envy*, I doubt, wou'd pow'rful prove,
And get the *better* of your *Love*;
'Twou'd please your Palate, *like a feast*,
To see him *mortify'd* at least—.                40

    'Tis true, we talk of *Friendship* much,
But, who are they that can *keep touch*—?
True *Friendship* in two breasts requires
The same *Aversions*, and *Desires*;
My *Friend* should have, when I complain,
A *Fellow-feeling* of my *Pain*.

    Yet, by *Experience*, oft we find,
Our *Friends* are of a *diff'rent* mind;
And, were I tortur'd with the *Gout*, ⎫
They'd *laugh*, to see me make a *rout*, ⎬    50
Glad, that themselves cou'd *walk* about. ⎭

    Let me suppose, two special Friends,
And, each to *Poetry* pretends:
Wou'd either *Poet* take it well,
To hear, the other *bore the Bell*—?
His *Rival*, for the *Chiefest* reckon'd,
*Himself*, pass only for the *Second*—?

    When you are *Sick*, your *Friends*, you say,
Will send their *Howd'ye's* ev'ry day:
Alas! that gives you small relief—!                60
They send for *Manners*—; not for *Grief*—:

Nor if you dy'd, wou'd fail to go
That Ev'ning to a *Puppet-Show*—:
Yet, come in time to *shew* their *Loves*,
And get a *Hatband, Scarf,* and *Gloves.*

To make these *Truths* the better known,
Let me suppose the *Case* my *own.*

The Day will come, when't shall be said,
"D'ye hear the *News*—? the *Dean* is dead—!
"*Poor Man!* he went, all on a sudden—!"       70
H'as drop'd, and *giv'n the Crow a Pudden!*
What *Money* was behind him found?
"I hear about *two thousand* Pound—
" 'Tis own'd he was a *Man* of *Wit*—,"
Yet many a *foolish thing* he writ—;
"And, sure he must be *deeply* learn'd—!"
That's more than ever I discern'd—;
"I know his *nearest Friends* complain,
"He was too *airy* for a *Dean*—.
"He was an *honest man* I'll swear—:"       80
Why Sir, I differ from you there,
For, I have heard another Story,
He was a most *confounded Tory*—!
"Yet here we had a strong report,
"That he was *well-receiv'd* at *Court*—."
Why, then it was, I do assert,
Their *Goodness,* more than his *Desert*—.
He grew, or else his *Comrades* ly'd,
Confounded *Dull*—, before he Dy'd—.

He hop'd to have a *Lucky Hit,*      }       90
Some *Medals* sent him for his *Wit;*    }
But, truly there the *Dean* was bit—.    }
"And yet, I think, for all your *Jokes,*
"His *Claim* as good as other *Folks*—.

"Must we the *Drapier* then forget?
"Is not our *Nation* in his Debt?
" 'Twas he that writ the *Drapier's Letters*—!"
He shou'd have left them for his *Betters;*

We had a Hundred *abler Men*,
Nor need *depend* upon his *Pen*—.                                   100
Say what you will about his *reading*,
You never can *defend* his *Breeding*!
Who, in his *Satyrs* running riot,
Cou'd never leave the *World* in *quiet*—;
Attacking, when he took the *Whim*,
Court, City, Camp, all one to him—.

   But, why wou'd he, except he *slobber'd*,
Offend our *Patriot*, Great Sir *Robert*,
Whose *Councils* aid the Sov'reign Pow'r,
To *save* the *Nation* ev'ry hour?                                    110
What *Scenes* of Evil he unravels,
In *Satyrs, Libels, lying Travels*!
Not sparing his own *Clergy-Cloth*,
But, *eats* into it, like a *Moth*—!

   "If he makes *Mankind* bad as *Elves*,
"I answer, they may thank themselves;
"If *Vice* can ever be abash'd,
"It must be *Ridicul'd*, or *Lash'd*."
But, if I chance to make a *slip*,
What right had he to hold the *Whip*?                                 120

   "If you *resent* it, who's to blame?
"He neither knew *you*, nor your *Name*;
"Shou'd *Vice* expect to 'scape rebuke,
"Because its *Owner* is a *Duke*?
"*Vice* is a *Vermin; Sportsm[e]n* say ⎫
"No *Vermin* can demand *fair Play*,    ⎬
"But, ev'ry Hand may justly slay."      ⎭

   I envy not the *Wits* who write
Meerly to *gratify* their *Spight*;
Thus did the *Dean*: his only scope                                   130
Was, to be held a *Misanthrope*.
This into gen'ral *Odium* drew him,
Which if he lik'd, *much good may do him*:
This gave him *Enemies* in plenty,
Throughout *two Realms* nineteen in twenty.

His *Zeal* was not to lash our *Crimes*,
But, *Discontent* against the Times;
For, had We made him *timely* Offers,
To *raise* his *Post*, or *fill* his *Coffers*,
Perhaps he might have truckled down,          140
Like other *Brethren* of his *Gown*,
For *Party* he would scarce have Bled—:
I say no more—, because he's *dead*—.


"But who cou'd charge him, to his face,
"That e'er he *cring'd* to *Men* in *Place*?
"His *Principles*, of antient date,
"Ill suit with those profess'd of late:
"The *Pope*, or *Calvin* he'd oppose,
"And thought they *Both* were *equal* Foes:
"That *Church* and *State* had suffer'd more          150
"By *Calvin*, than the *Scarlet Whore*:
"Thought *Popish* and *Fanatick Zeal*,
"*Both bitter* Foes to *Britain*'s Weal.
"The *Pope* would of our *Faith* bereave us,
"But, still our *Monarchy* wou'd leave us—.
"Not so, the vile *Fanatick Crew*;
"That Ruin'd *Church* and *Monarch* too.


"Supposing these Reflections just;
"We shou'd indulge the *Dean*'s disgust,
"Who saw this *Factious Tribe* caress'd,          160
"And *Lovers* of the *Church* distress'd—:
"The *Patrons* of the *good old Cause*,
"In *Senates* sit, at making Laws;
"The most *malignant* of the *Herd*,
"In surest way to be preferr'd—;
"And *Preachers*, find the better *quarter*,
"For *railing* at the *Royal Martyr*.


"Whole Swarms of *Sects*, with grief, he saw
"More favour'd, than the *Church by Law*:
"Thought *Protestant* too Good a Name          170
"For *canting Hypocrites* to claim,

"Whose *Protestation* hides a *Sting*
"Destructive to the *Church and King*:
"Which might as well, in his opinion,
"Become an *Atheist*, or *Socinian*.

"A *Protestant*'s a special *Clinker*;
"It serves for *Sceptick*, and *Free-thinker*,
"It serves for *Stubble, Hay*, and *Wood*,
"For ev'ry thing—, *but what it should.*"

What *Writings* had he left behind—?                180
"I hear, they're of a diff'rent kind:
"A few, in *Verse*; but most, in Prose—."
Some *high-flown Pamphlets*, I suppose—:
All scribbled in the *worst* of *times*,
To *palliate* his Friend *Oxford*'s Crimes,
To praise Queen *Anne*, nay more, defend her,
As never fav'ring the *Pretender*—:
Or *Libels* yet conceal'd from sight—,
Against the *Court* to shew his *Spight*—.
Perhaps, his *Travels, Part the Third*;             190
A *Lye*, at ev'ry *second* word:
Offensive to a *Loyal* Ear—:
But—*not one Sermon*, you may *swear*—.

"*Sir*, our *Accounts* are diff'rent quite,
"And your *Conjectures* are not right;
" 'Tis plain, his Writings were design'd
"To *please*, and to *reform* Mankind;
"And, if he often miss'd his Aim,
"The *World* must own it, to their *Shame*;
"The *Praise* is *His*, and *Theirs* the *Blame*.    200

"Then, since you *dread* no further *Lashes*,
"You freely may *forgive his Ashes*."

# VERSES ON THE
# Death of Dr. *Swift*, D.S.P.D.

### OCCASIONED
## By reading a Maxim in *Rochefoulcault*

Dans l'adversité de nos meilleurs amis nous trouvons quelque chose, qui ne nous deplaist pas.

In the Adversity of our best Friends, we find something that doth not displease us.

*The following Poem was printed and published in* London *with great Success. We are informed by the supposed Author's Friends that many Lines and Notes are omitted in the* English *Edition; therefore we hope, that such Persons who have seen the Original Manuscript, will help us to procure those Omissions, and correct any Things that may be amiss, and the Favour shall be gratefully acknowledged.*

AS *Rochefoucault* his Maxims drew
From Nature, I believe 'em true:
They argue no corrupted Mind
In him; the Fault is in Mankind.

THIS Maxim more than all the rest
Is thought too base for human Breast;
"In all Distresses of our Friends
"We first consult our private Ends,
"While Nature kindly bent to ease us,
"Points out some Circumstance to please us."        10

IF this perhaps your Patience move
Let Reason and Experience prove.

WE all behold with envious Eyes,
Our *Equal* rais'd above our *Size*;
Who wou'd not at a crowded Show,
Stand high himself, keep others low?
I love my Friend as well as you,
But would not have him stop my View;

Printed from Faulkner's Dublin edition, 1739, the text completed from the recension by Sir Harold Williams.

Then let me have the higher Post;
I ask but for an Inch at most.                                                            20

IF in a Battle you should find,
One, whom you love of all Mankind,
Had some heroick Action done,
A Champion kill'd, or Trophy won;
Rather than thus be over-topt,
Would you not wish his Lawrels cropt?

DEAR honest *Ned* is in the Gout,
Lies rackt with Pain, and you without:
How patiently you hear him groan!
How glad the Case is not your own!                                                       30

WHAT Poet would not grieve to see,
His Brethren write as well as he?
But rather than they should excel,
He'd wish his Rivals all in Hell.

HER End when Emulation misses,
She turns to Envy, Stings and Hisses:
The strongest Friendship yields to Pride,
Unless the Odds be on our Side.

VAIN human Kind! Fantastick Race!
Thy various Follies, who can trace?                                                      40
Self-love, Ambition, Envy, Pride,
Their Empire in our Hearts divide:
Give others Riches, Power, and Station,
'Tis all on me an Usurpation.
I have no Title to aspire;
Yet, when you sink, I seem the higher.
In POPE, I cannot read a Line,
But with a Sigh, I wish it mine:
When he can in one Couplet fix
More Sense than I can do in Six:                                                         50
It gives me such a jealous Fit,
I cry, Pox take him, and his Wit.

Why must I be outdone by Gay,
In my own hum'rous biting Way?

Arbuthnot is no more my Friend,
Who dares to Irony pretend;
Which I was born to introduce,
Refin'd it first, and shew'd its Use.

St. John, as well as Pultney knows,
That I had some repute for Prose;                60
And till they drove me out of Date,
Could maul a Minister of State:
If they have mortify'd my Pride,
And made me throw my Pen aside;
If with such Talents Heav'n hath blest 'em
Have I not Reason to detest 'em?

To all my Foes, dear Fortune, send
Thy Gifts, but never to my Friend:
I tamely can endure the first,
But, this with Envy makes me burst.              70

Thus much may serve by way of Proem,
Proceed we therefore to our Poem.

The Time is not remote, when I
Must by the Course of Nature dye:
When I foresee my special Friends,
Will try to find their private Ends:
Tho' it is hardly understood,
Which way my Death can do them good;
Yet, thus methinks, I hear 'em speak;
See, how the Dean begins to break:               80
Poor Gentleman, he droops apace,
You plainly find it in his Face:
That old Vertigo in his Head,
Will never leave him, till he's dead:
Besides, his Memory decays,
He recollects not what he says;
He cannot call his Friends to Mind;
Forgets the Place where last he din'd:

Plyes you with Stories o'er and o'er,
He told them fifty Times before.                                   90
How does he fancy we can sit,
To hear his out-of-fashion'd Wit?
But he takes up with younger Fokes,
Who for his Wine will bear his Jokes:
Faith, he must make his Stories shorter,
Or change his Comrades once a Quarter:
In half the Time, he talks them round;
There must another Sett be found.

   For Poetry, he's past his Prime,
He takes an Hour to find a Rhime:                                  100
His Fire is out, his Wit decay'd,
His Fancy sunk, his Muse a Jade.
I'd have him throw away his Pen;
But there's no talking to some Men.

   And, then their Tenderness appears,
By adding largely to my Years:
"He's older than he would be reckon'd,
"And well remembers *Charles* the Second.

   "He hardly drinks a Pint of Wine;
"And that, I doubt, is no good Sign.                               110
"His Stomach too begins to fail:
"Last Year we thought him strong and hale;
"But now, he's quite another Thing;
"I wish he may hold out till Spring."

   Then hug themselves, and reason thus;
"It is not yet so bad with us."

   In such a Case they talk in Tropes,
And, by their Fears express their Hopes:
Some great Misfortune to portend,
No Enemy can match a Friend;                                       120
With all the Kindness they profess,
The Merit of a lucky Guess,

(When daily Howd'y's come of Course,
And Servants answer; *Worse and Worse*)
Wou'd please 'em better than to tell,
That, GOD be prais'd, the Dean is well.
Then he who prophecy'd the best,
Approves his Foresight to the rest:
"You know, I always fear'd the worst,
"And often told you so at first:"          130
He'd rather chuse that I should dye,
Than his Prediction prove a Lye.
Not one foretels I shall recover;
But, all agree, to give me over.

YET shou'd some Neighbour feel a Pain,
Just in the Parts, where I complain;
How many a Message would he send?
What hearty Prayers that I should mend?
Enquire what Regimen I kept;
What gave me Ease, and how I slept?          140
And more lament, when I was dead,
Than all the Sniv'llers round my Bed.

MY good Companions, never fear,
For though you may mistake a Year;
Though your Prognosticks run too fast,
They must be verify'd at last.

"BEHOLD the fatal Day arrive!
"How is the Dean? He's just alive.
"Now the departing Prayer is read:
"He hardly breathes. The Dean is dead.          150
"Before the Passing-Bell begun,
"The News thro' half the Town has run.
"O, may we all for Death prepare!
"What has he left? And who's his Heir?
"I know no more than what the News is,
"'Tis all bequeath'd to publick Uses.
"To publick Use! A perfect Whim!
"What had the Publick done for him!

"Meer Envy, Avarice, and Pride!
"He gave it all:—But first he dy'd. 160
"And had the Dean, in all the Nation,
"No worthy Friend, no poor Relation?
"So ready to do Strangers good,
"Forgetting his own Flesh and Blood?"

Now Grub-Street Wits are all employ'd;
With Elegies, the Town is cloy'd:
Some Paragraph in ev'ry Paper,
To *curse* the *Dean*, or *bless* the *Drapier*.

THE Doctors tender of their Fame,
Wisely on me lay all the Blame: 170
"We must confess his Case was nice;
"But he would never take Advice:
"Had he been rul'd, for ought appears,
"He might have liv'd these Twenty Years:
"For when we open'd him we found,
"That all his vital Parts were sound."

FROM *Dublin* soon to *London* spread,
'Tis told at Court, the Dean is dead.

KIND Lady *Suffolk* in the Spleen,
Runs laughing up to tell the Queen. 180
The Queen, so Gracious, Mild, and Good,
Cries, "Is he gone? 'Tis time he shou'd.

168. The Author imagines, that the Scriblers of the prevailing Party, which he always opposed, will libel him after his Death; but that others will remember him with Gratitude, who consider the Service he had done to Ireland, under the Name of M. B. Drapier, by utterly defeating the destructive Project of Wood's Half-pence, in five Letters to the People of Ireland, at that Time read universally, and convincing every Reader.

178. The Dean supposeth himself to dye in Ireland.

179. Mrs. Howard, afterwards Countess of Suffolk, then of the Bed-chamber to the Queen, professed much Friendship for the Dean. The Queen then Princess, sent a dozen times to the Dean (then in London) with her Command to attend her; which at last he did, by Advice of all his Friends. She often sent for him afterwards, and always treated him very Graciously. He taxed her with a Present worth Ten Pounds, which she promised before he should return to Ireland, but on his taking Leave, the Medals were not ready.

"He's dead you say; why let him rot;
"I'm glad the Medals were forgot.
"I promis'd them, I own; but when?
"I only was the Princess then;
"But now as Consort of the King,
"You know 'tis quite a different Thing."

Now, *Chartres* at Sir *Robert*'s Levee,
Tells, with a Sneer, the Tidings heavy:                    190
"Why, is he dead without his Shoes?"
(Cries *Bob*) "I'm Sorry for the News;
"Oh, were the Wretch but living still,
"And in his Place my good Friend *Will*;
"Or, had a Mitre on his Head
"Provided *Bolingbroke* were dead."

184. The Medals were to be sent to the Dean in four Months, but she forgot
them, or thought them too dear. The Dean, being in Ireland, sent Mrs. Howard
a Piece of Indian Plad made in that Kingdom: which the Queen seeing took from
her, and wore it herself, and sent to the Dean for as much as would cloath herself
and Children, desiring he would send the Charge of it. He did the former. It cost
thirty-five Pounds, but he said he would have nothing except the Medals. He was
the Summer following in England, was treated as usual, and she being then
Queen, the Dean was promised a Settlement in England, but returned as he went,
and, instead of Favour or Medals, hath been ever since under her Majesty's
Displeasure.

189. Chartres is a most infamous, vile Scoundrel, grown from a Foot-Boy, or
worse, to a prodigious Fortune both in England and Scotland: He had a Way of
insinuating himself into all Ministers under every Change, either as Pimp, Flatterer,
or Informer. He was Tryed at Seventy for a Rape, and came off by sacrificing a
great Part of his Fortune (he is since dead, but this Poem still preserves the Scene
and Time it was writ in).

192. Sir Robert Walpole, Chief Minister of State, treated the Dean in 1726,
with great Distinction, invited him to Dinner at Chelsea, with the Dean's Friends
chosen on Purpose; appointed an Hour to talk with him of Ireland, to which
Kingdom and People the Dean found him no great Friend; for he defended Wood's
Project of Half-pence, &c. The Dean would see him no more; and upon his next
Year's return to England, Sir Robert on an accidental Meeting, only made a
civil Compliment, and never invited him again.

194. Mr. William Pultney, from being Mr. Walpole's intimate Friend, detesting
his Administration, opposed his Measures, and joined with my Lord Bolingbroke,
to represent his Conduct in an excellent Paper, called the Craftsman, which is
still continued.

196. Henry St. John, Lord Viscount Bolingbroke, Secretary of State to Queen
Anne of blessed Memory. He is reckoned the most Universal Genius in Europe;
Walpole dreading his Abilities, treated him most injuriously, working with King
George, who forgot his Promise of restoring the said Lord, upon the restless
Importunity of Walpole.

Now *Curl* his Shop from Rubbish drains;
Three genuine Tomes of *Swift*'s Remains.
And then to make them pass the glibber,
Revis'd by *Tibbalds, Moore, and Cibber*.                    200
He'll treat me as he does my Betters.
Publish my Will, my Life, my Letters.
Revive the Libels born to dye;
Which POPE must bear, as well as I.

HERE shift the Scene, to represent
How those I love, my Death lament.
Poor POPE will grieve a Month; and GAY
A Week; and ARBUTHNOTT a Day.

ST. JOHN himself will scarce forbear,
To bite his Pen, and drop a Tear.                            210
The rest will give a Shrug and cry
I'm sorry; but we all must dye.
Indifference clad in Wisdom's Guise,
All Fortitude of Mind supplies:
For how can stony Bowels melt,
In those who never Pity felt;
When *We* are lash'd, *They* kiss the Rod;
Resigning to the Will of God.

THE Fools, my Juniors by a Year,
Are tortur'd with Suspence and Fear.                         220

197. Curl hath been the most infamous Bookseller of any Age or Country: His Character in Part may be found in Mr. POPE's *Dunciad*. He published three Volumes all charged on the Dean, who never writ three Pages of them: He hath used many of the Dean's Friends in almost as vile a Manner.

200. Three stupid Verse Writers in London, the last to the Shame of the Court, and the highest Disgrace to Wit and Learning, was made Laureat. Moore, commonly called Jemmy Moore, Son of Arthur Moore, whose Father was Jaylor of Monaghan in Ireland. See the Character of Jemmy Moore, and Tibbalds, Theobald in the *Dunciad*.

202. Curl is notoriously infamous for publishing the Lives, Letters, and last Wills and Testaments of the Nobility and Ministers of State, as well as of all the Rogues, who are hanged at Tyburn. He hath been in Custody of the House of Lords for publishing or forging the Letters of many Peers; which made the Lords enter a Resolution in their Journal Book, that no Life or Writings of any Lord should be published without the Consent of the next Heir at Law, or Licence from their House.

Who wisely thought my Age a Screen,
When Death approach'd, to stand between:
The Screen remov'd, their Hearts are trembling,
They mourn for me without dissembling.


My female Friends, whose tender Hearts
Have better learn'd to act their Parts.
Receive the News in *doleful Dumps*,
"The Dean is dead, (*and what is Trumps?*)
"Then Lord have Mercy on his Soul.
"(Ladies I'll venture for the *Vole*.)          230
"Six Deans they say must bear the Pall.
"(I wish I knew what *King* to call.)
"Madam, your Husband will attend
"The Funeral of so good a Friend.
"No Madam, 'tis a shocking Sight,
"And he's engag'd To-morrow Night!
"My Lady *Club* wou'd take it ill,
"If he shou'd fail her at *Quadrill*.
"He lov'd the Dean. (*I lead a Heart*.)
"But dearest Friends, they say, must part.          240
"His Time was come, he ran his Race;
"We hope he's in a better Place."


WHY do we grieve that Friends should dye?
No Loss more easy to supply.
One Year is past; a different Scene;
No further mention of the Dean;
Who now, alas, no more is mist,
Than if he never did exist.
Where's now this Fav'rite of *Apollo*?
Departed; *and his Works must follow*:          250
Must undergo the common Fate;
His Kind of Wit is out of Date.
Some Country Squire to *Lintot* goes,
Enquires for SWIFT in Verse and Prose:
Says *Lintot*, "I have heard the Name:
"He dy'd a Year ago." The same.

253. Bernard Lintot, a Bookseller in London. *Vide* Mr. Pope's *Dunciad*.

He searcheth all his Shop in vain;
"Sir you may find them in *Duck-lane*:
"I sent them with a Load of Books,
"Last *Monday* to the Pastry-cooks.                    260
"To fancy they cou'd live a Year!
"I find you're but a Stranger here.
"The Dean was famous in his Time;
"And had a Kind of Knack at Rhyme:
"His way of Writing now is past;
"The Town hath got a better Taste:
"I keep no antiquated Stuff;
"But, spick and span I have enough.
"Pray, do but give me leave to shew 'em;
"Here's *Colley Cibber*'s Birth-day Poem.              270
"This Ode you never yet have seen,
"By *Stephen Duck*, upon the Queen.
"Then, here's a Letter finely penn'd
"Against the *Craftsman* and his Friend;
"It clearly shews that all Reflection
"On Ministers, is disaffection.
"Next, here's Sir *Robert*'s Vindication,
"And Mr. *Henly*'s last Oration:
"The Hawkers have not got 'em yet,
"Your Honour please to buy a Set?                      280

      "HERE's *Wolston*'s Tracts, the twelfth Edition;
      " 'Tis read by ev'ry Politician:
      "The Country Members, when in Town,
      "To all their Boroughs send them down:

258. A Place in London where old Books are sold.

277. Walpole hires a Set of Party Scriblers, who do nothing else but write in his Defence.

278. Henly is a Clergyman who wanting both Merit and Luck to get Preferment, or even to keep his Curacy in the Established Church, formed a new Conventicle, which he calls an Oratory. There, at set Times, he delivereth strange Speeches compiled by himself and his Associates, who share the Profit with him: Every Hearer pays a Shilling each Day for Admittance. He is an absolute Dunce, but generally reputed crazy.

281. Wolston was a Clergyman, but for want of Bread, hath in several Treatises, in the most blasphemous Manner, attempted to turn Our Saviour and his Miracles into Ridicule. He is much caressed by many great Courtiers, and by all the Infidels, and his Books read generally by the Court Ladies.

"You never met a Thing so smart;
"The Courtiers have them all by Heart:
"Those Maids of Honour (who can read)
"Are taught to use them for their Creed.
"The Rev'rend Author's good Intention,
"Hath been rewarded with a Pension:          290
"He doth an Honour to his Gown,
"By bravely running *Priest-craft* down:
"He shews, as sure as GOD's in *Gloc'ster*,
"That *Jesus* was a Grand Impostor:
"That all his Miracles were Cheats,
"Perform'd as Juglers do their Feats:
"The Church had never such a Writer:
"A Shame, he hath not got a Mitre!"

SUPPOSE me dead; and then suppose
A Club assembled at the *Rose*;          300
Where from Discourse of this and that,
I grow the Subject of their Chat:
And, while they toss my Name about,
With Favour some, and some without;
One quite indiff'rent in the Cause,
My Character impartial draws:

"THE Dean, if we believe Report,
"Was never ill receiv'd at Court:
"As for his Works in Verse and Prose,
"I own my self no Judge of those:          310
"Nor, can I tell what Criticks thought 'em;
"But, this I know, all People bought 'em;
"As with a moral View design'd
"To cure the Vices of Mankind:
"His Vein, ironically grave,
"Expos'd the Fool, and lash'd the Knave:
"To steal a Hint was never known,
"But what he writ was all his own.

"HE never thought an Honour done him,
"Because a Duke was proud to own him:          320

"Would rather slip aside, and chuse
"To talk with Wits in dirty Shoes:
"Despis'd the Fools with Stars and Garters,
"So often seen caressing *Chartres*:
"He never courted Men in Station,
"*Nor Persons had in Admiration;*
"Of no Man's Greatness was afraid,
"Because he sought for no Man's Aid.
"Though trusted long in great Affairs,
"He gave himself no haughty Airs:                    330
"Without regarding private Ends,
"Spent all his Credit for his Friends:
"And only chose the Wise and Good;
"No Flatt'rers; no Allies in Blood;
"But succour'd Virtue in Distress,
"And seldom fail'd of good Success;
"As Numbers in their Hearts must own,
"Who, but for him, had been unknown.

      "WITH Princes kept a due Decorum,
"But never stood in Awe before 'em:                    340
"And to her Majesty, God bless her,
"Would speak as free as to her Dresser,
"She thought it his peculiar Whim,
"Nor took it ill as come from him.
"He follow'd *David*'s Lesson just,
"*In Princes never put thy Trust.*
"And, would you make him truly sower;
"Provoke him with *a slave in Power*:
"The *Irish* Senate, if you nam'd,
"With what Impatience he declaim'd!                    350
"Fair LIBERTY was all his Cry;
"For her he stood prepar'd to die;

324. See the Notes before on Chartres.

349. The Huntington Library copy with manuscript additions has a marginal note against this line, which may have come originally from Swift himself: 'The Irish Parliament are reduced to yᵉ utmost Degree of Slavery, Flattery, Corruption, and Meaness of Spirit, & the worse they are treated, the more fawning and servile they grow; under the greatest & most contemptuous Grievances they dare not complain; by wᶜʰ Baseness and Tameness, unworthy Human Creatures, yᵉ Kingdom is irrecoverably ruin'd.' (Also in a copy of Faulkner's edition at the University of Texas Library.)

"For her he boldly stood alone;
"For her he oft expos'd his own.
"Two Kingdoms, just as Faction led,
"Had set a Price upon his Head;
"But, not a Traytor cou'd be found,
"To sell him for Six Hundred Pound.

"HAD he but spar'd his Tongue and Pen,
"He might have rose like other Men:                    360
"But, Power was never in his Thought;
"And, Wealth he valu'd not a Groat:
"Ingratitude he often found,
"And pity'd those who meant the Wound:
"But, kept the Tenor of his Mind,
"To merit well of human Kind:
"Nor made a Sacrifice of those
"Who still were true, to please his Foes.
"He labour'd many a fruitless Hour
"To reconcile his Friends in Power;                    370
"Saw Mischief by a Faction brewing,
"While they pursu'd each others Ruin.
"But, finding vain was all his Care,
"He left the Court in meer Despair.

"AND, oh! how short are human Schemes!
"Here ended all our golden Dreams.

355. In the Year 1713, the late Queen was prevailed with by an Address of the House of Lords in England, to publish a Proclamation, promising Three Hundred Pounds to whatever Person would discover the Author of a Pamphlet called, *The Publick Spirit of the Whiggs*; and in Ireland, in the Year 1724, my Lord Carteret at his first coming into the Government, was prevailed on to issue a Proclamation for promising the like Reward of Three Hundred Pounds, to any Person who could discover the Author of a Pamphlet called, *The Drapier's Fourth Letter*, &c. writ against that destructive Project of coining Half-pence for Ireland; but in neither Kingdom was the Dean discovered.

369. Queen ANNE's Ministry fell to Variance from the first Year after their Ministry began: Harcourt the Chancellor, and Lord Bolingbroke the Secretary, were discontented with the Treasurer Oxford, for his too much Mildness to the Whig Party; this Quarrel grew higher every Day till the Queen's Death: The Dean, who was the only Person that endeavoured to reconcile them, found it impossible; and thereupon retired to the Country about ten Weeks before that fatal Event: Upon which he returned to his Deanry in Dublin, where for many Years he was worryed by the new People in Power, and had Hundreds of Libels writ against him in England.

"What St. John's Skill in State Affairs,
"What Ormond's *Valour*, Oxford's Cares,
"To save their sinking Country lent,
"Was all destroy'd by one Event.　　　　380
"Too soon that precious Life was ended,
"On which alone, our Weal depended.
"When up a dangerous Faction starts,
"With Wrath and Vengeance in their Hearts:
"*By solemn League and Cov'nant bound,*
"To ruin, slaughter, and confound;
"To turn Religion to a Fable,
"And make the Government a *Babel*:
"Pervert the Law, disgrace the Gown,
"Corrupt the Senate, rob the Crown;　　　390
"To sacrifice old *England*'s Glory,
"And make her infamous in Story.
"When such a Tempest shook the Land,
"How could unguarded Virtue stand?


"With Horror, Grief, Despair the Dean
"Beheld the dire destructive Scene:
"His Friends in Exile, or the Tower,
"Himself within the Frown of Power;
"Pursu'd by base envenom'd Pens,
"Far to the Land of Slaves and Fens;　　　400
"A servile Race in Folly nurs'd,
"Who truckle most, when treated worst.

381. In the Height of the Quarrel between the Ministers, the Queen died.

383. Upon Queen ANNE's Death the Whig Faction was restored to Power, which they exercised with the utmost Rage and Revenge; impeached and banished the Chief Leaders of the Church Party, and stripped all their Adherents of what Employments they had, after which England was never known to make so mean a Figure in Europe. The greatest Preferments in the Church in both Kingdoms were given to the most ignorant Men, Fanaticks were publickly caressed, Ireland utterly ruined and enslaved, only great Ministers heaping up Millions, and so Affairs continue until this present third Day of May, 1732, and are likely to go on in the same Manner.

398. Upon the Queen's Death, the Dean returned to live in Dublin, at his Deanry-House: Numberless Libels were writ against him in England, as a Jacobite; he was insulted in the Street, and at Nights was forced to be attended by his Servants armed.

400. The Land of Slaves and Fens, is Ireland.

"By Innocence and Resolution,
"He bore continual Persecution;
"While Numbers to Preferment rose;
"Whose Merits were, to be his Foes.
"When, *ev'n his own familiar Friends*
"Intent upon their private Ends;
"Like Renegadoes now he feels,
"*Against him lifting up their Heels.*          410


"The Dean did by his Pen defeat
"An infamous destructive Cheat.
"Taught Fools their Int'rest how to know;
"And gave them Arms to ward the Blow.
"Envy hath own'd it was his doing,
"To save that helpless Land from Ruin,
"While they who at the Steerage stood,
"And reapt the Profit, sought his Blood.


"To save them from their evil Fate,
"In him was held a Crime of State.          420
"A wicked Monster on the Bench,
"Whose Fury Blood could never quench;
"As vile and profligate a Villain,
"As modern *Scroggs*, or old *Tressilian*;
"Who long all Justice had discarded,
"*Nor fear'd he GOD, nor Man regarded;*

412. One *Wood*, a Hardware-man from England, had a Patent for coining Copper Half-pence in Ireland, to the Sum of 108,000 l. which in the Consequence, must leave that Kingdom without Gold or Silver (See Drapier's *Letters*).

421. One *Whitshed* was then Chief Justice: He had some Years before prosecuted a Printer for a Pamphlet writ by the Dean, to perswade the People of Ireland to wear their own Manufactures. Whitshed sent the Jury down eleven Times, and kept them nine Hours, until they were forced to bring in a special Verdict. He sat as Judge afterwards on the Tryal of the Printer of the Drapier's *Fourth Letter*; but the Jury, against all he could say or swear, threw out the Bill: All the Kingdom took the Drapier's Part, except the Courtiers, or those who expected Places. The Drapier was celebrated in many Poems and Pamphlets: His Sign was set up in most Streets of Dublin (where many of them still continue) and in several Country Towns.

424. *Scroggs* was Chief Justice under King Charles the Second: His Judgment always varied in State Tryals, according to Directions from Court. *Tressilian* was a wicked Judge, hanged above three hundred Years ago.

"Vow'd on the Dean his Rage to vent,
"And make him of his Zeal repent;
"But Heav'n his Innocence defends,
"The grateful People stand his Friends:                    430
"Not Strains of Law, nor Judges Frown,
"Nor Topicks brought to please the Crown,
"Nor Witness hir'd, nor Jury pick'd,
"Prevail to bring him in convict.

"In Exile with a steady Heart,
"He spent his Life's declining Part;
"Where, Folly, Pride, and Faction sway,
"Remote from St. John, Pope, and Gay.

"His Friendship there to few confin'd,
"Were always of the midling Kind:                          440
"No Fools of Rank, a mungril Breed,
"Who fain would pass for Lords indeed:
"Where Titles give no Right or Power,
"And Peerage is a wither'd Flower,
"He would have held it a Disgrace,
"If such a Wretch had known his Face.
"On Rural Squires, that Kingdom's Bane,
"He vented oft his Wrath in vain:
"Biennial Squires, to Market brought;
"Who sell their Souls and Votes for Naught;                450
"The Nation stript go joyful back,
"To rob the Church, their Tenants rack,

435. In Ireland, which he had Reason to call a Place of Exile; to which Country nothing could have driven him, but the Queen's Death, who had determined to fix him in England, in Spight of the Dutchess of Somerset, &c.

438. Henry St. John, Lord Viscount Bolingbroke, mentioned before.

439. In Ireland the Dean was not acquainted with one single Lord Spiritual or Temporal. He only conversed with private Gentlemen of the Clergy or Laity, and but a small Number of either.

443. The Peers of Ireland lost a great Part of their Jurisdiction by one single Act, and tamely submitted to this infamous Mark of Slavery without the least Resentment, or Remonstrance.

449. The Parliament (as they call it) in Ireland meet but once in two Years; and, after giving five Times more than they can afford, return Home to reimburse themselves by all Country Jobs and Oppressions, of which some few only are here mentioned.

"Go Snacks with Thieves and Rapparees,
"And, keep the Peace, to pick up Fees:
"In every Jobb to have a Share,
"A Jayl or Barrack to repair;
"And turn the Tax for publick Roads
"Commodious to their own Abodes.

"Perhaps I may allow, the Dean
"Had too much Satyr in his Vein;                     460
"And seem'd determin'd not to starve it,
"Because no Age could more deserve it.
"Yet, Malice never was his Aim;
"He lash'd the Vice but spar'd the Name.
"No Individual could resent,
"Where Thousands equally were meant.
"His Satyr points at no Defect,
"But what all Mortals may correct;
"For he abhorr'd that senseless Tribe,
"Who call it Humour when they jibe:                  470
"He spar'd a Hump or crooked Nose,
"Whose Owners set not up for Beaux.
"True genuine Dulness mov'd his Pity,
"Unless it offer'd to be witty.
"Those, who their Ignorance confess'd,
"He ne'er offended with a Jest;
"But laugh'd to hear an Idiot quote,
"A Verse from *Horace*, learn'd by Rote.

"He knew an hundred pleasant Stories,
"With all the Turns of *Whigs* and *Tories*:          480
"Was chearful to his dying Day,
"And Friends would let him have his Way.

"He gave the little Wealth he had,
"To build a House for Fools and Mad:

453. The Highway-Men in Ireland are, since the late Wars there, usually called Rapparees, which was a Name given to those Irish Soldiers who in small Parties used, at that Time, to plunder the Protestants.

456. The Army in Ireland is lodged in Barracks, the building and repairing whereof, and other Charges, have cost a prodigious Sum to that unhappy Kingdom.

"And shew'd by one satyric Touch,
"No Nation wanted it so much:
"That Kingdom he hath left his Debtor,
"I wish it soon may have a Better."


# Helter Skelter

## OR

## The Hue and Cry after the ATTORNIES, going to ride the Circuit

NOW the active young Attornies
Briskly travel on their Journies,
Looking big as any Gyants,
On the Horses of their Clients;
Like so many little Mars's,
With their Tilters at their Arses,
Brazen hilted lately burnish'd,
And with Harness-Buckles furnish'd;
And with Whips and Spurs so neat,
And with Jockey-Coats compleat;                    10
And with Boots so very grazy
And with Saddles eke so easy
And with Bridles fine and gay,
Bridles borrow'd for a Day,
Bridles destin'd far to roam,
Ah! never to return Home;
And with Hats so very big, Sir,
And wi[t]h powder'd Caps and Wigs, Sir;
And with Ruffles to be shewn,
Cambrick Ruffles not their own;                    20
And with Holland Shirts so white,
Shirts becoming to the sight,

Printed from the original Broadside [Dublin 1731].

487. Meaning Ireland, where he now lives, and probably may dye.

Shirts be wrought with different Letters,
As belonging to their betters:
With their pretty tinsel'd Boxes,
Gotten from their dainty Doxies,
And with Rings so very trim,
Lately taken out of Lim—
And with very little Pence,
And as very little Sence:                               30
With some Law but little Justice,
Having stolen from mine Hostess,
From the Barber and the Cutler,
Like the Soldier from the Sutler;
From the Vintner and the Taylor,
Like the Felon from the Jailer,
Into this and t'other County,
Living on the publick Bounty;
Thorough Town and thorough Village,
All to plunder, all to pillage;                          40
Thorow Mountains thorow Vallies;
Thorow stinking Lanes and Allies;
Some to Cuckold Farmers Spouses,
And make merry in their Houses;
Some to tumble Country-Wenches
On their Rushy Beds and Benches,
And, if they begin a Fray,
Draw their Swords and run away:
All to murder Equity,
And to take a double Fee;                                50
Till the People all are quiet
And forget to broil and riot,
Low in Pocket, Cow'd in Courage,
Safely glad to sup their Porridge,
And Vacation's over—then
Hey for Dublin Town agen!

# THE

# PLACE

## OF THE

# DAMN'D

### By J. S. D. D. D. S. P. D.

ALL Folks who pretend to *Religion* and *Grace*,
  Allow there's a *HELL*, but dispute of the Place;
But if *HELL* may by *Logical* Rules be defin'd,
The Place of the *Damn'd*,—I will tell you my Mind.
  Wherever the Damn'd do Chiefly abound,
Most certainly there is *HELL* to be found,
Damn'd *Poets*, Damn'd *Criticks*, Damn'd *Block-Heads*, Damn'd
  *Knaves*,
Damn'd *Senators* brib'd, Damn'd prostitute *Slaves*;
Damn'd *Lawyers* and *Judges*, Damn'd *Lords* and Damn'd *Squires*,
Damn'd *Spies* and *Informers*, Damn'd *Friends* and Damn'd
  *Lyars*;                                                    10
Damn'd *Villains*, Corrupted in every *Station*,
Damn'd *Time-Serving Priests* all over the *Nation*;
And into the Bargain, I'll readily give you,
Damn'd Ignorant *Prelates*, and *Councellors Privy*.
Then let us no longer by *Parsons* be Flamm'd,
For We know by these *Marks*, the place of the Damn'd;
And *HELL* to be sure is at *Paris* or *Rome*,
How happy for *Us*, that it is not at *Home*.

Printed from the original Broadside, 1731, with corrections from *Poems*, 1735.

# THE
# DAY OF JUDGEMENT

WITH a Whirl of Thought oppress'd,
        I sink from Reverie to Rest.
An horrid Vision seiz'd my Head,
I saw the Graves give up their Dead.
Jove, arm'd with Terrors, burst the Skies,
And Thunder roars, and Light'ning flies!
Amaz'd, confus'd, its Fate unknown,
The World stands trembling at his Throne.
While each pale Sinner hangs his Head,
Jove, nodding, shook the Heav'ns, and said,          10
"Offending Race of Human Kind,
By Nature, Reason, Learning, blind;
You who thro' Frailty step'd aside,
And you who never fell—*thro' Pride*;
You who in different Sects have shamm'd,
And come to see each other damn'd;
(So some Folks told you, but they knew
No more of Jove's Designs than you)
The World's mad Business now is o'er,
And I resent these Pranks no more.          20
I to such Blockheads set my Wit!
I damn such Fools!—Go, go, you're bit."

Printed from the *St. James's Chronicle*, 9–12 April 1774.


# On PSYCHE

AT two Afternoon for our *Psyche* inquire,
        Her Tea-Kettle's on, and her Smock at the Fire:
So loitring, so active; so busy, so idle,
Which hath she most need of, a Spur or a Bridle?

Printed from *Works, Vol. VIII*, Dublin, 1762.

*Title:* PSYCHE. Mrs. Sican, a very ingenious well bred Lady, Wife to Mr.
John Sican, an eminent Grocer in Dublin.

Thus, a Greyhound out-runs the whole Pack in a Race,
Yet would rather be hang'd than he'd leave a warm Place.
She gives you such Plenty, it puts you in Pain;
But ever with Prudence takes Care of the Main.
To please you, she knows how to chuse a nice Bit;
For her Taste is almost as refin'd as her Wit.                    10
To oblige a good Friend, she will trace ev'ry Market,
It would do your Heart good, to see how she will cark it.
Yet beware of her Arts, for it plainly appears,
She saves Half her Victuals, by feeding your Ears.

# A BEAUTIFUL

# YOUNG NYMPH

## Going to BED

CORINNA, Pride of *Drury-Lane*,
  For whom no Shepherd sighs in vain;
Never did *Covent Garden* boast
So bright a batter'd, strolling Toast;
No drunken Rake to pick her up,
No Cellar where on Tick to sup;
Returning at the Midnight Hour;
Four Stories climbing to her Bow'r;
Then, seated on a three-legg'd Chair,
Takes off her artificial Hair:                                   10
Now, picking out a Crystal Eye,
She wipes it clean, and lays it by.
Her Eye-Brows from a Mouse's Hyde,
Stuck on with Art on either Side,
Pulls off with Care, and first displays 'em,
Then in a Play-Book smoothly lays 'em.
Now dextrously her Plumpers draws,
That serve to fill her hollow Jaws.
Untwists a Wire; and from her Gums
A Set of Teeth completely comes.                                 20

Printed from Roberts's quarto pamphlet of 1734.

Pulls out the Rags contriv'd to prop
Her flabby Dugs and down they drop.
Proceeding on, the lovely Goddess
Unlaces next her Steel-Rib'd Bodice;
Which by the Operator's Skill,
Press down the Lumps, the Hollows fill,
Up goes her Hand, and off she slips
The Bolsters that supply her Hips.
With gentlest Touch, she next explores
Her Shankers, Issues, running Sores,                    30
Effects of many a sad Disaster;
And then to each applies a Plaister.
But must, before she goes to Bed,
Rub off the Dawbs of White and Red;
And smooth the Furrows in her Front,
With greasy Paper stuck upon't.
She takes a *Bolus* e'er she sleeps;
And then between two Blankets creeps.
With Pains of Love tormented lies;
Or if she chance to close her Eyes,                     40
Of *Bridewell* and the *Compter* dreams,
And feels the Lash, and faintly screams;
Or, by a faithless Bully drawn,
At some Hedge-Tavern lies in Pawn;
Or to *Jamaica* seems transported,
Alone, and by no Planter courted;
Or, near *Fleet-Ditch*'s oozy Brinks,
Surrounded with a Hundred Stinks,
Belated, seems on watch to lye,
And snap some Cully passing by;                         50
Or, struck with Fear, her Fancy runs
On Watchmen, Constables and Duns,
From whom she meets with frequent Rubs;
But, never from Religious Clubs;
Whose Favour she is sure to find,
Because she pays them all in Kind.
    *CORINNA* wakes. A dreadful Sight!
Behold the Ruins of the Night!

46. —— *Et longam incomitata videtur*
        *Ire viam* ——

A wicked Rat her Plaister stole,
Half eat, and dragg'd it to his Hole.                    60
The Crystal Eye, alas, was miss't;
And *Puss* had on her Plumpers pisst.
A Pigeon pick'd her Issue-Peas;
And *Shock* her Tresses fill'd with Fleas.
    THE Nymph, tho' in this mangled Plight,
Must ev'ry Morn her Limbs unite.
But how shall I describe her Arts
To recollect the scatter'd Parts?
Or shew the Anguish, Toil, and Pain,
Of gath'ring up herself again?                           70
The bashful Muse will never bear
In such a Scene to interfere.
*Corinna* in the Morning dizen'd,
Who sees, will spew; who smells, be poison'd.


# STREPHON and CHLOE

OF *Chloe* all the Town has rung;
    By ev'ry size of Poets sung:
So beautiful a Nymph appears
But once in Twenty Thousand Years.
By Nature form'd with nicest Care,
And, faultless to a single Hair.
Her graceful Mein, her Shape, and Face,
Confest her of no mortal Race:
And then, so nice, and so genteel;
Such Cleanliness from Head to Heel:                      10
No Humours gross, or frowzy Steams,
No noisom Whiffs, or sweaty Streams,
Before, behind, above, below,
Could from her taintless Body flow.
Would so discreetly Things dispose,
None ever saw her pluck a Rose.

Printed from Roberts's quarto pamphlet of 1734.

Her dearest Comrades never caught her
Squat on her Hams, to make Maid's Water.
You'd swear, that so divine a Creature
Felt no Necessities of Nature.                    20
In Summer had she walkt the Town,
Her Arm-pits would not stain her Gown:
At Country Dances, not a Nose
Could in the Dog-Days smell her Toes.
Her Milk-white Hands, both Palms and Backs,
Like Iv'ry dry, and soft as Wax.
Her Hands the softest ever felt,
Tho' cold would burn, tho' dry would melt.
      Dear *Venus*, hide this wond'rous Maid,
Nor let her loose to spoil your Trade.            30
While she engrosseth ev'ry Swain,
You but o'er half the World can reign.
Think what a Case all Men are now in,
What ogling, sighing, toasting, vowing!
What powder'd Wigs! What Flames and Darts!
What Hampers full of bleeding Hearts!
What Sword-knots! What Poetic Strains!
What Billet-doux, and clouded Cains!
      But, *Strephon* sigh'd so loud and strong,
He blew a Settlement along:                       40
And, bravely drove his Rivals down
With Coach and Six, and House in Town.
The bashful Nymph no more withstands,
Because her dear Papa commands.
The charming Couple now unites;
Proceed we to the Marriage Rites.
      Imprimis, at the Temple Porch
Stood *Hymen* with a flaming Torch.
The smiling *Cyprian* Goddess brings
Her infant Loves with purple Wings;               50
And Pigeons billing, Sparrows treading,
Fair Emblems of a fruitful Wedding.
The Muses next in Order follow,
Conducted by their Squire, *Apollo*:

28. *Tho' cold* . . . Tho' deep, yet clear, &c. Denham.

Then *Mercury* with Silver Tongue,
And *Hebe*, Goddess ever young.
Behold the Bridegroom and his Bride,
Walk Hand in Hand, and Side by Side;
She by the tender Graces drest,
But, he by *Mars*, in Scarlet Vest.                    60
The Nymph was cover'd with her *Flammeum*,
And *Phœbus* sung th' *Epithalamium*.
And, last to make the Matter sure,
Dame *Juno* brought a Priest demure.
*Luna* was absent on Pretence
Her Time was not till Nine Months hence.
   The Rites perform'd, the Parson paid,
In State return'd the grand Parade;
With loud Huzza's from all the Boys,
That now the Pair must *crown their Joys*.              70
   But, still the hardest Part remains.
*Strephon* had long perplex'd his Brains,
How with so high a Nymph he might
Demean himself the Wedding-Night:
For, as he view'd his Person round,
Meer mortal Flesh was all he found:
His Hand, his Neck, his Mouth, and Feet
Were duly washt to keep 'em sweet;
(With other Parts that shall be nameless,
The Ladies else might think me shameless.)              80
The Weather and his Love were hot;
And should he struggle; I know what—
Why let it go, if I must tell it—
He'll sweat, and then the Nymph may smell it.
While she a Goddess dy'd in Grain
Was unsusceptible of Stain:
And, *Venus*-like, her fragrant Skin
Exhal'd *Ambrosia* from within:
Can such a Deity endure
A mortal human Touch impure?                            90

61. *Flammeum*. A Veil which the Roman Brides covered themselves with, when they were going to be married.
   62. *Epithalamium*. A Marriage Song at Weddings.
   65. *Luna*. Diana, Goddess of Midwives.

How did the humbled Swain detest
His prickled Beard, and hairy Breast!
His Night-Cap border'd round with Lace
Could give no Softness to his Face.

YET, if the Goddess could be kind,
What endless Raptures must he find!
And Goddesses have now and then
Come down to visit mortal Men:
To visit and to court them too;
A certain Goddess, God knows who,                    100
(As in a Book he heard it read)
Took Col'nel *Peleus* to her Bed.
But, what if he should lose his Life
By vent'ring *on* his heav'nly Wife?
For *Strephon* could remember well,
That, once he heard a School-boy tell,
How *Semele* of mortal Race,
By Thunder dy'd in *Jove*'s Embrace;
And what if daring *Strephon* dies
By Lightning shot from *Chloe*'s Eyes?                110

WHILE these Reflections fill'd his Head,
The Bride was put in Form to Bed;
He follow'd, stript, and in he crept,
But, awfully his Distance kept.

Now, *Ponder well ye Parents dear*;
Forbid your Daughters guzzling Beer;
And make them ev'ry Afternoon
Forbear their Tea, or drink it soon;
That, e'er to Bed they venture up,
They may discharge it ev'ry Sup;                      120
If not; they must in evil Plight
Be often forc'd to rise at Night,
Keep them to wholesome Food confin'd,
Nor let them taste what causes Wind;
('Tis this the Sage of *Samos* means,
Forbidding his Disciples Beans)
O, think what Evils must ensue;
Miss *Moll* the Jade will burn it blue:

125. A well known Precept of Pythagoras, not to eat Beans.

And when she once has got the Art,
She cannot help it for her Heart;                          130
But, out it flies, even when she meets
Her Bridegroom in the Wedding-Sheets.
*Carminative* and *Diuretick*,
Will damp all Passion Sympathetick;
And, Love such Nicety requires,
One *Blast* will put out all his Fires.
Since Husbands get behind the Scene,
The Wife should study to be clean;
Nor give the smallest Room to guess
The Time when Wants of Nature press;                       140
   BUT, after Marriage, practise more
Decorum than she did before;
To keep her Spouse deluded still,
And make him fancy what she will.
   IN Bed we left the married Pair;
'Tis Time to shew how Things went there.
*Strephon*, who had been often told,
That Fortune still assists the bold,
Resolv'd to make his first Attack:
But, *Chloe* drove him fiercely back.                      150
How could a Nymph so chaste as *Chloe*,
With Constitution cold and snowy,
Permit a brutish Man to touch her?
Ev'n Lambs by Instinct fly the Butcher.
Resistance on the Wedding-Night
Is what our Maidens claim by Right:
And, *Chloe*, 'tis by all agreed,
Was Maid in Thought, and Word, and Deed,
Yet, some assign a diff'rent Reason;
That *Strephon* chose no proper Season.                    160
   SAY, fair ones, must I make a Pause?
Or freely tell the secret Cause.
   TWELVE Cups of Tea, (with Grief I speak)
Had now constrain'd the Nymph to leak.
This Point must needs be settled first;
The Bride must either void or burst.

---

133. *Carminative*. Medicines to break Wind.   *Diuretick*. Medicines to provide
Urine.

Then, see the dire Effect of Pease,
Think what can give the Colick Ease,
The Nymph opprest before, behind,
As Ships are toss't by Waves and Wind,                    170
Steals out her Hand by Nature led,
And brings a Vessel into Bed:
Fair Utensil, as smooth and white
As *Chloe*'s Skin, almost as bright.
 *STREPHON* who heard the fuming Rill
As from a mossy Cliff distill;
Cry'd out, ye Gods, what Sound is this?
Can *Chloe*, heav'nly *Chloe* piss?
But, when he smelt a noysom Steam
Which oft attends that luke-warm Stream;                    180
(*Salerno* both together joins
As sov'reign Med'cines for the Loins)
And, though contriv'd, we may suppose
To slip his Ears, yet struck his Nose:
He found her, while the Scent increas'd,
As *mortal* as himself at least.
But, soon with like Occasions prest,
He boldly sent his Hand in quest,
(Inspir'd with Courage from his Bride,)
To reach the Pot on t'other Side.                    190
And as he fill'd the reeking Vase,
Let fly a Rouzer in her Face.
 THE little *Cupids* hov'ring round,
(As Pictures prove) with Garlands crown'd,
Abasht as what they saw and heard,
Flew off, nor evermore appear'd.
 ADIEU to ravishing Delights,
High Raptures, and romantick Flights;
To Goddesses so heav'nly sweet,
Expiring Shepherds at their Feet;                    200
To silver Meads, and shady Bow'rs,
Drest up with *Amaranthine* Flow'rs.
 How great a Change! how quickly made!
They learn to call a Spade, a Spade.

181. Vide. Schol. Salern. *Rules of health*, written by the School of Salernum.
*Mingere cum bumbis res est saluberrima lumbis.*

They soon from all Constraint are freed;
Can see each other *do their Need.*
On Box of Cedar sits the Wife,
And makes it warm for *Dearest Life.*
And, by the beastly way of Thinking,
Find great Society in Stinking.                    210
Now *Strephon* daily entertains
His *Chloe* in the homeli'st Strains;
And, *Chloe* more experienc'd grown,
With Int'rest pays him back his own.
No Maid at Court is less asham'd,
Howe'er for selling Bargains fam'd,
Than she, to name her Parts behind,
Or when a-bed, to let out Wind.

    FAIR *Decency,* celestial Maid,
Descend from Heav'n to Beauty's Aid;                220
Though Beauty may beget Desire,
'Tis thou must fan the Lover's Fire;
For, Beauty, like supreme Dominion,
Is best supported by Opinion;
If Decency brings no Supplies,
Opinion falls, and Beauty dies.

    To see some radiant Nymph appear
In all her glitt'ring Birth-day Gear,
You think some Goddess from the Sky
Descended, ready cut and dry:                       230
But, e'er you sell your self to Laughter,
Consider well what may come after;
For fine Ideas vanish fast,
While all the gross and filthy last.

    O *Strephon,* e'er that fatal Day
When *Chloe* stole your Heart away,
Had you but through a Cranny spy'd
On House of Ease your future Bride,
In all the Postures of her Face,
Which Nature gives in such a Case;                  240
Distortions, Groanings, Strainings, Heavings;
'Twere better you had lickt her Leavings,
Than from Experience find too late
Your Goddess grown a filthy Mate.

Your Fancy then had always dwelt
On what you saw, and what you smelt;
Would still the same Ideas give ye,
As when you spy'd her on the Privy.
And, spight of *Chloe*'s Charms divine,
Your Heart had been as whole as mine.          250

    AUTHORITIES both old and recent
Direct that Women must be decent;
And, from the Spouse each Blemish hide
More than from all the World beside.

    UNJUSTLY all our Nymphs complain,
Their Empire holds so short a Reign;
Is after Marriage lost so soon,
It hardly holds the Honey-moon:
For, if they keep not what they caught,
It is entirely their own Fault.          260
They take Possession of the Crown,
And then throw all their Weapons down;
Though by the Politicians Scheme
Whoe'er arrives at Pow'r supreme,
Those Arts by which at first they gain it,
They still must practise to maintain it.

    WHAT various Ways our Females take,
To pass for Wits before a Rake!
And in the fruitless Search pursue
All other Methods but the true.          270

    SOME try to learn polite Behaviour,
By reading Books against their Saviour;
Some call it witty to reflect
On ev'ry natural Defect;
Some shew they never want explaining,
To comprehend a double Meaning.
But, sure a Tell-tale out of School
Is of all Wits the greatest Fool;
Whose rank Imagination fills,
Her Heart, and from her Lips distills;          280
You'd think she utter'd from behind,
Or at her Mouth was breaking Wind.

    WHY is a handsome Wife ador'd
By ev'ry Coxcomb, but her Lord?

From yonder Puppet-Man inquire,
Whose wisely hides his Wood and Wire;
Shews *Sheba*'s Queen completely drest,
And *Solomon* in Royal Vest;
But, view them litter'd on the Floor,
Or strung on Pegs behind the Door;    290
*Punch* is exactly of a Piece
With *Lorraine*'s Duke, and Prince of *Greece*.
   A PRUDENT Builder should forecast
How long the Stuff is like to last;
And, carefully observe the Ground,
To build on some Foundation sound;
What House, when its Materials crumble,
Must not inevitably tumble?
What Edifice can long endure,
Rais'd on a Basis unsecure?    300
Rash Mortals, e'er you take a Wife,
Contrive your Pile to last for Life;
Since Beauty scarce endures a Day,
And Youth so swiftly glides away;
Why will you make yourself a Bubble
To build on Sand with Hay and Stubble?
   ON Sense and Wit your Passion found,
By Decency cemented round;
Let Prudence with Good Nature strive,
To keep Esteem and Love alive.    310
Then come old Age whene'er it will,
Your Friendship shall continue still:
And thus a mutual gentle Fire,
Shall never but with Life expire.

# CASSINUS and PETER

## A Tragical ELEGY

TWO College Sophs of *Cambridge* Growth,
Both special Wits, and Lovers both,
Conferring as they us'd to meet,
On Love and Books in Rapture sweet;
(Muse, find me Names to fix my Metre,
*Cassinus* this, and t'other *Peter*)
Friend *Peter* to *Cassinus* goes,
To chat a while, and warm his Nose:
But, such a Sight was never seen,
The Lad lay swallow'd up in Spleen;                     10
He seem'd as just crept out of Bed;
One greasy Stocking round his Head,
The t'other he sat down to darn
With Threads of diff'rent colour'd Yarn.
His Breeches torn exposing wide
A ragged Shirt, and tawny Hyde.
Scorcht were his Shins, his Legs were bare,
But, well embrown'd with Dirt and Hair.
A Rug was o'er his Shoulders thrown;
A Rug; for Night-gown he had none.                      20
His Jordan stood in Manner fitting
Between his Legs, to spew or spit in.
His antient Pipe in Sable dy'd,
And half unsmoakt, lay by his Side[.]
    HIM thus accoutred *Peter* found,
With Eyes in Smoak and Weeping drown'd:
The Leavings of his last Night's Pot
On Embers plac'd, to drink it hot.
    WHY, *Cassy*, thou wilt doze thy Pate:
What makes thee lie a'bed so late?                      30
The Finch, the Linnet and the Thrush,
Their Mattins chant in ev'ry Bush:

Printed from Roberts's quarto pamphlet of 1734.

And, I have heard thee oft salute
*Aurora* with thy early Flute.
Heaven send thou hast not got the Hypps.
How? Not a Word come from thy lips?
    THEN gave him some familiar Thumps,
A College Joke to cure the Dumps.
    THE Swain at last, with Grief opprest,
Cry'd, *Cælia!* thrice, and sigh'd the rest.      40
    DEAR *Cassy*, though to ask I dread,
Yet ask I must. Is *Cælia* dead?
    How happy I, were that the worst?
But I was fated to be curs'd.
    COME, tell us, has she play'd the Whore?
    OH *Peter*, wou'd it were no more!
    WHY, Plague confound her sandy Locks:
Say, has the small or greater Pox
Sunk down her Nose, or seam'd her Face?
Be easy, 'tis a common Case.      50
    OH *Peter!* Beauty's but a Varnish,
Which Time and Accidents will tarnish:
But, *Cælia* has contriv'd to blast
Those Beauties that might ever last.
Nor can Imagination guess,
Nor Eloquence Divine express,
How that ungrateful charming Maid,
My purest Passion has betray'd.
Conceive the most invenom'd Dart,
To pierce an injur'd Lover's Heart.      60
    WHY, hang her, though she seem'd so coy,
I know she loves the Barber's Boy.
    FRIEND *Peter*, this I could excuse;
For, ev'ry Nymph has Leave to chuse;
Nor, have I Reason to complain:
She loves a more deserving Swain.
But, oh! how ill hast thou divin'd
A Crime that shocks all human Kind;
A Deed unknown to Female Race,
At which the Sun should hide his Face.      70
Advice in vain you would apply---
Then, leave me to despair and dye.

Yet, kind *Arcadians*, on my Urn
These Elegies and Sonnets burn,
And on the Marble grave these Rhimes,
A Monument to after-Times:
"Here *Cassy* lies, by *Cælia* slain,
"And dying, never told his Pain."
   VAIN empty World farewel. But hark,
The loud *Cerberian* triple Bark.       80
And there —— behold *Alecto* stand,
A Whip of Scorpions in her Hand.
Lo, *Charon* from his leaky Wherry,
Beck'ning to waft me o'er the Ferry.
I come, I come,—*Medusa*, see,
Her Serpents hiss direct at me.
Begone; unhand me, hellish Fry;
Avaunt—ye cannot say 'twas I.
   DEAR *Cassy*, thou must purge and bleed;
I fear thou wilt be mad indeed.      90
But now, by Friendship's sacred Laws,
I here conjure thee, tell the Cause;
And *Cælia*'s horrid Fact relate;
Thy Friend would gladly share thy Fate.
   To force it out my Heart must rend;
Yet, when conjur'd by such a Friend—
Think, *Peter*, how my Soul is rack'd.
These Eyes, these Eyes beheld the Fact.
Now, bend thine Ear; since out it must:
But, when thou seest me laid in Dust,      100
The Secret thou shalt ne'er impart;
Not to the Nymph that keeps thy Heart;
(How would her Virgin Soul bemoan
A Crime to all her Sex unknown!)
Nor whisper to the tattling Reeds,
The blackest of all Female Deeds.
Nor blab it on the lonely Rocks,
Where Echo sits, and list'ning mocks.
Nor let the Zephyr's treach'rous Gale
Through *Cambridge* waft the direful Tale.      110

88. See *Mackbeth*.

Nor to the chatt'ring feather'd Race,
Discover *Cælia*'s foul Disgrace.
But, if you fail, my Spectre dread
Attending nightly round your Bed;
And yet, I dare confide in you;
So, take my Secret, and adieu.
    Nor wonder how I lost my Wits;
Oh! *Cælia, Cælia, Cælia* shits.

# *APOLLO:*

## OR,

## A PROBLEM solved

### Written in the Year 1731

A*POLLO*, God of Light and Wit,
  Could Verse inspire, but seldom writ:
Refin'd all Mettals with his Looks,
As well as Chymists by their Books:
As handsome as my Lady's Page;
Sweet Five and Twenty was his Age.
His Wig was made of sunny Rays,
He crown'd his youthful Head with Bays:
Not all the Court of Heav'n could shew
So nice and so compleat a Beau.        10
No Heir, upon his first Appearance,
With Twenty Thousand Pounds a Year Rents,
E'er drove, before he sold his Land,
So fine a Coach along the Strand;
The Spokes, we are by *Ovid* told,
Were Silver, and the Axel Gold.
(I own, 'twas but a Coach and Four,
For *Jupiter* allows no more.)

Printed from *Poems*, 1735.

YET, with his Beauty, Wealth, and Parts,
Enough to win ten Thousand Hearts;                    20
No Vulgar Deity above
Was so unfortunate in Love.

THREE weighty Causes were assign'd,
That mov'd the Nymphs to be unkind.
Nine Muses always waiting round him,
He left them Virgins as he found 'em.
His Singing was another Fault;
For he could reach to *B.* in *alt*:
And, by the Sentiments of *Pliny*,
Such Singers are like *Nicolini*.                    30
At last, the Point was fully clear'd;
In short; *Apollo* had no Beard.

# ON THE
# IRISH BISHOPS
## 1732

*We found the following Poem printed in Fog's Journal of the 1[5]th of Sept. 1733. It was written in the last Session, and many Copies were taken, but never printed here. The Subject of it is now over; but our Author's known Zeal against that Project made him generally supposed to be the Author. We reprint it just as it lyes in Fog's Journal.*

*The following Poem is the product of Ireland; it was occasioned by the Bishops of that Kingdom endeavouring to get an Act to divide the Church Livings, which Bill was rejected by the Irish House of Commons. It is said to be written by an honest Curate; the reader of Taste perhaps, may guess who the Curate could be, that was capable of writing it.*

OLD *Latimer* preaching did fairly describe
A Bishop who rul'd all the rest of his Tribe;
And who is this Bishop? And where does he dwell?
Why truly 'tis *Satan*, Arch-bishop of Hell:
And HE was a Primate, and HE wore a Mitre,
Surrounded with Jewels of Sulphur and Nitre.
How nearly this Bishop our Bishop resembles!
But his has the Odds, who *believes and who trembles.*

Printed from *Poems,* 1735.

30. *Nicolini.* A famous Italian Singer.

Cou'd you see his grim *Grace*, for a Pound to a Penny,
You'd swear it must be the *Baboon* of *Kilkenny*;     10
Poor *Satan* will think the Comparison odious;
I wish I could find him out one more commodious.
But this I am sure, the *Most Rev'rend old Dragon*,
Has got on the Bench many Bishops suffragan:
And all Men believe he presides there *incog.*
To give them by Turns an invisible Jog.

OUR Bishops puft up with Wealth and with Pride,
To Hell on the Backs of the Clergy wou'd ride;
They mounted, and labour'd with Whip and with Spur,
In vain—for the Devil a Parson wou'd stir.     20
So the *Commons* unhors'd them, and this was their Doom,
On their Crosiers to ride, like a Witch on a Broom.
Tho' they gallop so fast; on the Road you may find 'em,
And have left us but Three out of Twenty behind 'em.
Lord *Bolton*'s good Grace, Lord *Carr*, and Lord *Howard*,
In spite of the Devil would still be untoward.
They came of good Kindred, and cou'd not endure,
Their former Companions should beg at their Door.

WHEN *CHRIST* was betray'd to *Pilate*, the Prætor,
In a Dozen Apostles but one prov'd a Traytor!     30
One Traytor alone, and faithful Eleven;
But we can afford you Six Traytors in Seven.

WHAT a Clutter with Clippings, Dividings, and Cleavings!
And the Clergy, forsooth, must take up with their Leavings.
If making *Divisions* was all their Intent,
They've done it, we thank 'em, but not as they meant;
And so may such Bishops for ever *divide*,
That no honest Heathen would be on their side.
How shou'd we rejoice, if, like *Judas* the first,
Those Splitters of Parsons in sunder shou'd burst?     40

Now hear an Allusion!—A Mitre, you know,
Is divided above, but united below.
If this you consider, our Emblem is right;
The Bishops *divide*, but the Clergy *unite*.

Should the Bottom be split, our Bishops wou'd dread
That the Mitre wou'd never stick fast on their Head,
And yet they have learnt the chief Art of a Sov'reign,
As *Machiavel* taught 'em; *divide and ye govern.*
But, Courage, my Lords, tho' it cannot be said
That one *cloven Tongue*, ever sat on your Head;          50
I'll hold you a Groat, and I wish I cou'd see't,
If your Stockings were off, you cou'd show *cloven Feet.*

    BUT hold, cry the Bishops; and give us fair Play;
Before you condemn us, hear what we can say.
What truer Affection cou'd ever be shown,
Than saving your Souls, by damning our own?
And have we not practis'd all Methods to gain you;
With the Tyth of the Tyth of the Tyth to maintain you;
Provided a Fund for building you Spittles:
You are only to live four Years without Vittles!          60
Content, my good Lords; but let us change Hands;
First take you our Tyths, and give us your Lands.

    So GOD bless the Church, and three of our Mitres;
And GOD bless the *Commons* for *Biting* the *Biters.*

# *JUDAS*

### Written in the Year 1731[–2]

BY the just Vengeance of incensed Skies,
  Poor Bishop *Judas*, late repenting, dies;
The *Jews* engag'd him with a paultry Bribe,
Amounting hardly to a Crown a Tribe;
Which, though his Conscience forc'd him to restore,
(And, Parsons tell us, no Man can do more)
Yet, through Despair, of God and Man accurst,
He lost his Bishoprick, and hang'd, or burst.

Printed from *Poems*, 1735.

Those former Ages differ'd much from this:
*Judas* betrayed his Master with a Kiss:      10
But, some have kiss't the Gospel Fifty Times,
Whose Perjury's the least of all their Crimes:
Some who can perjure thro' a two-Inch Board;
Yet keep their Bishopricks, and 'scape the Cord.
Like *Hemp*, which by a skilful Spinster drawn
To slender Threads, may sometimes pass for *Lawn*.

  As antient *Judas by Transgression fell*,
And *burst asunder* e'er he went to Hell;
So, could we see a Set of new *Iscariots*,
Come headlong tumbling from their mitred Chariots,   20
Each modern *Judas* perish like the first;
Drop from the Tree with all his Bowels burst;
Who could forbear, that view'd each guilty Face,
To cry; Lo, *Judas, gone to his own Place*:
*His Habitation let all Men forsake,*
*And let his Bishoprick another take.*


# Advice to a PARSON

## *AN EPIGRAM*

WOU'D you rise in the *Church*, be *Stupid* and *Dull*,
  Be empty of *Learning*, of *Insolence* full:
Tho' Lewd and Immoral, be Formal and Grave,
In *Flatt'ry* an *Artist*, in *Fawning* a *Slave*,
No Merit, no Science, no Virtue is wanting
In him, that's accomplish'd in *Cringing* and *Canting*:
Be studious to practice true *Meanness of Spirit*;
For who but *Lord Bolton* was *mitred* for *Merit*?
Wou'd you wish to be wrap'd in a *Rochet*—In short[,]
Be as *Pox'd* and *Profane* as *Fanatical Hort*.   10

Printed from *The Lady's Dressing Room*, London, 1732.

# EPIGRAM

On seeing a worthy Prelate go out of Church in the
Time of *Divine Service*, to wait on his Grace the
Duke of *Dorset*

LORD *Pam* in the Church (cou'd you think it) kneel'd down,
When told the Lieutenant was just come to Town,
His *Station* despising, unaw'd by the *Place*,
He flies from his *God*, to attend on his *Grace*:
To the *Court* it was fitter to pay his *Devotion*,
Since *God* had no Hand in his Lordship's *Promotion*.

Printed from *Miscellanies. The Third Volume*, 1732.

# THE
# Beasts Confession
## TO THE
# PRIEST,
## ON
Observing how most Men mistake their own Talents

Written in the Year 1732

## The Preface

*I HAVE been long of Opinion, that there is not a more general and
greater Mistake, or of worse Consequences through the Commerce of
Mankind, than the wrong Judgments they are apt to entertain of their
own Talents: I knew a stuttering Alderman in* London, *a great*

Printed from the 8vo pamphlet, Faulkner, Dublin, 1738.

*Frequenter of Coffee-Houses; who, when a fresh News-Paper was brought in, constantly seized it first, and read it aloud to his Brother Citizens; but in a Manner, as little intelligible to the Standers-by as to himself. How many Pretenders to Learning expose themselves by chusing to discourse on those very Parts of Science wherewith they are least acquainted? It is the same case in every other Qualification. By the Multitude of those who deal in Rhimes from Half a Sheet to Twenty, which come out every Minute, there must be at least five hundred Poets in the City and Suburbs of* London; *half as many Coffee-House Orators, exclusive of the Clergy; forty thousand Politicians; and four thousand five hundred profound Scholars: Not to mention the Wits, the Railliers, the Smart Fellows, and Criticks; all as illiterate and impudent as a Suburb Whore. What are we to think of the fine dressed Sparks, proud of their own Personal Deformities, which appear the more hideous by the* Contrast *of wearing Scarlet and Gold, with what they call* \* Toupees *on their Heads, and all the Frippery of a modern Beau, to make a Figure before Women; some of them with Hump-Backs, others hardly five Foot high, and every Feature of their Faces distorted; I have seen many of these insipid Pretenders entering into Conversation with Persons of Learning, constantly making the grossest Blunders in every Sentence, without conveying one single Idea fit for a rational Creature to spend a Thought on; perpetually confounding all Chronology and Geography even of present Times. I compute, that* London *hath eleven native Fools of the Beau and Puppy-Kind, for one among us in* Dublin; *besides two thirds of ours transplanted thither, who are now naturalized; whereby that overgrown Capital exceeds ours in the Article of Dunces by forty to one; and what is more to our further Mortification, there is not one distinguished Fool of* Irish *Birth or Education, who makes any Noise in that famous Metropolis, unless the* London *Prints be very partial or defective; whereas* London *is seldom without a Dozen of their own educating, who engross the Vogue for half a Winter together, and are never heard of more, but give Place to a new Sett. This hath been the constant Progress for at least thirty Years past, only allowing for the Change of Breed and Fashion.*

## Advertisement

*The following Poem is grounded upon the universal Folly in Mankind of mistaking their Talents; by which the Author doth a great Honour*

\* Wigs with long black Tails, worn for some years past. *November* 1738.

*to his own Species, almost equalling them with certain Brutes; wherein,*
*indeed, he is too partial, as he freely confesseth: And yet he hath gone*
*as low as he well could, by specifying four Animals; the Wolf, the Ass,*
*the Swine and the Ape; all equally mischievous, except the last, who*
*outdoes them in the Article of Cunning: So great is the Pride of Man.*

THE

## Beasts Confession

TO THE

## PRIEST, &c.

WHEN Beasts could speak, (the Learned say
    They still can do so every Day)
It seems, they had Religion then,
As much as now we find in Men.
It happen'd when a Plague broke out,
(Which therefore made them more devout)
The King of Brutes (to make it plain,
Of Quadrupeds I only mean)
By Proclamation gave Command,
That ev'ry Subject in the Land                    10
Should to the Priest confess their Sins;
And, thus the pious Wolf begins:

    GOOD Father I must own with Shame,
That, often I have been to blame:
I must confess, on *Friday* last,
Wretch that I was, I broke my Fast:
But, I defy the basest Tongue
To prove I did my Neighbour wrong;
Or ever went to seek my Food
By Rapine, Theft, or Thirst of Blood.             20

    THE Ass approaching next, confess'd,
That in his Heart he lov'd a Jest:
A Wag he was, he needs must own,
And could not let a Dunce alone:
Sometimes his Friend he would not spare,
And might perhaps be too severe:

But yet, the worst that could be said,
He was a *Wit* both born and bred;
And if it be a Sin or Shame,
Nature alone must bear the Blame:                    30
One Fault he hath, is sorry for't,
His Ears are half a Foot too short;
Which could he to the Standard bring,
He'd shew his Face before the King:
Then, for his Voice, there's none disputes
That he's the Nightingal of Brutes.

THE Swine with contrite Heart allow'd,
His Shape and Beauty made him proud:
In Dyet was perhaps too nice,
But Gluttony was ne'er his Vice:                    40
In ev'ry Turn of Life content,
And meekly took what Fortune sent:
Inquire through all the Parish round
A better Neighbour ne'er was found:
His Vigilance might some displease;
'Tis true, he hated Sloth like Pease.

THE Mimick Ape began his Chatter,
How evil Tongues his Life bespatter:
Much of the cens'ring World complain'd,
Who said, his Gravity was feign'd:                    50
Indeed, the strictness of his Morals
Engag'd him in a hundred Quarrels:
He saw, and he was griev'd to see't,
His Zeal was sometimes indiscreet:
He found, his Virtues too severe
For our corrupted Times to bear;
Yet, such a lewd licentious Age
Might well excuse a Stoick's Rage.

THE Goat advanc'd with decent Pace;
And, first excus'd his youthful Face;                    60
Forgiveness begg'd, that he appear'd
('Twas Nature's Fault) without a Beard.

'Tis true, he was not much inclin'd
To fondness for the Female Kind;
Not, as his Enemies object,
From Chance, or natural Defect
Not by his frigid Constitution;
But, through a pious Resolution;
For, he had made a holy Vow
Of Chastity, as Monks do now;                    70
Which he resolv'd to keep for ever hence,
As strictly too; as doth his Reverence.

APPLY the Tale, and you shall find
How just it suits with human Kind.
Some Faults we own: But, can you guess?
Why?—Virtues carry'd to Excess;
Wherewith our Vanity endows us,
Though neither Foe nor Friend allows us.

THE Lawyer swears, you may rely on't,
He never squeez'd a needy Clyent:               80
And, this he makes his constant Rule;
For which his Brethren call him Fool:
His Conscience always was so nice,
He freely gave the Poor Advice;
By which he lost, he may affirm,
A hundred Fees last *Easter* Term.
While others of the learned Robe
Would break the Patience of a *Job*,
No Pleader at the Bar could match
His Diligence and quick Dispatch;                90
Ne'er kept a Cause, he well may boast,
Above a Term or two at most.

THE cringing Knave who seeks a Place
Without Success; thus tells his Case:
Why should he longer mince the Matter?
He fail'd, because he could not flatter:
He had not learn'd to turn his Coat,
Nor for a Party give his Vote:

72. *his Reverence.* The Priest his Confessor.

His Crime he quickly understood;
Too zealous for the Nation's Good:     100
He found, the Ministers resent it,
Yet could not for his Heart repent it.

THE Chaplain vows, he cannot fawn,
Though it would raise him to the Lawn:
He pass'd his Hours among his Books;
You find it in his meagre Looks:
He might, if he were worldly-wise,
Preferment get, and spare his Eyes:
But own'd, he had a stubborn Spirit
That made him trust alone in Merit:     110
Would rise by Merit to Promotion;
Alass! a meer Chymerick Notion.

THE Doctor, if you will believe him,
Confess'd a Sin, and God forgive him:
Call'd up at Mid-night, ran to save
A blind old Beggar from the Grave:
But, see how *Satan* spreads his Snares;
He quite forgot to say his Pray'rs.
He cannot help it for his Heart
Sometimes to act the Parson's Part:     120
Quotes from the Bible many a Sentence
That moves his Patients to Repentance:
And, when his Med'cines do no good,
Supports their Minds with heav'nly Food.
At which, however well intended,
He hears the Clergy are offended;
And grown so bold behind his Back
To call him Hypocrite and Quack.
In his own Church he keeps a Seat;
Says Grace before, and after Meat;     130
And calls, without affecting Airs,
His Household twice a Day to Pray'rs.
He shuns Apothecary's Shops;
And hates to cram the Sick with Slops:
He scorns to make his Art a Trade;
Nor bribes my Lady's fav'rite Maid.

Old Nurse-keepers would never hire
To recommend him to the Squire;
Which others, whom he will not name,
Have often practis'd to their Shame.          140


    THE Statesman tells you with a *Sneer*,
His Fault is to be too *Sincere*;
And, having no sinister Ends,
Is apt to disoblige his Friends.
The Nation's Good, his Master's Glory,
Without Regard to *Whig* or *Tory*,
Were all the Schemes he had in View;
Yet he was seconded by few:
Though some had spread a thousand Lyes;
'Twas *He* defeated the EXCISE.          150
'Twas known, tho' he had born Aspersion;
That, *Standing Troops* were his Aversion:
His Practice was, in ev'ry Station
To serve the King, and please the Nation.
Though hard to find in ev'ry Case
The fittest Man to fill a Place:
His Promises he ne'er forgot,
But took Memorials on the Spot:
His Enemies, for want of Charity,
Said, he affected Popularity:          160
'Tis true, the People understood,
That all he did was for their Good;
Their kind Affections he has try'd;
No Love is lost on either Side.
He came to Court with Fortune clear,
Which now he runs out every Year;
Must, at the Rate that he goes on,
Inevitably be undone.
Oh! if his Majesty would please
To give him but a Writ of Ease,          170
Would grant him Licence to retire,
As it hath long been his Desire,
By fair Accounts it would be found
He's poorer by ten thousand Pound.

He owns, and hopes it is no Sin,
He ne'er was partial to his Kin;
He thought it base for Men in Stations,
To crowd the Court with their Relations:
His Country was his dearest Mother,
And ev'ry virtuous Man his Brother:          180
Through Modesty, or aukward Shame,
(For which he owns himself to blame)
He found the wisest Men he could,
Without Respect to Friends, or Blood,
Nor ever acts on private Views,
When he hath Liberty to chuse.

THE Sharper swore he hated Play,
Except to pass an Hour away:
And, well he might; for to his Cost,
By want of Skill, he always lost:          190
He heard, there was a Club of Cheats
Who had contriv'd a thousand Feats;
Could change the Stock, or cog a Dye,
And thus deceive the sharpest Eye:
No Wonder how his Fortune sunk,
His Brothers fleece him when he's drunk.

I OWN, the Moral not exact;
Besides, the Tale is false in Fact;
And, so absurd, that could I raise up
From Fields *Elyzian*, fabling *Esop*;          200
I would accuse him to his Face
For libelling the *Four-foot* Race.
Creatures of ev'ry Kind but ours
Well comprehend their nat'ral Powers;
While We, whom *Reason* ought to sway,
Mistake our Talents ev'ry Day:
The Ass was never known so stupid
To act the Part of *Tray*, or *Cupid*;
Nor leaps upon his Master's Lap,
There to be stroak'd and fed with Pap;          210
As *Esop* would the World perswade;
He better understands his Trade:

Nor comes whene'er his Lady whistles;
But, carries Loads, and feeds on Thistles;
Our Author's Meaning, I presume, is
A Creature *bipes et implumis*;
Wherein the Moralist design'd
A Compliment on Human-Kind:
For, here he owns, that now and then
Beasts may *degen'rate* into Men.          220

# VERSES

## ON

## I KNOW NOT WHAT

M Y latest tribute here I send
With this let your Collection end
Thus I consign you down to Fame,
A Character to praise and blame,
And, if the whole may pass for true,
Contented rest; you have your due
Give future times the Satisfaction
To leave one handle for Detraction.

Printed from Swift's autograph in the Forster Collection, No. 526.

216. A Definition of Man, disapproved by all Logicians. *Homo est Animal bipes, implume, erecto vultu.*

220. *Vide* Gulliver in his Account of the Houyhnhnms.

To the Reverend

# Doctor SWIFT, D.S.P.D.

*With a Present of a Paper-Book,*
*finely bound, on his Birth-Day,*

November 30, 1732

*By the Right Hon.* JOHN *Earl of* ORRERY

TO thee, dear SWIFT, these spotless Leaves I send;
    Small is the Present, but sincere the Friend.
Think not so poor a Book below thy Care,
Who knows the Price that thou can'st make it bear?
Tho' tawdry now, and like *Tyrilla*'s Face,
The specious Front shines out with borrow'd Grace:
Tho' Paste-boards glitt'ring like a tinsel'd Coat,
A *Rasa Tabula* within denote;
Yet if a venal and corrupted Age,
And modern Vices, shou'd provoke thy Rage;              10
If warn'd once more by their impending Fate,
A sinking Country, and an injur'd State,
Thy great Assistance shou'd again demand,
And call forth Reason to defend the Land;
Then shall we view these Sheets with glad Surprize,
Inspir'd with Thought, and speaking to our Eyes:
Each vacant Space shall then, enrich'd, dispence
True Force of Eloquence, and nervous Sense;
Inform the Judgment, animate the Heart,
And sacred Rules of Policy impart.                      20
The spangled Cov'ring, bright with splendid Oar,
Shall cheat the Sight with empty Show no more;
But lead us inward to those golden Mines,
Where all thy Soul in native Lustre shines.
So when the Eye surveys some lovely Fair,
With Bloom of Beauty grac'd, with Shape and Air,
How is the Rapture heighten'd, when we find
Her Form excell'd by her Celestial Mind.

Printed from *Works, Vol. IV*, Dublin, 1735.

# Verses left with a Silver Standish, on the Dean of St. Patrick's Desk, on his Birth-Day

## [by Delany]

HITHER from *Mexico* I came,
To serve a proud *Iernian* Dame,
Was long submitted to her Will,
At length she lost me at Quadrille.
Thro' various Shapes I often pass'd,
Still hoping to have Rest at last;
And still ambitious to obtain
Admittance to the Patriot Dean.
And sometimes got within his Door,
But soon turn'd out to serve the Poor:          10
Not stroling Idleness to aid,
But honest Industry, decay'd.
At length an Artist purchas'd me,
And wrought me to the Shape you see.
    THIS done, to *Hermes* I apply'd:
'O *Hermes* gratify my Pride;
'Be it my Fate to serve a Sage,
'The greatest Genius of his Age:
'That matchless Pen let me supply,
'Whose living Lines will never die.'          20
    I GRANT your Suit, the God reply'd
And here he left me to reside.

## Verses written by Dr. SWIFT

A PAPER Book is sent by *Boyle*,
Too neatly guilt for me to soil.
*Delany* sends a Silver Standish,
When I no more a Pen can brandish.

10. Alluding to 500 l. a Year lent by the Dean, without Interest, to poor Tradesmen.

Let both around my Tomb be plac'd,
As Trophies of a Muse deceas'd:
And let the friendly Lines they writ
In praise of long departed Wit,
Be grav'd on either Side in Columns,
More to my Praise than all my Volumes;                    10
To burst with Envy, Spite, and Rage,
The *Vandals* of the present Age.


# A *New Simile*

## FOR THE

## LADIES

### WITH

*Useful Annotations*

[by Sheridan]

*To make a Writer miss his End,*
*You've nothing else to do but mend.*


I Often try'd in vain to find
  A *Simile* for Woman-kind,
A *Simile* I mean to fit 'em,
In ev'ry Circumstance to hit 'em,
Thro' ev'ry Beast and Bird I went,
I ransack'd ev'ry Element,
And after peeping thro' all Nature,
To find so whimsical a Creature,
A *Cloud* presented to my View,
And straight this Parallel I drew;                    10

Printed from the original pamphlet, Dublin, 1732.

2. Most Ladies in reading call this Word a Smile, but they are to note, it consists of three Syllables, Si-mi-le. In English, a Likeness.

4. Not to hurt them.        9. Not like a Gun or Pistol.

TSPW

*Clouds* turn with ev'ry Wind about,
They keep us in Suspense and Doubt,
Yet oft perverse like Woman-kind
Are seen to scud against the Wind,
And are not Women just the same?
For, who can tell at what they aim?

*Clouds* keep the stoutest Mortals under,
When bell'wing they discharge their Thunder;
So when the Alarm-Bell is rung,
Of *Xanti*'s everlasting Tongue,                    20
The Husband dreads its Loudness more,
Than Light'nings Flash, or Thunder's Roar.

*Clouds* weep as they do without Pain,
And what are Tears but Women's Rain?

The *Clouds* about the Welkin roam
And Ladies never stay at home.

16. This is not meaned as to Shooting, but resolving.

18. The Word bellowing is not here to be understood of a Bull; but a Cloud, which makes a Noise like a Bull when it Thunders.

20. *Xanti*, a Nick-Name for Xantippe, that Scold of glorious Memory, who never let poor Socrates have one Moment's Peace of Mind, yet with unexampled Patience, he bore her pestilential Tongue. I shall beg the Ladies Pardon, if I insert a few Passages concerning her, and at the same Time I assure them, it is not to lessen those of the present Age, who are possesst of the like laudable Talents; for I will confess that I know three in the City of Dublin, no way inferior to Xantippe, but that they have not as great Men to work upon.

When a Friend asked Socrates, How he could bear the Scolding of his Wife Xantippe, he retorted, and asked him, How he could bear the Gagling of his Geese; ay, but my Geese lay Eggs for me, reply'd his Friend, So does my Wife bear Children said Socrates. *Diog. Laert.*

Being asked at another Time by a Friend, how he could bear her Tongue, he said she was of this Use to him that she taught him to bear the Impertinencies of others with more Ease, when he went abroad. *Plut. de Capiend. ex host. utilit.*

Socrates invited his Friend Enthydemus to Supper. Xantippe in great Rage went in to them, and overset the Table. Enthydemus rising in a Passion to go off, my dear Friend, stay, said Socrates, Did not a Hen do the same Thing at your House the other Day, and did I shew any Resentment? *Plut. de irâ cohibendâ.*

I could give many more Instances of her Termagancy, and his Philosophy, if such a Proceeding might not look as if I were glad of an Opportunity to expose the fair Sex; but to shew I have no such Design, I declare solemnly, that I had much worse stories to tell of her Behaviour to her Husband, which I rather pass'd over on account of the great Esteem which I bear the Ladies, especially those in the honourable Station of Matrimony.

25. *roam*. Ramble.

> The *Clouds* build Castles in the Air,
> A Thing peculiar to the Fair;
> For all the Schemes of their Fore-casting,
> Are not more solid, nor more lasting.     30

> A *Cloud* is light by Turns, and dark,
> Such is a Lady with her Spark;
> Now, with a sudden pouting Gloom,
> She seems to darken all the Room;
> Again, she's pleas'd, his Fears beguil'd,
> And all is clear, when she has smil'd.
> In this they're wondrously alike,
> (I hope the *Simile* will strike)
> Tho' in the darkest Dumps you view 'em,
> Stay but a Moment you'll see through 'em.     40

> The *Clouds* are apt to make Reflection,
> And frequently produce Infection,
> So *Cælia*, with small Provocation,
> Blasts ev'ry Neighbour's Reputation.

> The *Clouds* delight in gaudy Shew,
> For they like Ladies have their Bow;
> The gravest Matron will confess,
> That she her self is fond of Dress.

> Observe the *Clouds* in Pomp array'd,
> What various Colours are display'd,     50
> The Pink, the Rose, the Vi'let's Dye,
> In that great Drawing-Room the Sky,
> How do these differ from our Graces,
> In gardin Silks, Brocades, and Laces?
> Are they not such another Sight,
> When met upon a Birth-Day Night?

29. Not vomiting.     33. Thrusting out the Lip.

35. This is to be understood not in the sense of Wort when Brewers put Yest or Barm in it; but it's true Meaning is Deceived, or Cheated.

38. Hit your Fancy.

39. Sullen Fits. We have a merry Jig call'd Dumpty Deary, invented to rouze Ladies from the Dumps.

41. Reflection of the Sun.     47. *Matron*. Motherly Women.

53. Not Grace before and after Meat, nor their Graces the Dutchesses, but the Graces which attended on Venus.

The *Clouds* delight to change their Fashion,
(Dear Ladies, be not in a Passion)
Nor let this Whim to you seem strange,
Who ev'ry Hour delight in change.          60

In them and you alike are seen
The sullen Symptoms of the Spleen,
The Moment that your Vapours rise,
We see them dropping from your Eyes.

In Ev'ning fair you may behold
The *Clouds* are fring'd with borrow'd Gold,
And this is many a Lady's Case,
Who flants about in borrow'd Lace.

Grave Matrons are like *Clouds* of Snow,
Their Words fall thick, and soft, and Slow,          70
While brisk Coquets, like rattling Hail,
Our Ears on ev'ry Side assayl.

*Clouds* when they intercept our Sight,
Deprive us of celestial Light:
So when my *Chloe* I pursue,
No Heav'n besides I have in View.

Thus on Comparison you see,
In every Instance they agree,
So like, so very much the same,
That one may go by t'other's Name,          80
Let me proclaim it then aloud,
That ev'ry Woman is a *Cloud*.

68. Not Flanders Lace, but Gold and Silver Lace. By borrowed I mean such as run honest Tradesmen's Debts, for what they were not able to pay, as many of them did for French Silver Lace against the Last Birth-Day. vid. the Shopkeepers Books.

71. *Coquets*. Girls who love to hear themselves prate, and put on a Number of Monkey Airs to catch Men.

77. I hope none will be so uncomplaisant to the Ladies as to think these Comparisons odious.

81. Tell it to the whole World, not to proclaim them as Robbers and Raparees.

# An Answer

To a late scandalous Poem, wherein the Author most audaciously presumes to compare a Cloud to a Woman

### By Dennis Nephelee, chief
### Cap of Howth

[p. 1]  PRESUMPTUOUS Poet, could you dare
    A Cloud with Woman kind compare?
Strange pride and insolence you shew,
Inferior mortals there below.
And is our thunder in your ears
As grating, or as loud as theirs?
We onely send our Thunder out
In hopes to make you more devout;
And is not femal clattring worse,
Which drives you not to pray, but curse?        10
    We hardly thunder thrice a year:
The bolt discharg'd, the sky grows clear;
But, ev'ry sublunary dowdy
The more she scolds, the more she's cloudy.
    How usefull were a womans thunder
If she like us would burst asunder!
[p. 2]    Yet, though her spouse hath often curst her,
And, whisp'ring wisht, the Devil burst her
For hourly thundring in his face,
She ne'er was known to burst a lace.        20
    Some Criticks may object perhaps,
That Clouds are blam'd for giving Claps:
But, what alas! are Claps ætherial
Compar'd for mischief, to Venereal?
Can Clouds give buboes, ulcers, blotches?
Or, from your noses dig out notches?

Printed from Swift's autograph in the Huntington Library, HM 14339. This is followed by the printed version, which was taken from a much revised copy.

We leave the body sweet and sound,
May kill perhaps, but never wound.
      You know, a cloudy sky bespeaks
Fair weather when the morning breaks,                    30
But, women in a cloudy plight
Foretell a storm to last till night.
      When Syrius o'er the welkin rages,
Our kindly help his fire assuages.
But, Woman is a curst inflamer;
No parish ducking-stool can tame her,
[p. 3]   To kindle strife Dame Nature taught her,
Like fire-works, she can burn in water.
      For Fickleness how durst you blame us?
Who, for our Steddyness are famous                       40
You men would be in wofull pickle
If Clouds were but like Femals fickle;
      You'll see a Cloud in gentle weather
Keep the same face an hour together,
While Women, if it could be reckon'd
Change ev'ry feature ev'ry second.
      Observe our visage in a morning;
Of foul and fair we give you warning;
But, can you guess from womens air
One minute whether foul or fair?                         50
      Go read in antient books enroll'd
What honors we possesst of old.
To disappoint Ixion's rape
Jove dresst a Cloud in Juno's shape,
Which when he had enjoy'd, he swore,
No Goddess could have pleas'd him more.
[p. 4]   No diff'rence could he find between
His Cloud, and Jove's imperiall Queen.
This Cloud produc'd a race of Centaurs
Fam'd for a thousand bold adventures                     60
From us descended ab origine,
By learned authors call'd Nubigenæ.
But say, what earthly nymph do you know,
So beautifull to pass for Juno?
      Before Æneas durst aspire
To court her Majesty of Tyre

His mother begg'd of us to dress him
That Dido smitt, might more caress him
A Coat we gave him dy'd in grain
A flaxen wig, and clouded cane,                    70
With which he made a tearing show:
And Dido quickly smoak't the Beau.
 Among your femals make inquiryes:
What nymph on earth so fair as Iris?
With heav'nly beauty so endow'd;
And yet her father is a Cloud:
We dresst her in a gold Brocade;
To rigg her out for Juno's mayd.

[p. 5]  Tis known, that Socrates the wise
Ador'd the Clouds as Deityes.                      80
To us he made his dayly pray'rs,
As Aristophanes declares;
From Jupiter took all dominion,
And dy'd defending his opinion.
By his authority tis plain,
You worship other Gods in vain
And from your own experience know
We govern all things there below.
You follow where we please to guide:
O'er all your passions we preside:                 90
Can raise them up, or sink them down,
As we think fit to smile or frown;
And, just as we dispose your brain,
Are witty, dull, rejoyce, complain.
 Compare us then to femal race!
We, to whom all the Gods give place.
They have no claim to Your allegiance
Because they live in lower regions
You find, the Gods in Homer dwell
In seas and woods, or low as hell                  100
[p. 6] Ev'n Jove, and Mercury his pimp
No higher climb than mount Olymp
(Who makes you think the Clouds he pierces:
He pierce the Clouds! he kiss our arses)
While we, o'er Tenariffa plac't,
Are lofty'r by a mile at least.

And, when Apollo struts on Pindus,
We see him from our kitchin windows,
Or, to Parnassus looking down,
Can piss upon his lawrel crown.　　　　　110
　　Fate never form'd the Gods to flye
They must be carryed through the Sky
When Jove would some fair nymph inveigle
He comes full gallop on his eagle:
Though Venus be as light as air,
She must have doves to draw her chair:
Though Mercury makes use of Wings
With which from earth to heav'n he springs;
He never honestly came by 'em,
And, e'er he flyes is forc'd to tye em.　　　　　120
Apollo stirs not out of dore
Without his taudry coach and four:
[p. 7]　And, jealous Juno, ever snarling,
Is drawn by peacocks in her Berlin
　　But, we can fly whene'er we please
O'er cityes, rivers, hills, and seas,
From East to west the world we roam,
And, in all clymates are at home:
Provide you duly as we go
With Sun-shine, rain, and hail, and snow.　　　　　130
　　Tis but by our peculiar grace
That Phebus ever shews his face;
For when we please, we open wide
Our curtains blue on either side;
You see how sawcily he shews
His carrot locks, and fiery nose;
And gives himself a haughty air,
As if he made the weather fair.
　　Tis sung; wherever Celia treeds,
The Vi'lets ope their purple heads,　　　　　140
The Roses blow, the Cowslip springs;
Tis sung. But we know better things.
Tis true; a Woman on her mettle
Will often piss upon a nettle;
Yet, though we grant she makes it wetter,
The nettle never thrives the better.

[p. 8]  But we by gentle April showers
Produce in May the sweetest flowrs.
   Your Poets Chloe's beauty heightning
Compare her radiant eyes to Lightning:     150
And yet, I hope 't will be allow'd,
No Lightning comes but from a Cloud.
However, we have too much sense
At Poets flights to take offence:
Nor can Hyperbole's demean us,
What Drabs have been compar'd to Venus?
Observe the case: I state it thus:
You may compare your Trull to us;
But think how damnably you err
When you compare us Clouds to her:     160
From whence you draw such bold conclusions;
But, Poets love profane allusions.
And, if you now so little spare us,
Who knows how soon you [will] compare us
To Chatres, Walpole, or a King,
If once we let you have your Swing.
Such wicked insolence appears
Offensive to all pious ears.
To flatter Woman by a Metaphor!
What profit could you hope to get of her     170
[p. 9]  And, for her sake turn base detractor
Against your greatest benefactor.
   But, we shall keep revenge in store
If ever you provoke us more.
For since we knew you walk a-foot,
We'll soundly drench your frize Sur-tout,
Or may we never thunder throw,
Nor souse to death a Birthday Beau.

   We own, Your verses are melodious,
But such Comparisons are odious.     180

# AN ANSWER

### To a SCANDALOUS

# POEM

#### WHEREIN

The AUTHOR most audaciously presumes to cast an
Indignity upon their HIGHNESSES the *CLOUDS*,
by comparing them to a *WOMAN*

*Written by* DERMOT O-NEPHELY, *Chief*
\* *Cap of* HOWTH
\* *The highest Point of* HOWTH *is called the Cap of* HOWTH

Written in the Year 1732

## ADVERTISEMENT

### From the *CLOUDS*

N.B. *The following Answer to that scurrilous Libel against us,
should have been published long ago in our own Justification: But it
was advised, that, considering the high Importance of the Subject, it
should be deferred until the Meeting of the Great Assembly of the
Nation.*

PRESUMPTUOUS Bard! How cou'd you dare
A Woman with a *Cloud* compare?
Strange Pride and Insolence you show,
Inferior Mortals *there* below.
And, is our Thunder in your Ears
So frequent or so loud as theirs?
Alas! our Thunder soon goes out;
And only makes you more devout.
Then, is not Female Clatter worse,
That drives you, not to *pray*, but *curse*?          10

Printed from *Works, Vol. VI*, Dublin, 1738.

WE hardly Thunder thrice a Year;
The Bolt discharg'd, the Sky grows clear:
But, ev'ry sublunary Dowdy,
The more she scolds, the more she's cloudy.

SOME Critick may object, perhaps,
That *Clouds* are blam'd for giving *Claps*;
But, what alas are *Claps* Ætherial,
Compar'd for Mischief, to Venereal?
Can *Clouds* give Bubo's, Ulcers, Blotches,
Or from your Noses dig out Notches?                    20
We leave the Body sweet and sound;
We kill, 'tis true, but never wound;

YOU know a *Cloudy* Sky bespeaks
Fair Weather, when the Morning breaks;
But, Women in a *Cloudy* Plight,
Foretel a Storm to last till Night.

A *Cloud*, in proper Seasons pours
His Blessings down in fruitful Show'rs;
But, Woman was by Fate design'd
To pour down Curses on Mankind.                        30

WHEN *Syrius* o'er the Welkin rages
Our kindly Help his Fire asswages;
But Woman is a curst Inflamer,
No Parish Ducking-Stool can tame her:
To kindle Strife, Dame-Nature taught her:
Like Fire-works, she can burn in Water.

FOR Fickleness how durst you blame us?
Who for our Constancy are famous.
You'll see a *Cloud* in gentle Weather
Keep the same Face an Hour together:                   40
While Women, if it could be reckon'd,
Change ev'ry Feature, ev'ry Second.

31. *Syrius*. The Dog-Star.

Observe our Figure in a Morning;
Of Foul or Fair we give you warning;
But, can you guess from Woman's Air,
One Minute, whether Foul or Fair?


Go read in antient Books enroll'd,
What Honours we possess'd of old!


To disappoint *Ixion*'s Rape,
*JOVE* drest a *Cloud* in *Juno*'s Shape:          50
Which when he had enjoy'd, he swore
No Goddess could have pleas'd him more,
No Diff'rence could he find between
His *Cloud*, and *JOVE*'s Imperial Queen:
His *Cloud* produc'd a Race of *Centaurs*,
Fam'd for a thousand bold Adventures;
From us descended *ab origine*;
By learned Authors call'd, *Nubigenæ*.
But say, what Earthly Nymph do you know,
So beautiful to pass for *Juno*?          60


Before *Æneas* durst aspire
To court her Majesty of *Tyre*,
His Mother begg'd of us to dress him,
That *Dido* might the more caress him:
A Coat we gave him, dy'd in Grain;
A *Flaxen* Wig, and *Clouded* Cane.
(The Wig was powder'd round with Sleet,
Which fell in *Clouds* beneath his Feet)
With which he made a tearing Show:
And *Dido* quickly *smoak'd the Beau*.          70


Among your Females make Inquiries;
What Nymph on Earth so fair as *Iris*?
With heav'nly Beauty so endow'd?
And yet her Father is a *Cloud*.
We dress'd her in a Gold Brocade,
Befitting *Juno*'s fav'rite Maid.

'TIS known, that *Socrates* the wise,
Ador'd us *Clouds* as Deities;
To us he made his daily Prayers,
As *Aristophanes* declares:                                    80
From *Jupiter* took all Dominion,
And dy'd defending his Opinion.
By his Authority, 'tis plain
You worship other Gods in vain:
And from your own Experience know,
We govern all Things there below.
You follow where we please to guide;
O'er all your Passions we preside;
Can raise them up, or sink them down,
As we think fit to smile or frown:                             90
And, just as we dispose your Brain,
Are witty, dull, rejoyce, complain.

COMPARE Us then to Female Race!
We, to whom all the Gods give Place:
Who better challenge your Allegiance,
Because we dwell in higher Regions:
You find, the Gods in *Homer* dwell,
In Seas, and Streams, or low as Hell:
Ev'n *Jove*, and *Mercury* his Pimp,
No higher climb than Mount *Olymp*,                           100
(Who makes you think, the *Clouds* he pierces:
He pierce the *Clouds*! He kiss their Arses.)
While we, o'er *Tenariffa* plac't,
Are loftier by a Mile at least:
And when *Apollo* struts on *Pindus*,
We see him from our Kitchen-windows:
Or, to *Parnassus* looking down,
Can piss upon his Lawrel Crown.

FATE never form'd the Gods to fly;
In Vehicles they mount the Sky:                               110
When *JOVE* would some fair Nymph inveigle,
He comes full gallop on his Eagle.
Though *Venus* be as light as Air,
She must have Doves to draw her Chair.

*Apollo* stirs not out of Door,
Without his lacker'd Coach and Four,
And, jealous *Juno*, ever snarling,
Is drawn by Peacocks in her Berlin:
But, we can fly where-e'er we please,
O'er Cities, Rivers, Hills, and Seas:                    120
From East to West, the World we roam;
And, in all Climates are at home;
With Care provide you as we go,
With Sun-shine, Rain, and Hail, or Snow.
You, when it rains, like Fools believe,
JOVE pisses on you through a Sieve;
An idle Tale, 'tis no such Matter;
We only dip a Spunge in Water;
Then, squeeze it close between our Thumbs,
And shake it well, and down it comes.                    130
As you shall to your Sorrow know;
We'll watch your Steps where-e'er you go:
And since we find, you walk a-foot
We'll soundly souce your Frize Surtout.

    'Tis but by our peculiar Grace,
That *Phœbus* ever shows his Face:
For, when we please, we open wide
Our Curtains blue, from Side to Side:
And then, how saucily he shows
His brazen Face, and fiery Nose:                         140
And gives himself a haughty Air,
As if He made the Weather fair.

    'Tis sung, where-ever *Celia* treads,
The Vi'lets ope their Purple Heads;
The Roses blow, the Cowslip springs;
'Tis sung, but we know better Things.
'Tis true; a Woman on her Mettle,
Will often piss upon a Nettle;
But, though we own, she makes it wetter,
The Nettle never thrives the better;                     150
While we, by soft prolifick Show'rs,
Can ev'ry Spring produce you Flow'rs.

YOUR Poets, *Chloe*'s Beauty height'ning,
Compare her radiant Eyes to Light'ning;
And yet, I hope, 'twill be allow'd,
That Light'ning comes but from a *Cloud*.

BUT, Gods like us, have too much Sense
At Poet's Flights to take Offence.
Nor can Hyperboles demean us;
Each Drab has been compar'd to *Venus*:                160

WE own, your Verses are melodious;
But such Comparisons are odious.


# AN EPISTLE

## TO

# A LADY,

Who desired the AUTHOR to make VERSES on Her,

### IN THE

## *HEROICK STILE*

AFTER venting all my Spight,
Tell me, what have I to write?
Ev'ry Error I could find
Thro' the Mazes of your Mind,
Have my busy Muse employ'd,
Till the Company was cloy'd.
Are you positive and fretful?
Heedless, ignorant, forgetful?
These, and twenty Follies more,
I have often told before.                10

Printed from the Folio, London, 1734, with corrections from *Poems*, 1735
(uncancelled state).

HEARKEN, what my *Lady* says—:
Have I nothing then to praise?
Ill it fits you to be witty,
Where a Fault shou'd move your Pity.
If you think me too conceited,
Or, to Passion quickly heated:
If my wand'ring Head be less
Set on Reading, than on Dress:
If I always seem too dull t'ye;
I can solve the Diffi—culty.                    20

YOU wou'd teach me to be wise;
Truth and Honour how to prize;
How to shine in Conversation,
And, with Credit fill my Station;
How to relish Notions high;
How to live, and how to die.

BUT it was decreed by Fate—;
Mr. DEAN, You come too late:
Well I know, you can discern,
I am now too old to learn:                       30
Follies, from my Youth instill'd,
Have my Soul entirely fill'd:
In my Head and Heart they center;
Nor will let your Lessons enter.

BRED a Fondling, and an Heiress;
Drest like any Lady May'ress;
Cocker'd by the Servants round,
Was too good to touch the Ground:
Thought the Life of ev'ry Lady
Shou'd be one continual Play-Day:                40
Balls, and Masquerades, and Shows,
Visits, Plays, and Powder'd Beaux.

THUS you have my Case at large,
And may now perform your Charge.
Those Materials I have furnish'd,
When, by you refin'd and burnish'd,

Must, that all the World may know 'em,
Be reduc'd into a Poem.
But, I beg, suspend a While,
That same paultry *Burlesque* Stile:     50
Drop, for once, your constant Rule,
Turning all to Ridicule:
Teaching others how to ape ye;
Court, nor Parli'ment, can 'scape ye;
Treat the Publick, and your Friends,
Both alike; while neither mends.

    SING my Praise in Strain sublime:
Treat not me with Doggrel Rhime.
'Tis but just, you shou'd produce,
With each Fault, each Fault's Excuse:     60
Not to publish ev'ry Trifle,
And my few Perfections stifle.
With some Gifts, at least endow me,
Which my very Foes allow me.
Am I spightful, proud, unjust?
Did I ever break my Trust?
Which, of all our modern Dames
Censures less, or less defames?
In Good Manners, am I faulty?
Can you call me rude, or haughty?     70
Did I e'er my Mite withold
From the Impotent and Old?
When did ever I omit
Due Regard for Men of Wit?
When have I Esteem express'd
For a Coxcomb gaily dress'd?
Do I, like the Female Tribe,
Think it Wit to fleer, and gibe?
Who, with less designing Ends,
Kindlier entertains her Friends?     80
With good Words and Count'nance sprightly,
Strive to treat them all politely.

    THINK not Cards my chief Diversion,
'Tis a wrong, unjust Aspersion:

Never knew I any Good in 'um,
But, to doze my Head, like *Lodanum.*
We, by Play, as Men by Drinking,
Pass our Nights, to drive out thinking.
From my Ailments give me Leisure,
I shall read and think with Pleasure:        90
Conversation learn to relish,
And with Books my Mind embellish.

    Now, methinks, I hear you cry;
Mr. DEAN, you must reply.

    MADAM, I allow 'tis true;
All these Praises are your Due.
You, like some acute Philosopher,
Ev'ry Fault have drawn a Gloss over:
Placing in the strongest Light,
All your Virtues to my Sight.        100

    THO' you lead a blameless Life,
Live an humble, prudent Wife;
Answer all domestick Ends,
What is this to us your Friends?
Tho' your Children by a Nod
Stand in Awe without the Rod:
Tho' by your obliging Sway
Servants love you, and obey:
Tho' you treat us with a Smile,
Clear your Looks, and smooth your Stile:        110
Load our Plates from ev'ry Dish;
This is not the Thing we wish.
Col'nel —— may be your Debtor;
We expect Employment better.
You must learn, if you would gain us,
With good sense to entertain us.

    SCHOLARS, when good Sense describing,
Call it *Tasting,* and *Imbibing*:
Metaphorick Meat and Drink,
Is to understand, and think:        120

We may *carve* for others thus;
And let others carve for us.
To discourse, and to attend,
Is to *help* yourself, and Friend.
Conversation is but *carving*,
Carve for all, yourself is starving.
Give no more to ev'ry Guest,
Than he's able to digest:
Give him always of the Prime,
And, but little at a Time.                              130
*Carve* to all but just enuff,
Let them neither starve, nor stuff:
And, that you may have your Due,
Let your Neighbours *carve* for you.

        To conclude this long Essay;
Pardon, if I disobey:
Nor, against my nat'ral Vein,
Treat you in Heroick Strain.
I, as all the Parish knows,
Hardly can be grave in Prose:                          140
Still to lash, and lashing Smile,
Ill befits a lofty Stile.
From the Planet of my Birth,
I encounter Vice with Mirth.
Wicked Ministers of State
I can easier scorn than hate:
And I find it answers right:
Scorn torments them more than Spight.
All the Vices of a Court,
Do but serve to make me Sport.                         150
Were I in some foreign Realm,
Which all Vices overwhelm;
Shou'd a Monkey wear a Crown,
Must I tremble at his Frown?
Could I not, thro' all his Ermin,
Spy the strutting chatt'ring Vermin?
Safely write a smart Lampoon,
To expose the brisk Baboon?

WHEN my Muse officious ventures
On the Nation's Representers;                    160
Teaching by what *Golden* Rules
Into Knaves they turn their Fools:
How the Helm is rul'd by *Walpole*
At whose Oars, like Slaves, they all pull:
Let the Vessel split on Shelves,
With the Freight enrich themselves:
Safe within my little Wherry,
All their Madness makes me merry:
Like the Watermen of *Thames,*
I row by, and call them Names.                   170
Like the ever-laughing Sage,
In a Jest I spend my Rage:
(Tho' it must be understood,
I would hang them if I cou'd:)
If I can but fill my Nitch,
I attempt no higher Pitch.
Leave to D'ANVERS and his Mate,
Maxims wise, to rule the State.
POULTNEY deep, accomplish'd ST. JOHNS,
Scourge the Villains with a Vengeance.           180
Let me, tho' the Smell be Noisom,
Strip their Bums; let CALEB hoyse 'em;
Then, apply ALECTO's Whip,
Till they wriggle, howl, and skip.

DEUCE is in you, Mr. DEAN;
What can all this Passion mean?
Mention Courts, you'll ne'er be quiet;
On Corruptions running Riot.
End, as it befits your Station;
Come to use, and Application:                    190
Nor with Senates keep a Fuss,
I submit; and answer thus.

IF the Machinations brewing,
To compleat the Publick Ruin,
Never once cou'd have the Pow'r
To affect me half an Hour;

(Sooner would I write in Buskins,
Mournful Elegies on *Bluskins*)
If I laugh at Whig and Tory;
I conclude *a Fortiori*,          200
All your Eloquence will scarce
Drive me from my fav'rite Farce.
This I must insist on. For, as
It is well observ'd by HORACE,
Ridicule has greater Pow'r
To reform the World, than Sour.
Horses thus, let Jockeys judge else,
Switches better guide than Cudgels.
Bastings heavy, dry, obtuse,
Only Dulness can produce,          210
While a little gentle Jerking
Sets the Spirits all a working.

    THUS, I find it by Experiment,
Scolding moves you less than Merriment.
I may storm and rage in vain;
It but stupifies your Brain.
But, with Raillery to nettle,
Set your Thoughts upon their Mettle:
Gives Imagination Scope,
Never lets your Mind elope:          220
Drives out Brangling, and Contention,
Brings in Reason and Invention.
For your Sake, as well as mine,
I the lofty Stile decline.
I Shou'd make a Figure scurvy,
And your Head turn Topsy-turvy.

    I, WHO love to have a Fling,
Both at Senate-House, and King;
That they might some better Way tread,
To avoid the publick Hatred;          230
Thought no Method more commodious,
Than to shew their Vices odious:

198. *Bluskins*. A famous Thief, who was hanged some Years ago.
204. —— Ridiculum Acri,
    Fortius & Melius, &c.

Which I chose to make appear,
Not by Anger, but a Sneer:
As my Method of Reforming,
Is by Laughing, not by Storming.
(For my Friends have always thought
Tenderness my greatest Fault.)
Wou'd you have me change my Stile,
On your Faults no longer smile?          240
But, to patch up all our Quarrels,
Quote you Texts from *Plutarch's Morals*;
Or from *Solomon* produce
Maxims teaching Wisdom's Use.

IF I treat you like a Crown'd Head
You have cheap enough compounded.
Can you put in higher Claims,
Then the Owners of *St. James*.
You are not so great a Grievance
As the Hirelings of *St. Stephens*.          250
You are of a lower Class
Than my Friend Sir *Robert Brass*.
None of these have Mercy found:
I have laugh'd, and lash'd them round.

HAVE you seen a *Rocket* fly?
You would swear it pierc'd the Sky;
It but reach'd the middle Air,
Bursting into Pieces there:
Thousand Sparkles falling down
Light on many a Coxcomb's Crown.          260
See, what Mirth the Sport creates;
Sindges Hair, but breaks no Pates.

THUS, Shou'd I attempt to climb,
Treat you in a Stile sublime,
Such a Rocket is my Muse,
Shou'd I lofty Numbers chuse,
E'er I reach'd *Parnassus* Top
I shou'd burst, and bursting drop.
All my *Fire* would fall in Scraps,
Give your Head some gentle Raps;          270

Only make it smart a while:
Then cou'd I forbear to smile,
When I found the tingling Pain,
Entring warm your frigid Brain:
Make you able upon Sight,
To decide of Wrong and Right?
Talk with Sense, whate'er you please on,
Learn to relish *Truth* and *Reason*.

Thus we both should gain our Prize:
I to laugh, and you grow wise.                    280


# ON POETRY:

## A *RAPSODY*

*The following Poem was published in London, and Dublin, and having been much admired,*
*we thought proper to include it in this Collection: And although the Author be not known, yet*
*we hope it will be acceptable to our Readers.*

ALL Human Race wou'd fain be *Wits*,
  And Millions miss, for one that hits.
*Young*'s universal Passion, *Pride*,
Was never known to spread so wide.
Say *Britain*, cou'd you ever boast,——
Three *Poets* in an Age at most?
Our chilling Climate hardly bears
A *Sprig* of Bays in Fifty Years:
While ev'ry Fool his Claim alledges,
As if it grew in common Hedges.                    10
What Reason can there be assign'd
For this Perverseness in the Mind?
*Brutes* find out where their Talents lie:
A *Bear* will not attempt to fly:
A founder'd *Horse* will oft debate,
Before he tries a five-barr'd Gate:

Printed from the Folio, London, 1733, with corrections from *Poems*, 1735.

A *Dog* by Instinct turns aside,
Who sees the Ditch too deep and wide.
But *Man* we find the only Creature,
Who, led by *Folly*, combats *Nature*;          20
Who, when *she* loudly cries, *Forbear*,
With Obstinacy fixes there;
And, where his *Genius* least inclines,
Absurdly bends his whole Designs.


  Not *Empire* to the Rising-Sun,
By Valour, Conduct, Fortune won;
Nor highest *Wisdom* in Debates
For framing Laws to govern States;
Nor Skill in Sciences profound,
So large to grasp the Circle round;          30
Such heavenly Influence require,
As how to strike the *Muses Lyre*.


  Not Beggar's Brat, on Bulk begot;
Not Bastard of a Pedlar *Scot*;
Not Boy brought up to cleaning Shoes,
The Spawn of *Bridewell*, or the Stews;
Not Infants dropt, the spurious Pledges
Of *Gipsies* littering under Hedges,
Are so disqualified by Fate
To rise in *Church*, or *Law*, or *State*,          40
As he, whom *Phebus* in his Ire
Hath *blasted* with poetick Fire.


  What hope of Custom in the *Fair*,
While not a Soul demands your Ware?
Where you have nothing to produce
For private Life, or publick Use?
*Court, City, Country* want you not;
You cannot bribe, betray, or plot.
For Poets, Law makes no Provision:
The Wealthy have you in Derision.          50
Of State-Affairs you cannot smatter,
Are awkward when you try to flatter.

Your Portion, taking *Britain* round,
Was just one annual Hundred Pound.
Now not so much as in Remainder
Since *Cibber* brought in an Attainder;
For ever fixt by Right Divine,
(A Monarch's Right) on *Grubstreet* Line.
Poor starv'ling Bard, how small thy Gains!
How unproportion'd to thy Pains!                    60

    And here a *Simile* comes Pat in:
Tho' *Chickens* take a Month to fatten,
The Guests in less than half an Hour
Will more than half a Score devour.
So, after toiling twenty Days,
To earn a Stock of Pence and Praise,
Thy Labours, grown the Critick's Prey,
Are swallow'd o'er a Dish of Tea;
Gone, to be never heard of more,
Gone, where the *Chickens* went before.              70

    How shall a new Attempter learn
Of diff'rent Spirits to discern,
And how distinguish, which is which,
The Poet's Vein, or scribling Itch?
Then hear an old experienc'd Sinner
Instructing thus a young Beginner.

    Consult yourself, and if you find
A powerful Impulse urge your Mind,
Impartial judge within your Breast
What Subject you can manage best;                    80
Whether your Genius most inclines
To Satire, Praise, or hum'rous Lines;
To Elegies in mournful Tone,
Or Prologue sent from Hand unknown.
Then rising with *Aurora*'s Light,
The Muse invok'd, sit down to write;
Blot out, correct, insert, refine,
Enlarge, diminish, interline;

54. Paid to the Poet Laureat, which Place was given to one Cibber, a Player.

Be mindful, when Invention fails,
To scratch your Head, and bite your Nails.          90

Your Poem finish'd, next your Care
Is needful, to transcribe it fair.
In modern Wit all printed Trash, is
Set off with num'rous *Breaks*——and *Dashes*——

To Statesmen wou'd you give a Wipe,
You print it in *Italick Type*.
When Letters are in vulgar Shapes,
'Tis ten to one the Wit escapes;
But when in *Capitals* exprest,
The dullest Reader smoaks a Jest:          100
Or else perhaps he may invent
A better than the Poet meant,
As learned Commentators view
In *Homer* more than *Homer* knew.

Your Poem in its modish Dress,
Correctly fitted for the Press,
Convey by Penny-Post to *Lintot*,
But let no Friend alive look into't.
If *Lintot* thinks 'twill quit the Cost,
You need not fear your Labour lost:          110
And, how agreeably surpriz'd
Are you to see it advertiz'd!
The Hawker shews you one in Print,
As fresh as Farthings from the Mint:
The Product of your Toil and Sweating;
A Bastard of your own begetting.

Be sure at *Will*'s the following Day,
Lie Snug, to hear what Criticks say.
And if you find the general Vogue
Pronounces you a stupid Rogue;          120
Damns all your Thoughts as low and little,
Sit still, and swallow down your Spittle.
Be silent as a Politician,
For talking may beget Suspicion:

107. *Lintot*. A Bookseller in London.          117. *Will's*. The Poet's Coffee-House.

Or praise the Judgment of the Town,
And help yourself to run it down.
Give up your fond paternal Pride,
Nor argue on the weaker Side;
For Poems read without a Name
We justly praise, or justly blame:     130
And Criticks have no partial Views,
Except they know whom they abuse.
And since you ne'er provok'd their Spight,
Depend upon't their Judgment's right:
But if you blab, you are undone;
Consider what a Risk you run.
You lose your Credit all at once;
The Town will mark you for a Dunce:
The vilest Doggrel *Grubstreet* sends,
Will pass for yours with Foes and Friends.     140
And you must bear the whole Disgrace,
'Till some fresh Blockhead takes your Place.


    Your Secret kept, your Poem sunk,
And sent in Quires to line a Trunk;
If still you be dispos'd to rhime,
Go try your Hand a second Time.
Again you fail, yet Safe's the Word,
Take Courage, and attempt a Third.
But first with Care imploy your Thoughts,
Where Criticks mark'd your former Faults.     150
The trivial Turns, the borrow'd Wit,
The *Similes* that nothing fit;
The *Cant* which ev'ry Fool repeats,
Town-Jests, and Coffee-house Conceits;
Descriptions tedious, flat and dry,
And introduc'd the Lord knows why;
Or where we find your Fury set
Against the harmless Alphabet;
On A's and B's your Malice vent,
While Readers wonder whom you meant.     160
A publick, or a private *Robber*;
A *Statesman*, or a South-Sea *Jobber*.

A *Prelate* who no God believes;
A Parliament, or Den of Thieves.
A Pick-purse, at the Bar, or Bench;
A Duchess, or a Suburb-Wench.
Or oft when Epithets you link,
In gaping Lines to fill a Chink;
Like stepping Stones to save a Stride,
In Streets where Kennels are too wide:          170
Or like a Heel-piece to support
A Cripple with one Foot too short:
Or like a Bridge that joins a Marish
To Moorlands of a diff'rent Parish.
So have I seen ill-coupled Hounds,
Drag diff'rent Ways in miry Grounds.
So Geographers in *Afric*-Maps
With Savage-Pictures fill their Gaps;
And o'er unhabitable Downs
Place Elephants for want of Towns.          180

But tho' you miss your third Essay,
You need not throw your Pen away.
Lay now aside all Thoughts of Fame,
To spring more profitable Game.
From Party-Merit seek Support;
The vilest Verse thrives best at Court.
A Pamphlet in Sir *Bob*'s Defence
Will never fail to bring in Pence;
Nor be concern'd about the Sale,
He pays his Workmen on the Nail.          190

A Prince the Moment he is crown'd,
Inherits ev'ry Virtue round,
As Emblems of the sov'reign Pow'r,
Like other Bawbles of the Tow'r.
Is gen'rous, valiant, just and wise,
And so continues 'till he dies.
His humble *Senate* this professes,
In all their *Speeches, Votes, Addresses.*
But once you fix him in a Tomb,
His Virtues fade, his Vices bloom;          200

And each Perfection wrong imputed
Is fully at his Death confuted.
The Loads of Poems in his Praise,
Ascending make one Funeral-Blaze.
As soon as you can hear his Knell,
This God on Earth turns *Devil* in Hell.
And lo, his Ministers of State,
Transform'd to Imps, his Levee wait.
Where, in the Scenes of endless Woe,
They ply their former Arts below.                    210
And as they sail in *Charon*'s Boat,
Contrive to bribe the Judge's Vote.
To *Cerberus* they give a Sop,
His triple-barking Mouth to Stop:
Or in the Iv'ry Gate of Dreams,
Project Excise and South-Sea Schemes:
Or hire their Party-Pamphleteers,
To set *Elysium* by the Ears.

Then *Poet*, if you mean to thrive,
Employ your Muse on Kings alive;                    220
With Prudence gath'ring up a Cluster
Of all the Virtues you can muster:
Which form'd into a Garland sweet,
Lay humbly at your Monarch's Feet;
Who, as the Odours reach his Throne,
Will smile, and think 'em all his own:
For *Law* and *Gospel* both determine
All Virtues lodge in royal Ermine.
(I mean the Oracles of Both,
Who shall depose it upon Oath.)                    230
Your Garland in the following Reign,
Change but the Names will do again.

But if you think this Trade too base,
(Which seldom is the Dunce's Case)
Put on the Critick's Brow, and sit
At *Wills* the puny Judge of Wit.

215.    Sunt geminæ Somni portæ—
Altera candenti perfecta nitens elephanto. Virg. 1.6.

A Nod, a Shrug, a scornful Smile,
With Caution us'd, may serve a-while.
Proceed no further in your Part,
Before you learn the Terms of Art:                    240
(For you can never be too far gone,
In all our modern Criticks Jargon.)
Then talk with more authentick Face,
Of *Unities, in Time and Place.*
Get Scraps of *Horace* from your Friends,
And have them at your Fingers Ends.
Learn *Aristotle*'s Rules by Rote,
And at all Hazards boldly quote:
Judicious *Rymer* oft review:
Wise *Dennis*, and profound *Bossu.*                   250
Read all the *Prefaces* of *Dryden*,
For these our Criticks much confide in,
(Tho' meerly writ at first for filling
To raise the Volume's Price, a Shilling.)

 A forward Critick often dupes us
With sham Quotations *Peri Hupsous*:
And if we have not read *Longinus*,
Will magisterially out-shine us.
Then, lest with *Greek* he over-run ye,
Procure the Book for Love or Money,                   260
Translated from *Boileau*'s Translation,
And quote *Quotation* on *Quotation.*

 At *Wills* you hear a Poem read,
Where *Battus* from the Table-head,
Reclining on his Elbow-chair,
Gives Judgment with decisive Air.
To him the Tribe of circling Wits,
As to an Oracle submits.
He gives Directions to the Town,
To cry it up, or run it down.                         270
(Like *Courtiers*, when they send a Note,
Instructing *Members* how to Vote.)

256. *Peri Hupsous.* A famous Treatise of Longinus.  261. By Mr. Welsted.

He sets the Stamp of Bad and Good,
Tho' not a Word be understood.
Your Lesson learnt, you'll be secure
To get the Name of *Conoisseur*.
And when your Merits once are known,
Procure Disciples of your own.

For Poets (you can never want 'em,
Spread thro' *Augusta Trinobantum*)          280
Computing by their Pecks of Coals,
Amount to just Nine thousand Souls.
These o'er their proper Districts govern,
Of Wit and Humour, Judges sov'reign.
In ev'ry Street a City-bard
Rules, like an Alderman his Ward.
His indisputed Rights extend
Thro' all the Lane, from End to End.
The Neighbours round admire his *Shrewdness*,
For songs of *Loyalty* and *Lewdness*.          290
Out-done by none in Rhyming well,
Altho' he never learnt to spell.

Two bordering Wits contend for Glory;
And one is *Whig*, and one is *Tory*.
And this, for Epicks claims the Bays,
And that, for Elegiack Lays.
Some famed for Numbers soft and smooth,
By Lovers spoke in *Punch*'s Booth.
And some as justly Fame extols
For lofty Lines in *Smithfield* Drols.          300
*Bavius* in *Wapping* gains Renown,
And *Mævius* reigns o'er *Kentish-Town*:
*Tigellius* plac'd in *Phœbus*' Car,
From *Ludgate* shines to *Temple-bar*.
Harmonius *Cibber* entertains
The Court with annual Birth-day Strains;
Whence *Gay* was banish'd in Disgrace,
Where *Pope* will never show his Face;
Where *Young* must torture his Invention,
To flatter *Knaves*, or lose his *Pension*.          310

280. *Augusta Trinobantum.* The antient Name of London.

But these are not a thousandth Part
Of Jobbers in the Poets Art,
Attending each his proper Station,
And all in due Subordination;
Thro' ev'ry Alley to be found,
In Garrets high, or under Ground:
And when they join their *Pericranies*,
Out skips a *Book of Miscellanies.*
*Hobbes* clearly proves that ev'ry Creature
Lives in a State of War by Nature.                320
The Greater for the Smaller watch,
But meddle seldom with their Match.
A Whale of moderate Size will draw
A Shole of Herrings down his Maw.
A Fox with Geese his Belly crams;
A Wolf destroys a thousand Lambs.
But search among the rhiming Race,
The Brave are worried by the Base.
If, on *Parnassus'* Top you sit,
You rarely bite, are always bit:                 330
Each Poet of inferior Size
On you shall rail and criticize;
And strive to tear you Limb from Limb,
While others do as much for him.
The Vermin only teaze and pinch
Their Foes superior by an Inch.
So, Nat'ralists observe, a Flea
Hath smaller Fleas that on him prey,
And these have smaller yet to bite 'em,
And so proceed *ad infinitum*:                   340
Thus ev'ry Poet in his Kind,
Is bit by him that comes behind;
Who, tho' too little to be seen,
Can teaze, and gall, and give the Spleen;
Call Dunces, Fools, and Sons of Whores,
Lay *Grubstreet* at each others Doors:
Extol the *Greek* and *Roman* Masters,
And curse our modern Poetasters.
Complain, as many an ancient Bard did,
How Genius is no more rewarded;                  350

How wrong a Taste prevails among us;
How much our Ancestors out-sung us;
Can personate an awkward Scorn
For those who are not Poets born:
And all their Brother Dunces lash,
Who crowd the Press with hourly Trash.

O, *Grubstreet*! how do I bemoan thee,
Whose graceless Children scorn to own thee!
This filial Piety forgot,
Deny their Country like a SCOT:     360
Tho' by their Idiom and Grimace
They soon betray their native Place:
Yet *thou* hast greater Cause to be
Asham'd of them, than they of thee.
Degenerate from their ancient Brood,
Since first the Court allow'd them Food.

Remains a Difficulty still,
To purchase Fame by writing ill:
From *Flecknoe* down to *Howard*'s Time,
How few have reach'd the *low Sublime*?     370
For when our high-born *Howard* dy'd,
*Blackmore* alone his Place supply'd:
And least a Chasm should intervene,
When Death had finish'd *Blackmore*'s Reign,
The *leaden Crown* devolv'd to thee,
Great Poet of the *Hollow-Tree*.
But, oh, how unsecure thy Throne!
Ten thousand Bards thy Right disown:
They plot to turn in factious Zeal,
*Duncenia* to a Common-Weal;     380
And with rebellious Arms pretend
An equal Priv'lege to *descend*.

In Bulk there are not more Degrees,
From *Elephants* to *Mites* in Cheese,
Than what a curious Eye may trace
In Creatures of the rhiming Race.

376. *Great Poet.* Lord Grimston, lately deceased. [fn. 1735].

USPW

From bad to worse, and worse they fall,
But, who can reach to Worst of all?
For, tho' in Nature Depth and Height
Are equally held infinite,                                    390
In Poetry the Height we know;
'Tis only infinite below.
For Instance: When you rashly think,
No Rhymer can like *Welsted* sink.
His Merits ballanc'd you shall find,
The Laureat leaves him far behind.
*Concannen,* more aspiring Bard,
Climbs downwards, deeper by a Yard:
Smart JEMMY MOOR with Vigor drops,
The Rest pursue as thick as Hops:                             400
With Heads to Points the Gulph they enter,
Linkt perpendicular to the Centre:
And as their Heels elated rise,
Their Heads attempt the nether Skies.

    O, what Indignity and Shame
To prostitute the Muse's Name,
By flatt'ring Kings whom Heaven design'd
The Plagues and Scourges of Mankind.
Bred up in Ignorance and Sloth,
And ev'ry Vice that nurses both.                              410

    Fair *Britain* in thy Monarch blest,
Whose Virtues bear the strictest Test;
Whom never *Faction* cou'd bespatter,
Nor *Minister,* nor *Poet* flatter.
What Justice in rewarding Merit?
What Magnanimity of Spirit?
What Lineaments divine we trace
Thro' all his Figure, Mien, and Face;
Tho' Peace with Olive bind his Hands,
Confest the conqu'ring Hero stands.                           420

393. *Vide* The Treatise on the Profound, and Mr. Pope's *Dunciad.*

396. In the London Edition, instead of *Laureat,* was maliciously inserted Mr. *Fielding,* for whose ingenious Writings the supposed Author hath manifested a great Esteem.

*Hydaspes*, *Indus*, and the *Ganges*,
Dread from his Hand impending Changes.
From him the *Tartar*, and *Chinese*,
Short by the Knees intreat for Peace.
The *Consort* of his Throne and Bed,
A perfect Goddess born and bred.
Appointed sov'reign Judge to sit
On Learning, Eloquence and Wit.
Our eldest Hope, divine *Iülus*,
(Late, very late, O, may he rule us.)     430
What early Manhood has he shown,
Before his downy Beard was grown!
Then think, what Wonders will be done
By going on as he begun;
An Heir for *Britain* to secure
As long as Sun and Moon endure.

    The Remnant of the royal Blood,
Comes pouring on me like a Flood.
Bright Goddesses, in Number five;
Duke *William*, sweetest Prince alive.     440

    Now sing the *Minister* of *State*,
Who shines alone, without a Mate.
Observe with what majestick Port
This *Atlas* stands to prop the Court:
Intent the Publick Debts to pay,
Like prudent *Fabius* by *Delay*.
Thou great Vicegerent of the King,
Thy Praises ev'ry Muse shall sing.
In all Affairs thou sole Director,
Of Wit and Learning chief Protector;     450
Tho' small the Time thou hast to spare,
The Church is thy peculiar Care.
Of pious Prelates what a Stock
You chuse to rule the Sable-flock.
You raise the Honour of the Peerage,
Proud to attend you at the Steerage.

424. Genibus minor.
446. *Fabius*. Unus Homo nobis Cunctando restituit rem.

You dignify the noble Race,
Content yourself with humbler Place.
Now Learning, Valour, Virtue, Sense,
To Titles give the sole Pretence.                    460
*St. George* beheld thee with Delight,
Vouchsafe to be an azure Knight,
When on thy Breast and Sides *Herculean*,
He fixt the *Star* and *String Cerulean*.


    Say, Poet, in what other Nation,
Shone ever such a Constellation.
Attend ye *Popes*, and *Youngs*, and *Gays*,
And tune your Harps, and strow your Bays.
Your Panegyricks here provide,
You cannot err on Flatt'ry's Side.                   470
Above the Stars exalt your Stile,
You still are low ten thousand Mile.
On *Lewis* all his Bards bestow'd,
Of Incense many a thousand Load;
But *Europe* mortify'd his Pride,
And swore the fawning Rascals ly'd:
Yet what the World refus'd to *Lewis*,
Apply'd to George exactly true is:
Exactly true! Invidious Poet!
'Tis fifty thousand Times below it.                  480


    Translate me now some Lines, if you can,
From *Virgil*, *Martial*, *Ovid*, *Lucan*;
They could all Pow'r in Heaven divide,
And do no Wrong to either Side:
They teach you how to split a Hair,
Give George and *Jove* an equal Share.
Yet, why should we be lac'd so straight;
I'll give my Monarch Butter-weight.
And Reason good; for many a Year
Jove never intermeddl'd here:                        490
Nor, tho' his Priests be duly paid,
Did ever we *desire* his Aid:

    486. Divisum Imperium cum Jove Cæsar habet.

We now can better do without him,
Since *Woolston* gave us Arms to rout him.
* * * * * *Cætera desiderantur* * * * * *

The following are cancelled lines of 'On Poetry: A Rapsody' given either
by Scott, or Orrery, or by both. The numbers indicate the line of the printed
version which, in each instance, precedes the position intended for the cancelled
passage. All six passages are found, except the third couplet, in a contemporary
transcript in the Huntington Library, Acc. No. 81494, Vol. II.

164 [Orrery only]
    A House of Peers, or Gaming Crew,
    A griping Monarch, or a Jew.
186 [Scott only]
    And may you ever have the luck
    To rhyme almost as ill as Duck;
    And, though you never learn'd to scan verse,
    Come out with some lampoon on D'Anvers.
190 [Orrery and Scott]
    Display the blessings of the Nation,
    And praise the whole Administration,
    Extoll yᵉ Bench of Bishops round,
    Who at them rail bid God Confound:
    To Bishop-Haters answer thus
    (The only Logick us'd by Us)
    What tho' they don't believe in Christ
    Deny them Protestants—thou ly'st.

204 [Scott only]
    His panegyrics then are ceased,
    He's grown a tyrant, dunce, and beast.

410 [Orrery and Scott]
    Perhaps you say Augustus shines
    Immortal made in Virgil's Lines,
    And Horace brought yᵉ tunefull Choir
    To sing his Virtues on yᵉ Lyre,
    Without reproach for flattery; true
    Because their Praises were his due

Printed from the Orrery papers in Harvard College Library; and the second
edition of Swift's *Works*, ed. Scott, 1824; with corrections from the Huntington
transcript.

For in those Ages Kings we find,
Were Animals of human kind,
But now go search all Europe round
Among y^e savage Monsters crown'd          [10]
With Vice polluting every Throne
(I mean all Kings except our own,)
In vain you make y^e strictest View
To find a King in all y^e Crew,
With whom a Footman out of Place
Wou'd not conceive a high disgrace
A burning Shame, a crying Sin
To take, his mornings Cup of Gin.
Thus all are destin'd to obey
Some Beast of Burthen or of Prey          [20]
Tis sung Prometheus forming Man
Thro' all the brutal Species ran,
Each proper Quality to find
Adapted for a human Mind,
A mingled Mass of Good & Bad,
The worst & best that could be had
Then from a Clay of Mixture base
He shap'd a King to rule y^e Race
Endow'd with Gifts from every Brute
Which best y^e regal Nature suit,          [30]
Thus think on Kings, y^e Name denotes
Hogs, Asses, Wolves, Baboons, & Goats
To represent in figure just
Sloth, Folly, Rapine, Mischief, Lust
O! were they all but Neb'chadnazzars
What Herds of Kings would turn to Grazers.

416 [Orrery only]
How well his publick Thrift is shewn?
All coffers full except his own.

# A *LOVE SONG*

## In the *MODERN* Taste

### Written in the Year 1733

### I

FLUTT'RING spread thy purple Pinions,
  Gentle *Cupid* o'er my Heart;
I a Slave in thy Dominions;
  Nature must give Way to Art.

### II

Mild *Arcadians*, ever blooming,
  Nightly nodding o'er your Flocks,
See my weary Days consuming,
  All beneath yon flow'ry Rocks.

### III

Thus the *Cyprian* Goddess weeping,
  Mourn'd *Adonis*, darling Youth:          10
Him the Boar in Silence creeping,
  Gor'd with unrelenting Tooth.

### IV

*Cynthia*, tune harmonious Numbers;
  Fair Discretion string the Lyre;
Sooth[e] my ever-waking Slumbers:
  Bright *Apollo* lend thy Choir.

### V

Gloomy *Pluto*, King of Terrors,
  Arm'd in adamantine Chains,
Lead me to the Chrystal Mirrors,
  Wat'ring soft *Elysian* Plains.          20

Printed from *Poems*, 1735.

## VI

Mournful Cypress, verdant Willow,
  Gilding my *Aurelia*'s Brows,
*Morpheus* hov'ring o'er my Pillow,
  Hear me pay my dying Vows.

## VII

Melancholly smooth *Meander*,
  Swiftly purling in a Round,
On thy Margin Lovers wander,
  With thy flow'ry Chaplets crown'd.

## VIII

Thus when *Philomela* drooping,
  Softly seeks her silent Mate;                30
See the Bird of *Juno* stooping.
  Melody resigns to Fate.

# THE
# Hardship put upon LADIES

### Written in the Year 1733

POOR Ladies! though their Bus'ness be to play,
  'Tis hard they must be busy Night and Day:
Why should they want the Privilege of Men,
And take some small Diversions now and then?
Had Women been the Makers of our Laws;
(And why they were not, I can see no Cause;)
The Men should slave at Cards from Morn to Night;
And Female Pleasures be to read and write.

Printed from *Poems*, 1735.

# On the Words—Brother Protestants, and Fellow Christians, *so familiarly used by the Advocates for the Repeal of the* Test Act *in* Ireland, 1733

*The following Poem having been printed in London, we have thought proper to insert it here, not doubting but it will be acceptable to our Readers; although we cannot say who is the Author.*

AN Inundation, says the Fable,
O'erflow'd a Farmer's Barn and Stable;
Whole Ricks of Hay and Stacks of Corn,
Were down the sudden Current born;
While Things of heterogeneous Kind,
Together float with Tide and Wind;
The generous Wheat forgot its Pride,
And sail'd with Litter Side by Side;
Uniting all, to shew their Amity,
As in a general Calamity.                                        10
A Ball of new-dropt Horse's Dung,
Mingling with Apples in the Throng,
Said to the Pippin, plump, and prim,
*See, Brother, how we Apples swim.*


THUS *Lamb*, renown'd for cutting Corns,
An offer'd Fee from *Radcliff* scorns;
*Not for the World—we Doctors, Brother,*
*Must take no Fee of one another.*
Thus to a Dean some Curate Sloven,
Subscribes, *Dear Sir, your Brother loving.*                    20
Thus all the Footmen, Shoe-boys, Porters,
About St. *James*'s, cry, *We Courtiers.*
Thus *Horace* in the House will prate,
*Sir, we the Ministers of State.*

Printed from *Poems*, 1735.

Thus at the Bar that Booby *Bettesworth,*
Tho' Half a Crown o'er-pays his Sweat's Worth;
Who knows in Law, nor Text, nor Margent,
Calls *Singleton* his Brother Serjeant.
And thus Fanatic Saints, tho' neither in
Doctrine, or Discipline our Brethren,  30
Are *Brother Protestants and Christians,*
As much as *Hebrews* and *Philistines*:
But in no other Sense, than Nature
Has made a Rat our Fellow-Creature.
Lice from your Body suck their Food;
But is a Louse your Flesh and Blood?
Tho' born of human Filth and Sweat, it
May well be said Man did beget it.
But Maggots in your Nose and Chin,
As well may claim you for their Kin.  40

YET Criticks may object, why not?
Since Lice are Brethren to a *Scot*:
Which made our Swarm of Sects determine
Employments for their Brother Vermin.
But be they *English, Irish, Scottish,*
What Protestant can be so sottish,
While o'er the Church these Clouds are gathering,
To call a Swarm of Lice his Brethren?

As *Moses,* by divine Advice,
In *Egypt* turn'd the Dust to Lice;  50
And as our Sects, by all Descriptions,
Have Hearts more harden'd than *Egyptians*;
As from the trodden Dust they spring,
And, turn'd to Lice, infest the King:
For Pity's Sake it would be just,
A *Rod* should turn them back to *Dust.*

LET Folks in high, or holy Stations,
Be proud of owning such Relations;
Let Courtiers hug them in their Bosom,
As if they were afraid to lose 'em:  60

While I, with humble *Job*, had rather,
Say to Corruption—*Thou'rt my Father*.
For he that has so little Wit,
To nourish Vermin, may be *bit*.

# EPIGRAMS

## ON THE

## BUSTS in RICHMOND HERMITAGE

*On the Hermitage at Richmond*

LEWIS the Living Learned fed,
And rais'd the scientific Head:
Our frugal Queen to save her Meat,
Exalts the Heads that cannot eat.

*A Conclusion*
*Drawn from an Epigram on the Queen*
*To the Drapier*

SINCE Anna, whose Bounty thy Merits had fed,
E'er her own was laid low, hath exalted thy Head,
And since our good Queen to the Wise is so just,
To raise Heads for such, as are humbled in Dust:
I wonder, good Man, that you are not envaulted:
Prithee, go, and be dead, and be doubly exalted.

Printed from Eng. MS. 659, John Rylands Library. This manuscript consists of two leaves addressed to Swift as Dean of St. Patrick's. The communication is undated. Above the address is written, apparently in Swift's hand, 'On the Hermitage'. On the recto of the inner leaf, in the same hand as the address, appear the first two of the epigrams printed by Deane Swift. Underneath Swift has written and scored out two lines,

'To bury me is not so just
I'm humbled e'er I meet the dust,'

and beneath these the third of the epigrams as printed by Deane Swift.

## SWIFT'S EPIGRAM

HER Majesty never shall be my Exalter
And yet she would raise me I know,—by a halter


THE

# YAHOO'S OVERTHROW;

## OR

The KEVAN BAYL'S NEW BALLAD,

upon Serjeant Kite's insulting the Dean

To the Tune of *Derry down*

JOLLY boys of St. Kevans, St. Patrick's, Donore,
    And Smithfield, I'll tell you, if not told before,
How Bettesworth, that booby, and Scoundrel in grain,
Hath insulted us all by insulting the Dean.
    *Knock him down, down, down, knock him down.*

The Dean and his merits we ev'ry one know,
But this skip of a Lawyer, where the De'el did he grow?
How greater's his merit at four Courts or House,
Than the barking of Towzer, or leap of a louse?
    *Knock him down, &c.*          10

That he came from the Temple, his morals do show,
But where his deep law is, few mortals yet know:
His rhet'ric, bombast, silly jests, are by far
More like to lampooning than pleading at bar.
    *Knock him down, &c.*

This pedlar, at speaking and making of laws,
Hath met with returns of all sorts but applause;

Printed from *Works, 4to, Vol. VIII* (2), London, 1765.

Has, with noise and odd gestures, been prating some years,
What honester folks never durst for their ears.
            *Knock him down*, &c.        20

Of all sizes and sorts, the Fanatical crew
Are his Brother Protestants, good men and true;
Red hat, and blue bonnet, and turbant's the same,
What the De'el is't to him whence the Devil they came?
            *Knock him down*, &c.

Hobbes, Tindal, and Woolston, and Collins, and Nayler,
And Muggleton, Toland, and Bradley the taylor,
Are Christians alike; and it may be averr'd,
He's a Christian as good as the rest of the herd.
            *Knock him down*, &c.        30

He only the rights of the clergy debates,
Their rights! their importance! We'll set on new rates
On their tythes at half-nothing, their priesthood at less:
What's next to be voted with ease you may guess.
            *Knock him down*, &c.

At length his Old Master (I need not him name)
To this damnable Speaker had long ow'd a shame;
When his speech came abroad, he paid him off clean,
By leaving him under the pen of the Dean.
            *Knock him down*, &c.        40

He kindled, as if the whole Satire had been
The oppression of Virtue, not wages of Sin:
He began as he bragg'd, with a rant and a roar;
He bragg'd how he bounc'd, and he swore how he swore.
            *Knock him down*, &c.

Tho' he cring'd to his Deanship in very low strains,
To others he boasted of knocking out brains,
And slitting of noses, and cropping of ears,
While his own ass's Zaggs were more fit for the shears.
            *Knock him down*, &c.        50

On this Worrier of Deans whene'er we can hit,
We'll show him the way how to crop and to slit;

We'll teach him some better address to afford
To the Dean of all Deans, tho' he wears not a sword.
　　　　　　*Knock him down, &c.*

We'll colt him thro' Kevan, St. Patrick's, Donore,
And Smithfield, as Rap was ne'er colted before;
We'll oil him with kennel, and powd'r him with grains,
A modus right fit for insulters of Deans.
　　　　　　*Knock him down, &c.*　　　　60

And, when this is over, we'll make him amends,
To the Dean he shall go; they shall kiss, and be friends:
But how? Why, the Dean shall to him disclose
A face for to kiss, without eyes, ears, or nose.
　　　　　　*Knock him down, &c.*

If you say this is hard, on a man that is reckon'd
That serjeant at law, whom we call Kite the Second,
You mistake; for a Slave, who will coax his superiors,
May be proud to be licking a great man's posteriors.
　　　　　　*Knock him down, &c.*　　　　70

What care we how high runs his passion or pride?
Tho' his soul he despises, he values his hide:
Then fear not his tongue, his sword, or his knife;
He'll take his revenge on his innocent wife.
　　　*Knock him down, down, down,—keep him down.*


# AN EPIGRAM

### Inscribed to the Honourable Sergeant Kite

IN your indignation what mercy appears,
While Jonathan's threaten'd with loss of his ears;
For who would not think it a much better choice,
By your knife to be mangled than rack'd with your voice.
If truly you [would] be reveng'd on the parson,
Command his attendance while you act your farce on,
Instead of your maiming, your shooting, or banging,
Bid *Povey* secure him while you are haranguing.

Printed from *Works*, ed. Scott, Vol. X, 1814.

Had this been your method to torture him, long since,
He had cut his own ears to be deaf to your nonsense.    10

# ON THE
# ARCHBISHOP of CASHEL, and
# BETTESWORTH

DEAR Dick, prithee tell by what passion you move?
    The world is in doubt, whether hatred or love;
And, while at good Cashel you rail with such spite,
They shrewdly suspect it is all but a bite.
You certainly know, tho' so loudly you vapour,
His spite cannot wound, who attempted the Drapier.
Then, prithee reflect, take a word of advice;
And, as your old wont is, change sides in a trice:
On his virtues hold forth; 'tis the very best way;
And say of the man what all honest men say.    10
But if, still obdurate, your anger remains,
If still your foul bosom more rancour contains;
Say then more than they; nay, lavishly flatter,
'Tis your gross panegyrics alone can bespatter.
For thine, my dear Dick, give me leave to speak plain,
Like a very foul mop, dirty more than they clean.

Printed from *Works, 4to, Vol. VIII* (2), London, 1765.

# *Written by the Reverend Dr.* Swift. *On his own* Deafness

VERTICOSUS, *inops, surdus, male gratus amicis;*
    *Non campana sonans, tonitru non ab Jove missum,*
*Quod mage mirandum, saltem si credere fas est,*
*Non clamosa meas mulier jam percutit aures.*

The Latin and English text is here printed from *Works, Vol. VIII*, Dublin, 1746. 'Verticosus' (originally 'Vertiginosus') is restored from the MS. draft, HM 14338, in the Huntington Library.

D EAF, giddy, helpless, left alone,
    To all my Friends a Burthen grown,
No more I hear my Church's Bell,
Than if it rang out for my Knell:
At Thunder now no more I start,
Than at the Rumbling of a Cart:
Nay, what's incredible, alack!
I hardly hear a Woman's Clack.

## Verses spoken extempore by Dean Swift on his Curate's Complaint of hard Duty

I MARCH'D three miles thro' scorching sand,
  With zeal in heart, and notes in hand;
I rode four more to great St. *Mary*;
Using four legs when two were weary.
To three fair virgins I did tie men
In the close bands of pleasing hymen.
I dipp'd two babes in holy-water,
And purify'd their mothers after.
Within an hour, and eke a half,
I preached three congregations deaf,                    10
Which, thundring out with lungs long-winded,
I chopp'd so fast, that few there minded.
My Emblem, the labourious sun,    ⎫
Saw all these mighty labours done,  ⎬
Before one race of his was run;    ⎭
All this perform'd by *Robert Hewit*,
What mortal else cou'd e'er go through it!

Printed from *The Gentleman's Magazine*, Dec. 1734.

# THE
# PARSON'S CASE

THAT you, friend *Marcus*, like a stoick
 Can wish to die, in strain heroick,
No real fortitude implies:
Yet, all must own, thy wish is wise.
 Thy curate's place, thy fruitful wife,
Thy busy, drudging scene of life,
Thy insolent illit'rate vicar,
Thy want of all-consoling liquor,
Thy thread-bare gown, thy cassock rent,
Thy credit sunk, thy money spent,       10
Thy week made up of fasting days,
Thy grate unconscious of a blaze,
And, to compleat thy other curses,
The quarterly demands of nurses,
Are ills you wisely wish to leave,
And fly for refuge to the grave:
And, O what virtue you express
In wishing such afflictions less!
 But, now shou'd fortune shift the scene,
And make thy curate-ship a dean;       20
Or some rich benefice provide,
To pamper luxury and pride;
With labour small, and income great;
With chariot less for use than state;
With swelling scarf, and glossy gown,
And license to reside in town;
To shine, where all the gay resort,
At consort, coffeehouse, or court;
And weekly persecute his grace
With visits, or to beg a place;       30
With underlings thy flock to teach,
With no desire to pray or preach;

Printed from *The Gentleman's Magazine*, Dec. 1734.

With haughty spouse in vesture fine,
With plenteous meals, and gen'rous wine;
Wou'dst thou not wish, in so much ease,
Thy years as num'rous as thy days?

# THE
# DEAN and DUKE

JAMES Bruges & the Dean had long been friends,
   James is be-duk'd; : of course their friendshp ends
But, sure the Dean deserves a sharp Rebuke
From knowing James, to boast he knows the Duke.
But, since just Heav'n the Dukes ambition mocks
Since all he got by Fraud, is lost by Stocks,
His wings are clipp't; he tryes no more in vain
With Bands of Fidlers to extend his Treyn.
Since he no more can build, and plant, & revell,
The Duke and Dean seem near upon a levell.      10
Oh! wer't thou not a Duke, my good Duke Humphry,
From Bayliffs claws thou scarce cou'd keep thy Bum free.
A Duke to know a Dean! go smooth your Frown,
Thy Brother (far thy Betters) wore a Gown.
Well: but a Duke thou art; so pleas'd the King
Oh! would His Majesty but add a String.

Printed from Swift's autograph, Forster Collection, No. 527.

# On Dr. RUNDLE

### Bishop of DERRY

MAKE *Rundle* Bishop; fye for Shame!
   An *Arrian* to usurp the Name!
A Bishop in the Isle of Saints!
How will his Brethren make Complaints?

Printed from *Works, Vol. X*, Dublin, 1762.

Dare any of the mitred Host,
Confer on him the HOLY GHOST;
In Mother Church to breed a Variance,
By coupling *Orthodox* with *Arrians*?

YET, were he *Heathen*, *Turk* or *Jew*,
What is there in it strange or new?     10
For, let us hear the weak Pretence,
His Brethren find to take Offence;
Of whom there are but four at most,
Who know there is an HOLY GHOST:
The rest, who boast they have conferr'd it,
Like *Paul*'s *Ephesians*, never heard it;
And, when they gave it, well 'tis known,
They gave what never was their own.

*RUNDLE* a Bishop! well he may;
He's still a *Christian* more than they.     20

WE know the Subject of their Quarrels;
The Man has Learning, Sense and Morals.

THERE is a Reason still more weighty;
'Tis granted he believes a Deity.
Has ev'ry Circumstance to please us,
'Though Fools may doubt his Faith in Jesus.
But why shou'd he with that be loaded,
Now twenty Years from Court exploded?
And, is not this Objection odd
From Rogues who ne'er believ'd a GOD?     30
For Liberty a Champion stout,
'Though not so Gospel-ward devout.
While others hither sent to save us,
Came but to plunder and enslave us;
Nor ever own'd a Pow'r Divine,
But *Mammon*, and the *German* Line.

SAY, how did *Rundle* undermine 'em;
Who shew'd a better *Jus divinum*?
From antient Canons would not vary,
But thrice refus'd *Episcopari*.     40

Our Bishop's Predecessor, *Magus*,
Would offer all the Sands of *Tagus*;
Or sell his Children, House, and Lands,
For that one Gift to lay on Hands:
But all his Gold could not avail
To have the *Spirit* set to Sale.
Said surly *Peter*, *Magus*, prithee
Be gone: Thy Money perish with thee.
Were *Peter* now alive, perhaps
He might have found a Score of Chaps,          50
Could he but make his Gift appear
In Rents three thousand Pounds a Year.

Some fancy this Promotion odd,
As not the Handy-work of God;
Though ev'n the Bishops disappointed,
Must own it made by God's *Anointed*.
And well we know, The *Congee Regal*
Is more secure as well as legal[,]
Because our Lawyers all agree,
That Bishopricks are held in Fee.          60

Dear *Baldwin* chaste, and witty *Crosse*,
How sorely I lament your Loss?
That such a pair of wealthy Ninnies
Should slip your Time of dropping Guineas;
For, had you made the King your Debtor,
Your Title had been so much better.


# AN EPIGRAM

Friend Rundall fell with grievous bump,
  Upon his reverential rump.
Poor rump, thou hadst been better sped,
Had thou been join'd to Boulter's head.
An head so weighty and profound,
Would needs have kept thee from the ground.

Printed from *Works, Vol. XVI*, Dublin, 1767.

## *On a* Printer's *being sent to Newgate, by* ——

BETTER we all were in our Graves
  Than live in Slavery to Slaves,
Worse than the Anarchy at Sea,
Where Fishes on each other prey;
Where ev'ry Trout can make as high Rants
O'er his Inferiors as our Tyrants;
And swagger while the Coast is clear:
But should a lordly Pike appear,
Away you see the Varlet scud,
Or hide his coward Snout in Mud.                    10
Thus, if a Gudgeon meet a Roach
He dare not venture to approach;
Yet still has Impudence to rise,
And, like *Domitian*, leap at Flyes.

Printed from *Works, Vol. VIII*, Dublin, 1746.

# ON

# NOISY TOM

— *Qui promittit, cives, urbem, sibi curæ,*
*Imperium fore, et Italiam, et delubra Deorum;*
*Quo patre sit natus, num ignota matre inhonestus*
*Omnes mortales curare, & quærere cogit.*
*Tune Syri, Damæ, aut Dionysi filius audes*
*Dejicere e saxo cives, aut tradere Cadmo?*
                    HOR. Lib. 1. Sat 6. l. 34–39

Translated literally

Whoever promiseth (in the Senate) to take the City (of *Rome*)
and the Citizens under his Care, nay, the whole Empire, *Italy,*

Printed from *Works, Vol. X*, Dublin, 1762.

and the Temples of the Gods; such a Man compelleth all
Mortals curiously to enquire from what Father he sprung, and
whether his Mother were some obscure dishonourable Female.
(The People would cry out) What, thou, the Son of *Cyrus**, or
*Damas**, or *Dionysius**, dare thou cast our Citizens down the
*Tarpeian* Rock, or deliver them Prisoners to *Cadmus*.†


## PARAPHRASED

IF noisy *Tom* should in the Senate prate,
   That he would answer both for Church and State;
And, further to demonstrate his Affection,
Would take the Kingdom into his Protection:
All Mortals must be curious to enquire,
Who could this Coxcomb be, and who his Sire?
What! thou the Spawn of him who sham'd our Isle,
That Traitor, Assassin, Informer vile.
Though by the Female Side you proudly bring,
To mend your Breed, the Murderer of a King.        10
What was thy Grandsire but a Mountaineer,
Who held a Cabbin for ten Groats a Year;
Whose Master, *Moore*, preserv'd him from the Halter,
For stealing Cows, nor could he read the Psalter.
Durst thou, ungrateful, from the Senate chace
Thy Founder's Grandson and usurp his Place.

\* Usual Names of Slaves at Rome.

† *Cadmus* was a Lictor, an Officer who seized on Criminals, like a Constable, or Messenger of the House of Commons.

1. Sir Thomas Prendergast.

7. The Father of Sir Thomas Prendergast, who engaged in a Plot to murder King William III but, to avoid being hanged, turned Informer against his Associates, for which he was rewarded with a good Estate, and made a Baronet.

9. Cadogan's Family, &c.

11. A poor thieving Cottager under Mr. Moore, condemned at Clonmell Assizes to be hanged for stealing Cows.

13. The Grandfather of Guy Moore, Esq; who procured him a Pardon.

16. Guy Moore was fairly elected Member of Parliament for Clonmell; but Sir Thomas depending upon his Interest with a certain Party then prevailing, and since known by the Title of Parson-hunters, petitioned the House against him, out of which he was turned upon Pretence of Bribery, which the paying of his lawful Debts was then voted to be.

Just Heaven! to see the Dunghill dastard Brood
Survive in thee, and make the Proverb good.
Then vote a worthy Citizen to Jail,
In Spight to Justice, and refuse his Bail.          20


# A CHARACTER, PANEGYRIC, and DESCRIPTION of the LEGION CLUB

### Written in the Year, 1736

AS I strole the City, oft I
Spy a Building large and lofty,
Not a Bow-shot from the College,
Half the Globe from Sense and Knowledge.
By the prudent Architect
Plac'd against the Church direct;
Making good my Grandames Jest,
*Near the Church*—you know the rest.

TELL us, what this Pile contains?
Many a Head that holds no Brains.          10
These Demoniacs let me dub
With the Name of *Legion Club*.
Such Assemblies, you might swear,
Meet when Butchers bait a Bear;
Such a Noise, and such haranguing,
When a Brother Thief is hanging.
Such a Rout and such a Rabble
Run to hear Jackpudding gabble;
Such a Croud their Ordure throws
On a far less Villain's Nose.          20

Printed from *Works, Vol. X*, Dublin, 1762.

18. Save a Thief from the Gallows, and he will cut your Throat.

19. Mr. George Faulkner, a very honest and eminent Printer in Dublin, who was voted to Newgate upon a ridiculous Complaint of one Serjeant Bettesworth.

Could I from the Building's Top
Hear the rattling Thunder drop,
While the Devil upon the Roof,
If the Devil be Thunder Proof,
Should with Poker fiery-red
Crack the Stones, and melt the Lead;
Drive them down on every Scull,
While the Den of Thieves is full,
Quite destroy that Harpies Nest,
How might then our Isle be blest?                    30
For Divines allow, that God
Sometimes makes the Devil his Rod:
And the Gospel will inform us,
He can punish Sins enormous.


Yet should *Swift* endow the Schools
For his Lunatics and Fools,
With a Rood or two of Land,
I allow the Pile may stand.
You perhaps will ask me, why so?
But it is with this Proviso,                    40
Since the House is like to last,
Let a royal Grant be pass'd,
That the Club have Right to dwell
Each within his proper Cell;
With a Passage left to creep in,
And a Hole above for peeping.


Let them, when they once get in
Sell the Nation for a Pin;
While they sit a picking Straws
Let them rave of making Laws;                    50
While they never hold their Tongue,
Let them dabble in their Dung;
Let them form a grand Committee,
How to plague and starve the City;
Let them stare and storm and frown,
When they see a Clergy-Gown.

Let them, 'ere they crack a Louse,
Call for th'Orders of the House;
Let them with their gosling Quills,
Scribble senseless Heads of Bills;                    60
We may, while they strain their Throats,
Wipe our Arses with their Votes.


LET Sir *Tom*, that rampant Ass,
Stuff his Guts with Flax and Grass;
But before the Priest he fleeces
Tear the Bible all to Pieces.
At the Parsons, *Tom*, Halloo Boy,
Worthy Offspring of a Shoeboy,
Footman, Traytor, vile Seducer,
Perjur'd Rebel, brib'd Accuser;                       70
Lay the paltry Priviledge aside,
Sprung from Papists and a Regicide;
Fall a Working like a Mole,
Raise the Dirt about your Hole.


COME, assist me, Muse obedient,
Let us try some new Expedient;
Shift the Scene for half an Hour,
Time and Place are in thy Power.
Thither, gentle Muse, conduct me,
I shall ask, and you instruct me.                     80


SEE, the Muse unbars the Gate;
Hark, the Monkeys, how they prate!


ALL ye Gods, who rule the Soul
*Styx*, through Hell whose Waters roll!
Let me be allow'd to tell
What I heard in yonder Hell.

83. *ALL ye Gods,* . . . Virg. *Aen.* vi. 264 ff.
              '*Dii, quibus imperium est animarum,* &c.
              *Sit mihi fas audita loqui,* &c.'

NEAR the Door an entrance gapes,
Crouded round with antic Shapes;
*Poverty*, and *Grief*, and *Care*,
Causeless *Joy*, and true *Despair*;                    90
*Discord* periwigg'd with Snakes,
See the dreadful Strides she takes.

BY this odious Crew beset,
I began to rage and fret
And resolv'd to break their Pates,
'Ere we enter'd at the Gates;
Had not *Clio* in the Nick,
Whisper'd me, let down your Stick;
What, said I, is this the Mad-House?
These, she answer'd, are but Shadows,                   100
Phantoms, bodiless and vain,
Empty Visions of the Brain.

IN the Porch *Briareus* stands,
Shews a Bribe in all his Hands:
*Briareus* the Secretary,
But we Mortals call him *Cary*.
When the Rogues their Country fleece,
They may hope for Pence a Piece.

*CLIO*, who had been so wise
To put on a Fool's Disguise,                            110
To bespeak some Approbation,
And be thought a near Relation;

87. *NEAR the Door* . . . Ib. 273:
          '*Vestibulum ante ipsum primisque in faucibus Orci*
          *Luctus & ultrices, &c.*'
91. *Discord* . . . Ib. 280:
                    '*Discordia demens,*
          *Vipereum crinem vittis innexa cruentis.*'
93. *BY this odious Crew* . . . Ib. 290:
          '*Corripit hic subita trepidus formidine ferrum*
          *Aeneas, strictamque aciem venientibus offert.*'
97. *Had not Clio* . . . Virg *Aen.* vi. 292:
          '— *ni docta comes tenues sine corpore vitas.*'
103. *In the Porch Briareus stands.* Ib. 287:
          '*Et centumgeminus Briareus.*'

When she saw three hundred Brutes,
All involv'd in wild Disputes;
Roaring till their Lungs were spent,
Privilege of Parliament,
Now a new Misfortune feels,
Dreading to be laid by th' Heels.
Never durst a Muse before
Enter that Infernal Door;                    120
*Clio* stifled with the Smell,
Into Spleen and Vapours fell;
By the *Stygian* Steams that flew,
From the dire infectious Crew.
Not the Stench of Lake *Avernus*,
Could have more offended her Nose;
Had she flown but o'er the Top,
She would feel her Pinions drop,
And by Exhalations dire,
Though a Goddess[,] must expire.             130
In a Fright she crept away,
Bravely I resolved to stay.


  WHEN I saw the Keeper frown,
Tipping him with Half a Crown;
Now, said I, we are alone,
Name your Heroes one, by one.


  WHO is that Hell-featur'd Brawler,
Is it Satan? No, 'tis *Waller.*
In what Figure can a Bard dress
*Jack*, the Grandson of Sir *Hardress*?       140
Honest Keeper, drive him further,
In his Looks are Hell and Murther;
See the Scowling Visage drop,
Just as when he murther'd *Throp.*


  KEEPER, shew me where to fix
On the Puppy Pair of *Dicks*;
By their lanthorn Jaws and Leathern,
You might swear they both are Brethren:

*Dick Fitz-Baker, Dick* the Player,
Old Acquaintance, are you there?            150
Dear Companions hug and kiss,
Toast *old Glorious* in your Piss.
Tye them Keeper in a Tether,
Let them stare and stink together;
Both are apt to be unruly,
Lash them daily, lash them duly,
Though 'tis hopeless to reclaim them,
Scorpion Rods perhaps may tame them.

KEEPER, yon old Dotard smoke,
Sweetly snoring in his Cloak.            160
Who is he? 'Tis hum-drum *Wynne*,
Half encompass'd by his Kin:
There observe the Tribe of *Bingham*,
For he never fails to bring 'em;
While he sleeps the whole Debate,
They submissive round him wait;
Yet would gladly see the Hunks
In his Grave, and search his Trunks.
See they gently twitch his Coat,
Just to yawn, and give his Vote;            170
Always firm in his Vocation,
For the Court against the Nation.

THOSE are *Allens, Jack* and *Bob*,
First in every wicked Jobb,
Son and Brother to a Queer,
Brainsick Brute, they call a Peer.
We must give them better Quarter,
For their Ancestor trod Mortar;
And at *Hoath* to boast his Fame,
On a Chimney cut his Name.            180

THERE sit *Clements, Dilkes,* and *Harrison,*
How they swagger from their Garrison.
Such a Triplet could you tell
Where to find on this Side Hell?

*Harrison*, and *Dilkes*, and *Clements*,
Souse them in their own Ex-crements.
Every Mischief in their Hearts,
If they fail 'tis Want of Parts.


BLESS us, *Morgan*! Art thou there Man?
Bless mine Eyes! Art thou the Chairman?          190
Chairman to yon damn'd Committee!
Yet I look on thee with Pity.
Dreadful Sight! What[,] learned *Morgan*
Metamorphos'd to a Gorgan!
For thy horrid Looks, I own,
Half convert me to a Stone.
Hast thou been so long at School,
Now to turn a factious Tool!
*Alma Mater* was thy Mother,
Every young Divine thy Brother.          200
Thou a disobedient Varlet,
Treat thy Mother like a Harlot!
Thou, ungrateful to thy Teachers,
Who are all grown reverend Preachers!
*Morgan!* Would it not surprise one?
Turn thy Nourishment to Poison!
When you walk among your Books,
They reproach you with their Looks;
Bind them fast, or from the Shelves
They'll come down to right themselves:          210
*Homer, Plutarch, Virgil, Flaccus*,
All in Arms prepare to back us:
Soon repent, or put to Slaughter
Every *Greek* and *Roman* Author.
While you in your Faction's Phrase
Send the Clergy all to graze;
And to make your Project pass,
Leave them not a Blade of Grass.


How I want thee, humorous *Hogart*?
Thou I hear, a pleasant Rogue art;          220
Were but you and I acquainted,
Every Monster should be painted;

You should try your graving Tools
On this odious Group of Fools;
Draw the Beasts as I describe 'em,
Form their Features, while I gibe them;
Draw them like, for I assure you,
You will need no *Car'catura*;
Draw them so that we may trace
All the Soul in every Face.                    230
Keeper, I must now retire,
You have done what I desire:
But I feel my Spirits spent,
With the Noise, the Sight, the Scent.

   PRAY be patient, you shall find
Half the best are still behind:
You have hardly seen a Score,
I can shew two hundred more.
Keeper, I have seen enough,
Taking then a Pinch of Snuff;                  240
I concluded, looking round 'em,
May their God, the Devil confound 'em.

# From Catullus

Lesbia mi dicit semper malè &c.

LESBIA for ever on me rails;
  To talk on me she never fails:
Yet, hang me, but for all her Art;
  I find that I have gain'd her Heart:
My proof is this: I plainly see
  The Case is just the same with me:
I curse her ev'ry hour sincerely;
  Yet, hang me, but I love her dearly.

Printed from Swift's autograph. Coll. Dr. Dallas Pratt.

# AY AND NO

## A TALE FROM DUBLIN

### Written in 1737

AT *Dublin's* high feast sat Primate and Dean,
Both dress'd like divines, with band and face clean.
Quoth *Hugh* of *Armagh*, "The mob is grown bold."
"Ay, ay," quoth the Dean, "the cause is old gold."
"No, no," quoth the Primate, "if causes we sift,
"This mischief arises from witty Dean *Swift*."
The smart-one replied, "There's no wit in the case;
"And nothing of that ever troubled your Grace.
"Though with your state-sieve your own notions you split,
"A *Boulter* by name is no *bolter* of wit.          10
"It's matter of weight, and a mere money-job;
"But the lower the coin, the higher the mob.
"Go tell your friend *Bob* and the other great folk,
"That sinking the coin is a dangerous joke.
"The *Irish* dear joys have enough common sense,
"To treat gold reduc'd like *Wood's* copper pence.
"It's a pity a Prelate should die without law;
"But if I say the word—take care of *Armagh*!"

Printed from *Supplement to Dr. Swift's Works*, ed. Nichols, 1776.

# RIDDLES

## BY
## SWIFT and his FRIENDS

# ÆNIGMA

### By Mr. *S. T.*

F*ROM* India'*s burning Clime I'm brought,*
  *With cooling Gales, like* Zephirs *fraught;*
*Not* Iris, *when she paints the Sky,*
*Can shew more different Hues than I;*
*Nor can she change her Form so fast,*
*I'm now a Sail, and now a Mast;*
*I here am Red, and there am Green,*
*A Begger there, and here a Queen.*
*I sometimes live in House of Hair,*
*And oft in Hand of Lady Fair;*            10
*I please the Young, I grace the Old,*
*And am at once both Hot and Cold:*
*Say what I am, then if you can*
*But find the Rhime, and you're the Man.*

## The *Ænigma* in the last Mercury explain'd

### By Mr. *S. W.*

Y*OUR House of Hair and Lady's Hand*
  *At first did put me to a stand;*
*I have it now —— 'Tis plain enough,*
*Your hairy Business is a Muff.*
*Your Engine fraught with cooling Gales,*
*At once so like to Masts or Sails,*
*Your Thing of various Shape and Hue,*
*Must be some painted Toy I knew;*
*And for the Rhime, to you're the Man,*
*What fits it better than a Fan.*            10

Printed from *The Muses Mercury*, April, May, 1707.

# ÆNIGMA

## I

I'M wealthy and poor,
    I'm empty and full,
I'm humble and proud,
I'm witty and dull.

## II

I'm foul, and yet fair,
I'm old, and yet young
I lie with Moll Kerr,
And toast Mrs. Long.

## The Ænigma in the last Mercury explain'd

### By Mr. F——

IN Rigging he's rich, tho in Pocket he's Poor.
    He cringes to Courtiers, and cocks to the Cits,
Like twenty he dresses, but looks like threescore,
    He's a Wit to the Fools, and a Fool to the Wits.

Of Wisdom he's empty, but full of Conceit,
    He paints and perfumes, while he rots with the Scab.
'Tis a Beau you may swear by his Sense and his Gate,
    He boasts of a Beauty, and lies with a Drab.

Printed from The Muses Mercury, May, June, 1707. Doubtfully by Swift.

# A RIDDLE

Written in the Year 1724

IN Youth exalted high in Air,
Or bathing in the Waters fair;
Nature to form me took Delight,
And clad my Body all in White:
My Person tall, and slender Waste,
On either Side with Fringes grac'd;
Till me that Tyrant Man espy'd,
And drag'd me from my Mother's Side:
No Wonder now I look so thin;
The Tyrant strip't me to the Skin:          10
My Skin he flay'd, my Hair he cropt:
At Head and Foot my Body lopt:
And then, with Heart more hard than Stone,
He pick't my Marrow from the Bone.
To vex me more, he took a Freak,
To slit my Tongue, and made me speak:
But, that which wonderful appears,
I speak to Eyes and not to Ears.
He oft employs me in Disguise,
And makes me tell a Thousand Lyes:          20
To me he chiefly gives in Trust
To please his Malice, or his Lust.
From me no Secret he can hide;
I see his Vanity and Pride:
And my Delight is to expose
His Follies to his greatest Foes.

Printed from *Poems*, 1735, which has the following note: 'About Nine or Ten Years ago, some ingenious Gentlemen, Friends to the Author, used to entertain themselves with writing Riddles, and send them to him and their other Acquaintance, Copies of which ran about, and some of them were printed both here and in England. The Author, at his leisure Hours, fell into the same Amusement; although it be said that he thought them of no great Merit, Entertainment, or Use. However, by the Advice of some Persons, for whom the Author hath a great Esteem, and who were pleased to send us the Copies, we have ventured to print the few following, as we have done two or three before, and which are allowed to be genuine; because, we are informed that several good Judges have a Taste for such Kind of Compositions.'

ALL Languages I can command,
Yet not a Word I understand.
Without my Aid, the best Divine
In Learning would not know a Line:        30
The Lawyer must forget his Pleading,
The Scholar could not shew his Reading.
Nay; Man, my Master, is my Slave:
I give Command to kill or save.
Can grant ten Thousand Pounds a Year,
And make a Beggar's Brat a Peer.

BUT, while I thus my Life relate,
I only hasten on my Fate.
My Tongue is black, my Mouth is furr'd,
I hardly now can force a Word.        40
I dye unpity'd and forgot;
And on some Dunghill left to rot.

42. A Pen.

# ANOTHER

ALL-ruling Tyrant of the Earth,
To vilest Slaves I owe my Birth.
How is the greatest Monarch blest,
When in my gaudy Liv'ry drest!
No haughty Nymph has Pow'r to run
From me; or my Embraces shun.
Stabb'd to the Heart, condemn'd to Flame,
My Constancy is still the same.
The fav'rite Messenger of *Jove*,
And *Lemnian* God consulting strove,        10
To make me glorious to the Sight
Of Mortals, and the Gods Delight.
Soon would their Altars Flame expire,
If I refus'd to lend them Fire.

14. Gold.

## ANOTHER

B Y Fate *exalted high* in Place;
  Lo, here I stand with *double Face*;
*Superior* none on Earth I find;
But see *below me* all Mankind.
Yet, as it oft attends the Great,
I almost *sink* with my own *Weight*;
At every *Motion* undertook,
The Vulgar all consult my *Look*.
I sometimes give Advice in *Writing*,
But never of my own *inditing*.                    10

  I AM a Courtier in my Way;
For those who *rais'd* me, I *betray*;
And some give out, that I entice
To Lust and Luxury, and Dice:
Who Punishments on me inflict,
Because they find their Pockets pick't.

  BY riding *Post* I lose my Health;
And only to get others Wealth.

18. Gold.

## ANOTHER

B ECAUSE I am by Nature *blind*,
  I wisely chuse to walk *behind*;
However, to avoid Disgrace,
I let no Creature see my *Face*.
My *Words* are few, but spoke with *Sense*:
And yet my *speaking* gives Offence:
Or, if to *whisper* I presume,
The Company will fly the Room.

By all the World I am *oppress't*,
And my *Oppression* gives them *Rest*.                    10


   THROUGH me, though sore against my Will,
*Instructors* ev'ry Art instill.
By Thousands I am *sold* and *bought*,
Who neither get, nor lose a Groat;
For none, alas, by me can gain,
But those who give me *greatest Pain*.
Shall Man presume to be my Master,
Who's but my *Caterer* and *Taster*?
Yet, though I always have my Will,
I'm but a meer *Depender* still:                          20
An humble *Hanger-on* at best;
Of whom all People *make a Jest*.


   IN me, Detractors seek to find
Two Vices of a diff'rent Kind:
I'm too *profuse* some Cens'rers cry,
And all I get, I *let it fly*:
While others give me many a Curse,
Because too *close* I hold my *Purse*.
But this I know, in either Case
They dare not *charge* me to my *Face*:                   30
'Tis true, indeed, sometimes I *save*,
Sometimes *run out* of all I have;
But when the Year is at an End,
Computing what I *get* and *spend*,
My *Goings out*, and *Comings in*,
I cannot find I lose or win,
And therefore, all that know me, say
I justly keep the *middle Way*.
I'm always by my Betters led;
I last *get up*, am first *a-bed*;                        40
Though, if I rise *before my Time*,
The Learn'd in Sciences sublime,
Consult the Stars, and thence foretell
*Good Luck* to those with whom I dwell.

44. The Posteriors.

# ANOTHER

THE Joy of Man, the Pride of Brutes,
Domestick Subject for Disputes,
Of Plenty thou the Emblem fair,
Adorn'd by Nymphs with all their Care:
I saw thee rais'd to high Renown,
Supporting half the *British* Crown;
And often have I seen thee grace
The chaste *Diana*'s infant Face;
And whensoe're you please to shine,
Less useful is her Light than thine; 10
Thy num'rous Fingers know their Way,
And oft in *Celia*'s Tresses play.

To place thee in another View,
I'll shew the World strange Things and true;
What Lords and Dames of high Degree,
May justly claim their Birth from thee;
The Soul of Man with Spleen you vex;
Of Spleen you cure the Female Sex.
Thee, for a Gift, the Courtier sends
With Pleasure to his special Friends: 20
He gives; and with a gen'rous Pride,
Contrives all Means the Gift to hide:
Nor oft can the Receiver know
Whether he has the Gift or no.
On Airy Wings you take your Flight,
And fly unseen both Day and Night;
Conceal your Form with various Tricks;
And few know how and where you fix.
Yet, some who ne'er bestow'd thee, boast
That they to others give thee most: 30
Mean Time, the Wise a Question start,
If thou a real Being art;

Or, but a Creature of the Brain,
That gives imaginary Pain:
But the sly Giver better knows thee;
Who feels true Joys when he bestows thee.

36. A Horn.


# ANOTHER

THOUGH I, alas! a Pris'ner be,
My Trade is, Pris'ners to set free.
No Slave his Lord's Commands obeys,
With such *insinuating* Ways.
My Genius *piercing, sharp* and *bright*,
Wherein the Men of Wit delight.
The Clergy keep me for their Ease,
And *turn* and *wind* me as they please.
A new and wond'rous Art I show
Of raising Spirits from below;                    10
In *Scarlet* some, and some in *White*;
They rise, walk round, yet never fright.
In at each *Mouth* the *Spirits* pass,
Distinctly seen as through a Glass:
O'er *Head* and *Body* make a Rout,
And drive at last all *Secrets* out:
And still, the more I show my Art,
The more they *open every Heart*.


A GREATER Chymist none, than I,
Who from *Materials hard and dry*,             20
Have taught Men to *extract* with Skill,
More precious Juice than from a Still.


ALTHOUGH I'm often *out of Case*,
I'm not asham'd to show my *Face*,
Though at the Tables of the Great,
I near the Side-board take my Seat;

Yet, the plain Squire, when Dinner's done,
Is never pleas'd till I make one:
He kindly bids me near him stand;
And often takes me by the *Hand*.　　　30

　I TWICE a Day a *hunting* go;
Nor ever fail to *seize my Foe*;
And, when I have him by the *Pole*,
I drag him upwards from his *Hole*.
Though some are of so stubborn Kind,
I'm forc'd to leave a *Limb* behind.

　I HOURLY wait some fatal End;
For, I can *break*, but scorn to *bend*.

38. A Corkscrew.

# ANOTHER

## *The* Gulph *of all* human Possessions

Written in the Year 1724

COME hither and behold the Fruits,
　Vain Man, of all thy vain Pursuits.
Take wise Advice, and *look behind*,
Bring all *past* Actions to thy Mind.
Here you may see, as in a Glass,
How soon all human Pleasures pass.
How will it mortify thy Pride,
To turn the true impartial Side!
How will your Eyes contain their Tears,
When all the sad *Reverse* appears!　　　10

　THIS Cave within its Womb confines
The last Result of all Designs:
Here lye deposited the Spoils
Of busy Mortals endless Toils:

Here, with an easy Search we find
The *foul Corruptions* of Mankind.
The wretched Purchase here behold
Of Traytors who their Country sold.

    THIS Gulph insatiable imbibes
The Lawyer's Fees, the Statesman's **Bribes**.     20
Here, in their proper Shape and Mien,
Fraud, Perjury, and Guilt are seen.

    NECESSITY, the Tyrant's Law,
All human Race must hither draw:
All prompted by the same *Desire*,
The vig'rous Youth, and aged Sire:
Behold, the Coward, and the Brave,
The haughty Prince, the humble Slave,
Physician, Lawyer, and Divine,
All make *Oblations* at this Shrine.     30
Some enter boldly, some by Stealth,
And leave *behind* their fruitless Wealth.
For, while the bashful Sylvan Maid,
As half asham'd, and half afraid,
Approaching, finds it hard to part
With that which dwelt so *near her Heart*;
The courtly Dame, unmov'd by Fear,
Profusely pours her *Off'rings* here.

    A TREASURE here of *Learning* lurks,
Huge Heaps of never-dying Works;     40
Labours of many an ancient Sage,
And Millions of the present Age.

    IN at this Gulph all Off'rings pass,
And lye an undistinguish'd Mass.
*Deucalion*, to restore Mankind
Was bid to throw the Stones *behind*;
So, those who here their Gifts convey,
Are forc't to *look another Way*;
For, few, a chosen few, must know,
The Mysteries that lye below.     50

SAD Charnel-house! a dismal Dome,
For which all Mortals leave their Home;
The Young, the Beautiful, and Brave,
Here bury'd in one common Grave;
Where each Supply of *Dead*, renews
Unwholsome *Damps*, *offensive Dews*:
And lo! the *Writing on the Walls*
Points out where each new *Victim* falls;
The *Food of Worms*, and Beasts obscene,
Who round the Vault luxuriant reign.                    60

SEE where those mangled Corpses lye;
Condemn'd by Female Hands to dye;
A comely Dame once clad in white,
Lyes there consign'd to endless Night;
By cruel Hands her Blood was spilt,
And yet her *Wealth* was all her Guilt.

AND here six Virgins in a Tomb,
All beauteous Offspring of one Womb,
Oft in the Train of *Venus* seen,
As fair and lovely as their Queen:                      70
In Royal Garments each was drest,
Each with a Gold and Purple Vest;
I saw them of their Garments stript,
Their Throats were cut, their Bellies ript,
*Twice* were they bury'd, *twice* were born,
*Twice* from their Sepulchres were torn;
But, now dismember'd here are cast,
And find a resting Place at last.

HERE, oft the Curious Trav'ller finds,
The Combat of *opposing Winds*:                         80
And seeks to learn the secret Cause,
Which alien seems from Nature's Laws;
Why at this *Cave*'s tremendous *Mouth*,
He feels at once both *North* and *South*:
Whether the Winds in Caverns pent
Through *Clefts* oppugnant force a Vent;
Or, whether *op'ning all his Stores*,
Fierce *Æolus* in Tempests roars.

Yᴇᴛ from this *mingled Mass* of Things,
In Time a new Creation springs.                    90
These *crude* Materials once shall rise,
To fill the Earth, and Air, and Skies:
In various Forms appear agen
Of Vegetables, Brutes, and Men.
So *Jove* pronounc'd among the Gods,
*Olympus* trembling as he nods.

96. A Privy.

# ANOTHER

*Louisa* to *Strephon*

Aʜ, *Strephon*, how can you despise
Her, who, without thy Pity, dies?
To *Strephon* I have still been true,
And of as noble Blood as you;
Fair Issue of the genial Bed,
A Virgin in thy Bosom bred;
Embrac'd thee closer than a Wife;
When thee I leave, I leave my Life.
Why should my Shepherd take amiss
That oft I wake thee with a Kiss?                  10
Yet you of ev'ry Kiss complain;
Ah, is not Love a pleasing Pain?
A Pain which ev'ry happy Night
You cure with Ease and with Delight;
With Pleasure, as the Poet sings,
Too great for Mortals less than Kings.

*CHLOE*, when on thy Breast I lye,
Observe me with revengeful Eye:
If *Chloe* o'er thy Heart prevails,
She'll tear me with her desp'rate Nails;           20

And with relentless Hands destroy
The tender Pledges of our Joy.
Nor have I bred a spurious Race;
They all were born from thy Embrace.

CONSIDER, *Strephon*, what you do;
For, should I dye for Love of you,
I'll haunt thy Dreams, a bloodless Ghost;
And all my Kin, a num'rous Host,
Who down direct our Lineage bring
From Victors o'er the *Memphian* King;　　　　30
Renown'd in Sieges and Campaigns,
Who never fled the bloody Plains,
Who in tempestuous Seas can sport,
And scorn the Pleasures of a Court;
From whom great *Sylla* found his Doom;
Who scourg'd to Death that Scourge of *Rome*,
Shall on thee take a Vengeance dire;
Thou, like *Alcides*, shalt expire,
When his envenom'd Shirt he wore,
And Skin and Flesh in Pieces tore.　　　　40
Nor less that Shirt, my Rival's Gift,
Cut from the Piece that made her Shift,
Shall in thy dearest Blood be dy'd,
And make thee tear thy tainted Hyde.

　　　44. Louse to his Patron [anagram].


# ANOTHER

## Written in the Year 1725

DEPRIV'D of Root, and Branch, and Rind,
　　Yet Flow'rs I bear of ev'ry Kind;
And such is my prolific Pow'r,
They bloom in less than half an Hour:
Yet Standers-by may plainly see
They get no Nourishment from me.

My Head, with Giddiness, goes round;
And yet I firmly stand my Ground:
All over naked I am seen,
And painted like an *Indian* Queen.                    10
No Couple-Beggar in the Land
E'er join'd such Numbers Hand in Hand;
I join them fairly with a *Ring*;
Nor can our Parson blame the Thing:
And tho' no Marriage Words are spoke,
They part not till the *Ring* is broke.
Yet hypocrite Fanaticks cry,
I'm but an Idol rais'd on high;
And once a Weaver in our Town,
A damn'd *Cromwellian*, knock'd me down.                    20
I lay a Prisoner twenty Years;
And then the Jovial Cavaliers
To their old Posts restor'd all Three,
I mean the Church, the King, and Me.

                    24. A Maypole.


# A RIDDLE

I WITH borrow'd Silver shine,
  What you see is none of mine,
First I shew you but a Quarter,
Like the Bow that guards the *Tartar*,
Then the Half, and then the Whole,
Ever dancing round a Pole.
And what will raise your Admiration,
I am not one of GOD's Creation,
But sprung (and I this Truth maintain)
Like *Pallas* from my Father's Brain.                    10
And after all, I chiefly owe
My Beauty to the Shades below.

Printed from *Works, Vol. VIII*, Dublin, 1746, with the following Note: 'The Author and his Friends used to divert themselves for Amusement in making Riddles, some of which have been printed in the second Volume of his Works, and were well received; as we hope, the following will be, although we cannot tell the Authors of each.'

Most wondrous Forms you see me wear
A Man, a Woman, Lion, Bear,
A Fish, a Fowl, a Cloud, a Field,
All Figures Heav'n or Earth can yield,
Like *Daphne* sometimes in a Tree,
Yet am not one of all you see.

18. The Moon.


# ANOTHER

B EGOTTEN, and Born, and dying with Noise,
   The Terror of Women, and Pleasure of Boys,
Like the Fiction of Poets concerning the Wind,
I'm chiefly unruly, when strongest confin'd.
For Silver and Gold I don't trouble my Head,
But all I delight in is Pieces of Lead;
Except when I trade with a Ship or a Town,
Why then I make pieces of Iron go down.
One Property more I would have you remark,
No Lady was ever more fond of a Spark;                    10
The Moment I get one my Soul's all a-fire,
And I roar out my Joy, and in Transport expire.

12. A Cannon.


# ANOTHER

T HERE is a Gate, we know full well,
   That stands 'twixt Heav'n, and Earth, and Hell,
Where many for a Passage venture,
But very few are found to enter;
Altho' 'tis open Night and Day,
They for that Reason shun this Way:
Both Dukes and Lords abhor its Wood,
They can't come near it for their Blood.

What other Way they take to go,
Another Time I'll let you know.                    10
Yet Commoners with greatest Ease,
Can find an Entrance when they please.
The poorest hither march in State,
(Or they can never pass the Gate)
Like *Roman* Generals triumphant,
And then they take a Turn and jump on't.
If gravest Parsons here advance,
They cannot pass before they dance;
There's not a Soul, that does resort here,
But strips himself to pay the Porter.              20

20. The Gallows.


# ANOTHER

FROM Heav'n I fall, tho' from Earth I begin,
No Lady alive can shew such a Skin.
I am bright as an Angel, and light as a Feather,
But heavy, and dark, when you squeeze me together.
Tho' Candor and Truth in my Aspect I bear,
Yet many poor Creatures I help to ensnare.
Tho' so much of Heav'n appears in my Make,
The foulest Impressions I easily take.
My Parent and I produce one another,
The Mother the Daughter, the Daughter the Mother.   10

10. Snow.


# ANOTHER

I'M up, and down, and round about,
Yet all the World can't find me out,
Tho' Hundreds have employ'd their Leisure,
They never yet cou'd find my Measure.

I'm found almost in ev'ry Garden,
Nay, in the Compass of a Farthing.
There's neither Chariot, Coach, or Mill,
Can move an Inch except I will.

8. A Circle.


# ANOTHER

I AM jet-Black, as you may see,
    The Son of Pitch, and gloomy Night;
Yet all that know me will agree,
    I'm dead except I live in Light.

Sometimes in Panegyrick high,
    Like lofty *Pindar* I can soar,
And raise a Virgin to the Sky,
    Or sink her to a pocky Whore.

My Blood this Day is very sweet,
    To-morrow of a bitter Juice,                    10
Like Milk 'tis cry'd about the Street,
    And so apply'd to diff'rent Use.

Most wond'rous is my Magick Power;
    For with one Colour I can paint;
I'll make the Dev'l a Saint this Hour,
    Next make a Devil of a Saint.

Thro' distant Regions I can fly,
    Provide me but with Paper Wings,
And fairly shew a Reason, why
    There shou'd be Quarrels among Kings.          20

And after all you'll think it odd,
    When learned Doctors will dispute,
That I shou'd point the Word of GOD,
    And shew where they can best confute.

Let Lawyers bawl and strain their Throats,
'Tis I that must the Lands convey,
And strip their Clients to their Coats;
Nay give their very Souls away.

28. Ink.

# ANOTHER

EVER eating, never cloying,
All devouring, all destroying,
Never finding full Repast,
Till I eat the World at last.

4. Time.

# ANOTHER

WE are little airy Creatures,
All of diff'rent Voice and Features,
One of us in Glass is set,
One of us you'll find in Jet,
T'other you may see in Tin,
And the fourth a Box within,
If the fifth you shou'd pursue
It can never fly from you.

8. The Vowels.

# ANOTHER

ALL of us in one you'll find,
Brethren of a wond'rous Kind,
Yet among us all no Brother
Knows one Tittle of the other;

We in frequent Councils are,
And our Marks of Things declare,
Where, to us unknown, a Clerk
Sits, and takes them in the Dark.
He's the Register of All
In our Ken, both great and small;                    10
By us forms his Laws, and Rules,
He's our Master, we his Tools;
Yet we can, with greatest Ease,
Turn and wind him where we please.
    One of us alone can sleep,
Yet no Watch the rest will keep,
But the Moment that he closes,
Ev'ry Brother else reposes.
    If Wine's bought, or Victuals drest
One enjoys them for the Rest.                         20
    Pierce us all with wounding Steel,
One for all of us will feel.
    Tho' ten thousand Canons roar,
Add to them ten thousand more,
Yet but one of us is found
Who regards the dreadful Sound.
    Do what is not fit to tell,
There's but one of us can smell.

28. The five Senses.

# ANOTHER

FONTINELLA* *to* FLORINDA

WHEN on my Bosom thy bright Eyes,
    *Florinda*, dart their Heav'nly Beams,
I feel not the least Love Surprize,
    Yet endless Tears flow down in Streams.
There's nought so beautiful in thee,
But you may find the same in me.

* FONTINELLA. A fountain.

The Lillies of thy Skin compare;
  In me you see them full as white,
The Roses of your Cheeks, I dare
  Affirm, can't glow to more Delight.                    10
Then, since I shew as fine a Face,
Can you refuse a soft Embrace.

Ah lovely Nymph, thou'rt in thy Prime!
  And so am I whilst thou art here;
But soon will come the fatal Time,
  When all we see shall disappear.
'Tis mine to make a just Reflection,
And yours to follow my Direction.

Then catch Admirers while you may;
  Treat not your Lovers with Disdain;                    20
For Time with Beauty flies away,
  And there is no return again.
To you the sad Account I bring,
Life's Autumn has no second Spring.


# ANOTHER

NEVER sleeping, still awake,
  Pleasing most when most I speak,
The Delight of old and young,
Tho' I speak without a Tongue.
Nought but one Thing can confound me,
Many Voices joining round me;
Then I fret, and rave and gabble,
Like the Labourers of *Babel*.
Now I am a Dog, or Cow,
I can bark, or I can low,                                10
I can bleat, or I can sing,
Like the Warblers of the Spring.

1. The word 'speaking' appears in the early editions, and should presumably be 'sleeping'. (H.W.)

Let the Love-sick Bard complain,
And I mourn the cruel Pain;
Let the happy Swain rejoice,
And I join my helping Voice;
Both are welcome, Grief or Joy,
I with either sport and toy.
Tho' a Lady, I am stout,
Drums and Trumpets bring me out;                    20
Then I clash and roar, and rattle,
Join in all the Din of Battle.
*Jove*, with all his loudest Thunder,
When I'm vext, can't keep me under;
Yet so tender is my Ear,
That the lowest Voice I fear;
Much I dread the Courtier's Fate,
When his Merit's out of Date,
For I hate a silent Breath,
And a Whisper is my Death.                          30

30. An Echo.


# ANOTHER

MOST Things by me do rise and fall,
And as I please they're great and small;
Invading Foes, without Resistance,
With Ease I make to keep their Distance;
Again, as I'm dispos'd, the Foe
Will come, tho' not a Foot they go.
Both Mountains, Woods, and Hills, and Rocks,
And gaming Goats, and fleecy Flocks,
And lowing Herds, and piping Swains,
Come dancing to me o'er the Plains.                 10
The greatest Whale, that swims the Sea
Does distantly my Pow'r obey.
In vain from me the Sailor flies,
The quickest Ship I can surprize,

And turn it as I have a Mind,
And move it against Tyde and Wind.
Nay, bring me here the tallest Man,
I'll squeeze him to a little Span,
Or bring a tender Child and pliant,
You'll see me stretch him to a Giant;                    20
Nor shall they in the least complain,
Because my Magick gives no Pain.

22. Reflection in a mirror.


# ANOTHER

WE are little Brethren twain,
   Arbiters of Loss and Gain,
Many to our Counters run,
Some are made, and some undone.
But, Men find it to their Cost,
Few are made, but Numbers lost.
Tho' we play them Tricks for ever,
Yet, they always hope, our Favour.

8. A Pair of Dice.


# ANOTHER

BY something form'd, I nothing am,
   Yet ev'ry Thing that you can name;
In no Place have I ever been,
Yet ev'ry where I may be seen;
In all Things false, yet always true,
I'm still the same —— but ever new.
Lifeless, Life's perfect Form I wear,
Can shew a Nose, Eye, Tongue, or Ear, }
Yet neither Smell, See, Taste, or Hear. 

Printed from *Miscellaneous Poems*, London, 1729.

All Shapes and Features I can boast,                    10
No Flesh, no Bones, no Blood —— no Ghost:
All Colours, without Paint, put on,
And change like the *Cameleon*.
Swiftly I come, and enter there,
Where not a Chink let's in the Air;
Like Thought I'm in a Moment gone,
Nor can I ever be alone;
All Things on Earth I imitate,
Faster than Nature can create;
Sometimes imperial Robes I wear,                    20
Anon in Beggar's Rags appear;
A Giant now, and strait an Elf,
I'm ev'ry one, but ne'er my self;
Ne'er sad I mourn, ne'er glad rejoice,
I move my Lips, but want a Voice;
I ne'er was born, nor e'er can die,
Then prythee tell me what am I.

27. Reflection in a mirror.

# ANOTHER

O F all inhabitants on earth,
    To Man alone I owe my birth,
And yet the Cow, the Sheep, the Bee,
Are all my parents more than he:
I, a virtue strange and rare,
Make the fairest look more fair;
And myself, which yet is rarer,
Growing old, grow still the fairer.
Like sots, alone I'm dull enough,
When dos'd with smoak, and smear'd with snuff:                    10
But, in the midst of mirth and wine,
I with double lustre shine.
Emblem of the Fair am I,
Polish'd neck, and radient eye;
In my eye my greatest grace,
Emblem of the *Cyclops'* race;

Printed from *Miscellaneous Poems*, London, 1729.

Metals I like them subdue,
Slave like them to *Vulcan* too.
Emblem of a monarch old,
Wise and glorious to behold; 20
Wasted he appears, and pale,
Watching for the public weal.
Emblem of the bashful dame,
That in secret feeds her flame,
Often aiding to impart
All the secrets of her heart.
Various is my bulk and hue,
Big like *Bess*, and small like *Sue*;
Now brown and burnish'd like a nut,
At other times a very slut; 30
Often fair, and soft, and tender,
Taper, tall, and smooth, and slender;
Like *Flora*, deck'd with fairest flowers;
Like *Phœbus*, guardian of the hours:
But, whatever be my dress,
Greater be my size or less,
Swelling be my shape or small,
Like thyself I shine in all.
Clouded if my face is seen,
My complexion wan and green, 40
Languid like a love-sick maid,
Steel affords me present aid.
Soon or late, my date is done,
As my thread of life is spun;
Yet to cut the fatal thread
Oft' revives my drooping head:
Yet I perish in my prime,
Seldom by the death of time;
Die like lovers as they gaze,
Die for those I live to please; 50
Pine unpitied to my urn,
Nor warm the fair for whom I burn;
Unpitied, unlamented too,
Die like all that look on you.

54. A Candle.

# A RIDDLE

### By DOCTOR DELANY

I Reach all Things near me, and far off to boot,
  Without stretching a Finger, or stirring a Foot.
I take them all in too, to add to your Wonder,
Tho' many and various, and large and asunder.
Without jostling or crowding they pass Side by Side,
Thro' a wonderful Wicket, not Half an Inch wide.
Then I lodge them at Ease in a very large Store,
Of no Breadth, or Length, with a thousand Things more.
All this I can do without Witchcraft or Charm,
Tho' sometimes they say I bewitch, and do Harm;      10
Tho' cold I inflame, and tho' quiet invade,
And nothing can shield from my Spell but a Shade.
A Thief that has robb'd you, or done you Disgrace,
In magical Mirrour I'll shew you his Face:
Nay, if you'll believe what the Poets have said,
They'll tell you I kill, and can call back the Dead.
Like Conjurors safe in my Circle I dwell,
I love to look black too, it heightens my Spell;
Tho' my Magick is mighty in every Hue,
Who see all my Power must see it in YOU.      20

# ANSWERED

### By DEAN SWIFT

WITH half an Eye
  Your *Riddle* I spy.
I observe your Wicket
Hemm'd in by a Thicket,
And whatever passes
Is strained thro' Glasses.

Printed from *Works, Vol. VIII*, Dublin, 1762.

You say it is quiet,
I flatly deny it:
It wanders about,
Without stirring out, 10
No Passion so weak
But gives it a Tweak;
Love, Joy, and Devotion
Set it always in Motion.
And as for the Tragick
Effects of its Magick,
Which you say it can kill,
Or revive at its Will,
The Dead are all sound
And revive above Ground, 20
After all you have writ,
It cannot be Wit.
Which plainly does follow,
Since it flies from *Apollo*.
Its Cowardice such,
It cries at a Touch,
'Tis a perfect Milksop,
Grows drunk with a Drop.
Another great Fault,
It cannot bear Salt; 30
And a Hair can disarm
It of every Charm.

# A LETTER

*SIR*,

PRAY discruciate what follows:

> The dullest Beast, and Gentleman's Liquor,
> When young is often due to the Vicar.
> The dullest Beast, and Swine's Delight
> Make up a Bird very swift of Flight.

Printed from *Works, Vol. VIII*, Dublin, 1746.

2. A swine.     4. A swallow.

The dullest Beast when high in Stature, ⎫
Add another of royal Nature.                       ⎬
For breeding is a useful Creature.              ⎭
    The dullest Beast, and a Party distrest,
When too long, is bad at best.
    The dullest Beast, and the Saddle it wears,      10
Is good for Partridge, not for Hares.
    The dullest Beast and kind Voice of a Cat,
Will make a Horse go, though he be not fat.
    The dullest of Beasts and of Birds in the Air,
Is that by which all *Irishmen* swear.
    The dullest Beast and fam'd College for *Teagues*
Is a Person very unfit for Intrigues.
    The dullest Beast and a Cobler's Tool, ⎫
With a Boy that is only fit for School,     ⎬
In Summer is very pleasant and cool.      ⎭     20
    The dullest Beast, and that which you kiss,
May break a Limb of Master or Miss.
    Of Serpent-Kind, and what at distance kills,
Poor Miss *Dingley* oft hath felt its Bills.
    The dullest Beast and Eggs unsound,
Without it I rather would walk on the Ground.
    The dullest Beast and what covers a House,
Without it a Writer is not worth a Louse.
    The dullest Beast, and scandalous Vermin
Of roast or boil'd, to the Hungry is charming.     30
    The dullest Beast, and what's cover'd with Crust,
There's nobody but a Fool that would trust.
    The dullest Beast mending Highways,
Is to a Horse an evil Disease.
    The dullest Beast and a Hole in the Ground,
Will dress a Dinner worth five Pound.
    The dullest Beast, and what Doctors pretend
The Cook-maid often hath by the End.

| | | |
|---|---|---|
| 7. A stallion. | 9. A sail. | 11. A spaniel. |
| 13. A spur. | 15. A soul. | 17. A sloven. |
| 20. A salad. | 22. A slip. | 24. A sparrow. |
| 26. A saddle. | 28. A style. | 30. A slice. |
| 32. A spy. | 34. A spavin. | 36. A spit. |
| 38. A skewer. | | |

The dullest Beast and Fish for Lent
May give you a Blow you'll for ever repent.      40
The dullest Beast and a shameful Jeer,
Without it a Lady should never appear.

40. Assault.      42. A smock.

## *Probatur Aliter*

A LONG-EAR'D Beast, and a Field-house for Cattle,
  Among the Coals does often rattle.
A long-ear'd Beast, a Bird that prates,
The Bridegrooms' first Gift to their Mates,
Is by all pious Christians thought,
In Clergymen the greatest Fault.
  A long-ear'd Beast, and Woman of Endor,
If your Wife be a Scold, that will mend her.
  With a long-ear'd Beast, and Med'cines Use,
Cooks make their Fowl look tight and spruce.      10
  A long-ear'd Beast and holy Fable,
Strengthens the Shoes of half the Rabble.
  A long-ear'd Beast, and Rhenish Wine,
Lies in the Lap of Ladies fine.
  A long-ear'd Beast and *Flanders* College,
Is Dr. *Tisdal* to my Knowledge.
  A long-ear'd Beast, and Building Knight;
Censorious People do in spight.
  A long-ear'd Beast, and Bird of Night,
We Sinners are too apt to slight.      20
  A long-ear'd Beast, and shameful Vermin,
A Judge will eat, tho' clad in Ermin.

Printed from *Works, Vol. VIII*, Dublin, 1746.

2. A shovel.      6. Aspiring.      8. A switch.      10. A skewer.
12. A sparable; abbreviated form of 'sparrow-bill', a small headless nail used by cobblers.
14. A shock.      16. A sloven (Ass-Louvain).      18. Asperse.
20. A soul.      22. A slice.

A long-ear'd Beast, and *Irish* Cart,
Can leave a Mark and give a Smart.
  A long-ear'd Beast, in Mud to lye,
No Bird in Air so swift can fly.
  A long-ear'd Beast, and a sputt'ring old Whig,
I wish he were in it a dancing a Jig.
  A long-ear'd Beast, and Liquor to write,
Is a damnable Smell both Morning and Night.          30
  A long-ear'd Beast, and the Child of a Sheep,
At Whist they will make a desperate Sweep.
  A Beast long-ear'd, and till Midnight you stay,
Will cover a House much better than Clay.
  A long-ear'd Beast, and the Drink you love best
You call him a Sloven in earnest or jest.
  A long-ear'd Beast, and the sixteenth Letter,
I'd not look at all, unless I look't better.
  A long-ear'd Beast give me, and Eggs unsound,
Or else I will not ride one Inch of Ground.          40
  A long-ear'd Beast, another Name for Jeer,
To Ladies Skins there's nothing comes so near.
  A long-ear'd Beast, and kind Noise of a Cat,
Is useful in Journies, take Notice of that.
  A long-ear'd Beast, and what seasons your Beef,
On such an Occasion the Law gives Relief.
  A long-ear'd Beast, a Thing that Force must drive in,
Bears up his House, that's of his own contriving.

| | | | |
|---|---|---|---|
| 24. A scar. | 26. A swallow. | 28. A sty. | 30. A sink. |
| 32. A slam. | 34 A slate. | 36. A swine. | 38. Askew. |
| 40. A saddle. | 42. A smock. | 44. A spur. | 46. Assault. |
| 48. A snail. | | | |

# POEMS
## OF
# DOUBTFUL DATE

# FABULA CANIS ET UMBRAE

ORE cibum portans catulus dum spectat in undis,
    Apparet liquido prædæ melioris imago:
Dum speciosa diu damna admiratur, et alte
Ad latices inhiat, cadit imo vortice præceps
Ore cibus, nec non simulachrum corripit unà.
Occupat ille avidus deceptis faucibus umbram;
Illudit species, ac dentibus aëra mordet.

Printed from *Works, 4to, Vol. VIII* (2), London, 1765.

# To Mrs. HOUGHTON of *Bormount*, upon praising her Husband to Dr. SWIFT

YOU always are making a God of your Spouse,
    But this neither Reason nor Conscience allows;
Perhaps you will say, 'tis in Gratitude due,
And you adore him, because he adores you.
Your Argument's weak, and so you will find,
For you, by this Rule, must adore all Mankind.

Printed from *Works, Vol. VIII*, Dublin, 1762.

# *Mr.* Jason Hassard, *a Woollen-Drapier in* Dublin, *put up the Sign of the* Golden Fleece, *and desired a Motto in Verse*

JASON, the valiant Prince of *Greece*,
    From *Colchos* brought the *Golden Fleece*:
We comb the Wool, refine the Stuff,
For modern *Jasons* that's enuff.
Oh! could we tame yon *watchful Dragon*,
Old *Jason* would have less to brag on.

Printed from *Works, Vol. VIII*, Dublin, 1746.

# EPIGRAM ON FASTING
## FROM THE FRENCH

*A* French *Gentleman dining with some Company on a Fast-day, called for some Bacon and Eggs. The rest were very angry, and reproved him for so heinous a Sin: Whereupon he writ the following Lines,* extempore, *which are here translated.*

P*EUT* on croire avec bon sens
  Qu'un lardon le mit en colère;
Ou, que manger un harang
C'est un secret pour luy plaire?
En sa gloire envelopé
Songe-t-il bien de nos soupés?

### In *ENGLISH*

WHO can believe with common Sense,
  A Bacon-slice gives God Offence?
Or, how a Herring hath a Charm
Almighty Anger to disarm?
Wrapt up in Majesty divine,
Does he regard on what we dine?

Printed from *Miscellanies, Vol. the Fifth,* London, 1735.

# *An* EPIGRAM *on* SCOLDING

GREAT Folks are of a finer Mold;
  Lord! how politely they can scold;
While a coarse *English* Tongue will itch,
For Whore and Rogue; and Dog and Bitch.

Printed from *Works, Vol. VIII,* Dublin, 1746.

# THE UPSTART

THE rascal! that's too mild a name;
Does he forget from whence he came?
Has he forgot from whence he sprung?
A mushroom in a bed of dung;
A maggot in a cake of fat,
The offspring of a beggar's brat.
As eels delight to creep in mud,
To eels, we may compare his blood;
His blood delights in mud to run;
Witness his lazy, lousy son!                    10
Puff'd up with pride and insolence,
Without a grain of common sense,
See with what consequence he stalks,
With what pomposity he talks;
See how the gaping crowd admire
The stupid blockhead and the liar.
How long shall vice triumphant reign?
How long shall mortals bend to gain?
How long shall virtue hide her face,
And leave her votaries in disgrace?             20
—Let indignation fire my strains,
Another villain yet remains—
Let purse-proud C—n next approach,
With what an air he mounts his coach!
A cart would best become the knave,
A dirty parasite and slave;
His heart in poison deeply dipt,
His tongue with oily accents tipt,
A smile still ready at command,
The pliant bow, the forehead bland—             30
     \*   \*   \*   \*   \*   \*   \*
     \*   \*   \*   \*   \*   \*   \*

Printed from Wilson's *Swiftiana*, 1804, with the following note: 'There was one
character which, through life, always kindled Swift's indignation, *the haughty,
presuming, tyrannizing upstart!* A person of this description chanced to reside in the
parish of Laracor. . . . The following lines have been found, written by Swift upon
this man.' [Internal evidence suggests, however, some affinity with *The Legion Club*.]

XSPW

# VERSES

*made for Women who cry Apples,* &c.

## APPLES

COME buy my fine Wares,
Plumbs, Apples and Pears,
A hundred a Penny,
In Conscience too many,
Come, will you have any;
My Children are seven,
I wish them in Heaven,
My Husband's a Sot,
With his Pipe and his Pot,
Not a Farthing will gain 'em,          10
And I must maintain 'em.

## ASPARAGUS

RIPE 'Sparagrass,
Fit for Lad or Lass,
To make their Water pass:
O, 'tis pretty Picking
With a tender Chicken.

## ONYONS

COME, follow me by the Smell,
Here's delicate Onyons to sell,
I promise to use you well.
They make the Blood warmer,
You'll feed like a Farmer:

Printed from *Works, Vol. VIII*, Dublin, 1746.

For this is ev'ry Cook's Opinion,
No sav'ry Dish without an Onyon;
But lest your Kissing should be spoyl'd,
Your Onyons must be th'roughly boyl'd;
    Or else you may spare         10
    Your Mistress a Share,
The Secret will never be known;
    She cannot discover
    The Breath of her Lover,
But think it as sweet as her own.

## OYSTERS

CHARMING Oysters I cry,
  My Masters come buy,
So plump and so fresh,
So sweet is their Flesh,
No *Colchester* Oyster,
Is sweeter and moyster,
Your Stomach they settle,
And rouse up your Mettle,
They'll make you a Dad
Of a Lass or a Lad;         10
And, Madam your Wife
They'll please to the Life;
Be she barren, be she old,
Be she Slut, or be she Scold,
Eat my Oysters, and lye near her,
She'll be fruitful, never fear her.

## HERRINGS

BE not sparing,
  Leave off swearing
Buy my Herring
Fresh from *Malahide*,
Better ne'er was try'd.

4. *Malahide.* Malahide, about five miles from Dublin, famous for Oysters.

Come eat 'em with pure fresh Butter and Mustard,
Their Bellies are soft, and as white as a Custard.
Come, Six-pence a Dozen to get me some Bread,
Or, like my own Herrings, I soon shall be dead.


## ORANGES

COME, buy my fine Oranges, Sauce for your Veal,
And charming when squeez'd in a Pot of brown Ale.
Well roasted, with Sugar and Wine in a Cup,
They'll make a sweet Bishop when Gentlefolks sup.


### *The* Author's *manner of Living*

ON rainy Days alone I dine,
Upon a Chick, and Pint of Wine.
On rainy Days, I dine alone,
And pick my Chicken to the Bone:
But this my Servants much enrages,
No Scraps remain to save Board-wages.
In Weather fine I nothing spend,
But often spunge upon a Friend:
Yet where He's not so rich as I;
I pay my Club, and so GOD b'y'——.                10

Printed from *Works, Vol. VIII*, Dublin, 1746.


# A PORTRAIT from the LIFE

COME sit by my side, while this picture I draw:
In chatt'ring a magpie, in pride a jackdaw;
A temper the Devil himself could not bridle,
Impertinent mixture of busy and idle.

Printed from *Works, 4to, Vol. VIII* (2), London, 1765.

As rude as a bear, no mule half so crabbed;
She swills like a sow, and she breeds like a rabbit:
A house-wife in bed, at table a slattern;
For all an example, for no one a pattern.
Now tell me, friend Thomas, Ford, Grattan, and merry Dan,
Has this any likeness to good Madam Sheridan? 10

# A CANTATA

Printed from *Works*, *Vol. VIII*, Dublin, 1746, with music by John Echlin, who advised on music at St. Patrick's.

Sleep - ing Weep, Weep - ing Sleep. Bo peep, 'bo peep, 'bo peep, bo peep, peep, bo bo peep.

# SOME POEMS ATTRIBUTED TO SWIFT

## Dunkirk *to be Let*

OLD Lewis *thus the Terms of Peace to Burnish,*
   *Has lately let out* Dunkirk *Ready Furnish'd;*
*But whether 'tis by* Lease, *or* Coppy-hold,
*Or* Tenure in Capite, *we've not been told:*
*But this we hope, if yet he pulls his Horns in,*
*He'll be oblig'd to give his Tenants Warning.*

Printed from the Broadside, containing also *A Hue-and-Cry after Dismal, etc.,*
published in July 1712.

# BLUE-SKIN'S BALLAD

*To the Tune of Packington's Pound*

### 1

YE Fellows of Newgate whose Fingers are nice
   In Diving in Pockets and Cogging of Dice;
Ye Sharpers so rich who can buy off the Noose,
Ye honester poor Rogues who Die in your Shoes,
       Attend and draw near,
       Good News you shall hear
How Honest *Wild*'s Throat was cut from Ear to Ear
Now *Blueskin*'s sharp Penknife has set you at Ease,
And ev'ry Man round me may rob if he please.

### 2

When to the Old Baily this *Blueskin* was led,        10
He held up his Hand, his Indictment was Read,
Loud rattled his Chains, near him honest *Wild* stood,
For full Forty Pounds was the Price of his Blood.
       Then hopeless of Life
       He drew his Penknife
And made a sad Widow of honest *Wild*'s Wife.
But forty Pounds paid her, her Grief shall appease
And ev'ry Man round me may, &c.

Printed from the Dublin Broadside, 1724–5, but never included by Faulkner
in any edition of Swift's *Poems*.

3

Some say there are Courtiers of highest Renown
Who steal the King's Gold and leave him but a Crown;    20
Some say there are Peers and some Parliament Men
Who meet once a Year to rob Courtiers again;
       But let them have their Swing
         To pillage the King,
And get a blue Ribbon instead of a String.
For *Blueskin*'s sharp, &c.


4

Knaves of old to hide Guilt by their cunning Inventions
Call Briberies Grants, and plain Robbery Pensions.
Physicians and Lawyers who take their Degrees     30
To be learned Rouges, call their pilferings Fees.
       Since this happy Day
        Now ev'ry one may
Rob (as safe as in Office) upon the High-way,
For, &c.


5

Some Rob in the *Customs*, some Cheat in the *'xcise*
But he who Robs *Both* is esteemed most wise
Church-Wardens who always have dreaded the Halter
As yet only venture to steal from the Altar.     40
       But now to get Gold
        They may be more bold.
And rob on the High-way since honest *Wild*'s cold,
For, &c.


6

Some by *Publick Revenues* which pass thro' their Hands
Have purchas'd *Clean Houses* and bought *Dirty Lands*;
Some to steal from a Charity think it no Sin
Which at home (says the Proverb) does always begin
       If ever you be     50
        Assign'd a Trustee
Treat not Orphans like Masters in the Chancery
For ev'ry Man round, &c.

### 7

What a Pother is here with *Woods* and his Brass
Who wou'd modestly make a few Halfpennies pass;
The Patent is good, and the Precedent's old,
For *Diomede* changed his Copper for Gold;
      But if *Ireland* despise
      The new Halfpennies      60
More safely to Rob on the Road I advise,
For *Blueskin*'s, &c.


## On Wisdom's Defeat In a Learned Debate

*Quid est Sapienta semper idem velle, atq; idem nolle*

MINERVA has vow'd since the Bishops do slight Her,
Shou'd the Reverend Peers, by chance e're invite Her,
She's resolv'd never more to be known by the MITRE.

The Temporal Lords, who Voted against Her,
She Frankly forgives, as not having incenst Her,
For securing their Pensions is best Proof of their Sense Sir.

At first putting the Question, their Lordships were for't,
And his Grace's wise Motion did bravely support,
Till positive Orders was Whisper'd from Court.

So this they Alledge in their Justification,      10
They Vote for their Bread in Undoing the Nation,
And the first Law of Nature is Self-Preservation.

                *Rose Common,*
                Shameless Woman.

Printed from the Dublin Broadside (Sarah Harding), 1725.

# A BALLAD

### I

PATRICK astore, what news upon the town?
  By my soul there's bad news, for the gold she was pulled
    down,
The gold she was pull'd down, of that I'm very sure,
For I saw'd them reading upon the towlsel doore.
                              Sing, och, och, hoh, hoh.

### II

Arrah! who was him reading? 'twas a *jauntleman* in ruffles,
And Patrick's bell she was ringing all in muffles;
She was ringing very sorry, her tongue tied up with rag;
Lorsha! and out of her shteeple there was hung a black flag.
                              Sing och, &c.    10

### III

Patrick astore, who was him made this law?
Some they do say, 'twas the big man of straw;
But others they do say, that it was Jug-Joulter,
The devil he may take her into hell and *Boult-her*!
                              Sing och, &c.

### IV

Musha! Why Parliament wouldn't you maul,
Those *carters*, and paviours, and footmen and all;
Those rascally paviours who did us undermine,
Och ma ceade millia mollighart, on the feeders of swine!
                              Sing och, &c.    20

Printed from *Works*, ed. Scott, Vol. X, 1814.

# EPIGRAM

BEHOLD! a proof of *Irish* sense!
　　Here *Irish* wit is seen!
When nothing's left, that's worth defence,
　　We build a magazine.

Printed from *Works*, *4to*, *Vol. IX* (2), London, 1775, ed. Nichols, who added the following footnote:

'The Dean, in his lunacy, had some intervals of sense; at which time his guardians, or physicians, took him out for the air. On one of these days, when they came to the Park, Swift remarked a new building, which he had never seen, and asked what it was designed for. To which Dr. Kingsbury answered, "That Mr. Dean, is the magazine for arms and powder, for the security of the city". "Oh! oh!" says the Dean, pulling out his pocket-book, "let me take an item of that. This is worth remarking: my tablets, as Hamlet says, my tablets—memory put down that!"—Which produced the above lines, said to be the last he ever wrote.'

# INDEX OF TITLES

# INDEX OF FIRST LINES